ARTIFICIAL INTELLIGENCE
Structures and Strategies for Complex Problem Solving
Second Edition

ARTIFICIAL INTELLIGENCE

Structures and Strategies for Complex Problem Solving

Second Edition

George F. Luger

William A. Stubblefield

University of New Mexico, Albuquerque

The Benjamin/Cummings Publishing Company, Inc.

Redwood City, California • Menlo Park, California
Reading, Massachusetts • New York • Don Mills, Ontario
Wokingham, U.K. • Amsterdam • Bonn • Sydney
Singapore • Tokyo • Madrid • San Juan

Sponsoring Editor: Carter Shanklin
Production Coordinator: Megan Rundel
Copyeditor: Anna Huff
Cover Designer: Rudy Zehnter
Compositor: GTS Graphics

Cover and part opener artwork by Thomas Barrow.

Library of Congress Cataloging-in-Publication Data
Luger, George F.
    Artificial intelligence: structures and strategies for complex problem solving
    George F. Luger, William A. Stubblefield.—2nd ed.
        p.   cm.
    Includes bibliographical references and index.
    ISBN 0-8053-4780-1
    1. Artificial intelligence. 2. Knowledge representation (Information theory) 3. Problem solving. 4. PROLOG (Computer program language) 5. LISP (Computer program language) I. Stubblefield, William A. II. Title.
Q335.L84 1992   92-26477
006.3—dc20   CIP

ISBN 0-8053-4780-1

2 3 4 5 6 7 8 9 10–DO–95 94 93

The Benjamin/Cummings Publishing Company, Inc.
390 Bridge Parkway
Redwood City, California 94065

For my wife, Kathleen, and our children Sarah, David, and Peter.

For my parents, George Fletcher Luger and Loretta Maloney Luger.

Si quid est in me ingenii, judices . . .

Cicero, Pro Archia Poeta

GFL

For my parents, William Frank Stubblefield and Maria Christina Stubblefield.
And for my wife, Merry Christina.

She is far more precious than jewels.

The heart of her husband trusts in her,

and he will have no lack of gain.

Proverbs 31:10–11

WAS

PREFACE

Purpose

This book is an introduction to artificial intelligence and its many applications. Our goal in writing it is to place AI within the larger context of engineering, science, and philosophy. This includes not only computer science, but the full range of scientific efforts to understand the nature of intelligent activity.

There are three features of this book that reflect our own attitudes towards teaching artificial intelligence and distinguish our book from others.

First, we unify the diverse branches of AI through a detailed discussion of its theoretical foundations. Throughout its history, AI has exhibited two major methodological schools, often called the *neats* and the *scruffies*. The neats emphasize formal treatment of the theory behind intelligent programs including the analysis of search algorithms, the establishment of a theory of knowledge representation using logic or other well-defined formalisms, and the careful characterization of the soundness and completeness of inference strategies. The scruffies take a more application-oriented approach, beginning with a problem to be solved and finding, through intuition and experiment, the best techniques for solving that particular problem.

A major goal in writing this text is to unify these two approaches; indeed, we believe that these schools have much more in common than is usually admitted. Theoretical work in AI leads to an increasing awareness that intelligent behavior relies on domain-specific knowledge, knowledge that is often obtained by observation, experimentation and revision.

Conversely, the best AI implementations are usually built on the knowledge representation and problem-solving techniques developed in theoretical research.

To construct a unified approach to AI, we start with a well-marked separation between theory and practice by formally considering search in Part II and later implementing search algorithms in PROLOG (Chapters 6 and 13) and LISP (Chapters 7, 14 and 15). However, even the more formal chapters use realistic examples to illustrate important issues. For instance, much of our theoretical discussion of representation and search is illustrated through an extended example of an expert system for financial advice, our chapter on expert systems is anchored by a case study of the MYCIN program, and our machine learning algorithms, in Chapter 12, are supported by numerous implemented examples. The chapter on natural language concludes with a detailed discussion of the implementation of a natural language front end for a data base system.

The second feature of this text is the development, justification, and use of advanced representational formalisms and search techniques. This begins with the classic approach to representation and problem solving using predicate calculus, recursion-based graph search, and heuristics. We then extend this model to the knowledge-intensive approaches used for modern intelligent systems. Much of the emphasis of AI reaserch is on the development of languages which directly support specific knowledge structures such as class hierarchies, frames and objects, and tools for describing the semantics of natural languages. We discuss the importance of structuring information and control with semantic nets, conceptual graphs, frames, inheritance systems, and other representational techniques.

Part V, and especially Chapter 15, introduces object-oriented programming and hybrid expert system design. We present three implementations of object-oriented representations, two in LISP, the first with OOPS, our own object system, the second with CLOS, the Common Lisp Object System; and one in PROLOG. Our presentation gives the reader the opportunity to design and build several simple object-based and hybrid applications.

Finally, we show how the algorithms and data structures of AI programming can be built using either LISP or PROLOG. We have covered both languages because they represent two very different but equally important AI programming paradigms: logic programming in PROLOG and functional programming in LISP. We feel that the skills of the programmer depend on a knowledge of all available tools, and each language has its representational strengths and search-based advantages. Indeed, in many modern programming environments the strengths of both languages are available.

The third feature of this book is that we place artificial intelligence within the context of empirical science. We do this in several ways. First, by introducing artificial intelligence in Chapter 1 as part of the long tradition of a science of intelligent systems. This context shows AI, not as some strange abberation from the scientific tradition, but as part of a general quest for knowledge about and understanding of intelligence. Furthermore, our AI programming tools, along with an exploratory programming methodology in Chapter 8, are ideal for exploring our environment. Our tools give us a medium for both understanding and questions. We come to appreciate and know phenomena constructively, that is, by progressive approximation.

Thus we see each design and program as an experiment with nature: we propose a representation, we generate a search algorithm, and then we question the adequacy of our characterization to account for part of the phenomenon of intelligence. And the natural world gives a response to our query. Our experiment can be deconstructed, revised, extended, and run again. Our model can be refined, our understanding extended. We consider artificial intelligence as empirical enquiry in detail in Chapter 16.

New in This Edition

Machine learning, currently a very important research topic in the AI community, is the first major addition to this edition. The ability to learn must be part of any system that would claim to possess general intelligence. Learning is also an important component of practical AI applications such as expert systems. The learning models presented in Chapter 12 include explicitly represented knowledge where information is encoded in a symbol system and learning takes place through algorithmic manipulation, or search, of these structures. We also present the sub-symbolic approach to learning. In a neural net, for instance, information is implicit in the organization and weights on a set of connected processors, and learning is a rearrangement and modification of the overall structure of the system. We also introduce genetic algorithms where learning is cast as an evolutionary and adaptive process. We compare and contrast the directions and results of each approach to machine learning and develop learning algorithms first in pseudocode and then in LISP and/or PROLOG.

Our second major addition is object-oriented design with CLOS, the Common Lisp Object System. CLOS is now the ANSI standard for object based design in Common LISP. We show the power of CLOS for building object systems, and in Chapter 15 we develop a simulation for a heating system that can be easily extended by the reader.

We have also extended the presentation of the other applications of the book. After presenting the knowledge representations for semantic meaning of natural language in Chapter 9, we discuss the integration of syntax and semantics in the implementation programs of Chapter 10. We design and build context-free, context-sensitive, and a recursive descent semantic net parser in Chapter 13. Other application areas explored in the text include planning (Chapter 5) and automated reasoning (Chapter 11). In addition to these traditional AI application areas, we briefly examine the role of AI in understanding human intelligence through a treatment of cognitive science (Chapter 16).

The Contents

Chapter 1 introduces artificial intelligence, beginning with a brief history of attempts to understand mind and intelligence in philosophy, psychology, and other areas of research. In a very important sense, AI is an old science, tracing its roots back at least to Aristotle. An appreciation of this background is essential for an understanding of the issues addressed in modern research. We also present an overview of some of the important application areas in AI. Our goal in Chapter 1 is to provide both background and a motivation for the theory and applications that follow.

Chapters 2, 3, 4, and 5 (Part II) introduce the research tools for AI problem solving. These include the predicate calculus to describe the essential features of a domain (Chapter 2), search to reason about these descriptions (Chapter 3) and the algorithms and data structures used to implement search. In Chapters 4 and 5, we discuss the essential role of heuristics in focusing and constraining search based problem solving. We also present a number of architectures, including the blackboard and production system, for building these search algorithms.

Part III presents AI languages. These languages are first compared to each other and to traditional programming languages to give an appreciation of the AI approach to problem solving. Chapter 6 covers PROLOG, and Chapter 7, LISP. We demonstrate these languages as tools for AI problem solving by building on the search and representation techniques of the earlier chapters, including breadth-first, depth-first and best-first search algorithms. We implement these search techniques in a problem-independent fashion so they may later be extended to form shells for search in rule based expert systems, semantic net and frame systems, as well as in other applications.

Chapters 8, 9, 10, 11, and 12 make up Part IV of the text: representations for knowledge-based systems. In Chapter 8 we present the rule-based expert system. This model for problem solving is a natural evolution of the material in the first five chapters: using a production system of predicate calculus expressions to orchestrate a graph search. Both data-driven and goal-driven search are presented in this context and the role of heuristics is demonstrated. We also discuss the unique problems encountered in applying expert systems. Examples are taken from the Stanford University research, including presentations of MYCIN and Teiresias.

Chapters 9 and 10 present AI techniques for modeling semantic meaning, with a particular focus on natural langauge understanding. We begin with a discussion of semantic networks and extend this model to include conceptual dependency theory, conceptual graphs, frames, and scripts. Class hierarchies and inheritance are important representation tools; we discuss both the benefits and difficulties of implementing inheritance systems for realistic taxonomies. This material is strengthened by an in-depth examination of a particular formalism, conceptual graphs. This discussion emphasizes the epistemological issues involved in representing knowledge and shows how these issues are addressed in a modern representation language. In Chapter 10, we also show how conceptual graphs can be used to implement a natural language data base front end.

Theorem proving, often referred to as automated reasoning, is one of the oldest areas of AI research. In Chapter 11, we discuss the first programs in this area, including the Logic Theorist and the General Problem Solver. The primary focus of the chapter is binary resolution proof procedures, especially resolution refutations. More advanced inferencing with hyper-resolution and paramodulation is also discussed.

In Chapter 12 we present a detailed look at algorithms for machine learning, a fruitful area of research spawning a number of different problems and solution approaches. The learning algorithms vary in their goals, the training data considered, the learning strategies, and the knowledge representations they employ. The symbol-based learning includes induction, concept learning, version space search, and ID3. The role of inductive bias is considered, as well as generalizations from patterns of data, and the effective use of knowledge to learn from a single example with explanation-based learning. Category learning, or conceptual clustering, is presented with unsupervised learning. We also present subsymbolic learning with genetic algorithms and neural nets. We take care to compare and contrast these diverse approaches to machine learning.

Part V, Chapters 13, 14, and 15, presents advanced AI programming in PROLOG and LISP. Here we discuss techniques for implementing the knowledge representation and problem-solving algorithms of Part IV. A major feature of these chapters is the implementation of expert system shells in both LISP and PROLOG. These shells include certainty measures, user queries, and complete explanation facilities. They illustrate the major architectural features of expert system shells and provide a useful tool for building such systems. We also implement the algorithms from Chapter 12 in machine learning, with several algorithms presented. Finally, we discuss the implementation of inheritance in frame and network representations. All three chapters discuss the formal underpinning of each language: resolution refutation systems for PROLOG and functional programming for LISP.

In Chapter 15, we discuss frame- or object-based design, showing how object-oriented techniques are used both for organizing traditional programs and for developing knowledge-based systems. We then give examples of the techniques used to implement object-oriented programming in both LISP and PROLOG. Finally, the chapter discusses the integration of rule- and frame-based approaches in hybrid knowledge engineering environments.

The final chapter, 16, serves as an epilogue for the text. It introduces the discipline of cognitive science, addresses contemporary challenges to AI, discusses AI's current limitations, and examines what we feel is its exciting future.

Using This Book

Artificial intelligence is a big field; consequently, this is a big book. Although it would require more than a single semester to cover all of the material in the text, we have designed it so that a number of paths may be taken through the material. By selecting subsets of the material, we have used this text for single semester and full year (two semester) courses.

Benjamin/Cummings (390 Bridge Parkway, Redwood City CA 94065) will provide an instructor's manual for this text. It includes suggestions for teaching topics, selected figures and formatted algorithms that can be used for making view graphs, and a selection of worked out exercises. The instructor's manual also suggests some paths through the book, depending on time allowed and topics chosen. A disk containing the programming examples is available from the publisher. This disk contains all the PROLOG and LISP code in the book as well as a public domain C-PROLOG interpreter.

We assume that most students will have had introductory courses in discrete mathematics, including predicate calculus and graph theory. If this is not true the instructor should spend more time on these concepts in the sections at the beginning of the text (2.1, 3.1). We also assume that students have had courses in data structures including trees, graphs, and recursion-based search using stacks, queues, and priority queues. If they have not, they should spend more time on the beginning sections of Chapters 3, 4, and 5.

The algorithms are described using a Pascal-like pseudo code. This notation uses the control structures of Pascal along with English descriptions of the tests and operations. We have added two useful constructs to the Pascal control structures. The first is a modified case statement that, rather than comparing the value of a variable with constant case labels, as in standard Pascal, lets each item be labeled with an arbitrary boolean test. The case evaluates these tests in order until one of them is true and then performs the associated action; all other actions are ignored. Those familiar with LISP will note that this has the same semantics as the LISP cond statement.

The other addition to the language is a return statement which takes one argument and can appear anywhere within a procedure or function. When the return is encountered, it causes the program to immediately exit the function, returning its argument as a result. Other than these modifications we used Pascal structure, with a reliance on the English descriptions, to make the algorithms clear.

Acknowledgments

First we would like to thank our reviewers, whose comments often suggested important additions of material and focus. These include Dennis Bahler, Skona Brittain, John Donald, Sarah Douglas, Ray Mooney, Bruce Porter, Jude Shavlik, Carl Stern, Marco Valtorta, and Bob Veroff. Carl Stern, a colleague at the University of New Mexico, has been especially helpful in the technical editing of this book. Mike Delleney, Jim Skinner, Steve Verzi, and numerous others participated in using and refining the code. We thank especially a decade of students who used this text in its preliminary stages and its first edition for their help in expanding its horizons, as well as in removing its typos and bugs.

We wish to thank Thomas Barrow, internationally recognized artist and University of New Mexico Professor of Art, who created the six photograms especially for this book after reading an early draft of the manuscript.

We would also like to thank Vivian McDougal, Lisa Moller, Megan Rundel, and Mary Tudor at Benjamin/Cummings for their work on the second edition of this text.

In a number of places, we have used figures or quotes from the work of other authors. We would like to thank the authors and publishers for their permission to use this material. These contributions are listed at the end of the text.

Artificial intelligence is an exciting and oftentimes rewarding discipline; may you enjoy your study as you come to appreciate its power and challenges.

George F. Luger
William A. Stubblefield
1 July 1992

TABLE OF CONTENTS

PART II
ARTIFICIAL INTELLIGENCE AS REPRESENTATION AND SEARCH   29

2   THE PREDICATE CALCULUS   41

3   STRUCTURES AND STRATEGIES FOR STATE SPACE SEARCH   75

PART III
LANGUAGES FOR AI PROBLEM SOLVING   195

6   AN INTRODUCTION TO PROLOG   210

PART IV
REPRESENTATIONS FOR KNOWLEDGE-BASED SYSTEMS   303

8   RULE-BASED EXPERT SYSTEMS   308

PART V
ADVANCED AI PROGRAMMING TECHNIQUES   535

15   Objects, Messages, and Hybrid Expert System Design   638

ARTIFICIAL INTELLIGENCE
Structures and Strategies for Complex Problem Solving
Second Edition

PART I

ARTIFICIAL INTELLIGENCE: ITS ROOTS AND SCOPE

Everything must have a beginning, to speak in Sanchean phrase; and that beginning must be linked to something that went before. The Hindus give the world an elephant to support it, but they make the elephant stand upon a tortoise. Invention, it must be humbly admitted, does not consist in creating out of void, but out of chaos; the materials must, in the first place, be afforded. . . .

—MARY SHELLEY, *Frankenstein*

Artificial Intelligence—An Attempted Definition

Artificial intelligence (AI) may be defined as the branch of computer science that is concerned with the automation of intelligent behavior. This definition is particularly appropriate to this text in that it emphasizes our conviction that AI is a part of computer science and, as such, must be based on sound theoretical and applied principles of that field. These principles include the data structures used in knowledge representation, the algorithms needed to apply that knowledge, and the languages and programming techniques used in their implementation.

However, this definition suffers from the fact that intelligence itself is not very well defined or understood. Although most of us are certain that we know intelligent behavior when we see it, it is doubtful that anyone could come close to defining intelligence in a way that would be specific enough to help in the evaluation of a supposedly intelligent computer program, while still capturing the vitality and complexity of the human mind.

Thus the problem of defining artificial intelligence becomes one of defining intelligence itself: is intelligence a single faculty, or is it just a name for a collection of distinct and unrelated abilities? To what extent is intelligence learned as opposed to having an a priori existence? Exactly what does happen when learning occurs? What is creativity? What is intuition? Can intelligence be inferred from observable behavior, or does it require evidence of a particular internal mechanism? How is knowledge represented in the nerve tissue of a living being, and what lessons does this have for the design of intelligent

1

machines? What is self-awareness, and what role does it play in intelligence? Is it necessary to pattern an intelligent computer program after what is known about human intelligence, or is a strict "engineering" approach to the problem sufficient? Is it even possible to achieve intelligence on a computer, or does an intelligent entity require the richness of sensation and experience that might be found only in a biological existence?

These are all unanswered questions, and all of them have helped to shape the problems and solution methodologies that constitute the core of modern AI. In fact, part of the appeal of artificial intelligence is that it offers a unique and powerful tool for exploring exactly these questions. AI offers a medium and a test-bed for theories of intelligence: such theories may be stated in the language of computer programs and consequently verified through the execution of these programs on an actual computer.

For these reasons, our initial definition of artificial intelligence seems to fall short of unambiguously defining the field. If anything, it has only led to further questions and the paradoxical notion of a field of study whose major goals include its own definition. But this difficulty in arriving at a precise definition of AI is entirely appropriate. Artificial intelligence is still a young discipline, and its structure, concerns, and methods are less clearly defined than those of a more mature science such as physics.

Artificial intelligence has always been more concerned with expanding the boundaries of computer science than with defining those borders. Keeping this exploration grounded in sound theoretical principles is one of the challenges facing AI researchers in general and this text in particular.

We need to summarize the major questions and assumptions that dominate the field of artificial intelligence to provide background and motivation for the methodologies presented in this text. This goal is better met with the following recursive definition: *artificial intelligence is the collection of problems and methodologies studied by artificial intelligence researchers.* This definition may seem silly and meaningless, but it makes an important point: artificial intelligence, like every science, is a human endeavor and may best be understood in that context.

There are reasons that any science, AI included, concerns itself with a certain set of problems and develops a particular body of techniques for approaching these problems. A short history of artificial intelligence and the people and assumptions that have shaped it will explain why a certain set of questions have come to dominate the field and why the methods discussed in this text have been taken for their solution.

AI: HISTORY AND APPLICATIONS

Hear the rest, and you will marvel even more at the crafts and resources I have contrived. Greatest was this: in the former times if a man fell sick he had no defense against the sickness, neither healing food nor drink, nor unguent; but through the lack of drugs men wasted away, until I showed them the blending of mild simples wherewith they drive out all manner of diseases. . . .

It was I who made visible to men's eyes the flaming signs of the sky that were before dim. So much for these. Beneath the earth, man's hidden blessing, copper, iron, silver, and gold—will anyone claim to have discovered these before I did? No one, I am very sure, who wants to speak truly and to the purpose. One brief word will tell the whole story: all arts that mortals have come from Prometheus.

—AESCHYLUS, *Prometheus Bound*

1.1 From Eden to ENIAC: Attitudes toward Intelligence, Knowledge, and Human Artifice

Prometheus speaks of the fruits of his transgression against the gods of Olympus: his purpose was not merely to steal fire for the human race but also to enlighten humanity through the gift of intelligence or *nous*: the "rational mind." This intelligence forms the foundation for all of human technology and ultimately all human civilization. The work of the classical Greek dramatist illustrates a deep and ancient awareness of the extraordinary power of knowledge. Artificial intelligence, in its very direct concern for Prometheus's gift, has been applied to all the areas of his legacy—medicine, psychology, biology, astronomy, geology—and many areas of scientific endeavor that Aeschylus could not have imagined.

Though Prometheus's action freed humanity from the sickness of ignorance, it also earned him the wrath of Zeus. Outraged over this theft of knowledge that previously belonged only to the gods of Olympus, Zeus commanded that Prometheus be chained to a barren rock to suffer the ravages of the elements for eternity. The notion that human efforts to gain knowledge constitute a transgression against the laws of God or nature is deeply ingrained in Western thought. It is the basis of the story of Eden and appears in the work of Dante and Milton. Both Shakespeare and the ancient Greek tragedians portrayed intellectual ambition as the cause of disaster. The belief that the desire for knowledge must ultimately lead to disaster has persisted throughout history, enduring the Renaissance, the Age of Enlightenment, and even the scientific and philosophical advances of the nineteenth and twentieth centuries. Thus, we should not be surprised that artificial intelligence inspires so much controversy in both academic and popular circles.

Indeed, rather than dispelling this ancient fear of the consequences of intellectual ambition, modern technology has only made those consequences seem likely, even imminent. The legends of Prometheus, Eve, and Faustus have been retold in the language of technological society. In her introduction to *Frankenstein* (subtitled, interestingly enough, *The Modern Prometheus*), Mary Shelley writes:

> Many and long were the conversations between Lord Byron and Shelley to which I was a devout and silent listener. During one of these, various philosophical doctrines were discussed, and among others the nature of the principle of life, and whether there was any probability of its ever being discovered and communicated. They talked of the experiments of Dr. Darwin (I speak not of what the doctor really did or said that he did, but, as more to my purpose, of what was then spoken of as having been done by him), who preserved a piece of vermicelli in a glass case till by some extraordinary means it began to move with a voluntary motion. Not thus, after all, would life be given. Perhaps a corpse would be reanimated; galvanism had given token of such things: perhaps the component parts of a creature might be manufactured, brought together, and endued with vital warmth.

Shelley shows us the extent to which scientific advances such as the work of Darwin and the discovery of electricity had convinced even nonscientists that the workings of nature were not divine secrets, but could be broken down and understood systematically. Frankenstein's monster is not the product of shamanistic incantations or unspeakable transactions with the underworld: it is assembled from separately "manufactured" components and infused with the vital force of electricity. Although nineteenth-century science was inadequate to realize the goal of understanding and creating a fully intelligent agent, it affirmed the notion that the mysteries of life and intellect might be brought into the light of scientific analysis.

1.1.1 Historical Foundations

By the time Mary Shelley finally and perhaps irrevocably joined modern science with the Promethean myth, the philosophical foundations of modern work in artificial intelligence had been developing for several thousand years. Although the moral and cultural issues raised by artificial intelligence are both interesting and important, our introduction is more properly concerned with AI's intellectual heritage. The logical starting point for such a history is the genius of Aristotle, or, as Dante refers to him, "the master of those who know." Aristotle wove together the insights, wonders, and fears of the early Greek tradition with the careful analysis and disciplined thought that were to become the standard for more modern science.

For Aristotle, the most fascinating aspect of nature was change. In his *Physics*, he defined his "philosophy of nature" as the "study of things that change." He distinguished between the "matter" and "form" of things: a sculpture is fashioned from the "material" bronze and has the "form" of a human. Change occurs when the bronze is molded to a new form. The matter/form distinction provides a philosophical basis for modern notions such as symbolic computing and data abstraction. In computing (even with numbers) we are manipulating patterns that are the forms of electromagnetic material, with the changes of form of this material representing aspects of the solution process. Abstracting the form from the medium of its representation not only allows these forms to be manipulated computationally but also provides the promise of a theory of data structures, the heart of modern computer science.

In his *Metaphysics* (located just after, *meta*, the *Physics* in his writing), Aristotle developed a science of things that never change, including his cosmology and theology. More relevant to artificial intelligence, however, was Aristotle's epistemology or science of knowing, discussed in his *Logic*. Aristotle referred to his logic as the "instrument" (*organon*), because he felt that the study of thought itself was at the basis of all knowledge. In his *Logic*, he investigated whether certain propositions can be said to be "true" because they are related to other things that are known to be true. Thus if we know that "all men are mortal" and that "Socrates is a man," then we can conclude that "Socrates is mortal." This argument is an example of what Aristotle referred to as a syllogism using the deductive form *modus ponens*. Although the formal axiomatization of reasoning needed another two thousand years for its full flowering in the works of Gottlob Frege, Bertrand Russell, Kurt Gödel, Alan Turing, Alfred Tarski, and others, its roots may be traced to Aristotle.

Renaissance thought, building on the Greek tradition, initiated the evolution of a different and powerful way of thinking about humanity and its relation to the natural world. Empiricism began to replace mysticism as a means of understanding nature. Clocks and, eventually, factory schedules superseded the rhythms of nature for thousands of city dwellers. Most of the modern social and physical sciences found their origin in the notion that processes, whether natural or artificial, could be mathematically analyzed and understood. In particular, scientists and philosophers realized that thought itself, the way that knowledge was represented and manipulated in the human mind, was a difficult but essential subject for scientific study. Efforts to understand the nature of intelligent thought go back much further than the digital computer, and even so modern a science as AI has much to gain from these centuries of philosophical activity.

Perhaps the major event in the development of the modern world view was the Copernican revolution, the replacement of the ancient Earth-centered model of the universe with the idea that the Earth and other planets actually rotate around the sun. After centuries of an "obvious" order, in which the scientific explanation of the nature of the cosmos was consistent with the teachings of religion and common sense, a drastically different and not at all obvious model was proposed to explain the motions of heavenly bodies. For perhaps the first time, *our ideas about the world were seen as fundamentally distinct from its appearance.* This split between the human mind and its surrounding reality, between ideas about things and things themselves, is essential to the modern study of the mind and its organization. This breach was widened by the writings of Galileo, whose scientific observations further contradicted the "obvious" truths about the natural world and whose development of mathematics as a tool for describing that world emphasized the distinction between the world and our ideas about it. It is out of this breach that the modern notion of the mind evolved: introspection became a common motif in literature, philosophers began to study epistemology and mathematics, and the systematic application of the scientific method rivaled the senses as tools for understanding the world.

Although the seventeenth and eighteenth centuries saw a great deal of work in epistemology and related fields, here we have space only to discuss the work of René Descartes. Descartes is a central figure in the development of the modern notion of thought and the mind. In his famous *Meditations*, Descartes attempted to find a basis for reality purely through cognitive introspection. Systematically rejecting the input of his senses as untrustworthy, Descartes was forced to doubt even the existence of the physical world and was left with only the reality of thought; even his own existence had to be justified in terms of thought: "Cogito ergo sum" (I think, therefore I am). After he established his own existence purely as a thinking entity, Descartes inferred the existence of God as an essential creator and ultimately reasserted the reality of the physical universe as the necessary creation of a benign God.

We can make two interesting observations here: first, the schism between the mind and the physical world had become so complete that the process of thinking could be discussed in isolation from any specific sensory input or worldly subject matter; second, the connection between mind and the physical world was so tenuous that it required the intervention of a benign God to allow reliable knowledge of the physical world. This view of the duality between the mind and the physical world underlies all of Descartes's thought, including his development of analytic geometry. How else could he have unified such a seemingly worldly branch of mathematics as geometry with such an abstract mathematical framework as algebra?

Why have we included this philosophical discussion in a text on artificial intelligence? There are two consequences of this analysis that are essential to the enterprise of AI:

1. By finally separating the mind and the physical world, Descartes and related thinkers established that the structure of ideas about the world was not necessarily the same as the structure of their subject matter. This underlies the methodology of the field of AI, along with the fields of epistemology, psychology, much of higher mathematics, and most of modern literature: mental processes had an existence of their own, obeyed their own laws, and could be studied in and of themselves.

2. Once the mind and the body were separated, philosophers found it necessary to find a way to reconnect the two, because some kind of interaction between the mental and the physical is essential for human existence.

Although millions of words have been written on the *mind-body problem*, and numerous solutions proposed, no one has successfully explained the obvious interactions between mental states and physical actions while affirming a fundamental difference between them. The most widely accepted response to this problem, and the one that provides an essential foundation for the study of AI, holds that the mind and the body are not fundamentally different entities at all. In this view, mental processes are indeed achieved by physical systems such as brains (or computers). Mental processes, like physical processes, can ultimately be characterized through formal mathematics. Or, as stated by the Scots philosopher David Hume, "Cognition is computation."

1.1.2 The Development of Logic

Once thinking had come to be regarded as a form of computation, its formalization and eventual mechanization were logical next steps. In the seventeenth century, Gottfried Wilhelm von Leibniz introduced the first system of formal logic and constructed machines for automating calculation (Leibniz 1887). Euler, in the eighteenth century, with his analysis of the "connectedness" of the bridges joining the riverbanks and islands of the city of Königsberg (see the introduction to Chapter 3), introduced the study of representations that abstractly capture the structure of relationships in the world (Euler 1735).

The formalization of graph theory also afforded the possibility of *state space search*, a major conceptual tool of artificial intelligence. This modern model of problem solving, based on Euler's graphs, looks for a solution by systematically searching through the various situations (states) of a problem. These situations are connected by the legal moves of a game or the inference rules of an expert reasoning system. In either case they form a graph of interconnected stages in a solution process. Searching this graph can construct the succession of steps that leads to a solution (Section 1.3 and Chapter 3). It is this philosophical heritage that Charles Babbage, Ada Lovelace, Gottlob Frege, George Boole, Bertrand Russell, and other Victorian and modern thinkers built upon to develop the science of computation.

As one of the originators of the science of operations research, as well as the designer of the first programmable mechanical computing machines, Charles Babbage is arguably the earliest practitioner of artificial intelligence (Morrison and Morrison 1961). Babbage's "difference engine" was a special-purpose machine for computing the values of certain polynomial functions and was the forerunner of his "analytical engine." The analytical engine, designed but not successfully constructed during Babbage's lifetime, was a general-purpose programmable computing machine that presaged many of the architectural assumptions underlying the modern computer.

In describing the analytical engine, Ada Lovelace, Babbage's friend, supporter, and collaborator, said:

> We may say most aptly that the Analytical Engine weaves algebraical patterns just as the Jacquard loom weaves flowers and leaves. Here, it seems to us, resides much more of originality than the difference engine can be fairly entitled to claim.

Babbage's inspiration was his desire to apply the technology of his day to liberate humans from the drudgery of arithmetic calculation. In this sentiment, as well as his conception of his computers as mechanical devices, Babbage was thinking in purely nineteenth-century terms. His analytical engine, however, included many modern notions, such as the separation of memory and processor (the "store" and the "mill" in Babbage's terms), the concept of a digital rather than analog machine, and programmability based on the execution of a series of operations encoded on punched pasteboard cards. The most striking feature of Ada Lovelace's description, and of Babbage's work in general, is its treatment of the "pattern" of an intellectual activity as an entity that may be studied, characterized, and finally implemented mechanically without concern for the particular values that are finally passed through the "mill" of the calculating machine. This is an implementation of the "abstraction and manipulation of form" first described by Aristotle.

The goal of creating a formal language for thought also appears in the work of George Boole, another nineteenth-century mathematician whose work must be included in any discussion of the roots of artificial intelligence (Boole 1847, 1854). Although he made contributions to a number of areas of mathematics, his best known work was in the mathematical formalization of the laws of logic, an accomplishment that forms the very heart of modern computer science. Though the role of Boolean algebra in the design of logic circuitry is well known, Boole's own goals in developing his system seem closer to those of contemporary AI researchers. In the first chapter of *An Investigation of the Laws of Thought, on which are founded the Mathematical Theories of Logic and Probabilities*, Boole described his goals as

> to investigate the fundamental laws of those operations of the mind by which reasoning is performed: to give expression to them in the symbolical language of a Calculus, and upon this foundation to establish the science of logic and instruct its method; . . . and finally to collect from the various elements of truth brought to view in the course of these inquiries some probable intimations concerning the nature and constitution of the human mind.

The greatness of Boole's accomplishment is in the extraordinary power and simplicity of the system he devised: three operations, "AND" (denoted by $*$ or $\wedge$), "OR" (denoted by $+$ or $\vee$), and "NOT" (denoted by $\neg$), formed the heart of his logical calculus. These operations have remained the basis for all subsequent developments in formal logic, including the design of modern computers. While keeping the meaning of these symbols nearly identical to the corresponding algebraic operations, Boole noted that "the Symbols of logic are further subject to a special law, to which the symbols of quantity, as such, are not subject." This law states that for any X, an element in the algebra, $X*X=X$ (or that once something is known to be true, repetition cannot augment that knowledge). This led to the characteristic restriction of Boolean values to the only two numbers that may satisfy this equation: 1 and 0. The standard definitions of Boolean multiplication (AND) and addition (OR) follow from this insight. Boole's system not only provided the basis of binary arithmetic but also demonstrated that an extremely simple formal system was adequate to capture the full power of logic. This assumption and the system Boole developed to demonstrate it form the basis of all modern efforts to formalize logic, from Russell and Whitehead's *Principia Mathematica* (Whitehead and Russell 1950), through the work of Turing and Gödel, up to modern automated reasoning systems.

Gottlob Frege, in his *Foundations of Arithmetic* (Frege 1879, 1884), created a mathematical specification language for describing the basis of arithmetic in a clear and precise fashion. With this language Frege formalized many of the issues first addressed by Aristotle's *Logic*. Frege's language, now called the *first-order predicate calculus*, offers a tool for describing the propositions and truth value assignments that make up the elements of mathematical reasoning and describes the axiomatic basis of "meaning" for these expressions. The formal system of the predicate calculus, which includes predicate symbols, a theory of functions, and quantified variables, was intended to be a language for describing mathematics and its philosophical foundations. It also plays a fundamental role in creating a theory of representation for artificial intelligence (Chapter 2). The first-order predicate calculus offers the tools necessary for automating reasoning: a language for expressions, a theory for assumptions related to the meaning of expressions, and a logically sound calculus for inferring new true expressions.

Russell and Whitehead's work (Whitehead and Russell, 1950) is particularly important to the foundations of AI, in that their stated goal was to derive the whole of mathematics through formal operations on a collection of axioms. Although many mathematical systems have been constructed from basic axioms, what is interesting is Russell and Whitehead's commitment to mathematics as a purely formal system. This meant that axioms and theorems would be treated solely as strings of characters: proofs would proceed solely through the application of well-defined rules for manipulating these strings. There would be no reliance on intuition or the meaning of theorems as a basis for proofs. Every step of a proof followed from the strict application of formal (syntactic) rules to either axioms or previously proven theorems, even where traditional proofs might regard such a step as "obvious." What "meaning" the theorems and axioms of the system might have in relation to the world would be independent of their logical derivations. This treatment of mathematical reasoning in purely formal (and hence mechanical) terms provided an essential basis for its automation on physical computers. The logical syntax and formal rules of inference developed by Russell and Whitehead are still a basis for automatic theorem-proving systems as well as for the theoretical foundations of artificial intelligence.

Alfred Tarski is another mathematician whose work is essential to the foundations of AI. Tarski created a *theory of reference* wherein the *well-formed formulae* of Frege or Russell and Whitehead can be said to refer, in a precise fashion, to the physical world (Tarski 1944, 1956). This insight underlies most theories of formal semantics. In his paper "The semantic conception of truth and the foundation of semantics," Tarski describes his theory of reference and truth value relationships. Modern computer scientists, especially Scott, Strachey, Burstall (Burstall and Darlington 1977), and Plotkin have related this theory of semantics to programming languages and other specifications for computing.

Although in the eighteenth, nineteenth, and early twentieth centuries the formalization of science and mathematics created the intellectual prerequisite for the study of artificial intelligence, it was not until the twentieth century and the introduction of the digital computer that AI became a viable scientific discipline. By the end of the 1940s electronic digital computers had demonstrated their potential to provide the memory and processing power required by intelligent programs. It was now possible to implement formal reasoning systems on a computer and empirically test their sufficiency for exhibiting intelligence. An essential component of the science of artificial intelligence is this commitment to digital computers as the vehicle of choice for creating and testing theories of intelligence.

Digital computers are not merely a vehicle for testing theories of intelligence. Their architecture also suggests a specific paradigm for such theories: intelligence is a form of information processing. The notion of search as a problem-solving methodology, for example, owes more to the sequential nature of computer operation than it does to any biological model of intelligence. Most AI programs represent knowledge in some formal language that is then manipulated by algorithms, honoring the separation of data and program fundamental to the von Neumann style of computing. Formal logic has emerged as the lingua franca of AI research, whereas graph theory plays an indispensable role in the analysis of problem spaces as well as providing a basis for semantic networks and similar models of semantic meaning. These techniques and formalisms are discussed in detail throughout the body of this text; we mention them here to emphasize the symbiotic relationship between the digital computer and the theoretical underpinnings of artificial intelligence.

We often forget that the tools we create for our own purposes tend to shape our conception of the world through their structure and limitations. Although seemingly restrictive, this interaction is an essential aspect of the evolution of human knowledge: a tool (and scientific theories are ultimately only tools) is developed to solve a particular problem. As it is used and refined, the tool itself seems to suggest other applications, leading to new questions and, ultimately, the development of new tools.

1.1.3   The Turing Test

One of the earliest papers to address the question of machine intelligence specifically in relation to the modern digital computer was written in 1950 by the British mathematician Alan Turing. "Computing machinery and intelligence" (Turing 1950) is still timely in both its assessment of the arguments against the possibility of creating an intelligent computing machine and its answers to those arguments. Turing, known mainly for his contributions to the theory of computability, considered the question of whether or not a machine could actually be made to think. Noting that the fundamental ambiguities in the question itself (what is thinking? what is a machine?) precluded any rational answer, he proposed that the question of intelligence be replaced by a more clearly defined empirical test.

The Turing test measures the performance of an allegedly intelligent machine against that of a human being, arguably the best and only standard for intelligent behavior. The test, which Turing called the "imitation game," places the machine and a human counterpart in rooms apart from a second human being, referred to as the interrogator (Figure 1.1). The interrogator is not able to see or speak directly to either of them, does not know which entity is actually the machine, and may communicate with them solely by use of a textual device such as a terminal. The interrogator is asked to distinguish the computer from the human being solely on the basis of their answers to questions asked over this device. If the interrogator cannot distinguish the machine from the human, then, Turing argues, the machine may be assumed to be intelligent.

By isolating the interrogator from both the machine and the other human participant, the test ensures that the interrogator will not be biased by the appearance of the machine or any mechanical property of its voice. The interrogator is free, however, to ask any questions, no matter how devious or indirect, in an effort to uncover the computer's identity. For example, the interrogator may ask both subjects to perform a rather involved arithmetic calculation, assuming that the computer will be more likely to get it correct than the human;

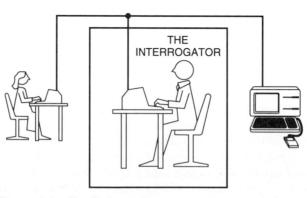

Figure 1.1   The Turing test.

to counter this strategy, the computer will need to know when it should fail to get a correct answer to such problems in order to seem like a human. To discover the human's identity on the basis of emotional nature, the interrogator may ask both subjects to respond to a poem or work of art; this strategy will require that the computer have knowledge concerning the emotional makeup of human beings.

The important features of this test are:

1. It gives us an objective notion of intelligence, i.e., the behavior of a known intelligent being in response to a particular set of questions. This provides a standard for determining intelligence that avoids the inevitable debates over the "true" nature of intelligence.

2. It prevents us from being sidetracked by such confusing and currently unanswerable questions as whether or not the computer uses the appropriate internal processes or whether or not the machine is actually conscious of its actions.

3. It eliminates any bias in favor of living organisms over machine intelligence by forcing the interrogator to focus solely on the content of the answers to questions.

Because of these advantages, the Turing test provides a basis for many of the schemes actually used to evaluate modern AI programs. A program that has potentially achieved intelligence in some area of expertise may be evaluated by comparing its performance on a given set of problems to that of a human expert. This evaluation technique is just a variation of the Turing test: a group of humans are asked to blindly compare the performance of a computer and a human being on a particular set of problems. As we will see, this methodology has become an essential tool in both the development and verification of modern expert systems.

The Turing test, in spite of its intuitive appeal, is vulnerable to a number of justifiable criticisms. One of the most important of these is aimed at its bias toward purely symbolic problem-solving tasks. It does not test abilities requiring perceptual skill or manual dexterity, even though these are important components of human intelligence. Conversely, it is sometimes suggested that the Turing test needlessly constrains machine intelligence to fit a human mold. Perhaps machine intelligence is simply different from human intelligence and trying to evaluate it in human terms is a fundamental mistake. Do we really wish the machine to do mathematics as slowly and inaccurately as the human does it? Shouldn't an intelligent machine capitalize on its own assets, such as an infallible memory, rather than trying to emulate human cognition?

Turing also addressed the feasibility of constructing such a program on a digital computer. By thinking in terms of a specific model of computation (an electronic discrete state computing machine), Turing made some well-founded conjectures concerning the storage capacity, program complexity, and basic design philosophy required for such a system. Finally, he addressed a number of moral, philosophical, and scientific objections to the possibility of constructing such a program in terms of an actual technology. The reader is referred to Turing's article for a perceptive and still relevant summary of the debate over the possibility of intelligent machines.

Two of the objections cited by Turing are worth considering further. "Lady Lovelace's Objection," first stated by Ada Lovelace, argues that computers can only do as they are told and consequently cannot perform original (hence, intelligent) actions. This objection has become a reassuring if somewhat dubious part of contemporary technological folklore.

Expert systems (Section 1.2.3 and Chapter 8), for example, have reached conclusions unanticipated by their designers. Indeed, a number of researchers now feel that human creativity can be expressed in a computer program.

The other related objection, the "Argument from Informality of Behavior," asserts the impossibility of creating a set of rules that will tell an individual exactly what to do under every possible set of circumstances. Certainly, the flexibility that enables a biological intelligence to respond to an infinite range of situations in a reasonable if not necessarily optimal fashion is a hallmark of intelligent behavior. While it is true that the control structure used in most traditional computer programs does not demonstrate great flexibility or originality, it is not true that all programs must be written in this fashion. Indeed, much of the work done in AI over the past 25 years has been in the development of programming languages and models such as production systems, object-based systems, network representations, and others discussed in this text that attempt to overcome this deficiency.

Modern AI programs generally consist of a collection of modular components, or rules of behavior, that do not execute in a rigid order but rather are invoked as needed in response to the structure of a particular problem instance. Pattern matchers allow general rules to apply over a range of instances. These systems have an extreme flexibility that enables relatively small programs to exhibit a vast range of possible behaviors in response to differing problems and situations.

Whether these systems can ultimately be made to exhibit the flexibility shown by a living organism is still the subject of much debate. Nobel laureate Herbert Simon has argued that much of the originality and variability of behavior shown by living creatures is due to the richness of their environment rather than the complexity of their own internal programs. In *The Sciences of the Artificial,* Simon (1981) describes an ant progressing circuitously along an uneven and cluttered stretch of ground. Although the ant's path seems quite complex, Simon argues that the ant's goal is very simple: to return to its colony as quickly as possible. The twists and turns in its path are caused by the obstacles it encounters on its way. Simon concludes that

> An ant, viewed as a behaving system, is quite simple. The apparent complexity of its behavior over time is largely a reflection of the complexity of the environment in which it finds itself.

This idea, if ultimately proved to apply to organisms of higher intelligence as well as to such simple creatures as insects, constitutes a powerful argument that such systems are relatively simple and, consequently, comprehensible. It is interesting to note that if one applies this idea to humans, it becomes a strong argument for the importance of culture in the forming of intelligence. Rather than growing in the dark like mushrooms, intelligence seems to depend on an interaction with a suitably rich environment. Culture is just as important in creating humans as human beings are in creating culture. Rather than denigrating our intellects, this idea emphasizes the miraculous richness and coherence of the cultures that have formed out of the lives of separate human beings.

Our preliminary discussion of the possibility of a theory of automated intelligence is in no way intended to overstate the progress made to date or minimize the work that lies ahead. As we emphasize throughout this text, it is important to be aware of our limitations and to be honest about our successes. For example, there have been only limited results with programs that in any interesting sense can be said to "learn." Our accomplishments in modeling the semantic complexities of a natural language such as English have also been very modest. Even fundamental issues such as organizing knowledge or fully managing the complexity and correctness of very large computer programs (such as large knowledge bases) require considerable further research. Expert systems, though they have achieved marketable engineering successes, still have many limitations in the quality and generality of their reasoning. These include their inability to perform *commonsense reasoning* or to exhibit knowledge of rudimentary physical reality, such as how things change over time.

But we must maintain a reasonable perspective. It is easy to overlook the accomplishments of artificial intelligence when honestly facing the work that remains. In the next section, we establish this perspective through an overview of several areas of artificial intelligence research and development.

1.2 Overview of AI Application Areas

The Analytical Engine has no pretensions whatever to originate anything. It can do whatever we know how to order it to perform.

—ADA BYRON, *Countess of Lovelace*

I'm sorry Dave; I can't let you do that.

—HAL 9000 in *2001: A Space Odyssey* by Arthur C. Clarke

We now return to our stated goal of defining artificial intelligence through an examination of the ambitions and accomplishments of workers in the field. The two most fundamental concerns of AI researchers are *knowledge representation* and *search*. The first of these addresses the problem of capturing in a formal language, i.e., one suitable for computer manipulation, the full range of knowledge required for intelligent behavior. Chapter 2 introduces predicate calculus as a language for describing the properties and relationships among objects in problem domains that require qualitative reasoning rather than arithmetic calculations for their solutions. Later chapters (9, 10, 11, and 15) discuss other languages that artificial intelligence has developed for better capturing the ambiguities and complexities of areas such as commonsense reasoning and natural language understanding.

Search is a problem-solving technique that systematically explores a space of *problem states*, i.e., successive and alternative stages in the problem-solving process. Examples of problem states might include the different board configurations in a game or intermediate steps in a reasoning process. This space of alternative solutions is then searched to find a final answer. Newell and Simon (1976) have argued that this is the essential basis of human problem solving. Indeed, when a chess player examines the effects of different moves or a doctor considers a number of alternative diagnoses, they are searching among alternatives. The implications of this model and techniques for its implementation are discussed in Chapters 3, 4, and 5.

Like most sciences, AI is decomposed into a number of subdisciplines that, while sharing an essential approach to problem solving, have concerned themselves with different applications. In this section we outline several of these major application areas and their contributions to artificial intelligence as a whole.

1.2.1 Game Playing

Much of the early research in state space search was done using common board games such as checkers, chess, and the 16-puzzle. In addition to their inherent intellectual appeal, board games have certain properties that made them ideal subjects for this early work. Most games are played using a well-defined set of rules: this makes it easy to generate the search space and frees the researcher from many of the ambiguities and complexities inherent in less structured problems. The board configurations used in playing these games are easily represented on a computer, requiring none of the complex formalisms needed to capture the semantic subtleties of more complex problem domains. As games can be easily played, testing a game-playing program presents no financial or ethical burden. State space search, the paradigm underlying most game-playing research, is presented in Chapters 3 and 4.

Games can generate extremely large search spaces. These are large and complex enough to require powerful techniques for determining what alternatives to explore in the problem space. These techniques are called *heuristics* and constitute a major area of AI research. A heuristic is a useful but potentially fallible problem-solving strategy, such as checking to make sure that an unresponsive appliance is plugged in before assuming that it is broken or trying to protect your queen from capture in a chess game. Much of what we call intelligence resides in the heuristics used by humans to solve problems.

Because most of us have some experience with these simple games, it is possible to devise and test the effectiveness of our own heuristics. We do not need to find and consult an expert in some esoteric problem area such as medicine or mathematics (chess is an obvious exception to this rule). For these reasons, games provide a rich domain for the study of heuristic search. Chapter 4 introduces heuristics using these simple games; Chapter 8 extends their application to expert systems.

Game-playing programs, in spite of their simplicity, offer their own challenges, including an opponent whose moves may not be reliably anticipated. This presence of the opponent further complicates program design by adding an element of unpredictability and the need to consider psychological as well as tactical factors in game strategy.

1.2.2 Automated Reasoning and Theorem Proving

We could argue that automatic theorem proving is the oldest branch of artificial intelligence, tracing its roots back through Newell and Simon's Logic Theorist (Newell and Simon 1963a) and General Problem Solver (Newell and Simon 1963b) to its origins in Russell and Whitehead's efforts to treat all of mathematics as the purely formal derivation of theorems from basic axioms. In any case, it has certainly been one of the most fruitful branches of the field. Theorem-proving research was responsible for much of the early work in formalizing search algorithms and developing formal representation languages such as predicate calculus (Chapter 2) and the logic programming language PROLOG (Chapters 6 and 13).

Most of the appeal of automated theorem proving lies in the rigor and generality of logic. Because it is a formal system, logic lends itself to automation. A wide variety of problems can be attacked by representing the problem description and relevant background information as logical axioms and treating problem instances as theorems to be proved. This insight is the basis of work in automatic theorem proving and mathematical reasoning systems (Chapter 11).

Unfortunately, early efforts at writing theorem provers failed to develop a system that could consistently solve complicated problems. This was due to the ability of any reasonably complex logical system to generate an infinite number of provable theorems: without powerful techniques (heuristics) to guide their search, automated theorem provers proved large numbers of irrelevant theorems before stumbling onto the correct one. In response to this inefficiency, many argue that purely formal, syntactic methods of guiding search are inherently incapable of handling such a huge space and that the only alternative is to rely on the informal, ad hoc strategies that humans seem to use in solving problems. This is the approach underlying the development of expert systems, and it has proved to be a fruitful one.

Still, the appeal of reasoning based in formal mathematical logic is too strong to ignore. Many important problems such as the design and verification of logic circuits, verification of the correctness of computer programs, and control of complex systems seem to respond to such an approach. In addition, the theorem-proving community has enjoyed success in devising powerful heuristics that rely solely on an evaluation of the syntactic form of a logical expression, reducing the complexity of the search space without resorting to the ad hoc techniques used by human problem solvers.

Another reason for the continued interest in automatic theorem provers is the realization that such a system does not have to be capable of independently solving extremely complex problems without human assistance. Many modern theorem provers function as intelligent assistants, letting humans perform the more demanding tasks of decomposing a large problem into subproblems and devising heuristics for searching the space of possible proofs. The theorem prover then performs the simpler but still demanding task of proving lemmas, verifying smaller conjectures, and completing the formal aspects of a proof outlined by its human associate (Boyer and Moore 1979).

1.2.3 Expert Systems

One major insight gained from early work in problem solving was the importance of domain-specific knowledge. A doctor, for example, is not effective at diagnosing illness solely because she possesses some innate general problem-solving skill; she is effective because she knows a lot about medicine. Similarly, a geologist is effective at discovering mineral deposits because he is able to apply a good deal of theoretical and empirical knowledge about geology to the problem at hand. Expert knowledge is a combination of a theoretical understanding of the problem and a collection of heuristic problem-solving rules that experience has shown to be effective in the domain. Expert systems are constructed by obtaining this knowledge from a human expert and coding it into a form that a computer may apply to similar problems.

This reliance on the knowledge of a human domain expert for the system's problem-solving strategies is a major feature of expert systems. Although some programs are written in which the designer is also the source of the domain knowledge, it is far more typical to see such programs growing out of a collaboration between a domain expert such as a doctor, chemist, geologist, or engineer and a separate artificial intelligence specialist. The domain expert provides the necessary knowledge of the problem domain through a general discussion of her problem-solving methods and by demonstrating those skills on a carefully chosen set of sample problems. The AI specialist, or *knowledge engineer*, as expert systems designers are often known, is responsible for implementing this knowledge in a program that is both effective and seemingly intelligent in its behavior. Once such a program has been written, it is necessary to refine its expertise through a process of giving it example problems to solve, letting the domain expert criticize its behavior, and making any required changes or modifications to the program's knowledge. This process is repeated until the program has achieved the desired level of performance.

One of the earliest systems to exploit domain-specific knowledge in problem solving was DENDRAL, developed at Stanford in the late 1960s (Lindsay et al. 1980). DENDRAL was designed to infer the structure of organic molecules from their chemical formulas and mass spectrographic information about the chemical bonds present in the molecules. Because organic molecules tend to be very large, the number of possible structures for these molecules tends to be huge. DENDRAL addresses the problem of this large search space by applying the heuristic knowledge of expert chemists to the structure elucidation problem. DENDRAL's methods proved remarkably effective, routinely finding the correct structure out of millions of possibilities after only a few trials. The approach has proved so successful that descendants of the system are used in chemical laboratories throughout the country.

Whereas DENDRAL was one of the first programs to effectively use domain-specific knowledge to achieve expert level problem-solving performance, MYCIN established the methodology of contemporary expert systems (Buchanan 1984). MYCIN uses expert medical knowledge to diagnose and prescribe treatment for spinal meningitis and bacterial infections of the blood.

MYCIN, developed at Stanford in the mid-1970s, was one of the first programs to address the problems of reasoning with uncertain or incomplete information. MYCIN provided clear and logical explanations of its reasoning, used a control structure appropriate to the specific problem domain, and identified criteria to reliably evaluate its performance. Many of the expert system development techniques currently in use were first developed in the MYCIN project (Chapter 8).

Other classic expert systems include the PROSPECTOR program for determining the probable location and type of ore deposits based on geological information about a site (Duda et al. 1979a, 1979b), the INTERNIST program for performing diagnosis in the area of internal medicine, the Dipmeter Advisor for interpreting the results of oil well drilling logs (Smith and Baker 1983), and XCON for configuring VAX computers. XCON has been in use since 1981; every VAX sold by Digital Equipment Corporation is now configured by XCON. Numerous other expert systems are currently solving problems in areas such as medicine, education, business, design, and science (Waterman 1986).

It is interesting to note that most expert systems have been written for relatively specialized, expert level domains. These domains are generally well studied and have clearly defined problem-solving strategies. Problems that depend on a more loosely defined notion of "common sense" are much more difficult to solve by these means (Part IV).

In spite of the promise of expert systems, it would be a mistake to overestimate the ability of this technology. Current deficiencies include:

1. Difficulty in capturing "deep" knowledge of the problem domain. MYCIN, for example, lacks any real knowledge of human physiology. It does not know what blood does or the function of the spinal cord. Folklore has it that once, when select-

ing a drug for treatment of meningitis, MYCIN asked whether the patient was pregnant, even though it had been told that the patient was male. Whether this actually occurred or not, it does illustrate the potential narrowness of expert systems.

2. Lack of robustness and flexibility. If humans are presented with a problem instance that they cannot solve immediately, they can generally return to an examination of first principles and come up with some strategy for attacking the problem. Expert systems generally lack this ability.

3. Inability to provide deep explanations. Because expert systems lack deep knowledge of their problem domains, their explanations are generally restricted to a description of the steps they took in finding a solution. They cannot tell "why" a certain approach was taken.

4. Difficulties in verification. Though the correctness of any large computer system is difficult to prove, expert systems are particularly difficult to verify. This is a serious problem, as expert systems technology is being applied to critical applications such as air traffic control, nuclear reactor operations, and weapons systems.

5. Little learning from experience. Current expert systems are handcrafted; once the system is completed, its performance will not improve without further attention from its programmers. This leads to severe doubts about the intelligence of such systems.

In spite of these limitations, expert systems are proving their value in a number of important applications. It is hoped that these limitations will only encourage the student to pursue this important new branch of computer science. Expert systems are a major topic in this text and are discussed in Chapters 5, 8, 13, 14, and 15.

1.2.4 Natural Language Understanding and Semantic Modeling

One of the long-standing goals of artificial intelligence is the creation of programs that are capable of understanding human language. Not only does the ability to understand natural language seem to be one of the most fundamental aspects of human intelligence, but also its successful automation would have an incredible impact on the usability and effectiveness of computers themselves. Much effort has been put into writing programs that understand natural language. Although these programs have achieved success within restricted contexts, systems that can use natural language with the flexibility and generality that characterize human speech are beyond current methodologies.

Understanding natural language involves much more than parsing sentences into their individual parts of speech and looking those words up in a dictionary. Real understanding depends on extensive background knowledge about the domain of discourse and the idioms used in that domain as well as an ability to apply general contextual knowledge to resolve the omissions and ambiguities that are a normal part of human speech.

Consider, for example, the difficulties in carrying on a conversation about baseball with an individual who understands English but knows nothing about the rules, players, or history of the game. Could this person possibly understand the meaning of the sentence: "With none down in the top of the ninth and the go-ahead run at second, the manager called his relief from the bull pen"? Even though all of the words in the sentence may be individually understood, this sentence would be gibberish to even the most intelligent non-baseball fan.

The task of collecting and organizing this background knowledge in such a way that it may be applied to language comprehension forms the major problem in automating natural language understanding. Responding to this need, researchers have developed many of the techniques for structuring semantic meaning used throughout artificial intelligence (Chapters 9 and 10).

Because of the tremendous amounts of knowledge required for understanding natural language, most work is done in well-understood, specialized problem areas. One of the earliest programs to exploit this "micro world" methodology was Winograd's SHRDLU, a natural language system that could "converse" about a simple configuration of blocks of different shapes and colors (Winograd 1973). SHRDLU could answer queries such as "what color block is on the blue cube?" and plan actions such as "move the red pyramid onto the green brick." Problems of this sort, involving the description and manipulation of simple arrangements of blocks, have appeared with surprising frequency in AI research and are known as "blocks world" problems.

In spite of SHRDLU's success in conversing about arrangements of blocks, its methods did not generalize from the blocks world. The representational techniques used in the program were too simple to capture the semantic organization of richer and more complex domains in a useful way. Much of the current work in natural language understanding is devoted to finding representational formalisms that are general enough to be used in a wide range of applications yet adapt themselves well to the specific structure of a given domain. A number of different techniques (most of which are extensions or modifications of *semantic networks*) are explored for this purpose and used in the development of programs that can understand natural language in constrained but interesting knowledge domains. General natural language understanding, however, remains beyond the current state of the art.

1.2.5 Modeling Human Performance

Although much of the above discussion uses human intelligence as a reference point in considering artificial intelligence, it does not follow that programs should pattern themselves after the organization of the human mind. Indeed, many AI programs are engineered to solve some useful problem without regard for their similarities to human mental architecture. Even expert systems, while deriving much of their knowledge from human experts, do not really attempt to simulate human internal mental processes. If performance is the only criterion by which a system will be judged, there may be little reason to attempt to simulate human problem-solving methods; in fact, programs that take nonhuman approaches to solving problems are often more successful than their human counterparts. Still, the design of systems that explicitly model some aspect of human problem solving has been a fertile area of research in both artificial intelligence and psychology.

Human performance modeling, in addition to providing AI with much of its basic methodology, has proved to be a powerful tool for formulating and testing theories of human cognition. The problem-solving methodologies developed by computer scientists have given psychologists a new metaphor for exploring the human mind. Rather than casting theories of cognition in the vague language used in early research or abandoning the problem of describing the inner workings of the human mind entirely (as suggested by the behaviorists), many psychologists have adopted the language and theory of computer science to formulate models of human intelligence. Not only do these techniques provide a new vocabulary for describing human intelligence, but also computer implementations of these theories offer psychologists an opportunity to empirically test, critique, and refine their ideas. Further discussion of the relationship between artificial intelligence and efforts to understand human intelligence is found throughout the text and summarized in Chapter 16.

1.2.6   Planning and Robotics

Planning is an important aspect of the effort to design robots that perform their task with some degree of flexibility and responsiveness to the outside world. Briefly, planning assumes a robot that is capable of performing certain atomic actions. It attempts to find a sequence of those actions that will accomplish some higher-level task such as moving across an obstacle-filled room.

Planning is a difficult problem for a number of reasons, not the least of which is the size of the space of possible sequences of moves. Even an extremely simple robot is capable of generating a vast number of potential move sequences. Imagine, for example, a robot that can move forward, backward, right, or left, and consider how many different ways that robot can possibly move around a room. Assume also that there are obstacles in the room and that the robot must select a path that moves around them in some efficient fashion. Writing a program that can intelligently discover the best path under these circumstances, without being overwhelmed by the huge number of possibilities, requires sophisticated techniques for representing spatial knowledge and controlling search.

One method that human beings use in planning is *hierarchical problem decomposition*. If you are planning a trip to London, you will generally treat the problems of arranging a flight, getting to the airport, making airline connections, and finding ground transportation in London separately, even though they are all part of a bigger overall plan. Each of these may be further decomposed into smaller subproblems such as finding a map of the city, negotiating the subway system, and finding a decent pub. Not only does this approach effectively restrict the size of the space that must be searched, but also allows saving of frequently used subplans for future use.

While humans plan effortlessly, creating a computer program that can do the same is a difficult challenge. A seemingly simple task such as breaking a problem into independent subproblems actually requires sophisticated heuristics and extensive knowledge about the planning domain. Determining what subplans should be saved and how they may be generalized for future use is an equally difficult problem.

A robot that blindly performs a sequence of actions without responding to changes in its environment or being able to detect and correct errors in its own plan could hardly be considered intelligent. Often, a robot will have to formulate a plan based on incomplete information and correct its behavior as it executes the plan. A robot may not have adequate sensors to locate all obstacles in the way of a projected path. Such a robot must begin moving through the room based on what it has "perceived" and correct its path as other obstacles are detected. Organizing plans in a fashion that allows response to environmental conditions is another major problem for planning. We present the elements of planning algorithms in Chapters 5 and 16.

1.2.7 Languages and Environments for AI

Some of the most important by-products of artificial intelligence research are advances in programming languages and software development environments. For a number of reasons, including the sheer size of most AI application programs, the tendency of search algorithms to generate huge spaces, and the difficulty of predicting the behavior of heuristically driven programs, AI programmers have been forced to develop a powerful set of programming methodologies.

Programming environments include knowledge-structuring techniques such as object-oriented programming and expert systems frameworks (these are discussed in Part IV). High-level languages, such as LISP and PROLOG, which strongly support modular development, help manage program size and complexity. Trace packages allow a programmer to reconstruct the execution of a complex algorithm and make it possible to unravel the complexities of heuristically guided search. Without such tools and techniques, it is doubtful that many significant AI systems could have been built.

Many of these techniques are now standard tools for software engineering and have little relationship to the core of AI theory. Others, such as object-oriented programming, are of significant theoretical and practical interest (Chapters 9 and 15).

The languages developed for artificial intelligence programming are intimately bound to the theoretical structure of the field. We cover both LISP and PROLOG in this text and prefer to remain apart from religious debates over the relative merits of these languages. Rather, we adhere to the adage "a good worker knows all the tools." The language chapters (6, 7, 13, 14, and 15) discuss the advantages of each language for specific programming tasks.

1.2.8 Machine Learning

Learning has remained a difficult problem for AI programs, in spite of their success as problem solvers. This shortcoming seems severe, particularly as the ability to learn is one of the most important components of intelligent behavior. An expert system may perform extensive and costly computations to solve a problem. Unlike a human being, however, if it is given the same or a similar problem a second time, it will not remember the solution. It performs the same sequence of computations again. This is true the second, third, fourth, and every time it solves that problem—hardly the behavior of an intelligent problem solver.

Most expert systems are hindered by the inflexibility of their problem-solving strategies and the difficulty of modifying large amounts of code. The obvious solution to these problems is for programs to learn on their own, either from experience, analogy, and examples or by being "told" what to do.

Although learning is a difficult area of research, several programs have been written that suggest that this is not an impossible goal. Perhaps the most striking such program is AM, the Automated Mathematician, designed to discover mathematical laws (Lenat 1977, 1982). Initially given the concepts and axioms of set theory, AM was able to induce such important mathematical concepts as cardinality and integer arithmetic and many of the results of number theory. AM conjectured new theorems by modifying its current knowledge base and used heuristics to pursue the most "interesting" of a number of possible alternatives.

Other influential work includes Patrick Winston's research on the induction of structural concepts such as "arch" from a set of examples in the blocks world (Winston 1975*a*). The ID3 algorithm has proved successful in learning general patterns from specific examples (Quinlan 1986a). Meta-DENDRAL learns rules for interpreting mass spectrographic data in organic chemistry from examples of data on compounds of known structure. Teiresias, an intelligent "front end" for expert systems, converts high-level advice into new rules for its knowledge base (Davis 1982). Hacker devises plans for performing blocks world manipulations through an iterative process of devising a plan, testing it, and correcting any flaws discovered in the candidate plan (Sussman 1975). Work in explanation-based learning has shown the effectiveness of prior knowledge in learning (Mitchell 1986, DeJong 1986).

The success of these and other machine learning programs suggests the existence of a set of general learning principles that will allow the construction of programs with the ability to learn in realistic domains. We discuss machine learning in detail with more complete references in Chapter 12.

1.2.9 Neural Networks or Parallel Distributed Processing (PDP)

Most of the techniques presented in this text use explicitly represented knowledge and carefully designed search algorithms to implement intelligence. A very different approach seeks to build intelligent programs using models that parallel the structure of neurons in the human brain.

A simple schematic of a neuron (Figure 1.2) consists of a cell body that has a number of branched protrusions, called *dendrites*, and a single branch called the *axon*. Dendrites

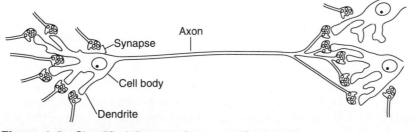

Figure 1.2   Simplified diagram of a neuron (Crick and Asanuma 1986).

receive signals from other neurons. When these combined impulses exceed a certain threshold, the neuron fires and an impulse, or "spike," passes down the axon. Branches at the end of the axon form *synapses* with the dendrites of other neurons. The synapse is the point of contact between neurons; synapses may be either *excitatory* or *inhibitory*. An excitatory synapse adds to the total of signals reaching the neuron; an inhibitory synapse subtracts from this total.

This description of a neuron is excessively simple, but it captures those features that are relevant to neural models of computation. In particular, each computational unit computes some function of its inputs and passes the result along to connected units in the network. Instead of using explicit symbols and operations, the knowledge of the system emerges out of the entire network of neural connections and threshold values.

Neural architectures are appealing as mechanisms for implementing intelligence for a number of reasons. Traditional AI programs tend to be brittle and overly sensitive to noise: rather than degrading gracefully, such programs tend to either be right or fail completely. Human intelligence is much more flexible; we are good at interpreting noisy input, such as recognizing a face in a darkened room from an odd angle or following a single conversation in a noisy party. Even where a human may not be able to solve some problem, we generally can make a reasonable guess as to its solution. Neural architectures, because they capture knowledge in a large number of fine-grained units, seem to have more potential for partially matching noisy and incomplete data.

Neural architectures are also more robust because knowledge is distributed somewhat uniformly around the network. Experience with people who have lost part of their brain from disease or accident has shown that they do not lose specific memories; rather they suffer more general degradations of their mental processes.

Neural architectures also provide a natural model for parallelism, because each neuron is an independent unit. Hillis (1985) has commented on the fact that humans get faster at a task as they acquire more knowledge, while computers tend to slow down. This slowdown is due to the cost of sequentially searching a knowledge base; a massively parallel architecture like the human brain would not suffer from this problem. Finally, something is intrinsically appealing about approaching the problems of intelligence from a neural point of view. After all, the brain achieves intelligence and it does so using a neural architecture.

We present neural networks, along with other models of machine learning, in Chapter 12.

1.2.10   AI and Philosophy

In Section 1.1 we presented the philosophical, mathematical, and sociological roots of artificial intelligence. It is important to realize that modern AI is not just a product of this rich intellectual tradition but also contributes to it.

For example, the questions that Turing posed about intelligent programs also reflect back on our understanding of intelligence itself. What is intelligence, and how may it be described? What is the nature of knowledge? Can knowledge be represented? What is skill? How does knowledge in an application area relate to problem-solving skill in that domain? How does *knowing what* is true, Aristotle's *theoria,* relate to *knowing how* to perform, his *praxis*?

Answers proposed to these questions make up an important part of what AI researchers and designers do. In the scientific sense, AI programs can be viewed as experiments. A design is made concrete in a program and the program is run as an experiment. The program designers observe the results and then redesign and rerun the experiment. In this manner we can determine whether our representations and algorithms are sufficient models of intelligent behavior. Newell and Simon (1976) proposed this approach to scientific understanding in their 1976 Turing Award lecture.

Newell and Simon (1976) also propose a stronger model for intelligence with their physical symbol system hypothesis: *the necessary and sufficient condition for a physical system to exhibit intelligence is that it be a physical symbol system.* What this hypothesis means in practice as well as how it may be criticized we take up in Chapter 16.

A number of AI's application areas also open up deep philosophical issues. In what sense can we say that a computer can understand natural language expressions? To produce or understand a language requires interpretation of symbols. It is not sufficient to be able to say that a string of symbols is well formed. A mechanism for understanding must be able to impute meaning or interpret symbols in context. What is meaning? What is interpretation? In what sense does interpretation require responsibility?

Similar philosophical issues emerge from many AI application areas, whether they be building expert systems to cooperate with human problem solvers, designing computer vision systems, or designing algorithms for machine learning. We look at many of these issues as they come up in the chapters of this book and address the general issue of relevance to philosophy again in Chapter 16.

1.3 Artificial Intelligence—A Summary

We have attempted to define artificial intelligence through discussion of its major areas of research and application. This survey reveals a young and promising field of study whose primary concern is finding an effective way to understand and apply intelligent problem-solving, planning, and communication skills to a wide range of practical problems. In spite of the variety of problems addressed in artificial intelligence research, a number of important features emerge that seem common to all divisions of the field; these include:

1. The use of computers to do symbolic reasoning.

2. A focus on problems that do not respond to algorithmic solutions. This underlies the reliance on heuristic search as an AI problem-solving technique.

3. A concern with problem solving using inexact, missing, or poorly defined information and the use of representational formalisms that enable the programmer to compensate for these problems.

4. An effort to capture and manipulate the significant qualitative features of a situation rather than relying on numeric methods.

5. An attempt to deal with issues of semantic meaning as well as syntactic form.

6. Answers that are neither exact nor optimal, but are in some sense "sufficient." This is a result of the essential reliance on heuristic problem-solving methods in situations where optimal or exact results are either too expensive or not possible.

7. The use of large amounts of domain-specific knowledge in solving problems. This is the basis of expert systems.

8. The use of meta-level knowledge to effect more sophisticated control of problem-solving strategies. Although this is a very difficult problem, addressed in relatively few current systems, it is emerging as an essential area of research.

We hope that this introduction provides some feel for the overall structure and significance of the field of artificial intelligence. We also hope that the brief discussions of such technical issues as search and representation were not excessively cryptic and obscure; they are developed in proper detail throughout the remainder of the text. They were included here to demonstrate their significance in the more general organization of the field.

As we mentioned in the discussion of knowledge representation, objects take on meaning through their relationships with other objects. This is equally true of the facts, theories, and techniques that constitute a field of scientific study. We have intended to give a sense of those interrelationships, so that when the separate technical themes of artificial intelligence are presented, they will find their place in a developing understanding of the overall substance and directions of the field. In writing this text we were guided by an observation made by Gregory Bateson, the psychologist and systems theorist (Bateson 1979):

> Break the pattern which connects the items of learning and you necessarily destroy all quality.

1.4 Epilogue and References

The challenging field of AI reflects some of the oldest concerns of Western civilization in the light of the modern computational model. The notions of rationality, representation, and reason are now under scrutiny as perhaps never before, because we computer scientists demand to understand them algorithmically! At the same time, the political, economic, and ethical situation of our species forces us to confront our responsibility for the effects of our artifices. The interplay between applications and the more humanistic aspirations for much of AI continues to inspire hosts of rich, challenging questions. We hope you will glean from the following chapters both a familiarity with the contemporary concepts and techniques of AI and an appreciation for the timelessness of the problems they address.

Several excellent sources available on the topics raised in this chapter are *Mind Design* (Haugheland 1981), *Artificial Intelligence: The Very Idea* (Haugheland 1985), *Brainstorms* (Dennett 1978), and *Elbow Room* (Dennett 1984). Several of the primary sources are also readily available, including Aristotle's *Physics, Metaphysics,* and *Logic;* papers by Frege; and the writings of Babbage, Boole, and Russell and Whitehead. Turing's papers are also very interesting, especially his discussions of the nature of intelligence and the possibility of designing intelligent programs (Turing 1950). Turing's biography, *Alan Turing: The Enigma* (Hodges 1983), also makes excellent reading.

Computer Power and Human Reason (Weizenbaum 1976) and *Understanding Computers and Cognition* (Winograd and Flores 1986) offer sobering comments on the limitations of and ethical issues in AI. *The Sciences of the Artificial* (Simon 1981) is a positive statement on the possibility of artificial intelligence and its role in society.

The AI applications mentioned in Section 1.2 are intended to introduce the reader to the broad interests of AI researchers and outline many of the important questions under investigation. The *Handbook of Artificial Intelligence* (Barr and Feigenbaum 1989) offers an introduction to each of these areas. Besides the *Handbook* we recommend, for extended treatment of game playing, *Principles of Artificial Intelligence* (Nilsson 1980) and *Heuristics* (Pearl 1984); this is also an important topic in our Chapters 2 through 5. We discuss automated reasoning in Chapters 2, 3, and 11; some of the highlights in the literature of automated reasoning are *Automated Reasoning* (Wos et al. 1984), "Non-resolution theorem proving" (Bledsoe 1977), and *A Computational Logic* (Boyer and Moore 1979).

After reading our Chapters 8 and 15, the reader can get a good feel of the area for expert systems in *Expert Systems: Artificial Intelligence in Business* (Harmon and King 1985), *Building Expert Systems* (Hayes-Roth et al. 1983), and *A Guide to Expert Systems* (Waterman 1986). Natural language understanding is a dynamic field of study; some important points of view are expressed in *Natural Language Understanding* (Allen 1987), *Language as a Cognitive Process* (Winograd 1983), *Inside Computer Understanding* (Schank and Riesbeck 1981), *Computer Models of Thought and Language* (Schank and Colby 1973), and *Grammar, Meaning and the Machine Analysis of Language* (Wilks 1972); an introduction to the field is presented in our Chapters 9 and 10.

Using computers to model human performance, which we present in Chapter 16, is discussed in some depth in *Human Problem Solving* (Newell and Simon 1972), *Computation and Cognition* (Pylyshyn 1984), and "Arguments concerning representations for mental imagery" (Anderson 1978). Planning and robotics (see our Chapters 5 and 13) are well surveyed in Volume 3 of the *Handbook of Artificial Intelligence* (Barr and Feigenbaum 1989).

The subject of AI-oriented languages and environments is explored in Chapters 6, 7, 13, 14, and 15 of this text; see also *Principles of Programming Languages* (MacLennan 1987) and *Smalltalk/V* (Anon. Digitalk 1986). Machine learning is discussed in some detail in Chapter 12; volumes I, II and III of *Machine Learning* (Michalski et al. 1983, 1986; Kodraloff et al. 1989) and the *Journal of Machine Learning* are important sources.

1.5   Exercises

1. Create and justify your own definition of artificial intelligence.

2. Give several other examples of Aristotle's distinction between "matter" and "form." Can you show how your examples might fit into a theory of abstraction?

3. Much traditional Western thought has dwelt on the mind-body relationship. Are the mind and body:

   a. distinct entities somehow interacting, or
   b. is mind an expression of "physical processes," or
   c. is body just an illusion of the rational mind?

   Discuss your thoughts on the mind-body problem and its importance for a theory of artificial intelligence.

4. Criticize Turing's criteria for computer software being "intelligent."

5. Describe your own criteria for computer software to be considered "intelligent."

6. Although computing is a relatively new discipline, philosophers and mathematicians have been thinking about the issues involved in automating problem solving for thousands of years. What is your opinion of the relevance of these philosophical issues to the design of a device for intelligent problem solving? Justify your answer.

7. Given the differences between the architectures of modern computers and that of the human brain, what relevance does research into the physiological structure and function of biological systems have for the engineering of AI programs? Justify your answer.

8. Pick one problem area that you feel would justify the energy required to design an expert system solution. Spell the problem out in some detail. Based on your own intuition, which aspects of this solution would be most difficult to automate?

9. Add two more benefits for expert systems to those already listed in the text. Discuss these in terms of intellectual, social, or financial results.

10. List and discuss two potentially negative effects on society of the development of artificial intelligence techniques.

PART II

ARTIFICIAL INTELLIGENCE AS REPRESENTATION AND SEARCH

All sciences characterize the essential nature of the systems they study. These characterizations are invariably qualitative in nature, for they set the terms with which more detailed knowledge can be developed. . . .

The study of logic and computers has revealed to us that intelligence resides in physical symbol systems. This is computer science's most basic law of qualitative structure. Symbol systems are collections of patterns and processes, the latter being capable of producing, destroying and modifying the former. The most important property of patterns is that they can designate objects, processes or other patterns, and that when they designate processes they can be interpreted. . . .

A second law of qualitative structure for artificial intelligence is that symbol systems solve problems by generating potential solutions and testing them—that is by searching. Solutions are usually sought by creating symbolic expressions and modifying them sequentially until they satisfy the conditions for a solution.

—NEWELL AND SIMON, ACM *Turing Award Lecture, 1976 (Newell and Simon 1976)*

In their Turing Award lecture, Newell and Simon argue that intelligent activity, in either human or machine, is achieved through the use of:

1. Symbol patterns to represent significant aspects of a problem domain.
2. Operations on these patterns to generate potential solutions to problems.
3. Search to select a solution from among these possibilities.

These assumptions form the basis for what is known as the *physical symbol system hypothesis* (Section 16.1). This hypothesis justifies our efforts to build intelligent machines and makes explicit the underlying assumptions of artificial intelligence research.

The physical symbol system hypothesis implicitly distinguishes between the *patterns* formed by an arrangement of symbols and the *medium* used to implement them. If intelligence derives only from the structure of a symbol system, then any medium that successfully implements the correct patterns and processes will achieve intelligence, regardless of whether it is composed of neurons, logic circuits, or Tinkertoys. The possibility of building a machine that will pass the Turing test depends on this distinction. According to the Church-Turing thesis (Machtey and Young 1979), computers are capable of implementing *any* effectively described symbolic process. It follows that a properly programmed digital computer will achieve intelligence.

The physical symbol system hypothesis also outlines the major foci of AI research and application development: defining the symbol structures and operations necessary for intelligent problem solving and developing strategies to efficiently and correctly search the potential solutions generated by these structures and operations. These are the interrelated issues of *knowledge representation* and *search*; together, they are at the heart of modern research in artificial intelligence.

The physical symbol system hypothesis is disputed by critics who argue that intelligence is inherently biological and existential and cannot be captured symbolically (Searle 1980; Winograd and Flores 1986). These arguments provide a well-considered challenge to the dominant direction of AI research, and we examine them in Chapter 16. In spite of these challenges, the assumptions of the physical symbol system hypothesis underlie nearly all practical and theoretical work in expert systems, planning, and natural language understanding.

Knowledge Representation

The function of any representation scheme is to capture the essential features of a problem domain and make that information accessible to a problem-solving procedure. It is obvious that a representation language must allow the programmer to express the knowledge needed for a problem solution. *Abstraction,* the representation of only that information needed for a given purpose, is an essential tool for managing complexity. Inheritance (Fig. II.4) is an important abstraction technique. It is also important that the resulting programs be computationally efficient. *Expressiveness* and *efficiency* are major dimensions for evaluating knowledge representation languages. As we will see (Chapters 9 and 10), many highly expressive representations are too inefficient for use in certain classes of problems. Sometimes, expressiveness must be sacrificed to improve efficiency. This must be done without limiting the representation's ability to capture essential problem-solving knowledge. Optimizing this trade-off is a major task for designers of intelligent systems.

Knowledge representation languages are also tools for helping humans solve problems. As such, a representation should provide a *natural* framework for expressing problem-solving knowledge; it should make that knowledge available to the computer and assist the programmer in its organization.

The computer representation of floating-point numbers illustrates these trade-offs (see Fig. II.1). In general, real numbers require an infinite string of digits to be fully described; this cannot be accomplished on a finite device, indeed a finite-state machine. The best answer to this dilemma is to represent the number in two pieces: its *significant* digits and the location within those digits of the decimal point. Although it is not possible to actually

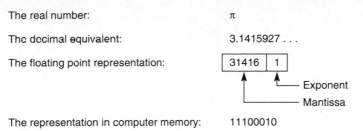

| The real number: | π |
| The decimal equivalent: | 3.1415927 . . . |

The floating point representation:

31416 | 1

— Exponent

— Mantissa

The representation in computer memory: 11100010

Figure II.1   Different representations of the real number π.

store a real number in a computer, it is possible to create a representation that functions adequately in most practical applications.

Floating-point representation thus sacrifices full expressive power to make the representation efficient, in this case to make it possible. The representation allows algorithms for multiple-precision arithmetic, giving effectively infinite precision by limiting round-off error to any prespecified tolerance. It also guarantees well-behaved round-off errors. Like all representations, it is only an abstraction, a symbol pattern that designates a desired entity and not the entity itself.

The array is another representation common in computer science. For many problems, it is more natural and efficient than the memory architecture implemented in computer hardware. This gain in naturalness and efficiency involves compromises in expressiveness, as illustrated by the following example from image processing. Figure II.2 is a digitized image of human chromosomes in a stage called metaphase. The image is processed to determine the number and structure of the chromosomes, looking for breaks, missing pieces, and other abnormalities.

The visual scene is made up of a number of picture points. Each picture point, or *pixel*, has both a location and a number value representing its gray level. It is natural, then, to collect the entire scene into a two-dimensional array where the row and column address gives the location of a pixel (X and Y coordinates) and the content of the array element is the gray level at that point. Algorithms are designed to perform operations like looking for isolated points to remove noise from the image, finding threshold levels for discerning objects and edges, summing contiguous elements to determine size or density, and in various other ways transforming the picture point data. Implementing these algorithms is straightforward, given the array representation and the FORTRAN language. This task would be quite cumbersome using other representations such as the predicate calculus, records, or assembly code, because these do not have a natural fit with the material being represented.

When we represent the picture as an array of pixel points, we sacrifice fineness of resolution (compare a photo in a newspaper to the original print of the same picture). In addition, pixel arrays cannot express the deeper semantic organization of the image. For example, a pixel array cannot represent the organization of chromosomes in a single cell nucleus, their genetic function, or the role of metaphase in cell division. This knowledge is more easily captured using a representation such as predicate calculus (Chapter 2) or semantic networks (Chapter 9).

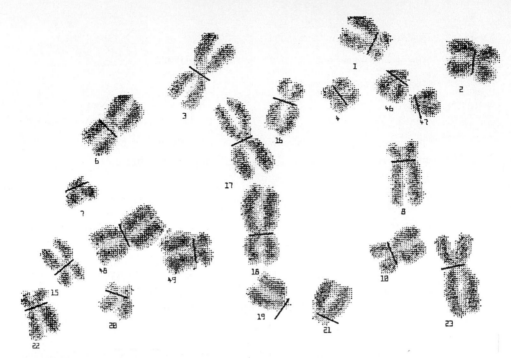

Figure II.2 Digitized image of chromosomes in metaphase.

A representational scheme should:

1. Be adequate to express all of the necessary information.
2. Support efficient execution of the resulting code.
3. Provide a natural scheme for expressing the required knowledge.

McDermott and others have stated that the key to writing a successful knowledge-based program is the selection of appropriate representational tools. Often, lower-level language (BASIC, FORTRAN, etc.) programmers fail in building expert systems simply because these languages do not provide the representational power and modularity required for knowledge-based programming (McDermott 1981).

In general, the problems AI attempts to solve do not lend themselves to the representations offered by more traditional formalisms such as arrays. Artificial intelligence is concerned with qualitative rather than quantitative problem solving, with reasoning rather than calculation, with organizing large and varied amounts of knowledge rather than implementing a single, well-defined algorithm. To support these needs, an AI representation language must:

A. Handle qualitative knowledge.
B. Allow new knowledge to be inferred from a set of facts and rules.
C. Allow representation of general principles as well as specific situations.
D. Capture complex semantic meaning.
E. Allow for meta-level reasoning.

These topics make up the remainder of our discussion of knowledge representation.

A. Handle qualitative knowledge.

Artificial intelligence programming requires a means of capturing and reasoning about the *qualitative* aspects of a problem. As a simple example, consider Figure II.3, the arrangement of blocks on a table:

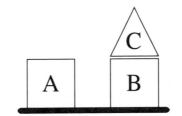

Figure II.3   A blocks world.

One way to represent this blocks arrangement would be to use a Cartesian coordinate system, giving the X and Y coordinates of each vertex of a block. Although this approach certainly describes the blocks world and is the correct representation for many tasks, it fails to capture directly the properties and relations required for qualitative reasoning. These include determining which blocks are stacked on other blocks and which blocks have clear tops so that they can be picked up. *Predicate calculus*, a subset of formal logic, directly captures this descriptive information. Using predicate calculus, the blocks world could be described by the logical assertions:

```
clear(c).
clear(a).
ontable(a).
ontable(b).
on(c, b).
cube(b).
cube(a).
pyramid(c).
```

The first word of each expression (**on, ontable,** etc.) is a *predicate* denoting some property or relationship among its arguments (appearing within parentheses). The arguments are symbols denoting objects (blocks) in the domain. The collection of logical clauses describes the important properties and relationships of the blocks world. Predicate calculus provides artificial intelligence programmers with a well-defined language for describing and reasoning about qualitative aspects of a system. Although it is not the only approach to representation, it is probably the best understood. In addition, it is sufficiently general to provide a foundation for other formal models of knowledge representation. Predicate calculus is discussed in detail in Chapter 2.

B. Allow new knowledge to be inferred from a set of facts and rules.

The ability to infer additional knowledge from a world description is essential to any intelligent entity. Humans, for example, do not store an inflexible description of every situation encountered; this would be impossible. Rather, we are able to formulate and reason from abstract descriptions of classes of objects and situations. A knowledge representation language must provide this capability.

In the blocks world example, we might like to define a test to determine whether a block is *clear*, that is, has nothing stacked on top of it. This is important if a robot hand is to pick it up or stack another block on top of it. It is not necessary to explicitly add this to our description for all such blocks. Instead, we define a general rule that allows the system to infer this information from the given facts. In predicate calculus, the rule can be written

$$\forall\, X \neg \exists\, Y\; on(Y,X) \Rightarrow clear(X)$$

or, "for all X, X is clear if there does not exist a Y such that Y is on X." This rule can be applied to a variety of situations by substituting different values for X and Y. By letting the programmer form general rules of inference, predicate calculus allows much greater economy of representation, as well as the possibility of designing systems that are flexible and general enough to respond intelligently to a range of situations.

C. Allow representation of general principles as well as specific situations.

In addition to demonstrating the use of logical rules to infer additional knowledge from basic facts, the blocks example introduced the use of variables in the predicate calculus. Because an intelligent system must be as general as possible, any useful representation language needs variables. The requirements of qualitative reasoning make the use and implementation of variables subtly different from their treatment in traditional programming languages. The assignment, type, and scope rules we find in calculation-oriented languages are too restrictive for reasoning systems. Good knowledge representation languages handle the bindings of variable names, objects, and values in a highly dynamic fashion (Chapters 2, 6, 7, and 15).

D. Capture complex semantic meaning.

Many artificial intelligence problem domains require large amounts of highly structured interrelated knowledge. It is not sufficient to describe a car by listing its component parts; a valid description must also describe the ways in which those parts are combined and the interactions between them. This view of structure is essential to a range of situations including taxonomic information, such as the classification of plants by genus and species, or a description of complex objects such as a diesel engine or a human body in terms of their component parts. In our blocks example, the interactions among predicates were the basis of a complete description of the arrangement.

Semantic relationships are also important in describing the causal relationships between events occurring over time. These are necessary to understand simple narratives such as a child's story or to represent a robot's plan of action as a sequence of atomic actions that must be executed in order.

Though all of these situations can ultimately be represented as collections of predicates or similar formalisms, some higher-level notion of structure is desirable to help both program and programmer deal with complex concepts in a coherent fashion. For example, a simple description of a bluebird might be "a bluebird is a small blue-colored bird and a bird is a feathered flying vertebrate." This may be represented as a set of logical predicates:

```
hassize(bluebird,small).
hascovering(bird,feathers).
hascolor(bluebird,blue).
hasproperty(bird,flies).
isa(bluebird,bird).
isa(bird,vertebrate).
```

This description could also be represented graphically by using the *arcs* (or *links*) in a graph instead of predicates to indicate relations (Fig. II.4). This description, called a *semantic network*, is a fundamental technique for representing semantic meaning.

Because relationships are explicitly denoted by the links of the graph, an algorithm for reasoning about the domain could make relevant associations simply by following links. In the bluebird illustration, a system need only follow two links in order to determine that a bluebird is a vertebrate. This is more efficient than exhaustively searching a data base of predicate calculus descriptions of the form isa(X, Y).

In addition, knowledge may be organized to reflect the natural class-instance structure of the domain. Certain links in a semantic network (the *ISA* links in Fig. II.4) indicate class membership and allow properties attached to a class description to be *inherited* by all members of the class. This inheritance mechanism is built into the language itself and allows knowledge to be stored at the highest possible level of abstraction. Inheritance is a natural tool for representing taxonomically structured information and ensures that all members of a class share common properties. Because of these gains in efficiency and naturalness of expression and because they make the power of graph theory available for reasoning about the structural organization of a knowledge base, semantic nets are an important alternative to predicate calculus. Semantic networks are discussed in detail in Chapter 9.

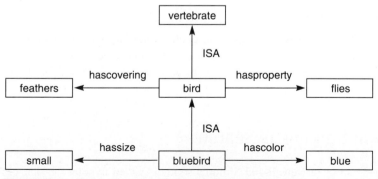

Figure II.4 Semantic network description of a bluebird.

We have just seen an example of a single problem description having two or more representations. Selecting the proper representation is a critical task for AI programmers. The benefits of a higher-level representation such as a semantic network are not unlike the advantages of a higher-level programming language such as Pascal over low-level machine code: although every Pascal program is ultimately compiled down to machine code, a higher-level language is almost essential for the creation of well-designed, coherent programs. Continuing this simile, predicate calculus or LISP s-expressions may be thought of as machine languages for AI representation. AI knowledge-structuring techniques such as frames, semantic networks, scripts, and plans provide more powerful constructs for organizing knowledge (Chapters 9 and 15).

E. Allow for meta-level reasoning.

An intelligent system not only should know things but also should know what it knows. It should be able not only to solve problems but also to explain how it solved the problems and why it made certain decisions. It should be able to describe its knowledge in both specific and general terms, recognize the limitations of its knowledge, and learn from its interactions with the world. This "knowing about what you know" constitutes a higher level of knowledge called *meta-knowledge*, and its automation is essential to the design and development of truly intelligent systems.

The problem of formalizing meta-knowledge was first explored by Bertrand Russell in his theory of logical types. Briefly, if sets are allowed to be members of other sets (a situation analogous to having knowledge about knowledge), it is possible to have sets that are members of themselves. As Russell discovered, this leads to irresolvable paradoxes. Russell disallowed these paradoxes by classifying sets as being of different types depending on whether they were sets of individuals, sets of sets of individuals, etc. Sets could not be members of sets of a smaller or equal type number. This corresponds to the distinctions between knowledge and meta-knowledge. As Russell discovered, numerous difficulties arise in attempting to formally describe this reasoning (Whitehead and Russell 1950).

The ability to learn from examples, from experience, or even from high-level instructions (as opposed to being programmed) depends on the application of meta-knowledge. The representational techniques developed for AI programming offer the flexibility and modifiability required of learning systems and form a basis for this research (Chapters 12 and 15).

To meet the needs of symbolic computing, artificial intelligence has developed representation languages such as the predicate calculus, semantic networks, frames (Chapter 9), and objects (Chapter 15). LISP and PROLOG are languages for implementing these and other representations. All of these tools are examined in detail throughout the text.

Problem Solving as Search

The second aspect of Newell and Simon's symbol system hypothesis, that problems are solved by searching among alternative choices, is supported by a commonsense view of human problem solving. Humans generally consider a number of alternative strategies on their way to solving a problem. A chess player typically considers a number of possible next moves, selecting the best according to such criteria as the opponent's possible responses or the degree to which various moves support some global game strategy. A player also considers short-term gain (such as taking the opponent's queen), opportunities to sacrifice a piece for positional advantage, or conjectures concerning the opponent's psychological makeup and level of skill. A mathematician will choose from a different but no less complex set of strategies to find a proof for a difficult theorem, a physician may systematically evaluate a number of possible diagnoses, and so on. This aspect of intelligent behavior underlies the problem-solving technique of *state space search*.

Consider, as a simple example, the game of tic-tac-toe. Given any board situation, there is only a finite number of moves that a player can make. Starting with an empty board, the first player may place an X in any one of nine places. Each of these moves yields a different board that will allow the opponent eight possible responses, and so on. We can represent this collection of possible moves and responses by regarding each board configuration as a *node* in a graph. The *links* of the graph represent legal moves from one board configuration to another. These nodes thus correspond to different *states* of the game board. The resulting structure is called a *state space graph*.

If we begin with an empty board (indicating the start of a game) and construct a graph through the process of drawing links from the board to all board states that may be reached through a legal move, we will construct the state space graph for the game of tic-tac-toe (Fig. II.5). The significance of this construction is that by starting at the node representing a new board and moving along arcs until we get to a state representing either a win or a tie, it is possible to trace the sequence of moves in any potential game. The state space representation thus enables us to treat all possible games of tic-tac-toe as different paths through this state space graph. Given this representation, an effective game strategy will search through the graph for the paths that lead to the most wins and fewest losses and play in a way that always tries to force the game along one of these optimal paths. Not only is this strategy an effective one but also, because of the regularity and precision of the state space representation, it is straightforward to implement on a computer.

As an example of how search is used to solve a more complicated problem, consider the task of diagnosing a mechanical fault in an automobile. Although this problem does not initially seem to lend itself to state space search as easily as tic-tac-toe or chess, it actually fits this strategy quite well. Instead of letting each node of the state space graph represent a "board state," we let it represent a state of partial knowledge about the automobile's mechanical problems. The process of examining the symptoms of the fault and inducing its cause may be thought of as searching through states of increasing knowledge. The starting node of the graph is empty, indicating that nothing is known about the cause of the problem. The first thing a mechanic might do is ask the customer which major system (engine, transmission, steering, brakes, etc.) seems to be causing the trouble. This is represented by a collection of arcs from the start states to states that indicate a focus on a single subsystem of the automobile (Fig. II.6).

Each of the states in the graph has arcs (corresponding to basic diagnostic checks) that lead to states representing further accumulation of knowledge in the diagnostic process. For example, the engine trouble node has arcs to nodes labeled engine starts and engine won't start. From the won't start node we may move to nodes labeled turns over and won't turn over. The won't turn over node has arcs to nodes labeled battery dead and battery ok (Fig. II.7).

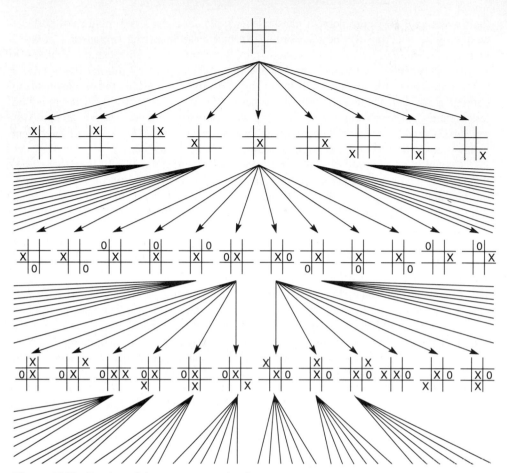

Figure II.5 Portion of the state space for tic-tac-toe.

We can construct a graph that includes all possible diagnostic checks and leads to a set of nodes that represent final diagnostic conclusions. A problem solver can diagnose car trouble by searching for a path through this graph that is consistent with the symptoms of a particular defective car. Note that the diagnostic checks performed in a given instance are determined by the path through the graph, with each decision eliminating certain tests from consideration. Although this problem is very different from that of finding an optimal way to play tic-tac-toe, it is equally amenable to solution by state space search.

In spite of this apparent universality, state space search is not, by itself, sufficient for automating intelligent problem-solving behavior; if it were, intelligent machines would already be a reality. It would be fairly simple, for example, to write a program that plays chess by searching through the entire state space for the sequence of moves most likely to bring a victory. This problem-solving method is known as *exhaustive search*. Though exhaustive search can be applied to any state space, the overwhelming size of the state space for interesting problems makes this approach a practical impossibility. The game of chess, for example, has approximately 10^{120} different board states. This is a number larger than the number of molecules in the universe or the number of nanoseconds that have

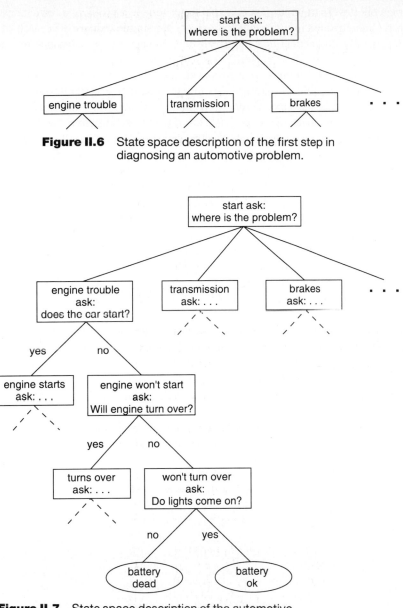

Figure II.6 State space description of the first step in diagnosing an automotive problem.

Figure II.7 State space description of the automotive diagnosis problem.

passed since the "big bang." Search of a space that large is well beyond the capabilities of any computing device whose dimensions must be confined to the known universe and whose execution must be completed before that universe succumbs to the ravages of entropy.

Throughout the text we show how state space search may be used to approach practically any problem. Search provides a framework for automating problem solving, but it is a framework devoid of intelligence. It enables us to give a problem a formal description that can be implemented in a computer program, but simple exhaustive search of a large space is generally impractical and intuitively fails to capture the substance of intelligent activity.

Humans use search: a chess player considers a number of possible moves, a doctor examines several possible diagnoses, a computer scientist entertains different designs before beginning to write code. Human beings do not use exhaustive search: the chess player examines only moves that experience has shown to be effective, the doctor does not require tests that are not somehow indicated by the symptoms at hand, software design is guided by experience and theoretical sophistication. Human problem solving seems to be based on judgmental rules that guide our search to those portions of the state space that seem somehow "promising."

These rules are known as *heuristics*, and they constitute one of the central topics of AI research. A heuristic (the name is taken from the Greek word "to discover") is a strategy for selectively searching a problem space. It guides our search along lines that have a high probability of success while avoiding wasted or apparently stupid efforts. Human beings use a large number of heuristics in problem solving. If you ask a mechanic why your car is overheating, she may say something like, "Usually that means the thermostat is bad." If you ask a doctor what could cause nausea and stomach pains, he might say it is "probably either stomach flu or food poisoning."

Heuristics are not foolproof: even the best game strategy can be defeated, diagnostic tools developed by expert physicians sometimes fail, experienced mathematicians sometimes fail to prove a difficult theorem. Although it does not always guarantee an optimal solution to a problem, a good heuristic can and should come close most of the time. Most important, it employs knowledge about the nature of a problem to find a solution efficiently.

If state space search gives us a means of formalizing the problem-solving process, then heuristics allow us to infuse that formalism with intelligence. These techniques are discussed in detail in the early chapters of this text and remain at the heart of most modern work in AI, including expert systems, natural language understanding, theorem provers and learning.

Throughout the text we explore the theoretical aspects of knowledge representation and search and the use of this theory in building effective programs. The treatment of knowledge representation begins with the predicate calculus (Chapter 2). Although the predicate calculus is only one of the schemes used in knowledge representation, it has the advantage of a well-defined semantics and provably correct *inference rules*. Using logic, we introduce the issues of knowledge representation and its relationship to search. Once the reader has gained experience in these issues, we demonstrate limitations of the predicate calculus and introduce alternative representation schemes (Chapters 9 and 15).

Chapter 3 introduces search in the context of simple games. By beginning with games, we can study the issues involved in state space search without the problems involved in representing real-world problems. This methodology is then applied to the more complex state spaces defined by logic problem solvers and expert systems (Chapters 4, 5, and 8).

In Chapter 4, we discuss the implementation of search algorithms, with particular attention to the use of heuristics to guide search. Chapter 5 looks at production systems, a general and powerful model of search-based problem solving. Chapter 5 also presents problem solving with triangle tables and the blackboard architecture.

THE PREDICATE CALCULUS

We come to the full possession of our power of drawing inferences, the last of our faculties; for it is not so much a natural gift as a long and difficult art.

— C. S. Pierce

The essential quality of a proof is to compel belief.

— Fermat

2.0 Introduction

In this chapter we introduce the predicate calculus as a representation language for artificial intelligence. The importance of the predicate calculus was discussed in the introduction to Part II; these advantages include a well-defined *formal semantics* and *sound* and *complete* inference rules. This chapter begins with a brief review of the propositional calculus (Section 2.1). Section 2.2 defines the syntax and semantics of the predicate calculus. In Section 2.3 we discuss predicate calculus inference rules and their use in problem solving. Finally, the chapter demonstrates the use of the predicate calculus to implement a knowledge base of financial investment advice.

2.1 The Propositional Calculus

2.1.1 Symbols and Sentences

The propositional calculus and, in the next subsection, the predicate calculus are first of all languages. Using their words, phrases, and sentences, we can represent and reason about properties and relationships in the world. The first step in describing a language is to introduce the pieces that make it up: its set of symbols.

PROPOSITIONAL CALCULUS SYMBOLS

The *symbols* of propositional calculus are the propositional symbols:

P, Q, R, S, T, ...

truth symbols:

true, false

and connectives:

∧, ∨, ¬, ⇒, =

Propositional symbols denote *propositions*, or statements about the world that may be either true or false, such as "the car is red" or "water is wet." Propositions are denoted by uppercase letters near the end of the English alphabet.

Sentences in the propositional calculus are formed from these atomic symbols according to the following rules:

DEFINITION

PROPOSITIONAL CALCULUS SENTENCES

Every propositional symbol and truth symbol is a sentence.

For example: true, P, Q, and R are sentences.

The *negation* of a sentence is a sentence.

For example: ¬P and ¬false are sentences.

The *conjunction*, or *and*, of two sentences is a sentence.

For example: P∧¬P is a sentence.

The *disjunction*, or *or*, of two sentences is a sentence.

For example: P∨¬P is a sentence.

The *implication* of one sentence for another is a sentence.

For example: P⇒Q is a sentence.

The *equivalence* of two sentences is a sentence.

For example: P∨Q=R is a sentence.

Legal sentences are also called *well-formed formulas* or *WFFs*.

In expressions of the form P∧Q, P and Q are called the *conjuncts*. In P∨Q, P and Q are referred to as *disjuncts*. In an implication, P⇒Q, P is the *premise* or *antecedent* and Q, the *conclusion* or *consequent*.

In propositional calculus sentences, the symbols ( ) and [ ] are used to group symbols into subexpressions and so control their order of evaluation and meaning. For example, (P∨Q)=R is quite different from P∨(Q=R), as can be demonstrated using truth tables (Section 2.1.2).

We can determine whether an expression is a sentence in the propositional calculus by using this inductive definition: "here are the basic units, here is how the basic units are composed. . . ." Only expressions that are formed of legal symbols through some sequence of these rules are well-formed formulas. For example,

((P∧Q)⇒R)=¬P∨¬Q∨R

is a well-formed sentence in the propositional calculus because:

P, Q, and R are propositions and thus sentences.

P∧Q, the conjunction of two sentences, is a sentence.

(P∧Q)⇒R, the implication of a sentence for another, is a sentence.

¬P and ¬Q, the negations of sentences, are sentences.

¬P∨¬Q, the disjunction of two sentences, is a sentence.

¬P∨¬Q∨R, the disjunction of two sentences, is a sentence.

((P∧Q)⇒R)=¬P∨¬Q∨R, the equivalence of two sentences, is a sentence.

This is our original sentence, which has been constructed through a series of applications of legal rules and is therefore well formed.

2.1.2 The Semantics of the Propositional Calculus

Section 2.1.1 presented the syntax of the propositional calculus by defining a set of rules for producing legal sentences. In this section we formally define the *semantics* or "meaning" of these sentences. Because AI programs must reason with their representational structures, it is important to demonstrate that the truth of their conclusions depends only on the truth of their initial knowledge, i.e., that logical errors are not introduced by the inference procedures. A precise treatment of semantics is essential to this goal.

A proposition symbol corresponds to a statement about the world. For example, P may denote the statement "it is raining" or Q, the statement "I live in a brown house." A proposition may be either true or false, given some state of the world. The truth value assignment to propositional sentences is called an *interpretation*, an assertion about their truth in some *possible world*.

Formally, an interpretation is a mapping from the propositional symbols into the set {T, F}. As mentioned in the previous section, the symbols true and false are part of the set of well-formed sentences of the propositional calculus; i.e., they are distinct from the truth value assigned to a sentence. To enforce this distinction, the symbols T and F are used for truth value assignment.

Each possible mapping corresponds to a possible world of interpretation. For example, if P denotes the proposition "it is raining" and Q denotes "I am at work," then the set of propositions {P, Q} has four different functional mappings into the truth values {T, F}. These correspond to four different possible worlds.

Given an interpretation of a set of propositions, it is necessary to define the truth values for compound expressions. These values depend on the operator used to form the expression and the truth values assigned to the operands. The semantics of propositional calculus, like its syntax, is defined inductively.

DEFINITION

PROPOSITIONAL CALCULUS SEMANTICS

An *interpretation* of a set of propositions is the assignment of a truth value, either T or F, to each propositional symbol.
The symbol true is always assigned T, and the symbol false is assigned F.
The interpretation or truth value for sentences is determined by:

The truth assignment of *negation*, ¬P, where P is any propositional symbol, is F if the assignment to P is T, and T if the assignment to P is F.

The truth assignment of *conjunction*, ∧, is T only when both conjuncts have truth value T; otherwise it is F.

The truth assignment of *disjunction*, ∨, is F only when both disjuncts have truth value F; otherwise it is T.

The truth assignment of *implication*, ⇒, is F only when the premise or symbol before the implication is T and the truth value of the consequent or symbol after the implication is F; otherwise it is T.

The truth assignment of *equivalence*, =, is T only when both expressions have the same truth assignment for all possible interpretations; otherwise it is F.

The truth assignments of compound propositions are often described in *truth tables*. A truth table lists all possible truth value assignments to the atomic propositions of an expression and gives the truth value of the expression for each assignment. In a sense, a truth table enumerates all possible worlds of interpretation that may be given to an expression.

The semantics of a connective may be defined using truth tables. For example, the truth table for P∧Q lists its truth value for each possible truth assignment to the operands. A conjunctive expression has four possible truth assignments:

1. Both P and Q are T, in which case P∧Q is T.

2. P is T in the world and Q is F, in which case P∧Q is F.

3. P is F and Q is T in the world, in which case P∧Q is F.

4. Both P and Q are F; P∧Q is also F.

The truth table for ∧ is given in Figure 2.1.
Or (∨), not (¬) implies (⇒), and equivalence (=) are defined in a similar fashion. The construction of these truth tables is left as an exercise.

Two expressions in the propositional calculus are equivalent if they have the same value under all truth value assignments. This may be proved using truth tables. For exam-

P	Q	P∧Q
T	T	T
T	F	F
F	T	F
F	F	F

Figure 2.1   Truth table for the operator ∧.

P	Q	¬P	¬P∨Q	P⇒Q	(¬P∨Q)=(P⇒Q)
T	T	F	T	T	T
T	F	F	F	F	T
F	T	T	T	T	T
F	F	T	T	T	T

Figure 2.2   Truth table demonstrating the equivalence of P
⇒ Q and ¬ P ∨ Q.

ple, a proof of the equivalence of P⇒Q and ¬P∨Q is given by the truth table of Figure 2.2.

By demonstrating that they have identical truth tables, we can prove the following propositional calculus equivalences. These expressions represent commonly used identities in the propositional calculus. The reader should confirm the truth of at least a few of them through the truth table method.

For propositional expressions P, Q, and R:

¬(¬P)=P

(P∨Q)=(¬P⇒Q)

de Morgan's law: ¬(P∨Q)=(¬P∧¬Q)

de Morgan's law: ¬(P∧Q)=(¬P∨¬Q)

distributive law: P∨(Q∧R)=(P∨Q)∧(P∨R)

distributive law: P∧(Q∨R)=(P∧Q)∨(P∧R)

commutative law: (P∧Q)=(Q∧P)

commutative law: (P∨Q)=(Q∨P)

associative law: ((P∧Q)∧R)=(P∧(Q∧R))

associative law: ((P∨Q)∨R)=(P∨(Q∨R))

contrapositive law: (P⇒Q)=(¬Q⇒¬P)

Identities such as these can be used to change predicate calculus expressions into a syntactically different but logically equivalent form. These identities may be used instead of truth tables to prove that two expressions are equivalent: find a series of identities that transform one expression into the other. An early AI program, the Logic Theorist (Newell and Simon 1956), designed by Newell, Simon, and Shaw, used transformations between equivalent forms of expressions to prove many of the theorems in Russell and Whitehead's *Principia Mathematica*. The ability to change a logical expression into a different form with equivalent truth values is also important when using inference rules (modus ponens, Section 2.4, and resolution, Chapter 11) that require expressions to be in a specific form.

2.2 The Predicate Calculus

In propositional calculus, each atomic symbol (P, Q, etc.) denotes a proposition of some complexity. There is no way to access the components of an individual assertion. Predicate calculus provides this ability. For example, instead of letting a single propositional symbol, P, denote the entire sentence "it rained on Tuesday," we can create a predicate **weather** that describes a relationship between a date and the weather: **weather(tuesday, rain)**. Through inference rules we can manipulate predicate calculus expressions, accessing their individual components and inferring new sentences.

Predicate calculus also allows expressions to contain variables. Variables let us create general assertions about classes of entities. For example, we could state that for all values of X, where X is a day of the week, the statement **weather(X, rain)** is true; i.e., it rains every day. As with propositional calculus, we will first define the syntax of the language and then discuss its semantics.

2.2.1 The Syntax of Predicates and Sentences

Before defining the syntax of correct expressions in the predicate calculus, we define an alphabet and grammar for creating the *symbols* of the language. This corresponds to the lexical aspect of a programming language definition. Predicate calculus symbols, like the *tokens* in a programming language, are irreducible syntactic elements: they cannot be broken into their component parts by the operations of the language.

Predicate calculus symbols are strings of letters and digits beginning with a letter. Blanks and nonalphanumeric characters cannot appear within the string, although the underscore, _, may be used to improve readability.

D E F I N I T I O N

PREDICATE CALCULUS SYMBOLS

The alphabet that makes up the symbols of the predicate calculus consists of:

1. The set of letters, both upper- and lowercase, of the English alphabet.
2. The set of digits, 0, 1, ..., 9.
3. The underscore, _.

Symbols in the predicate calculus begin with a letter and are followed by any sequence of these legal characters.

Legitimate characters in the alphabet of predicate calculus symbols include

```
a R 6 9 p _ z
```

Examples of characters not in the alphabet include

```
#  %  @  /  &  " "
```

Legitimate predicate calculus symbols include

```
George   fire3   tom_and_jerry  bill   XXXX   friends_of
```

Examples of strings that are not legal symbols are

```
3jack   "no blanks allowed"   ab%cd  ***71  duck!!!
```


Symbols, as we see in Section 2.2.2, are used to denote objects, properties, or relations in a world of discourse. As with most programming languages, the use of "words" that suggest the symbol's intended meaning assists us in understanding program code. Thus, even though l(g,k) and likes(george, kate) are formally equivalent (i.e., they have the same structure), the second can be of great help (for human readers) in indicating what relationship the expression represents. It must be stressed that these descriptive names are intended solely to improve the readability of expressions. The only meaning that predicate calculus expressions may be said to have is through their formal semantics.

Parentheses "( )", commas ",", and periods "." are used solely to construct well-formed expressions and do not denote objects or relations in the world. These are called *improper symbols*.

Predicate calculus symbols may represent either *variables*, *constants*, *functions*, or *predicates*.

Constants name specific objects or properties in the world. Constant symbols must begin with a lowercase letter. Thus george, tree, tall, and blue are examples of well-formed constant symbols. The constants true and false are reserved as *truth symbols*.

Variable symbols are used to designate general classes of objects or properties in the world. Variables are represented by symbols beginning with an uppercase letter. Thus George, BILL, and KAte are legal variables, whereas geORGE and bill are not.

Predicate calculus also allows functions on objects in the world of discourse. Function symbols (like constants) begin with a lowercase letter. Functions denote a mapping of one or more elements in a set (called the *domain* of the function) into a unique element of another set (the *range* of the function). Elements of the domain and range are objects in the world of discourse. In addition to common arithmetic functions such as addition and multiplication, functions may define mappings between nonnumeric domains.

Note that our definition of predicate calculus symbols does not include numbers or arithmetic operators. The number system is not included in the predicate calculus primitives; instead it is defined axiomatically using "pure" predicate calculus as a basis (Manna 1985). While the particulars of this derivation are of theoretical interest, they are less important to the use of predicate calculus as an AI representation language. For convenience, we assume this derivation and include arithmetic in the language.

Every function symbol has an associated *arity*, indicating the number of elements in the domain mapped onto each element of the range. Thus father could denote a function of arity 1 that maps people onto their (unique) male parent. plus could be a function of arity 2 that maps two numbers onto their arithmetic sum.

A *function expression* is a function symbol followed by its arguments. The arguments are elements from the domain of the function; the number of arguments is equal to the arity of the function. The arguments are enclosed in parentheses and separated by commas. For example,

```
f(X,Y)
father(david)
price(bananas)
```

are all well-formed function expressions.

Each function expression denotes the mapping of the arguments onto a single object in the range, called the *value* of the function. For example, if father is a unary function, then

```
father(david)
```

is a function expression whose value (in the authors' world of discourse) is george. If plus is a function of arity 2, with domain the integers, then

```
plus(2,3)
```

is a function expression whose value is the integer 5. The act of replacing a function with its value is called *evaluation*.

A predicate calculus *term* is either a constant, variable, or function expression. Terms denote objects and properties in a problem domain. Examples of terms are:

```
cat
times(2,3)
blue
X
mother(jane)
kate
```

These concepts are formalized in the following definition.

DEFINITION

SYMBOLS AND TERMS

Predicate calculus symbols include:

1. *Truth symbols* true and false (these are reserved symbols).

2. *Constant symbols*, which are symbol expressions having the first character lowercase.

3. *Variable symbols*, which are symbol expressions beginning with an uppercase character.

4. *Function symbols*, which are symbol expressions having the first character lowercase. Functions have an attached arity indicating the number of elements of the domain mapped onto each element of the range.

A *function expression* consists of a function constant of arity n, followed by n terms, $t_1, t_2, \cdots, t_n$, enclosed in parentheses and separated by commas.

A *term* is either a constant, variable, or function expression.

Symbols in predicate calculus may also represent predicates. Predicate symbols, like constants and function names, begin with a lowercase letter. A predicate names a relationship between zero or more objects in the world. The number of objects so related is the arity of the predicate. Examples of predicates are

likes   equals   on   near   part_of

An *atomic sentence* in predicate calculus is a predicate of arity n followed by n terms enclosed in parentheses and separated by commas. Predicate calculus sentences are delimited by a period. Examples of atomic sentences are

likes(george,kate).	likes(X,george).
likes(george,susie).	likes(X,X).
likes(george,sarah,tuesday).	friends(bill,richard).
friends(bill,george).	friends(father(david),father(andrew)).
helps(bill,george).	helps(richard,bill).

The predicate symbols in these expressions are likes, friends, and helps. Note that a predicate symbol may be used with different numbers of arguments. In this example there are two different likes, one with two and the other with three arguments. When a predicate symbol is used in sentences with different arities, it is considered to represent two different relations. Thus, a predicate relation is defined by its name and its arity. There is no reason that the two different likes cannot make up part of the same description of the world; however, good coding practice encourages us to avoid this whenever possible.

In the predicates above, bill, george, kate, etc., are constant symbols and represent objects in the problem domain. The arguments to a predicate are terms and may also include variables or function expressions. For example,

friends(father(david),father(andrew)).

is a predicate describing a relationship between two objects in a domain of discourse. These arguments are represented as function expressions whose mappings (given that the father of david is george and the father of andrew is allen) form the parameters of the predicate. After the function expressions are evaluated, the expression becomes friends(george,allen).

These ideas are formalized in the following definition.

DEFINITION

PREDICATES AND ATOMIC SENTENCES

Predicate symbols are symbols beginning with a lowercase letter.

Predicates have an associated positive integer referred to as the *arity* or "argument number" for the predicate. Predicates with the same name but different arities are considered distinct.

An atomic sentence is a predicate constant of arity n, followed by n terms, $t_1, t_2, \cdots, t_n$, enclosed in parentheses and separated by commas.

The truth values, true and false, are also atomic sentences.

Atomic sentences are also called *atomic expressions, atoms,* or *propositions.*

We may combine atomic sentences using logical operators to form *sentences* in the predicate calculus. These are the same logical connectives used in propositional calculus: $\wedge, \vee, \neg, \Rightarrow$, and $=$.

When a variable appears as an argument in a sentence, it refers to unspecified objects in the domain. Predicate calculus includes two symbols, the *variable quantifiers* $\forall$ and $\exists$, that constrain the meaning of a sentence containing a variable. A quantifier is followed by a variable and a sentence, such as,

∃ Y friends(Y, peter).
∀ X likes(X,ice_cream).

The *universal quantifier,* $\forall$, indicates that the sentence is true for all values of its variable. In the example above, likes(X, ice_cream) is true for all values in the domain of the definition of X. The *existential quantifier,* $\exists$, indicates that the sentence is true for some value(s) in the domain. friends(Y, peter) is true for some objects, indicated by the variable Y. Quantifiers are discussed in more detail in Section 2.2.2.

Sentences in the predicate calculus are defined inductively.

DEFINITION

PREDICATE CALCULUS SENTENCES

Every atomic sentence is a sentence.

1. If s is a sentence, then so is its negation, ¬s.
2. If s_1 and s_2 are sentences, then so is their conjunction, $s_1 \wedge s_2$.
3. If s_1 and s_2 are sentences, then so is their disjunction, $s_1 \vee s_2$.
4. If s_1 and s_2 are sentences, then so is their implication, $s_1 \Rightarrow s_2$.
5. If s_1 and s_2 are sentences, then so is their equivalence, $s_1 = s_2$.

6. If X is a variable and s a sentence, then ∀ X s is a sentence.

7. If X is a variable and s a sentence, then ∃ X s is a sentence.

Examples of well-formed predicate calculus sentences follow. Let times and plus be function symbols of arity 2 and let equal and foo be predicate symbols with arity 2 and 3, respectively.

plus(two,three) is a function and thus not an atomic sentence.

equal(plus(two,three), five) is an atomic sentence.

equal(plus(2, 3), seven) is an atomic sentence. Note that this sentence, given the standard interpretation of plus and equal, is false. Well-formedness and truth value are independent issues.

∃ X foo(X,two,plus(two,three)) ∧ equal(plus(two,three),five) is a sentence because both conjuncts are sentences.

(foo(two,two,plus(two,three))) ⇒ (equal(plus(three,two),five)=true) is a sentence because all its components are sentences, appropriately connected by logical operators.

The definition of predicate calculus sentences and the examples just presented suggest a method for verifying that an expression is a sentence. This is written as a recursive algorithm, verify_sentence. verify_sentence takes as argument a candidate expression and returns success if the expression is a sentence.

```
procedure verify_sentence(expression);

begin

  case

    expression is an atomic sentence: return(success);

    expression is of the form Q X s, where Q is either ∀ or ∃, X is a variable,
          and s is a sentence:
      if verify_sentence(s) returns success
      then return(success);

    expression is of the form ¬ s:
      if verify_sentence(s) returns success
      then return(success);

    expression is of the form s₁ op s₂, where op is a binary logical operator:
      if verify_sentence(s₁ ) returns success  and
        verify_sentence(s₂ ) returns success
      then return(success);

    otherwise: return(fail)

  end
end.
```

We conclude this section with an example of the use of predicate calculus to describe a simple world. The domain of discourse is a set of family relationships in a biblical genealogy:

```
mother(eve,abel).
mother(eve,cain).
father(adam,abel).
father(adam,cain).
```

$\forall$ X $\forall$ Y father(X, Y) $\lor$ mother(X, Y) $\Rightarrow$ parent(X, Y).
$\forall$ X $\forall$ Y $\forall$ Z parent(X, Y) $\land$ parent(X, Z) $\Rightarrow$ sibling(Y, Z).

In this example we use the predicates **mother** and **father** to define a set of parent-child relationships. The implications give general definitions of other relationships, such as parent and sibling, in terms of these predicates. Intuitively, it is clear that these implications can be used to infer facts such as **sibling(cain,abel)**. To formalize this process so that it can be performed on a computer, care must be taken to define inference algorithms and to ensure that such algorithms indeed draw correct conclusions from a set of predicate calculus assertions. In order to do so, we define the semantics of the predicate calculus (Section 2.2.2) and then address the issue of inference rules (Section 2.3).

2.2.2 A Semantics for the Predicate Calculus

Having defined well-formed expressions in the predicate calculus, it is important to determine their meaning in terms of objects, properties, and relations in the world. Predicate calculus semantics provide a formal basis for determining the truth value of well-formed expressions. The truth of expressions depends on the mapping of constants, variables, predicates, and functions into objects and relations in the domain of discourse. The truth of relationships in the domain determines the truth of the corresponding expressions.

For example, information about a person, George, and his friends Kate and Susie may be expressed by

```
friends(george,susie).
friends(george,kate).
```

If it is indeed true that George is a friend of Susie and George is a friend of Kate then these expressions would each have the truth value (assignment) T. If George is a friend of Susie but not of Kate, then the first expression would have truth value T and the second would have truth value F.

To use the predicate calculus as a representation for problem solving, we describe objects and relations in the domain of interpretation with a set of well-formed expressions. The terms and predicates of these expressions denote objects and relations in the domain. This data base of predicate calculus expressions, each having truth value T, describes the "state of the world." The description of George and his friends is a simple example of such a data base. Another example is the *blocks world* in the introduction to Part II.

Based on these intuitions, we formally define the semantics of predicate calculus. First, we define an *interpretation* over a domain D. Then we use this interpretation to determine the *truth value assignment* of sentences in the language.

DEFINITION

INTERPRETATION

Let the domain D be a nonempty set.

An *interpretation* over D is an assignment of the entities of D to each of the constant, variable, predicate, and function symbols of a predicate calculus expression, such that:

1. Each constant is assigned an element of D.
2. Each variable is assigned to a nonempty subset of D; these are the allowable substitutions for that variable.
3. Each function f of arity m is defined on m arguments of D and defines a mapping from D^m into D.
4. Each predicate p of arity n is defined on n arguments from D and defines a mapping from D^n into {T, F}.

Given an interpretation, the meaning of an expression is a truth value assignment over the interpretation.

DEFINITION

TRUTH VALUE OF PREDICATE CALCULUS EXPRESSIONS

Assume an expression E and an interpretation I for E over a nonempty domain D. The truth value for E is determined by:

1. The value of a constant is the element of D it is assigned to by I.
2. The value of a variable is the set of elements of D it is assigned to by I.
3. The value of a function expression is that element of D obtained by evaluating the function for the parameter values assigned by the interpretation.
4. The value of truth symbol "true" is T and "false" is F.
5. The value of an atomic sentence is either T or F, as determined by the interpretation I.
6. The value of the negation of a sentence is T if the value of the sentence is F and is F if the value of the sentence is T.
7. The value of the conjunction of two sentences is T if the value of both sentences is T and is F otherwise.
8.–10. The truth value of expressions using ∨, ⇒, and = is determined from the value of their operands as defined in Section 2.1.2.

Finally, for a variable X and a sentence S containing X:

11. The value of ∀ X S is T if S is T for all assignments to X under I, and it is F otherwise.

12. The value of ∃ X S is T if there is an assignment to X in the interpretation under which S is T; otherwise it is F.

Quantification of variables is an important part of predicate calculus semantics. When a variable appears in a sentence, such as X in likes(george,X) in the first example of Section 2.2.2, the variable functions as a placeholder. Any constant allowed under the interpretation can be substituted for it in the expression. By substituting for X in likes(george,X) we can form the statements likes(george,kate) and likes(george,susie).

The variable X stands for all constants that might appear as the second parameter of the sentence. This variable name might be replaced by any other variable name, such as Y or PEOPLE, without changing the meaning of the expression. In this sense the variable is said to be a *dummy*.

In predicate calculus, variables may be used or *quantified* in two ways. In the first, the sentence is true for all constants that can be substituted for the variable under the intended interpretation. The variable is said to be *universally* quantified.

The symbol indicating universal quantification is ∀. Parentheses are often used to indicate the *scope* of quantification, that is, the instances of a variable name over which a quantification holds. Thus

∀ X (p(X) ∧ q(Y) ⇒ r(X)).

indicates that X is universally quantified in both p(X) and r(X).

Universal quantification introduces problems in computing the truth value of a sentence, because all the possible values of a variable symbol must be tested to see whether the expression remains true. For example, to test the truth value of ∀ X likes(george,X), where X ranges over the set of all humans, all possible values for X must be tested. If the domain of an interpretation is infinite, exhaustive testing of all substitutions to a universally quantified variable is computationally impossible: the algorithm will never halt. Because of this problem, the predicate calculus is said to be *undecidable*.

As the propositional calculus does not use variables, sentences have only a finite number of possible truth assignments, and we can exhaustively test all possible assignments. This is what is done in a truth table.

Variables may also be quantified *existentially*. In this case the expression containing the variable is said to be true for at least one substitution from the domain of definition. The existential quantifier is indicated by ∃. The scope of an existentially quantified variable is also indicated by enclosing the quantified occurrences of the variable in parentheses.

Evaluating the truth of an expression containing an existentially quantified variable may be no easier than evaluating the truth of expressions containing universally quantified variables. Suppose we attempt to determine the truth of the expression by trying substitutions until one is found that makes the expression true. If the domain of the variable is infinite and the expression is false under all substitutions, the algorithm will never halt.

Several relationships between negation and the universal and existential quantifiers are given below. These relationships are used in resolution refutation systems described in Chapter 11. The notion of a variable name as a dummy symbol that stands for a set of constants is also noted. For predicates p and q and variables X and Y:

$$\neg \exists X \, p(X) = \forall X \neg p(X)$$

$$\neg \forall X \, p(X) = \exists X \neg p(X)$$

$$\exists X \, p(X) = \exists Y \, p(Y)$$

$$\forall X \, q(X) = \forall Y \, q(Y)$$

$$\forall X \, (p(X) \wedge q(X)) = \forall X \, p(X) \wedge \forall Y \, q(Y)$$

$$\exists X \, (p(X) \vee q(X)) = \exists X \, p(X) \vee \exists Y \, q(Y)$$

In the language we have defined, universal and existential quantified variables may refer only to objects (constants) in the domain of discourse. Predicate and function names may not be replaced by quantified variables. This language is called the first-order predicate calculus.

DEFINITION

FIRST-ORDER PREDICATE CALCULUS

First-order predicate calculus allows quantified variables to refer to objects in the domain of discourse and not to predicates or functions.

For example,

$\forall$ (Likes) Likes(george,kate).

is not a well-formed expression in the first-order predicate calculus. There are *higher-order* predicate calculi where such expressions are meaningful. Some researchers (McCarthy 1968; Appelt 1985) have used higher-order languages to represent knowledge in natural language understanding programs.

Almost any grammatically correct English sentence may be represented in first-order predicate calculus using the symbols, connectives, and variable symbols defined in this section. It is important to note that there is no unique mapping of sentences into predicate calculus expressions; in fact, an English sentence may have a number of different predicate calculus representations. A major challenge for AI programmers is to find a scheme for using these predicates that optimizes the expressiveness and efficiency of the resulting representation. Examples of English sentences represented in predicate calculus are:

If it doesn't rain tomorrow, Tom will go to the mountains.
$\neg$ weather(rain,tomorrow) $\Rightarrow$ go(tom,mountains)

Emma is a Doberman pinscher and a good dog.
gooddog(emma) ∧ isa(emma,doberman)

All basketball players are tall.
∀ X (basketball_player(X) ⇒ tall(X))

Some people like anchovies.
∃ X (person(X) ∧ likes(X,anchovies)).

If wishes were horses, beggars would ride.
equal(wishes,horses) ⇒ ride(beggars).

Nobody likes taxes.
¬ ∃ X likes(X,taxes).

We conclude this section by giving an extended example of a truth value assignment to a set of predicate calculus expressions. Suppose we want to model the blocks world of Figure 2.3 to design a control algorithm for a robot arm. We can use predicate calculus sentences to represent the qualitative relationships in the world: does a given block have a clear top surface? can we pick up block a? etc. Assume that the computer has knowledge of the location of each block and the arm itself and is able to keep track of these locations (perhaps in the form of three-dimensional coordinates) as the hand moves blocks about the table.

To pick up a block and stack it on another block, both blocks must be clear. In Figure 2.3, block a is not clear. Because the arm can move blocks, it can change the state of the world and clear a block. Suppose it removes block c from block a and updates the knowledge base to reflect this by deleting the assertion on(c,a). The program needs to be able to infer that block a has become clear.

The following rule describes when a block is clear:

∀ X (¬ ∃ Y on(Y,X) ⇒ clear(X)).

That is, for all X, X is clear if there does not exist a Y such that Y is on X.

This rule not only defines what it means for a block to be clear but also provides a basis for determining how to clear blocks that are not. For example, block d is not clear, because if variable X is given value d, substituting b for Y will make the statement false. Therefore, to make this definition true, block b must be removed from block d. This is easily done because the computer has a record of all the blocks and their locations.

Besides using implications to define when a block is clear, other rules may be added that describe operations such as stacking one block on top of another. For example: to stack X on Y first empty the hand, then clear X, then clear Y, and then pick_up X and put_down X on Y.

∀ X ∀ Y ((hand_empty ∧ clear(X) ∧ clear(Y) ∧ pick_up(X) ∧ put_down(X,Y))
⇒ stack(X,Y)).

Note that in implementing the above description it is necessary to "attach" an action of the robot arm to each predicate such as pick_up(X). It is also necessary for such an implementation to augment the semantics of predicate calculus by requiring that the actions be performed in the order in which they appear in a rule premise. However, much is gained

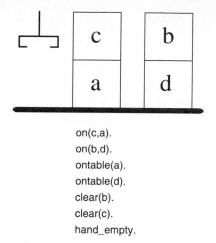

on(c,a).
on(b,d).
ontable(a).
ontable(d).
clear(b).
clear(c).
hand_empty.

Figure 2.3 A blocks world with its predicate calculus
description.

by separating these issues from the use of predicate calculus to define the relationships and
operations in the domain.

Figure 2.3 gives a semantic interpretation of these predicate calculus expressions. This
interpretation maps the constants and predicates in the set of expressions into a domain D,
here the blocks and relations between them. The interpretation gives truth value T to each
expression in the description. Another interpretation could be offered by a different set of
blocks in another location, or perhaps by a team of four acrobats. The important question
is not the uniqueness of interpretations, but whether the interpretation provides a truth value
for all expressions in the set and whether the expressions describe the world in sufficient
detail that all necessary inferences may be carried out by manipulating the symbolic expressions. The next section uses these ideas to provide a formal basis for predicate calculus
inference rules.

2.3 Using Inference Rules to Produce Predicate Calculus Expressions

2.3.1 Inference Rules

The semantics of predicate calculus provide a basis for a formal theory of *logical inference*.
The ability to infer new correct expressions from a set of true assertions is an important
feature of the predicate calculus. These new expressions are correct in that they are *consistent* with all previous interpretations of the original set of expressions. First we discuss
these ideas informally and then we create a set of definitions to make them precise.

An interpretation that makes a sentence true is said to *satisfy* that sentence. An interpretation that satisfies every member of a set of expressions is said to satisfy the set. An

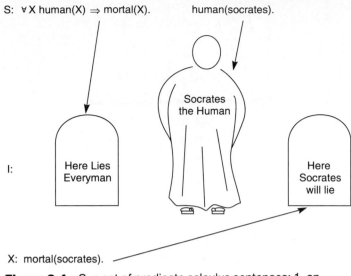

S: ∀X human(X) ⇒ mortal(X).   human(socrates).

Socrates
the Human

I:

Here Lies
Everyman

Here
Socrates
will lie

X: mortal(socrates).

Figure 2.4 S, a set of predicate calculus sentences; 1, an interpretation; and X, an expression logically following from S (also satisfied by 1).

expression X *logically follows* from a set of predicate calculus expressions S if every interpretation that satisfies S also satisfies X. The notation S ⊨ X indicates that X logically follows from S. The function of logical inference is to produce new sentences that logically follow a given set of predicate calculus sentences.

It is important that the precise meaning of "logically follow" be understood: the expression X is true for every interpretation that satisfies S (Figure 2.4).

The term itself, "logically follows," may be a bit confusing. It does not mean that X is deduced from or even that it is deducible from S. It simply means that X is true for every (potentially infinite) interpretation that satisfies S. However, because systems of predicates can have a potentially infinite number of possible interpretations, it is seldom practical to try all interpretations. Instead, *inference rules* provide a computationally feasible way to determine when an expression logically follows from another. The concept "logically follows" provides a formal basis for proofs of the soundness and correctness of inference rules.

An inference rule is essentially a mechanical means of producing new predicate calculus sentences from other sentences. That is, inference rules produce new sentences based on the syntactic form of given logical assertions. When every sentence X produced by an inference rule operating on a set S of logical expressions logically follows from S, the inference rule is said to be *sound*.

If the inference rule is able to produce every expression that logically follows from S, then it is said to be *complete*. *Modus ponens*, to be introduced below, and *resolution*, introduced in Chapter 11, are examples of inference rules that are sound and, when used with certain appropriate strategies, complete. Logical inference systems generally use sound rules of inference, although later chapters (5, 9, 10, and 14) examine heuristic reasoning and commonsense reasoning, both of which relax this requirement. It is less important, although often desirable, that inference procedures be complete.

We formalize these ideas through the following definitions.

DEFINITION

SATISFY, MODEL, VALID, INCONSISTENT

For a predicate calculus expression S and an interpretation I:

If S has a value of T under I and a particular variable assignment, then I is said to *satisfy* S.

If I satisfies S for all variable assignments, then I is a *model* of S.

S is *satisfiable* if and only if there exist an interpretation and variable assignment that satisfy it; otherwise, it is *unsatisfiable*.

A set of expressions is *satisfiable* if and only if there exist an interpretation and variable assignment that satisfy every element.

If a set of expressions is not satisfiable, it is said to be *inconsistent*.

If S has a value T for all possible interpretations, S is said to be *valid*.

In the blocks world example of Figure 2.3, the blocks world was a model for logical description. All of the sentences in the example were true under this interpretation. When a knowledge base is implemented as a set of true assertions about a problem domain, that domain is a model for the knowledge base.

The expression $\exists X (p(X) \land \neg p(X))$ is inconsistent, because it cannot be satisfied under any interpretation or variable assignment. On the other hand, the expression $\forall X (p(X) \lor \neg p(X))$ is valid.

The truth table method can be used to test validity for any expression not containing variables. Because it is not always possible to decide the validity of expressions containing variables (as mentioned above, the process may not terminate), the full predicate calculus is "undecidable." There are *proof procedures*, however, that can produce any expression that logically follows from a set of expressions. These are called *complete* proof procedures.

DEFINITION

PROOF PROCEDURE

A *proof procedure* is a combination of an inference rule and an algorithm for applying that rule to a set of logical expressions to generate new sentences.

We present proof procedures for the *resolution* inference rule in Chapter 11.

Using these definitions, we may formally define "logically follows."

LOGICALLY FOLLOWS, SOUND, AND COMPLETE

A predicate calculus expression X *logically follows* from a set S of predicate calculus expressions if every interpretation and variable assignment that satisfies S also satisfies X.

An inference rule is *sound* if every predicate calculus expression produced by the rule from a set S of predicate calculus expressions also logically follows from S.

An inference rule is *complete* if, given a set S of predicate calculus expressions, the rule can infer every expression that logically follows from S.

Modus ponens is a sound inference rule. If we are given an expression of the form $P \Rightarrow Q$ and another expression of the form P such that both are true under an interpretation I, then modus ponens allows us to infer that Q is also true for that interpretation. Indeed, because modus ponens is sound, Q is true for *all* interpretations for which P and $P \Rightarrow Q$ are true.

Modus ponens and a number of other useful inference rules are defined below.

DEFINITION

MODUS PONENS, MODUS TOLENS, AND ELIMINATION, AND INTRODUCTION, AND UNIVERSAL INSTANTIATION

If the sentences P and $P \Rightarrow Q$ are known to be true, then *modus ponens* lets us infer Q.

Under the inference rule *modus tolens*, if $P \Rightarrow Q$ is known to be true and Q is known to be false, we can infer $\neg P$.

And elimination allows us to infer the truth of either of the conjuncts from the truth of a conjunctive sentence. For instance, $P \wedge Q$ lets us conclude P and Q are true.

And introduction lets us infer the truth of a conjunction from the truth of its conjuncts. For instance, if P and Q are true, then $P \wedge Q$ is true.

Universal instantiation states that if any universally quantified variable in a true sentence is replaced by any appropriate term from the domain, the result is a true sentence. Thus, if a is from the domain of X, the $\forall X \, p(X)$ lets us infer $p(a)$.

As a simple example of the use of modus ponens in the propositional calculus, assume the following observations: "if it is raining then the ground will be wet" and "it is raining." If P denotes "it is raining" and Q is "the ground is wet" then the first expression becomes $P \Rightarrow Q$. Because it is indeed now raining (P is true), our set of axioms becomes

$P \Rightarrow Q$
P

Through an application of modus ponens, the fact that the ground is wet (Q) may be added to the set of true expressions.

Modus ponens can also be applied to expressions containing variables. Consider as an example the common syllogism "all men are mortal and Socrates is a man; therefore Socrates is mortal." "All men are mortal" may be represented in predicate calculus by

$$\forall X \, (man(X) \Rightarrow mortal(X)).$$

"Socrates is a man" is

man(socrates).

Because the X in the implication is universally quantified, we may substitute any value in the domain for X and still have a true statement under the inference rule of universal instantiation. By substituting socrates for X in the implication, we infer the expression

$$man(socrates) \Rightarrow mortal(socrates).$$

We can now apply modus ponens and infer the conclusion mortal(socrates). This is added to the set of expressions that logically follow from the original assertions. An algorithm called *unification* can be used by an automated problem solver to determine that socrates may be substituted for X in order to apply modus ponens. Unification is discussed in Section 2.3.2.

Chapter 11 discusses a more powerful rule of inference called resolution, which is the basis of many automated reasoning systems.

2.3.2 Unification

To apply inference rules such as modus ponens, an inference system must be able to determine when two expressions are the same or *match*. In propositional calculus, this is trivial: two expressions match if and only if they are syntactically identical. In predicate calculus, the process of matching two sentences is complicated by the existence of variables in the expressions. Universal instantiation allows universally quantified variables to be replaced by terms from the domain. This requires a decision process for determining the variable substitutions under which two or more expressions can be made identical (usually for the purpose of applying inference rules).

Unification is an algorithm for determining the substitutions needed to make two predicate calculus expressions match. We already saw this done in the previous subsection, where socrates in man(socrates) was substituted for X in $\forall X(man(X) \Rightarrow mortal(X))$. This allowed the application of modus ponens and the conclusion mortal(socrates). Another example of unification was seen previously when dummy variables were discussed. Because p(X) and p(Y) are equivalent, Y may be substituted for X to make the sentences match.

Unification and inference rules such as modus ponens allow us to make inferences on a set of logical assertions. To do this, the logical data base must be expressed in an appropriate form.

An essential aspect of this form is the requirement that all variables be universally quantified. This allows full freedom in computing substitutions. Existentially quantified variables may be eliminated from sentences in the data base by replacing them with the constants that make the sentence true. For example, ∃ X parent(X,tom) could be replaced by the expression parent(bob,tom) or parent(mary,tom), assuming that bob and mary are tom's parents under the interpretation.

The process of eliminating existentially quantified variables is complicated by the fact that the value of these substitutions may depend on the value of other variables in the expression. For example, in the expression ∀ X ∃ Y mother(Y,X), the value of the existentially quantified variable Y depends on the value of X. *Skolemization* replaces each existentially quantified variable with a function that returns the appropriate constant as a function of some or all of the other variables in the sentence. In the above example, because the value of Y depends on X, Y could be replaced by a *skolem function*, f, of X. This yields the predicate ∀ X mother(X,f(X)). Skolemization is discussed in more detail in Chapter 11.

Once the existentially quantified variables have been removed from a logical data base, unification may be used to match sentences in order to apply inference rules such as modus ponens.

Unification is complicated by the fact that a variable may be replaced by any term, including other variables and function expressions of arbitrary complexity. These expressions may themselves contain variables. For example, father(jack) may be substituted for X in man(X) to infer that jack's father is mortal.

Some instances of the expression

foo(X,a,goo(Y)).

generated by legal substitutions are given below:

1) foo(fred,a,goo(Z))
2) foo(W,a,goo(jack))
3) foo(Z,a,goo(moo(Z)))

In this example, the substitution instances or *unifications* that would make the initial expression identical to each of the other three are written as

1) {fred/X, Z/Y}
2) {W/X, jack/Y}
3) {Z/X, moo(Z)/Y}

The notation X/Y,... indicates that X is substituted for the variable Y in the original expression. Substitutions are also referred to as *bindings*. A variable is said to be *bound* to the value substituted for it.

In defining the unification algorithm that computes the substitutions required to match two expressions, a number of issues must be taken into account.

Although a constant may be systematically substituted for a variable, any constant is considered a "ground instance" and may not be replaced. Neither can two different ground instances be substituted for one variable.

A variable cannot be unified with a term containing that variable. X cannot be replaced by p(X) as this creates an infinite expression: p(p(p(p(...X)...). The test for this situation is called the *occurs check*.

Generally, a problem-solving process will require multiple inferences and, consequently, multiple successive unifications. Logic problem solvers must maintain consistency of variable substitutions. It is important that any unifying substitution be made consistently across all occurrences of the variable in both expressions being matched. This was seen before when socrates was substituted not only for the variable X in man(X) but also for the variable X in mortal(X).

Once a variable has been bound, future unifications and inferences must take the value of this binding into account. If a variable is bound to a constant, that variable may not be given a new binding in a future unification. If a variable X_1 is substituted for another variable X_2 and at a later time X_1 is replaced by a constant, then X_2 must also reflect this binding. The complete set of substitutions used in a sequence of inferences is important, because it may contain the answer to the original query (Section 11.2.5).

For example, if p(a,X) unifies with the premise of p(Y,Z) $\Rightarrow$ q(Y,Z) under the substitution {a/Y, X/Z}, modus ponens lets us infer q(a,X) under the same substitution. If we then match this result with the premise of q(W,b) $\Rightarrow$ r(W,b), we may infer r(a,b) under the substitution set {a/W, b/X}.

Another important concept is the *composition* of unification substitutions. If S and S' are two substitution sets, then the composition of S and S' (written S'S) is obtained by applying S to the elements of S' and adding the result to S.

Consider the example of composing the sequence of substitutions

{X/Y, W/Z}, {V/X}, {a/V, f(b)/W}.

These are equivalent to the single substitution

{a/Y, f(b)/Z}.

This was produced by composing {X/Y, W/Z} with {V/X} to yield {V/Y, W/Z} and then composing this with {a/V, f(b)/W} to produce {a/Y, f(b)/Z}.

Composition is the method by which unification substitutions are combined and returned in the recursive function unify, presented next. Composition can be shown to be associative but not commutative. The exercises present these issues in more detail.

A final requirement of the unification algorithm is that the unifier be as general as possible: that the *most general unifier* be found for the two expressions. This is important, as will be seen in the next example, because, if generality is lost in the solution process, it will lessen the scope of the eventual solution or even eliminate the possibility of a solution entirely.

For example, in unifying p(X) and p(Y) any constant expression such as {fred/X, fred/Y} will do the trick. However, fred is not the most general unifier; any variable would work and produce a more general expression: {Z/X, Z/Y}. The solutions obtained from the first substitution instance would always be restricted by having the constant fred limit the resulting inferences; i.e., fred would be a unifier, but it would lessen the generality of the result.

MOST GENERAL UNIFIER (mgu)

If s is any unifier of expressions E and g is the most general unifier of that set of expressions, then for s applied to E there exists another unifier s′ such that Es = Egs′ (where gs′ is the composition of unifiers, as seen above).

The most general unifier for a set of expressions is unique except for alphabetic variations; i.e., whether a variable is eventually called X or Y really does not make any difference to the generality of the resulting unifications.

Unification is critically important for any artificial intelligence problem solver that uses the predicate calculus as a representation language. Unification specifies the conditions under which two (or more) predicate calculus expressions may be said to be equivalent. This underlies the possibility of using inference rules such as modus ponens or resolution with logical representations such as PROLOG or the LISP-based logic programming language described in Chapter 13.

We conclude by presenting the pseudocode for a function, unify, that computes the unifying substitutions (when this is possible) between two predicate calculus expressions. Unify takes as arguments two expressions in the predicate calculus and returns either the most general unifying substitutions or the constant FAIL if no unification is possible. It is defined as a recursive function: first, it recursively attempts to unify the initial components of the expressions. If this succeeds, any substitutions returned by this unification are applied to the remainder of both expressions. These are then passed in a second recursive call to unify, which attempts to complete the unification. The recursion stops when either argument is a symbol (a predicate, function name, constant, or variable) or the elements of the expression have all been matched.

To simplify the manipulation of predicate calculus expressions, the algorithm assumes a slightly modified expression syntax. Because unify simply performs syntactic pattern matching, it can effectively ignore the predicate calculus distinction between predicates, functions, and arguments. By representing a sentence as a *list* (an ordered sequence of elements) with the predicate or function name as the first element followed by its arguments, we simplify the manipulation of expressions. Expressions in which an argument is itself a predicate or function expression are represented as lists within the list, thus preserving the structure of the expression. Lists are delimited by parentheses, ( ), and list elements are separated by spaces. Examples of expressions in both predicate calculus (PC) and list syntax are:

PC SYNTAX	LIST SYNTAX
p(a,b)	(p a b)
p(f(a),g(X,Y))	(p (f a) (g X Y))
equal(eve,mother(cain))	(equal eve (mother cain))
p(X) ∧ q(Y)	((p X) ∧ (q Y))

It should be stressed again that this modification of the syntax is done purely to simplify the definition of unify and implies no alteration of predicate calculus semantics. Alternative versions of the algorithm could be written that parse expressions in their original syntax. It is interesting to note that this form is based on the syntax of the LISP programming language. For reasons that are discussed later in the text, LISP is the most commonly used AI programming language, with many LISP implementations of predicate calculus using this syntax.

```
function unify(E1, E2);
  begin
    case
      both E1 and E2 are constants or the empty list:          %recursion stops
        if E1 = E2 then return {}
          else return FAIL;

      E1 is a variable:
        if E1 occurs in E2 then return FAIL
          else return {E2/E1};

      E2 is a variable:
        if E2 occurs in E1 then return FAIL
          else return {E1/E2}

      otherwise:                                               %both E1 and E2 are lists
        begin
            HE1 := first element of E1;
            HE2 := first element of E2;
            SUBS1 := unify(HE1,HE2);
            if SUBS1 = FAIL then return FAIL;
            TE1 := apply(SUBS1, rest of E1);
            TE2 := apply(SUBS1, rest of E2);
            SUBS2 := unify(TE1,TE2);
            if SUBS2 = FAIL then return FAIL;
                else return composition(SUBS1,SUBS2)
        end
    end                                                        %end case
  end
```

2.3.3   A Unification Example

The behavior of the preceding algorithm may be clarified by tracing the call

unify((parents X (father X) (mother bill)), (parents bill (father bill) Y)).

When unify is first called, because neither argument is an atomic symbol, i.e., a variable or constant, the function will attempt to recursively unify the first elements of each expression, calling

unify(parents, parents).

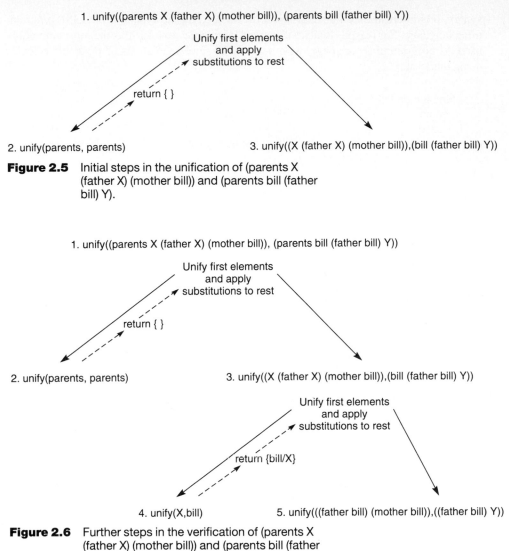

1. unify((parents X (father X) (mother bill)), (parents bill (father bill) Y))

Unify first elements
and apply
substitutions to rest

return { }

2. unify(parents, parents)   **3. unify((X (father X) (mother bill)),(bill (father bill) Y))**

Figure 2.5   Initial steps in the unification of (parents X
(father X) (mother bill)) and (parents bill (father
bill) Y).

1. unify((parents X (father X) (mother bill)), (parents bill (father bill) Y))

Unify first elements
and apply
substitutions to rest

return { }

2. unify(parents, parents)   **3. unify((X (father X) (mother bill)),(bill (father bill) Y))**

Unify first elements
and apply
substitutions to rest

return {bill/X}

4. unify(X,bill)   **5. unify(((father bill) (mother bill)),((father bill) Y))**

Figure 2.6   Further steps in the verification of (parents X
(father X) (mother bill)) and (parents bill (father
bill) Y).

This succeeds, returning the empty substitution, { }. Applying this to the remainder of the expressions creates no change; the algorithm then calls

unify((X (father X) (mother bill)), (bill (father bill) Y)).

A tree depiction of the execution at this stage appears in Figure 2.5.

In the second call to unify, neither expression is atomic, so the algorithm separates each expression into its first component and the remainder of the expression. This leads to the call unify(X, bill).

This call succeeds, because both expressions are atomic and one of them is a variable. The call returns the substitution {bill/X}. This substitution is applied to the remainder of each expression and unify is called on the results (Figure 2.6):

unify(((father bill) (mother bill)), ((father bill)Y)).

The first action of this call is to unify (father bill) with (father bill). This leads to the calls

unify(father, father)

unify(bill, bill)

unify((), ())

All of these succeed, returning the empty set of substitutions (Figure 2.7).
Unify is then called on the remainder of the expressions:

unify(((mother bill)), (Y)).

This, in turn, leads to calls

unify((mother bill), Y)

unify((),()).

In the first of these, (mother bill) unifies with Y. Notice that unification substitutes the whole *structure* (mother bill) for the variable Y. Thus, unification succeeds and returns the substitution {(mother bill)/Y}. The call

unify((),())

returns { }. These are composed, along with the earlier substitution {bill/X}, to return the answer {bill/X (mother bill)/Y}. A trace of the entire execution appears in Figure 2.7. Each call is numbered to indicate the order in which it was made; the substitutions returned by each call are noted on the arcs of the tree.

2.4   Application: A Logic-Based Financial Advisor

As a final example of the use of predicate calculus to represent and reason about problem domains, we design a simple financial advisor using predicate calculus. Although a simple example, it illustrates many of the issues involved in realistic applications.

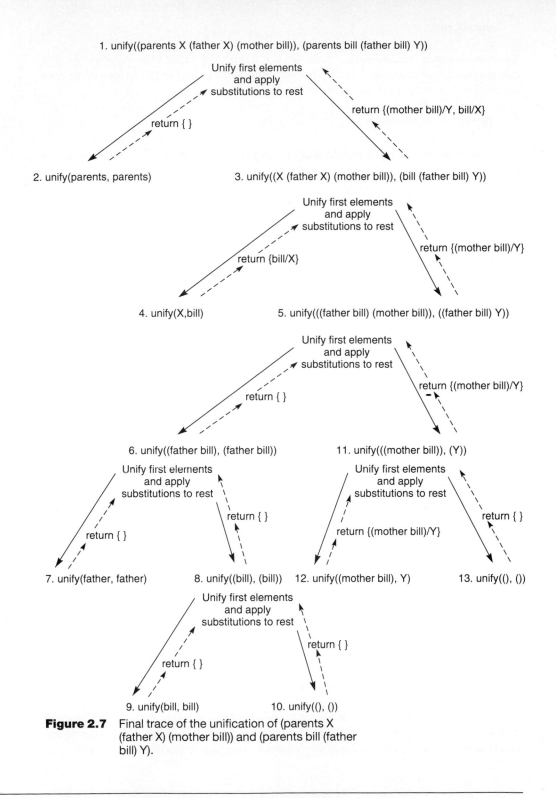

Figure 2.7 Final trace of the unification of (parents X (father X) (mother bill)) and (parents bill (father bill) Y).

The function of the advisor is to help a user decide whether to invest in a savings account or the stock market. Some investors may want to split their money between the two. The investment that will be recommended for individual investors depends on their income and the current amount they have saved according to the following criteria:

1. Individuals with an inadequate savings account should always make increasing the amount saved their first priority, regardless of their income.

2. Individuals with an adequate savings account and an adequate income should consider a riskier but potentially more profitable investment in the stock market.

3. Individuals with a lower income who already have an adequate savings account may want to consider splitting their surplus income between savings and stocks, to increase the cushion in savings while attempting to increase their income through stocks.

The adequacy of both savings and income is determined by the number of dependents an individual must support. Our rule is to have at least $5000 in the bank for each dependent. An adequate income must be a steady income and supply at least $15,000 per year plus an additional $4000 for each dependent.

To automate this advice, we translate these guidelines into sentences in the predicate calculus. The first task is to determine the major features that must be considered. Here, they are the adequacy of the savings and the income. These are represented by the predicates savings_account and income, respectively. Both of these are unary predicates, and their argument could be either adequate or inadequate. Thus,

savings_account(adequate).
savings_account(inadequate).
income(adequate).
income(inadequate).

are their possible values.

Conclusions are represented by the unary predicate investment, with possible values of its argument being stocks, savings, or combination (implying that the investment should be split).

Using these predicates, the different investment strategies are represented by implications. The first rule, that individuals with inadequate savings should make increased savings their main priority, is represented by

savings_account(inadequate) ⇒ investment(savings).

Similarly, the remaining two possible alternatives are represented by

savings_account(adequate) ∧ income(adequate) ⇒ investment(stocks).

savings_account(adequate) ∧ income(inadequate) ⇒ investment(combination).

Next, the advisor must determine when savings and income are adequate or inadequate. This will also be done using implication. The need to do arithmetic calculations requires the use of functions. To determine the minimum adequate savings, the function minsavings is defined. minsavings takes one argument, the number of dependents, and returns 5000 times that argument.

Using minsavings, the adequacy of savings is determined by the rules

∀ X amount_saved(X) ∧ ∃ Y (dependents(Y) ∧ greater(X, minsavings(Y))) ⇒
savings_account(adequate).

∀ X amount_saved(X) ∧ ∃ Y (dependents(Y) ∧ ¬ greater(X, minsavings(Y))) ⇒
savings_account(inadequate).

where minsavings(X) = 5000 * X.

In these definitions, amount_saved(X) and dependents(Y) assert the current amount in savings and the number of dependents of an investor; greater(X,Y) is the standard arithmetic test for one number being greater than another and is not formally defined in this example.

Similarly, a function minincome is defined as

minincome(X)=15000+(4000*X).

minincome is used to compute the minimum adequate income when given the number of dependents. The investor's current income is represented by a predicate, earnings. Because an adequate income must be both steady and above the minimum, earnings takes two arguments: the first is the amount earned, and the second must be equal to either steady or unsteady. The remaining rules needed for the advisor are

∀ X earnings(X, steady) ∧ ∃ Y (dependents(Y) ∧ greater(X, minincome(Y))) ⇒
income(adequate).

∀ X earnings(X, steady) ∧ ∃ Y (dependents(Y) ∧ ¬ greater(X, minincome(Y))) ⇒
income(inadequate).

∀ X earnings(X, unsteady) ⇒ income(inadequate).

In order to perform a consultation, a description of a particular investor is added to this set of predicate calculus sentences using the predicates amount_saved, earnings, and dependents. Thus, an individual with three dependents, $22,000 in savings, and a steady income of $25,000 would be described by

amount_saved(22000).
earnings(25000, steady).
dependents(3).

This yields a logical system consisting of the following sentences:

1. savings_account(inadequate) ⇒ investment(savings).
2. savings_account(adequate) ∧ income(adequate) ⇒ investment(stocks).

3. savings_account(adequate) ∧ income(inadequate) ⇒
   investment(combination).
4. ∀ X amount_saved(X) ∧ ∃ Y (dependents(Y) ∧
   greater(X, minsavings(Y))) ⇒ savings_account(adequate).
5. ∀ X amount_saved(X) ∧ ∃ Y (dependents(Y) ∧
   ¬ greater(X, minsavings(Y))) ⇒ savings_account(inadequate).
6. ∀ X earnings(X, steady) ∧ ∃ Y (dependents (Y) ∧
   greater(X, minincome(Y))) ⇒ income(adequate).
7. ∀ X earnings(X, steady) ∧ ∃ Y (dependents(Y) ∧
   ¬ greater(X, minincome(Y))) ⇒ income(inadequate).
8. ∀ X earnings(X, unsteady) ⇒ income(inadequate).
9. amount_saved(22000).
10. earnings(25000, steady).
11. dependents(3).

where minsavings(X) = 5000 * X and minincome(X) = 15000 + (4000 * X).

This set of logical sentences describes the problem domain. The assertions are numbered so that they may be referenced in the following trace.

Using unification and modus ponens, a correct investment strategy for this individual may be inferred as a logical consequence of these descriptions. A first step would be to unify the conjunction of 10 and 11 with the first two components of the premise of 7; i.e.,

earnings(25000,steady) ∧ dependents(3)

unifies with

earnings(X,steady) ∧ dependents(Y)

under the substitution {25000/X, 3/Y}. Performing this substitution yields the new implication

earnings(25000, steady) ∧ dependents(3) ∧ ¬ greater(25000, minincome(3)) ⇒
income(inadequate).

Evaluating the function minincome yields the expression

earnings(25000, steady) ∧ dependents(3) ∧ ¬ greater(25000, 27000) ⇒
income(inadequate).

Because all three components of the premise are individually true, by 10, 3, and the mathematical definition of greater, their conjunction is true and the entire premise is true. Modus ponens may therefore be applied, yielding the conclusion income(inadequate). This is added as assertion 12.

12. income(inadequate).

Similarly,

> amount_saved(22000) ∧ dependents(3)

unifies with the first two elements of the premise of assertion 4 under the substitution
{22000/X, 3/Y}, yielding the implication

> amount_saved(22000) ∧ dependents(3) ∧ greater(22000, minsavings(3)) ⇒
>   savings_account(adequate).

Here, evaluating the function minsavings(3) yields the expression

> amount_saved(22000) ∧ dependents(3) ∧ greater(22000, 15000) ⇒
>   savings_account(adequate).

Again, because all of the components of the premise of this implication are true, the
entire premise evaluates to true and modus ponens may again be applied, yielding the
conclusion savings_account(adequate), which is added as expression 13.

> 13. savings_account(adequate).

As an examination of expressions 3, 12, and 13 indicates, the premise of implication 3 is
also true. When we apply modus ponens a third time, the conclusion is invest-
ment(combination). This is the suggested investment for this individual.

This example illustrates how predicate calculus may be used to reason about a realistic
problem, drawing correct conclusions by applying inference rules to the initial problem
description. We have not discussed exactly how an algorithm can determine the correct
inferences to make to solve a given problem or the way in which this can be implemented
on a computer. These topics are discussed in Chapters 3 and 4.

2.5   Epilogue and References

In this chapter we introduced predicate calculus as a representation language for AI problem solving. The symbols, terms, expressions, and semantics of the language were
described and defined. Based on the semantics of predicate calculus, we defined inference
rules that allow us to derive sentences that logically follow a given set of expressions. We
defined a unification algorithm that determines the variable substitutions that make two
expressions match. Matching is essential to the application of inference rules. We concluded the chapter with the example of a financial advisor that represents financial knowledge in predicate calculus and demonstrates logical inference as a problem-solving
technique.

Predicate calculus is discussed in detail in a number of computer science books,
including *The Logical Basis for Computer Programming* by Zohar Manna and Richard
Waldinger (1985), *Logic for Computer Science* by Jean H. Gallier (1986), *Symbolic Logic
and Mechanical Theorem Proving* by Chin-liang Chang and Richard Char-tung Lee (1973),
and *An Introduction to Mathematical Logic and Type Theory* by Peter B. Andrews (1986).

Books that describe the use of predicate calculus as an artificial intelligence representation language include *Logical Foundations of Artificial Intelligence* by Michael Genesereth and Nils Nilsson (1987), *Principles of Artificial Intelligence* by Nils Nilsson (1980), *Automated Reasoning* by Larry Wos et al. (1984), and *Computer Modelling of Mathematical Reasoning* by Alan Bundy (1983). *Readings in Knowledge Representation* by Ronald Brachman and Hector Levesque (1985) includes a number of articles on the use of predicate calculus for knowledge representation.

2.6 Exercises

1. Using truth tables, prove the identities of Section 2.1.2.

2. A new operator, ⊕, or *exclusive-or*, may be defined by the following truth table:

P	Q	P ⊕ Q
T	T	F
T	F	T
F	T	T
F	F	F

   Create a propositional calculus expression using only ∧, ∨, and ¬ that is equivalent to P ⊕ Q. Prove their equivalence using truth tables.

3. The logical operator ⇔ is read "if and only if" P ⇔ Q is defined as being equivalent to (P ⇒ Q) ∧ (Q ⇒ P). Based on this definition, show that P ⇔ Q is logically equivalent to (P ∨ Q) ⇒ (P ∧ Q):

   a. By using truth tables.
   b. By a series of substitutions using the identities in Figure 2.2.

4. Prove that implication is transitive in the propositional calculus, that is, that ((P ⇒ Q) ∧ (Q ⇒ R)) ⇒ (P ⇒ R).

5. a. Prove that modus ponens is sound for propositional calculus. Hint: use truth tables to enumerate all possible interpretations.
   b. *Abduction* is an inference rule that infers P from P ⇒ Q and Q. Show that abduction is not sound.
   c. Show modus tollens ((P ⇒ Q) ∧ ¬ Q) ⇒ ¬ P is sound.

6. Assume that we have chosen to represent "Maria is Bill's mother" by mother(bill,maria) and "Amanda is one of Bill's ancestors" by ancestor(bill,amanda). Write a predicate calculus expression stating that every one of Bill's ancestors is either his mother, father, or one of their ancestors.

7. Attempt to unify the following pairs of expressions. Either show their most general unifiers or explain why they will not unify.
   a. p(X,Y) and p(a,Z)
   b. p(X,X) and p(a,b)
   c. ancestor(X,Y) and ancestor(bill,father(bill))
   d. ancestor(X,father(X)) and ancestor(david,george)
   e. q(X) and ¬ q(a)
   f. p(X,a,Y) and p(Z,Z,b)

8. a. Compose the substitution sets {a/X, Y/Z} and {X/W, b/Y}.
   b. Prove that composition of substitution sets is associative.
   c. Construct an example to show that composition is not commutative.

9. Implement the unification algorithm of Section 2.3.2 in the computer language of your choice.

10. Give two alternative interpretations for the blocks world description of Figure 2.3.

11. Jane Doe has four dependents, a steady income of $30,000, and $15,000 in her savings account. Add the appropriate predicates describing her situation to the general investment advisor of the example in Section 2.4 and perform the unifications and inferences needed to determine her suggested investment.

12. Write a set of logical predicates that will perform simple automobile diagnostics (e.g., if the engine won't turn over and the lights won't come on, then the battery is bad). Don't try to be too elaborate, but cover the cases of bad battery, out of gas, bad spark plugs, and bad starter motor.

13. The following story is quoted from N. Wirth's "Algorithms + data structures = programs" (Wirth 1976).

> I married a widow (let's call her W) who has a grown-up daughter (call her D). My father (F), who visited us quite often, fell in love with my step-daughter and married her. Hence my father became my son-in-law and my step-daughter became my mother. Some months later, my wife gave birth to a son (S_1), who became the brother-in-law of my father, as well as my uncle. The wife of my father, that is, my step-daughter, also had a son (S_2).

Using predicate calculus, create a set of expressions that represent the situation in the above story. Add expressions defining basic family relationships such as the definition of father-in-law and use modus ponens on this system to prove the conclusion that "I am my own grandfather."

STRUCTURES AND STRATEGIES FOR STATE SPACE SEARCH

In order to cope, an organism must either armor itself (like a tree or a clam) and "hope for the best," or else develop methods for getting out of harm's way and into the better neighborhoods of the vicinity. If you follow this later course, you are confronted with the primordial problem that every agent must continually solve: Now what do I do?

—DANIEL C. DENNETT, "Consciousness Explained"

Two roads diverged in a yellow wood,
And sorry I could not travel both
And be one traveler, long I stood
And looked down one as far as I could
To where it bent in the undergrowth;
Then took the other . . .

—ROBERT FROST, "The Road Not Taken"

3.0   Introduction

Chapter 2 introduced predicate calculus as an example of an artificial intelligence representation language. Well-formed predicate calculus expressions provide a means of describing objects and relations in a problem domain, and inference rules such as modus ponens allow us to infer new knowledge from these descriptions. These inferences define a space that is searched to find a problem solution. Chapter 3 introduces the theory of state space search.

To successfully design and implement search algorithms, a programmer must be able to analyze and predict their behavior. Questions that need to be answered include:

Is the problem solver guaranteed to find a solution?

Will the problem solver always terminate, or can it become caught in an infinite loop?

When a solution is found, is it guaranteed to be optimal?

What is the complexity of the search process in terms of time usage? Space usage?

How can the interpreter most effectively reduce search complexity?

How can an interpreter be designed to most effectively utilize a representation language?

The theory of *state space search* is our primary tool for answering these questions. By representing a problem as a *state space graph*, we can use *graph theory* to analyze the structure and complexity of both the problem and the procedures used to solve it.

A graph consists of a set of *nodes* and a set of *arcs* or *links* connecting pairs of nodes. In the state space model of problem solving, the nodes of a graph are taken to represent discrete *states* in a problem-solving process, such as the results of logical inferences or configurations of a game board. The arcs of the graph represent transitions between states. These transitions correspond to logical inferences or legal moves of a game. In expert systems, for example, states describe our knowledge of a problem instance at some stage of a reasoning process. Expert knowledge, in the form of *if . . . then* rules, allows us to generate new information; the act of applying a rule is represented as an arc between states.

Graph theory is our best tool for reasoning about the structure of objects and relations; indeed, this is precisely the need that led to its creation in the early eighteenth century. The Austrian mathematician Leonhard Euler invented graph theory to solve the "bridges of Königsberg problem." The city of Königsberg occupied both banks and two islands of a river. The islands and the riverbanks were connected by seven bridges, as indicated in Figure 3.1.

The bridges of Königsberg problem asks if there is a walk around the city that crosses each bridge exactly once. Although the residents had failed to find such a walk and doubted that it was possible, no one had proved its impossibility. Devising a form of graph theory, Euler created an alternative representation for the map, presented in Figure 3.2. The river-banks (rb1 and rb2) and islands (i1 and i2) are described by the nodes of a graph; the bridges are represented by labeled arcs between nodes (b1, b2, ..., b7). The graph representation preserves the essential structure of the bridge system, while ignoring extraneous features such as distance and direction.

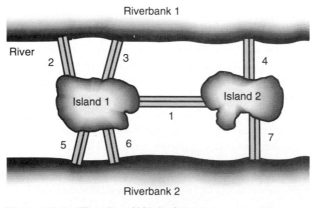

Figure 3.1 The city of Königsberg.

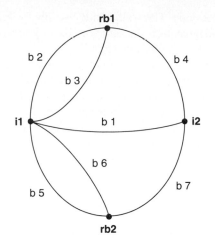

Figure 3.2 Graph of the Königsberg bridge system.

Alternatively, we may represent the Königsberg bridge system using predicate calculus. The connect predicate corresponds to an arc of the graph, asserting that two land masses are connected by a particular bridge. Each bridge requires two connect predicates, one for each direction in which the bridge may be crossed:

connect(i1,i2,b1).   connect(i2,i1,b1).
connect(rb1,i1,b2).   connect(i1,rb1,b2).
connect(rb1,i1,b3).   connect(i1,rb1,b3).
connect(rb1,i2,b4).   connect(i2,rb1,b4).
connect(rb2,i1,b5).   connect(i1,rb2,b5).
connect(rb2,i1,b6).   connect(i1,rb2,b6).
connect(rb2,i2,b7).   connect(i2,rb2,b7).

This is equivalent to the graph representation in that the connectedness is preserved. Indeed, an algorithm could translate between the two representations with no loss of information. However, the structure is made explicit in the graph representation, whereas it is left implicit in the predicate calculus version. Euler's proof illustrates this distinction.

In proving that the walk was impossible, Euler focused on the *degree* of the nodes of the graph, observing that a node could be of either *even* or *odd* degree. An *even* degree node has an even number of arcs joining it to neighboring nodes. An *odd* degree node has an odd number of arcs.

With the exception of its beginning and ending nodes, the desired walk would have to leave each node exactly as often as it entered it. Nodes of odd degree could be used only as the beginning or ending of the walk, because such nodes could be crossed only a certain number of times before they proved to be a dead end. The traveler could not exit the node without using a previously traveled arc.

Euler noted that unless a graph contained either exactly zero or two nodes of odd degree, the walk was impossible. If there were two odd-degree nodes, the walk could start at the first and end at the second; if there were no nodes of odd degree, the walk could begin and end at the same node. The walk is not possible for graphs containing any other number of nodes of odd degree, as is the case with the city of Königsberg. This problem is now called finding an *Euler path* through a graph.

Note that the predicate calculus representation, though it captures the relationships between bridges and land in the city, does not suggest the concept of the degree of a node. In the graph representation there is a single instance of each node with arcs between the nodes, rather than multiple occurrences of constants as arguments in a set of predicates. For this reason, the graph representation suggests the concept of node degree and the focus of Euler's proof. This illustrates graph theory's power for analyzing the structure of objects, properties, and relationships. In Chapter 9 we examine the advantages of graph theory for knowledge representation (semantic networks); this chapter uses graph theory to construct a computational theory of problem solving.

After reviewing basic graph theory, we present the state space description of problems, along with graph search as a problem-solving methodology. Depth-first and breadth-first search are two strategies for searching a state space. We compare these and make the added distinction between goal-driven and data-driven search. Section 3.3 demonstrates how state space search is used to characterize logical reasoning. Throughout the chapter, we use graph theory to analyze the structure and complexity of a variety of problems.

3.1 Graph Theory

3.1.1 Structures for State Space Search

A graph is a set of nodes and arcs that connect them. A *labeled* graph has one or more descriptors (labels) attached to each node that distinguish that node from any other node in the graph. In a state space graph, these descriptors identify states in a problem-solving process. If there are no descriptive differences between two nodes, they are considered the same. The arc between two nodes is indicated by the labels of the connected nodes.

The arcs of a graph may also be labeled. Arc labels are used to indicate that an arc represents a named relationship (as in a semantic network) or to attach weights to arcs (as in the traveling salesperson problem). If there are different arcs between the same two nodes (as in Figure 3.2), these can also be distinguished through labeling.

A graph is *directed* if arcs have an associated directionality. The arcs in a directed graph are usually drawn as arrows or have an arrow attached to indicate direction. Arcs that can be crossed in either direction may have two arrows attached but more often have no direction indicators at all. Figure 3.3 is a labeled, directed graph: arc ab may only be crossed from node a to node b, but arc bc is crossable in either direction.

A *path* through a graph connects a sequence of nodes through successive arcs. The path is represented by an ordered list that records the nodes in the order they occur in the path. In Figure 3.3, [a, b, c, d] represents the path through nodes a, b, c, and d, in that order.

A *rooted* graph has a unique node, called the *root*, such that there is a path from the root to all nodes within the graph. In drawing a rooted graph, the root is usually drawn at the top of the page, above the other nodes. The state space graphs for games are usually

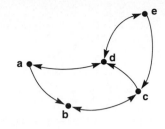

Nodes = {a,b,c,d,e}
Arcs = {(a,b),(a,d),(b,c),(c,b),(c,d),(d,a),(d,e),(e,c),(e,d)}

Figure 3.3   A labeled directed graph.

rooted graphs with the start of the game as the root. The initial moves of the tic-tac-toe game graph are represented by the rooted graph of Figure II.5. This is a directed graph with all arcs having a single direction. Note that this graph contains no cycles; players cannot (as much as they might sometimes wish!) undo a move.

A *tree* is a graph in which two nodes have at most one path between them. Trees often have roots, in which case they are usually drawn with the root at the top, like a rooted graph. Because each node in a tree has only one path of access from any other node, it is impossible for a path to *loop* or *cycle* continuously through a sequence of nodes.

Terms used to describe relationships between nodes include *parent, child,* and *sibling.* These are used in the usual familial fashion with the parent preceding its child along a directed arc. The children of a node are called *siblings.* Similarly, an *ancestor* comes before a *descendant* in some path of a directed graph. In Figure 3.4, b is a *parent* of nodes e and f (which are, therefore, *children* of b and *siblings* of each other). Nodes a and c are *ancestors* of states g, h, and i, and g, h, and i are *descendants* of a and c.

Before introducing the state space representation of problems we formally define these concepts.

D E F I N I T I O N

GRAPH

A graph consists of:

A set of *nodes* $N_1, N_2, N_3, \ldots N_n \ldots$, which need not be finite.

A set of *arcs* that connect pairs of nodes.

(Arcs are often described as an ordered pair of nodes; i.e., the arc (N_3, N_4) connects node N_3 to node N_4.)

A *directed* graph has an indicated direction for traversing each arc. For example, a directed graph might have (N_3, N_4) as an arc but not (N_4, N_3). This would indicate that a path through the graph could go from node N_3 to N_4 but not from N_4 to N_3.

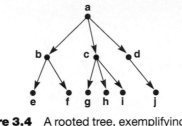

Figure 3.4   A rooted tree, exemplifying family relationships.

If a directed arc connects N_j and N_k, then N_j is called the *parent* of N_k and N_k, the *child* of N_j. If the graph also contains an arc (N_j, N_l), then N_k and N_l are called *siblings*.

A *rooted* graph has a unique node N_S from which all paths in the graph originate. That is, the root has no parent in the graph.

A *tip* or *leaf* node is a node that has no children.

An ordered sequence of nodes $[N_1, N_2, N_3, ..., N_n]$, where each N_i, N_{i+1} in the sequence represents an arc (N_i, N_{i+1}), is called a *path* of length $n-1$ in the graph.

On a path in a rooted graph, a node is said to be an *ancestor* of all nodes positioned after it (to its right) and a *descendant* of all nodes before it (to its left).

A path that contains any node more than once (some N_j in the definition of path above is repeated) is said to contain a *cycle* or *loop*.

A *tree* is a graph in which there is a unique path between every pair of nodes. (The paths in a tree, therefore, contain no cycles.)

The edges in a rooted tree are directed away from the root. Each node in a rooted tree has a unique parent.

Two nodes in a graph are said to be *connected* if a path exists that includes them both.

3.1.2   State Space Representation of Problems

In the *state space representation* of a problem, nodes of a graph correspond to partial problem solution *states* and the arcs correspond to steps in a problem-solving process. An *initial state*, corresponding to the given information in a problem instance, forms the root of the graph. The graph also defines a *goal* condition, which is the solution to a problem instance. *State space search* characterizes problem solving as the process of finding a *solution path* from the start state to a goal.

A goal may describe a state, such as a winning board in tic-tac-toe (Fig. II.5) or a goal configuration in the 8-puzzle (Fig. 3.6). Alternatively, a goal can describe some property of the solution path itself. In the traveling salesperson problem (Figs. 3.7 and 3.8), search terminates when the "shortest" path is found through all nodes of the graph. In the parsing problem (Section 3.3), the path of successful analysis of a sentence indicates termination.

Arcs of the state space correspond to steps in a solution process and paths through the space represent solutions in various stages of completion. Paths are searched, beginning at the start state and continuing through the graph, until either the goal description is satisfied or they are abandoned. The actual generation of new states along the path is done by applying operators, such as "legal moves" in a game or inference rules in a logic problem or expert system, to existing states on a path.

We now formally define the state space representation of problems.

DEFINITION

STATE SPACE SEARCH

A *state space* is represented by a four-tuple [N,A,S,GD], where:

N is the set of nodes or states of the graph. These correspond to the states in a problem-solving process.

A is the set of arcs (or links) between nodes. These correspond to the steps in a problem-solving process.

S, a nonempty subset of N, contains the start state(s) of the problem.

GD, a nonempty subset of N, contains the goal state(s) of the problem. The states in GD are described using either:

1. A measurable property of the states encountered in the search.
2. A property of the path developed in the search.

A *solution path* is a path through this graph from a node in S to a node in GD.

The task of a search algorithm is to find a solution path through such a problem space. Search algorithms must keep track of the paths from a start to a goal node, because these paths contain the series of operations that lead to the problem solution.

One of the general features of a graph, and one of the problems that arise in the design of a graph search algorithm, is that states can sometimes be reached through different paths. For example, in Figure 3.3 a path can be made from state a to state d either through b and c or directly from a to d. This makes it important to choose the *best* path according to the needs of a problem. In addition, multiple paths to a state can lead to loops or cycles in a solution path that prevent the algorithm from reaching a goal. A blind search for goal state e in the graph of Figure 3.3 might search the sequence of states abcdabcdabcd... forever!

If the space to be searched is a tree (as in Fig. 3.4), the problem of cycles does not occur. It is, therefore, important to distinguish between problems whose state space is a tree and those that may contain loops. General graph search algorithms must detect and eliminate loops from potential solution paths, whereas tree searches may gain efficiency by eliminating this test and its overhead.

Tic-tac-toe and the 8-puzzle exemplify the state spaces of simple games. Both of these examples demonstrate termination conditions of type 1 in the above definition. Example 3.1.3, the traveling salesperson problem, has a goal description of type 2.

The state space representation of tic-tac-toe appears in Figure II.5. The start state is an empty board, and the termination or goal description is a board state having three Xs in a row, column, or diagonal (assuming that the goal is a win for X). The path from the start state to a goal state gives the series of moves in a winning game.

The states in the space are all the different configurations of Xs and Os that the game can have. Of course, although there are 3^9 ways to arrange {blank, X, O} in nine spaces, most of them could never occur in an actual game. Arcs are generated by legal moves of the game, alternating between placing an X and an O in an unused location. The state space is a graph rather than a tree, as some states on the third and deeper levels can be reached by different paths. However, there are no cycles in the state space, because the directed arcs of the graph do not allow a move to be undone. It is impossible to "go back up" the structure once a state has been reached. No checking for cycles in path generation is necessary. A graph structure with this property is called a *directed acyclic graph*, or *DAG*, and is common in state space search.

The state space representation provides a means of determining the complexity of the problem. In tic-tac-toe, there are nine first moves with eight possible responses to each of them, followed by seven possible responses to each of these, and so on. It follows that $9 \times 8 \times 7 \times \ldots$ or 9! different paths can be generated. Although it is not impossible for a computer to search this number of paths (362,880) exhaustively, many important problems also exhibit factorial or exponential complexity, although on a much larger scale. Chess has 10^{120} possible game paths; checkers has 10^{40}, some of which may never occur in an actual game. These spaces are difficult or impossible to search exhaustively. Strategies for searching such large spaces rely on heuristics to reduce the complexity of the search (Chapter 4).

In the *15-puzzle* of Figure 3.5, 15 differently numbered tiles are fitted into 16 spaces on a grid. One space is left blank so that tiles can be moved around to form different patterns. The goal is to find a series of moves of tiles into the blank space that places the board in a goal configuration. This is a common game that most of us played as children. (The version we remember was about 3 inches square and had red and white tiles in a black frame.)

A number of interesting aspects of this game have made it useful to researchers in problem solving. The state space is large enough to be interesting but is not completely intractable (16! if symmetric states are treated as distinct). Game states are easy to repre-

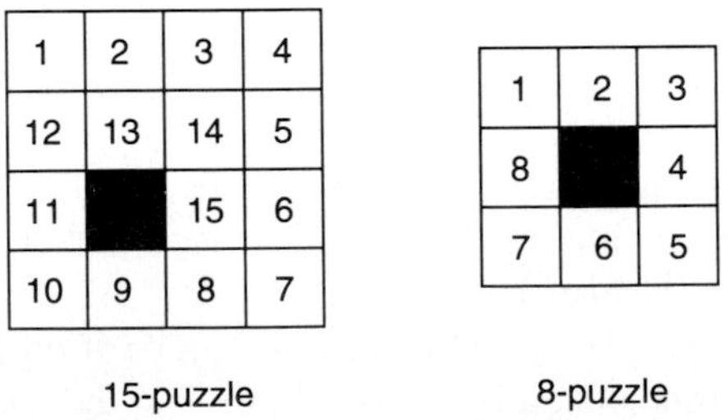

15-puzzle   8-puzzle

Figure 3.5   The 15-puzzle and the 8-puzzle.

sent. The game is rich enough to provide a number of interesting heuristics (see Chapter 4).

The *8-puzzle* is a 3 × 3 version of the 15-puzzle in which eight tiles can be moved around in nine spaces. Because it generates a smaller state space than the full 15-puzzle, it is used for many of the examples in this text.

Although in the physical puzzle moves are made by moving tiles ("move the 7 tile right, provided the blank is to the right of the tile" or "move the 3 tile down"), it is much simpler to think in terms of "moving the blank space" instead. This simplifies the definition of move rules because there are eight tiles but only a single blank. The legal moves are:

move the blank up   ↑
move the blank right   →
move the blank down   ↓
move the blank left   ←

In order to apply a move, we must make sure that it does not move the blank off the board. Therefore, all four moves are not applicable at all times; for example, when the blank is in one of the corners only two moves are possible.

If we specify a beginning state and a goal state for the 8-puzzle, it is possible to give a state space accounting of the problem-solving process (Figure 3.6). States could be rep-

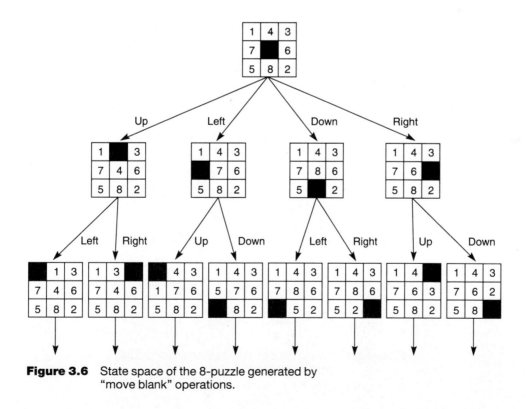

Figure 3.6   State space of the 8-puzzle generated by "move blank" operations.

resented using a simple 3 × 3 array. A predicate calculus representation could use a "state" predicate with nine parameters (for the locations of numbers in the grid). Four procedures, describing each of the possible moves of the blank, define the arcs in the state space.

As with tic-tac-toe, the state space for the 8-puzzle is a graph (with most states having multiple parents), but unlike tic-tac-toe, cycles are possible. The GD or goal description of the state space is a particular state or board configuration. When this state is found on a path, the search terminates. The path from the start to the goal is the desired series of moves.

It is interesting to note that the complete state space of the 8- and 15-puzzles consists of two disconnected (and in this case equal-sized) subgraphs. This makes half the possible states in the search space impossible to reach from any given start state. If we exchange (by prying loose!) two immediately adjacent tiles, states in the other component of the space become reachable.

EXAMPLE 3.1.3: THE TRAVELING SALESPERSON

Suppose a salesperson has five cities to visit and then must return home. The goal of the problem is to find the shortest path for the salesperson to travel, visiting each city, and then return to the starting city. Figure 3.7 gives an instance of this problem. The nodes of the graph represent cities, and each arc is labeled with a weight indicating the cost of traveling that arc. Let us assume the salesperson lives in city A and will return there.

The path [A,D,C,B,E,A], with associated cost of 450 miles, is an example of a possible circuit. The goal description requires a complete circuit with minimum cost. Note that the goal description is a property of the entire path, rather than of a single state. This is a goal description of type 2 from the definition of state space search.

Figure 3.8 shows one way in which possible solution paths may be generated and compared. Beginning with node A, possible next states are added until all cities are included and the path returns home. The goal is the lowest-cost path.

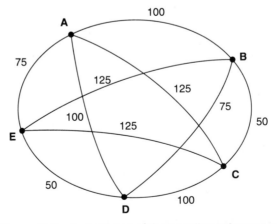

Figure 3.7　An instance of the traveling salesperson problem.

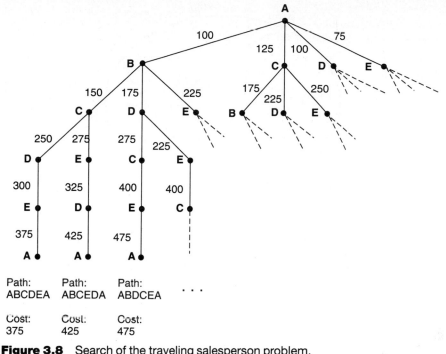

Figure 3.8 Search of the traveling salesperson problem. Each arc is marked with the total weight of all paths from the start node (A) to its endpoint.

As Figure 3.8 suggests, the complexity of exhaustive search in the traveling salesperson problem is $(N - 1)!$, where N is the number of cities in the graph. For 9 cities we may exhaustively try all paths, but for any problem instance of interesting size, such as 50 cities, simple exhaustive search cannot be performed within a practical length of time.

Several techniques can reduce the search complexity. One is called *branch and bound* (Horowitz and Sahni 1978). Branch and bound generates paths one at a time, keeping track of the best circuit found so far. This value is used as a *bound* on future candidates. As paths are constructed a city at a time, the algorithm examines each partially completed path. If it determines that the best possible extension to a path will have greater cost than the bound, it eliminates that partial path and *all* of its possible extensions. This reduces search considerably but still leaves an exponential number of paths (1.26^N rather than N!).

Another strategy for controlling search constructs the path according to the rule "go to the closest unvisited city." The "nearest neighbor" path through the graph of Figure 3.8 is [A,E,D,B,C,A], at a cost of 375 miles. This method is highly efficient, as there is only one path to be tried! The nearest neighbor heuristic is fallible, as graphs exist for which it does not find the shortest path (Figure 3.9), but it is a possible compromise when the time required makes exhaustive search impractical.

Section 3.2 examines strategies for state space search.

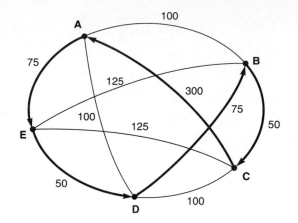

Figure 3.9 An instance of the traveling salesperson problem with the nearest neighbor path in bold. Note that this path (A, E, D, B, C, A), at a cost of 550, is not the shortest path. The comparatively high cost of arc (C, A) defeated the heuristic.

3.2 Strategies for State Space Search

3.2.1 Data-Driven and Goal-Driven Search

A state space may be searched in two directions: from the given data of a problem instance toward a goal or from a goal back to the data.

In *data-driven search*, sometimes called *forward chaining*, the problem solver begins with the given facts of the problem and a set of legal moves or rules for changing state. Search proceeds by applying rules to facts to produce new facts, which are in turn used by the rules to generate more new facts. This process continues until (we hope!) it generates a path that satisfies the goal condition.

An alternative approach is possible: take the goal that we want to solve. See what rules or legal moves could be used to generate this goal and determine what conditions must be true to use them. These conditions become the new goals, or *subgoals*, for the search. Search continues, working backward through successive subgoals until (we hope!) it works back to the facts of the problem. This finds the chain of moves or rules leading from data to a goal, although it does so in backward order. This approach is called *goal-driven* reasoning, or *backward chaining*, and is like the simple childhood trick of trying to solve a maze by working back from the finish to the start.

To summarize: data-driven reasoning takes the facts of the problem and applies the rules and legal moves to produce new facts that lead to a goal; goal-driven reasoning focuses on the goal, finds the rules that could produce the goal, and chains backward through successive rules and subgoals to the given facts of the problem.

In the final analysis, both data-driven and goal-driven problem solvers search the same state space graph; however, the order and actual number of states searched can differ. The preferred strategy is determined by the properties of the problem itself. These include the complexity of the rules, the "shape" of the state space, and the nature and availability of the problem data. All of these vary for different problems.

As an example of the effect a search strategy can have on the complexity of search, consider the problem of confirming or denying the statement "I am a descendant of Thomas Jefferson." A solution is a path of direct lineage between the "I" and Thomas Jefferson. This space may be searched in two directions, starting with the "I" and working along ancestor lines to Thomas Jefferson or starting with Thomas Jefferson and working through his descendants.

Some simple assumptions let us estimate the size of the space searched in each direction. Thomas Jefferson was born about 250 years ago; if we assume 25 years per generation, the required path will be about length 10. As each person has exactly two parents, a search back from the "I" would examine on the order of 2^{10} ancestors. A search that worked forward from Thomas Jefferson would examine more states, as people tend to have more than two children (particularly in the eighteenth and nineteenth centuries). If we assume an average of only three children per family, the search would examine on the order of 3^{10} nodes of the family tree. Thus, a search back from the "I" would examine fewer nodes. Note, however, that both directions yield exponential complexity.

Problem solvers have been written using each of the data- and goal-driven approaches; the decision is based on the structure of the problem to be solved. Goal-driven search is suggested if:

1. A goal or hypothesis is given in the problem statement or can easily be formulated. In a mathematics theorem prover, for example, the goal is the theorem to be proved. Many diagnostic systems, such as MYCIN, consider potential diagnoses in a systematic fashion, confirming or eliminating them using goal-driven reasoning.

2. There are a large number of rules that match the facts of the problem and thus produce an increasing number of conclusions or goals. Early selection of a goal can eliminate most of these branches, making goal-driven search more effective in pruning the space (Figure 3.10). In a mathematics theorem prover, for example, the number of rules that conclude a given theorem is much smaller than the number of rules that may be applied to the entire set of axioms.

3. Problem data are not given but must be acquired by the problem solver. In this case, goal-driven search can help guide data acquisition. In a medical diagnosis program, for example, a wide range of diagnostic tests can be applied. Doctors order only those that are necessary to confirm or deny a particular set of hypotheses.

Goal-driven search thus uses knowledge of the desired goal to guide the search through relevant rules and eliminate branches of the space.

Data-driven search is appropriate to problems in which:

1. All or most of the data are given in the initial problem statement. Interpretation problems often fit this mold by presenting a collection of data and asking the system to provide a high-level interpretation. Systems that analyze particular data (such as the PROSPECTOR or Dipmeter programs, which interpret geological

data or attempt to find what minerals are likely to be found at a site) fit the data-driven approach.

2. There are a large number of potential goals, but there are only a few ways to use the facts and given information of a particular problem instance (Figure 3.11). The DENDRAL program, an expert system that finds the molecular structure of organic compounds based on their formula, mass spectrographic data, and knowledge of chemistry, is an example of this. For any organic compound, there are an enormous number of possible structures. However, the mass spectrographic data on a compound allow DENDRAL to eliminate all but a few of these.

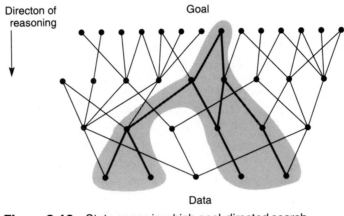

Figure 3.10 State space in which goal-directed search effectively prunes extraneous search paths.

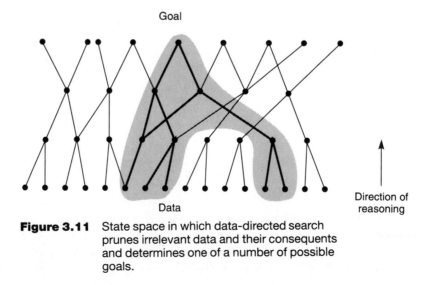

Figure 3.11 State space in which data-directed search prunes irrelevant data and their consequents and determines one of a number of possible goals.

3. It is difficult to form a goal or hypothesis. In a DENDRAL consultation, for example, little is initially known about the possible structure of a compound.

Data-driven search uses the knowledge and constraints found in the given data of a problem to guide search along lines known to be true.

To summarize, there is no substitute for careful analysis of the particular problem, considering such issues as the *branching factor* of rule applications (see Chapter 4; on average, how many new states are generated by rule applications in both directions?), availability of data, and ease of determining potential goals.

3.2.2 Implementing Graph Search

In solving a problem using either goal- or data-driven search, a problem solver must find a path from a start state to a goal through the state space graph. The sequence of arcs in this path corresponds to the ordered steps of the solution. If a problem solver were given an oracle or other infallible mechanism for choosing a solution path, search would not be required. The problem solver would move unerringly through the space to the desired goal, constructing the path as it went. Because oracles do not exist for interesting problems, a problem solver must consider different paths through the space until it finds a goal. *Backtracking* is a technique for systematically trying all paths through a state space.

Backtracking search begins at the start state and pursues a path until it reaches either a goal or a "dead end." If it finds a goal, it quits and returns the solution path. If it reaches a dead end, it "backtracks" to the most recent node on the path having unexamined siblings and continues down one of these branches. The algorithm's behavior at each node is described in the following recursive rule:

> If the present state S does not meet the requirements of the goal description, then generate its first descendant S_{child_1} and apply the backtrack procedure recursively to this node. If backtrack does not find a goal node in the subgraph rooted at S_{child_1}, repeat the procedure for its sibling S_{child_2}. This continues until either some descendant of a child is a goal node or all of the children have been so searched. If none of the children of S leads to a goal, then backtrack "fails back" to the parent of S, where it is applied to the siblings of S, and so on.

The algorithm continues in this fashion until it finds a goal or exhausts the state space. Figure 3.12 shows the backtrack algorithm applied to a hypothetical state space. The direction of the dashed arrows on the tree indicates the progress of search up and down the space. The number beside each node indicates the order in which it is visited.

Below, we define an algorithm that performs a backtracking search. It uses three lists to keep track of nodes in the state space:

> SL, for state list, lists the states in the current path being tried. If a goal is found, SL contains the ordered list of states on the solution path.

> NSL, for new state list, contains nodes awaiting evaluation, i.e., nodes whose descendants have not yet been generated and searched.

> DE, for dead ends, lists states whose descendants have failed to contain a goal node. If these states are encountered again, they will be detected as elements of DE and eliminated from consideration immediately.

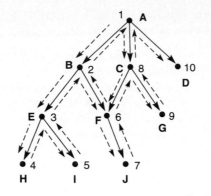

Figure 3.12 Depth-first backtracking search of a hypothetical state space.

In defining the backtrack algorithm for the general case (a graph rather than a tree), it is necessary to detect multiple occurrences of any state so that it will not be reentered and cause (infinite) loops in the path. This is accomplished by testing each newly generated state for membership in any of these three lists. If a new state belongs to any of these lists, then it has already been visited and may be ignored.

```
function backtrack;

begin
  SL := [Start];  NSL := [Start];  DE := [ ];  CS := Start;              % initialize:
  while NSL ≠ [ ]                                          % while there are states to be tried
    do begin
      if CS = goal (or meets goal description)
        then return(SL);                            % on success, return list of states in path.
      if CS has no children (excluding nodes already on DE, SL, and NSL)
        then begin
          while SL is not empty and CS = the first element of SL
            do begin
              add CS to DE;                                  % record state as dead end
              remove first element from SL;                              % backtrack
              remove first element from NSL;
              CS := first element of NSL;
            end
          add CS to SL;
        end
      else begin
        place children of CS (except nodes already on DE, SL, or NSL) on NSL;
        CS := first element of NSL;
        add CS to SL
      end
    end;
    return FAIL;                                          % state space is exhausted.
  end.
```

In backtrack, the state currently under consideration is called CS for current state. CS is always equal to the state most recently added to SL and represents the "frontier" of the solution path currently being explored. Inference rules, moves in the game, or other appropriate problem-solving operators are ordered and applied to CS. The result is an ordered set of new states, the children of CS. The first of these children is made the new current state and the rest are placed in order on NSL for future examination. The new current state is added to SL and search continues. If CS has no children, it is removed from SL (this is where the algorithm "backtracks") and any remaining children of its predecessor on SL are examined.

A trace of **backtrack** on the graph of Figure 3.12 is given by:

Initialize: SL = [A]; NSL = [A]; DE = [ ]; CS = A;

AFTER ITERATION	CS	SL	NSL	DE
0	A	[A]	[A]	[]
1	B	[B A]	[B C D A]	[]
2	E	[E B A]	[E F B C D A]	[]
3	H	[H E B A]	[H I E F B C D A]	[]
4	I	[I E B A]	[I E F B C D A]	[H]
5	F	[F B A]	[F B C D A]	[E I H]
6	J	[J F B A]	[J F B C D A]	[E I H]
7	C	[C A]	[C D A]	[B F J E I H]
8	G	[G C A]	[G C D A]	[B F J E I H]

As presented here, **backtrack** implements data-driven search, taking the root as a start state and evaluating its children to search for the goal. The algorithm can be restructured into a goal-driven search by letting the goal be the root of the graph and evaluating descendants back in an attempt to find a start state. Also, if the goal description is of type 2 (see Section 3.1.2), the algorithm must determine a goal state by examining the path on SL.

backtrack is an algorithm for searching state space graphs. The graph search algorithms in the remainder of the text, including depth-first, breadth-first, and best-first search, exploit the ideas used in backtrack, including:

1. The use of a list of unprocessed states (NSL) to allow the algorithm to return (backtrack) to any of these states.

2. A list of "bad" states (DE) to prevent the algorithm from retrying useless paths.

3. A list of nodes (SL) on the current solution path that is returned if a goal is found.

4. Explicit checks for membership of new states in these lists to prevent looping.

The next section introduces search algorithms that, like **backtrack**, use lists to keep track of states in a search space. These algorithms, including *depth-first*, *breadth-first*, and *best-first* (Chapter 4) search, differ from backtrack in providing a more flexible basis for implementing alternative graph search strategies.

3.2.3 Depth-First and Breadth-First Search

In addition to specifying a search direction (data-driven or goal-driven), a search algorithm determines the order in which states are examined in the tree or graph. This section considers two possibilities: *depth-first* and *breadth-first* search.

Consider the graph represented in Figure 3.13. States are labeled (A, B, C, . . .) so that they can be referred to in the discussion that follows. In depth-first search, when a state is examined, all of its children and their descendants are examined before any of its siblings. Depth-first search goes deeper into the search space whenever this is possible. Only when no further descendants of a state can be found are its siblings considered. Depth-first search examines the states in the graph of Figure 3.13 in the order A,B,E,K,S,L,T,F,M,C,G,N,H,O,P,U,D,I,Q,J,R. The backtrack algorithm of Section 3.2.2 implemented depth-first search.

Breadth-first search, in contrast, explores the space in a level-by-level fashion. Only when there are no more states to be explored at a given level does the algorithm move on to the next level. A breadth-first search of the graph of Figure 3.13 considers the states in the order A,B,C,D,E,F,G,H,I,J,K,L,M,N,O,P,Q,R,S,T,U.

We implement breadth-first search using lists, open and closed, to keep track of progress through the state space. open, like NSL in backtrack, lists states that have been generated but whose children have not been examined. The order in which states are removed from open determines the order of the search. closed records states that have already been examined. closed is the union of the DE and SL lists of the backtrack algorithm.

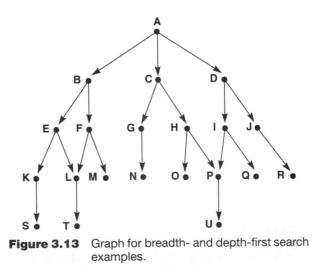

Figure 3.13 Graph for breadth- and depth-first search examples.

```
procedure breadth_first_search;

begin
    open := [Start];                                              % initialize
    closed := [];
    while open ≠ [] do                                           % states remain
        begin
            remove leftmost state from open, call it X;
            if X is a goal then return(success)                  % goal found
                else begin
                    generate children of X;
                    put X on closed;
                    eliminate children of X on open or closed;   % loop check
                    put remaining children on right end of open  % queue
                end
        end;

    return(failure)                                              % no states left

end.
```

Child states are generated by inference rules, legal moves of a game, or other state transition operators. Each iteration produces all children of the state X and adds them to open. Note that open is maintained as a *queue*, or first-in-first-out (FIFO) data structure. States are added to the right of the list and removed from the left. This biases search toward the states that have been on open the longest, causing the search to be breadth-first.

Child states that have already been discovered (already appear on either open or closed) are eliminated.

If the algorithm terminates because the condition of the "while" loop is no longer satisfied (open = [ ]) then it has searched the entire graph without finding the desired goal: the search has failed.

A trace of breadth_first_search on the graph of Figure 3.13 appears below. Each successive number, 2,3,4, . . . , represents an iteration of the "while" loop. U is the desired goal state.

1. open = [A]; closed = [ ]
2. open = [B,C,D]; closed = [A]
3. open = [C,D,E,F]; closed = [B,A]
4. open = [D,E,F,G,H]; closed = [C,B,A]
5. open = [E,F,G,H,I,J]; closed = [D,C,B,A]
6. open = [F,G,H,I,J,K,L]; closed = [E,D,C,B,A]
7. open = [G,H,I,J,K,L,M] (as L is already on open); closed = [F,E,D,C,B,A]
8. open = [H,I,J,K,L,M,N]; closed = [G,F,E,D,C,B,A]
9. and so on until either U is found or open = [ ]

Figure 3.14 illustrates the graph of Figure 3.13 after six iterations of breadth_first_search. The states on open and closed are highlighted. States not shaded have not been discovered by the algorithm. Note that open records the states on the "frontier" of the search at any stage and that closed records states already visited.

Because breadth-first search considers every node at each level of the graph before going deeper into the space, all states are first reached along the shortest path from the start state. Breadth-first search is therefore guaranteed to find the shortest path from the start state to the goal. Furthermore, because all states are first found along the shortest path, any states encountered a second time are found along a path of equal or greater length. Because there is no chance that duplicate states were found along a better path, the algorithm simply discards any duplicate states.

It is often useful to keep other information on open and closed besides the names of the states. For example, note that breadth_first_search does not maintain a list of states on the current path to a goal as backtrack did on the list SL; all visited states are kept on closed. If the path is required for a solution, it can be returned by the algorithm. This can be done by storing ancestor information along with each state. A state may be saved along with a record of its parent state, i.e., as an ordered pair (state, parent). If this is done in the search of the algorithm of Figure 3.13, the contents of open and closed at the fourth iteration would be:

open = [(D,A), (E,B), (F,B), (G,C), (H,C)]; closed = [(C,A), (B,A), (A,nil)]

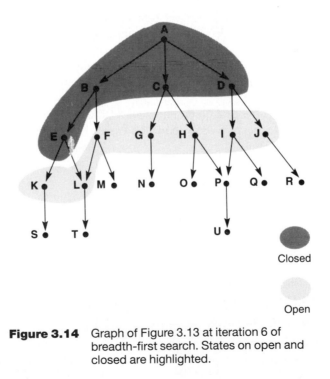

Closed

Open

Figure 3.14 Graph of Figure 3.13 at iteration 6 of breadth-first search. States on open and closed are highlighted.

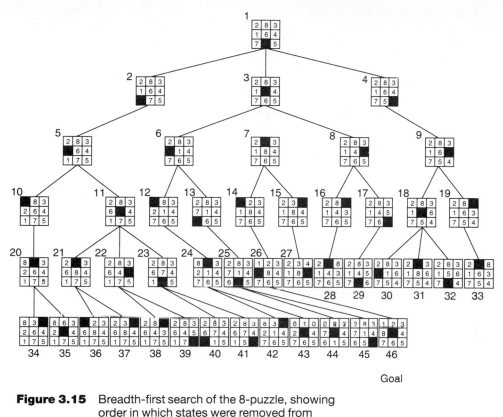

Figure 3.15 Breadth-first search of the 8-puzzle, showing order in which states were removed from open.

The path (A, B, F) that led from A to F could easily be constructed from this information. When a goal is found, the algorithm may construct the solution path by tracing back along parents from the goal to the start state. Note that state A has a parent of nil, indicating that it is a start state; this stops reconstruction of the path. Because breadth-first search finds each state along the shortest path and retains the first version of each state, this is the shortest path from a start to a goal.

Figure 3.15 shows the states removed from open and examined in a breadth-first search of the graph of the 8-puzzle. As before, arcs correspond to moves of the blank up, to the right, down, and to the left. The number next to each state indicates the order in which it was removed from open. States left on open when the algorithm halted are not shown.

Next we create a depth-first search algorithm. In examining the algorithm, note that the descendant states are both added and removed from the *left* end of open: open is maintained as a *stack*, or last-in-first-out (LIFO), structure. The organization of open as a stack biases search toward the most recently generated states, giving search a depth-first order.

Depth-first search is implemented by modifying the algorithm for breadth-first search:

```
procedure depth_first_search;

begin
    open := [Start];                                              % initialize
    closed := [];
    while open ≠ [] do                                           % states remain
        begin
            remove leftmost state from open, call it X;
            if X is a goal then return(success)                  % goal found
                else begin
                    generate children of X;
                    put X on closed;
                    eliminate children of X on open or closed;   % loop check
                    put remaining children on left end of open   % stack
                end
        end;
        return(failure)                                          % no states left
end.
```

A trace of **depth_first_search** on the graph of Figure 3.13 appears below. Each successive iteration of the "while" loop is indicated by a single line (2, 3, 4, ...). The initial states of **open** and **closed** are given on line 1. Assume U is the goal state.

1. open = [A]; closed = [ ]
2. open = [B,C,D]; closed = [A]
3. open = [E,F,C,D]; closed = [B,A]
4. open = [K,L,F,C,D]; closed = [E,B,A]
5. open = [S,L,F,C,D]; closed = [K,E,B,A]
6. open = [L,F,C,D]; closed = [S,K,E,B,A]
7. open = [T,F,C,D]; closed = [L,S,K,E,B,A]
8. open = [F,C,D]; closed = [T,L,S,K,E,B,A]
9. open = [M,C,D], as L is already on closed; closed = [F,T,L,S,K,E,B,A]
10. open = [C,D]; closed = [M,F,T,L,S,K,E,B,A]
11. open = [G,H,D]; closed = [C,M,F,T,L,S,K,E,B,A]

and so on until either U is discovered or **open** = [ ].

As with **breadth_first_search**, **open** lists all states discovered but not yet evaluated (the current "frontier" of the search), and **closed** records states already considered. Figure 3.16 shows the graph of Figure 3.13 at the sixth iteration of the **depth_first_search**. The contents of **open** and **closed** are highlighted. As with **breadth_first_search**, the algorithm could store a record of the parent along with each state, allowing the algorithm to reconstruct the path that led from the start state to a goal.

Unlike breadth-first search, a depth-first search is not guaranteed to find the shortest path to a state the first time that state is encountered. Later in the search, a different path may be found to any state. If path length matters in a problem solver, when the algorithm encounters a duplicate state, the algorithm should save the version reached along the short-

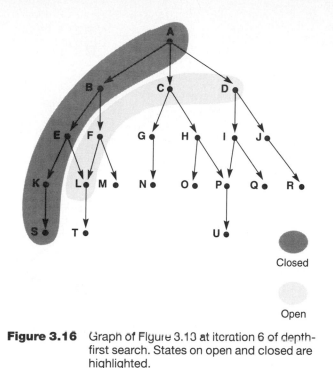

Closed

Open

Figure 3.16 Graph of Figure 3.13 at iteration 6 of depth-
first search. States on open and closed are
highlighted.

est path. This could be done by storing each state as a triple: (state, parent, length_of_path). When children are generated, the value of the path length is simply incremented by one and saved with the child. If a child is reached along multiple paths, this information can be used to retain the best version. This is treated in more detail in the discussion of *algorithm A* in Chapter 4. Note that retaining the best version of a state in a simple depth-first search does not guarantee that a goal will be reached along the shortest path.

Figure 3.17 gives a depth-first search of the 8-puzzle. As noted previously, the space is generated by the four "move blank" rules (up, down, left, and right). The numbers next to the states indicate the order in which they were considered, i.e., removed from open. States left on open when the goal is found are not shown. A depth bound of 5 was imposed on this search to keep it from getting lost deep in the space.

As with choosing between data- and goal-driven search for evaluating a graph, the choice of depth-first or breadth-first search depends on the specific problem being solved. Significant features include the importance of finding the shortest path to a goal, the branching of the state space, the available time and space resources, the average length of paths to a goal node, and whether we want all solutions or only the first solution. In making these decisions, there are advantages and disadvantages for each approach.

Breadth First   Because it always examines all the nodes at level n before proceeding to level n + 1, breadth-first search always finds the shortest path to a goal node. In a problem

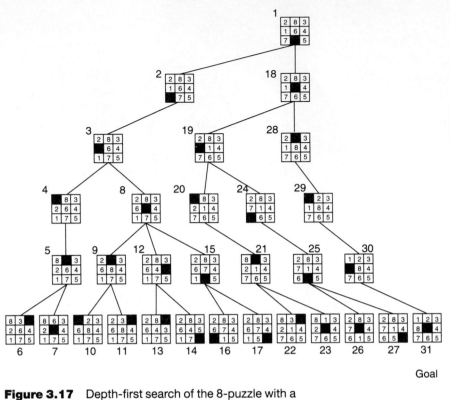

Figure 3.17 Depth-first search of the 8-puzzle with a depth bound of 5.

where it is known that a simple solution exists, this solution will be found. Unfortunately, if there is a bad branching factor, i.e., states have a high average number of descendants, the combinatorial explosion may prevent the algorithm from finding a solution using the available space. This is due to the fact that all unexpanded nodes for each level of the search must be kept on **open**. For deep searches, or state spaces with a high branching factor, this can become quite cumbersome.

The space utilization of breadth-first search, measured in terms of the number of states on **open**, is an exponential function of the length of the path at any time. If each state has an average of B children, the number of states on a given level is B times the number of states on the previous level. This gives B^n states on level n. Breadth-first search would place all of these on **open** when it begins examining level n. This can be prohibitive if solution paths are long.

Depth First   Depth-first search gets quickly into a deep search space. If it is known that the solution path will be long, depth-first search will not waste time searching a large number of "shallow" states in the graph. On the other hand, depth-first search can get "lost" deep in a graph, missing shorter paths to a goal or even becoming stuck in an infinitely long path that does not lead to a goal.

Depth-first search is much more efficient for search spaces with many branches because it does not have to keep all the nodes at a given level on the open list. The space usage of depth-first search is a linear function of the length of the path. At each level, open retains only the children of a single state. If a graph has an average of B children per state, this requires a total space usage of B × n states to go n levels deep into the space.

The best answer to the "depth-first versus breadth-first" issue is to examine the problem space carefully and consult experts in the area. In chess, for example, breadth-first search simply is not possible. In simpler games, breadth-first search not only may be possible but also may be the only way to avoid losing.

3.2.4 Depth-First Search with Iterative Deepening

A nice compromise on these trade-offs is to use a depth bound on depth-first search. The depth bound forces a failure on a search path once it gets below a certain level. This causes a breadth-like sweep of the search space at that depth level. When it is known that a solution lies within a certain depth or when time constraints, such as occur in an extremely large space like chess, limit the number of states that can be considered; then a depth-first search with a depth bound may be most appropriate. Figure 3.17 showed a depth-first search of the 8-puzzle in which a depth bound of 5 caused the sweep across the space at that depth.

This insight leads to a search algorithm that remedies many of the drawbacks of both depth-first and breadth-first search. *Depth-first iterative deepening* (Korf 1987) performs a depth-first search of the space with a depth bound of 1. If it fails to find a goal, it performs another depth-first search with a depth bound of 2. This continues, increasing the depth bound by one at each iteration. At each iteration, the algorithm performs a complete depth-first search to the current depth bound. No information about the state space is retained between iterations.

Because the algorithm searches the space in a level-by-level fashion, it is guaranteed to find a shortest path to a goal. Because it does only depth-first search at each iteration, the space usage at any level n is B × n, where B is the average number of children of a node.

Interestingly, although it seems as if depth-first iterative deepening would be much less time efficient than either depth-first or breadth-first search, its time complexity is actually of the same order of magnitude as either of these: $O(B^n)$. An intuitive explanation for this seeming paradox is given by Korf (1987):

> Since the number of nodes in a given level of the tree grows exponentially with depth, almost all the time is spent in the deepest level, even though shallower levels are generated an arithmetically increasing number of times.

Unfortunately, all the search strategies discussed in this chapter—depth-first, breadth-first, and depth-first iterative deepening—may be shown to have worst-case exponential time complexity. This is true for all *uninformed* search algorithms. The only approaches to search that reduce this complexity employ heuristics to guide search. *Best-first search* is a search algorithm that is similar to the algorithms for depth- and breadth-first search just presented. However, best-first search orders the states on the open list, the current fringe of the search, according to some measure of their heuristic merit. At each iteration, it considers neither the deepest nor the shallowest but the "best" state. Best-first search is the main topic of Chapter 4.

3.3 Using the State Space to Represent Reasoning with the Predicate Calculus

3.3.1 State Space Description of a Logical System

When we defined state space graphs in Section 3.1, we noted that nodes must be distinguishable from one another, with each node representing some state of the solution process. Predicate calculus can be used as the formal specification language for making these distinctions and for mapping the nodes of a graph onto the states of a problem-solving process. Furthermore, inference rules can be used to create and describe the arcs between states. In this fashion, problems in the predicate calculus, such as determining whether a particular expression is a logical consequence of a given set of assertions, may be solved using search.

The soundness and completeness of predicate calculus inference rules guarantee the correctness of conclusions derived through this form of graph-based reasoning. This ability to produce a formal proof of the integrity of a solution through the same algorithm that produces the solution is a unique attribute of much artificial intelligence and theorem proving based problem solving.

Although many problems (such as tic-tac-toe) may be more naturally described by other data structures (such as arrays), the power and generality of logical representation allow most AI problem solving to use predicate calculus descriptions and inference rules as just described. Other representations such as rules (Chapter 8), semantic networks, or frames (Chapters 9 and 15) employ similar search strategies and may also be understood using the graph search algorithms introduced in this chapter.

EXAMPLE 3.3.1.

The first example of how a set of logical assertions may be viewed as defining a graph is from the propositional calculus. Assume the following set of assertions:

$$q \Rightarrow p$$
$$r \Rightarrow p$$
$$v \Rightarrow q$$
$$s \Rightarrow r$$
$$t \Rightarrow r$$
$$s \Rightarrow u$$
$$s$$
$$t$$

From this set of assertions and the inference rule modus ponens, certain propositions (p, r, and u) may be inferred; others (such as v and q) may not be so inferred and indeed do not logically follow from these assertions. The relationship between the initial assertions and these inferences is expressed in the directed graph in Figure 3.18.

In Figure 3.18 the arcs correspond to logical implications ($\Rightarrow$). Propositions that are given as true (s and t) correspond to the given data of the problem. Propositions that are logical consequences of this set of assertions correspond to the nodes that may be reached along a directed path from a state representing a true proposition; such a path corresponds to a sequence of applications of modus ponens. For example, the path [s, r, p] corresponds to the sequence of inferences:

s and s $\Rightarrow$ r yields r.

r and r $\Rightarrow$ p yields p.

Given this representation, determining whether a given proposition is a logical consequence of a set of propositions becomes a problem of finding a path from a boxed node (the start node) to the proposition (the goal node). It has been cast as a graph search problem. The search strategy used here is data-driven, because it proceeds from what is known (the true propositions) toward the goal. Alternatively, a goal-directed strategy could be applied to the same state space by starting with the proposition to be proved (the goal) and searching back along arcs to find support for the goal among the true propositions. In addition, we can search this space of inferences in either a depth-first or breadth-first fashion.

3.3.2   And / Or Graphs

In Example 3.3.1, all of the assertions were simple implications of the form p $\Rightarrow$ q. We did not discuss the way in which the logical operators and and or could be represented in such a graph. Expressing the logical relationships defined by these operators requires an extension to the basic graph model known as an *and/or graph*. And/or graphs are an important tool for describing the search spaces generated by many AI problems, including those solved by logical theorem provers and expert systems.

In expressions of the form q $\wedge$ r $\Rightarrow$ p, both q and r must be true for p to be true. In expressions of the form q $\vee$ r $\Rightarrow$ p, the truth of either q or r is sufficient to prove p is true. Because implications containing disjunctive premises may be written as separate implications, this expression is often written as q $\Rightarrow$ p, r $\Rightarrow$ p. To represent these different relationships graphically, and/or graphs distinguish between and nodes and or nodes. If the

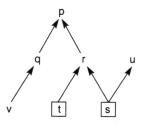

Figure 3.18   State space graph of a set of implications in the propositional calculus.

In the example of Figure 3.21, a goal-directed strategy for determining the truth of h first attempts to prove both a and e. The truth of a is immediate, but the truth of e requires the truth of both c and a; these are given as true. Once the problem solver has traced all these arcs down to true propositions, the true values are recombined at the and nodes to verify the truth of h.

A data-directed strategy for determining the truth of h, on the other hand, begins with the known facts (c, a, and b) and begins adding new propositions to this set of known facts according to the constraints of the and/or graph. e or d might be the first proposition added to the set of facts. These additions make it possible to infer new facts. This process continues until the desired goal, h, has been proved.

One way of looking at and/or graph search is that the ∧ operator (hence the and nodes of the graph) indicates a problem decomposition in which the problem is broken into subproblems such that all of the subproblems must be solved to solve the original problem. An ∨ operator in the predicate calculus representation of the problem indicates a selection, a point at which a choice may be made between alternative problem-solving strategies, any of which, if successful, is sufficient to solve the problem.

3.3.3 Further Examples and Applications

EXAMPLE 3.3.3.

One natural example of an and/or graph is a program for symbolically integrating mathematical functions. MACSYMA is a well-known program that is used extensively by mathematicians. The reasoning of MACSYMA can be represented as an and/or graph. In performing integrations, one important class of strategies involves breaking an expression into sub-expressions that may be integrated independently of one another, with the result being combined algebraically into a solution expression. Examples of this strategy include the rule for integration by parts and the rule for decomposing the integral of a sum into the sum of the integrals of the individual terms. These strategies, representing the decomposition of a problem into independent subproblems, can be represented by and nodes in the graph.

Another class of strategies involves the simplification of an expression through various algebraic substitutions. Because any given expression may allow a number of different substitutions, each representing an independent solution strategy, these strategies are represented by or nodes of the graph. Figure 3.22 illustrates the space searched by such a problem solver. The search of this graph is goal-directed, in that it begins with the query "find the integral of ???" and searches back to the algebraic expressions that define that integral. Note that this is an example in which goal-directed search is the obvious strategy. It would be practically impossible for a problem solver to determine the algebraic expressions that formed the desired integral without working back from the query.

EXAMPLE 3.3.4.

This example is taken from the predicate calculus and represents a goal-driven graph search where the goal to be proved true is a predicate calculus expression, often containing variables. The axioms are the logical descriptions of a relationship between a dog, Fred, and his master, Sam.

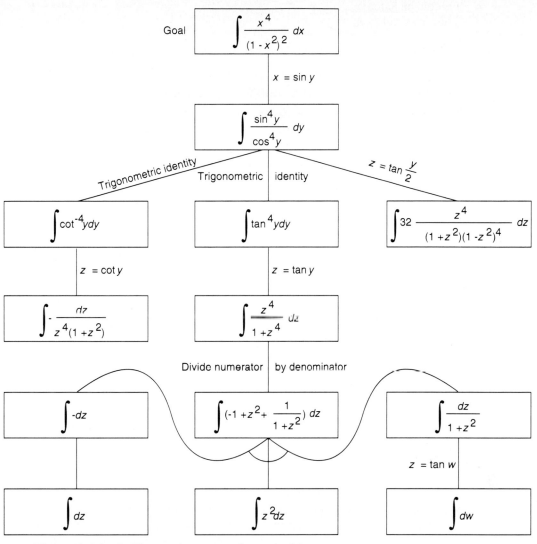

Goal $\displaystyle\int \frac{x^4}{(1-x^2)^2}\,dx$

$x = \sin y$

$\displaystyle\int \frac{\sin^4 y}{\cos^4 y}\,dy$

Trigonometric identity   Trigonometric identity $z = \tan \dfrac{y}{2}$

$\displaystyle\int \cot^{-4}y\,dy$ $\displaystyle\int \tan^4 y\,dy$ $\displaystyle\int 32\,\frac{z^4}{(1+z^2)(1-z^2)^4}\,dz$

$z = \cot y$ $z = \tan y$

$\displaystyle\int -\frac{dz}{z^4(1+z^2)}$ $\displaystyle\int \frac{z^4}{1+z^4}\,dz$

Divide numerator by denominator

$\displaystyle\int -dz$ $\displaystyle\int \left(-1+z^2+\frac{1}{1+z^2}\right)dz$ $\displaystyle\int \frac{dz}{1+z^2}$

$z = \tan w$

$\displaystyle\int dz$ $\displaystyle\int z^2 dz$ $\displaystyle\int dw$

Figure 3.22   And/or graph representing part of the state space for integrating a function.

The facts and rules of this example are given as English sentences followed by their predicate calculus equivalents:

1. Fred is a collie.
   collie(fred).

2. Sam is Fred's master.
   master(fred,sam).

3. It is Saturday.
   day(saturday).

4. It is cold on Saturday.
   ¬ (warm(saturday)).

5. Fred is a trained dog.
   trained(fred).

6. Spaniels or collies that are trained are good dogs.
   ∀ X[spaniel(X) ∨ (collie(X) ∧ trained(X)) ⇒ gooddog(X)]

7. If a dog is a good dog and has a master then he will be with his master.
   ∀ (X,Y,Z) [gooddog(X) ∧ master(X,Y) ∧ location(Y,Z) ⇒ location(X,Z)]

8. If it is Saturday and warm, then Sam is at the park.
   day(saturday) ∧ warm(saturday) ⇒ location(sam,park).

9. If it is Saturday and not warm, then Sam is at the museum.
   day(saturday) ∧ ¬(warm(saturday)) ⇒ location(sam,museum).

The goal is the expression ∃ X location(fred,X), meaning "where is fred?" A backward search algorithm examines alternative means of establishing this goal: "if fred is a good dog and fred has a master and fred's master is at a location then fred is at that location also." The premises of this rule are then examined: what does it mean to be a "good dog," etc.? This process continues, constructing the and/or graph of Figure 3.23.

Let us examine the search of Example 3.3.4 in more detail, particularly because it is the first example of goal-driven search using the predicate calculus and it illustrates the role of unification in the generation of the search space. The problem to be solved is "where is fred?" More formally, it may be seen as determining a substitution for the variable X, if such a substitution exists, under which location(fred,X) is a logical consequence of the initial assertions.

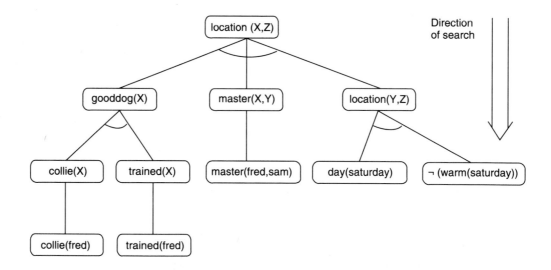

Substitutions = {fred/X, sam/Y, museum/Z}

Figure 3.23   And/or graph showing fred is at the museum.

When it is desired to determine Fred's location, clauses are examined that have location as their conclusion. The first of these is clause 7. This conclusion, location(P,Q), is then unified with location(fred, X) by the substitutions {fred/P, X/Q}. The premises of this rule, under the same substitution, form the and descendants of the top goal in the graph:

gooddog(fred) ∧ master(fred,Y) ∧ location(Y,Z).

This expression may be interpreted as meaning that one way to find Fred is to see if Fred is a good dog, find out who Fred's master is, and find out where the master is. The initial goal has thus been replaced by three subgoals. These are and nodes and all of them must be solved.

To solve these subgoals, the problem solver first determines whether Fred is a good dog. This matches the conclusion of clause 6. The premise of clause 6 is the or of two expressions:

∀ X spaniel(X) ∨ (collie(X) ∧ trained(X))

The first of these or nodes is spaniel(X). The data base does not contain this assertion, so the problem solver must assume it is false. The other or node is (collie(X) ∧ trained(X)), i.e., is Fred a collie and is Fred trained. Both of these need to be true, which they are by clauses 1 and 5.

This proves that gooddog(fred) is true. The problem solver then examines the second of the premises of clause 7: master(X,Y). Under the substitution {fred/X}, this becomes master(fred,Y), which unifies with the fact (clause 2) of master(fred,sam). This produces the unifying substitution of {sam/Y}, which also gives the value of sam to the third subgoal of clause 7, creating the new goal location(sam,Z).

In solving this, assuming the problem solver tries rules in order, the goal location(sam,Z) will first unify with the conclusion of clause 7. Note that the same rule is being tried with different bindings for X. Recall (Chapter 2) that X is a "dummy" variable and could have any name (any string beginning with an uppercase letter). Because the extent of the meaning of any variable name is contained within the clause in which it appears, the predicate calculus has no global variables. Another way of saying this is that values of variables are passed to other clauses as parameters and have no fixed (memory) locations. Thus, the multiple occurrences of X in different rules in this example indicate *different* formal parameters (Section 12.3).

In attempting to solve the premises of rule 7 with these new bindings, the problem solver will fail because sam is not a good dog. Here, the search will backtrack to the goal location(sam,Z) and try the next match, the conclusion of rule 8. This will also fail, causing another backtrack and a unification with the conclusion of clause 9, at(sam,museum).

Because the premises of clause 9 are supported in the set of assertions (clauses 3 and 4), it follows that the conclusion of clause 9 may be taken as true. This final unification goes all the way back up the tree to finally answer location(fred,X)? with location(fred,museum).

It is important to examine carefully the nature of the goal-driven search of a graph and compare it with the data-driven search of Example 3.3.2. Further discussion of this issue, including a more rigorous comparison of these two methods of searching a graph, continues in the next example but is seen in full detail only in the discussion of production systems in Chapter 5 and in the application to expert systems in Part IV. Another point implicit in this example is that the order of clauses affects the order of search. In the example above, the multiple location clauses were tried in order, with backtracking search eliminating those that failed to be proved true.

EXAMPLE 3.3.5.

In the last example of Chapter 2 we used predicate calculus to represent a set of rules for giving investment advice. In that example, modus ponens was used to infer a proper investment for a particular individual. We did not discuss the way in which a program might determine the appropriate inferences. This is, of course, a search problem; the present example illustrates one approach to implementing the logic-based financial advisor, using goal-directed, depth-first search with backtracking. The discussion uses the predicates found in Section 2.4; these predicates are not duplicated here.

Assume that the individual has two dependents, $20,000 in savings, and a steady income of $30,000. As discussed in Chapter 2, we can add predicate calculus expressions describing these facts to the set of predicate calculus expressions. Alternatively, the program may begin the search without this information and ask the user to add it as needed. This has the advantage of not requiring data that may not prove necessary for a solution. This approach, often taken in expert systems, is illustrated in this example.

In performing a consultation, the goal is to find an investment; this is represented as the predicate calculus expression investment(X). Note the use of the unbound variable X in the goal. This goal is also referred to as a *query*. There are three rules (1, 2, and 3) that conclude about investments, because the query will unify with the conclusion of these rules. If we select rule 1 for initial exploration, its premise savings_account(inadequate) becomes the subgoal, i.e., the child node that will be expanded next.

In generating the children of savings_account(inadequate), the only rule that may be applied is rule 5. This produces the and node:

amount_saved(X) ∧ dependents(Y) ∧ ¬greater(X,minsavings(Y))

If we attempt to satisfy these in left-to-right order, amount_saved(X) is taken as the first subgoal. Because the system contains no rules that conclude this subgoal, it will query the user. When amount_saved(20000) is added the first subgoal will succeed, with unification substituting 20000 for X. Note that because an and node is being searched, a failure here would eliminate the need to examine the remainder of the expression.

Similarly, the subgoal dependents(Y) leads to a user query, and the response, dependents(2), is added to the logical description. The subgoal matches this expression with the substitution {2/Y}. The search will then evaluate the truth of

¬ greater(X, minsavings(Y)).

This evaluates to false, causing failure of the entire and node. The search then backtracks to the parent node, savings_account(inadequate), and attempts to find an alternative way to prove that node true. This corresponds to the generation of the next child in the search. Because no other rules conclude this subgoal, search fails back to the top-level goal, investment(X). The next rule whose conclusions unify with this goal is rule 2, producing the new subgoals

savings_account(adequate) ∧ income(adequate).

Continuing the search, savings_account(adequate) is proved true as the conclusion of rule 4, and income(adequate) follows as the conclusion of rule 6. Although the details of the remainder of the search will be left to the reader, the and/or graph that is ultimately searched appears in Figure 3.24.

EXAMPLE 3.3.6.

The final example is not from the predicate calculus but consists of a set of rewrite rules for parsing sentences in a subset of English grammar. Rewrite rules take an expression and transform it into another by replacing the pattern on one side of the arrow (↔) with the pattern on the other side. For example, a set of rewrite rules could be defined to change an expression in one language, such as English, into another language (perhaps French or a predicate calculus clause). The rewrite rules given here transform a subset of English sentences into higher level grammatical constructs such as noun phrase, verb phrase, and sentence. These rules are used to *parse* sequences of words, i.e., to determine whether they are well-formed sentences (are grammatically correct or not) and to model the linguistic structure of the sentences.

Five rules for a simple subset of English grammar are:

1. A sentence is a noun phrase followed by a verb phrase.
   sentence ↔ np vp
2. A noun phrase is a noun.
   np ↔ n
3. A noun phrase is an article followed by a noun.
   np ↔ art n
4. A verb phrase is a verb.
   vp ↔ v
5. A verb phrase is a verb followed by a noun phrase.
   vp ↔ v np

In addition to these grammar rules, a parser needs a dictionary of words in the language. These words are called the *terminals* of the grammar. They are defined by their parts of speech using rewrite rules. In the following "dictionary," "a," "the," "man," "dog," "likes," and "bites" are the terminals of our simple grammar:

6. art ↔ a
7. art ↔ the

("a" and "the" are articles)

8. n ↔ man
9. n ↔ dog

("man" and "dog" are nouns)

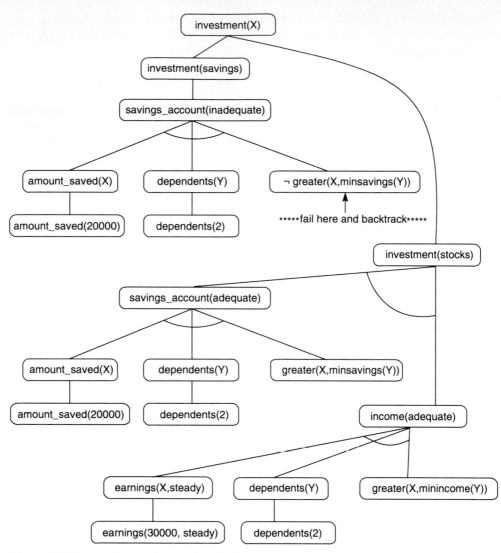

Figure 3.24 And/or graph searched by the financial advisor.

10. v ↔ likes

11. v ↔ bites

("likes" and "bites" are verbs)

These rewrite rules define the and/or graph of Figure 3.25. **Sentence** is the root. The elements on the left of a rewrite rule correspond to and nodes in the graph. Multiple rules with the same conclusion form the or nodes. Notice that the leaf or terminal nodes of this graph are the English words in the grammar (hence, they are called *terminals*).

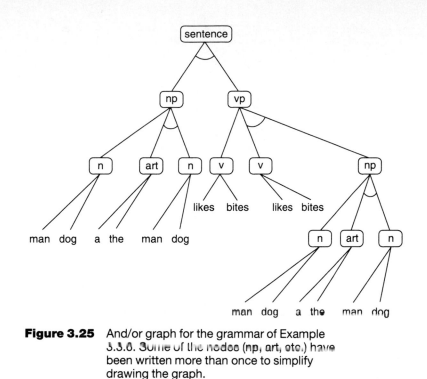

Figure 3.25 And/or graph for the grammar of Example 3.3.6. Some of the nodes (np, art, etc.) have been written more than once to simplify drawing the graph.

An expression is *well formed* in a grammar if it consists entirely of terminal symbols and there is a series of substitutions in the expression using rewrite rules that reduce it to the sentence symbol. Alternatively, this may be seen as constructing a *parse tree* that has the words of the expression as its leaves and the sentence symbol as its root.

For example, we may parse the sentence the dog bites the man, constructing the parse tree of Figure 3.26. This tree is a subtree of the and/or graph of Figure 3.25 and is constructed by searching this graph. A *data-driven parsing* algorithm would implement this by matching right-hand sides of rewrite rules with patterns in the sentence, trying these matches in the order in which the rules are written. Once a match is found, the part of the expression matching the right-hand side of the rule is replaced by the pattern on the left-hand side. This continues until the sentence is reduced to the symbol sentence (indicating a successful parse) or no more rules can be applied (indicating failure). A trace of the parse of the dog bites the man is:

1. The first rule that will match is 7, rewriting the as art. This yields: art dog bites the man.
2. The next iteration would find a match for 7, yielding art dog bites art man.
3. Rule 8 will fire, producing art dog bites art n.
4. Rule 3 will fire to yield art dog bites np.
5. Rule 9 produces art n bites np.

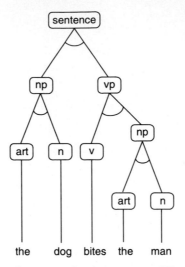

Figure 3.26 Parse tree for the sentence "The dog bites the man." Note that this is a subtree of the graph of Figure 3.25.

6. Rule 3 may be applied, giving np bites np.
7. Rule 11 yields np v np.
8. Rule 5 yields np vp.
9. Rule 1 reduces this to sentence, accepting the expression as correct.

The above example implements a data-directed depth-first parse, as it always applies the highest-level rule to the expression; e.g., art n reduces to np before bites reduces to v. Parsing could also be done in a goal-directed fashion, taking sentence as the starting string and finding a series of replacements of patterns that match left-hand sides of rules leading to a series of terminals that match the target sentence.

Parsing is important, not only for natural language (Chapter 10) but also for constructing compilers and interpreters for computer languages (Aho 1977). The literature is full of parsing algorithms for all classes of languages. These use various techniques to manage the combinatorics of complex grammars. For example, many goal-directed parsing algorithms will look ahead in the actual input stream to determine which rule to apply next.

In this example we have taken a very simple approach of searching the and/or graph in an uninformed fashion. One thing that is interesting in this example is the implementation of the search. This approach of keeping a record of the current expression and trying to match the rules in order is an example of using the *production system* to implement search. This is a major topic of the Chapter 5.

Another way in which rewrite rules are used is to generate legal sentences according to the rules of the grammar. Legal sentences may be generated by a goal-driven search, beginning with sentence as the top-level goal and ending when no more rules can be applied. This produces a string of terminal symbols that is a legal sentence in the grammar. For example:

A sentence is a np followed by a vp (rule 1).

np is replaced by n (rule 2), giving n vp.

man is the first n available (rule 8), giving man vp.

Now np is satisfied and vp is attempted. Rule 3 replaces vp with v, man v.

Rule 10 replaces v with likes.

man likes is found as the first acceptable sentence.

If it is desired to create all acceptable sentences, this search may be systematically repeated until all possibilities are tried and the entire state space has been searched exhaustively. This generates sentences including a man likes, the man likes, and so on. There are 84 correct sentences that are produced by an exhaustive search. These include such semantic anomalies as the man bites the dog.

Parsing and generating rules can be used together in a variety of ways to handle different problems. For instance, if it is desired to find all sentences to complete the string the man, then the problem solver may be given an incomplete string the man . . . . It can work upward in a data-driven fashion to produce the goal of completing the sentence rule (rule 1), where np is replaced by the man, and then work in a goal-driven fashion to determine all possible vps that will complete the sentence. This would create sentences such as the man likes, the man bites the man, and so on. Again, this example deals only with syntactic correctness. The issue of semantics (whether the string has a mapping into some "world" with "truth") is entirely different. Chapter 2 examined the issue of constructing a semantics for expressions in formal logic; for expressions in natural language, the issue is much more difficult and is discussed in Chapters 9 and 10.

This last example illustrates the extreme flexibility with which state spaces may be searched. In the next chapter we discuss the use of heuristics to focus search on the smallest possible portion of the state space. Chapter 5 discusses the production system, a formalism for controlling the application of problem-solving rules and other techniques for implementing search in a variety of problems and representation languages.

3.4   Epilogue and References

Chapter 3 introduced the theoretical foundations of state space search, using graph theory to analyze the structure and complexity of problem-solving strategies. In reviewing the basics of graph theory, we showed how it may be used to model problem solving as a search through a graph of problem states. The chapter compared data-driven and goal-driven reasoning and depth-first and breadth-first search.

And/or graphs allow us to apply state space search to the implementation of logical reasoning. The search strategies of Chapter 3 were demonstrated on a number of examples, including the financial advisor introduced in Chapter 2.

Basic graph search is discussed in a number of textbooks on computer algorithms. These include *Introduction to Algorithms* by Thomas Cormen, Charles Leiserson, and Ronald Rivest (1990), *Walls and Mirrors* by Paul Helman and Robert Veroff (1986), *Algorithms* by Robert Sedgewick (1983), and *Fundamentals of Computer Algorithms* by Ellis Horowitz and Sartaj Sahni (1978). More complete algorithms for and/or graph search are presented in Chapter 11, "Automated Reasoning," and are built in the PROLOG and LISP chapters.

The use of graph search to model intelligent problem solving is presented in *Human Problem Solving* by Alan Newell and Herbert Simon (1972). Artificial intelligence texts that discuss search strategies include Nils Nilsson's *Principles of Artificial Intelligence* (1980), Patrick Winston's *Artificial Intelligence* (1992), and *Artificial Intelligence* by Eugene Charniak and Drew McDermott (1985). *Heuristics* by Judea Pearl (1984) presents search algorithms and lays a groundwork for the material we present in Chapter 4. Alternative perspectives on search may be found in Rich and Knight (1991).

3.5   Exercises

1. Define a hamiltonian path as a path that uses every node of the graph exactly once. What conditions are necessary for such a path to exist? Is there such a path in the Königsberg map?

2. Give the graph representation for the farmer, wolf, goat, and cabbage problem of Figures 6.1 and 6.2. Let the nodes represent states of the world; e.g., the farmer and the goat are on the west bank and the wolf and cabbage, on the east. Discuss the advantages of each alternative for searching this space.

3. Write a graph representation for the relationships in Exercise 13 of Chapter 2. Let the nodes correspond to the people and the arcs to the relationships. Informally discuss what it might mean to perform inferences on such a graph and how a system might make the conclusion "I am my own grandfather" from this representation. Contrast the logical and the graph-based representations.

4. Give an instance of the traveling salesperson problem for which the nearest-neighbor strategy fails to find an optimal path. Suggest another heuristic for this problem.

5. "Hand run" the backtrack algorithm on the graph in Figure 3.27. Begin from state A. Keep track of the successive values of NSL, SL, CS, etc.

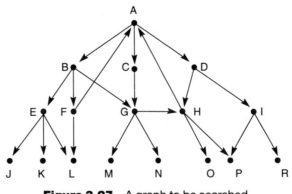

Figure 3.27   A graph to be searched.

6. Implement a backtrack algorithm in
   a. Pascal or C.
   b. FORTRAN.

7. Determine whether goal-driven or data-driven search would be preferable for solving each of the following problems. Justify your answer.
   a. Diagnosing mechanical problems in an automobile.
   b. You have met a person who claims to be your distant cousin, with a common ancestor named John Doe. You would like to verify her claim.
   c. Another person claims to be your distant cousin. He does not know the common ancestor's name but knows that it was no more than eight generations back. You would like to either find this ancestor or determine that she did not exist.
   d. A theorem prover for plane geometry.
   e. A program for examining sonar readings and interpreting them, such as telling a large submarine from a small submarine from a whale from a school of fish.
   f. An expert system that will help a human classify plants by species, genus, etc.

8. Extend the graphs of Figures 3.15 and 3.17 to show the states left on open when the algorithms halt.

9. In depth-first search, the children of each node are generated and expanded in some order. What criteria should be considered in determining the best order in which to generate the child nodes?

10. Would you use breadth-first or depth-first search for each of the following problems? What would you base your choice on?
    a. A chess playing program.
    b. A medical diagnostic program.
    c. A planner to find a path to get a robot from A to B.
    d. A program to determine the best sequence of manufacturing steps to go from raw materials to a finished product.
    e. A program that attempts to determine whether two expressions in the propositional calculus are equivalent.

11. Answer questions 1 through 4 from Example 3.3.2.

12. Write a backtrack algorithm for and/or graphs.

13. Trace the good-dog problem of Example 3.3.4 in a data-driven fashion.

14. Give another example of an and/or graph search problem. Develop part of the search space.

15. Trace a data-driven execution of the financial advisor of Example 3.3.5 for the case of an individual with four dependents, $18,000 in the bank, and a steady income of $25,000 per year. Based on a comparison of this problem and the example in the text, suggest a generally "best" strategy for solving the problem.

16. Add rules defining adjectives and adverbs to the grammar of Example 3.3.6.

17. Add rules for (multiple) prepositional phrases to Example 3.3.6.

HEURISTIC SEARCH

The task that a symbol system is faced with, then, when it is presented with a problem and a problem space, is to use its limited processing resources to generate possible solutions, one after another, until it finds one that satisfies the problem defining test. If the symbol system had some control over the order in which potential solutions were generated, then it would be desirable to arrange this order of generation so that actual solutions would have a high likelihood of appearing early. A symbol system would exhibit intelligence to the extent that it succeeded in doing this. Intelligence for a system with limited processing resources consists in making wise choices of what to do next. . . .

—NEWELL AND SIMON, 1976 Turing Award Lecture

I been searchin' . . .
Searchin' . . . Oh yeah
Searchin' every which-a-way . . .

—LIEBER AND STOLLER

4.0 Introduction

George Polya defines *heuristic* as "the study of the methods and rules of discovery and invention" (Polya 1945). This meaning can be traced to the term's Greek root, the verb *eurisco*, which means "I discover." When Archimedes emerged from his famous bath clutching the golden crown, he shouted "Eureka!" meaning "I have found it!" In state space search, *heuristics* are formalized as rules for choosing those branches in a state space that are most likely to lead to an acceptable problem solution.

AI problem solvers employ heuristics in two basic situations:

1. A problem may not have an exact solution because of inherent ambiguities in the problem statement or available data. Medical diagnosis is an example of this. A

given set of symptoms may have several possible causes; doctors use heuristics to choose the most likely diagnosis and formulate a plan of treatment. Vision is another example of an inherently inexact problem. Visual scenes are often ambiguous, allowing multiple interpretations of the connectedness, extent, and orientation of objects. Optical illusions exemplify these ambiguities. Vision systems use heuristics to select the most likely of several possible interpretations of a given scene.

2. A problem may have an exact solution, but the computational cost of finding it may be prohibitive. In many problems (such as chess), state space growth is combinatorially explosive, with the number of possible states increasing exponentially or factorially with the depth of the search. In these cases, exhaustive, *brute-force* search techniques such as depth-first or breadth-first search may fail to find a solution within any practical length of time. Heuristics attack this complexity by guiding the search along the most "promising" path through the space. By eliminating states and their descendants from consideration, a heuristic algorithm can (its designer hopes) defeat this combinatorial explosion and find an acceptable solution.

Unfortunately, like all rules of discovery and invention, heuristics are fallible. A heuristic is only an informed guess of the next step to be taken in solving a problem. It is often based on experience or intuition. Because heuristics use limited information, such as the descriptions of the states currently on the open list, they are seldom able to predict the exact behavior of the state space farther along in the search. A heuristic can lead a search algorithm to a suboptimal solution or fail to find any solution at all. This is an inherent limitation of heuristic search. It cannot be eliminated by "better" heuristics or more efficient search algorithms (Garey and Johnson 1979).

Heuristics and the design of algorithms to implement heuristic search have long been a core concern of artificial intelligence research. Game playing and theorem proving are two of the oldest applications in artificial intelligence; both of these require heuristics to prune spaces of possible solutions. It is not feasible to examine every inference that can be made in a mathematics domain or every possible move that can be made on a chessboard. Heuristic search is often the only practical answer.

More recently, expert systems research has affirmed the importance of heuristics as an essential component of problem solving. When a human expert solves a problem, he or she examines the available information and makes a decision. The "rules of thumb" that a human expert uses to solve problems efficiently are largely heuristic in nature. These heuristics are extracted and formalized by expert systems designers.

It is useful to think of heuristic algorithms as consisting of two parts: the heuristic measure and an algorithm that uses it to search the state space. In Section 4.1.1 we present an algorithm for heuristic or "best-first" search. The design and evaluation of effective heuristics are covered in the remainder of the chapter.

Consider the game of tic-tac-toe (Fig. II.5). The combinatorics for exhaustive search are high but not insurmountable. Each of the nine first moves has eight possible responses, which in turn have seven continuing moves, and so on. A simple counting principle puts the total number of states that need to be considered in an exhaustive search at $9 \times 8 \times 7 \times 6 \cdots$ or 9!

Symmetry reduction can decrease the search space a little. Many configurations are actually equivalent under symmetric operations on the game board. For example, there are really only three initial moves: to a corner, to the center of a side, and to the center of the grid. Symmetry reductions on the second level of states further reduce the number of possible paths through the space to a total of $12 \times 7!$ This reduced space is seen in Figure 4.1. It is smaller than the original space but is still factorial in its growth.

A simple heuristic, however, can almost eliminate search entirely: we may move to the board in which X has the most winning lines. (The first three states in the tic-tac-toe

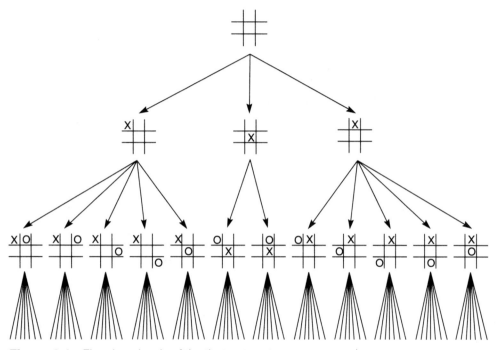

Figure 4.1   First three levels of the tic-tac-toe state space reduced by symmetry.

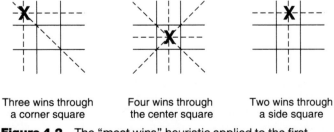

Three wins through
a corner square

Four wins through
the center square

Two wins through
a side square

Figure 4.2   The "most wins" heuristic applied to the first children in tic-tac-toe.

game are so measured in Figure 4.2.) In case of states with equal numbers of potential wins, take the first such state found. The algorithm then selects and moves to the state with the highest heuristic value. In this case X takes the center of the grid. Note that not only are the other alternatives eliminated, but so are all their descendants. Two-thirds of the space is pruned away with the first move (Fig. 4.3).

After the first move, the opponent can choose either of two alternatives (as seen in Fig. 4.3). Whichever is chosen, the heuristic can be applied to the resulting board, selecting among the possible moves. As search continues, each move evaluates the children of a single node; brute-force search is not required. Figure 4.3 shows the reduced search after three steps in the game. States are marked with their heuristic values.

Although it is difficult to compute the exact number of states that must be so examined, a crude upper bound can be computed by assuming a maximum of nine moves in a game and an average of eight possible children per move. This yields an upper bound of 4.5×9 or about 40 states, a considerable improvement over 9!

The next section (4.1) presents an algorithm for implementing heuristic search and demonstrates its performance using various heuristics to solve the 8-puzzle. In Section 4.2 we discuss some theoretical issues related to heuristic search, such as *admissibility* and

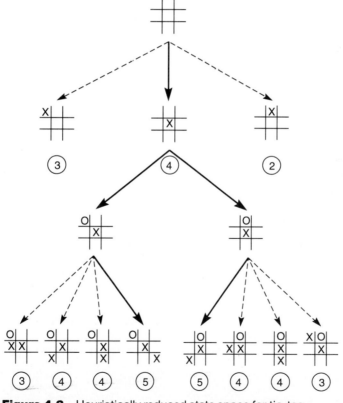

Figure 4.3 Heuristically reduced state space for tic-tac-toe.

monotonicity. Section 4.3 examines the use of *minimax* and *alpha-beta pruning* to apply heuristics to multiple-person games. The final section examines the complexity of heuristic search and reemphasizes its essential role in intelligent problem solving.

4.1 An Algorithm for Heuristic Search

4.1.1 Implementing ``Best-First'' Search

The simplest way to implement heuristic search is through a procedure called *hill climbing* (Pearl 1984). Hill-climbing strategies expand the current node in the search and evaluate its children. The best child is selected for further expansion; neither its siblings nor its parent are retained. Search halts when it reaches a state that is better than any of its children. Hill climbing is named for the strategy that might be used by an eager, but blind mountain climber: go uphill along the steepest possible path until you can go no farther. The problem with hill-climbing strategies is that an erroneous heuristic can lead along infinite paths that fail. Because it keeps no history, the algorithm cannot recover from these failures.

Hill-climbing strategies can also become stuck at local maxima. If they reach a state that has a better evaluation than any of its children, the algorithm halts. If this state is not a goal, but just a local maximum, the algorithm fails to find a solution. That is, performance might well improve in a limited setting, but because of the shape of the entire space, it may never reach the overall best. An example of local maxima in games occurs in the 8-puzzle. Very often, in order to move a particular tile to its destination, other tiles that are already in goal position have to be moved. This is necessary to solve the puzzle but temporarily worsens the board state. Because ``better'' need not be ``best'' in an absolute sense, hill-climbing methods are unable to distinguish between local and global maxima. There are various approaches to getting around this problem, such as randomly perturbing the evaluation function to break out of local maxima, but in general there is no way of guaranteeing optimal performance with hill-climbing techniques. We give an example of hill climbing with Samuel's checker-playing program in Section 4.3.2.

In spite of its limitations, hill climbing can be used effectively if the evaluation function is sufficiently informative to avoid local maxima and infinite paths. In general, however, heuristic search requires a more informed algorithm; this is provided by *best-first search*.

Like the depth-first and breadth-first search algorithms of Chapter 3, best-first search uses lists to maintain states: open to keep track of the current fringe of the search and closed to record states already visited. An added step in the algorithm orders the states on open according to some heuristic estimate of their ``closeness'' to a goal. Thus, each iteration of the loop considers the most ``promising'' state on the open list. The pseudocode for best-first search appears below.

```
procedure best_first_search;
begin
    open := [Start];                                                    % initialize
    closed := [];
    while open ≠ [] do                                                  % states remain
        begin
            remove the leftmost state from open, call it X;
            if X = goal then return the path from Start to X
            else begin
                generate children of X;
                for each child of X do
                case
                    the child is not on open or closed:
                        begin
                            assign the child a heuristic value;
                            add the child to open
                        end;
                    the child is already on open:
                        if the child was reached by a shorter path
                        then give the state on open the shorter path
                    the child is already on closed:
                        if the child was reached by a shorter path then
                            begin
                                remove the state from closed;
                                add the child to open
                            end;
                end;                                                    % case
                put X on closed;
                re-order states on open by heuristic merit (best leftmost)
            end;
    return failure                                                      % open is empty
end.
```

At each iteration, best_first_search removes the first element from the open list. If it meets the goal conditions, the algorithm returns the solution path that led to the goal. Note that this assumes each state retains ancestor information to allow the algorithm to return the final solution path. (See Section 3.2.3.)

If the first element on open is not a goal, the algorithm applies all matching production rules or operators to generate its descendants. If a child state is already on open or closed, the algorithm checks to make sure that the state records the shorter of the two partial solution paths. Duplicate states are not retained. By updating the ancestor history of nodes on open and closed when they are rediscovered, the algorithm is more likely to find a shorter path to a goal.

best_first_search then applies a heuristic evaluation to the states on open, and the list is sorted according to the heuristic values. This brings the "best" state to the front of open. Note that because these estimates are heuristic in nature, the next state to be examined may be from any level of the state space. open, when maintained as a sorted list, is often referred to as a *priority queue*.

Figure 4.4 shows a hypothetical state space with heuristic evaluations attached to

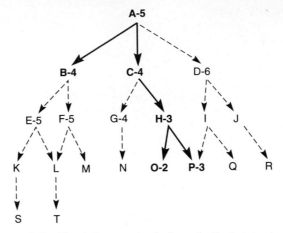

Figure 4.4 Heuristic search of a hypothetical state space.

some of its states. The states with attached evaluations are those actually generated in best-first search. The states expanded by the heuristic search algorithm are indicated in **bold**; note that it does not search all of the space. The goal of best-first search is to find the goal state by looking at as few states as possible; the more *informed* (Section 4.2.3) the heuristic, the fewer states are processed in finding the goal.

A trace of the execution of best_first_search on this graph appears below. Suppose P is the goal state in the graph of Figure 4.4. Because P is the goal, states along the path to P tend to have low heuristic values. The heuristic is fallible: the state O has a lower value than the goal itself and is examined first. Unlike hill climbing, the algorithm recovers from this error and finds the correct goal.

1. open = [A5]; closed = [ ]
2. evaluate A5; open = [B4,C4,D6]; closed = [A5]
3. evaluate B4; open = [C4,E5,F5,D6]; closed = [B4,A5]
4. evaluate C4; open = [H3,G4,E5,F5,D6]; closed = [C4,B4,A5]
5. evaluate H3; open = [O2,P3,G4,E5,F5,D6]; closed = [H3,C4,B4,A5]
6. evaluate O2; open = [P3,G4,E5,F5,D6]; closed = [O2,H3,C4,B4,A5]
7. evaluate P3; the solution is found!

Figure 4.5 shows the space as it appears after the fifth iteration of the while loop. The states contained in open and closed are indicated. open records the current frontier of the search and closed records states already considered. Note that the frontier of the search is highly uneven, reflecting the opportunistic nature of best-first search.

The best-first search algorithm always selects the most promising state on open for further expansion. However, as it is using a heuristic that may prove erroneous, it does not abandon all the other states but maintains them on open. In the event a heuristic leads the search down a path that proves incorrect, the algorithm may retrieve some previously generated "next best" state from open and shift its focus to another part of the space. In the

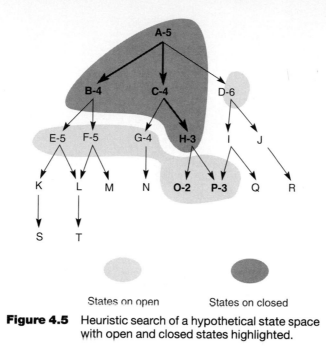

States on open   States on closed

Figure 4.5   Heuristic search of a hypothetical state space
with open and closed states highlighted.

example of Figure 4.4, after the children of state **B** were found to have poor heuristic evaluations, the search shifted its focus to state **C**. The children of **B** were kept on **open** in case the algorithm needed to return to them later. In **best_first_search**, as in the algorithms of Chapter 3, the **open** list allows backtracking from paths that fail to produce a goal.

4.1.2   Implementing Heuristic Evaluation Functions

We now evaluate the performance of several different heuristics for solving the 8-puzzle. Figure 4.6 shows a start and goal state for the 8-puzzle, along with the first three states generated in the search.

The simplest heuristic is to count the tiles out of place in each state when it is compared with the goal. This is intuitively appealing, because it would seem that, all else being equal, the state that had fewest tiles out of place is probably closer to the desired goal and would be the best to examine next.

However, this heuristic does not use all of the information available in a board configuration, because it does not take into account the distance the tiles must be moved. A "better" heuristic would sum all the distances by which the tiles are out of place, one for each square a tile must be moved to reach its position in the goal state.

Both of these heuristics can be criticized for failing to acknowledge the difficulty of tile reversals. That is, if two tiles are next to each other and the goal requires their being in

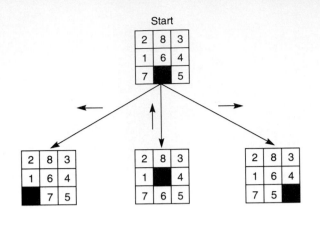

Start

Goal

Figure 4.6 The start state, first set of moves, and goal state for an 8-puzzle instance.

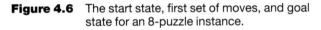

Goal

Figure 4.7 An 8-puzzle state with a goal and two reversals: 1 and 2, 5 and 6.

opposite locations, it takes (many) more than two moves to put them back in place, as the tiles must "go around" each other (Fig. 4.7).

A heuristic that takes this into account multiplies a small number (2, for example) times each direct tile reversal (where two adjacent tiles must be exchanged to be in the order of the goal). Figure 4.8 shows the result of applying each of these three heuristics to the three child states of Figure 4.6.

In the example of Figure 4.8, the "sum of distances" heuristic does indeed seem to provide a more accurate estimate of the work to be done than the simple count of the number of tiles out of place. Also, note that the tile reversal heuristic fails to distinguish between these states, giving each an evaluation of 0. Although it is an intuitively appealing heuristic, it breaks down since none of these states have any direct reversals. A fourth

	Tiles out of place	Sum of distances out of place	2 x the number of direct tile reversals
2 8 3 / 1 6 4 / ■ 7 5	**5**	**6**	**0**
2 8 3 / 1 ■ 4 / 7 6 5	**3**	**4**	**0**
2 8 3 / 1 6 4 / 7 5 ■	**5**	**6**	**0**

Goal

Figure 4.8 Three heuristics applied to states in the 8-puzzle.

heuristic, which may overcome the limitations of the tile reversal heuristic, adds the sum of the distances out of place and 2 times the number of direct reversals.

This example illustrates the difficulty of devising good heuristics. Our goal is to use the limited information available in a single state descriptor to make intelligent choices. Each of the heuristics proposed above ignores some critical bit of information and is subject to improvement. The design of good heuristics is an empirical problem; judgment and intuition help, but the final measure of a heuristic must be its actual performance on problem instances.

Because heuristics are fallible, it is possible that a search algorithm can be misled down some path that fails to lead to a goal. This problem arose in depth-first search, where a depth count was used to detect fruitless paths. This idea may also be applied to heuristic search. If two states have the same or nearly the same heuristic evaluations, it is generally preferable to examine the state that is nearest to the root state of the graph. This state will have a greater probability of being on the *shortest* path to the goal. The distance from the starting state to its descendants can be measured by maintaining a depth count for each state. This count is 0 for the beginning state and is incremented by 1 for each level of the search. It records the actual number of moves that have been used to go from the starting state in the search to each descendant. This can be added to the heuristic evaluation of each state to bias search in favor of states found shallower in the graph.

This makes our evaluation function, f, the sum of two components:

$$f(n) = g(n) + h(n)$$

where $g(n)$ measures the actual length of the path from any state n to the start state and $h(n)$ is a heuristic estimate of the distance from state n to a goal.

In the 8-puzzle, for example, we can let h(n) be the number of tiles out of place. When this evaluation is applied to each of the child states in Figure 4.6, their f values are 6, 4, and 6, respectively (Fig. 4.9).

The full best-first search of the 8-puzzle graph, using f as defined above, appears in Figure 4.10. Each state is labeled with a letter and its heuristic weight, $f(n) = g(n) + h(n)$. The number at the top of each state indicates the order in which it was taken off the open list. Some states (h, g, b, d, n, k, and i) are not so numbered, because they were still on open when the algorithm terminated.

The successive stages of open and closed that generate this graph are:

1. open = [a4];
   closed = [ ]
2. open = [c4, b6, d6];
   closed = [a4]
3. open = [e5, f5, g6, b6, d6];
   closed = [a4, c4]
4. open = [f5, h6, g6, b6, d6, I7];
   closed = [a4, c4, e5]
5. open = [j5, h6, g6, b6, d6, k7, I7];
   closed = [a4, c4, e5, f5]
6. open = [I5, h6, g6, b6, d6, k7, I7];
   closed = [a4, c4, e5, f5, j5]
7. open = [m5, h6, g6, b6, d6, n7, k7, I7];
   closed = [a4, c4, e5, f5, j5, I5]
8. success, m = goal!

In step 3 of the execution, both e and f have a heuristic evaluation of 5. State e is examined first, producing its children, h and i. Although state h, the immediate child of e, has the same number of tiles out of place as f, it is one level deeper in the state space. The depth measure, g(n), therefore causes the algorithm to select f for evaluation in step 4. The algorithm goes back to the shallower state and continues to the goal. The state space graph at this stage of the search, with open and closed highlighted, appears in Figure 4.11. Notice the opportunistic nature of best-first search.

In effect, the g(n) component of the evaluation function gives the search more of a breadth-first flavor. This prevents it from being misled by an erroneous evaluation: if a heuristic continuously returns "good" evaluations for states along a path that fails to reach a goal, the g value will grow to dominate h and force search back to a shorter solution path. This guarantees that the algorithm will not become permanently lost, descending an infinite branch. Section 4.2 examines the conditions under which best-first search using this evaluation function can actually be guaranteed to produce the shortest path to a goal.

When used in conjunction with the procedure best_first_search, the evaluation function f provides a general formulation of heuristic search. To summarize:

1. Other operations on states generate the children of the state currently under examination.

2. Each state is checked to see whether it has occurred before (is on either **open** or **closed**), thereby preventing loops.

3. Each state **n** is given an **f** value equal to the sum of its depth in the search space $g(n)$ and a heuristic estimate of its distance to a goal $h(n)$. The **h** value guides search toward heuristically promising states while the **g** value prevents search from persisting indefinitely on a fruitless path.

4. States on **open** are sorted by their **f** values. By keeping all states on **open** until they are examined or a goal is found, the algorithm can go back from fruitless paths. At any one time, **open** may contain states at different levels of the state space graph, allowing full flexibility in changing the focus of the search.

5. The efficiency of the algorithm can be improved by careful maintenance of the **open** and **closed** lists. For example, implementing **open** as a *heap* or *leftist tree* (Helman and Veroff 1986) can reduce sorting time.

Best-first search is a general algorithm for heuristically searching any state space graph (as were the breadth- and depth-first algorithms presented earlier). It is equally applicable to data- and goal-driven searches and supports a variety of heuristic evaluation functions. It will continue (Section 4.2) to provide a basis for examining the behavior of heuristic search. Because of its generality, best-first search can be used with a variety of

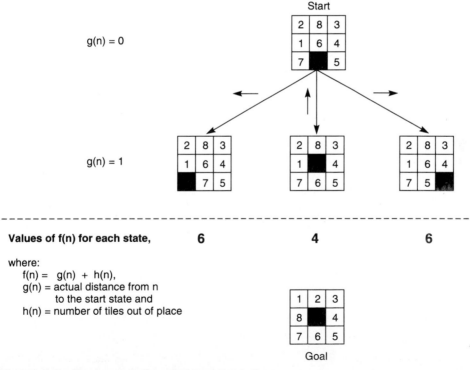

Figure 4.9 The heuristic **f** applied to states in the 8-puzzle.

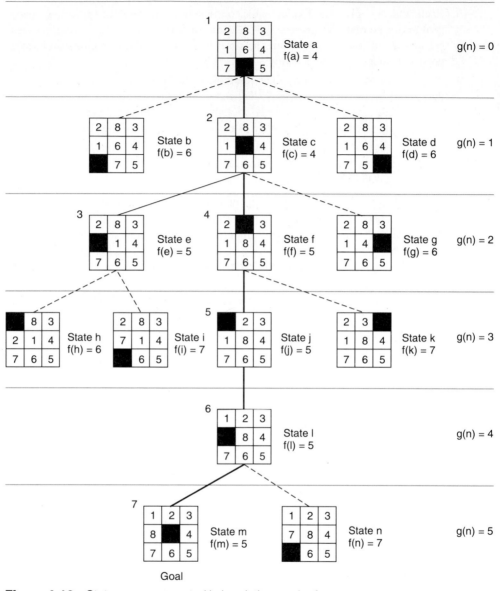

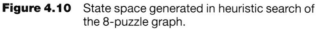

Figure 4.10 State space generated in heuristic search of the 8-puzzle graph.

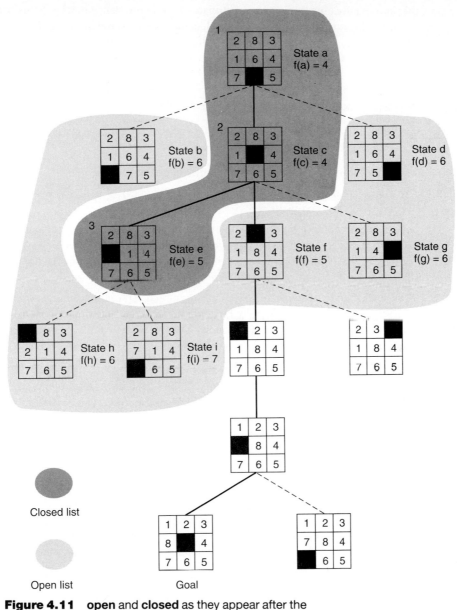

Figure 4.11 **open** and **closed** as they appear after the third iteration of heuristic search.

heuristics, ranging from subjective estimates of a state's "goodness" to sophisticated measures based on the probability of a state leading to a goal. Bayesian statistical measures (Chapter 8) offer an important example of this approach.

Another interesting approach to implementing heuristics is the use of confidence measures by expert systems to weigh the results of a rule. When human experts employ a heuristic, they are usually able to give some estimate of their confidence in its conclusions. Expert systems employ *confidence measures* to select the conclusions with the highest likelihood of success. States with extremely low confidences can be eliminated entirely. This approach to heuristic search is examined in the next section and again in Chapter 8.

4.1.3 Heuristic Search and Expert Systems

Simple games such as the 8-puzzle are ideal vehicles for exploring the design and behavior of heuristic search algorithms for a number of reasons:

1. The search spaces are large enough to require heuristic pruning.

2. Most games are complex enough to suggest a rich variety of heuristic evaluations for comparison and analysis.

3. Games generally do not involve complex representational issues. A single node of the state space is just a board description and usually can be captured in a straightforward fashion. This allows researchers to focus on the behavior of the heuristic, rather than the problems of knowledge representation.

4. Because each node of the state space has a common representation (e.g., a board description), a single heuristic may be applied throughout the search space. This contrasts with systems such as the financial advisor, where each node represents a different subgoal with its own distinct description.

More realistic problems greatly complicate the implementation and analysis of heuristic search. However, the insights gained from simple games generalize to problems such as those found in expert systems applications. Unlike the 8-puzzle, a single heuristic may not apply to each state in these spaces. Instead, the problem-solving heuristics are in the content of the rules themselves. Each rule is a heuristic that may be applied in a particular case; the pattern matcher matches the appropriate rule (heuristic) with the relevant state in the space.

EXAMPLE 4.1.1: THE FINANCIAL ADVISOR

Reconsider the financial advisor presented in Chapters 2 and 3. So far, the knowledge base has been treated as a set of logical implications, whose conclusions are either true or false, depending on the truth value of the premises. In actuality, these rules are highly heuristic in nature. For example, one rule states that an individual with adequate savings and income should invest in stocks:

savings_account(adequate) $\wedge$ income(adequate) $\Rightarrow$ investment(stocks).

In reality, it is possible that such an individual may prefer the added security of a combination strategy or even that of placing all investment money in savings. Thus, the rule is a heuristic, and the problem solver should try to account for this uncertainty. We could take additional factors, such as the age of the investor and the long-term prospects for security and advancement in the investor's profession, into account to make the rules more informed and capable of finer distinctions. However, this does not change the fundamentally heuristic nature of financial advice.

One way in which expert systems have addressed this issue is to attach a numeric weight (called a *confidence measure* or *certainty factor*) to the conclusion of each rule. This measures the confidence that may be placed in their conclusions.

Each rule conclusion is given a confidence measure, a real number between -1 and 1, with 1 corresponding to certainty (true) and -1 to a definite value of false. Values in between reflect varying confidence in the conclusion. For example, the preceding rule may be given a confidence of, say, 0.8, reflecting a small possibility that it may not be correct. Other conclusions may be drawn with different confidence weights:

savings_account(adequate) ∧ income(adequate) ⇒ investment(stocks)
    with confidence = 0.8.

savings_account(adequate) ∧ income(adequate) ⇒ investment(combination)
    with confidence = 0.5.

savings_account(adequate) ∧ income(adequate) ⇒ investment(savings)
    with confidence = 0.1.

These rules now reflect the judgment that although an individual with adequate savings and income would be most strongly advised to invest in stocks, there is some possibility that a combination strategy should be pursued and a very slight chance that they may want to continue investing in savings.

Heuristic search algorithms can use these certainty factors in a number of ways. For example, the results of all applicable rules could be produced along with their associated confidences. This is an exhaustive search, with varying certainties placed on multiple conclusions. Alternatively, the program might return only the result with the strongest confidence value. This would allow the program to ignore other rules, radically pruning the search space. A more conservative pruning strategy could ignore rules that draw a conclusion with a confidence less than a certain value (0.2 for example).

A number of important issues must be addressed in using confidence measures to weight rule conclusions. What does it really mean to have a "numeric confidence measure"? For example, how are the confidences handled if the conclusion of one rule is used as the premise of others? How are confidences combined in the event that more than one rule draws the same conclusion? How are the proper confidence measures assigned to rules in the first place? These issues are discussed in detail in Chapter 8.

4.2 Admissibility, Monotonicity, and Informedness

We may evaluate the behavior of heuristics along a number of dimensions. For instance, we may not only desire a solution but also may require the algorithm to find the shortest path to the goal. This could be important when an application might have an excessive cost for extra solution steps, such as planning a path for an autonomous robot through a dangerous environment. Heuristics that find the shortest path to a goal whenever it exists are said to be *admissible*. In other applications a minimal solution path might not be as important as overall problem-solving efficiency.

We may want to ask whether any better heuristics are available. In what sense is one heuristic "better" than another? This is the *informedness* of a heuristic.

When a state is discovered by using heuristic search, is there any guarantee that the same state won't be found later in the search at a cheaper cost (with a shorter path from the start state)? This is the property of *monotonicity*. The answers to these and other questions related to the effectiveness of heuristics make up the content of this section.

4.2.1 Admissibility Measures

A search algorithm is *admissible* if it is guaranteed to find a minimal path to a solution whenever such a path exists. Breadth-first search is an admissible search strategy. Because it looks at every state at level n of the graph before considering any state at the level $n + 1$, any goal nodes are found along the shortest possible path. Unfortunately, breadth-first search is often too inefficient for practical use.

Using the evaluation function $f(n) = g(n) + h(n)$ that was introduced in the last section, we may characterize a class of admissible heuristic search strategies. Before doing so, we formalize some definitions from the first part of this chapter:

DEFINITION

ALGORITHM A, ADMISSIBILITY

Consider the evaluation function $f(n) = g(n) + h(n)$,

where

      n is any state encountered in the search.

      $g(n)$ is the cost of n from the start state.

      $h(n)$ is the heuristic estimate of the cost of going from n to a goal.

If this evaluation function is used with the best_first_search algorithm of Section 4.1, the result is called *algorithm A*.

A search algorithm is *admissible* if, for any graph, it always terminates in the optimal solution path whenever a path from the start to a goal state exists.

If n is a node in the state space graph, $g(n)$ measures the depth at which that state has been found in the graph, and $h(n)$ is the heuristic estimate of the distance from n to a goal. In this sense $f(n)$ estimates the total cost of the path from the start state through n to the goal state.

In determining the properties of admissible heuristics, it is useful to define first an evaluation function f^*:

$$f^*(n) = g^*(n) + h^*(n)$$

where $g^*(n)$ is the cost of the *shortest* path from the start node to node n and h^* returns the *actual* cost of the shortest path from n to the goal. It follows that $f^*(n)$ is the actual cost of the optimal path from a start node to a goal node that passes through node n.

If we employ best_first_search with the evaluation function f^*, the resulting search strategy is admissible. (Proof is left to the reader.)

Although *oracles* such as f^* do not exist for most real problems, we would like the evaluation function f to be a close estimate of f^*. In algorithm A, $g(n)$, the cost of the current path to state n, is a reasonable estimate of g^*, but they may not be equal: $g(n) \geq g^*(n)$. These are equal only if the graph search has discovered the optimal path to state n.

Similarly, we replace $h^*(n)$ with $h(n)$, a heuristic estimate of the minimal cost to a goal state. Although we usually may not compute h^*, it is often possible to determine whether or not the heuristic estimate, $h(n)$, is bounded from above, i.e., is always less than, the actual cost of a minimal path, $h^*(n)$. If algorithm A uses an evaluation function f in which $h(n) \leq h^*(n)$, it is called algorithm A*.

DEFINITION

ALGORITHM A*

If algorithm A is used with an evaluation function in which $h(n)$ is less than or equal to the cost of the minimal path from n to the goal, the resulting search algorithm is called algorithm A* (pronounced "A STAR").

It is now possible to state a property of A* algorithms:

All A* algorithms are admissible.

This property is a theorem and the exercises at the end of the chapter give hints for its proof. The theorem says that any A* algorithm, i.e., one that uses a heuristic $h(n)$ such that $h(n) \leq h^*(n)$ for all n, is guaranteed to find the minimal path from n to the goal, if such a path exists.

Note that breadth-first search may be characterized as an A* algorithm in which $f(n) = g(n) + 0$. The decision for considering a state is based solely on its distance from the start state. We will show (Section 4.2.3) that the set of nodes considered by an A* algorithm is a subset of the states examined in breadth-first search.

Several heuristics from the 8-puzzle provide examples of A* algorithms. Although we may not be able to compute the value of $h^*(n)$ for the 8-puzzle, we may determine when a heuristic is bounded from above by the actual cost of the shortest path to a goal.

For instance, the heuristic of counting the number of tiles not in the goal position is certainly less than or equal to the number of moves required to move them to their goal position. Thus, this heuristic is admissible and guarantees an optimal (or shortest) solution path. The sum of the direct distances of tiles out of place is also less than or equal to the minimum actual path. Even using small multipliers for direct tile reversals gives an admissible heuristic.

This approach to proving admissibility of 8-puzzle heuristics may be applied to any heuristic search problem. Even though the actual cost of the shortest path to a goal may not always be computed, we can often prove that a heuristic is bounded from above by this value. When this can be done, the resulting search will terminate in the discovery of the shortest path when such a path exists.

4.2.2 Monotonicity

Recall that the definition of A^* algorithms did not require that $g(n) = g^*(n)$. This means that admissible heuristics may initially reach nongoal states along a suboptimal path, as long as the algorithm eventually finds an optimal path to all states on the path to a goal. It is natural to ask if there are heuristics that are "locally admissible," i.e., that consistently find the minimal path to each state they encounter in the search. This property is called *monotonicity*.

DEFINITION

MONOTONICITY

A heuristic function h is monotone if

1. For all states n_i and n_j, where n_j is a descendant of n_i,

   $$h(n_i) - h(n_j) \leq cost(n_i, n_j),$$

   where $cost(n_i, n_j)$ is the actual cost (in number of moves) of going from state n_i to n_j.
2. The heuristic evaluation of the goal state is zero, or $h(Goal) = 0$.

One way of describing the monotone property is that the search space is everywhere locally consistent with the heuristic employed. The difference between the heuristic measure for a state and any one of its successors is bound by the actual cost of going between that state and its successor. This is to say that the heuristic is everywhere admissible, reaching each state along the shortest path from its ancestors.

If the graph search algorithm for best-first search is used with a monotonic heuristic, an important step may be omitted. Because the heuristic finds the shortest path to any state the first time that state is discovered, when a state is rediscovered, it is not necessary to check whether the new path is shorter. It won't be! This allows any state that is rediscovered in the space to be dropped immediately without updating the path information retained on open or closed.

When using a monotonic heuristic, as the search moves through the space, the heuristic measure for each state n is replaced by the actual cost for generating that piece of the path to n. Because the actual cost is equal to or larger than the heuristic in each instance, f will not decrease; i.e., f is monotonically nondecreasing (hence the name).

A simple argument can show that any monotonic heuristic is admissible. This argument considers any path in the space as a sequence of states $s_1, s_2, \ldots, s_g$, where s_1 is the start state and s_g is the goal. For the sequence of moves in this arbitrarily selected path:

s_1 to s_2	$h(s_1) - h(s_2) \leq cost(s_1,s_2)$	by monotone property
s_2 to s_3	$h(s_2) - h(s_3) \leq cost(s_2,s_3)$	by monotone property
s_3 to s_4	$h(s_3) - h(s_4) \leq cost(s_3,s_4)$	by monotone property
.	. . .	by monotone property
.	. . .	by monotone property
s_{g-1} to s_g	$h(s_{g-1}) - h(s_g) \leq cost(s_{g-1}, s_g)$	by monotone property

Summing each column and using the monotone property of $h(s_g) = 0$:

path s_1 to s_g $h(s_1) \leq cost(s_1,s_g)$

This means that monotone heuristic h is A* and admissible.

It is left as an exercise whether the admissibility property of a heuristic implies monotonicity.

4.2.3   When One Heuristic Is Better: More Informed Heuristics

The final issue of this subsection is the notion of one heuristic being somehow better than another for finding the minimal path. An interesting case occurs when both heuristics are A*

DEFINITION

INFORMEDNESS

For two A* heuristics h_1 and h_2, if $h_1(n) \leq h_2(n)$, for all states n in the search space, heuristic h_2 is said to be *more informed* than h_1.

We can use this definition to compare the heuristics proposed for solving the 8-puzzle. As pointed out previously, breadth-first search is equivalent to the A* algorithm with heuristic h_1 such that $h_1(x) = 0$ for all states x. This is, trivially, less than h*. We have also shown that h_2, the number of tiles out of place with respect to the goal state, is a lower bound for h*. In this case $h_1 \leq h_2 \leq h^*$. It follows that the "number of tiles out of place" heuristic is more informed than breadth-first search. Figure 4.12 compares the spaces searched by these two heuristics. Both h_1 and h_2 find the optimal path, but h_2 evaluates many fewer states in the process.

Similarly, we can argue that the heuristic that calculates the sum of the direct distances by which all the tiles are out of place is again more informed than the calculation of the number of tiles that are out of place with respect to the goal state, and indeed this is the case. One can visualize a sequence of search spaces, each smaller than the previous one, converging on the direct optimal path solution.

If a heuristic h_2 is more informed than h_1, then the set of states examined by h_2 is a subset of those expanded by h_1. This can be verified by assuming the opposite (that there is one state expanded by h_2 and not by h_1). However, because h_2 is more informed than h_1, for all n, $h_2(n) < h_1(n)$, which is contradicted by our assumption.

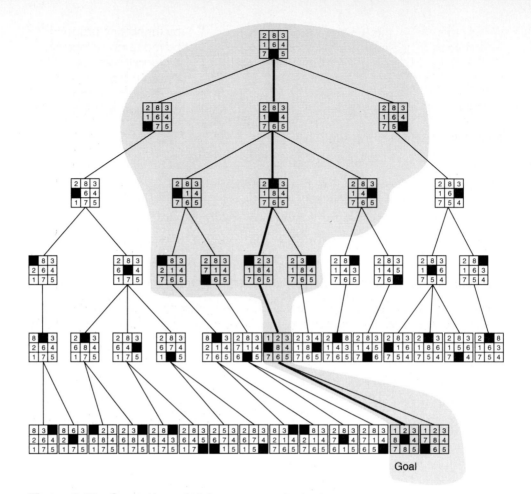

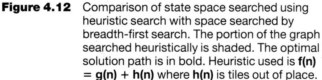

Goal

Figure 4.12 Comparison of state space searched using heuristic search with space searched by breadth-first search. The portion of the graph searched heuristically is shaded. The optimal solution path is in bold. Heuristic used is **f(n)** = **g(n)** + **h(n)** where **h(n)** is tiles out of place.

In general, then, the more informed an A* algorithm, the less of the space it needs to expand to get the optimal solution. We must be careful, however, that the computations necessary to employ the more informed heuristic are not so inefficient as to offset the gains from reducing the number of states searched.

Computer chess programs provide an interesting example of this trade-off. One school of thought uses simple heuristics and relies on the speed of the computer to search as deeply as possible into the search space. These programs often use specialized hardware to increase the depth of the search. Another school relies upon more sophisticated heuristics to reduce the number of board states searched. These heuristics include calculations of piece advantages, control of board geography, possible attack strategies, defensive strategies, passed pawns, and so on. Calculation of these heuristics can itself involve exponential complexity. As the total time for the first 40 moves of the game is limited, it is extremely important to optimize this trade-off between search and evaluation of heuristics (see also Fig. 4.22). The optimal blend of search and heuristics remains an open empirical question in computer chess.

4.3 Using Heuristics in Games

4.3.1 The Minimax Procedure on Exhaustively Searchable Graphs

Games have always been an important application area for heuristic algorithms. Two-person games are more complicated than simple puzzles because of the existence of a "hostile" and essentially unpredictable opponent. Thus, they provide some interesting opportunities for developing heuristics, as well as greater difficulties in developing search algorithms.

First we consider games whose state space is small enough to be exhaustively searched to find winning states; here the problem is systematically searching the space of possible moves and countermoves by the opponent. Then we look at games in which it is either impossible or undesirable to exhaustively represent and search the game graph. Because only a portion of the state space can be generated and searched, the game player must use heuristics to guide play along a path to a winning state.

Consider *nim*, a game whose state space may be exhaustively searched. To play nim, a number of matches are placed on a table between the two opponents; at each move, the player must divide a pile of matches into two nonempty piles with different numbers of matches in each pile. Thus, 6 matches may be divided into piles of 5 and 1 or 4 and 2, but not 3 and 3. The first player who can no longer make a move loses the game. For a reasonable number of matches, the state space can be exhaustively searched. Figure 4.13 illustrates the space for a game with 7 matches.

In playing games whose state space may be exhaustively delineated, the primary difficulty is in accounting for the actions of the opponent. A simple way to handle this is to assume that your opponent uses the same knowledge of the state space as you use and applies that knowledge in a consistent effort to win the game. Although this assumption has its limitations (which are discussed in Section 4.3.2), it provides a reasonable basis for predicting an opponent's behavior. *Minimax* implements game search under this assumption.

The opponents in a game are referred to as MIN and MAX. Although this is partly for historical reasons, the significance of these names is straightforward: MAX represents the player trying to win, or to MAXimize her advantage. MIN is the opponent who attempts to MINimize MAX's score. We assume that MIN uses the same information and always attempts to move to a state that is worst for MAX.

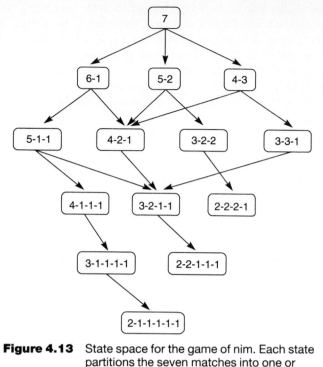

Figure 4.13 State space for the game of nim. Each state partitions the seven matches into one or more piles.

In implementing minimax, we label each level in the search space according to whose move it is at that point in the game, MIN or MAX. In the example of Figure 4.14, MIN is allowed to move first. Each leaf node is given a value of 1 or 0, depending on whether it is a win for MAX or for MIN. Minimax propagates these values up the graph through successive parent nodes according to the rule:

If the parent state is a MAX node, give it the maximum value among its children.

If the parent is a MIN node, give it the minimum value of its children.

The value that is thus assigned to each state indicates the value of the best state that this player can hope to achieve (assuming the opponent plays as predicted by the minimax algorithm). These derived values are used to choose among possible moves. The result of applying minimax to the state space graph for nim appears in Figure 4.14.

The values of the leaf nodes are propagated up the graph using minimax. Because all of MIN's possible first moves lead to nodes with a derived value of 1, the second player, MAX, always can force the game to a win, regardless of MIN's first move. MIN could win only if MAX played foolishly. In Figure 4.14, MIN may choose any of the first move alternatives, with the resulting win paths for MAX in bold arrows.

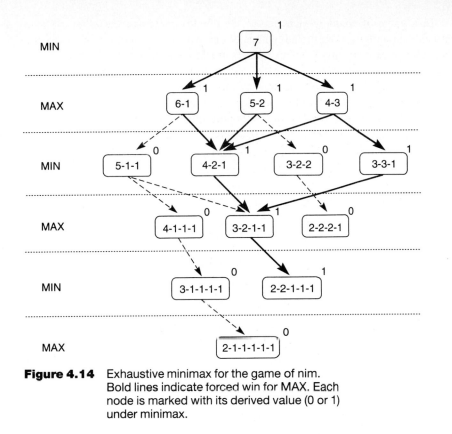

Figure 4.14 Exhaustive minimax for the game of nim.
Bold lines indicate forced win for MAX. Each
node is marked with its derived value (0 or 1)
under minimax.

Although there are many games where it is also possible to enumerate and exhaustively search the state space (as was done in Figure 4.14), the most interesting cases do not allow exhaustive search. We examine the heuristic application of minimax in the next section.

4.3.2 Minimaxing to Fixed Ply Depth

In applying minimax to more complicated games, it is seldom possible to expand the state space graph out to the leaf nodes. Instead, the state space is searched to a predefined number of levels, as determined by available resources of time and memory. This strategy is called an *n-move look-ahead*, where n is the number of levels explored. As the leaves of this subgraph are not final states of the game, it is not possible to give them values that reflect a win or a loss. Instead, each node is given a value according to some heuristic evaluation function. The value that is propagated back to the root node is not an indication of whether or not a win can be achieved (as in the previous example) but is simply the heuristic value of the best state that can be reached in n moves from this start node. Look-ahead increases the power of a heuristic by allowing it to be applied over a greater area of the state space. Minimax consolidates these separate evaluations into a single value of an ancestor state.

In a game of conflict, each player attempts to overcome the other, so many game heuristics directly measure the advantage of one player over another. In checkers or chess, piece advantage is important, so a simple heuristic might take the difference in the number of pieces belonging to MAX and MIN and try to maximize the difference between these piece measures. A more sophisticated strategy might assign different values to the pieces, depending on their value (e.g., queen vs. pawn or king vs. ordinary checker) or location on the board. Most games provide limitless opportunities for designing heuristics.

Game graphs are searched by level, or *ply*. As we saw in Figure 4.14, MAX and MIN alternately select moves. Each move by a player defines a new ply of the graph. Game-playing programs typically look ahead a fixed ply depth, often determined by the space/time limitations of the computer. The states on that ply are measured heuristically and the values are propagated back up the graph using minimax. The search algorithm then uses these *derived values* to select among possible next moves.

After assigning an evaluation to each state on the selected ply, the program propagates a value up to each parent state. If the parent is on a MIN level, the minimum value of the children is backed up. If the parent is a MAX node, minimax assigns it the maximum value of its children.

Maximizing for MAX parents and minimizing for MIN, the values go back up the graph to the children of the current state. These values are then used by the current state to select among its children. Figure 4.15 shows minimax on a hypothetical state space with a four-ply look-ahead.

The earliest AI work in this area was Samuel's checker-playing program (1959). This program was exceptional for its time and the limitations of the 1950s computers and is still a classic. Not only did Samuel's checker player apply heuristic search to checker playing, but it also implemented a simple form of learning.

Samuel's program evaluated board states with a weighted sum of several different heuristic measures:

$$\sum_i a_i x_i$$

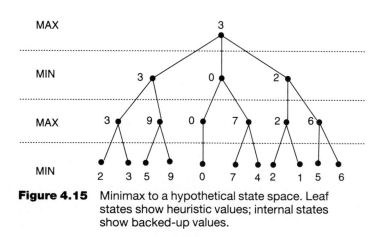

Figure 4.15 Minimax to a hypothetical state space. Leaf states show heuristic values; internal states show backed-up values.

The x_i in this sum was a feature of the game board such as piece advantage, piece location, control of center position, opportunities to sacrifice players in order to jump more of the opponent's pieces, and even a calculation of moments of inertia of one player's pieces about an axis of the board. The coefficients of these x_i were specially tuned weights that tried to model the importance of that factor in the overall board evaluation. Thus, if piece advantage was more important than control of the center, the piece advantage coefficient would be greater.

Samuel's program would look ahead in the search space the desired number of plies (usually imposed by space and/or time limitations of the computer) and evaluate all the states at that level with the evaluation polynomial. Using a variation on minimax, it propagated these values back up the graph. The checker player would then move to the best state; after the opponent's move, the process would be repeated for the new board state.

If the evaluation polynomial led to a losing series of moves, the program adjusted its coefficients in an attempt to improve performance. Evaluations with large coefficients were given most of the blame for losses and had their weights decreased, while smaller weights were increased to give these evaluations more influence. If the program won, the opposite was done. The program trained by playing either against a human partner or against another version of itself.

Samuel's program thus took a hill-climbing approach to learning, attempting to improve performance through local improvements on the evaluation polynomial. Samuel's checker player was able to improve its performance until it played a very good game of checkers. However, because it relied on hill climbing, it retained certain interesting limitations. For example, because it had no notion of a global strategy, it was vulnerable to strategies that used the evaluation function to lead the program into traps. The learning component of the program was vulnerable to inconsistencies in the opponent's play; for example, if the opponent used widely varying strategies, or simply played foolishly, the weights on the evaluation polynomial might begin to take on "random" values, leading to an overall degradation of performance.

We can make several final points about the minimax procedure. First, and most important, evaluations to any (previously decided) fixed ply depth may be seriously misleading. When a heuristic is applied with a limited look-ahead, it is possible that the depth of the look-ahead may not detect that a heuristically promising path leads to a bad situation later in the game. If your opponent in chess offers a rook as a lure to take your queen, and the evaluation only looks ahead to the ply where the rook is offered, the evaluation is going to be biased toward this state. Unfortunately, selection of the state may cause the entire game to be lost! This is referred to as the *horizon effect*. It is usually countered by searching several plies deeper from states that look exceptionally good. This selective deepening of search in important areas will not make the horizon effect go away, however. The search must stop somewhere and therefore will be blind to states beyond that point.

There is another effect that occurs in minimaxing backups. The evaluations that take place very deep in the space can be biased by their very depth (Pearl 1984). In the same way that the average of products differs from the product of averages, the estimate of minimax (which is what we desire) is different from the minimax of estimates (which is what we are doing). In this sense, deeper search with evaluation and minimax need not always mean better search. Further discussion of these issues and possible remedies is found in Pearl (1984).

In concluding the discussion of minimax, we present its application to tic-tac-toe (Section 4.1) (Nilsson 1980). We use a slightly more complex heuristic, one that attempts to measure the conflict in the game. The heuristic takes a state to be measured, counts all winning lines open to MAX, and then subtracts the total number of winning lines open to MIN. The search attempts to maximize this difference. If a state is a forced win for MAX, it is evaluated as $+\infty$; a forced win for MIN, as $-\infty$; Figure 4.16 shows this heuristic applied to several sample states.

The three figures that follow show the heuristic of Figure 4.16 with a two-ply minimax. MAX (X) has the first move in the game. The next three figures show the heuristic evaluation, the minimax backup, and MAX's choice of move.

4.3.3 The Alpha-Beta Procedure

Straight minimax requires a two-pass analysis of the search space, the first to descend to the ply depth and there apply the heuristic and the second to propagate values back up the tree. Minimax pursues all branches in the space, including many that could be ignored or pruned by a more intelligent algorithm. Researchers in game playing have developed a

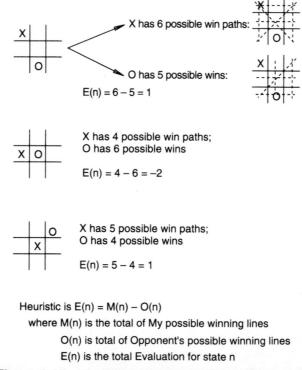

Heuristic is E(n) = M(n) – O(n)

where M(n) is the total of My possible winning lines

O(n) is total of Opponent's possible winning lines

E(n) is the total Evaluation for state n

Figure 4.16 Heuristic measuring conflict applied to states of tic-tac-toe.

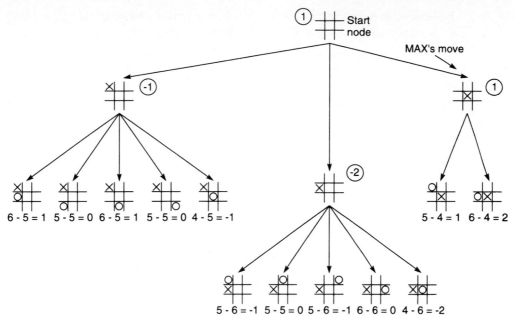

Figure 4.17 Two ply minimax applied to the opening move of tic-tac-toe.

class of search techniques called *alpha-beta* pruning to improve the efficiency of search in two-person games (Pearl 1984).

The idea for alpha-beta search is simple: rather than searching the entire space to the ply depth, alpha-beta search proceeds in a depth-first fashion. Two values, called *alpha* and *beta*, are created during the search. The alpha value, associated with MAX nodes, can never decrease, and the beta value, associated with MIN nodes, can never increase. Suppose a MAX node's alpha value is 6. Then MAX need not consider any backed-up value less than or equal to 6 that is associated with any MIN node below it. Alpha is the worst that MAX can "score" given that MIN will also do its "best." Similarly, if MIN has a beta value of 6, it need not consider further any MAX node below it that has a value of 6 or more.

To begin alpha-beta search, we descend to full ply depth in a depth-first fashion and apply our heuristic evaluation to a state and all its siblings. Assume these are MIN nodes. The maximum of these MIN values is then backed up to the parent (a MAX node, just as in minimax). This value is then offered to the grandparent of these MINs as a potential beta cutoff.

Next, the algorithm descends to other grandchildren and terminates exploration of their parent if any of their values is equal to or larger than this beta value. Similar procedures can be described for alpha pruning over the grandchildren of a MAX node.

Two rules for terminating search, based on alpha and beta values, are:

1. Search can be stopped below any MIN node having a beta value less than or equal to the alpha value of any of its MAX ancestors.

2. Search can be stopped below any MAX node having an alpha value greater than or equal to the beta value of any of its MIN node ancestors.

Alpha-beta pruning thus expresses a relation between nodes at ply n and nodes at ply n + 2 under which entire subtrees rooted at level n + 1 can be eliminated from consideration.

As an example, Figure 4.20 takes the space of Figure 4.15 and applies alpha-beta pruning. Note that the resulting backed-up value is identical to the minimax result and the search saving is considerable.

With a fortuitous ordering of states in the search space, alpha-beta can effectively double the depth of the search space considered with a fixed space/time computer commitment (Nilsson 1980). If there is a particular unfortunate ordering, alpha-beta searches no more of the space than normal minimax; however, the search is done in only one pass.

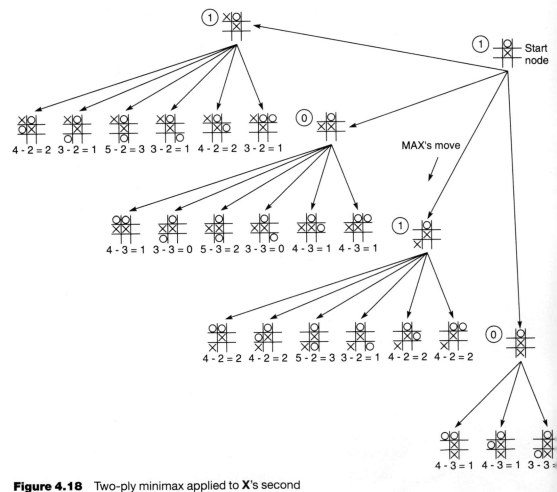

Figure 4.18 Two-ply minimax applied to **X**'s second move of tic-tac-toe.

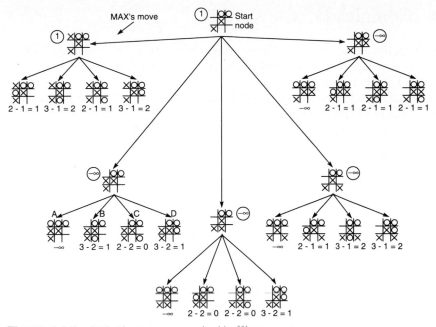

Figure 4.19 Two-ply minimax applied to **X**'s move near end game.

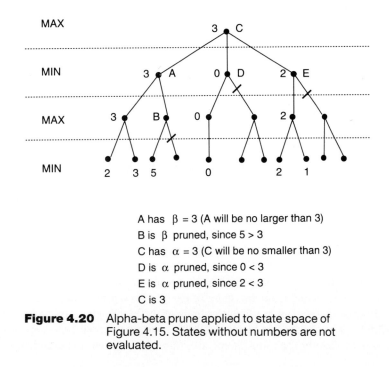

A has β = 3 (A will be no larger than 3)

B is β pruned, since 5 > 3

C has α = 3 (C will be no smaller than 3)

D is α pruned, since 0 < 3

E is α pruned, since 2 < 3

C is 3

Figure 4.20 Alpha-beta prune applied to state space of Figure 4.15. States without numbers are not evaluated.

4.4 Complexity Issues

The most difficult aspect of combinatorial problems is that the "explosion" often takes place without program designers realizing that it is happening. Because most activity, computing and otherwise, takes place in a world of linear algorithms and processing, we have difficulty appreciating the full meaning of exponential growth. The complaint is too often heard, "If only I had a larger (or faster or highly parallel . . .) computer my problem would be solved." Such claims, often made in the aftermath of the explosion, are usually rubbish. The problem wasn't understood properly and/or appropriate steps were not taken to address the combinatorics of the situation.

The full extent of combinatorial growth staggers the imagination. It has been estimated that the number of states produced by a full search of the space of possible chess moves is about 10^{120}. If this seems "just another large number," it is comparable to the number of molecules in the universe or the number of nanoseconds since the "big bang." It is simply not going to be computed!!

Several measures have been developed to help calculate complexity. One of these is the *branching factor* of a space. This is defined as the average number of descendants that emerge from any state in the space. The number of states at depth n of the search is equal to the branching factor raised to the nth power. Once the branching factor is computed for a space it is possible to estimate the search cost to generate a path of any particular length. Figure 4.21 gives the relationship between B (branching), L (path length), and T (total states in the search) for small values. The figure is logarithmic in T, so L is not the straight line it looks in the graph.

Several examples using this figure show how bad things can get. If the branching factor is 2 (in a binary tree, for example), it takes a search of about 100 states to examine all paths that extend six levels deep into the search space. It takes a search of about 10,000 states to consider paths 12 moves deep. If the branching can be cut down to 1.5 (by some heuristic or reformulation of the problem), then a path twice as long can be considered for the same amount of states searched.

The mathematical formula that produced the relationships of Figure 4.21 is straightforward:

$$T = B + B^2 + B^3 + \cdots + B^L$$

where T is total states, L is path length, and B is branching factor. This equation reduces to:

$$T = B(B^L - 1)/(B - 1)$$

Determining measurement aspects for a search space is by and large empirical and done by considerable playing about with and testing of a problem. Suppose, for example, we wish to establish the branching factor of the 8-puzzle. We calculate the total number of possible moves: 2 from each corner for a total of 8 corner moves, 3 from the center of each side for a total of 12, and 4 from the center of the grid for a grand total of 24. This divided by 9, the different number of possible locations of the blank, gives an average branching factor of 2.67. As can be seen in Figure 4.21, this is not very good for a deep search. If we eliminate moves directly back to a parent state (already built into the search algorithms of

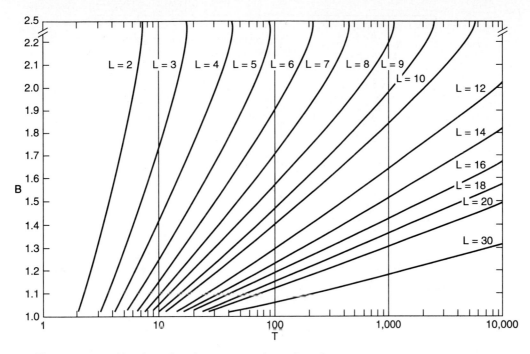

Figure 4.21 Number of nodes generated as a function of branching factor, B, for various lengths, L, of solution paths. The relating equation is: $T = B(B^L - 1)/(B - 1)$.

this chapter) there is one less move from each state. This gives a branching factor of 1.67, a considerable improvement, which might (in some state spaces) make exhaustive search possible.

As we considered in Chapter 3, the complexity cost of an algorithm can also be measured by the sizes of the open and closed lists. One method of keeping the size of open reasonable is to save on open only a few of the (heuristically) best states. This can produce a better focused search but has the danger of possibly eliminating the best, or even the only, solution path. This technique of maintaining a size bound, often a function of the number of steps taken in the search, is called *beam search*.

In the attempt to bring down the branching of a search or otherwise constrain the search space, we presented the notion of *more informed* heuristics. The more informed the search, the less the space must be searched to get the minimal path solution. As we pointed out in Section 4.3, the computational costs of the additional information needed to further cut down the search space may not always be acceptable. In solving problems on a computer, it is not enough to find a minimum path. We must also minimize total cpu costs.

Figure 4.22, taken from an analysis by Nilsson (1980), is an informal attempt to get at these issues. The "informedness" coordinate marks the amount of information that is included in the evaluation heuristic to improve its performance. The cpu coordinate marks the cpu costs for implementing aspects of the search. As the information included in the

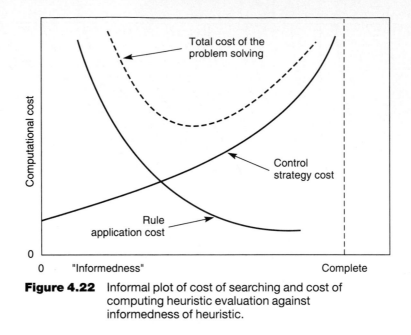

Figure 4.22   Informal plot of cost of searching and cost of
computing heuristic evaluation against
informedness of heuristic.

heuristic increases, the cpu cost of the heuristic increases. Similarly, as the heuristic gets more informed, the cpu cost of evaluating states gets smaller, because fewer states are considered. The critical cost, however, is the total cost of computing the heuristic PLUS evaluating states, and it is usually desirable that this cost be minimized.

Finally, heuristic search of and/or graphs is also an important area of concern, as the state spaces for expert systems are often of this form. The fully general search of these structures is made up entirely of the components already discussed in this and the preceding chapter. Because all and children must be searched to find a goal, the heuristic estimate of the cost of searching an and node is the sum of the estimates of searching the children.

More comments are made on heuristic-based and/or search in Section 8.3, where we present the design of expert systems and the implementation of appropriate search strategies.

4.5   Epilogue and References

The search spaces for interesting problems tend to grow exponentially; heuristic search is a primary tool for managing this combinatorial explosion. After presenting an algorithm for implementing best-first search, the chapter analyzed the behavior of heuristic algorithms, considering properties such as admissibility, monotonicity, and informedness.

Heuristic search was introduced using simple games such as the 8-puzzle and extended to the more complex problem spaces generated by rule-based expert systems

(Chapter 8). The chapter also applied heuristic search to two-person games, using minimax and alpha-beta pruning to implement look-ahead and predict the behavior of the opponent.

The discipline of complexity theory has essential ramifications for virtually every branch of computer science, especially the analysis of state space growth and heuristic pruning. Complexity theory examines the inherent complexity of problems (as opposed to algorithms). The key conjecture in complexity theory is that there exists a class of inherently intractable problems. This class, referred to as NP (Nondeterministically Polynomial), consists of problems that may not be solved in less than exponential time without resorting to the use of heuristics. Almost all search problems belong to this class. We especially recommend *Computers and Intractability* by Michael R. Garey and David S. Johnson (1979) and *Algorithms from P to NP, Vol. I: Design and Efficiency* by Bernard Moret and Henry Shapiro (1991) for this material.

Heuristics by Judea Pearl (1984) provides a comprehensive treatment of the design and analysis of heuristics for computer problem solving. R. E. Korf (1987) has continued to examine search algorithms. His work includes a thorough analysis of iterative deepening and the development of the IDA* algorithm, which integrates iterative deepening with the heuristic control of A* to obtain linear bounds on open for heuristic search. We are also indebted to Nils Nilsson (1980) for the general approach and many of the particular examples presented in this chapter.

4.6 Exercises

1. Give a heuristic that a block-stacking program might use to solve problems of the form "stack block X on block Y." Is it admissible? Monotonic?

2. The sliding-tile puzzle consists of three black tiles, three white tiles, and an empty space in the configuration shown in Figure 4.23.

   The puzzle has two legal moves with associated costs:

   > A tile may move into an adjacent empty location. This has a cost of 1. A tile can hop over one or two other tiles into the empty position. This has a cost equal to the number of tiles jumped over.

   The goal is to have all the white tiles to the left of all the black tiles. The position of the blank is not important.

   a. Analyze the state space with respect to complexity and looping.
   b. Propose a heuristic for solving this problem and analyze it with respect to admissibility, monotonicity, and informedness.

B	B	B		W	W	W

Figure 4.23   The sliding block puzzle.

3. Compare the three 8-puzzle heuristics of Figure 4.8 and the fourth heuristic of adding the sum of distances out of place to 2 times the number of direct reversals. Compare them in terms of:

    a. Accuracy in estimating distance to a goal. This requires that you first derive the shortest path solution and use it as a standard.
    b. Informedness. Which heuristic most effectively prunes the state space?
    c. Admissibility. Which of these heuristics are bounded from above by the actual cost of a path to the goal? Either prove your conclusions for the general case or give a counterexample.

4. a. As presented in the text, best-first search uses the closed list to implement loop detection. What would be the effect of eliminating this test and relying on the depth test, g(n), to detect loops? Compare the efficiencies of the two approaches.
    b. best_first_search does not test a state to see whether it is a goal until it is removed from the open list. This test could be performed when new states are generated. What effect would doing so have on the efficiency of the algorithm? Admissibility?

5. Prove A* is admissible. Hint: the proof should show that:

    a. During its execution there is always a node on open that lies on an optimal path to the goal.
    b. If there is a path to a goal, A* will terminate by finding the optimal path.

6. Does (or when does) admissibility imply monotonicity of a heuristic?

7. Prove that the set of states expanded by algorithm A* is a subset of those examined by breadth-first search.

8. Prove that more informed heuristics develop the same or less of the search space. Hint: formalize the argument presented in Section 4.2.3.

9. A Caesar cipher is a simple encryption scheme based on cyclic permutations of the alphabet, with the ith letter of the alphabet replaced by the $(i + n)$th letter of the alphabet. For example, in a Caesar cipher with a shift of 4, "Caesar" would be encrypted as "Giewev."

    a. Give three heuristics that might be used for solving Caesar ciphers.
    b. In a simple substitution cipher, each letter is replaced by another letter under some arbitrary one-to-one mapping. Which of the heuristics proposed for the Caesar cipher may be used to solve substitution ciphers? Explain. (Thanks to Don Morrison for this problem.)

10. Perform minimax on the tree shown in Figure 4.24.

11. Perform a left-to-right alpha-beta prune on the tree of Exercise 10. Perform a right-to-left prune on the same tree. Discuss why different pruning occurs.

12. Another way in which Samuel's checker player learned was to maintain a data base of previously encountered board states along with their derived evaluation under minimax. When a board was to be evaluated, the program first looked in the data base of board states. Discuss the effect this would have on the effectiveness of minimax. Give some "ballpark" estimates of the growth of this data base as a function of games played. Discuss ways in which this implementation may be made more efficient and more effective.

13. Why do game-playing programs work from a current state to a goal, rather than backward from a goal? What properties of a game might suggest using a backward strategy?

14. It was mentioned in the text that extending a heuristic minimax to extreme depths of the state space could degrade the effectiveness of the algorithm. Formalize this argument. Hint: see Chapter 10 of Pearl (1984).

15. Samuel's checker-playing program employed up to 16 different parameters in its evaluation polynomial. Suggest three evaluation functions for checkers that were not mentioned in the text.

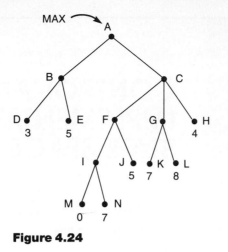

Figure 4.24

16. Consider three-dimensional tic-tac-toe. Discuss representational issues; analyze the complexity of the state space. Propose a heuristic for playing this game.

17. Perform the alpha-beta pruning on the tic-tac-toe search of Figures 4.17–4.19. How many leaf nodes can be eliminated in each case?

18. a. Define an algorithm for heuristically searching and/or graphs. Note that all descendants of an **and** node must be solved to solve the parent. Thus, in computing heuristic estimates of costs to a goal, the estimate of the cost to solve an **and** node must be at least the sum of the estimates to solve the different branches.
    b. Use this algorithm to search the graph in Figure 4.25.

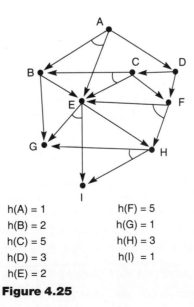

h(A) = 1 h(F) = 5
h(B) = 2 h(G) = 1
h(C) = 5 h(H) = 3
h(D) = 3 h(I) = 1
h(E) = 2

Figure 4.25

CONTROL AND IMPLEMENTATION OF STATE SPACE SEARCH

If we carefully factor out the influences of the task environments from the influences of the underlying hardware components and organization, we reveal the true simplicity of the adaptive system. For, as we have seen, we need postulate only a very simple information processing system in order to account for human problem solving in such tasks as chess, logic, and cryptarithmetic. The apparently complex behavior of the information processing system in a given environment is produced by the interaction of the demands of the environment with a few basic parameters of the system, particularly characteristics of its memories . . .

—A. NEWELL AND H. A. SIMON, "Human Problem Solving"

What we call the beginning is often the end
And to make an end is to make a beginning.
The end is where we start from . . .

—T. S. ELIOT, *Four Quartets*

5.0 Introduction

Chapters 3 and 4 represented problem solving as search through a set of problem states. The state space model of problem solving allows graph theory to be used as a tool for designing and analyzing intelligent programs. Chapter 3 defined a general backtracking graph search algorithm as well as algorithms for both depth-first and breadth-first search. Chapter 4 presented algorithms for heuristic search. The following definitions characterize the data and control structures used to implement state space search:

1. Representation of a problem solution as a path from a start state to a goal.

2. Search to test systematically alternative paths to a goal.

3. Backtracking to allow an algorithm to "recover" from paths that fail to lead to a goal.
4. Lists to keep explicit records of states under consideration.
   a. The *open* list allows the algorithm to backtrack to untried states if necessary.
   b. The *closed* list of visited states allows the algorithm to implement loop detection and avoid repeating fruitless paths.
5. Use of a *stack* to implement depth-first search, a *queue* to implement breadth-first search, and a *priority queue* to implement best-first search.

Chapter 5 introduces higher-level techniques for implementing search algorithms. The first of these, *recursive search*, implements depth-first search with backtracking in a more concise, natural fashion than in Chapter 3 and forms the basis for many of the algorithms in this text. Recursive search is augmented through the use of *unification* to search the state space generated by predicate calculus assertions. This *pattern-directed search* algorithm is the basis of PROLOG (Chapter 6) and many of the expert system shells discussed in Chapters 8 and 14.

Next, in Section 5.3 we introduce *production systems*, a general architecture for pattern-directed problem solving that has been used extensively both to model human problem solving and to build expert systems and other AI applications. In Section 5.4 we show how predicate calculus and pattern matching may be used in robot planning or problem solving across time periods. Finally we present another AI problem-solving technique, the blackboard.

5.1 Recursion-Based Search

5.1.1 Recursion

In mathematics, a recursive definition uses the term being defined as part of its own definition. In computer science, recursion is used to define and analyze both data structures and procedures. A recursive procedure consists of:

1. A recursive step in which the procedure calls itself to repeat a sequence of actions.
2. A terminating condition that stops the procedure from recurring endlessly (the recursive version of an endless loop).

Both of these components are essential and appear in all recursive definitions and algorithms. Recursion is a natural control construct for data structures that have no definite size, such as lists, trees, and graphs. This makes it particularly appropriate for state space search.

A simple example of recursion is an algorithm for determining if an item is a member of a list. Lists are ordered sequences of elements and fundamental building blocks for computer science data structures. Lists have already been used as an alternative syntax for predicate calculus expressions (Chapter 2) and to implement the open and closed lists in the search algorithms of Chapter 3. A procedure for testing whether an element is a member of a list is defined recursively by:

```
function member (item, list);

begin
  if list is empty
      then return (fail)                                    % terminate
      else
        if item = first element of list
            then return (success)                          % terminate
            else
              begin
                tail := list with its first item removed;
                member(item, tail)                         % recur
              end
end.
```

This procedure first tests whether list is empty; if so, the algorithm returns fail. Otherwise, it compares item to the first element of list; if these are equal, the procedure halts with success. These are the terminating conditions of the procedure. If neither terminating condition is met, member removes the first element from list and calls itself on the shortened list. In this fashion, member examines each element of the list in turn. Note that because list is finite and each step reduces its size by one element, the algorithm always halts.

This algorithm uses two fundamental list operations: one that returns the first element (the *head*) of a list and a *tail* operation, which returns the list with its first element removed. When coupled with recursion, these operations are the basis for higher-level list operations such as member. These operations are supported by both LISP and PROLOG and are described in detail in the chapters on each language.

When supported by a programming language, recursion offers all the power of more traditional control constructs such as loops and conditional branching. In other words, *anything* that can be done using explicit iteration can be done recursively. The benefit of recursive formulations is greater clarity and compactness of expression. Mathematical notations such as logic or functions do not support such concepts as sequencing, branching, and iteration; instead, they use recursion to indicate repetition. As recursion is easier to describe mathematically than explicit iteration, it is easier to analyze formally the correctness and complexity of recursive algorithms. Recursive formulations are also used frequently by systems that automatically generate or verify programs, and they play an important role in implementing compilers and interpreters. More important, however, is the power and naturalness of recursion as a tool for implementing AI problem-solving strategies such as graph search.

5.1.2   Recursive Search

A direct translation of the depth-first search algorithm of Chapter 3 into recursive form illustrates the equivalence of recursion and iteration. This algorithm uses global variables closed and open to maintain lists of states:

```
function depthsearch;                              % open & closed global

begin
  if open is empty
      then return(fail);
  current_state := the first element of open;
  if current_state is a goal state
      then return(success)
      else
        begin
          open := the tail of open;
          closed := closed with current_state added;
          for each child of current_state
              if not on closed or open                  % build stack
                  then add the child to the front of open
        end;
      depthsearch                                        % recur
  end.
```

Breadth-first search can be implemented with the same algorithm, simply by implementing open as a queue rather than a stack.

The implementation of depth-first search just presented does not utilize the full power of recursion. It is possible to simplify the procedure further by using recursion itself (rather than an explicit open list) to organize states and paths through the state space. In this version of the algorithm, closed is still maintained as a global variable and used to detect duplicate states and prevent loops.

```
function depthsearch (current_state);               % closed is global

begin
  if current_state is a goal
      then return(success);
  add current_state to closed;
  while current_state has unexamined children
      begin
        child := next unexamined child;
        if child not member of closed
            then if depthsearch(child) = success
                    then return(success)
      end;
  return(fail)                                       % search exhausted
  end.
```

Rather than generating all children of a state and placing them on an open list, this algorithm produces the child states one at a time and recursively searches the descendants of each child before generating its sibling. Note that the algorithm assumes an order to the state generation operators. In recursively searching a child state, if some descendant of that state is a goal, the recursive call returns success and the algorithm ignores the siblings. If the recursive call on the child state fails to find a goal, the next sibling is generated and all of its descendants are searched. In this fashion, the algorithm searches the entire graph in a depth-first order. The reader should verify that it actually searches the graph in the same order as the depth-first search algorithm of Section 3.2.3.

The omission of an explicit open list is made possible through recursion. The mechanisms by which a programming language implements recursion include a separate *activation record* (Aho 1977) of each recursive call. These record the local variables and state of execution of each procedure call. When the procedure is called recursively with a new state, a new activation record stores its parameters (the state), any local variables, and the current state of execution. In a recursive search algorithm, the series of states on the current path are recorded in the sequence of activation records of the recursive calls. The record of each call also indicates the last operation used to generate a child state; this allows the next sibling to be generated when needed.

Backtracking is effected when all descendants of a state fail to include a goal, causing the recursive call to fail. This returns fail to the procedure expanding the parent state, which generates and recurs on the next sibling. The internal mechanisms of recursion thus do the work of the open list used in the iterative version. The recursive implementation allows the programmer to restrict his or her point of view to a single state and its children rather than having to explicitly maintain an open list of states. The ability of recursion to express global concepts in a closed form is a major source of its power.

State space search is an inherently recursive process. To find a path from a current state to a goal, move to a child state and recur. If that child state does not lead to a goal, try its siblings in order. Recursion breaks a large and difficult problem (searching the whole space) into smaller, simpler pieces (generate the children of a single state) and applies this strategy (recursively) to each of them. This process continues until a goal state is discovered or the space is exhausted.

Symbolic integration, discussed in Section 3.3.3, is an excellent example of the power of a recursive approach to search problems. When attempting to integrate an expression, it applies either a substitution or a decomposition to the expression, replacing it with one (in the case of a substitution) or more (in the case of a decomposition) simpler subproblems. These subproblems are then solved recursively, with the separate solutions being recombined into a final answer. For example, after applying the rule that the integral of a sum equals the sum of the integrals of the terms, it recursively attempts to integrate each term. This may lead to further decompositions or substitutions, until each term has been integrated. These results are then combined (summed) to produce the final result. Recursion is a natural tool for systematically decomposing a problem and recombining partial solutions into a final answer.

In the next section, this recursive approach to problem solving is extended into a controller for a logic-based problem solver that uses unification and inference to generate and search a space of logical relations.

5.2 Pattern-Directed Search

The recursive search algorithm of Section 5.1 does not specify the representation of states or the operations that produce new states. Chapter 2 discussed the advantages of predicate calculus as an AI representation; Chapter 3 showed how inferences on predicate calculus assertions define a state space that may be searched. This section applies recursive search to a space of logical inferences; the result is a general search procedure for predicate calculus.

Suppose, for example, we want to write an algorithm that determines whether a predicate calculus expression is a logical consequence of some set of assertions. The algorithm must find a sequence of inferences that produce the goal expression. This suggests a goal-directed search with the initial query forming the goal and modus ponens the transitions between states. Given a goal (such as p(a)), the algorithm uses unification to select the implications whose conclusions match the goal (e.g., q(X) → p(X)). Because the algorithm treats implications as potential rules for solving the query, they are often simply called *rules*. After unifying the goal with the conclusion of the implication (or rule) and applying the resulting substitutions throughout the rule, the rule premise becomes a new goal (q(a)). This is called a *subgoal*. The algorithm then recurs on the subgoal. If a subgoal matches a fact in the knowledge base, search terminates. The series of inferences that led from the initial goal to the given facts prove the truth of the original goal.

```
function pattern_search (current_goal);
begin
   if current_goal is a member of closed                        % test for loops
      then return fail
      else add current_goal to closed;
   while there remain in data base unifying facts or rules do
      begin
      case
         current_goal unifies with a fact:
            return success;
         current_goal is a conjunction (p ∧ ...):
            begin
               for each conjunct do
                  call pattern_search on conjunct;
               if pattern_search succeeds for all conjuncts
                  then return success
                  else return fail
            end;
         current_goal unifies with rule conclusion (p in q → p):
            begin
               apply goal unifying substitutions to premise (q);
               call pattern_search on premise;
               if pattern_search succeeds
                  then return success
                  else return fail
            end;
      end;                                                       % end case
      return fail
end.
```

In the function pattern_search, search is performed by a modified version of the recursive search algorithm that uses unification, Section 2.3.2, to determine when two expressions match and modus ponens to generate the children of states. The current focus of the search is represented by the variable current_goal. If current_goal matches with a fact, the algorithm returns success. Otherwise the algorithm attempts to match current_goal with the conclusion of some rule, recursively attempting to solve the premise. If current_goal does not match any of the given assertions, the algorithm returns fail. This algorithm also handles conjunctive goals such as are often found in the premise of a rule:

For simplicity, this algorithm does not address the problem of maintaining consistency among the variable substitutions produced by unification. This is important when solving conjunctive queries with shared variables (as in p(X) ∧ q(X)). Not only must both conjuncts succeed, but they must succeed with unifiable bindings for X, Section 2.3.2. This problem is addressed at the end of this section.

The major advantage of using general methods such as unification and modus ponens to generate states is that the resulting algorithm may search *any* space of logical inferences. The specifics of a problem are described using predicate calculus assertions. Thus, we have a means of separating problem-solving knowledge from its control and implementation on the computer. pattern_search provides our first implementation of the separation of knowledge and control.

The use of predicate calculus with a general controller to solve search problems is illustrated through an example: a reduced version of the *knight's tour problem*. In the game of chess, a knight can move two squares either horizontally or vertically followed by one square in an orthogonal direction as long as it does not move off the board. There are thus at most eight possible moves that the knight may make (Fig. 5.1).

As traditionally defined, the knight's tour problem attempts to find a series of legal moves in which the knight lands on each square of the chessboard exactly once. This problem has been a mainstay in the development and presentation of search algorithms. The example given in this chapter is a simplified version of the knight's tour problem: is there

Figure 5.1   Legal moves of a chess knight.

a series of legal moves that will take the knight from one square to another on a reduced-size (3 × 3) chessboard? (The details of the full knight's tour problem on an 8 × 8 chessboard are discussed in examples 5.3.2 and 5.3.3.)

Figure 5.2 shows a 3 × 3 chessboard with each square labeled with integers 1 to 9. This labeling scheme is used instead of the more general approach of giving each space a row and column number in order to further simplify the example. Because of the reduced size of the problem, we simply enumerate the alternative moves rather than developing a general move operator. The legal moves on the board are then described in predicate calculus using a predicate called move, whose parameters are the starting and ending squares of a legal move. For example, move(1,8) takes the knight from the upper left-hand corner to the middle of the bottom row. The predicates of Figure 5.2 enumerate all possible moves for the 3 × 3 chessboard.

These predicates form the knowledge base for the knight's tour problem. As an example of how unification is used to access this knowledge base, we test for the existence of various moves on the board. To determine whether there is a move from 1 to 8, call pattern_search(move(1,8)). Because this goal unifies with move(1,8) in the knowledge base, the result is success, with no variable substitutions required.

Another request might be to find where the knight can move from a particular location, such as square 2. The goal move(2,X) unifies with two different predicates in the knowledge base, with the substitutions of {7/X} and {9/X}. Given the goal move(2,3), the response is fail, because no move(2,3) exists in the knowledge base. The goal query move(5,Y) also fails because no assertions exist that define a move from square 5.

The next task in constructing a search algorithm is to devise a general definition for a path of successive moves around the board. This is done through the use of predicate calculus implications. These are added to the knowledge base as *rules* for creating paths of successive moves. To emphasize the goal-directed use of these rules, we have reversed the direction of the implication arrow; i.e., the rules are written as Conclusion ← Premise.

For example, a two-move path could be formulated as:

$$\forall X,Y \ [path2(X,Y) \leftarrow \exists Z \ [move(X,Z) \land move(Z,Y)]]$$

This rule says that for all locations X and Y, a two-move path exists between them if there exists a location Z such that the knight can move from X to Z and then move from Z to Y.

move(1,8).	move(6,1).
move(1,6).	move(6,7).
move(2,9).	move(7,2).
move(2,7).	move(7,6).
move(3,4).	move(8,3).
move(3,8).	move(8,1).
move(4,9).	move(9,2).
move(4,3).	move(9,4).

1	2	3
4	5	6
7	8	9

Figure 5.2 A 3 × 3 chessboard with move rules.

The general path2 rule can be applied in a number of ways. First, it may be used to determine whether there is a two-move path from one location to another. If pattern_search is called with the goal path2(1,3), it matches the goal with the consequence of the rule path2(X,Y), and the substitutions are made in the rule's premise; the result is a specific rule that defines the conditions required for the path:

$$\text{path2}(1,3) \leftarrow \exists Z [\text{move}(1,Z) \wedge \text{move}(Z,3)]$$

Pattern_search then calls itself on this premise. Because this is a conjunction of two expressions, pattern_search will attempt to solve each subgoal separately. This requires not only that both subgoals succeed but also that any variable bindings be consistent across subgoals. Substituting 8 for Z allows both subgoals to succeed.

Another request might be to find all locations that can be reached in two moves from location 2. This is accomplished by giving pattern_search the goal path2(2,Y). Through a similar process, a number of such substitutions may be found, including {6/Y} and {2/Y} (with intermediate Z being 7) and {2/Y} and {4/Y} (with intermediate location 9). Further requests could be to find a two-move path from a number to itself, from any number to 5, and so on. Notice here one of the advantages of pattern-driven control: a variety of queries may be taken as the initial goal.

Similarly, a three-move path is defined as including two intermediate locations that are part of the path from the initial location to the goal. This is defined by:

$$\forall X,Y [\text{path3}(X,Y) \leftarrow \exists Z,W [\text{move}(X,Z) \wedge \text{move}(Z,W) \wedge \text{move}(W,Y)]]$$

This clause can solve such goals as path3(1,2), path3(1,X), or even path3(X,Y). Tracing the results of these queries is left as an exercise.

Similar path rules can be constructed for four or more move paths. It soon becomes evident that the path moves are the same for a path of any length, simply requiring the proper number of intermediate places to "land." It is also evident that the path moves could be stated in terms of each other, such as:

$$\forall X,Y [\text{path3}(X,Y) \leftarrow \exists Z [\text{move}(X,Z) \wedge \text{path2}(Z,Y)]]$$

This suggests the single, general recursive rule:

$$\forall X,Y [\text{path}(X,Y) \leftarrow \exists Z[\text{move}(X,Z) \wedge \text{path}(Z,Y)]]$$

The last path rule can be used to determine whether a path of any length exists. The rule may be stated as "to find a path from one square to another, first make a move from the starting square to an intermediate location and then find a path from the intermediate to the final square."

This recursive "path" rule is incomplete in that it includes no terminating condition. Any attempt to solve a goal involving the path predicate would fail to halt because each attempt to solve the rule premise would lead to another recursive call on path(Z,Y). There is no test in the rule to determine whether the desired goal state is ever reached. This can be remedied by adding the clause path(X,X) to the knowledge base. Because path(X,X) will unify only with predicates such as path(3,3) or path(5,5), it defines the desired terminating condition. The general recursive path definition is then given by two predicate calculus formulas:

∀ X path(X,X)

∀ X,Y [path(X,Y) ← ∃ Z [move(X,Z) ∧ path(Z,Y)]]

Note once again the elegance and simplicity of the recursive formulation. When combined with the recursive control provided by pattern_search, these rules will search the space of possible paths in the knight's tour problem. Combined with the move rules, this yields the complete problem description (or knowledge base):

move(1,8).　　move(1,6).　　move(2,9).　　move(2,7).
move(3,4).　　move(3,8).　　move(4,9).　　move(4,3).
move(6,1).　　move(6,7).　　move(7,2).　　move(7,6).
move(8,3).　　move(8,1).　　move(9,2).　　move(9,4).

∀ X path(X,X)
∀ X,Y [path(X,Y) ← ∃ Z [move(X,Z) ∧ path(Z,Y)]]

It is important to note that the solution to the problem is implemented through *both* the logical descriptions that define the state space and the use of pattern_search to control search of that space. Although the path rule is a satisfactory definition of a path, it does not tell us how to find that path. Indeed, many undesirable or meaningless paths around the chessboard also fit this definition. For example, without some way to prevent loops, the goal path(1,3) could lead to a path that simply goes back and forth between 1 and 8, instead of finding the correct path from 1 to 8 to 3. Both the loop and the correct path are logical consequences of the knowledge base. Similarly, if the recursive rule is tried before the terminating condition, the fact that path(3,3) should terminate the search could be overlooked, allowing the search to continue meaninglessly.

Although the initial version of pattern_search defined the behavior of a search algorithm for predicate calculus expressions, several subtleties must still be addressed. These include the order with which the algorithm tries alternative matches and proper handling of the full set of logical operators (∧, ∨, and ¬).

Logic is nondeterministic: it defines a space of possible inferences but does not tell a problem solver how to make the useful ones. To reason with predicate calculus, we need a control regime that systematically searches the space, avoiding meaningless paths and loops. A control algorithm such as pattern_search must try alternative matches in some sequential order. Knowing this order allows the program designer to control search by properly ordering rules in the knowledge base. The simplest way to define such an order is to require that the algorithm try rules and facts in the order in which they appear in the knowledge base. In the knight's tour, this ensures that the terminating condition (path(X,X)) is tried before the recursive step.

A second issue is the existence of logical connectives in the rule premises: e.g., implications of the form "p ← q ∧ r" or "p ← q ∨ (r ∧ s)." As will be recalled from the discussion of and/or graphs, an ∧ operator indicates that both expressions must be shown to be true for the entire premise to be true. In addition, the conjuncts of the expression must be solved with consistent variable bindings. Thus, to solve p(X) ∧ q(X), it is not sufficient to solve p(X) with the substitution {a/X} and q(X) with the substitution {b/X}. Both must be solved with the same or unifiable bindings for X. An or operator, on the other hand, indicates that either expression must be found to be true. The search algorithm must take this into account.

The last addition to the algorithm is the ability to solve goals involving logical negation (¬). Pattern_search handles negated goals by first solving the operand of the ¬. If this subgoal succeeds, then pattern_search returns fail. If the operand fails, then pattern_search returns an empty substitution set, indicating success. Note that even though a subgoal may contain variables, the result of solving its negation may not contain any substitutions. This is because ¬ can succeed only if its operand *fails*; hence, it cannot return any bindings for the operand.

Finally, the algorithm should not return success but should return the bindings involved in the solution. Consider the goal move(1,X); the substitutions {6/X} and {8/X} are an essential part of the solution.

The complete version of pattern_search, which takes these into account is:

```
function pattern_search(current_goal);

begin
    if current_goal is a member of closed                          % test for loops
        then return fail else add current_goal to closed;
    while there remain unifying facts or rules do
        begin
        case
            current_goal unifies with a fact:
                return unifying substitutions;
            current_goal is negated (¬ p):
                begin
                    call pattern_search on p;
                    if pattern_search returns fail
                        then return {}                             % negation is true
                        else return fail
                end;
            current_goal is a conjunction (p ∧ ...):
                begin
                    for each conjunct do
                        begin
                            call pattern_search on conjunct;
                            if pattern_search returns fail
                                then return fail
                                else apply substitutions to other conjuncts
                        end;
                    if pattern_search succeeds for all conjuncts
                        then return composition of unifications
                        else return fail
                end;
```

```
        current_goal is a disjunction (p ∨ ...):
          begin
            repeat for each disjunct
              call pattern_search on disjunct
            until no more disjuncts or success;
            if pattern_search succeeds
              then return substitutions
              else return fail
          end;
        current_goal unifies with rule conclusion (p in p ← q):
          begin
            apply goal unifying substitutions to premise (q);
            call pattern_search on premise;
            if pattern_search succeeds
              then return composition of p and q substitutions
              else return fail
          end;
        end;                                              % end case
      return fail
    end.
```

This algorithm for searching a space of predicate calculus rules and facts is the basis of PROLOG and many goal-directed expert system shells. Its behavior is further illustrated in Chapters 6, 8, and 13, as well as in a LISP implementation in Chapter 14. An alternative control structure for pattern-directed search is provided by the *production system*, discussed in the next section.

5.3   Production Systems

5.3.1   Definition and History

The *production system* is a model of computation that has proved particularly important in AI, both for implementing search algorithms and for modeling human problem solving. A production system provides pattern-directed control of a problem-solving process and consists of a set of *production rules*, a *working memory*, and a *recognize-act* control cycle (Brownston et al. 1985).

DEFINITION

PRODUCTION SYSTEM

A *production system* is defined by:

1. *The set of production rules.* These are often simply called *productions.* A production is a *condition-action* pair and defines a single chunk of problem-solving knowledge. The *condition part* of the rule is a pattern that determines

when that rule may be applied to a problem instance. The *action part* defines the associated problem-solving step.

2. *Working memory* contains a description of the *current state of the world* in a reasoning process. This description is a pattern that is matched against the condition part of a production to select appropriate problem-solving actions. When the condition element of a rule is matched by the contents of working memory, the action associated with that condition may then be performed. The actions of production rules are specifically designed to alter the contents of working memory.

3. *The recognize-act cycle.* The control structure for a production system is straightforward: the current state of the problem-solving process is maintained as a set of patterns in *working memory*. Working memory is initialized with the beginning problem description. The patterns in working memory are matched against the conditions of the production rules; this produces a subset of the productions, called the *conflict set*, whose conditions match the patterns in working memory. The productions in the conflict set are said to be *enabled*. One of the productions in the conflict set is then selected (*conflict resolution*) and the production is *fired*. That is, the action of the rule is performed, changing the contents of working memory. After the selected production rule is fired, the control cycle repeats with the modified working memory. The process terminates when no rule conditions are matched by the contents of working memory.

Conflict resolution chooses a rule from the conflict set for firing. Conflict resolution strategies may be simple, such as selecting the first rule whose condition matches the state of the world, or may involve complex rule selection heuristics. This is an important way in which a production system allows the addition of heuristic control to a search algorithm.

The *pure* production system model has no mechanism for recovering from dead ends in the search; it simply continues until no more productions are enabled and halts. Many practical implementations of production systems allow backtracking to a previous state of working memory in such situations.

A schematic drawing of a production system is presented in Figure 5.3.

A very simple example of production system execution appears in Figure 5.4. This is a production system program for sorting a string composed of the letters a, b, and c. In this example, a production is enabled if its condition matches a portion of the string in working memory. When a rule is fired, the substring that matched the rule condition is replaced by the string on the right-hand side of the rule. As this example suggests, production systems are a general model of computation that can be programmed to do anything that can be done on a computer. Their real strength, however, is as an architecture for knowledge-based systems.

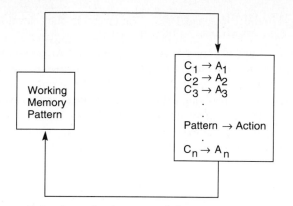

Figure 5.3 A production system. Control loops until working memory pattern no longer matches the conditions of any productions.

Production set:

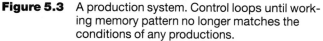

1. ba → ab
2. ca → ac
3. cb → bc

Iteration #	Working memory	Conflict set	Rule fired
0	cbaca	1, 2, 3	1
1	cabca	2	2
2	acbca	3, 2	2
3	acbac	1, 3	1
4	acabc	2	2
5	aacbc	3	3
6	aabcc	Ø	Halt

Figure 5.4 Trace of a simple production system.

The idea for the "production"-based design for computing came originally from writings of Post (1943), who proposed a production rule model as a formal theory of computation. The main construct of this theory was a set of rewrite rules for strings in many ways similar to the parsing rules in Example 3.3.6. It is also closely related to the approach taken by markov algorithms (Markov 1954) and, like them, is equivalent in power to a Turing machine.

An interesting application of production rules to modeling human cognition is found in the work of Newell and Simon at the Carnegie Institute of Technology (now Carnegie

Mellon University) in the 1960s and 1970s. The programs they developed, including the *General Problem Solver*, are largely responsible for the importance of production systems in AI. In this research, human subjects were monitored in various problem-solving activities such as solving problems in predicate logic and playing games like chess. The *protocol* (behavior patterns, including verbal descriptions of the problem-solving process, eye movements, etc.) of problem-solving subjects was recorded and broken down to its elementary components. These components were regarded as the basic bits of problem-solving knowledge in the human subjects and were composed as a search through a graph (called the *problem behavior graph*). A production system was then used to implement search of this graph.

The production rules represented the set of problem-solving skills of the human subject. The present focus of attention was represented as the current state of the world. In executing the production system, the "attention" or "current focus" of the problem solver would match a production rule, which would change the state of "attention" to match another production-encoded skill, and so on.

It is important to note that in this work Newell and Simon used the production system not only as a vehicle for implementing graph search but also as an actual model of human problem-solving behavior (Chapter 16). The productions corresponded to the problem-solving skills in the human's *long-term memory*. Like the skills in long-term memory, these productions are not changed by the execution of the system; they are invoked by the "pattern" of a particular problem instance, and new skills may be added without requiring "recoding" of the previously existing knowledge. The production system's working memory corresponds to *short-term memory* or current focus of attention in the human and describes the current stage of solving a problem instance. The contents of working memory are generally not retained after a problem has been solved.

This research is described in *Human Problem Solving* by Newell and Simon (1972) and in Luger (1978). Newell, Simon, and others have continued to use production rules to model the difference between novices and experts (Larkin et al. 1980; Simon and Simon 1978) in areas such as solving algebra word problems and physics problems. Production systems also form a basis for studying learning in both humans and computers (Klahr et al. 1987); ACT* (Anderson 1983) and SOAR (Newell 1991) build on this tradition.

Production systems provide a model for encoding human expertise in the form of rules and designing pattern-driven search algorithms, tasks that are central to the design of the rule-based expert system. In expert systems, the production system is not necessarily assumed to actually model human problem-solving behavior; however, the aspects of production systems that make them useful as a potential model of human problem solving (modularity of rules, separation of knowledge and control, separation of working memory and problem-solving knowledge) make them an ideal tool for building expert systems.

An important family of AI languages comes directly out of the production system language research at Carnegie Mellon. These are the OPS languages; OPS stands for Official Production System. Although their origins are in modeling human problem solving, these languages have proved highly effective for programming expert systems and for other AI applications. OPS5 is the implementation language for the VAX configurer XCON and other expert systems developed at Digital Equipment Corporation (McDermott 1981, 1982; Soloway et al. 1987; Barker and O'Connell 1989). OPS interpreters are widely available for PCs and workstations.

In the next section we give examples of how the production system may be used to solve a variety of search problems.

5.3.2   Examples of Production Systems

EXAMPLE 5.3.1: THE 8-PUZZLE

The search space generated by the 8-puzzle, introduced in Chapter 3, is both complex enough to be interesting and small enough to be tractable, so it is frequently used to explore different search strategies, such as depth-first and breadth-first search, as well as the heuristic strategies discussed in Chapter 4. It also lends itself to solution using a production system.

Recall that we gain generality by thinking of "moving the blank space" rather than moving a numbered tile. Legal moves are defined by the productions in Figure 5.5. Of course, all four of these moves are applicable only when the blank is in the center; when it is in one of the corners only two moves are possible. If a beginning state and a goal state for the 8-puzzle are now specified, it is possible to make a production system accounting of the problem's search space.

An actual implementation of this problem might represent each board configuration with a "state" predicate with nine parameters (for nine possible locations of the eight tiles

Production set:

Condition	Action
goal state in working memory	$\rightarrow$ halt
blank is not on the top edge	$\rightarrow$ move the blank up
blank is not on the right edge	$\rightarrow$ move the blank right
blank is not on the bottom edge	$\rightarrow$ move the blank down
blank is not on the left edge	$\rightarrow$ move the blank left

Working memory is the present board state and goal state.

Control regime:

1. Try each production in order.
2. Do not allow loops.
3. Stop when goal is found.

Figure 5.5   The 8-puzzle as a production system.

and the blank); rules could be written as implications whose premise performs the required condition check. Alternatively, arrays or list structures could be used for board states.

An example of the space searched in finding a solution for the problem given in Figure 5.5 follows in Figure 5.6. Because this solution path can go very deep if unconstrained, a depth bound has been added to the search. (A simple means for adding a depth bound is to keep track of the length of the current path and to force backtracking if this bound is exceeded.) A depth bound of 5 is used in the solution of Figure 5.6. Note that the number of possible states of working memory grows exponentially with the depth of the search.

EXAMPLE 5.3.2: THE KNIGHT'S TOUR PROBLEM

The 3×3 knight's tour problem presented in Section 5.2 may be solved using a production system approach. Here each move would be represented as a production whose condition is the location of the knight on a particular square and whose action moves the knight to another square. Sixteen productions represent all possible moves of the knight:

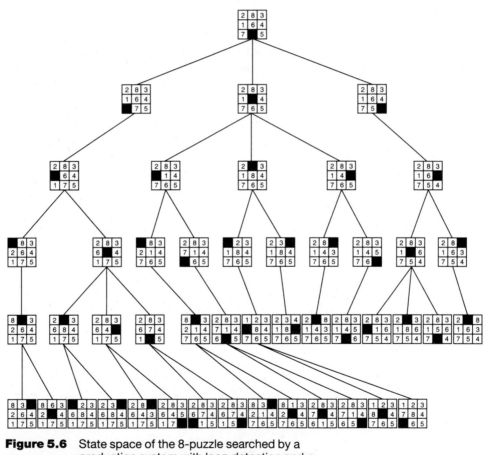

Figure 5.6 State space of the 8-puzzle searched by a production system with loop detection and a depth bound of 5.

RULE #	CONDITION		ACTION
1	knight on square 1	→	move knight to square 8
2	knight on square 1	→	move knight to square 6
3	knight on square 2	→	move knight to square 9
4	knight on square 2	→	move knight to square 7
5	knight on square 3	→	move knight to square 4
6	knight on square 3	→	move knight to square 8
7	knight on square 4	→	move knight to square 9
8	knight on square 4	→	move knight to square 3
9	knight on square 6	→	move knight to square 1
10	knight on square 6	→	move knight to square 7
11	knight on square 7	→	move knight to square 2
12	knight on square 7	→	move knight to square 6
13	knight on square 8	→	move knight to square 3
14	knight on square 8	→	move knight to square 1
15	knight on square 9	→	move knight to square 2
16	knight on square 9	→	move knight to square 4

Working memory contains both the current board state and the goal state. The control regime applies rules until the current state equals the goal state and then halts. A simple conflict resolution scheme would fire the first rule that did not cause the search to loop. Because the search may lead to dead ends (from which every possible move leads to a previously visited state and, consequently, a loop), the control regime should also allow backtracking. An execution of this production system that determines whether a path exists from square 1 to square 2 is charted in Figure 5.7.

It is interesting to note that in implementing the path predicate in the knight's tour example of Section 5.2, we have actually implemented this production system solution! From this point of view, pattern_search is simply an interpreter, with the actual search implemented by the path definition. The productions are the move facts, with the first parameter specifying the condition (the square the piece must be on to make the move) and

Iteration #	Working memory		Conflict set (rule #'s)	Fire rule
	Current square	Goal square		
0	1	2	1, 2	1
1	8	2	13, 14	13
2	3	2	5, 6	5
3	4	2	7, 8	7
4	9	2	15, 16	15
5	2	2		Halt

Figure 5.7 Production system solution to the 3 × 3 knight's tour problem.

the second parameter, the action (the square to which it can move). The recognize-act cycle is implemented by the recursive path predicate. Working memory contains the current state and the desired goal state and is represented as the parameters of the path predicate. On a given iteration, the conflict set is all of the move expressions that will unify with the goal move(X,Z). This program uses the simple conflict resolution strategy of selecting and firing the first move predicate encountered in the knowledge base that does not lead to a repeated state. The controller also backtracks from dead-end states. This characterization of the path definition as a production system is given in Figure 5.8.

Production systems are capable of generating infinite loops when searching a state space graph. These loops are particularly difficult to spot in a production system because the rules can fire in any order. That is, looping may appear in the execution of the system, but it cannot easily be found from a syntactic inspection of the rule set. For example, with the "move" rules of the knight's tour problem ordered as in Section 5.2 and a conflict resolution strategy of selecting the first match, the pattern move(2,X) would match with move(2,9), indicating a move to square 9. On the next iteration, the pattern move(9,X) would match with move(9,2), taking the search back to square 2, causing a loop.

To prevent looping, pattern_search checked a global list (closed) of visited states. The actual conflict resolution strategy was therefore: select the first matching move *that leads to an unvisited state.*

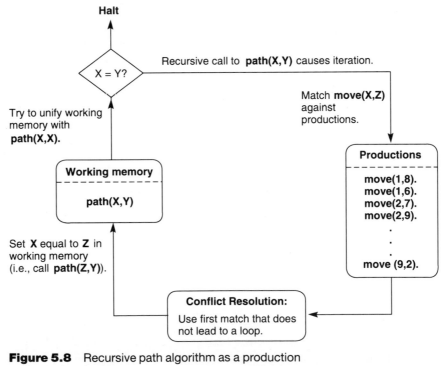

Figure 5.8 Recursive path algorithm as a production system.

In a production system, the proper place for recording such case-specific data as a list of previously visited states is not a global closed list but the working memory itself. We can alter the path predicate to use working memory for loop detection.

Assume that pattern_search does not maintain a global closed list or otherwise perform loop detection. Assume that our predicate calculus language is augmented by the addition of a special construct, assert(X), which causes its argument X to be entered into the working memory. assert is not an ordinary predicate but an action that is performed; hence, it always succeeds.

assert is used to place a "marker" in working memory to indicate when a state has been visited. This marker is represented as a unary predicate, been(X), which takes as its argument a square on the board. been(X) is added to working memory when a new state X is visited. Conflict resolution may then require that been(Z) must not be in working memory before move(X,Z) can fire. For a specific value of Z this can be tested by matching a pattern against working memory.

The modified recursive path definition is written:

$\forall$ X path(X,X).
$\forall$ X,Y path(X,Y) $\leftarrow \exists$ Z move(X,Z) $\wedge \neg$(been(Z)) $\wedge$ assert(been(Z)) $\wedge$ path(Z,Y).

In this definition, move(X,Z) succeeds on the first match with a move predicate. This binds a value to Z. If been(Z) matches with an entry in working memory, (been (Z)) will cause a failure (i.e., it will be false). pattern_search will then backtrack and try another match for move(X,Z). If square Z is a new state, the search will continue, with been(Z) asserted to the working memory to prevent future loops. The actual firing of the production takes place when the path algorithm recurs. Thus, the presence of been predicates in working memory implements loop detection in this production system.

Note that although predicate calculus is used as the language for both productions and working memory entries, the procedural nature of production systems requires that the goals be tested in left-to-right order in the path definition. This order of interpretation is provided by pattern_search.

EXAMPLE 5.3.3: THE FULL KNIGHT'S TOUR

We may generalize the knight's tour solution to the full 8 $\times$ 8 chessboard. Because it makes little sense to enumerate moves for such a complex problem, we replace the 16 move facts with a set of 8 rules to generate legal knight moves. These moves (productions) correspond to the 8 possible ways a knight can move (Figure 5.1).

If we index the chessboard by row and column numbers, we can define a production rule for moving the knight down two squares and right one square:

CONDITION: current row $\leq$ 6 $\wedge$ current column $\leq$ 7

ACTION: new row = current row + 2 $\wedge$ new column = current column + 1

If we use predicate calculus to represent productions, then a board square could be defined by the predicate square(R,C), representing the Rth row and Cth column of the board. The above rule could be rewritten in predicate calculus as:

$$\text{move(square(Row,Column),square(Newrow,Newcolumn))} \leftarrow$$
$$\text{less\_than\_or\_equals(Row,6)} \land$$
$$\text{equals(Newrow,plus(Row,2))} \land$$
$$\text{less\_than\_or\_equals(Column,7)} \land$$
$$\text{equals(Newcolumn,plus(Column,1))}$$

plus is a function for addition; less_than_or_equals and equals have the obvious arithmetic interpretations. Seven additional rules can be designed that similarly compute the remaining possible moves. These eight rules replace the move facts in the 3 × 3 version of the problem.

The path definition from the 3 × 3 example defines the control loop for this problem. As we have seen, when predicate calculus descriptions are interpreted procedurally, such as through the pattern_search algorithm, subtle changes are made to the semantics of predicate calculus. One such change is the sequential fashion in which goals are solved. This imposes an ordering, or *procedural semantics*, on predicate calculus expressions. Another change is the introduction of *meta-logical* predicates such as assert, which indicate actions beyond the truth value interpretation of predicate calculus expressions. These issues are discussed in more detail in the PROLOG chapters (6 and 13) and in the LISP implementation of a logic programming engine (Chapter 14).

EXAMPLE 5.3.4: THE FINANCIAL ADVISOR AS A PRODUCTION SYSTEM

In Chapters 2 and 3, we developed a small financial advisor, using predicate calculus to represent the financial knowledge and graph search to make the appropriate inferences in a consultation. The production system provides a natural vehicle for its implementation. The implications of the logical description form the productions. The case-specific information (an individual's salary, dependents, etc.) is loaded into working memory. Rules are enabled when their premises are satisfied. A rule is chosen from this conflict set and fired, adding its conclusion to working memory. This continues until all possible top-level conclusions have been added to the working memory. Indeed, many expert system "shells" are production systems with added features for supporting the user interface, handling uncertainty in the reasoning, editing the knowledge base, and tracing execution (see Sections 13.2.1 and 14.4).

5.3.3 Control of Search in Production Systems

The production system model offers a range of opportunities for adding heuristic control to a search algorithm. These include the choice of data-driven or goal-driven strategies, the structure of the rules themselves, and the choice of strategies for conflict resolution.

Control through Choice of Data-Driven or Goal-Driven Search Strategy. Data-driven search begins with a problem description (such as a set of logical axioms, symptoms of an illness, or a body of data that needs interpretation) and infers new knowledge from the data. This is done by applying rules of inference, legal moves in a game, or other state-generating operations to the current description of the world and adding the results to that problem description. This process continues until a goal is reached.

This description of data-driven reasoning emphasizes its close fit with the production system model of computation. The "current state of the world" (data that have been either assumed to be true or deduced as true with previous use of production rules) is placed in working memory. The recognize-act cycle then matches the current state against the (ordered) set of productions. When these data match (are unified with) the condition(s) of one of the production rules, the action of the production adds (by modifying working memory) a new piece of information to the current state of the world.

All productions have the form CONDITION → ACTION. When the CONDITION matches some elements of working memory, its ACTION is performed. If the production rules are formulated as logical implications and the ACTION adds assertions to working memory, then the act of firing a rule corresponds to an application of modus ponens. This creates a new state of the graph.

Figure 5.9 presents a simple data-driven search on a set of productions expressed as propositional calculus implications. The conflict resolution strategy is a simple one of choosing the enabled rule that has fired least recently (or not at all); in the event of ties, the first rule is chosen. Execution halts when a goal is reached. The figure also presents the sequence of rule firings and the stages of working memory in the execution, along with a graph of the space searched.

Although we have treated production systems in a data-driven fashion, they may also be used to characterize goal-driven search. As defined in Chapter 3, goal-driven search

Production set:

1. $p \wedge q \rightarrow goal$
2. $r \wedge s \rightarrow p$
3. $w \wedge r \rightarrow q$
4. $t \wedge u \rightarrow q$
5. $v \quad \rightarrow s$
6. start $\rightarrow v \wedge r \wedge q$

Trace of execution:

Iteration #	Working memory	Conflict set	Rule fired
0	start	6	6
1	start, v, r, q	6, 5	5
2	start, v, r, q, s	6, 5, 2	2
3	start, v, r, q, s, p	6, 5, 2, 1	1
4	start, v, r, q, s, p, goal	6, 5, 2, 1	halt

Space searched by execution:

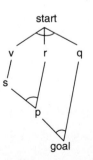

Direction of search

Figure 5.9 Data-driven search in a production system.

begins with a goal and works backward to establish its truth. To implement this in a production system, the goal is placed in working memory and matched against the ACTIONs of the production rules. These ACTIONs are matched (by unification, for example) just as the CONDITIONs of the productions were matched in the data-driven reasoning. All production rules whose conclusions (ACTIONs) match the goal form the conflict set.

When the ACTION of a rule is matched, the CONDITIONs are added to working memory and become the new subgoals (states) of the search. The new states are then matched to the ACTIONs of other production rules. The process continues until a fact is found, usually in the problem's initial description or, as is often the case in expert systems, by directly asking the user for specific information. The search stops when the CONDITIONs of all the productions fired in this backward fashion are found to be true. These CONDITIONs and the chain of rule firings leading to the original goal form a proof of its truth through successive inferences such as modus ponens. See Figure 5.10 for an instance of goal-driven reasoning on the same set of productions used in Figure 5.9. Note that the goal-driven search fires a different series of productions and searches a different space than the data-driven version.

As this discussion illustrates, the production system offers a natural characterization of both goal-driven and data-driven search. The production rules are the encoded set of inferences (the "knowledge" in a rule-based expert system) for changing state within the

Production set:

1. $p \wedge q \rightarrow goal$
2. $r \wedge s \rightarrow p$
3. $w \wedge r \rightarrow p$
4. $t \wedge u \rightarrow q$
5. $v \rightarrow s$
6. $start \rightarrow v \wedge r \wedge q$

Trace of execution:

Iteration #	Working memory	Conflict set	Rule fired
0	goal	1	1
1	goal, p, q	1, 2, 3, 4	2
2	goal, p, q, r, s	1, 2, 3, 4, 5	3
3	goal, p, q, r, s, w	1, 2, 3, 4, 5	4
4	goal, p, q, r, s, w, t, u	1, 2, 3, 4, 5	5
5	goal, p, q, r, s, w, t, u, v	1, 2, 3, 4, 5, 6	6
6	goal, p, q, r, s, w, t, u, v, start	1, 2, 3, 4, 5, 6	halt

Space searched by execution:

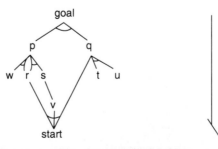

Direction of search

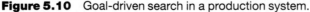

Figure 5.10 Goal-driven search in a production system.

graph. When the current state of the world (the set of true statements describing the world) matches the CONDITIONs of the production rules and this match causes the ACTION part of the rule to create another (true) descriptor for the world, it is referred to as data-driven search.

Alternatively, when the goal is matched against the ACTION part of the rules in the production rule set and their CONDITIONs are then set up as subgoals to be shown to be "true" (by matching the ACTIONs of the rules on the next cycle of the production system), the result is goal-driven problem solving.

Because a set of rules may be executed in either a data-driven or goal-driven fashion, we can compare and contrast the efficiency of each approach in controlling search. The complexity of search for either strategy is measured by such notions as *branching factor* or *penetrance* (Section 4.4). These measures of search complexity can provide a cost estimate for both the data-driven and goal-driven versions of a problem solver and therefore help in selecting the most effective strategy.

We can also employ combinations of strategies. For example, we can search in a forward direction until the number of states becomes large and then switch to a goal-directed search to use possible subgoals to select among alternative states. The danger in this situation is that, when heuristic or best-first search (Chapter 4) is used, the parts of the graphs actually searched may "miss" each other and ultimately require more search than a simpler approach (Figure 5.11). However, when the branching of a space is constant and exhaustive search is used, a combined search strategy can cut back drastically the amount of space searched. (See Figure 5.12.)

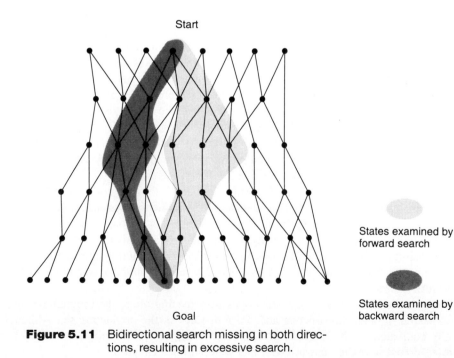

Start

Goal

States examined by
forward search

States examined by
backward search

Figure 5.11   Bidirectional search missing in both directions, resulting in excessive search.

Start

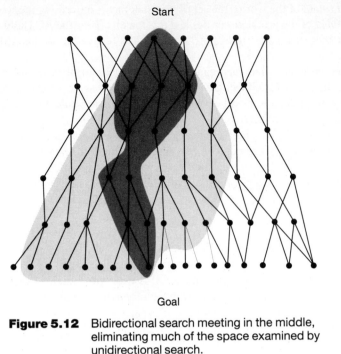

States examined by
forward search only

States examined by
combination of
forward and
backward search

Goal

Figure 5.12   Bidirectional search meeting in the middle,
eliminating much of the space examined by
unidirectional search.

Control of Search through Rule Structure.   The structure of rules in a production system, including the distinction between the condition and the action and the order in which conditions are tried, determines the fashion in which the space is searched. In introducing predicate calculus as a representation language, we emphasized the *declarative* nature of its semantics. That is, predicate calculus expressions simply define true relationships in a problem domain and make no assertion about the order in which their components are interpreted. Thus, an individual rule might be $\forall X (foo(X) \wedge goo(X) \rightarrow moo(X))$. Under the rules of predicate calculus, an alternative form of the same rule is $\forall X (foo(X) \rightarrow moo(X) \vee \neg goo(X))$. The equivalence relationship between these two clauses can be demonstrated by the truth table method of Section 2.1.

Although these formulations are logically equivalent, they do not lead to the same results when interpreted as productions because the production system implementation imposes an order on the matching and firing of rules. For this reason, the specific form of the rules determines the ease (or possibility) of matching a rule against a problem instance. This is a result of differences in the way in which the production system *interprets* the rules. The production system imposes a *procedural semantics* on the declarative language used to form the rules.

Because the production system tries rules in a specific order, the programmer may control search through the structure and order of rules in the production set. Although logically equivalent, $\forall X (foo(X) \wedge goo(X) \rightarrow moo(X))$ and $\forall X (foo(X) \rightarrow moo(X) \vee \neg goo(X))$ do not have the same behavior in a search implementation.

Human experts encode crucial heuristics within their rules of expertise. The order of premises encodes important procedural information for solving the problem. It is important that this form be preserved in building a program that "solves problems like the expert." When a mechanic says, "If the engine won't turn over and the lights don't come on, then check the battery," he or she is suggesting a specific sequence of actions. This information is not captured by the logically equivalent statement "the engine turns over or the lights come on or check the battery." This form of the rules is critical in controlling search, making the system behave logically, making traces of rule firings more understandable, etc.

Control of Search through Conflict Resolution.   Though production systems (like all architectures for knowledge-based systems) allow heuristics to be encoded in the knowledge content of rules themselves, they offer other opportunities for heuristic control through conflict resolution. Although the simplest such strategy is to choose the first rule that matches the contents of working memory, any strategy may potentially be applied to conflict resolution. For example, conflict resolution strategies supported by OPS5 (Brownston et al. 1985) include:

1. *Refraction.* Refraction specifies that once a rule has fired, it may not fire again until the working memory elements that match its conditions have been modified. This discourages looping.

2. *Recency.* The recency strategy prefers rules whose conditions match with the patterns most recently added to working memory. This focuses the search on a single line of reasoning.

3. *Specificity.* This strategy assumes that a more specific problem-solving rule is preferable to a general rule. A rule is more specific than another if it has more conditions. This implies that it will match fewer potential working memory patterns.

These are representative of the general strategies that may be used in conflict resolution.

5.3.4   Advantages of Production Systems for AI

As illustrated by the preceding examples, the production system offers a general framework for implementing search. Because of its simplicity, modifiability, and flexibility in applying problem-solving knowledge, the production system has proved to be an important tool for the construction of expert systems and other AI applications. The major advantages of production systems for artificial intelligence include:

Separation of Knowledge and Control.   The production system is an elegant model of separation of knowledge and control in a computer program. Control is provided by the recognize-act cycle of the production system loop, and the problem-solving knowledge is encoded in the rules themselves. The advantages of this separation include ease of modifying the knowledge base without requiring a change in the code for program control and, conversely, the ability to alter the code for program control without changing the set of production rules.

A Natural Mapping onto State Space Search. The components of a production system map naturally into the constructs of state space search. The successive states of working memory form the nodes of a state space graph. The production rules are the set of possible transitions between states, with conflict resolution implementing the selection of a branch in the state space. These rules simplify the implementation, debugging, and documentation of search algorithms.

Modularity of Production Rules. An important aspect of the production system model is the lack of any syntactic interactions between production rules. Rules may only effect the firing of other rules by changing the pattern in working memory; they may not "call" another rule directly as if it were a subroutine, nor may they set the value of variables in other production rules. The scope of the variables of these rules is confined to the individual rule. This syntactic independence supports the incremental development of expert systems by successively adding, deleting, or changing the knowledge (rules) of the system.

Pattern-Directed Control. The problems addressed by AI programs require particular flexibility in program execution. This goal is served by the fact that the rules in a production system may fire in any sequence. The descriptions of a problem that make up the current state of the world determine the conflict set and, consequently, the particular search path and solution.

Opportunities for Heuristic Control of Search. These were described in the preceding section.

Tracing and Explanation. The modularity of rules and the iterative nature of their execution make it easier to trace execution of a production system. At each stage of the recognize-act cycle, the selected rule may be displayed. Because each rule corresponds to a single "chunk" of problem-solving knowledge, the rule content should provide a meaningful explanation of the system's current state and action (Chapter 8). In contrast, a single line of code in a traditional language such as Pascal or FORTRAN is virtually meaningless.

Language Independence. The production system control model is independent of the representation chosen for rules and working memory, as long as that representation supports pattern matching. We described production rules as predicate calculus implications of the form $A \Rightarrow B$, where the truth of A and the inference rule modus ponens allow us to conclude B. Although there are many advantages to using logic as both the basis for representation of knowledge and the source of sound inference rules, the production system model may be used with other representations.

Although predicate calculus offers the advantage of logically sound inference, many problems require reasoning that is not sound in the logical sense. Instead, they involve probabilistic reasoning, use of uncertain evidence, and default assumptions. Later chapters (8, 9, and 11) discuss alternative inference rules that provide these capabilities. Regardless of the type of inference rules employed, however, the production system provides a vehicle for searching the state space.

A Plausible Model of Human Problem Solving.   Modeling human problem solving was among the first uses of production systems; they continue to be used as a model for human performance in much cognitive science research (Chapter 16).

Pattern-directed search gives us the ability to explore the space of logical inferences in the predicate calculus. Many problems build on this technique by using predicate calculus to model specific aspects of the world such as time and change. *Robot planning*, or often simply *planning*, must model the changes in the state of a world caused by actions of a robot or other agent. We use *add* and *delete* lists to represent these changes to the world and to specify new states of the search space.

5.4   Predicate Calculus and Planning

The task of a planner is to find a sequence of actions that allow a problem solver, often a robot, to accomplish some specific task. In addition to its obvious robotics applications, planning plays a role in expert systems when they must reason about events occurring over time. Planning has many applications in manufacturing, such as automatic process control. It is also important in natural language understanding, where humans frequently discuss plans, goals, and intentions.

In this discussion, we use examples from robotics. The component steps in a plan are the *atomic actions* of a robot. For planning purposes, we do not describe these capabilities in hardware or micro-level terms such as "turn the sixth stepper motor one revolution." Instead, planners specify actions at a higher level, in terms of their effect on the world. For example, a planner for a blocks world robot might include such actions as "pick up object a" or "go to location x." The micro control of steps to actually make a robot perform the plans is built into these higher-level actions.

Thus, a sequence of actions to "go get block a from room b" might be:

1. put down what you have
2. go to room b
3. go over to block a
4. pick up block a
5. leave room b
6. return to original location

Plans are created by searching through a space of possible actions until the sequence necessary to accomplish the task is discovered. This space represents states of the world that are changed by applying each of the actions. The search terminates when the goal state (the description of the world) is produced. Thus, many of the issues of heuristic search, including finding A* algorithms, are also appropriate in this domain.

The act of planning does not necessarily depend on the existence of an actual robot to carry out the plans. In the early years of computer planning (1960s), entire plans were formulated before the robot performed its first act. Thus plans were devised without the presence of a robot at all! Only more recently, with the implementation of more sophisticated sensing devices, has research focused on more integrated plan/action sequencing.

Planning relies on search techniques, and raises a number of unique issues. For one, the description of the states of the world may be considerably more complex than in previous examples of search. Consider the number of predicates necessary to describe rooms and corridors and objects in the robot's environment. Not only must we represent the robot's world; we must also represent the effect of atomic actions on that world. The full description of each state of the problem space can be quite extensive.

Another difference in planning is the need to characterize what is *not* changed by a particular action. Picking up an object does change (a) the location of the object and (b) the fact that the robot hand is now grasping the object. It does not change (a) the locations of the doors and the rooms or (b) the locations of other objects. The specification of what is true in one state of the world and exactly what is changed by performing some action in the world has become known as the *frame problem* (McCarthy 1980; McCarthy and Hayes 1969). As the complexity of the problem space increases, the issue of keeping track of the changes that occur with each action and the features of a state description that remain unchanged becomes more important. We present two solutions for coping with the frame problem, but, as will be seen, neither of these is totally satisfactory.

Other important issues include generating plans, saving and generalizing good plans, recovering from unexpected plan failures (part of the world might not be as expected, perhaps by being accidentally moved from its anticipated location), and maintaining consistency between the world and a program's internal model of the world.

In the examples of this section, we limit our robot's world to a set of blocks on a tabletop and the robot's actions to an arm that can stack, unstack, and otherwise move the blocks about the table. In Figure 5.13 we have five blocks, labeled a, b, c, d, e, sitting on the top of a table. The blocks are all cubes of the same size, and stacks of blocks, as in the figure, have blocks directly on top of each other. The robot arm has a gripper that can grasp any clear block (one with no block on top of it) and move it to any location on the tabletop or place it on top of any other clear block.

We assume the robot arm can perform the following tasks (U, V, W, X, Y, and Z are variables):

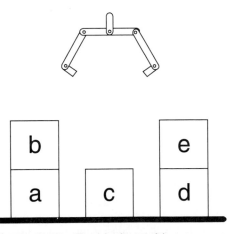

Figure 5.13   The blocks world.

goto (X,Y,Z)	Goto location described by coordinates X, Y, and Z. This location might be implicit in the command pickup (W) where block W has location X, Y, Z.
pickup (W)	Pick up block W from its current location and hold it. It is assumed that the block has nothing on top, the gripper is empty at the time of the pickup order, and the computer knows the location of block W.
putdown (W)	Place block W down at some location on the table and record the new location for block W. W must be held by the gripper at the time.
stack (U,V)	Place block U on top of block V. The gripper must be holding U and the top of V must be clear of other blocks.
unstack (U,V)	Remove block U from the top of V. U must be clear of other blocks, V must have block U on top of it, and the hand must be empty before this command can be executed.

We represent the state of the world using a set of predicates and predicate relationships:

location (W,X,Y,Z)	Block W is at coordinates X, Y, Z.
on (X,Y)	Block X is immediately on top of block Y.
clear (X)	Block X has nothing on top of it.
gripping (X)	The robot arm is holding block X.
gripping ( )	The robot gripper is empty.
ontable (W)	Block W is on the table.

ontable (W) is a short form for the predicate location (W,X,Y,Z), where Z is the table level. Similarly, on (X,Y) indicates that block X is located with its bottom coincident with the top of block Y. We can greatly simplify the world descriptions by having the computer record the present location (X,Y,Z) of each block and keep track of its movements to new locations. With this location assumption, the goto command becomes unnecessary; a command such as pickup (X) or stack (X) implicitly contains the location of X.

A number of truth relations (in the declarative sense) or rules for performance (in the procedural sense) are implicit in the blocks world descriptions seen so far, including specifications for clear (X), ontable(X), and gripping ( ):

1. $(\forall X) (clear (X) \leftarrow \neg (\exists Y) (on (Y,X)))$
2. $(\forall Y) (\forall X) \neg (on (Y,X) \leftarrow ontable (Y))$
3. $(\forall Y) gripping ( ) \leftrightarrow \neg (gripping (Y))$

The first statement says that if block X is clear, there does not exist any block Y such that Y is on top of X. Interpreted procedurally, this can be read "to clear block X go and remove any block Y that might be on top of X." The second relationship says that if any block is on the table, it is not on top of any other block.

The blocks world of Figure 5.13 may now be represented by the following predicates. We call this collection of predicates *STATE 1* for our continuing example.

ontable (a).	on (b,a).	clear (b).
ontable (c).	on (e,d).	clear (c).
ontable (d).	gripping ( ).	clear (e).

Because these predicates describing the state of the world for Figure 5.13 are all true at the same time, the full state description is the conjunction (∧) of these predicates. To produce new states from this description, we design rules for operating on states. The four operators (pickup, putdown, stack, unstack) are described by predicate calculus rules:

4. (∀ X) (pickup (X) → (gripping (X) ← (gripping ( ) ∧ clear (X)))).

5. (∀ X) (putdown(X) → ((gripping ( ) ∧ ontable (X) ∧ clear (X)) ← gripping (X))).

6. (∀ X) (∀ Y) (stack (X,Y) → ((on(X,Y) ∧ gripping ( ) ∧ clear (X)) ← (clear (Y) ∧ gripping (X)))).

7. (∀ X)(∀ Y) (unstack (X,Y) → ((clear (Y) ∧ gripping (X)) ← (on (X,Y) ∧ clear (X) ∧ gripping ( )))).

The fourth rule states that for all blocks X, pickup (X) means gripping (X) if the hand is empty and X is clear. Note the form of these rules: A → (B ← C). This says that operator A allows us to produce new predicate(s) B when condition(s) C is true. We use these rules to generate new states in a space. That is, if predicates C are true in a state, then B is true in its child state. In other words, operator A can be used to create a new state described by predicates B when predicates C are true.

But we must first address the *frame problem* before we can use these rule relationships to generate new states of the blocks world. *Frame relations* are rules to tell what predicates describing a state are *not* changed by rule applications and are thus carried over intact to help describe the new state of the world. For example, if we apply the operator pickup block b in Figure 5.13, then all predicates related to the rest of the blocks remain true in the child state. For our world of blocks we can specify several such frame rules:

8. (∀ X) (∀ Y) (∀ Z) (unstack (Y,Z) → (ontable (X) ← ontable (X))).

9. (∀ X) (∀ Y) (∀ Z) (stack (Y,Z) → (ontable (X) ← ontable (X))).

These two rules say that ontable is not affected by the stack and unstack operators. This is true even when X and Z are identical; if Y = Z either 6 or 7 above won't be true.

Other frame axioms say that on and clear are affected by stack and unstack operators only when that particular on relation is unstacked or when a clear relation is stacked. Thus, in our example, on (b,a) is not affected by unstack (c,d).

Similarly, frame axioms say that clear (X) relations are unaffected by gripping (Y) even when X = Y or gripping ( ) is true. More axioms say that gripping does not affect on(X,Y) relations but affects only the ontable (X) relation where X is gripped. Thus, a number of other frame relations need to be specified for our example.

Together, these operators and frame axioms define a state space, as illustrated by the operator unstack. unstack (X,Y) requires three conditions to be true, namely that on (X,Y) and gripping ( ) and clear (X) are all true. When these conditions are met the new predicates gripping (X) and clear (Y) are produced by unstack. A number of other predicates also true for *STATE 1* will remain true in *STATE 2*. These states are preserved by the frame axioms. We now produce the nine predicates describing *STATE 2* by applying the unstack operator and the frame axioms to the nine predicates of *STATE 1*:

STATE 2

ontable(a).	on(b,a).	clear(b).
ontable(c).	clear(c).	clear(d).
ontable(d).	gripping(e).	clear(e).

To summarize:

1. Planning may be seen as a state space search.

2. New states are produced by general operators such as stack and unstack plus frame rules.

3. The techniques of graph search may be applied to find a path from the start state to the goal state. The operations on this path constitute a plan.

Figure 5.14 shows an example of a state space searched by applying the operators as described above. If a goal description is added to this problem-solving process, then a plan may be seen as a set of operators that produces a path that leads from the present state of this graph to the goal. (See Section 3.1.2.)

This characterization of the planning problem defines its theoretical roots in state space search and predicate calculus representation and inferencing. However, it is important to note how complex this manner of solution can be. In particular, using the frame rules to calculate what remains unchanged between states can add exponentially to the search, as can be seen from the complexity of the very simple blocks problem. In fact, when any new predicate descriptor is introduced, for color, shape, or size, new frame rules must be defined to relate it to all appropriate actions!

This discussion also assumes that the subproblems that make up a task are independent and may thus be solved in an arbitrary order. This very seldom is the case in interesting problem areas, where the actions required to achieve one subgoal can conflict with the actions required to achieve another. Next we illustrate these problems and discuss an approach to planning that greatly assists in handling this complexity.

STRIPS, developed at what is now SRI International, stands for Stanford Research Institute Planning System (Fikes and Nilsson 1971, 1972). This controller was used to drive the *SHAKEY* robot of the early 1970s. STRIPS addressed the problem of efficiently representing and implementing the operations of a planner. It addressed the problem of conflicting subgoals and provided an early model of learning; successful plans were saved and generalized as *macro operators*, which could be used in similar future situations. In the remainder of this section, we present a version of STRIPS-style planning and *triangle tables*, the data structure used to organize and store macro operations.

Using the blocks example, the four operators pickup, putdown, stack, and unstack are represented as triples of descriptions. The first element of the triple is the set of *preconditions* (P), or conditions the world must meet for an operator to be applied. The second element of the triple is the *add* list (A), or the additions to the state description that are a result of applying the operator. Finally, there is the *delete* list (D), or the items that are

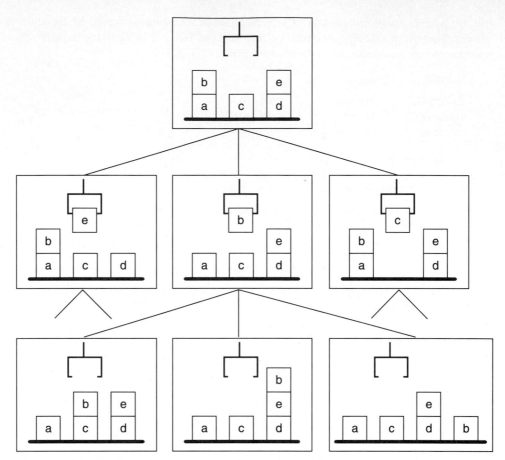

Figure 5.14 Portion of the state space for a portion of the blocks world.

removed from a state description to create the new state when the operator is applied. These lists eliminate the need for separate frame axioms.

We can represent the four operators in this fashion:

pickup (X)
P: gripping ( ) ∧ clear (X) ∧ ontable (X)
A: gripping (X)
D: ontable (X) ∧ gripping ( )

putdown (X)
P: gripping (X)
A: ontable (X) ∧ gripping ( ) ∧ clear (X)
D: gripping (X)

stack (X,Y)
P: clear (Y) ∧ gripping (X)
A: on (X,Y) ∧ gripping ( ) ∧ clear (X)
D: clear (Y) ∧ gripping (X)

$$\text{unstack (X,Y)} \quad \begin{aligned} &\text{P: clear (X)} \wedge \text{gripping ( )} \wedge \text{on (X,Y)} \\ &\text{A: gripping (X)} \wedge \text{clear (Y)} \\ &\text{D: gripping ( )} \wedge \text{on (X,Y)} \end{aligned}$$

The important thing about the add and delete lists is that they specify *everything* that is necessary to satisfy the frame axioms! Some redundancy exists in the add and delete list approach. For example, in unstack the *add* of gripping (X) could imply the *delete* of gripping ( ). But the gain of this redundancy is that every descriptor of a state that is not mentioned by the *add* or *delete* remains the same in the new state description.

A related weakness of the precondition-add-delete list approach is that we are no longer using a theorem-proving process to produce (by inference) the new states. This is not a serious problem, however, as proofs of the equivalence of the two approaches can guarantee the correctness of the precondition-add-delete method.

The precondition-add-delete list approach may be used to produce the same results we produced with the inference rules and frame axioms in our earlier example. The state space search, as in Figure 5.14, would be identical for both approaches.

A number of other problems inherent in planning are not solved by either of the two approaches presented so far. In solving a goal we often divide it into subproblems, for instance, unstack (e,d) and unstack (b,a). Attempting to solve these subgoals independently can cause problems if the actions needed to achieve one goal actually undo the other. Incompatible subgoals may result from a false assumption of *linearity* (independence) of subgoals. This can make solution searches unnecessarily difficult or even impossible.

We now show a very simple example of an incompatible subgoal using the start state *STATE 1* of Figure 5.13. Suppose the goal of the plan is *STATE G* as in Figure 5.15, with on (b,a) ∧ on (a,c) and blocks d and e remaining as in *STATE 1*. It may be noted that one of the parts of the conjunctive goal on (b,a) ∧ on (a,c) is true in *STATE 1*, namely on (b,a). This already satisfied part of the goal must be undone before the second subgoal, on (a,c), can be accomplished.

The *triangle table* representation (Fikes and Nilsson 1972; Nilsson 1980) is aimed at alleviating some of these anomalies. A triangle table is a data structure for organizing

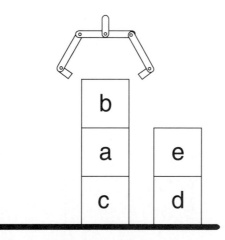

Figure 5.15   Goal state for the blocks world.

sequences of actions, including potentially incompatible subgoals, within a plan. It addresses the problem of conflicting subgoals by representing the global interaction of sequences of operations. A triangle table relates the preconditions of one action with the postconditions, the combined add and delete lists, of all the actions preceding it.

Triangle tables are used to determine when that macro operator could be used in building a plan. By saving these macro operators and reusing them, STRIPS increases the efficiency of its planning search. Indeed, we can generalize a macro operator, using variable names to replace the block names in a particular example. Then we can call the new generalized macro to prune search. In Chapter 12, with our presentation of learning, we discuss techniques for generalizing macro operations.

The reuse of macro operators also helps to solve the problem of conflicting subgoals. As the following example illustrates, once the planner has developed a plan for goals of the form stack (X,Y) ∧ stack (Y,Z), it may store and reuse that plan. This eliminates the need to break the goal into subgoals and avoids the complications that may follow.

Figure 5.16 presents a sample triangle table for the macro action stack (X,Y) ∧ stack (Y,Z). This macro action can be applied to states where on(X,Y) ∧ clear(X) ∧ clear(Z) is true. This triangle table is appropriate for starting *STATE 1* with X = b, Y = a, and Z = c.

The atomic acts of the plan are recorded along the diagonal. These are the four actions, pickup, putdown, stack, and unstack, discussed in this section. The preconditions of each of these acts are in the row preceding that act, and the postconditions of each act are in the column below the act. For example, row 5 lists the preconditions for pickup (X), and column 6 lists the postconditions (the add and delete lists) of pickup (X). These postcon-

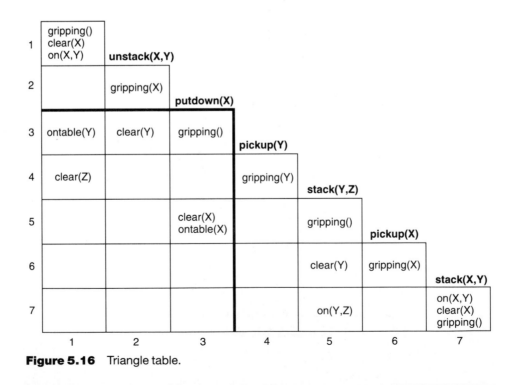

Figure 5.16 Triangle table.

ditions are placed in the row of the action that uses them as its preconditions, organizing them in a manner relevant to succeeding actions. Thus, the triangle table's purpose is to properly interleave the preconditions and postconditions of each of the smaller actions that make up the larger goal.

One advantage of triangle tables is the assistance they can offer in attempting to recover from unexpected happenings, such as a block being slightly out of place, or accidents, such as dropping a block. Often an accident can require backing up several steps before the plan can be resumed. When something goes wrong with a solution the planner can go back into the rows and columns of the triangle table to check what is still true. Once the planner has figured out what is still true within the rows and columns, it then knows what the next step must be if the larger solution is to be restarted. This is formalized with the notion of a *kernel*.

The *nth kernel* is the intersection of all rows below and including the nth row and all columns to the left of and including the nth column. In Figure 5.16 we have outlined the third kernel in bold. In carrying out a plan represented in a triangle table, the ith operation (that is, the operation in row i) may be performed only if all predicates contained in the ith kernel are true. This offers a straightforward way of verifying that a step can be taken and also allows us to recover systematically from any disruption of a plan. Given a triangle table, we find and execute the highest-numbered action whose kernel is enabled. This not only lets us back up in a plan but also allows for the possibility that an unexpected event might let us jump forward in a plan.

The conditions in the leftmost column are the preconditions for the macro action as a whole. The conditions in the bottom row are the conditions added to the world by the macro operator. A triangle table may be saved as a *macro operator* with its own set of preconditions and add and delete lists.

Of course, the triangle table approach does lose some of the semantic purity of the previous planning models. Notice, for example, that only those postconditions of an act are retained that are also preconditions of later acts. Thus, if guaranteed correctness is a desired result, further verification of the triangle tables, perhaps with additional information that might allow sequences of triangle tables to be composed, might be desirable.

Other problems arise with the use of macro operators in planning. As the number of macro operators increases, the planner has more powerful operations to use, decreasing the size of the state space that must be searched. Unfortunately, at each step of the search, all of these operators must be examined. The pattern matching needed to determine whether an operator may be applied can add considerable overhead to the search process, counteracting the gains made by saving macro operations. The problems of determining when a macro operation should be saved and the best way to determine the next operator to use remain the subject of much research.

5.5   The Blackboard Architecture for Problem Solving

The *blackboard* is the final control mechanism presented in this chapter. Where pattern search examined the states in a space of logical inferences in a very deterministic fashion, production systems provide greater flexibility by allowing us to represent multiple partial solutions simultaneously in working memory and to select the next state through conflict resolution. Blackboards extend production systems by allowing us to organize working memory into separate modules, each of which corresponds to a different subset of the production rules. Blackboards allow us to integrate separate sets of production rules in a single agent or to coordinate the actions of multiple cooperating problem solvers in a single global structure.

Many problems require the coordination of a number of different types of knowledge. For example, a speech understanding program must first manipulate an utterance represented as a digitized waveform. As the understanding process continues, it must find words in this utterance, form these into sentences, and finally produce a semantic representation of the utterance's meaning.

A related problem occurs when multiple processes must cooperate to solve a single problem. An example of this is the distributed sensing problem (Lesser and Corkill 1983). Assume that we have a network of sensors, each of which is monitored by a separate process. Assume also that the processes can communicate and that proper interpretation of each sensor's data depends on the data received by other sensors in the network. This problem arises in situations as diverse as tracking an airplane across multiple radar sites and combining the readings of multiple sensors in a manufacturing process.

The *blackboard architecture* is a model of control that has been applied to these and other problems requiring the coordination of multiple processes or knowledge sources. A *blackboard* is a central global data base for the communication of independent asynchronous knowledge sources focusing on related aspects of a particular problem. Figure 5.17 gives a schematic of the blackboard design.

In Figure 5.17 each *knowledge source* KS_i gets its data from the blackboard, processes the data, and returns its results to the blackboard to be used by the other knowledge sources. Each KS_i is independent in that it is a separate process operating according to its own specifications and, when a multiprocessing or multiprocessor system is used, it is independent of the other processing in the problem. It is an asynchronous system in that each KS_i begins its operation whenever it finds appropriate input data posted on the blackboard. When it finishes its processing it posts its results and awaits new input data.

The blackboard approach to organizing a large program was first presented in the HEARSAY-II research (Erman et al. 1980; Reddy 1976). HEARSAY-II was a speech understanding program; it was initially designed as the front end for a library data base of

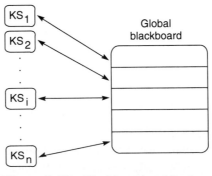

Figure 5.17 Blackboard architecture.

computer science articles. The user of the library would address the computer in spoken English with queries such as, "Are any by Feigenbaum and Feldman?" and the computer would answer the question with information from the library data base. Speech understanding requires that we integrate a number of different processes, all of which require very different knowledge and algorithms, all of which can be exponentially complex. Signal processing; recognition of phonemes, syllables, and words; syntactic parsing; and semantic analysis mutually constrain each other in interpreting speech.

The blackboard architecture allowed HEARSAY to coordinate the several different knowledge sources required for this complex task. The blackboard is usually organized along two dimensions. With HEARSAY these dimensions were the time as the speech act was produced and the level of analysis of the utterance. Each level of analysis was processed by a different class of knowledge sources. The levels of analysis of the utterance were:

KS_1. The waveform of the acoustic signal.

KS_2. The phonemes or possible sound segments of the acoustic signal.

KS_3. The syllables that the phonemes could produce.

KS_4. The possible words as analyzed by one KS.

KS_5. The possible words as analyzed by a second KS (usually considering words from different parts of the data).

KS_6. A KS to try to generate possible word sequences.

KS_7. A KS that puts word sequences into possible phrases.

We can visualize these processes as components of Figure 5.17. In processing spoken speech, the waveform of the spoken signal is entered at the lowest level. Knowledge sources for processing this entry are enabled and post their interpretations to the blackboard, to be picked up by the appropriate process. Because of the ambiguities of spoken language, multiple competing hypotheses may be present at each level of the blackboard. The knowledge sources at the higher levels attempt to disambiguate these competing hypotheses.

The analysis of HEARSAY-II should not be seen as simply one lower level producing data that the higher levels can then analyze. It is much more complex than that. If a KS at one level cannot process (make sense of) the data sent to it, that KS can request the KS that sent it the data to go back for another try or to make another hypothesis about the data. Furthermore, different KSs can be working on different parts of the utterance at the same time. All the processes, as mentioned previously, are asynchronous and data driven; they act when they have input data, continue acting until they have finished their task, and then post their results and wait for their next task.

One of the KSs, called the *scheduler*, handles the "consume-data post-result" communication between the KSs. This scheduler has ratings on the results of each KS's activity and thus is able to supply, by means of a priority queue, some direction in the problem solving. If no KS is active, the scheduler determines that the task is finished and shuts down.

When the HEARSAY program had a data base of about 1,000 words it worked quite well, although a bit slowly. When the data base was further extended, the data for the knowledge sources got more complex than they could handle. HEARSAY-III (Balzer et al. 1980; Erman et al. 1981) is a generalization of the approach taken by HEARSAY-II. The time dimension of HEARSAY-II is no longer needed, but the multiple KSs for levels of analysis are retained. The blackboard for HEARSAY-III is intended to interact with a general-purpose relational data base system. Indeed, HEARSAY-III is a general shell for the design of expert systems.

An important change in HEARSAY-III has been to split off the scheduler KS (as described above for HEARSAY-II) and to make it a separate blackboard controller for the first (or domain) blackboard. This second blackboard allows the scheduling process to be broken down, just as the domain of the problem is broken down, into separate KSs concerned with different aspects of the solution procedure (for example, when and how to apply the domain knowledge). The second blackboard can thus compare and balance *different* solutions for each problem (Nii and Aiello 1979; Nii 1986*a*, 1986*b*).

An alternative model of the blackboard scheme retains important parts of the knowledge base in the blackboard, rather than distributing it across multiple knowledge sources (Skinner and Luger 1991; 1992).

5.6   Epilogue and References

Chapter 5 discussed the implementation of the search strategies of Chapters 3 and 4. It presented recursion as an important tool for programming graph search, implementing the backtrack algorithm of Chapter 3 in recursive form. Pattern-directed search using unification and inference rules (Chapter 2) simplifies the implementation of search through a space of logical inferences.

The production system was shown as a natural architecture for modeling problem solving and implementing search algorithms. The chapter concluded with examples of production system implementations of data-driven and goal-driven search.

The references listed in the epilogue to Chapter 3 are also appropriate to this chapter. For references on recursion see Chapter 5.

The production system has always been an important paradigm for AI programming, beginning with work by Newell and Simon and their colleagues at Carnegie Mellon University (Newell and Simon 1972; Klahr et al. 1987). Two references on current implementations of production systems are *Programming Expert Systems in OPS5* by Lee Brownston et al. (1985) and *Pattern Directed Inference Systems* by Donald Waterman and Frederick Hayes-Roth (1978).

The planning section demonstrates some of the data structures and search techniques used for general-purpose planners. Further references include ABSTRIPS or ABstract specification for STRIPS generator relationships (Sacerdotti 1974) and NOAH for nonlinear or hierarchical planning (Sacerdotti 1975, 1977).

Meta-planning is a technique for reasoning not just about the plan but also about the process of planning. This can be important in expert systems solutions. References include Meta-DENDRAL for DENDRAL solutions (Lindsay et al. 1980) and Teiresias for MYCIN solutions (Chapter 8). For plans that interact continuously with the world, that is, model a changing environment, see McDermott (1978).

Further research includes *opportunistic planning* using blackboards and planning based on an object-oriented specification (Smolier 1985). Finally, there are several surveys of planning research in the *Handbook of Artificial Intelligence* (Barr and Feigenbaum 1989; Cohen and Feigenbaum 1989) and the *Encyclopedia of Artificial Intelligence* (Shapiro 1987).

Early work in blackboard models is described in HEARSAY-II research (Reddy 1976; Erman et al. 1980). Later work is described in the HEARSAY-III work (Lesser and Corkill 1983; Nii 1986). Current research may be found in Skinner and Luger (1992).

Research in production systems, planning, and blackboard architectures remains an active part of artificial intelligence. We recommend that the interested reader consult recent proceedings of the American Association for Artificial Intelligence Conference and the International Joint Conference on Artificial Intelligence. Morgan Kaufmann has published other conference proceedings, as well as collections of readings on AI topics. *Readings in Planning* (Allen 1990) is particularly relevant to the material in this chapter.

5.7 Exercises

1. The member algorithm of Section 5.1.1 recursively determines whether a given element is a member of a list.

   a. Write an algorithm to count the number of *elements* in a list.
   b. Write an algorithm to count the number of *atoms* in a list.

   (The distinction between atoms and elements is that an element may itself be a list.)

2. Write a recursive algorithm (using open and closed lists) to implement breadth-first search. Does recursion allow the omission of the open list when implementing breadth-first search? Explain.

3. Trace the execution of the recursive depth-first search algorithm (the version that does not use an open list) on the state space of Figure 3.10.

4. In an ancient Hindu tea ceremony, there are three participants: an elder, a servant, and a child. The four tasks they perform are feeding the fire, serving cakes, pouring tea, and reading poetry; this order reflects the decreasing importance of the tasks. At the beginning of the ceremony, the child performs all four tasks. They are passed one at a time to the servant and the elder until, at the end of the ceremony, the elder is performing all four tasks. No one can take on a less important task than those they already perform. Generate a sequence of moves to transfer all the tasks from the child to the elder. Write a recursive algorithm to perform the move sequence.

5. Using the move and path definitions for the knight's tour of Section 5.2, trace the execution of pattern_search on the goals:

   a. path(1,9).
   b. path(1,5).
   c. path(7,6).

   When the move predicates are attempted in order, there is often looping in the search. Discuss loop detection and backtracking in this situation.

6. Write the pseudocode definition for a breadth-first version of pattern_search (Section 5.2). Discuss the time and space efficiency of this algorithm.

7. Using the rule in Example 5.3.3 as a model, write the eight move rules needed for the full 8 × 8 version of the knight's tour.

8. Using the goal and start states of Figure 5.5, hand run the production system solution to the 8-puzzle:

   a. In goal-driven fashion.
   b. In data-driven fashion.

9. Consider the financial advisor problem discussed in Chapters 2, 3, and 4. Using predicate calculus as a representation language:

   a. Write the problem explicitly as a production system.
   b. Generate the state space and stages of working memory for the data-driven solution to the example in Chapter 3.
   c. Repeat b for a goal-driven solution.

10. Section 5.3.3 presented the general conflict resolution strategies of refraction, recency, and specificity. Propose and justify two more such strategies.

11. Create the remaining *frame axioms* necessary for the four operators pickup, putdown, stack, and unstack described in rules 4 through 7 of Section 5.4.

12. Use the operators and frame axioms of the previous question to generate the search space of Figure 5.14.

13. Show how the *add* and *delete* lists can be used to replace the frame axioms in the generation of *STATE 2* from *STATE 1* in Section 5.4.

14. Use *add* and *delete* lists to generate the search space of Figure 5.14.

15. Suggest an automated controller that could use *add* and *delete* lists to generate a graph search similar to that of Figure 5.14.

16. Show two more incompatible (precondition) subgoals in the blocks world operators of Figure 5.14.

17. Read the ABSTRIPS research (Sacerdotti 1974) and show how it handles the linearity (or incompatible subgoal) problem in planning.

18. Suggest two applications appropriate for solution using the blackboard architecture. Briefly characterize the organization of the blackboard and knowledge sources for each implementation.

PART III

LANGUAGES FOR AI PROBLEM SOLVING

---

looking through a glass onion . . .

—LENNON AND MCCARTNEY

for now we see as through a glass darkly . . .

—PAUL TO THE CORINTHIANS

The map is not the territory; the name is not the thing named.

—ALFRED KORZYBSKI

What have I learned but the proper use of several tools?

—GARY SNYDER, "What Have I Learned"

In Part III we discuss the major issues in selecting a language for artificial intelligence programming. The primary function of an AI language is to implement the representation and control structures needed for symbolic computing. The nature of these structures to a great extent determines the features that an implementation language should provide. In this introduction, we enumerate the programming language features desired for symbolic programming and give an overview of LISP and PROLOG, two of the major languages currently used in AI.

Chapters 6 and 7 treat LISP and PROLOG in detail; later in the text (Chapters 9 and 15), we introduce *object-oriented programming*, which structures programs in terms of messages passed between objects in a class hierarchy. Object-oriented programming, the underlying model for Smalltalk, Flavors, Common Objects, and a number of other languages, has emerged as an important programming methodology. It is also the basis of a number of expert system development environments currently available on the commercial market. The evolution of the object-oriented paradigm is presented in Chapter 9, and the design of object-oriented programming languages is discussed in Chapter 15.

Languages, Understanding, and Levels of Abstraction

The ability to form higher-level abstractions from the particulars of experience is one of the most powerful and fundamental abilities of the human mind. Abstraction allows us to consolidate the details of a complicated domain into a general characterization of its organization and behavior; these abstractions allow us to understand the full range of instances in that domain. If we enter a strange house, for example, we will be able to find our way around; the organization of the living room, bedrooms, kitchen, and bathrooms generally conforms to a standard model of a house. The abstraction lets us manage the particulars of different houses. A picture may be worth a thousand words, but an abstraction can define the important features of an entire class of pictures.

When we form theories to describe classes of phenomena, the significant qualitative and quantitative features of the class are abstracted out from the details that characterize its individual members. This loss of detail is compensated by the descriptive and predictive power of a valid theory. Abstraction is an essential tool for understanding and managing the complexity of the world around us, as well as that of our own mental structures. Indeed, this process of abstraction occurs continuously and recursively in the act of knowing: knowledge is built in layers of abstraction, from the mechanisms that extract structure from the chaos of raw sensory stimuli all the way up to the most subtle of scientific theories. Ultimately, most of our ideas are about other ideas.

Hierarchical abstraction, the organization of experience into increasingly abstract classes and descriptions, is an essential tool for understanding the behavior and organization of complex systems, including computer programs. Just as the behavior of an animal may be studied without concern for the underlying physiology of its nervous system, an algorithm has a characterization of its own, quite separate from the program that implements it.

Consider, for example, two different implementations of binary search, one written in FORTRAN using arrays and calculations on array indices and the other written in Pascal using pointers to implement binary search trees; in a very deep sense, these programs are the same. This separation of an algorithm from the code used to implement it is only one example of hierarchical abstraction in computer science.

Allen Newell has distinguished between the *knowledge level* and the *symbol level* of describing an intelligent system (Newell 1982). The symbol level is concerned with the particular formalisms used to represent problem-solving knowledge; the discussion of predicate logic as a representation language in Chapter 2 is an example of such a symbol-level consideration. Above the symbol level is the knowledge level, which is concerned with the knowledge content of the program and the way in which that knowledge is used.

This analysis is particularly appropriate to knowledge-based systems. Because the knowledge base is separate from the control aspects of the program, it is natural to separate the knowledge level of the program from its other aspects. Similarly, the symbol level is manifested through the choice of a representation language, such as logic or production rules, for the knowledge base. The implementation of the symbol-level representation constitutes a still lower level.

The capabilities of a knowledge-based system are largely determined at the knowledge level. The knowledge content is independent of the formalisms used to represent it, as long as the representation language is sufficiently expressive. Knowledge-level concerns include such questions as: What objects and relations are important in the domain? What queries will be made of the system? How is new knowledge added to the system? Will the facts change over time? Will the system need to reason about its own knowledge? Does the domain of discourse have a well-understood taxonomy? Does the domain involve uncertain or missing knowledge? Careful analysis at this level is an important step in designing the overall architecture of the program and in choosing the particular method of representation used at the symbol level.

At the symbol level, decisions are made about the structures used to represent and organize knowledge. The selection of a representation language is a symbol-level concern. As we shall see in Chapters 8, 9, and 15, logic is only one of many formalisms currently available for knowledge representation; others include network representations such as frames or semantic networks, procedural representations that capture knowledge as a body of instructions describing how to perform a certain task, and numerous extensions and variations on standard logic such as multivalued and temporal logics.

Each of these formalisms has its strengths and weaknesses. Not only must a representation language be able to express the knowledge required for an application, but it also must be concise, modifiable, and computationally efficient and must assist the programmer in acquiring and organizing the knowledge base. These goals often conflict and necessitate trade-offs in the design of representation languages.

Just as we have distinguished between the knowledge and symbol levels of a program, we can also distinguish between the symbol level and the algorithms and data structures used to implement it. For example, with the exception of efficiency, the behavior of a logic-based problem solver should be unaffected by the choice between a hash table and a binary tree to implement a table of its symbols. These are implementation decisions and should be invisible at the symbol level. Many of the algorithms and data structures used in implementing representation languages for AI are common computer science techniques such as binary trees and tables. Others are more specific to AI and are presented in pseudocode throughout the text and in the chapters on LISP and PROLOG programming techniques.

Below the algorithm/data structure level is the language level. It is here that the implementation language for the program becomes significant. Other levels exist below this one, including the assembly language level, possible microcode extensions to the machine architecture, and others leading to the underlying hardware.

These levels (Fig. III.1) are relatively independent. In consulting a knowledge base, users generally ignore the representation used at the symbol level and are concerned only with the system's knowledge and its ability to solve their problem. Similarly, in building the knowledge base, the programmer is very conscious of the representations used at the symbol level but usually ignores the lower levels of the system. The importance of these distinctions cannot be overemphasized: they allow a user or programmer to ignore the complexity hidden at lower levels and focus on issues appropriate to the current level of abstraction. They allow the theoretical foundations of artificial intelligence to be kept free of the nuances of a particular implementation or programming language. They allow us to modify an implementation, improving its efficiency or porting it to another machine, without affecting its behavior at higher levels.

Some thought about the nature of these higher levels and the demands they place on an implementation language is useful in understanding why certain languages and language

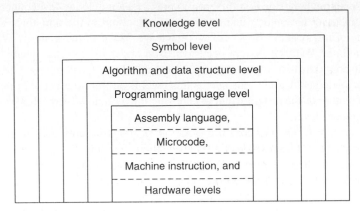

Figure III.1   Levels of a knowledge-based system.

features have proved important in AI programming. In the remainder of this section, we present requirements for AI languages based on the needs of AI problem solving. We then introduce the major AI programming languages: LISP and PROLOG.

Requirements for AI Languages

An important feature of these levels of abstraction is a degree of insensitivity of higher levels to the underlying implementation language. This observation has been verified in practice, with successful knowledge-based systems implemented in languages as diverse as LISP, PROLOG, C, Pascal, or even FORTRAN. Similarly, several systems have originally been implemented in LISP or PROLOG and later ported to C to improve their efficiency and portability. In both cases, behavior at the symbol level was largely unaffected.

However, these levels are not completely independent: the nature of the higher-level structures does influence the commitments we make at lower levels. In particular, the demands that AI programming places on the symbol level are repeated at the language level. For example, the data structures for symbolic computation do not lend themselves to such highly regular formalisms as arrays; lists are a much more flexible and natural implementation tool. In addition, AI is still a very new science, and many projects are started without a full understanding of the final form the program will assume. For this reason, much AI development is necessarily experimental and exploratory in nature. This requirement also places demands on a language and the tools it must provide. A language not only should be adequate to implement higher-level structures; it also should provide a natural and efficient tool for program development.

In the cases mentioned above, LISP and PROLOG were used to implement the original versions of the programs; only when these versions had been tested and reached a final form were they translated to C. In other cases where a traditional language such as Pascal, C, or FORTRAN was used to implement an AI system, the particular symbol-level structures being implemented were well understood. For these reasons, most AI programming is done in LISP and PROLOG, and these languages remain essential tools for work in artificial intelligence.

In the next five subsections, we discuss the requirements that the symbol-level structures of AI programs place on an implementation language:

Support of symbolic computation.

Flexibility of control.

Support of exploratory programming methodologies.

Late binding and constraint propagation.

A clear and well-defined semantics.

Support of Symbolic Computation. Although there are numerous ways of organizing knowledge at the symbol level, all of them are ultimately implemented as actions on patterns of symbols. This methodological commitment is summarized in Newell and Simon's physical symbol system hypothesis, discussed in the introduction to Part II. The physical symbol system hypothesis not only characterizes the dominant direction of AI research but also underscores the need for a programming language that simplifies the implementation of a range of operations on symbolic rather than numeric data. The numeric data types and operations emphasized by traditional programming languages are not well suited for implementing search algorithms or AI representation languages. Instead, an AI programming language should simplify the creation of arbitrary symbol structures and operations on these structures. This is the most fundamental requirement for an AI programming language.

Predicate calculus, described in Chapter 2, is a powerful and general tool for constructing qualitative descriptions of a domain. The significant features of a domain may be represented as sets of logical assertions: through the use of variables, it is possible to create general assertions about classes of entities; logical implications allow the representation of dependencies and other relationships between objects in a domain. PROLOG, discussed in Chapter 6, is a general programming language based on the first-order predicate calculus.

PROLOG programs are collections of descriptive facts about a domain and rules for deriving conclusions from those facts. Because PROLOG is based on concise mathematical notation, the programs tend to be compact, capturing problem-solving knowledge in a few statements. As an implementation of formal logic, PROLOG is sometimes used directly as a representation language at the symbol level. However, its real power is as a language for implementing more specialized and complex representations such as frames and networks in a concise and systematic fashion. Many symbol-level structures are easily built using the higher-level constructs of PROLOG. In Chapters 6, 13, and 15, we show how PROLOG may be used to implement various search algorithms, an expert system shell, and a simple semantic network.

Another important tool for building symbol structures is the list. A list is a sequence of elements in which each element may be either another list or an atomic symbol. Several examples of lists, using the syntax of the LISP programming language, are:

(this is a list)

((this is) (a list) (of lists))

(times (plus 1 3) (plus 2 3))

((1 2 3) (4 5 6) (7 8 9))

Note that several of these examples include lists nested within lists; this allows us to represent structural relations. The power of lists is largely a result of their ability to represent any symbol structure, regardless of its complexity or dimensionality or the operations it must support. This includes trees, arbitrary graphs, collections of logical predicates, arrays, data bases allowing keyword retrieval—in short, any conceivable structure may be captured in an appropriate arrangement of lists and lists within lists. Lists are such important representational building blocks that both LISP and PROLOG provide the user with the data elements and operations for manipulating and composing them into more complicated structured types. The exact way in which these structures may be built up from the list is discussed in the chapters on the individual languages.

Whereas PROLOG is based directly in the predicate calculus and includes lists as an additional representational tool, LISP uses the list as the basis of both data types and programs. All LISP structures are built from lists, and the language provides a rich set of tools for manipulating these structures and defining new functions for creating, accessing, and changing them. LISP's syntactic uniformity and extensibility make it easy to construct interpreters for any representation language. By taking an abstract data type approach, the LISP programmer can define the symbol structures and operations needed for any higher-level formalism, including search controllers, logic theorem provers, and other high-level representations.

Flexibility of Control. One of the hallmarks of intelligent behavior is its flexibility. Indeed, critics of AI have argued that intelligence cannot be achieved by the step-by-step execution of fixed instruction sequences exhibited by traditional computer programs. Fortunately, this is not the only way of organizing computation.

One of the oldest and most important paradigms for building an AI program is the production system, described in Chapter 5. In a production system, the program is a set of rules; these rules are executed in an order determined by the pattern of the data in a given problem instance. Production rules can fire in virtually any order in response to a given situation. In this fashion, a production system can provide both the flexibility and the coherency required for intelligent behavior.

Though AI uses a number of different control structures, many of them are related to production systems, and virtually all of them involve pattern matching. Pattern-directed control allows knowledge to be applied opportunistically in response to the features of a particular problem instance. Pattern matchers, such as unification, determine when the features of a problem instance match a particular chunk of program knowledge, selecting that knowledge for application to the problem. It is important that an AI language either provide this directly or simplify the development of pattern-directed control.

In PROLOG, unification (Chapter 2) and search algorithms are built into the language itself, forming the heart of the PROLOG interpreter. Using this built-in unification algorithm, it is simple to construct any pattern-driven control regime: depth-first search is given as a default, and other regimes such as breadth-first or best-first search may be constructed with a few lines of code (Chapter 6).

LISP does not provide a pattern-matching algorithm directly, but the sophistication of its symbolic computing facilities and the easy extensibility of the language make it simple to write pattern matchers and interpreters of arbitrary complexity and organization (Chapter 7). One advantage of this approach is that the pattern matcher and associated control structures may easily be tailored to fit the demands of a particular problem or representation.

Support of Exploratory Programming Methodologies. The problems that AI addresses do not always respond to such standard software engineering approaches as top-down design, successive refinement, and program development from detailed formal specifications. Because of the very nature of AI problems, it is seldom possible to give a correct and complete specification of the final form of an AI program before building at least a prototype. Often, our understanding of the problem the program is intended to solve changes through the course of program development. Reasons for this include:

1. **Most AI problems are initially poorly specified.** Because of the extreme youth of the field, it is seldom possible to examine a problem and determine conclusively the exact approach that should be taken to its solution. By contrast, in more familiar domains we have developed methods for creating complete and accurate problem specifications and generating code that meets these specifications.

   A complex reasoning task is inherently more difficult to characterize formally than is a task such as sorting a list or maintaining a file system. Exactly what does it mean, for example, to design a circuit or diagnose an illness? How does a human expert perform these tasks? What is a satisfactory level of performance for a given problem domain? What knowledge is required to solve the problem? The role and importance of such things as common sense, for example, are difficult to define or delineate in most domains. For these reasons, most AI problems are initially stated in very general terms and made more specific as code development illuminates the nature of the problem.

2. **The approaches taken to solving problems tend to be very domain specific.** Although there are general frameworks for AI problem solving such as production systems, search, and representation languages, each problem domain tends to require unique strategies. This means that successful solutions to problems seldom generalize fully to new domains: each application is, to some extent, a new ballgame.

3. **Heuristic methods are inherently empirical.** Even the techniques used by human experts have been developed through trial and error. This means that heuristic strategies, unlike algorithms, must be implemented and tested before their value can be fully known.

4. **Knowledge-based programming seems to be fundamentally incremental.** This is really just a different way of stating the previous point, but it stresses the facts

that intelligent systems use knowledge to solve problems and that knowledge is acquired by degree.

5. **The structures and formalisms for AI representations are new and not completely understood.** Although experience helps greatly in choosing and applying a representation, there is currently no substitute for trying an idea and seeing how it works.

For these reasons, AI programming is inherently exploratory; the program is often the vehicle through which we explore the problem domain and discover solution strategies. The challenge for AI programming is finding ways to do exploratory programming that are efficient, systematic, and well structured. Among the features that an exploratory programming language should provide are:

1. Modularity.
2. Extensibility.
3. Useful high-level constructs.
4. Support of early prototyping.
5. Program "readability."
6. Interpreted and compiled modes.
7. Software support for exploratory programming.

We discuss these topics in the following paragraphs:

1. **Modularity and modifiability of code.** It is important that a language for exploratory programming support frequent modifications of its code. This implies that programs should consist of small, well-bounded chunks rather than large bodies of complex code. The interactions between program components should be limited and clearly defined. This includes avoiding side effects and global variables and ensuring that the role of any single chunk in the program execution is easily determined.

LISP programs are written as collections of individual functions; in a well-written LISP program, each function is small and performs a single, well-defined task. Thus, it is usually simple to locate and correct the cause of any deficiencies. The parameter passing (a variation of "pass by value") and variable scoping rules of LISP also serve to reduce function side effects. Global variables, although supported by the language, are avoided in good LISP code.

In PROLOG the basic unit of the program is the rule. PROLOG rules, like LISP functions, tend to be small and specialized. Because the scope of variables in PROLOG is always restricted to a single rule and the language does not allow global variables, modifiability is simplified. Both LISP and PROLOG include trace facilities, which, when combined with a clear program structure, simplify the assignment of blame and credit in debugging.

2. **Extensibility and embedded languages.** Exploratory programming usually proceeds in a bottom-up fashion, with the higher-level structures of the program emerging as the code is developed. An important technique for doing this in a systematic and well-structured fashion is the development of an *embedded language*.

Often it is not possible to specify the final form of an AI program, but it is possible to determine the higher-level structures useful for exploring the domain. These structures can include pattern matchers, search controllers, and functions for defining a representation language. Essentially, this approach says "if you can't determine the final structure a program will take, attempt to define the language constructs that help develop that structure."

To support this methodology, a programming language should be easily extensible and should simplify the development of interpreters. By extensibility, we mean the ability to define new language constructs with maximum freedom and flexibility. LISP, PROLOG, and the object-oriented languages all allow easy definition of new functions, predicates, and objects, respectively. Once defined, these user-created constructs behave exactly like the built-in components of the language. One programs these languages by extending their basic capabilities from the bottom up until a solution is achieved. In a sense, traditional programs are "constructed" but AI programs are "grown."

This contrasts with the sharp distinction that traditional languages make between built-in features and user-developed programs. In Pascal, for example, we may define new functions or procedures, but their syntax is more restricted than the syntax of the built-in constructs of the language; this limits the flexibility and utility of these extensions. Consider, for example, the difficulty of writing a new control structure, such as a production system, in Pascal.

LISP and PROLOG also simplify the writing of interpreters. In LISP, both programs and data are syntactically represented as lists. This makes it very easy to write programs that manipulate LISP code as if they were data, greatly simplifying the development of interpreters. Many historically and commercially important AI languages such as PLANNER, ROSIE, KEE, and OPS were built on these capabilities of LISP. (We design a meta-interpreter in LISP in Chapter 14.) PROLOG provides this capability through a number of "meta-predicates," predicates for manipulating other PROLOG predicates, again simplifying the writing of arbitrary interpreters. As with LISP, a number of higher-level AI languages have been built on PROLOG using this methodology. (We present several meta-interpreters for PROLOG in Chapter 13.)

3. **Existence of useful high-level constructs.** Exploratory programming is aided by the existence of powerful high-level constructs in the language. These powerful but general abstractive constructs allow the programmer to quickly develop specialized structures for knowledge representation and program control.

In LISP, these include the basic list data type, which allows the construction of arbitrarily complex data structures, as well as powerful functions for defining operations on these structures. Because LISP is extensible and has been used for several decades, the most general and powerful of these user-defined functions have become standard features of the language. Most modern LISPs have evolved in this fashion to include literally hundreds of functions for creating data structures, building user interfaces, tracing program execution, and editing LISP structures.

PROLOG has remained a comparatively small language, partly because of its newness and partly out of a commitment to simplicity and compactness. However, PROLOG allows users to create their own library of specialized predicates, and the most useful of these have found their way into standard implementations.

4. **Support for early prototyping.** Another important exploratory programming methodology is early prototyping. Here, the programmer builds a "quick and dirty" solution to the problem and uses it to explore the problem space. Once we have explored the problem and outlined a viable solution strategy, we throw the prototype away and build a final program that emphasizes correctness and efficiency of implementation. Although it is generally difficult to throw away something that has required as much work to build as a computer program, doing so often saves time in the long run and improves the quality of the final program. The structures and methods provided by AI languages greatly speed up the development of prototypes.

5. **Program readability and documentation.** Because most AI programs are modified extensively through their lifetime, it is important that the code be readable and well documented. While there is no substitute for clear natural language comments in the code, AI languages, by yielding highly modular code composed of high-level constructs, greatly simplify this goal.

6. **Interpretation versus compilation.** Most AI languages are interpreted rather than compiled during program development. This means the programmer does not have to wait for lengthy recompilations every time the code is changed. In addition, the interactive interpreters provided for AI languages include extensive trace and debug facilities (discussed next). Because interpreted code runs slowly, modern AI languages usually allow the compilation of final versions of programs.

7. **Software support for exploratory programming.** Modern AI languages include rich programming environments, providing tools for tracing the execution of either whole programs or sections of programs. Debuggers allow the programmer to step through program execution incrementally, to temporarily change the value of program variables or even the code itself, to insert break points that halt program execution at prespecified points, and to freeze the execution environment at the point where an error is detected so that the program state may be examined. In addition, many language implementations include intelligent editors that spot syntax errors as code is being written. Because of the complexity of AI programs and the difficulty of predicting the behavior of such flexible control regimes as production systems, the importance of these support facilities cannot be overestimated.

Late Binding and Constraint Propagation.   Constraint propagation is an important AI programming methodology that should be supported by an implementation language. Often, the problems addressed by an AI program require that the values of certain entities remain unknown until sufficient information has been gathered to determine an assignment. This information may be seen as a series of constraints on the values that a variable may assume; as constraints are accumulated, the set of possible values is reduced, ultimately converging on a solution that satisfies all the constraints.

A simple example of this approach may be seen in a medical diagnostic system that gathers information about a patient's symptoms until the possible explanations have been reduced to a single diagnosis. The programming language analog of this methodology is late variable binding, or the ability to maintain a variable as explicitly unbound while manipulating it in the program code. Both LISP and PROLOG allow variables to be defined and manipulated as explicitly unbound, while defining the relationships and dependencies between those variables and other program units. This enables the easy and natural implementation of constraint propagation.

A Clear and Well-Defined Semantics.   This is a need that AI languages share with any programming language intended for the development of large, complicated, yet reliable systems. Unfortunately, traditional programming languages such as FORTRAN and Pascal tend to have complex and difficult semantic definitions. This shortcoming can be traced to the fact that such languages are essentially higher-level characterizations of the architecture of the underlying von Neumann computer and inherit many of the complexities of that physical system. Because AI languages have often been based on mathematical formalisms such as logic (PROLOG) or recursive function theory (LISP), they tend to have simpler semantics, inheriting much of the notational power and elegance of formal mathematics. This makes these languages particularly useful for researchers in areas such as implementing knowledge representation languages, formalizing the process of code development, proving programs correct, and automating the generation of efficient code from formal specifications. These research areas require that the semantics of the programming languages be clearly and formally specified.

It should also be noted that although the *function* of most AI programs is highly complex, the code that *implements* that function should strive for simplicity and clarity. Large blocks of complex opaque code do not imply good AI. A well-defined language semantics is an important tool for achieving these ends.

The Primary AI Languages: LISP and PROLOG

By meeting the needs outlined in the previous section, LISP, PROLOG, and to a lesser extent object-oriented programming have emerged as the dominant languages for AI research and development. When learning these languages, the student should keep these needs in mind and think about the ways in which they are supported by the specific features of each language.

These languages exemplify three of the most important alternative approaches to programming language design. Traditional languages are procedural and treat programming in terms of a separation of data and executable code. The code is a body of sequentially executed statements acting on a store of passive data. Because of a number of limitations that seem to be inherent in this model of programming (Backus 1978), researchers continue to explore alternative ways of designing programming languages. AI, because of the demands it places on an implementation language, has always played an important role in this research. Currently, three of the most important alternative approaches to programming are functional programming, logic programming, and object-oriented programming; these approaches are exemplified by LISP, PROLOG, and Smalltalk or CLOS (the Common LISP Object System), respectively.

PROLOG

The first PROLOG program was written in Marseille, France, in the early 1970s as part of a project in natural language understanding (Colmerauer et al. 1973; Roussel 1975; Kowalski 1979*a*). The theoretical background for the language PROLOG is discussed in the work of Kowalski, Hayes, and others (Kowalski 1979*a*, 1979*b*; Hayes 1977; Lloyd 1984).

PROLOG is the best-known example of a *logic programming language*. A logic program is a set of specifications in formal logic; PROLOG uses the first-order predicate calculus. An interpreter executes the program by systematically making inferences from these specifications. Indeed, the name itself comes from PROgramming in LOGic. The idea of using the representational power of the first-order predicate calculus to express specifications for problem solving is one of the central contributions of PROLOG to computer science in general and to artificial intelligence in particular. The benefits of using first-order predicate calculus for a programming language include a clean and elegant syntax and well-defined semantics.

The implementation of PROLOG has its roots in research on theorem proving by J. A. Robinson (1965). Robinson designed a proof procedure called *resolution*, which is the primary method for computing with PROLOG. The chapter on automated theorem proving demonstrates this implementation as a *resolution refutation system* (Sections 11.2 and 13.3).

Because of these features, PROLOG has proved to be a useful vehicle for investigating such experimental programming issues as automatic code generation, program verification, and design of high-level specification languages. PROLOG and other logic-based languages support a declarative programming style—that is, constructing a program in terms of high-level descriptions of a problem's constraints—rather than a procedural programming style—writing programs as a sequence of instructions for performing an algorithm. This mode of programming essentially tells the computer "what is true" and "what needs to be done" rather than "how to do it." This allows programmers to focus their energies on problem-solving specifications rather than the details of writing low-level control code.

The major development of the PROLOG language was carried out from 1975 to 1979 at the department of artificial intelligence of the University of Edinburgh. The group in Edinburgh responsible for the implementation of PROLOG were David H. D. Warren and Fernando Pereira. They produced the first PROLOG interpreter robust enough for delivery to the general computing community. This product was built on the DEC-system 10 and could operate in both interpretive and compiled modes (Warren et al. 1979). Further descriptions of this early code and comparisons of PROLOG with LISP may be found in Warren et al. (1977). This "Warren and Pereira" PROLOG became the early standard, and the book *Programming in PROLOG* (Clocksin and Mellish 1984) was the chief vehicle for delivering this PROLOG to the computing community. This text uses this standard, which has come to be known as the Edinburgh syntax.

During the period of development of the Warren-Pereira interpreter, a number of other projects at Edinburgh investigated the expressive power of this new language. These were:

1. A plan formation program (see Chapter 15) called WARPLAN, also developed by Warren (1976).

2. A program to solve algebraic equations and to prove theorems in geometry (Welham 1976; Bundy and Welham 1981).

3. A "compiler writing" program (Warren 1980).

4. A program to solve "mechanics" problems from their English language specifications (Bundy et al. 1979).

Originally developed in Europe, PROLOG attracted considerable interest in the United States as a result of its adoption as the language for the Japanese Fifth Generation Computing Project. The advantages of the language have been further demonstrated by a number of research projects designed to evaluate and extend the expressive power of logic programming. The Alvey program in Britain is a primary contributor to this research. PROLOG has also enjoyed increasing success in the development of artificial intelligence applications, as can be found in the Proceedings of the International Joint Conference on Artificial Intelligence and the Symposium on Logic Programming. See also the references at the end of Chapters 6 and 13.

LISP

LISP was first proposed by John McCarthy in the late 1950s. The language was originally intended as an alternative model of computation based on the theory of recursive functions. In an early paper, McCarthy (1960) outlined his goals: to create a language for symbolic rather than numeric computation, to implement a model of computation based on the theory of recursive functions (Church 1941), to provide a clear definition of the language's syntax and semantics, and to demonstrate formally the completeness of this computational model. Although LISP is one of the oldest computing languages still in existence (along with FORTRAN and COBOL), the careful thought given to its original design and the extensions made to the language through its history have kept it in the vanguard of programming languages. In fact, this programming model has proved so effective that a number of other languages have been based on functional programming (e.g., SCHEME, ML, FP).

The list is the basis of both programs and data structures in LISP: LISP is an acronym for LISt Processing. The power of lists for symbolic computing had been demonstrated in earlier work such as the Logic Theorist of Newell and Simon (1956). LISP provides a powerful set of list-handling functions implemented internally as linked pointer structures. LISP gives programmers the full power and generality of linked data structures while freeing them from the responsibility for explicitly managing pointers and pointer operations.

Originally, LISP was a very small and simple language, consisting of functions for constructing and accessing lists, defining new functions, detecting equality, and evaluating expressions. The only means of program control were recursion and a single conditional. More complicated functions, when needed, were defined in terms of these primitives. Through time, the best of these new functions became part of the language itself. This process of extending the language by adding new functions has led to the development of numerous dialects of LISP, often including hundreds of specialized functions for data structuring, program control, real and integer arithmetic, input/output (I/O), editing LISP functions, and tracing program execution. These dialects are the vehicle by which LISP has evolved from a simple and elegant theoretical model of computing into a rich, powerful, and practical environment for building large software systems. Because of the proliferation of early LISP dialects, the Defense Advanced Research Projects Agency in 1983 proposed a standard dialect of the language, known as Common LISP.

Although Common LISP has emerged as the lingua franca of LISP dialects, it is unlikely that all of the other dialects will disappear. Indeed, Common LISP has been criticized as excessively complicated and unwieldy, sacrificing elegance and clarity in an attempt to be "all things to all people." A number of simpler dialects continue to be widely used. These dialects include SCHEME, an elegant rethinking of the language that has been used both for AI development and for teaching the fundamental concepts of computer science, and XLISP, a compact dialect that also supports object-oriented programming. The dialect we use throughout the remainder of our text is Common LISP (Steele 1984). See also the references at the end of Chapters 7 and 14.

Selecting an Implementation Language

LISP and PROLOG are both capable of implementing any representation and control structures required by a given program. Each of them is based on a different model of computation. Currently, there is some debate over the relative merits of the different languages used for AI programming. We feel that both languages are an essential part of the AI programmer's skills and deserve treatment in an artificial intelligence text. However, this debate does call for some comment:

1. The important issue is to be familiar with the trade-offs involved in selecting an AI language, not to take a stand on which language is best.

2. Good programmers should be familiar with all the available tools; different jobs will often require the features of one language over another.

3. Different languages are used in the literature, and programmers must be familiar with these different languages to keep up with the field.

4. Each of the languages discussed in the text exemplifies one or more very important high-level language concepts such as functional programming, list-based data structures, formal logic, pattern-directed control, and object-oriented programming. These concepts not only are important tools for writing correct, understandable code in any language but also exemplify some of the major directions currently being explored in the design of future languages.

Given the current state of the art, it is certain that AI professionals will find themselves programming in one or more of the languages discussed in this text. It is also certain that given limitations of all currently available programming languages and the challenges and the vitality found in the field of AI language design, students will be programming in a very different and much improved language by the end of their careers. The treatment of languages in this text prepares students for both eventualities.

More detailed analysis of the languages of this chapter and full references are presented in Chapters 6, 7, 13, 14, and 15. A more complete analysis of object-oriented languages and their use is in Chapters 9, 14, and 15.

To support the study and comparison of these languages, we summarize their features in Table III.1. We include Pascal to provide a comparison with a more "traditional" programming language. Although many of the entries in the table will not be completely clear until you learn the languages, the table provides an overview of their major features to keep in mind while you study them.

TABLE III.1 COMPARISON OF FEATURES OF MAJOR LANGUAGE PARADIGMS

	PASCAL	LISP	PROLOG	OBJECT-ORIENTED LANGUAGES
Language model	Procedural programming	Functional programming	Logic programming	Object-oriented programming
Data types	Scalars, arrays, and records	Symbolic and numeric atoms, list structures, property and association lists	Symbolic and numeric atoms, predicates, lists and list structures	Symbolic and numeric atoms, slots and values, classes and instances
Data manipulation	Assignment, parameter passing by value and reference, function returns	Function returns, parameter passing binding of local and global variables	Variable binding through unifications	Message passing, instantiating slot values in objects
Program control	Sequencing, branching, looping, recursion	Function evaluation, recursion, looping	Pattern-directed search, recursion	Method invocation through message passing
Program structure	Block structure, nested procedure definitions	Functions in a global environment, let blocks	Rules and facts in a data base	Objects in a class hierarchy, inheritance
Variable scoping	Global and nested local scopes	Bound variables, lexical or dynamic scoping, local variables using let blocks	Variable scope confined to a single rule or fact	Object's slot values, visible to subclasses and instances through inheritance
Mode of interaction	Interpreted or compiled in batch mode	Interactive interpreter, compiler	Interactive interpreter, compiler	Interactive interpreter, compiler

AN INTRODUCTION TO PROLOG

All the objects of human reason or inquiry may naturally be divided into two kinds, to wit, "Relations of Ideas" and "Matters of Fact."

—DAVID HUME, "An Inquiry Concerning Human Understanding"

The only way to rectify our reasonings is to make them as tangible as those of the mathematicians, so that we can find our error at a glance, and when there are disputes among persons we can simply say, "Let us calculate . . . to see who is right."

—LEIBNIZ, *The Art of Discovery*

6.0 Introduction

As an implementation of logic as a programming language, PROLOG has made many interesting contributions to AI problem solving. These include its *declarative semantics*, a means of directly expressing problem relationships in AI, as well as, with built-in unification, some high-powered techniques for pattern matching and search. We address many of the important issues of *logic programming* in this chapter and in Chapter 13.

In Section 6.1 we present the basic PROLOG syntax and several simple programs. These programs demonstrate the use of the predicate calculus as a representation language. We show how to monitor the PROLOG environment and demonstrate the use of the *cut* with PROLOG's implicit depth-first control to improve efficiency.

In Section 6.2 we create *abstract data types* (ADTs) in PROLOG. These ADTs include *stacks, queues,* and *priority queues*, which are then used to build a production system in Section 6.3 and to design control structures for the search algorithms of Chapters 3 and 4 in Section 6.4. In Section 6.5 we create a planner, after the material presented in Section 5.4.

In Section 6.6 we examine PROLOG as a nonprocedural problem-solving representation and give several small examples to emphasize this important concept. The chapter ends with the discussion of the general issues of programming in logic and procedural versus declarative problem solving.

6.1   Syntax for Predicate Calculus Programming

6.1.1   Representing Facts and Rules

Although there are numerous dialects of PROLOG, the syntax used throughout this text is the original Warren and Pereira C-PROLOG (Clocksin and Mellish 1984). To simplify our presentation of PROLOG, our version of predicate calculus syntax in Chapter 2 used many PROLOG conventions. There are, however, a number of differences between PROLOG and predicate calculus syntax. In C-PROLOG, for example, the symbol :- replaces the ← of first-order predicate calculus. Several other symbols differ from those used in Chapter 2:

ENGLISH	PREDICATE CALCULUS	PROLOG
and	∧	,
or	∨	;
only if	←	:-
not	¬	not

As in Chapter 2, predicate names and bound variables are expressed as a sequence of alphanumeric characters beginning with an alphabetic. Variables are represented as a string of alphanumeric characters beginning (at least) with an uppercase alphabetic. Thus:

    likes(X, susie).

or, better,

    likes(Everyone, susie).

could represent the fact that "everyone likes Susie." Or,

    likes(george,Y), likes(susie,Y).

could represent the set of things (or people) that are liked by both George and Susie.

Similarly, suppose it was desired to represent in PROLOG the following relationships: "George likes Kate and George likes Susie." This could be stated as:

    likes(george, kate), likes(george, susie).

Likewise, "George likes Kate or George likes Susie":

likes(george, kate); likes(george, susie).

"George likes Susie if George likes Kate":

likes(george, susie) :- likes(george, kate).

Finally, the negation of a predicate, "Kate does not like Susie":

not(likes(kate, susie)).

These examples show how the predicate calculus connectives ∧, ∨, ¬, and ← are expressed in PROLOG. The predicate names (likes), the number or order of parameters, and even whether a given predicate always has the same number of parameters are determined by the design requirements (the implicit "semantics") of the problem. There are no expressive limitations other than the syntax of well-formed formulas in the language.

A PROLOG program is a set of specifications in the first-order predicate calculus describing the objects and relations in a problem domain. The set of specifications, or what is true about a particular problem situation, is referred to as the *data base* for that problem. The PROLOG interpreter responds to questions about this set of specifications. Queries to the data base are patterns in the same logical syntax as the data base entries. The PROLOG interpreter uses pattern-directed search to find whether these queries logically follow from the contents of the data base (see the abstract specification of PROLOG search in Section 13.3).

The interpreter processes queries, searching the data base to find out whether the query is a logical consequence of the data base of specifications. PROLOG is primarily an interpreted language. Some versions of PROLOG run in interpretive mode only, while others allow compilation of part or all of the set of data base specifications for faster execution. PROLOG is an interactive language; the user enters queries in response to the PROLOG prompt: ?-. This prompt appears in all PROLOG examples in this chapter.

Suppose that we would like to describe a "world" consisting of George's, Kate's, and Susie's likes and dislikes in a PROLOG data base. The data base would contain the following set of predicates:

likes(george, kate).
likes(george, susie).
likes(george, wine).
likes(susie, wine).
likes(kate, gin).
likes(kate, susie).

This set of specifications has the obvious interpretation, or mapping, into the world of George and his friends. This world is a model for the data base (Section 2.3). The interpreter may then be asked questions:

```
?- likes(george, kate).
yes
?- likes(kate, susie).
yes
?- likes(george, X).
X = kate
;
X = susie
;
X = wine
;
no
?- likes(george, beer).
no
```

Note several things in these examples. First, in the request likes(george, X), successive user prompts (;) cause the interpreter to return all the terms in the data base specification that may be substituted for the X in the query. They are returned in the order in which they are found in the data base: kate before susie before wine. Although it goes against the philosophy of nonprocedural specifications, a determined order of evaluation is a property of most interpreters implemented on sequential machines. The PROLOG programmer must be aware of the order in which PROLOG searches entries in the data base.

Also note that further responses to queries are produced when the user prompts with the ; (or). This forces a backtrack on the most recent result. Continued prompts force PROLOG to find all possible solutions to the query. When no further solutions exist, the interpreter responds no.

The above example also illustrates the *closed world assumption* or *negation as failure*. PROLOG assumes that "anything is false whose opposite is not provably true." In the query likes(george, beer), the interpreter looks for the predicate likes(george, beer) or some rule that could establish that likes(george, beer) is true. Failing in this task, it asserts that the request is false. Thus, PROLOG assumes that all knowledge of the world is present in the data base.

The closed world assumption introduces a number of practical and philosophical difficulties in the language (presented in detail in Section 13.3). For example, failure to include a fact in the data base often means that its truth is unknown; the closed world assumption treats it as false. If a predicate were omitted or there were a misspelling, such as likes(george, beer), the response remains no. The negation-as-failure issue is a very important topic in AI research. Though negation as failure is a simple way to deal with the problem of unspecified knowledge, more sophisticated approaches, such as multivalue logics (true, false, unknown) and nonmonotonic reasoning (Section 8.3.4), provide a richer interpretive context. Several of these issues are addressed again in the chapters on advanced representations.

The PROLOG expressions used in the data base above are examples of *fact* specifications. PROLOG also lets us define *rules* to describe relationships between facts using the logical implication, :-. In creating a PROLOG rule, only one predicate is permitted on the left-hand side of the if symbol, :-; this predicate must be a *positive literal*, which means it cannot be negated (Section 13.3). All predicate calculus expressions that contain implication or equivalence relationships (←, →, and ↔) must be reduced to this form, referred to as *Horn clause* logic. In Horn clause form, the left-hand side (conclusion) of an implication must be a single positive literal. The *Horn clause calculus* is equivalent to the full first-order predicate calculus for proofs by refutation. (See Chapters 11 and 13.)

Suppose we add to the specifications of the previous data base a rule for determining whether two people are friends. This may be defined:

```
friends(X, Y) :- likes(X, Z), likes(Y, Z).
```

This expression might be interpreted as "X and Y are friends if there exists a Z such that X likes Z and Y likes Z." Two issues are important here. First, because neither the predicate calculus nor PROLOG has global variables, the scope (extent of definition) of X, Y, and Z is limited to the friends rule. Second, values bound to, or unified with, X, Y, and Z are consistent across the entire expression. The treatment of the friends rule by the PROLOG interpreter is seen in the following example.

With the friends rule added to the set of specifications of the preceding example, we can query the interpreter:

```
?- friends(george, susie).
yes
```

In solving the query, the PROLOG interpreter searches the data base using the backtrack algorithm presented in Chapters 3 and 5. The query friends(george, susie) is matched or unified with the conclusion of the rule friends(X, Y) :- likes(X, Z), likes(Y, Z), with X as george and Y as susie. The interpreter then tries to find a Z such that likes(george, Z) is true. This is first attempted using the first fact in the data base, with Z as kate.

The interpreter then tries to determine whether likes(susie, kate) is true. When it is found to be false, using the closed world assumption, the value for Z (kate) is rejected. The interpreter then goes back to the data base (backtracks) to find a second value for Z in likes(george, Z).

likes(george, Z) then matches the second clause in the data base, with Z bound to susie. The interpreter then tries to match likes(susie, susie). When this also fails, the interpreter goes back to the data base (backtracks) for yet another value for Z. This time wine is found in the third predicate, and the interpreter goes on to show that likes(susie, wine) is true. In this case wine is the binding that ties george and susie. Note that PROLOG tries to match goals with patterns in the order in which these patterns are entered in the data base.

It is important to state the relationship between universal and existential quantification in the predicate calculus and the treatment of variables in a PROLOG program. When a variable is placed in the specifications of a PROLOG data base, the variable is assumed to be universally quantified. For example, likes(susie, Y) means, according to the semantics of the previous examples, "Susie likes everyone." In the course of interpreting some query, any term, or list or predicate, may be bound to Y. Similarly, in the rule friends(X, Y) :- likes(X, Z), likes(Y, Z), any X, Y, and Z that meet the specifications of the expression are acceptable variable bindings.

To represent an existentially quantified variable in PROLOG, we may take two approaches. First, if the existential value of a variable is known, that value may be entered directly into the data base. Thus, likes(george, wine) is an instance of likes(george, Z) and may be thus entered into the data base, as it was in the previous examples.

Second, to find an instance of a variable that makes an expression true, we may make a query to the interpreter. For example, to find whether a Z exists such that likes(george, Z) is true, we put this query directly to the interpreter. It will find whether a value of Z exists under which the expression is true. Some PROLOG interpreters find all such existentially quantified values; C-PROLOG requires repeated user prompts (;) to get all values.

6.1.2   Creating, Changing, and Monitoring the PROLOG Environment

In creating a PROLOG program the data base of specifications must first be created. In the interactive PROLOG environment the PROLOG predicate assert is used to add a new predicate to the present set of specifications. Thus:

```
?- assert(likes(david, sarah)).
```

adds this predicate to the computing specifications. Now:

```
?- likes(david, X).
```

will return:

```
?- X = sarah.
```

assert allows further control in adding new specifications to the data base: asserta(P) asserts the predicate P at the beginning of all the predicates P, and assertz(P) adds P at the end of all the predicates named P. This is important for search priorities and building heuristics, as is discussed in Chapters 8, 9, 13, and 14. To remove a predicate P from the data base of specifications retract(P) may be used.

It soon becomes tedious to create a set of specifications using the predicates assert and retract. Instead, the programmer usually takes her favorite editor and creates a file containing all the PROLOG specifications. Once this file is created (let's call it myfile) and PROLOG is called, then the file is placed in the data base by the PROLOG command consult. Thus:

```
?- consult(myfile).
yes
```

will add all the predicates in myfile to the database. A short form of the consult predicate, and better for adding multiple files to the set of specifications, uses the list notation, to be seen shortly:

```
?- [myfile].
yes
```

The predicates **read** and **write** are important for user communication. **read(X)** takes the next term from the current input stream and binds it to **X**. Input expressions are terminated with a "**.**". **write(X)** puts **X** in the output stream. If **X** is unbound then an integer preceded by an underline is printed (_69). This integer represents the internal bookkeeping on all variables necessary in a theorem-proving environment (see Chapter 11) and can be useful in debugging.

The PROLOG predicates **see** and **tell** are used to read information from and place information into files. **see(X)** opens the file **X** and defines the current input stream as originating in **X**. If **X** is not bound to an available file **see(X)** fails. Similarly, **tell(X)** opens a file for the output stream. If no file **X** exists, **tell(X)** creates a file named by the bound value of **X**. **seen(X)** and **told(X)** close the respective files.

A number of PROLOG predicates are important in helping us keep track of the state of the PROLOG database as well as the state of computing about the data base; the most important of these are **listing**, **trace**, and **spy**. If we use **listing(predicate_name)** where **predicate_name** is the name of a predicate, such as **member**, above, all the clauses with that predicate name in the data base are returned by the interpreter. Note that the number of arguments of the predicate is not indicated; in fact, all uses of the predicate, regardless of the number of arguments, are returned.

trace allows the user to monitor the progress of the PROLOG interpreter. This is accomplished by printing to the output file every goal that PROLOG attempts. The tracing facilities in many PROLOG environments are rather cryptic and take some study to understand. The information available in a trace usually includes the following:

1. The depth level of recursive calls (marked left to right on line).
2. When a goal is tried for the first time (sometimes **call** is used).
3. When a goal is successfully satisfied (with an **exit**).
4. When a goal has further matches possible (a **retry**).
5. When a goal fails because all attempts to satisfy it have failed (**fail** is often used).
6. The goal **notrace** stops the exhaustive tracing.

When a more selective trace is required the goal **spy** is useful. This predicate usually takes a predicate name as argument but sometimes is defined as a prefix operator where the predicate to be monitored is listed after the operator. Thus, **spy member** causes the interpreter to print to output all uses of the predicate **member**. **spy** can also take a list of predicates followed by their arities: **spy[member/2,append/3]** sets monitoring of the interpreter on all uses of the goals **member** with two arguments and **append** with three. **nospy** removes these spy points. Some interpreters use the predicate **trace** with arguments to perform spying.

6.1.3 Recursion-Based Search in PROLOG

The previous subsections presented PROLOG syntax in several simple examples. These examples introduced PROLOG as an engine for computing with predicate calculus expressions (in Horn clause form). This is consistent with all the principles of predicate calculus inference presented in Chapter 2. PROLOG uses unification for pattern matching and returns the bindings that make an expression true. These values are unified with the variables in a particular expression and are not bound in the global environment.

Recursion is the primary control mechanism for PROLOG programming. We demonstrate this with the knight's tour problem by designing a PROLOG-based production system to search its graph. But first we consider some simple list-processing examples.

The list is a data structure consisting of ordered sets of elements (or, indeed, lists). Recursion is the "natural" way to process the list structure. Unification and recursion come together in list processing in PROLOG.

In PROLOG, list elements are enclosed by brackets [ ] and are separated by commas. Examples of PROLOG lists are:

[1, 2, 3, 4]
[[george, kate], [allen, amy], [don, pat]]
[tom, dick, harry, fred]
[]

The first elements of a list may be separated from the tail of the list by the bar operator, |. The tail of a list is the list with its first element removed. For instance, when the list is [tom,dick,harry,fred], the first element is tom and the tail is the list [dick, harry, fred]. Using the vertical bar operator and unification, we can break a list into its components:

If [tom,dick,harry,fred] is matched to [X|Y], then X = tom and Y = [dick,harry,fred].

If [tom,dick,harry,fred] is matched to [X,Y|Z], then X = tom, Y = dick, and Z = [harry,fred].

If [tom,dick,harry,fred] is matched to [X,Y,Z|W], then X = tom, Y = dick, Z = harry, and W = [fred].

If [tom,dick,harry,fred] is matched to [W,X,Y,Z|V], then W = tom, X = dick, Y = harry, Z = fred, and V = [ ].

[tom,dick,harry,fred] will not match [V,W,X,Y,Z|U].

[tom,dick,harry,fred] will match [tom,X|[harry,fred]], to give X = dick.

and so on.

Besides "tearing lists apart" to get at particular elements, unification can be used to "build" the list structure. For example, if X = tom, Y = [dick], and L unifies with [X|Y], then L will be bound to [tom,dick]. To summarize, the terms separated by commas before the | are all elements of the list, and the structure after the | is always a list, often referred to as the tail of the list.

Let's take a simple example of recursive processing of lists: the member check. We define a predicate to determine whether an item, represented by X, is in a list. This predicate member takes two arguments, an element and a list, and is true if the element is a member of the list. For example:

?- member(a, [a, b, c, d, e]).
yes
?- member(a, [1, 2, 3, 4]).
no

```
?- member(X, [a, b, c]).
X = a
;
X = b
;
X = c
;
no
```

To define **member** recursively, we begin by testing whether the element X is the first item in the list. We define this check in the following manner:

```
member(X,[X|T]).
```

This tests whether X and the first element of the list are identical. If they are not, then it is natural to check whether X is an element of the rest (T) of the list. This is defined by:

```
member(X,[Y|T]) :- member(X,T).
```

The two lines of PROLOG for checking list membership are, then:

```
member(X,[X|T]).
member(X,[Y|T]) :- member(X,T).
```

The first line asks whether X and the head of the list are identical. If this fails, when X is not the head of the list, **member** checks whether X is a member of the tail of the list.

This example illustrates the importance of PROLOG's built-in order of search to programming in the language. The terminating condition is usually placed in the data base before the recursive call; this guarantees that the terminating condition will be tested before the algorithm recurs. If the order of the predicates is reversed, the terminating condition may never be checked. The trace of the call, member(c,[a,b,c]), follows.

For this example,

```
1: member(X,[X|T]).
2: member(X,[Y|T]) :- member(X,T).
```

```
?- member(c,[a,b,c]).
        call 1. fail, since c ≠ a
        call 2. X = c, Y = a, T = [b,c], member(c,[b,c])?
            call 1. fail, since c ≠ b
            call 2. X = c, Y = b, T = [c], member(c,[c])?
                call 1. success, c = c
            yes (to second call 2.)

        yes (to first call 2.)
    yes
```

An important addition to our list membership specification is the use of *anonymous variables*. The use of these variables serves as an indication to the programmer and interpreter that certain variables are used solely for pattern-matching purposes, with the variable binding itself not part of the computation process. Thus, when we test whether the element X is the same as the first item in the list we usually say: member(X,[X|_]). The use of the _ indicates that even though the tail of the list plays a crucial part in the unification of a query, the content of the tail of the list is unimportant. In the member check the anonymous variable should be used in the recursive statement as well, where the value of the head of the list is unimportant:

```
member(X,[X|_]).
member(X,[_|T]) :- member(X,T).
```

Of course, many programmers also prefer more specific variable names, such as Item rather than X and Tail rather than T.

Writing out a list, one element to a line, is a nice exercise for understanding both lists and recursive control. Suppose we wish to write out the list [a,b,c,d]. We could define the recursive command:

```
writelist([ ]).
writelist([H|T]) :- write(H), nl, writelist(T).
```

This predicate writes one element of the list on each line, as nl requires the output stream controller to begin a new line. If we wish to write out a list in reversed order the recursive predicate must come before the write command. This guarantees that the list is traversed to the end before any element is written. At that time the last element of the list is written followed by each preceding element as the recursive control comes back up to the top. A reverse write of a list would be:

```
reverse_writelist([ ]).
reverse_writelist([H|T]) :- reverse_writelist(T), write(H), nl.
```

The reader should run writelist and reverse_writelist with trace to observe the behavior of these predicates.

6.1.4   Recursive Search in PROLOG

In Section 5.2 we represented the 3×3 knight's tour problem in the predicate calculus. We numbered the board squares like this:

1	2	3
4	5	6
7	8	9

The legal moves are represented in PROLOG using a move predicate. The path predicate defines an algorithm for finding a path of zero or more moves between its arguments. Note that path is defined recursively:

```
move(1,6).     move(3,4).     move(6,7).     move(8,3).
move(1,8).     move(3,8).     move(6,1).     move(8,1).
move(2,7).     move(4,3).     move(7,6).     move(9,4).
move(2,9).     move(4,9).     move(7,2).     move(9,2).
```

```
path(Z,Z).
path(X,Y) :- move(X,W), not(been(W)), assert(been(W)), path(W,Y).
```

This definition of path is a PROLOG implementation of the algorithm defined in Chapter 5. As noted above, assert is a built-in PROLOG predicate that always succeeds and has the side effect of placing its argument in the data base of specifications. The been predicate is used to record previously visited states and avoid loops.

This use of the been predicate violates the program designer's goal of creating predicate calculus specifications that do not use global variables. Thus been(3), when asserted into the data base, is indeed a fact available to any other procedure in the data base and, as such, has global extension. Even more important, creating global structures to alter program control violates the basic tenet of the production system model, where the logic (of problem specifications) is kept separate from the control of the program. Here been structures were created as global specifications to modify the program execution.

As we proposed in Chapter 3, a list may be used to keep track of visited states and thus keep the path call from looping. The member predicate is used to detect duplicate states (loops). This approach remedies the problems of using global been(W) assertions. The PROLOG-based specification of the following clauses exactly implements the depth-first graph search with the backtracking algorithm of Chapters 3 and 5:

```
path(Z,Z,L).
path(X,Y,L) :- move(X,Z), not(member(Z,L)), path(Z,Y,[Z|L]).
```

where:

```
member(X,[X|T]).
member(X,[Y|T]) :- member(X,T).
```

The third parameter of path is the local variable representing the list of states that have already been visited. When a new state is generated (using the move predicate) and this state is not already on the list of visited states, not(member(Z,L)), it is placed on the front of the state list [Z|L] for the next path call.

It should be noted that all the parameters of path are local and their current values depend on where they are called in the graph search. Each recursive call adds a state to this list. If all continuations from a certain state fail, then that particular path call fails. When the interpreter backs up to the parent call, the third parameter, representing the list of states visited, has its previous value. Thus, states are added to and deleted from this list as the backtracking search moves through the graph.

When the path call finally succeeds, the first two parameters are identical. The third parameter is the list of states visited on the path from the start state to the goal state (in reverse order). Thus we can print out the solution path. The PROLOG specification for the knight's tour problem using lists and a depth-first search employing backtrack may be obtained by using this definition of path with the move specifications and member predicates just presented.

The call to the PROLOG interpreter path(X,Y,[X]), where X and Y are replaced by numbers between 1 and 9, finds a path from state X to state Y, if the path exists. The third parameter initializes the path list with the starting state X. Note that there is no typing distinction in PROLOG: the first two parameters are any representation of states in the problem space and the third is a list of states. Unification makes this generalization of pattern matching across data types possible. Thus, path is a general depth-first search algorithm that may be used with any graph. In Section 6.3 we use this to implement a production system solution to the farmer, wolf, goat, and cabbage problem, with state specifications replacing square numbers in the call to path.

We now present the trace of a solution for the 3 × 3 knight's tour. It is left as an exercise for the reader to design the set of specifications for the full 8 × 8 knight's tour problem in PROLOG. (See exercises in Chapters 5 and 6.)

For this example we refer to the two parts of the path algorithm by number:

```
1. is path(Z,Z,L).
2. is path(X,Y,L) :- move(X,Z), not (member(Z,L)), path(Z,Y,[Z|L]).

   ?- path(1,3,[1]).

   path(1,3,[1]) attempts to match 1.  fail 1 ≠ 3.
   path(1,3,[1]) matches 2. X is 1, Y is 3, L is [1]
     move(1,Z) matches Z as 6, not(member(6,[1])) is true, call path(6,3,[6,1])

     path(6,3,[6,1]) attempts to match 1.  fail 6 ≠ 3.
     path(6,3,[6,1]) matches 2. X is 6, Y is 3, L is [6,1].
       move(6,Z) matches Z as 7, not(member(7,[6,1])) is true, path(7,3,[7,6,1])

       path(7,3,[7,6,1]) attempts to match 1.  fail 7 ≠ 3.
       path(7,3,[7,6,1]) matches 2. X is 7, Y is 3, L is [7,6,1].
         move(7,Z) is Z = 6, not(member(6,[7,6,1])) fails, backtrack!
         move(7,Z) is Z = 2, not(member(2,[7,6,1])) true, path(2,3,[2,7,6,1])

         path call attempts 1, fail, 2 ≠ 3.
         path matches 2, X is 2, Y is 3, L is [2,7,6,1]
           move matches Z as 7, not(member(...)) fails, backtrack!
           move matches Z as 9, not(member(...)) true, path(9,3,[9,2,7,6,1])

           path fails 1, 9 ≠ 3.
           path matches 2, X is 9, Y is 3, L is [9,2,7,6,1]
             move is Z = 4, not(member(...)) true, path(4,3,[4,9,2,7,6,1])
```

```
                                    path fails 1, 4 ≠ 3.
                                    path matches 2, X is 4, Y is 3, L is [4,9,2,7,6,1]
                                      move Z = 3, not(member(...)) true, path(3,3,[3,4,9,2,7,6,1])

                                    path attempts 1, true, 3 = 3, yes

                              yes

                          yes

                      yes

                  yes

              yes

          yes
```

In summary, the recursive **path** call is a *shell* or general control structure for search in a graph. All the checks are made for a graph search algorithm: in **path(X,Y,L)**, **X** is the present state; **Y** is the goal state. When **X** and **Y** are identical, the recursion terminates. **L** is the list of states on the current path to state **Y**, and as each new state **Z** is found with the call **move(X,Z)** it is placed on the list: **[Z|L]**. The state list is checked, using **not(member(Z,L))**, to be sure the path does not loop.

The difference between the state list **L** in the **path** call above and **closed** in Chapter 5 is that **closed** records all states visited, while the state list **L** keeps track of only the present path. It is quite straightforward to expand the record keeping in the **path** call along the lines presented in Chapter 5, and we do this in Section 6.4.

6.1.5   The Use of Cut to Control Search in PROLOG

The *cut* is represented by an exclamation point, !. The syntax for cut is that of a goal with no arguments. It has several side effects: first, it always succeeds and, second, if it is "failed back to" in the normal course of backtracking, it causes the entire goal in which it is contained to fail.

For a simple example of the effect of the cut, recall the two-move **path** call from the knight's tour example (Section 4.2). There the predicate **path2** could be created:

    path2(X,Y) :- move(X,Z), move(Z,Y).

(There is a two-move path between **X** and **Y** if there exists an intermediate stop **Z** between them.) For this example, assume part of the knight's data base:

    move(1,6).
    move(1,8).
    move(6,7).

```
move(6,1).
move(8,3).
move(8,1).
```

When the interpreter is asked to find all the two-move paths from 1, there are four answers:

```
?- path2(1,W).
W = 7
;
W = 1
;
W = 3
;
W = 1
;
no
```

When path2 is altered to contain the cut:

```
path2(X,Y) :- move(X,Z), !, move(Z,Y).
```

and the same goal is presented:

```
?- path2(1,W).
```

only two answers result:

```
W = 7
;
W = 1
;
no
```

This happens because variable Z takes on only one value (the first value it is bound to), namely 6. Once the first subgoal succeeds, Z is bound to 6 and the cut is encountered. This prohibits further backtracking to the first subgoal; no further bindings for the Z parameter are tried.

There are several uses for the cut in programming. First, as this example demonstrated, it allows the programmer to control explicitly the shape of the search tree. When further (exhaustive) search is not required, the tree can be explicitly pruned at that point. This allows PROLOG code to have the flavor of function calling: when one set of values (bindings) is "returned" by a PROLOG predicate (or set of predicates) and the cut is encountered, the interpreter does not search for other unifications. If that set of values does not lead on to a solution then no further values are attempted.

A second use of cut is to control recursive calls. In the recursive path call in Section 6.2, cut may be added after the recursive call:

```
path(Z,Z,L).
path(X,Z,L) :- move(X,Y), not(member(Y,L)), path(Y,Z,[Y|L]), !.
```

This addition of cut means that (at most) one solution to the graph search is produced. Only one solution is produced because further solutions occur after the clause path(Z,Z,L) is satisfied. If the user asks for more solutions, path(Z,Z,L) fails, and the second path call is reinvoked to continue the (exhaustive) search of the graph. When the cut is placed after the recursive path call, the call cannot be reentered (backed into) for further search.

Important side effects of the cut are to make the program run faster and to conserve memory locations. When cut is used within a predicate, the pointers in memory needed for backtracking to predicates to the left of the cut are not created. This is, of course, because they will never be needed. Thus, cut produces the desired solution, and only the desired solution, with more efficient use of memory.

The cut can also be used with recursion to reinitialize the path call for further search within the graph. When searching through a series of rules, PROLOG stores an activation record of each unification on an internal stack. This stack keeps track of the successive calls to a recursive predicate. Sometimes in a recursive predicate we need to retain only the most recent bindings of the parameters. The cut is then placed after the recursive call to keep the interpreter from recording all parent calls on the stack. This prevents the stack from getting too cumbersome and makes the program more efficient. We will use the cut in this fashion when we build the open and closed lists with breadth-first and best-first search algorithms in Section 6.4.

6.2   Abstract Data Types (ADTs) in PROLOG

Programming in any environment is enhanced by procedural abstractions and information hiding. Because the set, stack, queue, and priority queue data structures were the support constructs for the graph search algorithms of Chapters 3, 4, and 5, we build them in PROLOG in the present section and then use them in the design of the PROLOG search algorithms that round out this chapter.

Recursion, lists, and pattern matching, as emphasized throughout this book, are the primary tools for building and searching graph structures. These are the pieces with which we build our ADTs. All list handling and recursive processing are "hidden" within the ADT abstraction.

6.2.1   The ADT Stack

A stack is a linear structure with access at one end only. Thus all elements must be added to, pushed, and removed, popped, from the structure at that end of access. The stack is sometimes referred to as a last-in-first-out (LIFO) data structure. We saw its use with depth-first search in Section 3.2.3. The operators defined for a stack are:

1. Test whether the stack is empty.
2. Push an element onto the stack.

3. **Pop**, or remove, an element from the stack.

4. **Peek** at the next element on the stack without popping it.

Stack operators are sometimes augmented by:

5. **Member_stack**, which checks whether an element is in the stack.

6. **Add_list**, which adds a list of elements to the stack.

Both 5 and 6 may be built from 1–4.

We now build these operators in PROLOG. As just noted, we use the list primitives:

1. **empty_stack([ ])**. This predicate can be used either to test a stack to see whether it is empty or to generate a new empty stack.

2–4. **stack(Top, Stack, [Top|Stack])**. This predicate performs the **push, pop,** and **peek** predicates depending on the variable bindings of its arguments. For instance, **push** produces a new stack as the third argument when the first two arguments are bound. Likewise, **pop** produces the next element of the stack when the third argument is bound to the original stack. Furthermore, the second argument will then be bound to the new stack, once the top element is popped. Finally, if we keep the stack as the third argument, the first argument lets us peek at its top element.

5. **member_stack(Element, Stack) :- member(Element,Stack)**. This allows us to determine whether an element is a member of the stack. Of course, the same result could be produced by creating a recursive call that peeked at the next element of the stack and then, if this element did not match **Element**, popped the stack. This would continue until the empty stack predicate was **true**.

6. **add_list_to_stack(List,Stack,Result) :- append(List,Stack,Result)**. This adds **List** to **Stack** to produce **Result**, a new stack. Of course, the same result could be obtained by popping **List** and pushing each element onto a temporary stack until empty stack is true of **List**. We then pop the temporary stack and push each element onto the **Stack** until empty stack is true of the temporary stack. **append** is described in detail in Section 6.6.

A final predicate for printing a stack in reverse order is **reverse_print_stack**. This is very useful when a stack has, in reversed order, the current path from the start state to the present state of the graph search. We see several examples of this in the next subsections.

```
reverse_print_stack(S) :-
    empty_stack(S).
reverse_print_stack(S) :-
    stack(E, Rest, S),
    reverse_print_stack(Rest),
    write(E), nl.
```

6.2.2   The ADT Queue

A queue is a first-in-first-out (FIFO) data structure. It is often characterized as a list where elements are taken off (dequeued) from one end and added to (enqueued) at the other end. The queue was used for defining breadth-first search in Chapters 3 and 4. The queue operators are:

1. empty_queue([ ]). This predicate either tests whether a queue is empty or initializes a new empty queue.

2. enqueue(E,[ ],[E]).
   enqueue(E,[H|T],[H|Tnew]) :- enqueue(E,T,Tnew). This recursive predicate adds the element E to a queue, the second argument. The new augmented queue is the third argument.

3. dequeue(E,[E|T],T). This predicate produces a new queue, the third argument, that is the result of taking the next element, the first argument, off the original queue, the second argument.

4. dequeue(E,[E|T], _). This predicate lets us peek at the next element, E, of the queue.

5. member(Element,Queue). This allows us to determine whether Element is a member of Queue.

6. add_list_to_queue(List,Queue,Newqueue) :-
   append(Queue,List,Newqueue). This lets us enqueue an entire list of elements.

Of course, 5 and 6 can be created using only 1–4; append is presented in Section 6.6.

6.2.3 The ADT Priority Queue

A priority queue orders the elements of a regular queue so that each new entrant to the priority queue is placed in its sorted order. The dequeue operator removes the "best" sorted element from the priority queue. We used the priority queue in the design of best-first search in Chapter 4.

Because the priority queue is a sorted queue, many of its operators are the same as the queue operators, in particular, empty_queue, member_queue, dequeue (the "best" of the sorted elements will be next for the dequeue), and peek. We will call enqueue in a priority queue the insert_pq operator, as each new item must be placed in its proper sorted order.

```
insert_pq(State,[ ],[State]).
insert_pq(State,[H|Tail],[State,H|Tail]):-
    precedes(State,H).
insert_pq(State,[H|T],[H|Tnew]):-
    insert_pq(State,T,Tnew).
```

The first argument of this predicate is the new element that is to be inserted. The second argument is the previous priority queue, and the third argument is the augmented priority queue. The precedes predicate that checks the order of elements is defined by the application.

Another useful priority queue operator is insert_list_pq. This predicate may be used to merge an unsorted list or set of elements into the priority queue, as is necessary when adding the children of a state to the priority queue for best-first search (see Section 6.4.4). insert_list_pq uses insert_pq to put each individual new item into the priority queue:

```
insert_list_pq([], L, L).
insert_list_pq([State|Tail], L, New_L) :-
    insert_pq(State, L, L2),
    insert_list_pq(Tail, L2, New_L).
```

6.2.4   The ADT Set

Finally, we describe the ADT set. A set is a collection of elements with no element repeated. Sets can be used for collecting all the children of a state or for maintaining **closed** in a search algorithm, as in Chapters 3 and 4. The set operators include empty_set, member, delete_if_in, and add_if_not_in. We also have operators for combining and comparing sets: union, intersection, set_difference, subset, and equal_set.

```
empty_set([]).


member_set(E,S) :-
    member(E,S).


delete_if_in_set(E,[],[]).
delete_if_in_set(E,[E|T],T) :- !.
delete_if_in_set(E,[H|T],[H|T_new]) :-
    delete_if_in_set(E,T,T_new), !.


add_if_not_in_set(X,S,S) :-
    member(X,S), !.
add_if_not_in_set(X,S,[X|S]).



intersection([],_,[]).
intersection([H|T],S,[H|S_new]) :-
    member_set(H,S),
    intersection(T,S,S_new), !.
intersection([_|T],S,S_new) :-
    intersection(T,S,S_new), !.


union([],S,S).
union([H|T],S,S_new) :-
    union(T,S,S2),
    add_if_not_in_set(H,S2,S_new).


subset([],_).
subset([H|T],S) :-
    member_set(H,S),
    subset(T,S).
```

```
set_diff([],_,[]).
set_diff([H|T],S,T_new) :-
    member_set(H,S),
    set_diff(T,S,T_new), !.
set_diff([H|T],S,[H|T_new]) :-
    set_diff(T,S,T_new), !.



equal_set(S1,S2) :-
    subset(S1,S2),
    subset(S2,S1).
```

6.3   A Production System Example in PROLOG

In this section we write a production system solution to the farmer, wolf, goat, and cabbage problem. This problem is stated as follows:

> A farmer with his wolf, goat, and cabbage come to the edge of a river they wish to cross. There is a boat at the river's edge, but, of course, only the farmer can row. The boat also can carry only two things (including the rower) at a time. If the wolf is ever left alone with the goat, the wolf will eat the goat; similarly, if the goat is left alone with the cabbage, the goat will eat the cabbage. Devise a sequence of crossings of the river so that all four characters arrive safely on the other side of the river.

In the next paragraphs we present a production system solution to this problem. First, we observe that the problem may be represented as a search through a graph. To do this we consider the possible moves that might be available at any time in the solution process. Some of these moves are eventually ruled out because they produce states that are unsafe (something will be eaten).

For the moment, suppose that all states are safe, and simply consider the graph of possible states. The boat can be used in four ways: to carry the farmer and wolf, the farmer and goat, the farmer and cabbage, and the farmer alone. A state of the world is some combination of the characters on the two banks. Several states of the search are represented in Figure 6.1. States of the world are represented using a predicate, state(F, W, G, C), with the location of the farmer as first parameter, location of the wolf as second parameter, the goat as third, and the cabbage as fourth. We assume that the river runs "north to south" and that the characters are on either the east, e, or west, w, bank. Thus, state(w, w, w, w) has all characters on the west bank to start the problem.

It must be pointed out that these choices are conventions that have been arbitrarily chosen by the authors. Indeed, as researchers in AI continually point out, the selection of an appropriate representation is often the most critical aspect of problem solving. These conventions are selected to fit the predicate calculus representation in PROLOG. Different states of the world are created by different crossings of the river, represented by changes in the values of the parameters of the state predicate (Figure 6.1). Other representations are certainly possible.

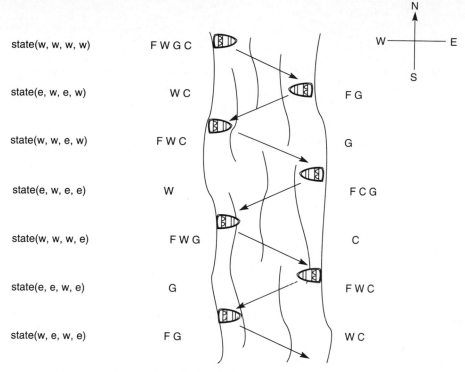

state(w, w, w, w)   F W G C

state(e, w, e, w)   W C   F G

state(w, w, e, w)   F W C   G

state(e, w, e, e)   W   F C G

state(w, w, w, e)   F W G   C

state(e, e, w, e)   G   F W C

state(w, e, w, e)   F G   W C

Figure 6.1   Sample crossings for the farmer, wolf, goat, and cabbage problem.

We now describe a general graph for this river-crossing problem. For the time being, we ignore the fact that some states are unsafe. In Figure 6.2 we see the beginning of the graph of possible moves back and forth across the river. Note that in this graph it is not necessary to have a separate representation for the location of the boat (why?). Figure 6.2 represents part of the graph that is to be searched for a solution path.

The recursive **path** call previously described provides the control mechanism for the production system search. The production rules are the rules for changing state in the search. We define these as **move** rules in PROLOG form.

Because PROLOG uses Horn clauses, a production system designed in PROLOG must either represent production rules directly in Horn clause form or translate rules to this format. We take the former option here and the latter in Section 12.2. Horn clauses require that the pattern for the present state and the pattern for the next state both be placed in the head of the Horn clause (or to the left of :-). These are the arguments to the **move** predicate. The conditions that the production rule requires to fire (and return the next state) are placed to the right of :- . As shown in the following example, these conditions are also expressed as unification constraints.

The first rule we define is for the farmer to take the wolf across the river. This rule must account for both the transfer from east to west and the transfer from west to east, and

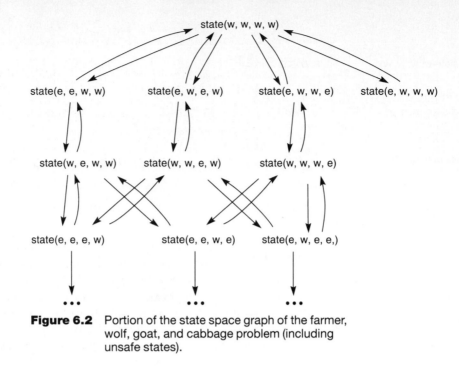

Figure 6.2 Portion of the state space graph of the farmer, wolf, goat, and cabbage problem (including unsafe states).

it must not be applicable when the farmer and wolf are on opposite sides of the river. Thus, it must transform state(e,e,G,C) to state(w,w,G,C) and state(w,w,G,C) to state(e,e,G,C). It must also fail for state(e,w,G,C) and state(w,e,G,C). The variables G and C represent the fact that the third and fourth parameters can be bound to either e or w. Whatever their values, they remain the same after the move of the farmer and wolf. Some of the states produced may indeed be "unsafe."

The following move rule operates only when the farmer and wolf are in the same location and takes them to the opposite side of the river. Note that the goat and cabbage do not change their present location (whatever it might be).

```
move(state(X,X,G,C), state(Y,Y,G,C)) :- opp(X,Y).


opp(e,w).
opp(w,e).
```

This rule fires when a state (the present location in the graph) is presented to the first parameter of move in which the farmer and wolf are at the same location. When the rule fires, a new state, the second parameter of move, is produced with the value of X opposite, opp, the value of Y. Two conditions are satisfied to produce the new state: first, that the values of the first two parameters are the same and, second, that their new location is opposite the old.

The first condition was checked implicitly in the unification process, in that move is not even called unless the first two parameters are the same. This test may be done explicitly by using the following rule:

```
move(state(F,W,G,C), state(Z,Z,G,C)) :- F = W, opp(F,Z).
```

This equivalent move rule first tests whether F and W are the same and, only if they are, assigns the opposite value of F to Z. Note that the closest that PROLOG comes to "assignment" is through the binding of variable values in unification. Bindings are shared by all occurrences of a variable in a clause, and the scope of a variable is limited to the clause in which it occurs.

Pattern matching, a powerful tool in AI programming, is especially important in pruning search. States that do not fit the patterns in the rule are automatically pruned. In this sense, the first version of the move rule presented is a more efficient representation, because unification does not even consider the clause if the first two parameters are not identical.

Next, we create a predicate to test whether each new state is safe, so that nothing is eaten in the process of getting across the river. Again, unification plays an important role in this definition. Any state where the second and third parameters are the same and opposite the first parameter is unsafe; the wolf eats the goat. Alternatively, if the third and fourth parameters are the same and opposite the first parameter, the state is unsafe: the goat eats the cabbage.

These unsafe situations may be represented with the following rules.

```
unsafe(state(X,Y,Y,C)) :- opp(X,Y).
unsafe(state(X,W,Y,Y)) :- opp(X,Y).
```

Several points should be mentioned here. First, if a state is to be not unsafe (i.e., safe), according to the definition of not in PROLOG, neither of these unsafe predicates can be true. Thus, both of these predicates must not unify with the current state or, if they do unify, their conditions must not be satisfied. Second, not in PROLOG is not exactly equivalent to the logical ¬ of the first-order predicate calculus; not is rather "negation by failure of its opposite." The reader should test a number of states to verify that unsafe does what it is intended to do.

Now, a not unsafe test may be added to the previous production rule:

```
move(state(X,X,G,C), state(Y,Y,G,C))
            :- opp(X,Y), not(unsafe(state(Y,Y,G,C))).
```

The not unsafe test calls unsafe, as mentioned above, to see whether the generated state is an acceptable new state in the search. When all criteria are met, including the check in the path algorithm that the new state is not a member of the visited-state list, path is (recursively) called on this state to go deeper into the graph. When path is called, the new state is added to the visited-state list.

In a similar fashion, we can create the three other production rules to represent the farmer taking the goat, cabbage, and himself across the river. We have added a writelist command to each production rule to print a trace of the current rule.

The reverse_print_stack command is used in the terminating condition of path to print out the final solution path. Finally, we add a fifth "pseudorule" that always fires, because no conditions are placed on it, when all previous rules have failed; it indicates that the path call is backtracking from the current state, and then it itself fails. This pseudorule is added only to assist the user in seeing what is going on as the production system is running.

We now present the full production system program in PROLOG to solve the farmer, wolf, goat, and cabbage problem. The PROLOG stack predicates may be found in Section 6.2.1:

```
move(state(X,X,G,C), state(Y,Y,G,C)) :-
 opp(X,Y), not(unsafe(state(Y,Y,G,C))),
 writelist(['try farmer takes wolf',Y,Y,G,C]).


move(state(X,W,X,C), state(Y,W,Y,C)) :-
 opp(X,Y), not(unsafe(state(Y,W,Y,C))),
 writelist(['try farmer takes goat',Y,W,Y,C]).


move(state(X,W,G,X), state(Y,W,G,Y)) :-
 opp(X,Y), not(unsafe(state(Y,W,G,Y))),
 writelist(['try farmer takes cabbage',Y,W,G,Y]).


move(state(X,W,G,C), state(Y,W,G,C)) :-
 opp(X,Y), not(unsafe(state(Y,W,G,C))),
 writelist(['try farmer takes self',Y,W,G,C]).


move(state(F,W,G,C), state(F,W,G,C)) :-
 writelist(['    BACKTRACK from:',F,W,G,C]), fail.


path(Goal, Goal, Been_stack) :-
 write('Solution Path Is: '), nl,
 reverse_print_stack(Been_stack).


path(State, Goal, Been_stack) :-
 move(State,Next_state),
 not(member_stack(Next_state, Been_stack)),
 stack(Next_state, Been_stack, New_been_stack),
 path(Next_state, Goal, New_been_stack), !.
```

path(_, _, _) :- write('No solution found with the given moves!').

opp(e,w).
opp(w,e).

We now present a trace of program execution. The code is called by requesting go, which initializes the recursive path call. For easier input, we present a predicate, test, that may be used to make repeated testing easier:

```
go(Start, Goal) :-
    empty_stack(Empty_been_stack),
    stack(Start, Empty_been_stack, Been_stack),
    path(Start, Goal, Been_stack).


test :- go(state(w,w,w,w), state(e,e,e,e)).
```

The algorithm backtracks from states that allow no further progress. You may also use trace to monitor the various variable bindings local to each call of path. It may also be noted that this program is a general program for moving the four creatures from any (legal) position on the banks to any other (legal) position, including asking for a path from the goal back to the start state. Several other interesting features of production systems, including the fact that different orderings of the rules can produce different searches through the graph, are presented in the exercises. A trace of the execution of the program is:

```
?- test.
try farmer takes goat e w e w
try farmer takes self w w e w
try farmer takes wolf e e e w
try farmer takes goat w e w w
try farmer takes cabbage e e w e
try farmer takes wolf w w w e
try farmer takes goat e w e e
    BACKTRACK from e,w,e,e
    BACKTRACK from w,w,w,e
try farmer takes self w e w e
try farmer takes goat e e e e
Solution Path Is:
state(w,w,w,w)
state(e,w,e,w)
state(w,w,e,w)
state(e,e,e,w)
state(w,e,w,w)
state(e,e,w,e)
state(w,e,w,e)
state(e,e,e,e)
```

In summary, this PROLOG program implements a production system solution to the farmer, wolf, goat, and cabbage problem. The move rules make up the content of the production memory. The working memory is represented by the arguments of the path call. The production system control mechanism is defined by the recursive path call. We show how this control may be altered in the next subsections. Finally, the ordering of rules for generation of children from each state (conflict resolution) is determined by the order in which the rules are placed in the production memory.

6.4   Designing Alternative Search Strategies

As the previous subsection demonstrated, and as is made more precise in Section 13.3, PROLOG itself uses depth-first search with backtracking. We now show how the alternative search strategies of Chapters 3, 4, and 5 can be implemented in PROLOG. Our implementations of breadth-first and best-first search use open and closed lists to record states in the search. When search fails at any point we do not go back to the preceding values of open and closed, as found on the stack. Instead, open and closed are updated within the path call and the search continues with these new values. The cut is used to keep PROLOG from storing the old versions of open and closed.

6.4.1   Depth-First Search Using the Closed List

Because the values of variables are restored when recursion backtracks, the list of visited states in the depth-first path algorithm records states only on the current path to the goal. Although the test for membership in this list prevents loops, it still allows branches of the space to be reexamined if they are reached along paths generated earlier but abandoned as unfruitful. A more efficient implementation would keep track of all the states that have ever been encountered. This more complete collection of states made up the list called closed in Chapter 3.

closed holds all states on the current path plus the states that were rejected when we backtracked out of them; thus, it no longer represents the path from the start to the current state. We now present a shell structure for depth-first search in PROLOG, keeping track of closed and checking each new state to be sure it was not previously visited. path has four arguments, the Open_stack, Closed_set (maintained as a set), a Path_stack (the path from the start to the present state), and the Goal state. The current state, Top, is the next state on the Open_stack. The stack and set operators are found in Section 6.2. We assume a set of move rules according to the application:

```
move(Present, Next_state) :- ...                    % test first rule.
move(Present, Next_state) :- ...                    % test second rule.
    ....
    ....
```

```
path(Open_stack, _, _) :-
    stack_empty(Open_stack),
    write('No solution found with these rules').


path(Open_stack, Closed_set, Path_stack, Goal) :-
    stack(Top, _, Open_stack), Top = Goal,
    write('A Solution Is Found!'),
    reverse_print_stack(Path_stack).


path(Open_stack, Closed_set, Path_stack, Goal) :-
    stack(Top, Rest_open_stack, Open_stack),
    move(Top, Next_state),
    not(member_stack(Next_state, Open_stack)),
    not(member_set(Next_state, Closed_set)),
    stack(Next_state, Rest_open_stack, New_open_stack),
    stack(Next_state, Path_stack, New_path_stack),
    add_if_not_in_set(Next_state, Closed_set, New_closed_set),
    path(New_open_stack, New_closed_set, Path_stack, Goal), !.
```

The first path call terminates search when the Open_stack is empty, which means there are no more states on open to continue the search. This usually indicates that the graph has been exhaustively searched. The search is started by a go predicate that initializes the path call:

```
go(Start, Goal) :-
    empty_stack(Open), empty_stack(Path),
    empty_set(Closed),
    stack(Start, Open, Open_stack),
    stack(Start, Path, Path_stack),
    add_if_not_in_set(Start, Closed, Closed_set),
    path(Open_stack, Closed_set, Path_stack, Goal).
```

6.4.2 Breadth-First Search in PROLOG

We now present the *shell* of an algorithm for breadth-first search using explicit open and closed lists. The shell can be used with the move rules for any search problem. This algorithm is called by:

```
go(Start, Goal) :-
    empty_queue(Empty_open_queue),
    add_to_queue([Start, nil], Empty_open_queue, Open_queue),
    empty_set(Closed_set),
    path(Open_queue, Closed_set, Goal).
```

Start and Goal have their obvious values. We create the ordered pair [State, Parent] to keep track of each state and its parent; the Start state is represented by [Start, nil]. This will be used to re-create the solution path from the Closed_set. The first parameter of path is the Open_queue, the second is the Closed_set, and the third is the Goal. *Don't care* variables, those whose values are not used in a clause, are written as _.

```
path(Open_queue, _, _) :-
    empty_queue(Open_queue),
    write('Graph searched, no solution found.').

path(Open_queue, Closed_set, Goal) :-
    dequeue([State, Parent],Open_queue,_),
    State = Goal,
    write('Solution path is: '), nl,
    printsolution([State, Parent],Closed).

path(Open_queue, Closed_set, Goal) :-
    dequeue([State, Parent],Open_queue, Rest_open_queue),
    get_children(State, Rest_open_queue, Closed_set, Children),
    add_list_to_queue(Children, Rest_open_queue, New_open_queue),
    union([[State, Parent]], Closed_set, New_closed_set),
    path(New_open_queue, New_closed_set, Goal), !.

get_children(State, Rest_open_queue, Closed_set, Children) :-
    bagof(Child, moves(State, Rest_open_queue,
        Closed_set, Child), Children).

moves(State, Rest_open_queue, Closed_set, [Next,State]) :-
    move(State,Next),
    not(unsafe(Next)),                              % test depends on problem
    not(member_queue([Next,_], Rest_open_queue)),
    not(member_set([Next,_], Closed_set)).

printsolution([State, nil], _) :-
    write(State), nl.

printsolution([State, Parent], Closed_set) :-
    member_set([Parent, Grandparent], Closed_set),
    printsolution([Parent, Grandparent], Closed_set),
    write(State), nl.
```

The algorithm is a shell in that no move rules are given. These must be supplied to fit the specific problem domain. The queue and set operators are found in Section 6.2.

The first termination condition is defined for the case that path is called with its first argument, Open_queue, empty. This happens only when no more states in the graph remain to be searched and the solution has not been found. A successful solution is found in the second termination condition when the head of open and the goal state are identical. A useful debugging aid is to print open and closed after each call to path to watch the progress of the search.

The algorithm uses bagof, a PROLOG predicate standard to most interpreters. bagof lets us gather all the unifications of a pattern into a single list. The second parameter to bagof is the pattern to be matched in the data base. The first parameter specifies the components of the second parameter that we wish to collect. For example, we may be interested in the values bound to a single variable of a predicate. All bindings of the first parameter resulting from these matches are collected in a list and bound to the third parameter.

In this program, bagof collects the states reached by firing *all* of the enabled production rules. Of course, this is necessary to gather all descendants of a particular state so that we can add them, in proper order, to open. The second argument of bagof, a new predicate named moves, calls the move predicates to generate all the states that may be reached using the production rules. The arguments to moves are the present state, the open list, the closed list, and a variable that is the state reached by a good move. Before returning this state, moves checks that the state is not a member of either open or closed. bagof calls moves and collects all the states that meet these conditions. The third argument of bagof thus represents the new states that are placed on the Open_queue.

In some implementations, bagof fails when no matches exist for the second argument and thus the third argument is empty. This can be remedied by substituting (bagof(X, moves(S,T,C,X), List); List = [ ]) for the current calls to bagof in the code.

6.4.3   Best-First Search in PROLOG

Our shell for best-first search is a modification of the breadth-first algorithm in which the open queue is replaced by a priority queue, ordered by heuristic merit, for each new call to path.

In our algorithm, we attach a heuristic measure permanently to each new state on open and use this measure for ordering states on open. We also retain the parent of each state. This information is used by printsolution to build the solution path once the goal is found.

Thus each state is represented as a list of five elements: the state description, the parent of the state, an integer giving the depth in the graph of its discovery, an integer giving the heuristic measure of the state, and the integer sum of the third and fourth elements. The first and second elements are found in the usual way; the third is determined by adding one to the depth of its parent; the fourth is determined by the heuristic measure of the particular problem. The fifth element, eventually used for ordering the states on the open_pq, is $f(n) = g(n) + h(n)$, as presented in Chapter 4.

As before, the move rules are not specified; they are defined to fit the specific problem. The ADT operators for set and priority queue are presented in Section 6.2. heuristic, also specific to each problem, is a measure applied to each state to determine its heuristic weight, the value of the fourth parameter in its descriptive list.

This algorithm, as with breadth-first search above, has two termination conditions. The algorithm is called by:

```
go(Start, Goal) :-
    empty_set(Closed_set),
    empty_pq(Open),
    heuristic(Start, Goal, H),
    insert_pq([Start, nil, 0, H, H], Open, Open_pq),
    path(Open_pq, Closed_set, Goal).
```

nil is the parent of Start and H is the heuristic evaluation of Start. The code for best-first search is:

```
path(Open,_,_) :-
    empty_pq(Open),
    write('Graph searched, no solution found.').


path(Open_pq, Closed_set, Goal) :-
    dequeue_pq([State,Parent,_,_,_], Open_pq, _),
    State = Goal,
    write('The solution path is: '), nl,
    printsolution([State,Parent,_,_,_], Closed_set).


path(Open_pq, Closed_set, Goal) :-
    dequeue_pq([State, Parent, D, H, S], Open_pq,Rest_open_pq),
    get_children([State, Parent, D, H, S], Rest_open_pq, Closed_set, Children, Goal),
    insert_list_pq(Children, Rest_open_pq, New_open_pq),
    add_if_not_in_set([State, Parent, D, H, S], Closed_set, New_closed_set),
    path(New_open_pq, New_closed_set, Goal), !.
```

get_children is a predicate that generates all the children of State. It uses bagof and moves predicates as in breadth-first search. Details are found in Section 6.4.3. Move rules, a safe check for legal moves, and a heuristic must be specifically defined for each application.

```
get_children([State,_,D,_,_],Rest_open_pq,Closed_set,Children,Goal):-
    bagof(Child, moves([State,_,D,_,_], Rest_open_pq,
    Closed_set, Child, Goal), Children).


moves([State,_,Depth,_,_], Rest_open_pq, Closed_set,
        [Next, State, New_D, H, S], Goal) :-
    move(State, Next),
    not(unsafe(Next)),                          % determined by application
    not(member_pq([Next,_,_,_,_], Rest_open_pq)),
    not(member_set([Next,_,_,_,_], Closed_set)),
    New_D is Depth + 1,
    heuristic(Next, Goal, H),                    % determined by application
    S is New_D + H.
```

Finally, printsolution prints the solution path. It recursively finds State Parent pairs by matching the first two elements in the state description with all the descriptions in the Closed_set. The start state has nil as its parent.

```
printsolution([State,nil,_,_,_],_) :-
    write(State), nl.
```

```
printsolution([State,Parent, _,_,_], Closed_set) :-
    member_set([Parent,Grandparent,_,_,_], Closed_set),
    printsolution([Parent,Grandparent,_,_,_], Closed_set),
    write(State), nl.
```

6.5   A PROLOG Planner

In Section 5.4 we described a predicate calculus–based planning algorithm. It was predicate calculus (PC) based in that the PC representation was chosen for both the state of the
planning world descriptions as well as the change of state rules. In this section we create a
PROLOG version of that algorithm.

We represent the states of the world, including the begin and goal states, as lists of
predicates. Two states, the start and goal states for our example, are described:

```
start = [handempty, ontable(b), ontable(c), on(a,b), clear(c), clear(a)]
goal = [handempty, ontable(c), on(a,b), on(b,c), clear(a)]
```

These states are seen, along with a portion of the search space, in Figures 6.3 and 6.4.

The moves in this world are described using add and delete lists, as in Section 5.4.
Four of the moves within this world may be described:

```
move(pickup(X),[handempty, clear(X), on(X,Y)],
    [del(handempty), del(clear(X)), del(on(X,Y)),
    add(clear(Y)), add(holding(X))]).

move(pickup(X), [handempty, clear(X), ontable(X)],
    [del(handempty), del(clear(X)), del(ontable(X)),
    add(holding(X))]).

move(putdown(X), [holding(X)],
    [del(holding(X)), add(ontable(X)),
    add(clear(X)), add(handempty)]).

move(stack(X, Y), [holding(X), clear(Y)],
    [del(holding(X)), del(clear(Y)), add(handempty),
    add(on(X,Y)), add(clear(X))]).
```

The move predicates have three arguments. First is the move predicate name with its arguments. The second argument is the list of preconditions: the predicates that must be true in
the description of the state of the world for the move rule to be applied to that state. The
third argument is the add and delete list: the predicates that are added to and deleted from
the state of the world to create the new state of the world that results from applying the
move rule. Notice how useful the ADT set operators of union, intersection, set difference,
etc., will be in manipulating the preconditions and the add and delete lists.

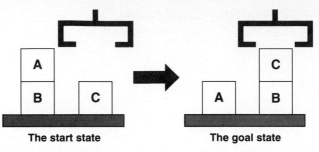

The start state   **The goal state**

Figure 6.3   The start and goal states for the blocks world problem.

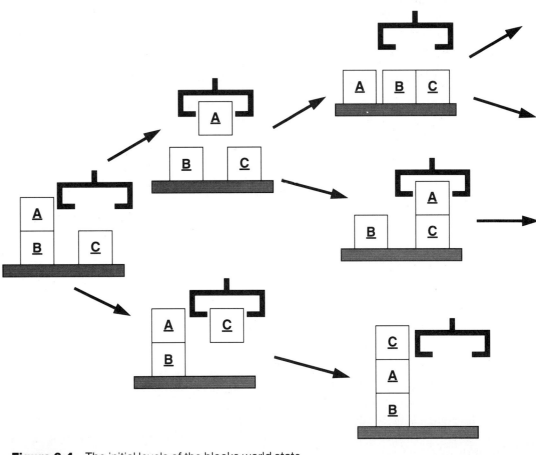

Figure 6.4   The initial levels of the blocks world state space.

Finally, we have the recursive controller for the plan generation. The first plan predicate gives the successful termination conditions for the plan, namely, when the goal is produced. The final plan predicate states that after exhaustive search, no plan is possible. The recursive plan generator:

1. Searches for a move relationship.
2. Checks, using the subset operator, whether the state's Preconditions are met.
3. The change_state predicate produces a new Child_state using the add and delete list.
4. member_stack makes sure the new state has not been visited before.
5. The stack operator pushes the new Child_state onto the New_moves_stack.
6. The stack operator pushes the original Name state onto the New_been_stack.
7. The recursive plan call searches for the next state using the Child_state and an updated New_move_stack and Been_stack.

A number of supporting utilities, built on the stack and set ADTs (Sections 6.2.1 and 6.2.4) are included. Of course, the search, being stack based, is depth first with backtracking and terminates with the first path found to a goal. It is left as an exercise to build breadth-first and best-first planners.

```
plan(State, Goal, _, Move_stack) :-
    equal_set(State, Goal),
    write('moves are'), nl,
    reverse_print_stack(Move_stack).

plan(State, Goal, Been_stack, Move_stack) :-
    move(Name, Preconditions, Actions),
    conditions_met(Preconditions, State),
    change_state(State, Actions, Child_state),
    not(member_stack(Child_state, Been_stack)),
    stack(Name, Been_stack, New_been_stack),
    stack(Child_state, Move_stack, New_move_stack),
    plan(Child_state, Goal, New_been_stack, New_move_stack), !.

plan(_, _, _) :- write('No plan possible with these moves!').

conditions_met(P, S) :-
    subset(P, S).

change_state(S, [ ], S).
change_state(S, [add(P)|T], S_new) :-
    change_state(S, T, S2),
    add_if_not_in_set(P, S2, S_new), !.

change_state(S, [del(P)|T], S_new) :-
    change_state(S, T, S2),
    delete_if_in_set(P, S2, S_new), !.
```

```
reverse_print_stack(S) :-
    empty_stack(S).
reverse_print_stack(S) :-
    stack(E, Rest, S),
reverse_print_stack(Rest),
    write(E), nl.
```

Finally we create a go predicate to initialize the arguments for plan, as well as a test predicate to demonstrate an easy method to save repeated creation of the same input string.

```
go(Start,Goal) :-
    empty_stack(Move_stack)
    empty_stack(Been_stack),
    stack(Start, Been_stack, New_been_stack),
    plan(Start, Goal, New_been_stack, Move_stack).
```

```
test :-
    go([handempty,ontable(b),ontable(c), on(a,b),clear(c),clear(a)],
        [handempty,ontable(c),on(a,b), on(b,c),clear(a)]).
```

6.6   PROLOG: Toward a Nonprocedural Computing Language

In traditional computer languages such as FORTRAN and C, the logic for the problem's specification and the control for executing the solution algorithm are inextricably mixed together. A program in these languages is simply a sequence of things to be done to get an answer. This is the accepted notion of a *procedural* language.

One of the goals of the designers of PROLOG has been to separate the logic or specification for a problem from the execution of that specification. There are several reasons for this separation, not the least of which is the ability to determine after the specifications are created what might be the best control for executing them.

Another goal of this separation of logic from control is that each aspect of the problem may be analyzed separately. The specifications may themselves be translated to other specifications before execution. Specifications may be checked for correctness or otherwise evaluated independently of their execution.

In the future, it might even be possible to send a logic specification to a number of processors, where the number of processors and the distribution of the specification predicates among the processors are seen as a deterministic aspect of the specifications themselves.

Needless to say, PROLOG has not yet achieved this state of computing nirvana! It is still possible, however, to show how logic programming, as represented by the PROLOG language, exhibits some benefits of a nonprocedural semantics. How the interpreter achieves these features can be clearly understood only after the subsection on Horn clause resolution in Chapters 11 and 13. We now present several examples of the declarative nature of PROLOG.

For the first example consider the predicate **append**. This predicate is defined:

```
append([], L, L).
append([X|T], L, [X|NL]) :- append(T, L, NL).
```

append is nonprocedural in that it defines a relationship between lists rather than a series of operations for joining two lists. Consequently, different queries will cause it to compute different aspects of this relationship. We can understand **append** by tracing its execution in joining two lists together. If the following call is made:

```
?- append([a,b,c], [d,e], Y).
```

the response is:

```
Y = [a,b,c,d,e]
```

The execution of **append** is not tail recursive, in that the local variable values are accessed after the recursive call has succeeded. In this case, X is placed on the head of the list ([X|NL]) after the recursive call has finished. This requires that a record of each call be kept on the PROLOG stack. Here is the trace of **append** on the above query:

```
For purposes of reference in this trace:
    1 is append([], L, L).
    2 is append([X|T], L, [X|NL]) :- append(T, L, NL).

?- append([a,b,c], [d,e], Y).

    try match 1, fail [a, b, c] ≠ []
    match 2, X is a, T is [b, c], L is [d, e], call append([b, c], [d, e], NL)

        try match 1, fail [b, c] ≠ []
        match 2, X is b, T is [c], L is [d, e], call append([c], [d, e], NL)

            try match 1, fail [c] ≠ []
            match 2, X is c, T is [], L is [d,e], call append([], [d, e], NL)

                match 1, L is [d, e] (for BOTH parameters), yes

            yes, N is [d, e], [X|NL] is [c,d,e]

        yes, NL is [c, d, e], [X|NL] is [b, c, d, e]

    yes, NL is [b, c, d, e], [X|NL] is [a, b, c, d, e]

Y = [a, b, c, d, e], yes
```

In the PROLOG algorithms shown in this chapter, the parameters of the predicates seem to be intended as either "input" or "output"; most definitions assume that certain parameters would be bound in the call and others would be unbound. This need not be so. In fact, there is no commitment at all to parameters being input or output in PROLOG!

PROLOG code is intended to be simply a set of specifications of what is true, a statement of the logic of the situation. Thus, append specifies the relationship between three lists, such that the third list is the catenation of the first onto the front of the second.

To demonstrate this fact we can give append a different set of goals:

```
?- append([a,b], [c], [a,b,c]).
yes
?- append([a], [c], [a,b,c]).
no
```

We can also use an unbound variable for different parameters of the call to append:

```
?- append(X, [b,c], [a,b,c]).
X = [a]
?- append(X, Y, [a,b,c]).
X = []
Y = [a, b, c]
;
X = [a]
Y = [b, c]
;
X = [a, b]
Y = [c]
;
X = [a, b, c]
Y = []
;
no
```

In the last query, PROLOG returns all the lists X and Y that, appended together, give [a, b, c]—four pairs of lists in all. As mentioned above, append is a statement of the logic of a relationship among three lists. What the interpreter produces depends on the specific query it is given.

Our second example of the nonprocedural nature of logic programming is a simple program that is both a parser and a generator of sentences. We selected this example both to demonstrate nonprocedurality and to show a common method of parsing and generating sentences using PROLOG. This is also a direct implementation of the "parser" in the applications section of Chapter 3 and a precursor of parsing and grammars in Chapter 10.

Consider the subset of English grammar rules below. These rules are nonprocedural in that they simply define relationships among parts of speech. With this subset of rules a large number of simple sentences can be judged as well formed or not.

```
Sentence ↔ NounPhrase VerbPhrase
NounPhrase ↔ Noun
```

NounPhrase ↔ Article Noun
VerbPhrase ↔ Verb
VerbPhrase ↔ Verb NounPhrase

Adding some vocabulary to the grammar rules:

Article(a)
Article(the)
Noun(man)
Noun(dog)
Verb(likes)
Verb(bites)

The parse tree of a simple sentence ("the man bites the dog") is shown in Figure 6.5.
The specification rules of the grammar are transcribed into PROLOG rules in a natural fashion. For example, a **sentence** is a **nounphrase** and a **verbphrase**. This is represented as the PROLOG rule:

sentence(Start, End) :- nounphrase(Start, Rest), verbphrase(Rest, End).

Each PROLOG rule takes two parameters. The first is a sequence of words in list form. The rule attempts to determine whether some initial part of the list is a legal part of speech. Any remaining suffix of the list not parsed will match the second parameter. Thus, we are implementing a left-to-right parse of the sentence. If the sentence rule succeeds, the second parameter of **sentence** will have the value of what remains after the **nounphrase** and

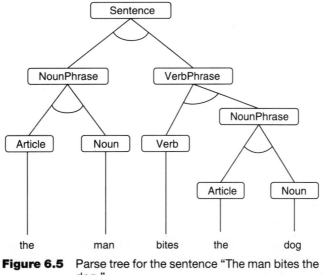

Figure 6.5   Parse tree for the sentence "The man bites the dog."

verbphrase parse; if the list is a correct sentence, this is []. The two alternative forms of noun phrases and verb phrases are similarly defined.

The sentence itself, for simplicity, is cast as a list: [the,man,likes, the,dog]. The list is now broken up and passed to the various grammar rules to be examined for syntactic correctness. Note how the "pattern matching" works on the list in question: pulling off the head, or the head and second element; passing on what is left over; and so on.

The complete grammar is defined below. The utterance predicate takes the list to be parsed as its argument and calls the sentence rule. It initializes the second parameter of sentence to [], indicating that nothing should remain in the list after a successful parse.

```
utterance(X) :- sentence(X,[]).

sentence(Start, End) :- nounphrase(Start, Rest), verbphrase(Rest, End).

nounphrase([Noun|End], End) :- noun(Noun).
nounphrase([Article, Noun|End], End) :- article(Article), noun(Noun).

verbphrase([Verb|End], End) :- verb(Verb).
verbphrase([Verb|Rest], End) :- verb(Verb), nounphrase(Rest, End).

article(a).
article(the).
noun(man).
noun(dog).
verb(likes).
verb(bites).
```

Example sentences may be tested for well-formedness:

```
?- utterance([the,man,bites,the,dog]).
yes
?- utterance([the,man,bites,the]).
no
```

New, partial sentences may be proposed and the interpreter asked to fill in potential remaining words so that the sentence is syntactically correct:

```
?- utterance([the,man,likes,X]).
X = man
;
X = dog
;
no
```

PROLOG finds all legitimate ways in which the sentence may be concluded!

Finally, the same code may be used to generate the set of all well-formed sentences using this limited dictionary and set of grammar rules:

```
?- utterance(X).
[man, likes]
;
[man, bites]
;
[man, likes, man]
;
[man, likes, dog]
etc.
```

If the user continues asking for more solutions, eventually all possible well-formed sentences that can be generated from the grammar rules and our vocabulary are returned as values for X. Note that the PROLOG search is left to right and depth-first.

The grammar rules are the specification set for well-formedness of expressions in this subset of legitimate sentences of English. The PROLOG code represents this set of logic specifications. The interpreter is asked questions about this set of specifications. Thus, the answer is a function of the specifications and the question asked. This is a major advantage of computing with a language that is itself a theorem prover operating on specifications! Further details on PROLOG as a theorem prover are provided in Chapter 13.

The previous example can be extended in a straightforward fashion. Suppose we desire to have proper noun-verb agreement in sentences. In the dictionary entry for each word its singular or plural form can be noted as such. Then in the grammar specifications for nounphrase and verbphrase a further parameter can be entered to signify the number of each phrase. Thus, a singular noun has to be associated with a singular verb.

This modification increases the power of the grammar considerably. Whereas the first version implemented a context-free grammar, this version implements a context-sensitive grammar (Chapter 10). It retains the contextual information needed to check number agreement. These additions are made to the previous code:

```
utterance(X) :- sentence(X, []).

sentence(Start, End) :- nounphrase(Start, Rest, Number),
    verbphrase(Rest, End, Number).

nounphrase([Noun|End], End, Number) :- noun(Noun, Number).
nounphrase([Article, Noun|End], End, Number) :- noun(Noun, Number),
        article(Article, Number).

verbphrase([Verb|End], End, Number) :- verb(Verb, Number).
verbphrase([Verb|Rest], End, Number) :- verb(Verb, Number),
        nounphrase(Rest, End, _).

article(a, singular).
article(these, plural).
article(the, singular).
article(the, plural).
```

```
noun(man, singular).
noun(men, plural).
noun(dog, singular).
noun(dogs, plural).
verb(likes, singular).
verb(like, plural).
verb(bites, singular).
verb(bite, plural).
```

New sentences may now be tested:

```
?- utterance([the,men,like,the,dog]).
yes
?- utterance([the,men,likes,the,dog]).
no
```

The answer to the second query is no, because the subject (men) and the verb (likes) do not agree in number. If we enter the goal:

```
?- utterance([the,men|X]).
```

X returns all well-formed verb phrases for completing the sentence "the men. . ." with noun-verb number agreement! As before, we may request all legitimate sentences, according to the grammar and dictionary:

```
?- utterance(X).
```

The present example uses the parameters on dictionary entries to introduce more information on the meanings in the sentence. This approach may be generalized to a powerful parser for natural language. More and more information may be included in the dictionary about the items described in the sentences, implementing a knowledge base of the meaning of English words. For example, men are animate and human. Similarly, dogs may be described as animate and nonhuman. With these descriptions new rules may be added for parsing, such as "humans do not bite animate nonhumans" to eliminate sentences such as [the,man,bites,the,dog]. If the nonhuman is no longer animate, of course, it might be eaten in a restaurant! These ideas are developed further in Chapters 9, 10, and 13.

Semantic networks and other representational formalisms of this sort have played an important role in artificial intelligence research. These topics are seen again in some detail in Chapters 9, 13, and 14.

6.7   Epilogue and References

PROLOG is a general-purpose language, and we ignored a great number of its important concepts because of the space limitations of our book. We recommend that the interested reader pursue some of the many excellent texts available, such as *Programming in PRO-*

LOG (Clocksin and Mellish 1984), *Computing with Logic* (Maier and Warren 1988), *The Art of PROLOG* (Sterling and Shapiro 1986), *The Craft of PROLOG* (O'Keefe 1990), or *Advanced PROLOG: Techniques and Examples* (Ross 1989).

We focused our introduction to PROLOG on developing the representation and search topics introduced in Chapters 2, 3, 4, and 5 of this text. The reader should do many of the exercises presented at the end of the chapter for exactly this reason.

The most important topic of this chapter, however, is the introduction of the language itself. The notion of solving a problem based on a set of specifications for correct relationships in a domain area coupled with the action of a theorem prover is exciting and important. Some say this way of casting a problem and its solution influenced the Japanese adoption of the concepts of logic programming, seen in PROLOG, as the core of their Fifth Generation project.

Of course, PROLOG is not a pure "nonprocedural" language. Such a language probably will not be created using computing architectures as they are currently known. However, the move that PROLOG offers toward a fully declarative specification language is important. Indeed, a strength of PROLOG interpreters is that they are open to a procedural as well as a declarative conceptualization (Kowalski 1979*b*). Thus a clause such as:

A :- B, C, D.

might in one instance be a specification logic:

A is true if B and C and D are true.

and in another instance be a procedure for doing something:

To accomplish A go out and first do B and then do C and finally do D.

This procedural interpretation lends representational flexibility to the PROLOG language.

How the PROLOG interpreter works cannot be properly understood without the concepts of resolution theorem proving, especially the Horn clause refutation process. This is presented in detail in Chapters 11 and 13.

The intellectual roots of PROLOG reside in the theoretical concepts of using logic for problem specification and solution. The main commentator on these issues is Robert Kowalski. Especially recommended are *Logic for Problem Solving* (Kowalski 1979*b*) and "Algorithm = logic + control" (Kowalski 1979*a*). Further references are found in the introduction to Part III.

6.8.   Exercises

1. Create a relational data base in PROLOG. Represent the data tuples as facts and the constraints on the data tuples as rules. Suitable examples might be from stock in a department store or records in a personnel office. For example, the facts may include the cost, supplier, part number, and amount in stock for each product sold. Constraints might include rules for when to reorder

items, the ability to calculate the total value of the inventory, and optimal reorder amounts for best price.

2. Write a PROLOG program to answer Wirth's "I am my own grandfather" problem (Chapter 2, Exercise 13).

3. Write the "member check" program in PROLOG. What happens when an item is not in the list? Form a query to the "member" specification that would cause it to break a list into all its component elements.

4. Design a PROLOG program unique(Bag,Set) that takes a Bag (a list that may contain duplicate elements) and returns a Set (no elements are repeated).

5. Write a PROLOG program to count the elements in a list (a list within the list counts as one element). Write a program to count the atoms in a list (count the elements within any sublist). (Hint: several meta-predicates such as atom() can be helpful.)

6. Write the PROLOG code for the farmer, wolf, goat, and cabbage problem.
   a. Execute this code and draw a graph of the search space.
   b. Alter the rule ordering to produce alternative solution paths.
   c. Use the shell in the text to produce a breadth-first solution.
   d. Describe a heuristic that might be appropriate for this problem.
   e. Build the heuristic search solution.

7. Do a to e as in Exercise 6 for the missionary and cannibal problem:

   > Three missionaries and three cannibals come to the bank of a river they wish to cross. There is a boat that will hold only two, and any of the group is able to row it. If there are ever more missionaries than cannibals on any side of the river the cannibals will get converted. Devise a series of moves to get all the people across the river with no conversions.

8. Use your code to check alternative forms of the missionary and cannibal problem—for example, when there are four missionaries and four cannibals and the boat holds only two. What if the boat can hold three? Try to generalize solutions for the whole class of missionary and cannibal problems.

9. Write PROLOG code to solve the full 8 × 8 knight's tour problem. Use the production system architecture proposed in this chapter and Chapter 5. Create the code so that you can get the program to solve a number of different tasks, such as getting from any one square to another. Do tasks a to e described with Exercise 6 above.

10. Do a to e as in Exercise 6 for the water jugs problem:

    > There are two jugs, one holding 3 and the other 5 gallons of water. A number of things can be done with the jugs: they can be filled, emptied, and dumped one into the other either until the poured-into jug is full or until the poured-out-of jug is empty. Devise a sequence of actions that will produce 4 gallons of water in the larger jug. (Hint: only integer values of water will be used.)

11. Use your explorations of Exercise 10 to create the full graph of the water jugs problem. Discuss this graph: which nodes can be reached from where, which are impossible states, and when can breadth-first search be an advantage?

12. Take the path algorithm presented for the knight's tour problem in the text. Rewrite the path call in the recursive code to the following form:

    path(X,Y) :- path(X,W), move(W,Y).

Examine the trace of this execution and describe what is happening. Can you generalize these results to the missionary and cannibal and water jugs problems?

13. Write the PROLOG code for a subset of English grammar rules, as in Section 6.6. Add:
    a. Adjectives and adverbs that can modify verbs and nouns, respectively.
    b. Prepositional phrases. (Can you do this with a recursive call?)
    c. Compound sentences (two sentences joined by a conjunction).

14. The simple natural language parser presented in this chapter will accept grammatically correct sentences that may not have a commonsense meaning, such as "the man bites the dog." These sentences may be eliminated from the grammar by augmenting the parser to include some notion of what is semantically plausible. Design a small "semantic network" in PROLOG (see comments in text) to allow you to reason about some aspect of the possible interpretations of the English grammar rules, such as when it is reasonable for "the man to bite the dog."

15. Write a program to pass values up to the top level of a game tree or graph:
    a. Using MIN-MAX.
    b. Using alpha-beta pruning of the tree.
    c. Using both of these on the game of tic-tac-toe.

16. Write a PROLOG program to build the search process for the financial advisor program that was used in Chapters 2–5. Use the production system architecture. Add several more advisory rules to make the program more interesting.

17. Complete the partition predicates in the following quicksort algorithm. Demonstrate the algorithm by (a) sorting a list and (b) sorting a list of predicates by their fourth argument. In quicksort, the second argument is the sorted first argument:

```
quicksort([X|Xs], Ys) :- partition(Xs, X, Small, Large),
    quicksort(Small, Ss),
    quicksort(Large, Ls),
    append(Ss, [X|Ls], Ys).


quicksort([], []).


partition([X|Xs], Y, [X|Ss], Ls) :- X <= Y, partition..........
partition([X|Xs], Y, Ss, [X|Ls]) :- X > Y, partition....
partition([], Y, [], []).
```

18. Finish and run the code for the planner of Section 6.5. Add the code for a situation that would require a new set of moves, such as adding a pyramid or sphere that could not be stacked on.

19. Design a breadth-first search planner for the planner of Section 6.5.

20. Add heuristics to the search of your planning algorithm. Can you specify a heuristic that is admissible?

21. Create a triangle table–like structure to use with your planner. Use it to save, and generalize, where possible, successful move sequences.

22. Create the full set of ADT predicates for the priority queue in Section 6.2.

23. Create a set of ADT predicates for bagof, like set, except that multiple copies of an element are allowed.

LISP

7.0 Introduction

For the 35 years of its existence, LISP has been the dominant language for artificial intelligence programming. Originally designed for symbolic computing, LISP has been extended and refined over its lifetime in direct response to the needs of AI programming. Like most traditional programming languages, LISP is *procedural*; LISP programs describe *how* to perform an algorithm. This contrasts with *declarative* languages such as PROLOG, whose programs are declarative assertions about a problem domain. However, unlike traditional procedural languages (FORTRAN, Pascal, etc.), LISP is *functional*: its syntax and semantics are derived from the mathematical theory of recursive functions. The power of functional programming, illustrated in the examples of this chapter, combined with a powerful set of high-level tools for building symbolic data structures, is largely responsible for LISP's popularity in the AI community.

In the early days of artificial intelligence, many programs were implemented directly in LISP, taking advantage of its built-in facilities for manipulating symbolic data structures.

In the early days of artificial intelligence, many programs were implemented directly in LISP, taking advantage of its built-in facilities for manipulating symbolic data structures. Later, as higher-level formalisms such as production systems, logic theorem provers, and rule-based expert systems emerged, LISP became a primary language for their implementation. Today, LISP continues to be used as a language for implementing AI tools and models, particularly in the research community, where its high-level functionality and rich development environment make it an ideal language for building and testing prototype systems.

In this chapter we introduce the syntax and semantics of Common LISP, with particular emphasis on the features of the language that make it useful for AI programming: the use of lists to create symbolic data structures and the implementation of interpreters and search algorithms to manipulate these structures. In Chapters 13 and 14 we use LISP to implement high-level tools including theorem provers, rule-based expert system shells, frames, semantic networks, and object-oriented programming languages. It is not our goal to provide a complete introduction to LISP; a number of excellent texts (see the epilogue to this chapter) do this in far greater detail than our space allows. Instead, we focus on using LISP to implement the representation languages and algorithms of artificial intelligence programming, especially those presented in Chapters 1–5.

7.1   LISP: A Brief Overview

7.1.1   Symbolic Expressions, the Syntactic Basis of LISP

The syntactic elements of the LISP programming language are *symbolic expressions*, also known as *s-expressions*. Both programs and data are represented as s-expressions. An s-expression may be either an *atom* or a *list*. LISP atoms are the basic syntactic units of the language and include both numbers and symbols. Symbolic atoms are composed of letters, numbers, and certain nonalphanumeric characters:

```
* - + / @ $ % ^ & _ < > ~ .
```

Examples of LISP atoms include:

```
3.1416
100
x
hyphenated-name
?some-predicate
nil
```

A list is a sequence of either atoms or other lists separated by blanks and enclosed in parentheses. Examples of lists include:

```
(1 2 3 4)
(tom mary john joyce)
()
```

```
(on block-1 table)
(likes bill ?X)
(( 2467 (lovelace ada) programmer) ( 3592 (babbage charles) computer-designer))
((key-1 value-1) (key-2 value-2) (key-3 value-3))
(* 7 9)
(- (+ 3 4) 7)
```

Note that lists may be elements of lists. This nesting may be arbitrarily deep and allows us to create symbol structures of any desired form and complexity. The empty list, "()", plays a special role in the construction and manipulation of LISP data structures and is given the special name nil. nil is the only s-expression that is considered to be both an atom and a list. Two of the examples, (on block-1 table) and (likes bill ?X), may be interpreted as trivial syntactic variants on expressions in the predicate calculus. This syntax is used for predicate calculus expressions in the unification algorithm of this chapter. The next two examples suggest ways in which lists may be used to implement the data structures needed in a data base application.

The last two of the above examples are of particular interest in that they may be interpreted as arithmetic expressions in a prefix notation. This is exactly how LISP treats these expressions, with (* 7 9) representing the product of 7 and 9. When LISP is invoked on the computer, the user enters an interactive dialogue with the LISP interpreter. The interpreter prints a prompt (in the examples in this text, a >), reads the user input, attempts to evaluate that input, and, if successful, prints the result. For example:

```
> (* 7 9)
63
>
```

Here, the user enters (* 7 9) and LISP responds with 63, i.e., the *value* associated with that expression. LISP then prints another prompt and waits for more user input. This cycle is known as the *read-eval-print loop* and is the heart of the LISP interpreter.

When given a list, the LISP evaluator attempts to interpret the first element of the list as the name of a function and the remaining elements of the list as its arguments. Thus, the s-expression (f x y) is equivalent to the more traditional mathematical function notation f(x,y). The value printed by LISP is the result of *applying* the function to its arguments. LISP expressions that may be meaningfully evaluated are called *forms*. If the user enters an expression that may not be correctly evaluated, LISP prints an error message and allows the user to trace and correct the problem. A sample LISP session appears below:

```
> (+ 14 5)
19
> (+ 1 2 3 4)
10
> (- (+ 3 4) 7)
0
> (* (+ 2 5) (- 7 (/ 21 7)))
28
> (= (+ 2 3) 5)
t
```

> (> (* 5 6) (+ 4 5))
t

Several of the examples have arguments that are themselves lists, such as (- (+ 3 4) 7). This indicates the composition of functions, in this case "subtract 7 from the *result* of adding 3 to 4." The word "result" is emphasized here to indicate that the function - is not passed the s-expression "(+ 3 4)" as an argument but rather the result of *evaluating* that expression.

In evaluating a function, LISP first evaluates its arguments and then applies the function indicated by the first element of the expression to the results of these evaluations. If the arguments are themselves function expressions, LISP applies this rule recursively to their evaluation. Thus, LISP allows nested function calls of arbitrary depth. It is important to remember that by default, LISP evaluates everything. LISP uses the convention that numbers always evaluate to themselves. If, for example, 5 is typed into the LISP interpreter, LISP will respond with 5. Symbols, such as x, may have a value *bound* to them. If a symbol is bound, the binding is returned when the symbol is evaluated (one way in which symbols become bound is in a function call; see Section 7.1.2). If a symbol is unbound, it is an error to evaluate that symbol.

For example, in evaluating the expression (+ (* 2 3) (* 3 5)), LISP first evaluates the arguments, (* 2 3) and (* 3 5). In evaluating (* 2 3), LISP evaluates the arguments 2 and 3, which return their respective arithmetic values; these values are multiplied to yield 6. Similarly, (* 3 5) evaluates to 15. These results are then passed to the top-level addition, which is evaluated, returning 21. A diagram of this evaluation appears in Figure 7.1.

In addition to arithmetic operations, LISP includes a large number of functions that operate on lists. These include functions to construct and combine lists, to access elements of lists, and to test various properties. For example, list takes any number of arguments and constructs a list of those elements. nth takes a number and a list as arguments and returns the indicated element of the list. By convention nth begins counting with 0. Examples of these and other list manipulation functions include:

> (list 1 2 3 4 5)
(1 2 3 4 5)

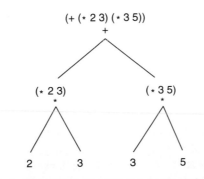

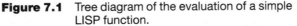

Figure 7.1 Tree diagram of the evaluation of a simple LISP function.

```
> (nth 0 '(a b c d))
a
> (nth 2 (list 1 2 3 4 5))
3
> (nth 2 '((a 1) (b 2) (c 3) (d 4)))
(c 3)
> (length '(a b c d))
4
> (member 7 '(1 2 3 4 5))
nil
> (null ())
t
```

We discuss list-handling functions in greater detail in Section 7.5. The concepts of this section are summarized in the following definition.

DEFINITION

S-EXPRESSION

An s-expression is defined recursively:

1. An atom is an s-expression.

2. If $s_1, s_2, \ldots, s_n$ are s-expressions,
    then so is the list ($s_1 \, s_2 \, \ldots \, s_n$).

A list is a nonatomic s-expression.

A form is an s-expression that is intended to be evaluated. If it is a list, the first element is treated as the function name and the subsequent elements are evaluated to obtain the function arguments.

In evaluating an s-expression:

If the s-expression is a number, return the value of the number.

If the s-expression is an atomic symbol, return the value bound to that symbol; if it is not bound it is an error.

If the s-expression is a list, evaluate the second through the last arguments and apply the function indicated by the first argument to the results.

It is important to note that both programs and data in LISP are represented as s-expressions. Not only does this simplify the syntax of the language but also, when combined with the ability to control the evaluation of s-expressions, it makes it easy to write programs that treat other LISP programs as data. This simplifies the implementation of interpreters in LISP.

7.1.2 Control of LISP Evaluation: quote and eval

In the previous section, several of the examples included arguments that were lists preceded by a single quotation mark: '. The purpose of the quote is to prevent evaluation of an s-expression that should be treated as data rather than an evaluable form. When evaluating an s-expression, LISP will first try to evaluate all of its arguments. If the interpreter is given the expression (nth 0 (a b c d)), it will first try to evaluate the argument (a b c d). This attempted evaluation will result in an error, because a, the first element of this s-expression, does not represent any known LISP function.

To prevent this, LISP provides the user with the built-in function quote. quote takes one argument and returns that argument without evaluating it. For example:

```
> (quote (a b c))
(a b c)
> (quote (+ 1 3))
(+ 1 3)
```

Because quote is used so often, LISP allows it to be abbreviated by a single quotation mark, '. Thus, the preceding examples could be written:

```
> '(a b c)
(a b c)
> '(+ 1 3)
(+ 1 3)
```

In general, quote is used to prevent the evaluation of arguments to a function when these arguments are intended to be treated as data rather than evaluable forms. In the earlier examples of simple LISP arithmetic, quote was not needed, because numbers always evaluate to themselves. Consider the effect of quote in the following two calls to the list function:

```
> (list (+ 1 2) (+ 3 4))
(3 7)
> (list '(+ 1 2) '(+ 3 4))
((+ 1 2) (+ 3 4))
```

In the first example, the arguments are not quoted; they are therefore evaluated and passed to list according to the default evaluation scheme. In the second example, quote prevents this evaluation, with the s-expressions themselves being passed on to list. Even though (+ 1 2) is a meaningful LISP form, quote prevents its evaluation. The ability to prevent evaluation of programs and manipulate them as data is an important feature of LISP.

As a complement to quote, LISP also provides a function, eval, that allows the programmer to evaluate an s-expression at will. eval takes one s-expression as an argument: this argument is evaluated as is usual for arguments to functions; however, the result is then evaluated *again* and this final result is returned as the value of the eval expression. Examples of the behavior of eval and quote include:

```
> (quote (+ 2 3))
(+ 2 3)
> (eval (quote (+ 2 3)))                          ; eval undoes the effect of quote
5
> (list '* 2 5)                                   ; this constructs an evaluable s-expression
(* 2 5)
> (eval (list '* 2 5))                            ; this constructs and evaluates it
10
```

The eval function is precisely what is used in the ordinary evaluation of s-expressions. By making this function available to the programmer, LISP greatly simplifies the development of *meta-interpreters*. This important programming methodology is illustrated in the "infix-interpreter" of Section 7.6 and the design of an expert system shell in Chapter 14.

7.1.3   Programming in LISP: Creating New Functions

All modern LISP dialects support a large number of built-in functions, including:

A full range of arithmetic functions, supporting both integers and real numbers.

A variety of looping and program control functions.

List manipulation and other data structuring functions.

Input/output functions.

Forms for the control of function evaluation.

Functions for the control of the environment and operating system.

LISP includes too many functions to list in this chapter; for a more detailed discussion, consult a specialized LISP text or the manual for your particular implementation.

In LISP, we program by defining new functions in the LISP environment, constructing programs from this already rich repertoire of built-in functions. These new functions are defined in terms of existing functions using defun, which is short for define function. Once a function is defined it may be used in the same fashion as functions that are built into the language.

Suppose, for example, the user would like to define a function called square that takes a single argument and returns the square of that argument. square may be created by having LISP evaluate the following expression:

```
(defun square (x)
    (* x x))
```

The first argument to defun is the name of the function being defined; the second is a list of the formal parameters for that function, which must all be symbolic atoms; the remaining arguments are zero or more s-expressions, which constitute the body of the new function, the LISP code that actually defines its behavior. Unlike most LISP functions, defun does not evaluate its arguments; instead, it uses them as specifications to create a new function. As with all LISP functions, however, defun returns a value, although the value returned is simply the name of the new function.

The important result of evaluating a defun is the side effect of creating a new function and adding it to the LISP environment. In the above example, square is defined as a function that takes one argument and returns the result of multiplying that argument by itself. Once a function is defined, it must be called with the same number of arguments, or "actual parameters," as there are formal parameters specified in the defun. When a function is called, the actual parameters are bound to the formal parameters. The body of the function is then evaluated with these bindings. For example, the call (square 5) causes 5 to be bound to the formal parameter x in the body of the definition. When the body (* x x) is evaluated, LISP first evaluates the arguments to the function. Because x is bound to 5 by the call, this leads to the evaluation of (* 5 5).

More concisely, the syntax of a defun expression is:

```
(defun <function name> (<formal parameters>) <function body>)
```

(This notational convention is used throughout this text to define LISP forms, with descriptions of the elements of a form being enclosed in angle brackets, < >.) Note that the formal parameters in a defun are enclosed in a list.

A newly defined function may be used just like any built-in function. Suppose, for example, that we need a function to compute the length of the hypotenuse of a right triangle given the lengths of the other two sides. This function may be defined according to the Pythagorean theorem, using the previously defined square function along with the built-in function sqrt. Comments are included in the example. LISP supports "end of line comments"; it ignores all text from the first ";" to the end of the same line.

```
(defun hypotenuse (x y)            ; the length of the hypotenuse is
    (sqrt  (+ (square x)            ; the square root of the sum of
            (square y))))          ; the squares of the other sides.
```

This example is typical in that most LISP programs are built up of relatively small functions, each performing a single well-defined task. Once defined, these functions are used to implement higher-level functions until the desired "top-level" function has been defined.

7.1.4 Program Control in LISP: Conditionals and Predicates

LISP branching is based on function evaluation; control functions perform tests and, depending on the results, selectively evaluate alternative forms. Consider, for example, the following definition of the absolute value function using cond (note that LISP has a built-in function, abs, that computes absolute value):

```
(defun absolute-value (x)
    (cond  ((< x 0)   (- x))                           ; if x is less than 0, return -x
           ((>= x 0)  x)))                             ; otherwise, return x unchanged
```

cond takes as arguments a number of *condition-action pairs*:

```
( cond ( <condition₁>  <action₁> )
       ( <condition₂>  <action₂> )
       . . .
       ( <conditionₙ>  <actionₙ> ))
```

These pairs may be arbitrary s-expressions, and each pair is enclosed in parentheses. Like defun, cond does not evaluate all of its arguments. Instead, it evaluates the conditions in order until one of them returns a non-nil (for "true") value. When this occurs, the associated action is evaluated and this result is returned as the value of the cond expression. None of the other actions and none of the subsequent conditions are evaluated. If all of the conditions evaluate to nil (for "false"), the cond returns nil.

An alternative definition of absolute-value is:

```
(defun absolute-value (x)
    (cond  ((< x 0)   (- x))                           ; if x is less than 0, return -x
           (t         x)))                             ; otherwise, return x unchanged
```

This version notes that the second condition, $(>= x\ 0)$, is always true if the first is false. The "t" atom in the final condition of the cond statement is a LISP atom that roughly corresponds to "true." By convention, t always evaluates to itself; this causes the last action to be evaluated if "$(< x\ 0)$" returns nil. This construct is extremely useful, as it provides a way of giving a cond statement a default action that is evaluated if and only if preceding conditions all return nil. It is used frequently in LISP code as a way of giving a conditional a final "else" action.

Although any evaluable s-expressions may be used as the conditions of a cond, generally these are a particular kind of LISP function called a *predicate*. A predicate is simply a function that returns a value of either true or false depending on whether or not its arguments possess some property. The most obvious examples of predicates are the relational operators typically used in arithmetic such as $=$, $>$, and $>=$. Here are some examples of arithmetic predicates in LISP:

```
> (= 9 (+ 4 5))
t
> (>= 17 4)
t
> (< 8 (+ 4 2))
nil
> (oddp 3)                          ; oddp tests whether its argument is odd or not
t
> (minusp 6)                        ; minusp tests whether its argument is less than 0
nil
```

```
> (numberp 17)              ; numberp tests whether its argument is numeric
t
> (numberp nil)
nil
> (zerop 0)
t
> (plusp 10)
t
> (plusp -2)
nil
```

One interesting thing about the above examples is that the predicates do not return "true" or "false" but rather t or nil. LISP is defined so that a predicate may return nil to indicate "false" and anything other than nil (not necessarily t) to indicate "true." An example of this is the member predicate. member takes two arguments, the second of which must be a list, and determines whether the first s-expression is a member of the second. If it is not, member returns nil; if it is, member returns the suffix of the second argument, which contains the first argument as its initial element. For example:

```
>  (member 3 '(1 2 3 4 5))
(3 4 5)
```

One rationale for this convention is that it allows a predicate to return a value that, in the "true" case, may be of use in further processing. It also allows any LISP function to be used as a condition in a cond form.

As an alternative to cond, the if form takes three arguments. The first is a test. If evaluates the test; if it returns a non-nil value, the if form evaluates its second argument and returns the result, otherwise it returns the result of evaluating the third argument. In cases involving a two-way branch, the if construct generally provides cleaner, more readable code than cond. For example, absolute-value could be defined using the if form:

```
(defun absolute-value (x)
  (if (< x 0) (- x)  x))
```

In addition to if and cond, LISP offers a wide selection of alternative branching constructs, including a number of iterative constructs such as do and while loops. Although these functions provide LISP programmers with a wide range of control structures that fit almost any situation and programming style, we will not discuss them in this section; the reader is again referred to a more specialized LISP text for this information.

One of the more interesting program control techniques in LISP involves the use of the logical connectives and, or, and not. not takes one argument and returns t if its argument is nil and nil otherwise. Both and and or may take any number of arguments and behave as you would expect from the definitions of the corresponding logical operators. It is important to note, however, that and and or are based on *conditional evaluation*.

In evaluating an and form, LISP evaluates its arguments in left-to-right sequence, stopping when any one of the arguments evaluates to nil or the last argument has been evaluated. Upon completion, the and form returns the value of the last argument evaluated.

It therefore returns non-nil only if all its arguments return non-nil. Similarly, the or form evaluates its arguments only until a non-nil value is encountered, returning this value as a result. Both functions may leave some of their arguments unevaluated, as may be seen by the behavior of the print statements in the following example. Note that in addition to printing its argument, print returns a value of nil on completion.

```
> (and (oddp 2) (print "second statement was evaluated "))
nil
> (and (oddp 3) (print "second statement was evaluated "))
second statement was evaluated nil
> (or (oddp 3) (print "second statement was evaluated "))
nil
> (or (oddp 2) (print "second statement was evaluated "))
second statement was evaluated nil
```

Because (oddp 2) evaluates to nil in the first of the above expressions, the and simply returns nil without evaluating the print form. In the second expression, however, (oddp 3) evaluates to t and the and form then evaluates the print. A similar analysis may be applied to the or examples. It is important to be aware of this behavior, particularly if some of the arguments are forms whose evaluations have side effects. (Sources of possible side effects, in addition to the print function, may include changes in a global variable, as discussed in Section 7.1.8.)

The conditional evaluation of logical connectives makes them useful in controlling the flow of execution of LISP programs. For example, an or form may be used to try several alternative solutions to a problem, evaluating them in order until one of them returns a non-nil result. An example of this may be found in the implementation of the farmer, wolf, goat, and cabbage problem at the end of this chapter.

7.1.5 Functions, Lists, and Symbolic Computing

Although the preceding sections introduced LISP syntax and demonstrated a few useful LISP functions, they did so in the context of simple arithmetic examples. The real power of LISP, however, is in symbolic computing and is based on the use of lists to construct arbitrarily complex data structures of symbolic and numeric atoms, along with the forms needed for manipulating them. We illustrate the ease with which LISP handles symbolic data structures, as well as the naturalness of data abstraction techniques in LISP, with a simple data base example. Our data base application requires the manipulation of employee records containing name, salary, and employee number fields.

These records are represented as lists, with the name, salary, and number fields as the first, second, and third elements of a list. Using nth, it is possible to define access functions for the various fields of a data record. For example:

```
(defun name-field (record)
  (nth 0 record))
```

will have the behavior:

```
> (name-field '((Ada Lovelace) 45000.00 38519))
(Ada Lovelace)
```

Similarly, the functions **salary-field** and **number-field** may be defined to access the appropriate fields of a data record. Also, because a name is itself a list containing two elements, a first name and a last name, it is useful to define functions that take a **name** as argument and return either the first or last name as a result.

```
(defun first-name (name)
  (nth 0 name))
```

will have the behavior:

```
> (first-name (name-field '((Ada Lovelace) 45000.00 338519)))
Ada
```

In addition to accessing individual fields of a data record, it is also necessary to implement functions to create and modify data records. These are defined using the built-in LISP function: **list**. **list** takes any number of arguments, evaluates them, and returns a list containing those values as its elements. For example:

```
> (list 1 2 3 4)
(1 2 3 4)
> (list '(Ada Lovelace) 45000.00 338519)
((Ada Lovelace) 45000.00 338519)
```

As the second of these examples suggests, **list** may be used to define a record constructor for the data base, which is a function that takes a name, salary, and employee number as arguments and returns an employee record as a result:

```
(defun build-record (name salary emp-number)
  (list name salary emp-number))
```

will have the behavior:

```
> (build-record '(Alan Turing) 50000.00 135772)
((Alan Turing) 50000.00 135772)
```

Now, using **build-record** and the access functions, we may construct functions that return a modified copy of a record. For example:

```
(defun replace-salary-field (record new-salary)
  (build-record (name-field record)
                new-salary
                (number-field record)))
```

will behave:

```
> (replace-salary-field '((Ada Lovelace) 45000.00 338519) 50000.00)
((Ada Lovelace) 50000.00 338519)
```

Notice that this function does not actually update the record itself but produces a modified copy of the record, sort of a "copy-update." This updated version may be saved by binding it to a global variable using setf (Section 7.1.8). Although LISP provides forms that allow a particular element in a list to be modified "in place," these operations are somewhat tricky and are not covered in this text. For LISP applications involving all but extremely large structures, modifications are generally done by creating a new copy of the structure.

In the above examples, we created an abstract data type for employee records. Later sections of this chapter introduce the functions and techniques needed to write code for searching and maintaining large collections of such records. By using the various access and update functions defined in this section, this code may be implemented using a specialized language appropriate to the meaning of the records, without requiring that the programmer be constantly aware of the actual list structures being used to implement the records. This simplifies the later development of higher-level code, as well as making that code much easier to maintain and understand.

Generally, AI programs use large amounts of varied knowledge about problem domains. The data structures used to represent this knowledge, such as frames and semantic networks, are complex, and humans generally find it easier to relate to this knowledge in terms of its meaning rather than the particular syntax of its internal representation. Therefore, data abstraction techniques, always good computer science, are essential tools for the AI programmer. Because of the ease with which LISP supports the definition of new functions, it is an ideal language for data abstraction.

7.1.6   Lists as Recursive Structures

In the previous section, we used nth and list to implement access functions for records in a simple "employee" data base. Because all employee records were of a determinate length (three elements), these two functions were sufficient to access the fields of records. However, these functions are not adequate for performing operations on lists of unknown length, such as searching through an unspecified number of employee records. To do this, we must be able to scan a list iteratively or recursively, terminating when certain conditions are met (e.g., the desired record is found) or the list is exhausted. In this section we introduce list operations, along with the use of recursion to create list-processing functions. Although LISP includes a number of constructs for doing explicit iteration, the fundamentally recursive structure of lists makes recursion a natural vehicle for list manipulation.

The basic functions for accessing the components of lists are car and cdr. car takes a single argument, which must be a list, and returns the first element of that list. cdr also takes a single argument, which must be a list, and returns that list with its first argument removed. For example:

```
> (car '(a b c))                                    ; note that the list is quoted
a
> (cdr '(a b c))
(b c)
> (car '((a b) (c d)))                              ; the first element of a list may be a list
(a b)
> (cdr '((a b) (c d)))
((c d))
> (car (cdr '(a b c d)))
b
```

The way in which car and cdr operate suggests a recursive approach to manipulating list structures:

To perform an operation on each of the elements of a list:

1. *If the list is empty, quit.*

2. *Perform the operation on the first element of the list and recur on the remainder of the list.*

Using this scheme, we can define a number of useful list-handling functions. For example, Common LISP includes the predicates member, which determines whether one s-expression is a member of a list, and length, which determines the length of a list. We may define our own versions of these functions. my-member takes two arguments, an arbitrary s-expression and a list. It returns nil if the s-expression is not a member of the list; otherwise it returns the portion of the list containing the s-expression as its first element:

```
(defun my-member (element list)
    (cond ((null list) nil)                         ; element not in list
          ((equal element (car list)) list)         ; element found
          (t (my-member element (cdr list)))))      ; recursive step
```

my-member has the behavior

```
> (my-member 4 '(1 2 3 4 5 6))
(4 5 6)
> (my-member 5 '(a b c d))
nil
```

Similarly, we may define our own versions of length and nth:

```
(defun my-length (list)
   (cond ((null list) 0)
         (t (+ (my-length (cdr list) 1)))))
```

```
(defun my-nth (n list)
   (cond ((zerop n) (car list))                     ; zerop tests if its argument is zero
         (t (my-nth (- n 1) (cdr list)))))
```

It is interesting to note that these examples, though presented here to illustrate the use of car and cdr, reflect the historical development of LISP. Early versions of the language did not include as many built-in functions as Common LISP does; programmers defined their own functions for checking list membership, length, etc. Over time, the most generally useful of these functions have been incorporated into the language standard. As an easily extensible language, Common LISP makes it easy for programmers to create and use their own library of reusable functions.

In addition to the functions car and cdr, LISP provides a number of functions for constructing lists. One of these, list, which takes as arguments any number of s-expressions, evaluates them, and returns a list of the results, was introduced in Section 7.1.1. A more primitive list constructor is the function cons. cons takes two s-expressions as arguments, evaluates them, and returns a list whose car is the value of the first argument and whose cdr is the value of the second:

```
> (cons 1 '(2 3 4))
(1 2 3 4)
> (cons '(a b) '(c d e))
((a b) c d e)
```

cons bears an inverse relationship to car and cdr in that the car of the value returned by a cons form is always the first argument to the cons and the cdr of the value returned by a cons form is always the second argument to that form:

```
> (car (cons 1 '(2 3 4)))
1
> (cdr (cons 1 '(2 3 4)))
(2 3 4)
```

An example of the use of cons is seen in the definition of the function filter-negatives, which takes a list of numbers as an argument and returns that list with any negative numbers removed. filter-negatives recursively examines each element of the list; if the first element is negative, it is discarded and the function returns the result of filtering the negative numbers from the cdr of the list. If the first element of the list is positive, it is "consed" onto the result of filtering negatives from the rest of the list:

```
(defun filter-negatives (number-list)
  (cond ((null number-list) nil)                                    ; termination condition
        ((plusp (car number-list)) (cons (car number-list)
                                    (filter-negatives (cdr number-list))))
        (t (filter-negatives (cdr number-list)))))
```

which behaves:

```
> (filter-negatives '(1 -1 2 -2 3 -4))
(1 2 3)
```

This example is typical of the way cons is often used in recursive functions on lists. car and cdr tear lists apart and "drive" the recursion; cons selectively constructs the result as the recursion "unwinds." Another example of this use of cons is in redefining the built-in function append:

```
(defun my-append (list1 list2)
   (cond ((null list1) list2)
          (t (cons (car list1) (my-append (cdr list1) list2)))))
```

which yields the behavior:

```
> (my-append '(1 2 3) '(4 5 6))
(1 2 3 4 5 6)
```

Note that the same recursive scheme is used in the definitions of my-append, my-length, and my-member. Each definition uses the cdr function to remove an element from the list, allowing a recursive call on the shortened list; the recursion "bottoms out" on the empty list. Recursion is used to scan the list, element by element; as the recursion unwinds, the cons function reassembles the solution. This particular scheme is known as cdr *recursion*, because it uses the cdr function to linearly scan the elements of a list.

7.1.7   Nested Lists, Structure, and car / cdr Recursion

Although both cons and append may be used to combine smaller lists into a single list, it is important to note the difference between these two functions. If cons is called with two lists as arguments, it makes the first of these a new first element of the second list, whereas append returns a list whose elements are the elements of the two arguments:

```
> (cons '(1 2) '(3 4))
((1 2) 3 4)
> (append '(1 2) '(3 4))
(1 2 3 4)
```

It is important to distinguish between the lists (1 2 3 4) and ((1 2) 3 4), which have fundamentally different structures.

This difference may be noted graphically by exploiting the isomorphism between lists and trees. The simplest way to map lists onto trees is to create an unlabeled node for each list, with descendants equal to the elements of that list. This rule is applied recursively to the elements of the list that are themselves lists; elements that are atoms are mapped onto leaf nodes of the tree. Thus, the two lists mentioned above generate the different tree structures illustrated in Figure 7.2.

This example illustrates the representational power of lists, particularly as a means of representing any tree structure such as a search tree or a parse tree (Fig. 7.1). In addition, nested lists provide a way of hierarchically structuring complex data. In the employee records example of Section 7.1.4, the name field was itself a list consisting of a first name

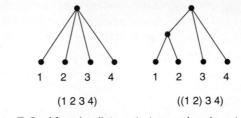

Figure 7.2 Mapping lists onto trees, showing structural differences.

and a last name. This list could be treated as a single entity or its individual components could be accessed.

The simple cdr-recursive scheme discussed in the previous section is not sufficient to implement all manipulations on nested lists, because it does not distinguish between items that are lists and those that are simple atoms. Suppose, for example, that the length function defined in Section 7.1.6 is applied to a nested list structure:

```
> (length '((1 2) 3 (1 (4 (5)))))
3
```

In the above example, length returns 3 because the list has 3 elements, (1 2), 3, and (1 (4 (5))). This is, of course, the correct and desired behavior for a length function. If we want the function to count the number of *atoms* in the list, however, we need a different recursive scheme, one that, in addition to scanning along the elements of the list, "opens up" non-atomic list elements and recursively applies itself to the task of counting their atoms. This function, which will be called count-atoms, is defined:

```
(defun count-atoms (list)
  (cond ((null list) 0)
        ((atom list) 1)
        (t (+ (count-atoms (car list))          ; open up an element
              (count-atoms (cdr list))))))       ; scan down the list
```

which behaves:

```
> (count-atoms '((1 2) 3 (((4 5 (6)))))
6
```

The above definition is an example of car-cdr *recursion*. Instead of just recurring on the cdr of the list, count-atoms also recurs on the car of its argument, with the + function combining the two components into an answer. Recursion halts when it encounters an atom or empty list. One way of thinking of this scheme is that it adds a second dimension to simple cdr recursion, that of "going down into" each of the list elements. Compare the diagrams of calls to length and count-atoms in Figure 7.3. Note the similarity between

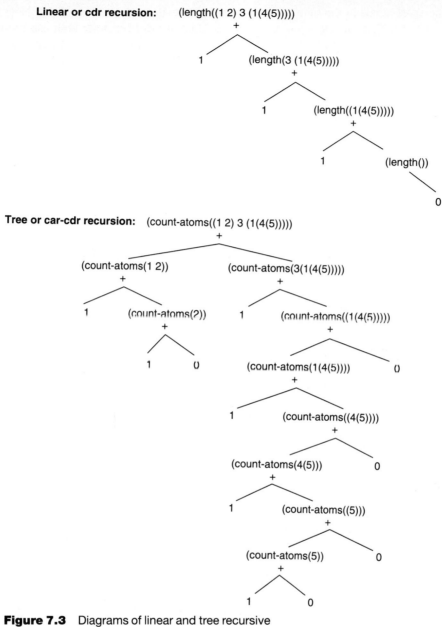

Linear or cdr recursion: (length((1 2) 3 (1(4(5)))))

Tree or car-cdr recursion: (count-atoms((1 2) 3 (1(4(5)))))

Figure 7.3 Diagrams of linear and tree recursive executions.

the structure of **car-cdr** recursion and the recursive definition of s-expressions given in Section 7.1.1.

Another example of the use of **car-cdr** recursion is in the definition of the function **flatten. flatten** takes as argument a list of arbitrary structure and returns a list that consists of the same atoms in the same order but with all the atoms at the same level. Note the similarity between the definition of **flatten** and that of **count-atoms**: both use **car-cdr** recursion to tear apart lists and drive the recursion, both terminate when the argument is either null or atomic, and both use a second function (**append** or $+$) to construct an answer from the results of the recursive calls.

```
(defun flatten (lst)
  (cond ((null lst) nil)
        ((atom lst) (list lst))
        (t (append (flatten (car lst))(flatten (cdr lst))))))
```

Examples of calls to **flatten** include:

```
> (flatten '(a (b c) (((d) e f))))
(a b c d e f)
> (flatten '(a b c))                              ; this list is already flattened
(a b c)
> (flatten '(1 (2 3) (4 (5 6) 7)))
(1 2 3 4 5 6 7)
```

car-cdr recursion is the basis of our implementation of unification in Section 7.6.

7.1.8 Functional Programming, Side Effects, **set**, and **let**

LISP is based on the theory of recursive functions; early LISP was the first example of a functional or *applicative* programming language. An important aspect of purely functional languages is the lack of any side effects as a result of function execution. This means that the value returned by a function call depends only on the function definition and the value of the parameters in the call. Although LISP is based on mathematical functions, it is possible to define LISP forms that violate this important property. Consider the following LISP interaction:

```
> (f 4)
5
> (f 4)
6
> (f 4)
7
```

Note that **f** does not behave as a true function in that its output is not determined solely by the calling parameter; each time it is called with 4, it returns a different value. Execution of the function creates a side effect that influences the behavior of future calls. **f** is implemented using a LISP built-in function called **set**:

```
(defun f (x)
  (set 'inc (+ inc 1))
  (+ x inc))
```

set takes two arguments. The first must evaluate to a symbol; the second may be an arbitrary s-expression. set evaluates the second argument and binds this value to the symbol defined by the first argument. In the above example, if inc is first set to 0 (by the call (set 'inc 0)), each subsequent evaluation will increment its parameter by one more than the previous evaluation.

set requires that its first argument evaluate to a symbol. In most cases, the first argument is simply a quoted symbol. Because this is done so often, LISP provides an alternative form, setq, that does not evalute its first argument. Instead, setq requires that the first argument be a symbol; this eliminates the need to quote the symbol being bound. For example, the following forms are equivalent:

```
> (set 'x 0)
0
> (setq x 0)
0
```

Although this makes it possible to create LISP objects that are not pure functions in the mathematical sense, the ability to bind a value to a variable in the global environment is a useful feature. Many programming tasks are most naturally implemented using this ability to define objects whose state persists across function calls. The classic example of this is the "seed" in a random number generator: each call to the function changes and saves the value of the seed. Similarly, it would be natural for a data base program (such as was described in Section 7.1.3) to store the data base by binding it to a variable in the global environment.

So far, we have seen two ways of binding a value to a symbol: explicitly using set or setq or implicitly when a function call binds the calling parameters to the formal parameters in the definition. In the examples seen so far, all variables in a function body were either *bound* or *free*. A bound variable is one that appears as a formal parameter in the definition of the function, while a free variable is one that appears in the body of the function but is not a formal parameter. When a function is called, any bindings that a bound variable may have in the global environment are saved and the variable is rebound to the calling parameter. After the function has completed execution, the original bindings are restored. Thus, setting the value of a bound variable inside a function body has no effect on the global bindings of that variable, as illustrated by the following LISP interaction:

```
> (defun foo (x)
    (setq x (+ x 1))              ; increment bound variable x
    x)                           ; return its value
foo
> (setq y 1)
1
```

```
> (foo y)
2
> y                                                    ; note that value of y is unchanged
1
```

In the earlier example, x was bound in the function f, whereas inc was free in that function. As we demonstrated in the example, free variables in a function definition are the primary source of side effects in functions.

An interesting alternative to set and setq is the generalized assignment function, setf. Where set and setq treat their first argument as a symbol, setf regards it as naming a memory location. For example, instead of treating x as a symbol to be bound to a value, setf treats x as naming a location in memory. Instead of binding a value to a symbol, setf evaluates its first argument to obtain a memory location and places the value of the second argument in that location. When binding a value to a symbol, setf behaves like setq:

```
> (setq x 0)
0
> (setf x 0)
0
```

However, because setf treats its first argument as naming a location, it allows a more general semantics. We may call setf with any form that corresponds to a memory location. If we make the first argument to setf a call to the car function, setf will replace the first element of that list. If the first argument to setf is a call to the cdr function, setf will replace the tail of that list. For example:

```
> (setf x '(a b c))                                    ; x is bound to a list
(a b c)
> x                                                    ; the value of x is a list
(a b c)
> (setf (car x) 1)                        ; the car of x corresponds to a location in memory
1
> x                                       ; note that setf changed the value of the car of x
(1 b c)
> (setf (cdr x) '(2 3))
(2 3)
> x                                                    ; note that x now has a new tail
(1 2 3)
```

We may call setf with most LISP forms that correspond to a memory location; these include symbols and calls functions such as car, cdr, and nth. Thus, setf allows us great flexibility in replacing components of LISP data structures.

Another useful function for explicitly controlling the binding of variables is the let function. let allows the creation of local variables. As an example of the use of let, consider a function to compute the roots of a quadratic equation. This function takes as arguments the three parameters (a, b, and c) of the equation

$$ax^2+bx+c=0$$

and returns a list of the two roots of the equation. For example:

```
> (quad-roots 1 2 1)
(-1.0 -1.0)
> (quad-roots 1 6 8)
(-2.0 -4.0)
```

These roots would be calculated from the formula

$$x = \frac{-b \pm \sqrt{b^2 - 4ac}}{2a}$$

In computing the two roots, the value of

$$\sqrt{b^2 - 4ac}$$

is used twice. For reasons of efficiency, as well as elegance, we should compute this value only once, saving it in a variable for use in computing the two roots. Based on this idea, an initial implementation of quad-roots might be:

```
(defun quad-roots-1 (a b c)
   (setq temp (sqrt (- (* b b) (* 4 a c))))
   (list (/ (+ (- b) temp) (* 2 a))
         (/ (- (- b) temp) (* 2 a))))
```

Note that the above implementation assumes that the equation does not have imaginary roots, as attempting to take the square root of a negative number would cause the sqrt function to halt with an error condition. Modifying the code to handle this case is straightforward and not relevant to this discussion.

Although, with this exception, the code is correct, evaluation of the function body will have the side effect of setting the value of temp in the global environment:

```
> (quad-roots-1 1 2 1)
(-1.0 -1.0)
> temp
0.0
```

It is much more desirable to make temp local to the function quad-roots, thereby eliminating this side effect. This can be done through the use of a let block. A let expression has the syntax:

```
(let (<local-variables>) <expressions>)
```

where the elements of (<local-variables>) are either symbolic atoms or pairs of the form:

```
(<symbol> <expression>)
```

When a let form (or block) is evaluated, it establishes a local environment consisting of all of the symbols in (<local-variables>). If a symbol is the first element of a pair, the second element is evaluated and the symbol is bound to this result; symbols that are not included in pairs are bound to nil. If any of these symbols are already bound in the global environment, these global bindings are saved and restored when the let block terminates.

After these local bindings are established, the <expressions> are evaluated in order within this environment. When the let statement terminates, it returns the value of the last expression evaluated within the block.

The behavior of the let block is illustrated by the following example:

```
> (setq a 0)
0
> (let ((a 3) b)
      (setq b 4)
      (+ a b))
7
> a
0
> b
ERROR - b is not bound at top level.
```

In this example, before the let block is executed, a is bound to 0 and b is unbound at the top-level environment. When the let is evaluated, a is bound to 3 and b is bound to nil. The setq binds b to 4, and the sum of a and b is returned by the let statement. Upon termination of the let, a and b are restored to their previous values, including the unbound status of b.

Using the let statement, quad-roots is implemented with no global side effects:

```
(defun quad-roots-2 (a b c)
   (let (temp)
      (setq temp (sqrt (- (* b b) (* 4 a c))))
      (list (/ (+ (- b) temp) (* 2 a))
            (/ (- (- b) temp) (* 2 a)))))
```

Alternatively, temp may be bound when it is declared in the let statement, giving a somewhat more concise implementation of quad-roots. In this final version, the denominator of the formula, 2a, is also computed once and saved in a local variable, denom:

```
(defun quad-roots-3 (a b c)
   (let ((temp (sqrt (- (* b b) (* 4 a c))))
         (denom (* 2 a)))
      (list (/ (+ (- b) temp) denom)
            (/ (- (- b) temp) denom))))
```

In addition to avoiding side effects, quad-roots-3 is the most efficient of the three versions, because it does not recompute values unnecessarily.

7.1.9   Data Types in Common LISP

LISP provides the user with a number of built-in data types. These include integers, floating point numbers, strings, and characters. LISP also includes such structured types as arrays, hash tables, sets, and structures (which correspond to Pascal records). All of these types include the appropriate operations on the type and predicates for testing whether an object is a member of the type. For example, lists are supported by such functions as listp, which identifies an object as a list; null, which identifies the empty list, and constructors and accessors such as list, nth, car, and cdr.

However, unlike such strongly typed languages as Pascal, it is the data objects that are typed, rather than variables. Any LISP symbol may bind to any object; the object itself is typed. This provides the programmer with the power of strong typing but also with a great deal of flexibility in manipulating types. For example, because variables are not typed, we may bind any object to any variable at run time; this means that we may define data structures such as frames (Chapter 9) and not specify the type of the values stored in them.

Consequently, LISP implements run-time type checking. Although we may bind any value to a symbol, if we attempt to use the value in an erroneous fashion, LISP will complain. For example:

```
> (setq x 'a)
a
> (+ x 2)
>> Error: a is not a valid argument to + .
>> While executing: +
```

It is important to note that this flexibility requires that all type checking be done at run time, rather than compile time. This provides further overhead for LISP execution, but it also provides flexibility. For example, users may implement their own type checking using either built-in or user-defined type predicates. This allows the programmer to trap type errors and manage these errors as they see fit.

In addition to the built-in types, the ease of defining functions makes it simple for the programmer to define abstract data types. We have already done this with the simple data base example of Section 7.1.5, and we continue to do it in the remaining examples of the text.

The preceding few pages are not a complete description of LISP. Instead, they supplement the reader's knowledge of LISP with a discussion of interesting features of the language that will be of use in implementing AI data structures and algorithms. These features include:

1. The naturalness with which LISP supports a data abstraction approach to programming.

2. The use of lists to create symbolic data structures.

3. The use of cond and recursion to control program flow.

4. The recursive nature of list structures and the recursive schemes involved in their manipulation.

5. The use of quote and eval to control function evaluation.

6. The use of set and let to control variable bindings and side effects.

The remainder of this chapter builds on these ideas to demonstrate the use of LISP for typical AI programming tasks such as pattern matchers and search algorithms.

7.2 Search Algorithms in LISP: A Functional Approach to the Farmer, Wolf, Goat, and Cabbage Problem

As an introduction to AI programming in LISP, we solve the farmer, wolf, goat, and cabbage problem:

> A farmer with his wolf, goat, and cabbage come to the edge of a river they wish to cross. There is a boat at the river's edge, but, of course, only the farmer can row it. The boat also can carry only two things (including the rower) at a time. If the wolf is ever left alone with the goat, the wolf will eat the goat; similarly, if the goat is left alone with the cabbage, the goat will eat the cabbage. Devise a sequence of crossings of the river so that all four characters arrive safely on the other side of the river.

This problem was first presented and solved in PROLOG in Chapter 6. The LISP version searches the same space and has structural similarities to the PROLOG solution; however, it differs in ways that reflect LISP's procedural orientation. The LISP solution searches the state space in a depth-first fashion and uses a list of visited states to avoid loops.

The heart of the program is a set of functions that define states of the world as an abstract data type. These functions hide the internals of state representation from higher-level components of the program. Allowing the programmer to ignore the internals of state representation is, of course, just good software engineering; although such abstraction is not really necessary for this simple example, most AI programs involve complex representations that require this approach.

Internally, states are represented as lists of four elements, where each element denotes the location of the farmer, wolf, goat, or cabbage, respectively. Thus, (e w e w) represents the problem state in which the farmer (the first element) and the goat (the third element) are on the east bank and the wolf and cabbage are on the west bank. The basic functions defining the state data type will be a constructor, make-state, which takes as arguments the locations of the farmer, wolf, goat, and cabbage and returns a state, and four access functions, farmer-side, wolf-side, goat-side, and cabbage-side, which take a state and return the location of an individual. These functions are defined:

```
(defun make-state (f w g c) (list f w g c))

(defun farmer-side (state)
  (nth 0 state))
```

```
(defun wolf-side (state)
  (nth 1 state))

(defun goat-side (state)
  (nth 2 state))

(defun cabbage-side (state)
  (nth 3 state))
```

The rest of the program is built on these state access and construction functions. In particular, they are used to implement the four possible actions the farmer may take: rowing across the river either alone or with either the wolf, goat, or cabbage.

These functions use the access functions to tear a state apart into its components. A function called **opposite** (to be defined shortly) determines the new location of the individuals that cross the river, and **make-state** reassembles these into the new state. For example, the function farmer-takes-self may be defined:

```
(defun farmer-takes-self (state)
  (make-state (opposite (farmer-side state))
              (wolf-side state)
              (goat-side state)
              (cabbage-side state)))
```

Note that this function returns the new state, regardless of whether it is safe or not. A state is unsafe if the farmer has left the goat alone with the cabbage or left the wolf alone with the goat. The program must find a solution path that does not contain any unsafe states. Although this "safe" check may be done at a number of different stages of the program, our approach is to perform it in the move functions. This is implemented by using a function called **safe**; **safe**, which is also defined shortly, has the following behavior:

```
> (safe '(w w w w))                            ; safe state, return unchanged.
(w w w w)
> (safe '(e w w e))                            ; wolf eats goat, return nil.
nil
> (safe '(w w e e))                            ; goat eats cabbage, return nil.
nil
```

safe is used in each move function to filter out the unsafe states. Thus, any move that moves to an unsafe state will return nil instead of that state. The recursive path algorithm can check for this nil and use it to prune that state. Using **safe**, a final definition of farmer-takes-self is:

```
(defun farmer-takes-self (state)
  (safe (make-state (opposite (farmer-side state))
                    (wolf-side state)
                    (goat-side state)
                    (cabbage-side state))))
```

The remaining move functions are defined similarly but include a conditional test to determine whether the farmer and the prospective passenger are on the same side of the river. If a move cannot be made because the farmer and the passenger are not on the same bank, these functions return nil:

```
(defun farmer-takes-wolf (state)
  (cond ((equal (farmer-side state) (wolf-side state))
            (safe (make-state (opposite (farmer-side state))
                              (opposite (wolf-side state))
                              (goat-side state)
                              (cabbage-side state))))
        (t nil)))


(defun farmer-takes-goat (state)
  (cond ((equal (farmer-side state) (goat-side state))
            (safe (make-state (opposite (farmer-side state))
                              (wolf-side state)
                              (opposite (goat-side state))
                              (cabbage-side state))))
        (t nil)))

(defun farmer-takes-cabbage (state)
  (cond ((equal (farmer-side state) (cabbage-side state))
            (safe (make-state (opposite (farmer-side state))
                              (wolf-side state)
                              (goat-side state)
                              (opposite (cabbage-side state)))))
        (t nil)))
```

These definitions use the state manipulation functions from above and a function **opposite**, which returns the opposite of a given side:

```
(defun opposite (side)
  (cond ((equal side 'e) 'w)
        ((equal side 'w) 'e)))
```

It is worth noting the use of the predicate **equal** in the previous definitions. LISP provides a number of different predicates for testing equality. The most stringent, **eq**, is true only if its arguments evaluate to the same object, which means they point to the same memory location. **equal** is less strict: it requires that its arguments be syntactically identical. The following transcript illustrates the difference between these two definitions of equality:

```
> (setq l1 '(1 2 3))
(1 2 3)
> (setq l2 '(1 2 3))
(1 2 3)
```

```
> (equal l1 l2)
t
> (eq l1 l2)
nil
> (setq l3 l1)
(1 2 3)
> (eq l1 l3)
t
```

safe is defined using a cond to check for the two unsafe conditions: (1) the farmer on the opposite bank from the wolf and the goat and (2) the farmer on the opposite bank from the goat and the cabbage. If the state is safe, it is returned unchanged:

```
(defun safe (state)
  (cond ((and (equal (goat-side state) (wolf-side state))          ; wolf eats goat
              (not (equal (farmer-side state) (wolf-side state))))  nil)
        ((and (equal (goat-side state) (cabbage-side state))        ; goat eats cabbage
              (not (equal (farmer-side state) (goat-side state)))) nil)
    (t state)))
```

path implements the backtracking search of the state space. It takes as arguments a state and a goal and first checks to see whether they are equal, indicating a successful termination of the search. If they are not equal, path generates all four of the neighboring states in the state space graph, calling itself recursively on each of these neighboring states in turn to try to find a path from them to a goal. Translating this simple definition directly into LISP yields something like:

```
(defun path (state goal)
  (cond ((equal state goal) 'success)
        (t (or (path (farmer-takes-self state) goal)
               (path (farmer-takes-wolf state) goal)
               (path (farmer-takes-goat state) goal)
               (path (farmer-takes-cabbage state) goal)))))
```

This version of the path function is a simple translation of the recursive path algorithm from English into LISP and has several "bugs" that need to be corrected. It does, however, capture the essential structure of the algorithm and should be examined before continuing. The first test in the cond statement is for a successful completion. If this occurs, the recursion stops and the atom success is returned. Otherwise, path generates the four descendant nodes of the graph and calls itself on each of them in turn.

In particular, note the use of the or form to control evaluation of its arguments. Recall that an or evaluates its arguments in turn until one of them returns a non-nil value. When this occurs, the or terminates without evaluating the other arguments and returns this non-nil value as a result. Thus, the or not only is used as a logical operator but also provides a way of controlling branching. It is used here instead of a cond because the value that is being tested and the value that should be returned if the test is non-nil are the same.

One problem with this definition is that a move function may return a value of nil if the move may not be made or if it leads to an unsafe state. To prevent path from attempting to generate the children of a nil state, it must first check whether the current state is nil. If it is, path should return nil.

The other issue that needs to be addressed in the implementation of path is that of loops in the search space. If the above implementation of path is run, the farmer will soon find himself going back and forth alone between the two banks; i.e., the algorithm will be stuck in an infinite loop between identical states. To prevent this from happening, path is given a third parameter, been-list, a list of all the states that have already been visited. Each time that path is called recursively on a new state of the world, the parent state will be added to been-list. path uses the member predicate to make sure the current state is not a member of been-list, i.e., that it has not already been visited. This is accomplished by checking the current state for membership in been-list before generating its descendants. path is now defined:

```
(defun path (state goal been-list)
  (cond ((null state) nil)
     ((equal state goal) (reverse (cons state been-list)))
     ((not (member state been-list :test #'equal))
        (or (path (farmer-takes-self state) goal (cons state been-list))
            (path (farmer-takes-wolf state) goal (cons state been-list))
            (path (farmer-takes-goat state) goal (cons state been-list))
            (path (farmer-takes-cabbage state) goal (cons state been-list))))))
```

In the above implementation, member is a Common LISP built-in function that behaves in essentially the same way as the my-member function defined in this chapter. The only difference is the inclusion of :test #'equal in the argument list. Unlike our "home-grown" member function, the Common LISP built-in form allows the programmer to specify the function that is used in testing for membership. This wrinkle increases the flexibility of the function and should not cause too much concern in this discussion.

Rather than having the function return just the atom success, it is better to have it return the actual solution path. Because the series of states on the solution path is already contained in the been-list, this list is returned instead. Because the goal is not already on been-list, it is consed onto the list. Also, because the list is constructed in reverse order (with the start state as the last element), the list is reversed (constructed in reverse order using another LISP built-in function, reverse) prior to being returned.

Finally, because the been-list parameter should be kept "hidden" from the user, a top-level calling function may be written that takes as arguments a start and a goal state and calls path with a nil value of been-list:

```
(defun solve-fwgc (state goal) (path state goal nil))
```

Let us compare the LISP version of the farmer, wolf, goat, and cabbage problem with the PROLOG solution presented in Chapter 6. Not only does the LISP program solve the same problem, but it also searches exactly the same state space as the PROLOG version. This underscores the point that the state space conceptualization of a problem is independent of the implementation of a program for searching that space. Because both programs search the same space, the two implementations have strong similarities; the differences tend to be subtle but provide an interesting contrast between declarative and procedural programming styles.

States in the PROLOG version are represented using a predicate, state(e,e,e,e), and the LISP implementation uses a list. These two representations are more than syntactic variations on one another. The LISP representation of state is defined not only by its list syntax but also by the access and move functions that constitute the abstract data type "state." In general, the extensibility of LISP, combined with the representational flexibility of lists, makes data abstraction natural in LISP programs. In the PROLOG version, states are patterns; their meaning is determined by the way in which they match other patterns in PROLOG rules, which indeed, could also be lists.

The LISP version of path is slightly longer than the PROLOG version. One reason for this is that the LISP version must implement a search strategy whereas the PROLOG version takes advantage of PROLOG's built-in search algorithm. The control algorithm is explicit in the LISP version but is implicit in the PROLOG version.

In conclusion, a comparison of LISP and PROLOG is more a matter of understanding the trade-offs made in each language than of selecting one language as "better" than the other. Because PROLOG is built on declarative representation and theorem-proving techniques, the PROLOG program is more concise and has a flavor of describing the problem domain, without directly implementing the search algorithm. The price paid for this conciseness is that much of the program's behavior is hidden, determined by PROLOG's built-in inference strategies. Programmers may also feel more pressure to make the problem solution conform to PROLOG's representational formalism and search strategies. LISP, on the other hand, allows greater flexibility for the programmer. The price paid here is that the programmer cannot draw on a built-in representation or search strategy and must implement this explicitly in the algorithm.

7.3 Higher-Order Functions and Procedural Abstraction

7.3.1 Maps and Filters

A *filter* is a function that applies a test to the elements of a list, eliminating those that fail the test. filter-negatives, presented earlier in this chapter, was an example of a filter. *Maps* take a list of data objects and apply a function to each one, returning a list of the results. This idea may be further generalized through the development of general maps and filters that take as arguments both lists and the functions or tests that are to be applied to their elements. Functions that take other functions as parameters or return them as results are called *higher-order functions* and constitute an important tool for procedural abstraction.

To begin with an example, recall the function filter-negatives from Section 7.1.6. This function took as its argument a list of numbers and returned that list with all negative values deleted. For example, a function to filter out all the even numbers in a list may be defined:

```
(defun filter-evens (number-list)
  (cond ((null number-list) nil)                            ; termination condition
        ((oddp (car number-list))
          (cons (car number-list) (filter-evens (cdr number-list))))
        (t (filter-evens (cdr number-list)))))
```

Because these two functions differ *only* in the name of the predicate used to filter elements from the list, it is natural to think of generalizing them into a single function that takes the filtering predicate as a second parameter.

This may be defined using a LISP form called funcall, which takes as arguments a function and a series of arguments and applies that function to those arguments:

```
(defun filter (list-of-elements test)
  (cond ((null list-of-elements) nil)
        ((funcall test (car list-of-elements))
          (cons (car list-of-elements) (filter (cdr list-of-elements) test)))
        (t (filter (cdr list-of-elements) test))))
```

The function, filter, applies the test to the first element of the list. If the test returns non-nil it conses the element onto the result of filtering the cdr of the list; otherwise, it just returns the filtered cdr. This function may be used with different predicates passed in as parameters to perform a variety of filtering tasks:

```
> (filter '(1 3 -9 5 -2 -7 6) #'plusp)
(1 3 5 6)
> (filter '(1 2 3 4 5 6 7 8 9) #'evenp)
(2 4 6 8)
> (filter '(1 a b 3 c 4 7 d) #'numberp)
(1 3 4 7)
```

When a function is passed as a parameter, as in the above examples, it should be preceded by a #' instead of just a '. The purpose of this convention is to flag arguments that are functions so that they may be given appropriate treatment by the LISP interpreter. In particular, when a function is passed as an argument in Common LISP, the bindings of free variables (if any) must be included with that function. This combination of function definition and bindings of free variables is called a *lexical closure*; the #' informs LISP that the lexical closure must be constructed and passed with the function.

More formally, funcall is defined as having the syntax:

$$(\text{funcall} <\text{function}> <\text{arg}_1> <\text{arg}_2> ... <\text{arg}_n>)$$

In this definition, <function> is a LISP function and $<\text{arg}_1> ... <\text{arg}_n>$ are zero or more arguments to the function. The result of evaluating a funcall is the same as the result of evaluating <function> with the specified arguments as actual parameters.

A similar function is apply, which performs the same task as funcall but requires that the arguments be in a list. Except for this syntactic difference, apply and funcall behave the same; the programmer can choose the function that seems more convenient for a given application. These two functions are similar to eval in that all three of these functions allow the user to specify that function evaluation should take place. The difference is that eval requires its argument to be an s-expression that is evaluated, while funcall and apply take a function and its arguments as separate parameters. Examples of the behavior of these functions are:

```
> (funcall #'plus 2 3)
5
> (apply #'plus '(2 3))
5
> (eval '(plus 2 3))
5
> (funcall #'car '(a b c))
a
> (apply #'car '((a b c)))
a
```

Another important class of higher-order functions consists of *mapping functions*, functions that will apply a given function to all the elements of a list. Using funcall, the simple mapping function map-simple, which returns a list of the results of applying a functional argument to all the elements of a list, is defined:

```
(defun map-simple (func list)
  (cond ((null list) nil)
        (t (cons (funcall func (car list)) (map-simple func (cdr list))))))
```

For example, map-simple has the behavior:

```
> (map-simple '1+ '(1 2 3 4 5 6))
(2 3 4 5 6 7)
> (map-simple 'listp '(1 2 (3 4) 5 (6 7 8)))
(nil nil t nil t)
```

map-simple is actually a simplified version of a LISP built-in function called map-car. mapcar extends map-simple by allowing more than one argument list. This enables functions of more than one argument to be applied to corresponding elements of several lists:

```
> (mapcar '1+ '(1 2 3 4 5 6))                    ; this is the same as map-simple
(2 3 4 5 6 7)
> (mapcar '+ '(1 2 3 4) '(5 6 7 8))
(6 8 10 12)
> (mapcar 'max '(3 9 1 7) '(2 5 6 8))
(3 9 6 8)
```

mapcar is only one of many mapping functions provided by LISP, as well as only one of many higher-order functions built into the language.

7.3.2 Functional Arguments and Lambda Expressions

In the preceding examples, function arguments were passed in by their name and applied to a series of arguments. This requires that the functions be previously defined in the global environment. Frequently, however, it is desirable to pass a simple function definition directly, without first defining it globally. This is made possible through the lambda expression.

Essentially, the lambda expression allows us to separate a function definition from the function name. The origin of lambda expressions is in the *lambda calculus*, a mathematical model of computation that provides (among other things) a particularly thoughtful treatment of this distinction between an object and its name. The syntax of a lambda expression is similar to the function definition in a defun, except that the function name is replaced by the term lambda. That is,

    (lambda (<formal-parameters>) <body>)

Lambda expressions may be used in place of a function name in a funcall. The funcall will execute the body of the lambda expression with the arguments bound to the parameters of the funcall. As with named functions, the number of formal parameters and the number of actual parameters must be the same. For example:

    > (funcall #'(lambda (x) (* x x)) 4)
    16

Here, x is bound to 4 and the body of the lambda expression is then evaluated. The result, the square of 4, is returned by funcall. Other examples of the use of lambda expressions with funcall and apply are:

    > (apply #'(lambda (x y) (+ (* x x) y)) (2 3))
    7
    > (funcall #'(lambda (x) (append x x)) '(a b c))
    (a b c a b c)
    > (funcall #'(lambda (x1 x2) (append (reverse x1) x2)) '(a b c) '(d e f))
    (c b a d e f)

Lambda expressions may be used in a higher-order function such as mapcar in place of the names of globally defined functions. For example:

    > (mapcar #'(lambda (x) (* x x)) '(1 2 3 4 5))
    (1 4 9 16 25)
    > (mapcar #'(lambda (x) (* x 2)) '(1 2 3 4 5))
    (2 4 6 8 10)
    > (mapcar #'(lambda (x) (and (> x 0) (< x 10))) '(1 24 5 -9 8 23))
    (t nil t nil t nil)

Without lambda expressions the programmer must define every function in the global environment using a defun, even though that function may be used only once. Lambda expressions free the programmer: if it is desired to square each element in a list, the lambda form is passed to mapcar as the first of the above examples illustrates. It is not necessary to define a squaring function first.

7.4   Search Strategies in LISP

The use of higher-order functions provides LISP with a powerful tool for procedural abstraction. In this section, we use this abstraction technique to implement general algorithms for breadth-first, depth-first, and best-first search. These algorithms implement the search algorithms from Chapters 3 and 4, using open and closed lists to manage search through the state space. The moves for a given problem are a parameter to the search algorithm; the algorithms apply moves to states using funcall.

7.4.1   Breadth-First and Depth-First Search

The LISP implementation of breadth-first search maintains the open list as a first-in-first-out (FIFO) structure. We define open and closed as global variables. This is done for reasons of efficiency, avoiding the overhead of passing large lists as parameters to each call to breadth-first search. Though this approach digresses from the purely functional style, efficiency often dictates such an approach. In this situation, because open and closed may be large and are of global importance to the algorithm, their use as global variables seems justified. In addition, since the code is using global variables, we will make the goal global. By convention, global variables in Common LISP are written to begin and end with *.

Breadth-first search is defined:

```
(defun breadth-first ()
  (cond ((null *open*) nil)
    (t (let ((state (car *open*)))
        (cond ((equal state *goal*) 'success)
          (t (setq *closed* (cons state *closed*))
            (setq *open* (append (cdr *open*) (generate-descendants state *moves*)))
            (breadth-first)))))))


(defun run-breadth (start goal)
    (setq *open* (list start))
    (setq *closed* nil)
    (setq *goal* goal)
    (breadth-first))
```

In this algorithm, the *open* list is tested: if it is nil, the algorithm returns nil, indicating failure; otherwise it examines the first element of *open*. If this is equal to the goal, the algorithm halts and returns success; otherwise, it calls generate-descendants to produce the children of the current state, adds them to the *open* list, and recurs. run-breadth is an initialization function that sets the initial values of *open*, *closed*, and *goal*. Note that generate-descendants is passed both the state and *moves* as parameters. *moves* is a list of the functions that generate moves. In the farmer, wolf, goat, and cabbage problem, assuming the move definitions of Section 7.2, *moves* would be defined by

```
(setq *moves*
  '(farmer-takes-self farmer-takes-wolf farmer-takes-goat farmer-takes-cabbage))
```

generate-descendants takes a state and returns a list of its children. In addition to generating child states, it disallows duplicates in the list of children and eliminates any children that are already in the open or closed list. In addition to the state, generate-descendants is given a list of moves. These are functions that compute child states; they may be the names of defined functions, or they may be lambda definitions. generate-descendants uses a let block to save the result of a move in the local variable child. We define generate-descendants:

```
(defun generate-descendants (state moves)
  (cond ((null moves) nil)
    (t (let ((child (funcall (car moves) state))
         (rest (generate-descendants state (cdr moves))))
      (cond ((null child) rest)
        ((member child rest :test #'equal) rest)
        ((member child *open* :test #'equal) rest)
        ((member child *closed* :test #'equal) rest)
        (t (cons child rest)))))))
```

Note that the member functions use an additional parameter: :test #'equal. The member function allows the user to specify any test for membership. This allows us to use predicates of arbitrary complexity and semantics to test membership. Though LISP does not require that we specify the test, the default comparison is the predicate eq. eq requires that two objects be identical, which means they have the same location in memory; we are using a weaker comparison, equal, that only requires that the objects have the same value.

By binding the global variable *moves* to an appropriate set of move functions, this search algorithm may be used to search any state space in a breadth-first fashion.

One difficulty that remains with this algorithm is its inability to print the list of states along the path from a start to a goal. Although all the states that lead to the goal are present in the closed list when the algorithm halts, these are mixed with all other states from earlier levels of the search space. The algorithm can be modified to save a list containing the state and its parent. For example, if the state (e e e e) generates the state (w e w e), a record of both states, ((w e w e) (e e e e)), is placed on both *open* and *closed*.

When the current state is found to equal the goal, this ancestor information can be used to reconstruct the path from the goal back to the start state by tracing back along successive parents. This augmented version of breadth-first search begins by defining state records as an abstract data type:

```
(defun build-record (state parent) (list state parent))

(defun get-state (state-tuple) (nth 0 state-tuple))

(defun get-parent (state-tuple) (nth 1 state-tuple))

(defun retrieve-by-state (state list)
  (cond ((null list) nil)
    ((equal state (get-state (car list))) (car list))
    (t (retrieve-by-state state (cdr list)))))
```

build-record constructs a state/parent pair. get-state and get-parent access the appropriate fields of a record. retrieve-by-state takes a state and a list of state records and returns the record whose state field matches that state.

build-solution uses retrieve-by-state to chain back from state to parent, constructing a list of successive states that led to a goal. When initializing *open*, we will give the starting state a parent of nil; build-solution stops when passed a null state.

```
(defun build-solution (state)
  (cond ((null state) nil)
    (t (cons state (build-solution (get-parent (retrieve-by-state state *closed*)))))))
```

The remainder of the algorithm is a straightforward modification of the simple breadth-first search algorithm:

```
(defun run-breadth (start goal)
  (setq *open* (list (build-record start nil)))
  (setq *closed* nil)
  (setq *goal* goal)
  (breadth-first))

(defun breadth-first ()
  (cond ((null *open*) nil)
    (t (let ((state (car *open*)))
      (setq *closed* (cons state *closed*))
      (cond ((equal (get-state state) *goal*) (build-solution *goal*))
        (t (setq *open* (append (cdr *open*)
              (generate-descendants (get-state state) *moves*)))
          (breadth-first)))))))

(defun generate-descendants (state moves)
  (cond ((null moves) nil)
    (t (let ((child (funcall (car moves) state))
        (rest (generate-descendants state (cdr moves))))
      (cond ((null child) rest)
        ((retrieve-by-state child rest) rest)
        ((retrieve-by-state child *open*) rest)
        ((retrieve-by-state child *closed*) rest)
        (t (cons (build-record child state) rest)))))))
```

Depth-first search may be implemented by modifying breadth-first search to maintain open as a stack. This simply involves reversing the order of the arguments to append and is left to the reader.

7.4.2 Best-First Search

Best-first search may be implemented through straightforward modifications to the breadth-first search algorithm. Specifically, the heuristic evaluation is saved along with each state. The tuples on *open* are then sorted according to this evaluation. The data type definitions for state records are a simple extension of those used in breadth-first search:

```
(defun build-record (state parent depth weight)
  (list state parent depth weight))

(defun get-state (state-tuple) (nth 0 state-tuple))

(defun get-parent (state-tuple) (nth 1 state-tuple))

(defun get-depth (state-tuple) (nth 2 state-tuple))


(defun get-weight (state-tuple) (nth 3 state-tuple))

(defun retrieve-by-state (state list)
  (cond ((null list) nil)
    ((equal state (get-state (car list))) (car list))
    (t (retrieve-by-state state (cdr list)))))
```

best-first and generate-descendants are defined:

```
(defun best-first ()
  (cond ((null *open*) nil)
    (t (let ((state (car *open*)))
        (setq *closed* (cons state *closed*))
        (cond ((equal (get-state state) *goal*) (build-solution *goal*))
          (t (setq *open*
              (insert-by-weight
                (generate-descendants (get-state state)
                      (1+ (get-depth state)) *moves*) (cdr *open*)))
            (best-first)))))))

(defun generate-descendants (state depth moves)
  (cond ((null moves) nil)
    (t (let ((child (funcall (car moves) state))
          (rest (generate-descendants state depth (cdr moves))))
      (cond ((null child) rest)
```

```
                    ((retrieve-by-state child rest) rest)
                    ((retrieve-by-state child *open*) rest)
                    ((retrieve-by-state child *closed*) rest)
                    (t (cons (build-record child state depth (+ depth (heuristic child))) rest))))))))
```

The only differences between best-first and breadth-first search are the use of **insert-by-weight** to sort the records on *open* by heuristic weights and the computation of search depth and heuristic weights in **generate-descendants**.

Completion of **best-first** requires a definition of **insert-by-weight**. This function takes an unsorted list of state records and inserts them, one at a time, into their appropriate positions in *open*. It also requires a problem-specific definition of **heuristic**. This function takes a state and, using the global *goal*, computes a heuristic weight for that state. We leave the definition of these functions as an exercise for the reader.

7.5   Pattern Matching in LISP

Pattern matching is an important AI methodology that has already been discussed in the PROLOG chapters and the discussion of production systems. In this section we implement a recursive pattern matcher and use it to build a pattern-directed retrieval function for a simple data base.

The heart of this retrieval system is a function called **match**, which takes as arguments two s-expressions and returns **t** if the expressions match. Matching requires that both expressions have the same *structure*, as well as having identical atoms in corresponding positions. In addition, **match** allows the inclusion of variables, denoted by **?**, in an s-expression. Variables are allowed to match with any s-expression, either a list or an atom, but do not save bindings, as with full unification. Examples of the desired behavior for **match** appear below. If the examples seem reminiscent of the PROLOG examples in Chapter 6, this is because **match** is actually a simplified version of the unification algorithm that forms the heart of PROLOG, as well as many other pattern-directed AI systems. In Section 7.6 we expand **match** into the full unification algorithm by allowing named variables and returning a list of bindings required for a match.

```
> ( match '(likes bill wine) '(likes bill wine))
t
> (match '(likes bill wine) '(likes bill milk))
nil
> (match '(likes bill ?) '(likes bill wine))              ; example with a variable
t
> (match '(likes ? wine) '(likes bill ?))                 ; note variables in both expressions
t
> (match '(likes bill ?) '(likes bill (prolog lisp smalltalk))
t
> (match '(likes ?) '(likes bill wine))
nil
```

match is used to define a function called get-matches, which takes as arguments two s-expressions. The first argument is a pattern to be matched against elements of the second s-expression, which must be a list. get-matches returns a list of the elements of the list that match the first argument. In effect, the second argument is a data base of s-expressions, with get-matches implementing pattern-directed retrieval from that data base. In the example below, get-matches is used to retrieve records from an employee data base as described earlier in this chapter.

Because the data base is a large and relatively complex s-expression, we have bound it to the global variable *database* and use that variable as an argument to get-matches. This was done to improve readability of the examples.

```
> (setq *database*'((((lovelace ada) 50000.00 1234)
((turing alan) 45000.00 3927)
((shelley mary) 35000.00 2850)
((vonNeumann john) 40000.00 7955)
((simon herbert) 50000.00 1374)
((mccarthy john) 48000.00 2864)
((russell bertrand) 35000.00 2950))
*database*
> (get-matches '((turing alan) 45000.00 3927) *database*)
((turing alan) 45000.00 3927)
> (get-matches '(? 50000.00 ?) *database*)              ; all people who make 50000
(((lovelace ada) 50000.00 1234) ((simon herbert) 50000.00 1374))
> (get-matches '((? john) ? ?) *database*)              ; all people named john

(((vonNeumann john) 40000.00 7955) ((mccarthy john) 48000.00 2864))
```

We implement get-matches through a straightforward use of cdr recursion to scan down the data base looking for elements that match with the first argument (the pattern). All elements of the data base that match the pattern are consed together to form the answer. get-matches is defined:

```
(defun get-matches (pattern database)
  (cond ((null data-base) ())
    ((match pattern (car data-base))                    ; match found, add to result
      (cons (car data-base) (get-matches pattern (cdr data-base))))
    ( t (get-matches pattern (cdr data-base)))))         ; no match
```

The heart of the system is the match function, a predicate that determines whether or not two s-expressions containing variables actually match. match is based on the idea that two lists match if and only if their respective cars and cdrs match. This suggests a car-cdr recursive scheme for the algorithm. The recursion terminates when either of the arguments is atomic (this includes the empty list, nil, which is both an atom and a list). If both patterns are the same atom or if one of the patterns is a variable atom, ?, which can match with anything, then termination is with a successful match; otherwise, the match will fail. Notice that if either of the patterns is a variable, the other pattern may or may not be atomic; variables may match with s-expressions of arbitrary complexity.

PART III / LANGUAGES FOR AI PROBLEM SOLVING

Because the handling of the terminating conditions is complex, the implementation of match uses a function called **match-atom** that takes two arguments, one or both of which is an atom, and checks to see whether the patterns match. Also, by hiding this complexity in match-atom the car-cdr recursive structure of match is more apparent:

```
(defun match (pattern1 pattern2)
   (cond (or (atom pattern1) (atom pattern2))       ; one of the patterns is atomic
            (match-atom pattern1 pattern2))          ; call match-atom, otherwise
         (t (and (match (car pattern1) (car pattern2))   ; match both car and cdr
               (match (cdr pattern1) (cdr pattern2))))))
```

The implementation of **match-atom** makes use of the fact that when it is called, at least one of the arguments is an atom. Because of this assumption, a simple test for equality of patterns is all that is needed to test that both patterns are the same atom (including both being a variable); it will fail either if the two patterns are different atoms or if one of them is nonatomic. If the first test fails, the only way a match can succeed is if one of the patterns is a variable. This check constitutes the remainder of the function definition. Finally, a function **variable** is defined to test whether or not a pattern is a variable. Treating variables as an abstract data type now will simplify later extensions to the function (e.g., named variables as in PROLOG). The following definitions complete the pattern-matching retrieval system:

```
(defun match-atom (pattern1 pattern2)
   (or (equal pattern1 pattern2)        ; both patterns are the same, or
       (variable pattern1)              ; one of them is a variable.
       (variable pattern2)))

(defun variable (x) (equal x '?))
```

7.6   A Recursive Unification Function

In Section 7.5 we implemented a recursive pattern-matching algorithm that allowed the inclusion of unnamed variables (denoted by **?**) in patterns. Now we extend this simple pattern matcher into the full unification algorithm presented in Chapter 2. The function, unify, allows named variables in both of the patterns to be matched and returns a list of the variable bindings required for the match. This unification function is the basis of the inference systems developed in Chapter 14.

7.6.1   Implementing the Unification Algorithm

As in Section 7.5, patterns are either constants, variables, or list structures. In a full unifier, variables may be distinguished from one another by their names. Named variables are represented as lists of the form (var <name>), where <name> is usually an atomic symbol. (var x), (var y), and (var newstate) are all examples of legal variables.

The function unify takes as arguments two patterns to be matched and a set of variable substitutions (bindings) to be employed in the match. Generally, this set will be empty (nil) when the function is first called. On a successful match, unify returns a (possibly empty) set of substitutions required for a successful match. If no match was possible, unify returns the symbol failed; nil is used to indicate an empty substitution set, i.e., a match in which no substitutions were required. The representation of substitution sets is discussed in Section 7.6.2.

An example of the behavior of unify, with comments, appears below.

```
> (unify '(p a (var x)) '(p a b) ())              ; returns substitution of b for (var x)
(((var x) . b))
> (unify '(p (var y) b) '(p a (var x)) ())        ; variables appear in both patterns
(((var x) . b) ((var y) . a))
> (unify '(p (var x)) '(p (q a (var y))) ())      ; variable bound to more complex pattern
(((var x) q a (var y)))
> (unify '(p a) '(p a) ())                         ; nil indicates no substitution required
nil
> (unify '(p a) '(q a) ())                         ; returns the atom failed to indicate failure
failed
```

We explain the "." notation, as in ((var x).6), in section 7.6.2. unify, like the pattern matcher of Section 7.5, uses a car-cdr recursive scheme and is defined by:

```
(defun unify (pattern1 pattern2 substitution-list)
  (cond ((equal substitution-list 'failed) 'failed)
        ((varp pattern1) (match-var pattern1 pattern2 substitution-list))    ; varp tests
        ((varp pattern2) (match-var pattern2 pattern1 substitution-list))    ; if variable
        ((is-constant-p pattern1)
          (cond ((equal pattern1 pattern2) substitution-list)
                (t 'failed)))
        ((is-constant-p pattern2) 'failed)
        (t (unify (cdr pattern1) (cdr pattern2)
          (unify (car pattern1) (car pattern2) substitution-list)))))
```

On entering unify, the algorithm first checks whether the substitution list is equal to failed. This could occur if a prior attempt to unify the cars of two patterns had failed. If this condition is met, the function returns failed.

Next, if either pattern is a variable, the function match-var is called to perform further checking and possibly add a new binding to the substitution list. If neither pattern is a variable, unify tests whether either is a constant, returning the unchanged substitution list if they are the same constant, failed otherwise.

The last item in the cond statement implements the tree-recursive decomposition of the problem: first the cars of the patterns are unified using the bindings in substitution-list. The result is passed as the third argument to the call of unify on the cdrs of both patterns. This allows the variable substitutions made in matching the cars to be applied to other occurrences of those variables in the cdrs of both patterns.

match-var, which handles the case of matching a variable and a pattern, is defined by:

```
(defun match-var (var pattern substitution-list)
  (cond ((equal var pattern) substitution-list)
    (t (let ((binding (get-binding var substitution-list)))
        (cond (binding (unify (get-binding-value binding) pattern substitution-list))
              ((occursp var pattern) 'failed)
              (t (add-substitution var pattern substitution-list))))))))
```

match-var first checks whether the variable and the pattern are the same; unifying a variable with itself requires no added substitutions, so substitution-list is returned unchanged.

If var and pattern are not the same, match-var checks whether the variable is already bound. If a binding exists, unify is called recursively to match the *value* of the binding with pattern. Note that this binding value may be a constant, a variable, or a pattern of arbitrary complexity; this requires a call to the full unification algorithm to complete the match.

If no binding currently exists for var, the function calls occursp to test whether var appears in pattern. The *occurs check* is needed to prevent attempts to unify a variable with a pattern containing that variable, leading to a circular structure. For example, if (var x) was bound to (p (var x)), any attempt to apply those substitutions to a pattern would result in an infinite loop. If var appears in pattern, match-var returns failed; otherwise, it adds the new substitution pair to substitution-list using add-substitution.

unify and match-var are the heart of the unification algorithm. occursp (which performs a tree walk on a pattern to find any occurrences of the variable in that pattern), varp, and is-constant-p (which test whether their argument is a variable or a constant, respectively) appear below. Functions for handling substitution sets are discussed in the next section.

```
(defun occursp (var pattern)
  (cond ((equal var pattern) t)
    ((or (varp pattern) (is-constant-p pattern)) nil)
    (t (or (occursp var (car pattern))
           (occursp var (cdr pattern))))))

(defun is-constant-p (item)
  (atom item))

(defun varp (item)
  (and (listp item)
    (equal (length item) 2)
    (equal (car item) 'var)))
```

7.6.2 Implementing Substitution Sets Using Association Lists

Sets of substitutions are represented using a built-in LISP data type called the *association list* or *a-list*. This is the basis for the functions add-substitutions, get-binding, and binding-value. An association list is a list of data records, or *key/data* pairs. The car of each record is a *key* for its retrieval; the cdr of each record is called the *datum*. The datum may be a list of values or a single atom. Retrieval is implemented by the function assoc, which takes as arguments a key and an association list and returns the first member of the association list that has the key as its car. An optional third argument to assoc specifies the test to be used in comparing keys. The default test is the Common LISP function eql, a form of equality test that requires that two arguments be exactly the same object (i.e., either the same memory location or the same numeric value). In implementing substitution sets, we will specify a less strict test, equal, which requires only that the arguments match syntactically (i.e., are designated by identical names). An example of assoc's behavior appears below:

```
> (assoc 3 '((1 a) (2 b) (3 c) (4 d)))
(3 c)
> (assoc 'd '((a b c) (b c d e) (d e f) (c d e)) :test #'equal)
(d e f)
> (assoc 'c '((a . 1) (b . 2) (c . 3) (d . 4)) :test #'equal)
(c . 3)
> (assoc 'jimmy '((ron . nancy) (jimmy . ros) (jerry . betty) (dick . pat)) :test #'equal)
(jimmy . ros)
```

Note that assoc returns the entire record matched on the key; the datum may be retrieved from this list by the cdr function. Also, notice that in the last two calls the members of the a-list are not lists but a structure called *dotted pairs* (e.g., (a . 1), (ron . nancy)).

The dotted pair, or *cons pair*, is actually the fundamental constructor in LISP. It is the result of consing one s-expression onto another; the list notation that we have used throughout the chapter is just a notational variant of dotted pairs. For example, the value returned by (cons 1 nil) is actually (1 . nil); this is equivalent to (1). Similarly, the list (1 2 3) may be written in dotted pair notation as (1 . (2 . (3 . nil))). Although the actual effect of a cons is to create a dotted pair, the list notation is cleaner and is generally preferred.

If two atoms are consed together, the result is always written using dotted pair notation. The cdr of a dotted pair is the second element in the pair, rather than a list containing the second atom. For example:

```
> (cons 'a 'b)
(a . b)
> (car '(a . b))
a
> (cdr '(a . b))
b
```

Dotted pairs occur naturally in association lists when one atom is used as a key for retrieving another atom, as well as in other applications that require the formation and manipulation of pairs of atomic symbols. Because unifications often substitute a single atom for a variable, dotted pairs appear often in the association list returned by the unification function.

Along with assoc, Common LISP defines the function acons, which takes as arguments a key, a datum, and an a-list and returns a new association list whose first element is the result of consing the key onto the datum. For example:

```
> (acons 'a 1 nil)
((a . 1))
```

Note that when acons is given two atoms, it adds a dotted pair to the association list:

```
> (acons 'george 'barb '((ron . nancy) (jimmy . ros) (jerry . betty) (dick . pat)))
((george . barb) (ron . nancy) (jimmy . ros) (jerry . betty) (dick . pat))
> (acons 'pets' (emma jack clyde)
     '((name . bill) (hobbies music skiing movies) (job . programmer)))
((pets emma jack clyde) (name . bill) (hobbies music skiing movies) (job . programmer))
```

Members on an association list may be either dotted pairs or lists.

Association lists provide a convenient way to implement a variety of tables and other simple data retrieval schemes. In implementing the unification algorithm, we use association lists to represent sets of substitutions: the keys are the variables, and the data are the values of their bindings. The datum may be a simple variable or constant or a more complicated structure.

Using association lists, the substitution set functions are defined:

```
(defun get-binding (var substitution-list)
  (assoc var substitution-list :test #'equal))

(defun get-binding-value (binding) (cdr binding))

(defun add-substitution (var pattern substitution-list)
  (acons var pattern substitution-list))
```

This completes the implementation of the unification algorithm.

7.7   Interpreters and Embedded Languages

The top level of the LISP interpreter is known as the *read-eval-print* loop. This describes the interpreter's behavior in reading, evaluating, and printing the value of s-expressions entered by the user. The eval function, defined in Section 7.1.4, is the heart of the LISP interpreter; using eval, it is possible to write the top-level read-eval-print loop in LISP itself. In the next example, we develop a simplified version of this loop. This version is simplified chiefly in that it does not have the error-handling abilities of the built-in loop, although LISP does provide the functionality needed to implement such capabilities.

To write the read-eval-print loop, we use two more LISP functions, read and print. read is a function that takes no parameters; when it is evaluated, it simply returns the next s-expression entered at the keyboard. print is a function that takes a single argument, evaluates it, and then prints that result to standard output. On completion, print returns a value of nil. Another function that will prove useful is terpri, a function of no arguments that causes a newline character to be sent to standard output. terpri also returns a value of nil on completion.

Using these functions, the read-eval-print loop is based on a simple nested s-expression:

```
(print (eval (read)))
```

When this is evaluated, the innermost s-expression, (read), is evaluated first. The value returned by the read, the next s-expression entered by the user, is passed to eval, where it is evaluated. The result of this evaluation is passed to print, where it is sent to the display screen. To complete the loop we add a print expression to output the prompt, a terpri to output a newline after the result has been printed, and a recursive call to repeat the cycle. Thus, the final read-eval-print loop is defined:

```
(defun my-read-eval-print ()              ; this function takes no arguments
  (print ':)                              ; output a prompt, ours is a ":"
  (print (eval (read)))                   ; read-eval-print
  (terpri)                                ; output a newline
  (my-read-eval-print))                   ; do it all again
```

This may be used "on top of" the built-in interpreter:

```
> (my-read-eval-print)
:(+ 1 2)                                  ; note the new prompt
3
:                                         ; etc.
```

As this example illustrates, by making functions such as quote and eval available to the user, LISP gives the programmer a high degree of control over the handling of functions. Because LISP programs and data are both represented as s-expressions, we may write programs that perform any desired manipulations of LISP expressions prior to evaluating them. This underlies much of LISP's power as a procedural representation language, because it allows arbitrary LISP code to be stored, modified, and evaluated when needed. It also makes it simple to write specialized interpreters that may extend or modify the behavior of the built-in LISP interpreter in some desired fashion. This capability is at the heart of many LISP-based expert systems, where the system is basically a loop that reads user queries and responds to them according to the expertise contained in its knowledge base.

As an example of the way in which such a specialized interpreter may be implemented in LISP, we may modify my-read-eval-print so that it evaluates arithmetic expressions in an infix rather than a prefix notation. That is, the loop should function as an interpreter for arithmetic expressions in an infix notation, as in the following example (note the modified prompt, infix->):

```
infix-> (1 + 2)
3
infix-> (7 - 2)
5
infix-> ((5 + 2) * (3 - 1))          ; the loop should allow nesting of expressions
14
```

To simplify the example, the infix interpreter handles only arithmetic expressions. A further simplification restricts the interpreter to binary operations and requires that all expressions be fully parenthesized, eliminating the need for more sophisticated parsing techniques or worries about operator precedence. However, it does allow expressions to be nested to arbitrary depth and handles all the binary arithmetic operators supported by LISP.

Our approach is to modify the previously developed read-eval-print loop by adding a function that translates infix expressions into prefix expressions prior to passing them on to eval. A first attempt at writing this function might look like:

```
(defun simple-in-to-pre (exp)
   (list (nth 1 exp)          ; middle element (operator) becomes first element.
      (nth 0 exp)                                        ; first operand
      (nth 2 exp)))                                     ; second operand
```

simple-in-to-pre is effective in translating simple expressions; however, it is not able to correctly translate nested expressions, that is, expressions in which the operands are themselves infix expressions. To handle this situation properly, the operands must also be translated into prefix notation. Recursion is halted by testing the argument to determine whether it is a number, returning it unchanged if it is. The completed version of the infix-to-prefix translator is:

```
(defun in-to-pre (exp)
  (cond ((numberp exp) exp)
     (t (list (nth 1 exp)
           (in-to-pre (nth 0 exp))
           (in-to-pre (nth 2 exp))))))
```

Using this translator, the read-eval-print loop may be modified to interpret infix expressions, as defined below:

```
(defun in-eval ()
    (print 'infix->)
    (print (eval (in-to-pre (read))))
    (terpri)
    (in-eval))
```

This allows the interpretation of binary expressions in infix form:

```
> (in-eval)
infix->(2 + 2)
4
infix->((3 * 4) - 5)
7
```

In the above example, we have implemented a new language, the language of infix arithmetic, in LISP. Because of the powerful facilities LISP provides for symbolic computing (lists and functions for their manipulation) along with the ability to control evaluation, this was much easier to do than in most programming languages. This example is important in that it illustrates an important AI programming methodology, that of *embedded languages*. Very often in AI programming, a problem is not completely understood, or the program required to solve a problem is extremely complex. So it becomes desirable to place another conceptual layer between LISP and the final solution to the problem. This layer is either a collection of functions or a higher-level language that, though it does not directly solve the problem, provides a more powerful tool for exploring the problem and eventually implementing a full solution to it. In effect, rather than being used to code a problem solution, LISP is used to implement a language that seems more directly applicable to the development of such a program. Features that typically appear in embedded languages in AI include pattern matchers, production system controllers, and access functions for data structures such as frames and semantic networks (Chapter 14).

7.8   Epilogue and References

Though this chapter has given some examples of using LISP to solve a number of AI problems, it has discussed only a few of the rich ideas included in the language. A number of texts provide further discussion of the language. *Common LISP: The Language*, 2d edition, by Guy L. Steele, Jr. (1990), is the standard reference on the syntax and semantics of the language. Other books, which give a more tutorial treatment of the language and its use, include *Lisp* by Patrick Winston and Berthold K. P. Horn (1984), *Common Lispcraft* by Robert Wilensky (1986), and *Introduction to Common LISP* by Taiichi Yuasa and Masami Hagiya (1986).

A comprehensive book on AI programming techniques using LISP is *Artificial Intelligence Programming*, 2d edition, by Charniak, Riesbeck, and McDermott (1987).

The Structure and Interpretation of Computer Programs by Abelson and Sussman (1985) is a particularly interesting book based on the LISP dialect SCHEME. This is much more than a book on a programming language: it is a rethinking of computer science based on techniques suggested by the SCHEME dialect.

Finally, for an interesting theoretical discussion of functional programming, including the implementation issues involved in LISP-like languages, *Functional Programming* by Henderson (1980) is recommended.

7.9 Exercises

1. Newton's method for solving roots takes an estimate of the value of the root and tests it for accuracy. If the guess does not meet the required tolerance, it computes a new estimate and repeats. Pseudocode for using Newton's method to take the square root of a number is:

   function root-by-newtons-method (x, tolerance)

   begin
     guess := 1;
     repeat
       guess := 1/2(guess + x/guess)
     until absolute-value(x - guess*guess) < tolerance

   Write a recursive LISP function to compute square roots by Newton's method.

2. a. Write a recursive LISP function that will reverse the elements of a list. (Do not use the built-in reverse function.) What is the complexity of your implementation? It is possible to reverse a list in linear time; can you do so?

   b. Write a LISP function that will take a list nested to any depth and print the mirror image of that list. For instance, the function should have the behavior:

   > (mirror '((a b) (c (d e))))
   (((e d) c) (b a))

3. Write a random number generator in LISP. This function must maintain a global variable, seed, and return a different random number each time it is called. For a description of a reasonable random number algorithm, consult any basic algorithms text.

4. Write the functions initialize, push, top, pop, and list-stack to maintain a global stack. These functions should behave:

   > (initialize)
   nil
   > (push 'foo)
   foo
   > (push 'bar)
   bar
   > (top)
   bar
   > (list-stack)
   (bar foo)
   > (pop)
   bar
   > (list-stack)
   (foo)

5. Sets may be represented using lists. Note that these lists should not contain any duplicate elements. Write LISP implementations of the set operations union, intersection, and difference. (Do not use Common LISP's built-in versions of these functions.)

6. The tower of Hanoi problem is based on the following legend:

In a Far Eastern monastery, there is a puzzle consisting of three diamond needles and 64 gold disks. The disks are of graduated sizes. Initially, the disks are all stacked on a single needle in decreasing order of size. The monks are attempting to move all the disks to another needle under the following rules:

a. Only one disk may be moved at a time.
b. No disk can ever rest on a smaller disk.

Legend has it that when the task has been completed, the universe will end.

Write a LISP program to solve this problem. For safety's sake (and to write a program that will finish in your lifetime) do not attempt the full 64-disk problem. Three or four disks is more reasonable.

7. Write a compiler for arithmetic expressions of the form:

(op operand1 operand2)

where op is either +, −, *, or / and the operands are either numbers or nested expressions. An example of a legal expression is (* (+ 3 6) (- 7 9)). Assume that the target machine has instructions:

(move value register)
(add register-1 register-2)
(subtract register-1 register-2)
(times register-1 register-2)
(divide register-1 register-2)

All the arithmetic operations will leave the result in the first register argument. To simplify, assume an unlimited number of registers. Your compiler should take an arithmetic expression and return a list of these machine operations.

8. Implement a depth-first backtracking solution (such as was used to solve the farmer, wolf, goat, and cabbage problem in Section 7.2) to the missionary and cannibal problem:

Three missionaries and three cannibals come to the bank of a river they wish to cross. There is a boat that will hold only two, and any of the group is able to row it. If there are ever more missionaries than cannibals on any side of the river the cannibals will get converted. Devise a series of moves to get all the people across the river with no conversions.

9. Implement a depth-first solution to the water jugs problem:

There are two jugs, one holding 3 and the other 5 gallons of water. A number of things that can be done with the jugs: they can be filled, emptied, and dumped one into the other either until the poured-into jug is full or until the poured-out-of jug is empty. Devise a sequence of actions that will produce 4 gallons of water in the larger jug. (Hint: only integer values of water are used.)

10. Use the breadth-first search algorithm of Exercise 10 to solve:

    a. The farmer, wolf, goat, and cabbage problem (see Section 7.2).

    b. The missionary and cannibal problem (see Exercise 8).

    c. The water jugs problem (see Exercise 9).

    Compare the breadth-first results to the depth-first results. The differences will probably be the most telling for the water jugs problem. Why?

11. Finish implementing best-first search using the general path algorithm described in Section 7.3.3. Use this along with appropriate heuristics to solve each of the three problems mentioned in Exercise 11.

12. Write a LISP program to solve the full 8 × 8 version of the knight's tour problem.

13. Write a LISP program to solve the 8-queens problem. (This problem is to find a way to place eight queens on a chessboard so that no queen may capture any other through a single move.)

14. Although we have implemented breadth-first and best-first search using a recursive function, these algorithms are suited to an iterative implementation. Using the generalized looping function do (see a LISP manual for its definition), implement iterative versions of these functions.

15. The implementations of breadth-first, depth-first, and best-first search using open and closed lists are all very similar; they differ only in the way in which open is maintained. Write a general search function that can implement any of these three searches by defining the function for maintaining open as a parameter.

16. Using the unification function of this chapter, implement a simple data base retrieval system that will retrieve records using pattern matching.

PART IV

REPRESENTATIONS FOR KNOWLEDGE-BASED SYSTEMS

Nam et ipsa scientia potestas est (Knowledge is power).

—FRANCIS BACON

Horatio: O day and night but this is wondrous strange!

Hamlet: And therefore as a stranger give it welcome.
  There are more things in heaven and earth, Horatio,
  Than are dreamt of in your philosophy.
  But come . . .

—WILLIAM SHAKESPEARE, *Hamlet*

In the late 1950s and early 1960s, Alan Newell and Herbert Simon wrote several computer programs to test the hypothesis that intelligent behavior resulted from heuristic search. Their first major program, the Logic Theorist, developed in conjunction with J. C. Shaw (Newell and Simon 1963*a*), proved theorems in elementary logic using the notation and axioms provided by Russell and Whitehead's *Principia Mathematica*. The authors describe their research as being

> aimed at understanding the complex processes (heuristics) that are effective in problem solving. Hence, we are not interested in methods that guarantee solutions, but which require vast amounts of computation. Rather we wish to understand how a mathematician, for example, is able to prove a theorem even though he does not know when he starts how, or if, he is going to succeed.

A later program, Newell and Simon's General Problem Solver (GPS) (Newell and Simon 1963*b*, 1972), continued this effort to find general principles of intelligent problem solving. The GPS solved problems formulated as state space search; legal problem-solving steps were a set of operations for modifying state representations. The General Problem Solver searched for a sequence of operations that would transform the start state into the goal state, searching a space of possible state transformations in the same fashion as the search algorithms discussed in earlier chapters of this text.

GPS used *means-ends analysis,* a general heuristic for selecting among alternative state transformation operations, to guide search through the problem space. Means-ends analysis examines the *syntactic* differences between the current state and the goal state and selects an operator that reduces these differences. Suppose, for example, that GPS is attempting to prove the equivalence of two logical expressions. If the current state contains an ∧ operator and the goal does not contain an ∧, then means-ends analysis would select a transformation such as de Morgan's law, to remove ∧ from expressions.

Like all heuristics, means-ends analysis is not foolproof; it fails, for example, when given expressions that must first have their differences temporarily increased in order to find a solution path. Consider, for example, the 8-puzzle board of Figure IV.1. Although only one tile, 3, is out of place, the only possible next step is to move either tile 2 or tile 4. Because either of these moves increases the difference between the board and the goal, a strictly applied difference reduction heuristic cannot select either of them. In fact, it would be difficult for means-ends analysis to determine whether a solution exists in this case.

A fundamental aspect of the GPS is its restriction to a heuristic based solely on the syntactic form of state descriptors. By using a heuristic that examines only the syntactic form of states, it was hoped that GPS would indeed prove to be a *general* architecture for intelligent problem solving, no matter what the domain. Programs like the GPS, which restrict themselves to strategies that can be applied across a wide variety of applications, are known as *weak problem solvers.* Because they attempt to implement general strategies, such as those described in Chapters 2 through 5, weak problem solvers may only examine the syntactic form of state descriptions. They may not use theoretical or empirical knowledge about a specific problem domain.

Weak methods are an important class of problem-solving techniques that are used where general search strategies are required or where it is difficult to extract a suitable body of strong heuristics. Besides the problem solving described in Chapters 2 through 5, automatic theorem proving (Chapter 11) depends heavily on weak methods, as does much research in machine learning (Chapter 12).

Unfortunately, there does not seem to be a single heuristic that can successfully be applied to all problem domains. In general, the methods we use to solve problems employ a great deal of knowledge about the domain. Doctors are able to diagnose illness because they have extensive knowledge of medicine, in addition to their general problem-solving abilities. Architects are able to design houses because they know about architecture. The heuristics used in medical diagnosis would be useless in designing an office building.

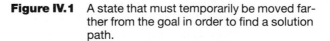

Current state   Goal

Figure IV.1   A state that must temporarily be moved farther from the goal in order to find a solution path.

Weak methods stand in sharp contrast to *strong methods*, which use knowledge of a particular problem domain. For example, a strong heuristic for diagnosing automotive problems might be:

if
the engine does not turn over, and
the lights do not come on
then
the problem is battery or cables

This heuristic, phrased as an *if . . . then . . .* rule, focuses search on the battery/cable subsystem of the automobile, eliminating other components and pruning the search space. Notice that this particular heuristic, unlike means-ends analysis, uses empirical knowledge of how automobiles function, such as knowledge of the relationships among the battery, lights, and starter. It is useless in any problem domain except auto repair.

Many important problems depend on domain-specific knowledge for their solution. These include most of the problem areas that we associate with expert-level performance in humans, such as medicine, engineering, science, and business. This knowledge-intensive approach contrasts sharply with GPS's goal of finding a single general heuristic for solving all problems.

Not only do strong problem solvers use domain-specific heuristics, but also they generally require large amounts of such knowledge to be effective. The bad-battery heuristic, for example, would not be of much use in diagnosing a bad carburetor; an automotive diagnostic program must have a number of such specific rules to handle a range of possible diagnoses. The major challenge in designing a knowledge-based program is the acquisition and organization of large amounts of specific problem-solving knowledge.

Most of the techniques that AI has developed for solving these problems depend on the separation of the knowledge and control aspects of the program. Levesque (Levesque and Brachman 1985) has given a simple illustration of the benefits of this separation in the form of two PROLOG programs:

```
% Version 1

print_color(rose) :- write(red),nl,!.
print_color(sky) :- write(yellow),nl,!.
print_color(grass) :- write(green),nl,!.
print_color(_) :- write('color not known'),nl,!.


% Version 2

print_color(X) :- color(X,Y),write(Y),nl,!.
print_color(_) :- write('color not known'),nl,!.

color(rose,red).
color(sky,yellow).
color(grass,green).
```

Although both of these programs have identical behavior, the second has represented the relationship between an object and its color explicitly using the color predicate. These color predicates constitute a *knowledge base* that is distinct from the control and implementation details found in the definition of print_color. A *knowledge-based system* is one that uses a separate base of explicitly represented problem-solving knowledge.

Because it is separate from the control aspects of the program, the knowledge base is highly modular and modifiable. The programmer does not have to worry about the implementation of the control aspects of the program but may focus on the acquisition and organization of the knowledge itself. Another benefit of this separation is that it allows knowledge to be represented in a concise and intuitively appealing form, such as the color predicate.

Note, however, that both versions of the program allow incorrect knowledge (the sky is yellow) to be included. Although this approach assists the programmer by making the contents of the knowledge base explicit, it does not guarantee correctness of the knowledge.

The separation of knowledge and control is so intuitively appealing and so common in AI that it is often taken for granted as the best way to design an intelligent program. Before proceeding with Part IV, we would like to emphasize that in following this approach, we are making certain assumptions about the nature of intelligent systems. In addition to its benefits, the knowledge-based approach has subtle implications for the questions proposed in AI research and the paths taken toward their solution.

These assumptions have been formalized by Brian Smith (1985) as the *knowledge representation hypothesis*. This hypothesis states that

> any mechanically embodied intelligent process will be comprised of structural ingredients that (a) we as external observers naturally take to represent a propositional account of the knowledge that the overall process exhibits, and (b) independent of such external semantical attribution, play a formal role in engendering the behavior that manifests that knowledge.

The important aspects of this hypothesis include the assumption that knowledge will be represented *propositionally*, that is, in a form that explicitly represents the knowledge in question and that may be seen by an outside observer as a "natural" description of that knowledge. The second major assumption is that the behavior of the system should be directly caused by the propositions in the knowledge base and that this behavior should be consistent with our perceived meaning of those propositions. Note that this assumption does not require a particular syntax for the representation, such as expressions in formal logic; it only requires that we be able to understand the intended meaning by examining the contents of the knowledge base. This eliminates programs that represent knowledge implicitly in a formalism such as arrays of numbers or circuits. For examples of the non-propositional approach to AI, the reader is referred to work in neural networks or connectionist models of intelligence (Chapter 12).

The knowledge representation hypothesis makes explicit the assumptions underlying the majority of work in artificial intelligence.

One of the major benefits of the separation of knowledge and control is greater freedom in the design of knowledge representation languages. In Part II, we introduced the predicate calculus as a representation language for AI. Another important representation is found in the *rule-based expert system*. Much of the pioneering work in knowledge-based programming was done using rule-based representations, and this approach continues to be used in numerous applications. In Chapter 8 we discuss this work and examine the problems involved in the acquisition, formalization, and debugging of a knowledge base.

In spite of the benefits of logical and rule-based representations, the demands of knowledge-based problem solving have continued to stimulate work in the design of knowledge representation languages. In Chapter 9 we examine the major alternatives to rules and logic, including *semantic networks*, *frames*, and *objects*.

Because enormous amounts of knowledge are needed to unravel the complexity and ambiguity of human language, *natural language understanding* has remained one of the most difficult areas of AI research and has motivated much of this research in knowledge representation. Using a knowledge-based approach, researchers have successfully developed programs that understand natural language in specific domains. In Chapter 10 we introduce some techniques for writing natural language understanding programs.

In spite of the successes of expert systems and similar strong problem solvers, many domains require general methods. In fact, the control strategies of expert systems themselves depend on good weak problem-solving methods. Much promising work on weak problem solvers has been done in the automatic theorem proving community. These techniques have found application in a number of important areas including integrated circuit design and proofs of program correctness. In Chapter 11 we examine work in automated reasoning and continue the presentation of formal reasoning we started in Chapter 2.

Chapter 12 introduces machine learning. Not only is machine learning currently an exciting focus for AI researchers, but it is also an area where we must make progress if we are going to consider machines intelligent. We present several approaches to machine learning that can each be classified by their relationship to weak and strong problem solving methods.

RULE-BASED EXPERT SYSTEMS

The first principle of knowledge engineering is that the problem solving power exhibited by an intelligent agent's performance is primarily the consequence of its knowledge base, and only secondarily a consequence of the inference method employed. Expert systems must be knowledge-rich even if they are methods-poor. This is an important result and one that has only recently become well understood in AI. For a long time AI has focused its attentions almost exclusively on the development of clever inference methods; almost any inference method will do. The power resides in the knowledge.

—EDWARD FEIGENBAUM, Stanford University

It is a capital mistake to theorize in advance of the facts . . .

—ARTHUR CONAN DOYLE, "Sherlock Holmes"

The imagination loses vitality as it ceases to adhere to what is real . . .

—WALLACE STEVENS

8.0   Introduction

An *expert system* is a knowledge-based program that provides "expert quality" solutions to problems in a specific domain. Generally, its knowledge is extracted from human experts in the domain and it attempts to emulate their methodology and performance. As with skilled humans, expert systems tend to be specialists, focusing on a narrow set of problems. Also, like humans, their knowledge is both theoretical and practical, having been perfected through experience in the domain. Unlike a human being, however, current programs cannot learn from their own experience; their knowledge must be extracted from humans and encoded in a formal language. This encoding is the major task facing expert system builders.

Expert systems should not be confused with cognitive modeling programs, which attempt to simulate human mental architecture in detail. These are discussed in Chapter 16. Expert systems neither copy the structure of the human mind nor are mechanisms for general intelligence. They are practical programs that use heuristic strategies developed by humans to solve specific classes of problems.

Because of the heuristic, knowledge-intensive nature of expert-level problem solving, expert systems are generally:

1. Open to inspection, both in presenting intermediate steps and in answering questions about the solution process.

2. Easily modified, both in adding and in deleting skills from the knowledge base.

3. Heuristic, in using (often imperfect) knowledge to obtain solutions.

An expert system is "open to inspection" in that the user may, at any time during program execution, inspect the state of its reasoning and determine the specific choices and decisions that the program is making. This is desirable for several reasons: first, if a human expert such as a doctor or an engineer is to accept a recommendation from the computer, he or she must be satisfied the solution is correct. "The computer said so" is not sufficient reason to follow its advice. Indeed, few human experts will accept advice from another human without understanding the reasons for that advice. This need to have answers explained is more than mistrust on the part of users; explanations help people relate the advice to their existing understanding of the domain and apply it in a more confident and flexible manner.

Second, when a solution is open to inspection, we can evaluate every decision taken during the solution process, allowing for partial agreement and the addition of new information or rules to improve performance. This plays an essential role in the refinement of a knowledge base.

The exploratory nature of AI and expert system programming requires that programs be easily prototyped, tested, and changed. These abilities are supported by AI programming languages and environments and the use of good programming techniques by the designer. In a pure production system, for example, the modification of a single rule has no global syntactic side effects. Rules may be added or removed without requiring further changes to the larger program. Expert system designers have commented that easy modification of the knowledge base is a major factor in producing a successful program (McDermott 1981).

The third feature of expert systems is their use of heuristic problem-solving methods. As expert system designers have discovered, informal "tricks of the trade" and "rules of thumb" are often more important than the standard theory presented in textbooks and classes. Sometimes these rules augment theoretical knowledge; occasionally they are simply shortcuts that seem unrelated to the theory but have been shown to work.

The heuristic nature of expert problem-solving knowledge creates problems in the evaluation of program performance. Although we know that heuristic methods will occasionally fail, it is not clear exactly how often a program must be correct to be accepted: 98% of the time? 90%? 80%? Perhaps the best way to evaluate a program is to compare its results to those obtained by human experts in the same area. This suggests a variation of the Turing test (Chapter 1) for evaluating the performance of expert systems: a program has achieved expert-level performance if people working in the area cannot differentiate, in a blind evaluation, between the best human efforts and those of the program. In evaluating the MYCIN program for diagnosing meningitis infections, Stanford researchers had a number of infectious-disease experts blindly evaluate the performance of both MYCIN and human specialists in infectious diseases. Similarly, Digital Equipment Corporation decided that XCON, a program for configuring VAX computers, was ready for commercial use when its performance was comparable to that of human engineers.

Expert systems have been built to solve a range of problems in domains such as medicine, mathematics, engineering, chemistry, geology, computer science, business, law, defense, and education. These programs have addressed a wide range of problem types; the following list, adapted from Waterman (1986), is a useful summary of general expert system problem categories.

1. *Interpretation*—forming high-level conclusions or descriptions from collections of raw data.
2. *Prediction*—projecting probable consequences of given situations.
3. *Diagnosis*—determining the cause of malfunctions in complex situations based on observable symptoms.
4. *Design*—determining a configuration of system components that meets certain performance goals while satisfying a set of constraints.
5. *Planning*—devising a sequence of actions that will achieve a set of goals given certain starting conditions.
6. *Monitoring*—comparing the observed behavior of a system to its expected behavior.
7. *Debugging and Repair*—prescribing and implementing remedies for malfunctions.
8. *Instruction*—detecting and correcting deficiencies in students' understanding of a subject domain.
9. *Control*—governing the behavior of a complex environment.

8.1 Overview of Expert System Technology

8.1.1 Design of Rule-Based Expert Systems

Figure 8.1 shows the most important modules that make up a rule-based expert system. The user interacts with the expert system through a user interface that makes access more comfortable for the human and hides much of the system complexity (e.g., the internal structures of the rule base). Expert systems employ a variety of interface styles, including question-and-answer, menu-driven, natural language, or graphics interfaces.

The program must keep track of *case-specific data*: the facts, conclusions, and other relevant information of the case under consideration. This includes the data given in a problem instance, partial conclusions, confidence measures of conclusions, and dead ends in the search process. This information is separate from the general knowledge base.

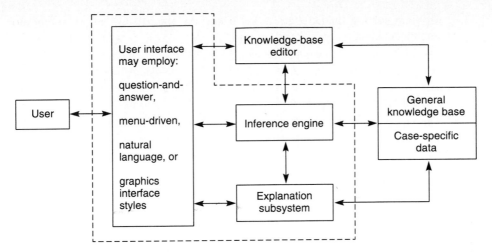

Figure 8.1 Architecture of a typical expert system.

The *explanation subsystem* allows the program to explain its reasoning to the user. These explanations include justifications for the system's conclusions (*how queries*, as discussed in Section 8.2.2), explanations of why the system needs a particular piece of data (*why queries*), and, in some experimental systems, tutorial explanations or deeper theoretical justifications of the program's actions.

Many systems also include a *knowledge-base editor*. Knowledge-base editors can access the explanation subsystem and help the programmer locate bugs in the program's performance. They also may assist in the addition of new knowledge, help maintain correct rule syntax, and perform consistency checks on the updated knowledge base. An example of the Teiresias knowledge-base editor is presented in Section 8.4.5.

The heart of the expert system is the general knowledge base, which contains the problem-solving knowledge of the particular application. In a rule-based expert system this knowledge is represented in the form of *if . . . then . . .* rules, as in the auto battery/cable example of Section 8.2. Other ways of representing this knowledge are discussed in Chapters 9 and 15.

The *inference engine* applies the knowledge to the solution of actual problems. It is the interpreter for the knowledge base. In the production system, the inference engine performs the recognize-act control cycle. The procedures that implement the control cycle are separate from the production rules themselves. It is important to maintain this separation of knowledge base and inference engine for several reasons:

1. The separation of the problem-solving knowledge and the inference engine makes it possible to represent knowledge in a more natural fashion. "If . . . then" rules, for example, are closer to the way in which human beings describe their own problem-solving techniques than a program that embeds this knowledge in lower-level computer code.

2. Because the knowledge base is separated from the program's lower-level control structures, expert system builders can focus directly on capturing and organizing

problem-solving knowledge rather than on the details of its computer implementation.

3. The separation of knowledge and control, along with the modularity of rules and other representational structures used in building knowledge bases, allows changes to be made in one part of the knowledge base without creating side effects in other parts of the program code.

4. The separation of the knowledge and control elements of the program allows the same control and interface software to be used in a variety of systems. The *expert system shell* has all the components of Figure 8.1 except that the knowledge base and, of course, the case-specific data contain no information. Programmers can use the "empty shell" and create a new knowledge base appropriate to their application. The broken lines of Figure 8.1 indicate the shell modules.

5. As illustrated in the discussion of production systems (Chapter 5), this modularity allows us to experiment with alternative control regimes for the same rule base.

The use of an expert system shell can reduce the design and implementation time of a program considerably. As may be seen in Figure 8.3, MYCIN was developed in about 20 person-years. EMYCIN (Empty MYCIN) is a general expert system shell that was produced by removing the specific domain knowledge from the MYCIN program. Using EMYCIN, knowledge engineers implemented PUFF, a program to analyze pulmonary problems in patients, in about 5 person-years. This is a remarkable saving and an important aspect of the commercial viability of expert system technology. Expert system shells have become increasingly common, with commercially produced shells available for all classes of computers.

It is important that the programmer choose the proper expert system shell. Different problems often require different reasoning processes: goal-driven rather than data-driven search, for instance. The control strategy provided by the shell must be appropriate to the new application. The medical reasoning in the PUFF application was much like that of the original MYCIN work; this made the use of the EMYCIN shell appropriate. If the shell does not support the appropriate reasoning processes, its use can be a mistake and worse than starting from nothing. As we shall see, part of the responsibility of the expert system builder is to correctly characterize the reasoning processes required for a given problem domain and to either select or construct an inference engine that implements these structures.

Unfortunately, shell programs do not solve all of the problems involved in building expert systems. Although the separation of knowledge and control, the modularity of the production system architecture, and the use of an appropriate knowledge representation language all help with the building of an expert system, the acquisition and organization of the knowledge base remain difficult tasks.

8.1.2 Selecting a Problem for Expert System Development

Expert systems tend to involve a considerable investment in money and human effort. Attempts to solve a problem that is too complex, poorly understood, or otherwise unsuited to the available technology can lead to costly and embarrassing failures. Researchers have developed an informal set of guidelines for determining whether a problem is appropriate for expert system solution:

1. *The need for the solution justifies the cost and effort of building an expert system.* For example, Digital Equipment Corporation had experienced considerable financial expense because of errors in configuring VAX and PDP-11 computers. If a computer is shipped with missing or incompatible components, the company is obliged to correct this situation as quickly as possible, often incurring added shipping expense or absorbing the cost of parts not taken into account when the original price was quoted. Because this expense was considerable, DEC was extremely interested in automating the configuration task; the resulting system, XCON, has paid for itself in both financial savings and customer goodwill. Similarly, many expert systems have been built in domains such as mineral exploration, business, defense, and medicine where a large potential exists for savings in either money, time, or human life. In recent years, the cost of building expert systems has gone down as software tools and expertise in AI have become more available. The range of potentially profitable applications has grown correspondingly.

2. *Human expertise is not available in all situations where it is needed.* Much expert system work has been done in medicine, for example, because the specialization and technical sophistication of modern medicine have made it difficult for doctors to keep up with advances in diagnostics and treatment methods. Specialists with this knowledge are rare and expensive, and expert systems are seen as a way of making their expertise available to a wider range of doctors. In geology, there is a need for expertise at remote mining and drilling sites. Often, geologists and engineers find themselves traveling large distances to visit sites, with resulting expense and wasted time. By placing expert systems at remote sites, many problems may be solved without needing a visit by a human expert. Similarly, loss of valuable expertise through employee turnover or pending retirement may justify building an expert system. Many other jobs in our society require expertise that is not always available. These jobs include insurance claims adjustment, credit approval, regulatory compliance, and forms handling.

3. *The problem may be solved using symbolic reasoning techniques.* This means the problem should not require physical dexterity or perceptual skill. Although robots and vision systems are available, they currently lack the sophistication and flexibility of human beings. Expert systems are generally restricted to problems that humans can solve through symbolic reasoning.

4. *The problem domain is well structured and does not require commonsense reasoning.* Although expert systems have been built in a number of areas requiring specialized technical knowledge, more mundane commonsense reasoning is well beyond our current capabilities. Highly technical fields have the advantage of being well studied and formalized; terms are well defined and domains have clear and specific conceptual models. Most significantly, however, the amount of knowledge required to solve such problems is small in comparison to the amount of knowledge used by human beings in commonsense reasoning.

5. *The problem may not be solved using traditional computing methods.* Expert system technology should not be used to "reinvent the wheel." If a problem can be solved satisfactorily using more traditional techniques such as numerical, statistical, or operations research techniques, then it is not a candidate for an expert system. Because expert systems

rely on heuristic approaches, it is unlikely that an expert system will outperform an algorithmic solution if such a solution exists.

6. *Cooperative and articulate experts exist.* The knowledge used by expert systems is often not found in textbooks but comes from the experience and judgment of humans working in the domain. It is important that these experts be both willing and able to share that knowledge. This implies that the experts should be articulate and believe that the project is both practical and beneficial. If, on the other hand, the experts feel threatened by the system, fearing that they may be replaced by it or that the project cannot succeed and is therefore a waste of time, it is unlikely that they will give it the necessary time and effort. It is also important that management be supportive of the project and allow the domain experts to take time away from their usual responsibilities to work with the program implementers.

7. *The problem is of proper size and scope.* It is important that the problem not exceed the capabilities of current technology. For example, a program that attempted to capture all of the expertise of a medical doctor would not be feasible; a program that advised MDs on the use of a particular piece of diagnostic equipment would be more appropriate. As a rule of thumb, problems that require days or weeks for human experts to solve are probably too complex for current expert system technology.

Although a large problem may not be amenable to expert system solution, it may be possible to break it into smaller, independent subproblems that are. Or we may be able to start with a simple program that solves a portion of the problem and gradually increase its functionality to handle more of the problem domain. This was done successfully in the creation of XCON: initially the program was designed only to configure VAX 780 computers; later it was expanded to include the full VAX and PDP-11 series (Bachant and McDermott 1984).

8.1.3 The Knowledge Engineering Process

The primary people involved in building an expert system are the *knowledge engineer*, the *domain expert*, and the *end user*.

The knowledge engineer is the AI language and representation expert. His or her main task is to select the software and hardware tools for the project, help extract the necessary knowledge from the domain expert, and implement that knowledge in a correct and efficient knowledge base. The knowledge engineer may initially be ignorant of the application domain.

The domain expert provides the knowledge of the problem area. The domain expert is generally someone who has worked in the domain area and understands its problem-solving techniques, such as using shortcuts, handling imprecise data, evaluating partial solutions, and all the other skills that mark a person as an expert. The domain expert is primarily responsible for spelling out these skills to the knowledge engineer.

As in most applications, the end user determines the major design constraints. Unless the user is happy, the development effort is by and large wasted. The skills and needs of the user must be considered throughout the design cycle: What level of explanation does the user need? Can the user provide correct information to the system? Is the user interface appropriate? Are there environmental restrictions on the program's use? An interface that required typing, for example, would not be appropriate for use in the cockpit of a jet fighter. Will the program make the user's work easier, quicker, more comfortable?

Like most AI programming, expert system development requires a nontraditional development cycle based on early prototyping and incremental revision of the code. This exploratory programming methodology (described in the introduction to Part III) is complicated by the interaction between the knowledge engineer and the domain expert.

Generally, work on the system begins with the knowledge engineer attempting to gain some familiarity with the problem domain. This helps in communicating with the domain expert. This is done in initial interviews with the expert or by reading introductory texts in the domain area. Next, the knowledge engineer and expert begin the process of extracting the expert's problem-solving knowledge. This is often done by giving the domain expert a series of sample problems and having him or her explain the techniques used in their solution.

Here, it is often useful for the knowledge engineer to be a novice in the problem domain. Human experts are notoriously unreliable in explaining exactly what goes on in solving a complex problem. Often they forget to mention steps that have become obvious or even automatic to them after years of work in their field. Knowledge engineers, by virtue of their relative naïveté in the domain, should be able to spot these conceptual jumps and ask for clarification.

Once the knowledge engineer has obtained a general overview of the problem domain and gone through several problem-solving sessions with the domain expert, he or she is ready to begin actual design of the system: selecting a way to represent the knowledge, such as rules or frames, determining the search strategy (forward, backward, etc.), and designing the user interface (see Section 8.1.4.). After making these design commitments, the knowledge engineer builds a prototype.

This prototype should be able to solve problems in a small area of the domain and provides a test bed for preliminary design assumptions. Once the prototype has been implemented, the knowledge engineer and domain expert test and refine its knowledge by giving it problems to solve and correcting its shortcomings. Should the assumptions made in designing the prototype prove correct, it can be built into a complete system.

Expert systems are built by progressive approximations, with the program's mistakes leading to corrections or additions to the knowledge base. In a sense, the knowledge base is "grown" rather than constructed. Figure 8.2 presents a flow chart describing the exploratory programming development cycle. This approach to programming was proposed by Seymour Papert with his LOGO language (Papert 1980). The LOGO philosophy argues that watching the computer respond to the improperly formulated ideas represented by the code leads to their correction (being debugged) and clarification with more precise code. Other researchers have verified this notion that design proceeds through a process of trying and correcting candidate designs, rather than by such neatly hierarchical processes as top-down design.

It is also understood that the prototype may be thrown away if it becomes too cumbersome or if the designers decide to change their basic approach to the problem. The prototype lets program builders explore the problem and its important relationships by actually constructing a program to solve it. After this progressive clarification is complete, they can often write a cleaner version, usually with fewer actual rules.

The second major feature of expert system programming is that the program need

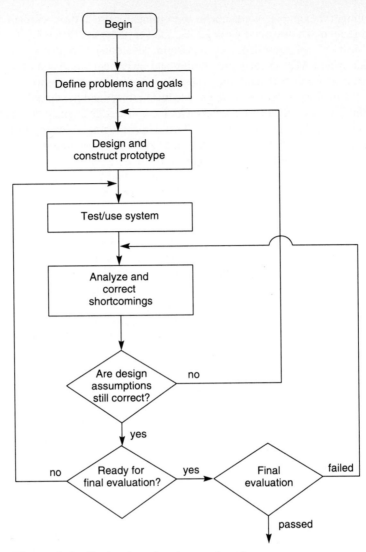

Figure 8.2 Exploratory development cycle.

never be considered "finished." A large heuristic knowledge base will always have limitations. The modularity and ease of modification available in the production system model make it natural to add new rules or make up for the shortcomings of the present rule base at any time. DEC, for example, has continued to add new rules to the XCON program to extend its capabilities to the rest of their product line. In 1981, XCON had about 500 rules and could configure the VAX 780; it was progressively refined until, currently, with over 6,000 rules, XCON configures most of the DEC product line. Furthermore, as DEC changed the specifications for its computers, previously correct rules needed updating. One report noted that up to 50% of the XCON rules were changed each year just to keep up with changes in the product line (Soloway et al. 1987).

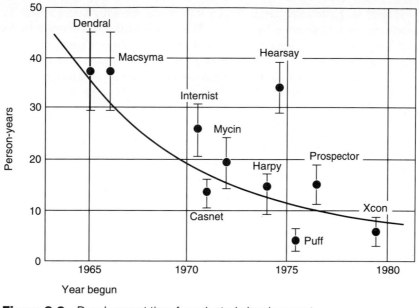

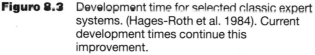

Figure 8.3 Development time for selected classic expert systems. (Hages-Roth et al. 1984). Current development times continue this improvement.

Even though expert systems of commercial quality have been available since 1980, research in the development of expert systems has gone on since the middle 1960s. The major development activity for these early programs took place at three universities: Stanford, MIT, and Carnegie Mellon. The main research and development thrust for the rule-based expert system was at Stanford, under the direction of Edward Feigenbaum, although other work in the area certainly took place at, for instance, Rutgers and the University of Pittsburgh. The early development of the production system model for problem solving, including the development of the OPS languages, took place primarily at Carnegie Mellon University.

Figure 8.3 presents another important aspect of the evolution of expert system programs: the average development time for expert systems has been drastically reduced across the decades of evolution. The emergence of expert system shells was instrumental in reducing the design time. This is perhaps the most important reason for current commercial successes.

8.1.4 Conceptual Models and Their Role in Knowledge Acquisition

Figure 8.4 presents the common view of knowledge acquisition. There is a domain of knowledge and skill in an application area; this knowledge is often vague or only partially articulated. The knowledge engineer must translate this into a formal language. This process brings with it several important problems:

1. Human skill is practice based. As Aristotle points out in his *Ethics*, "what we have to learn to do, we learn by doing." Skills such as those possessed by medical doctors are learned as much in years of internship and residency, with their constant focus on patients, as they are in physiology lectures, where emphasis is on experiment and theory. Delivery of medical care is to a great extent practice driven. And after years of performance these skills are highly integrated and often not explicitly retrievable.

2. Human expertise often takes the form of knowing *how* to cope in a situation rather than knowing *what* a rational characterization of the situation might be, of developing skilled performance mechanisms rather than a fundamental understanding of what these mechanisms are. An obvious example of this is riding a unicycle: the successful rider is not, in real time, consciously solving multiple sets of simultaneous differential equations to keep in balance; rather she or he is using an intuitive combination of feelings of "gravity," "momentum," and "inertia" to form a usable control procedure. In fact, we find a huge gap often exists between human expertise in an application area and any precise accounting of this skill. Many of the reasons behind this have been considered by cognitive scientists and philosophers, as we present in Chapter 16.

3. We often think of knowledge acquisition as gaining factual knowledge of an objective reality, the so-called "real world." As both theory and practice have shown, human expertise represents an individual's or community's model of the world. Such models are as influenced by convention, social processes, and hidden agendas as they are by empirical methodologies.

4. Expertise changes. Not only do human experts gain new knowledge, but also existing knowledge may be subject to radical reformulation, as evidenced by ongoing controversies in both scientific and nonscientific fields.

Knowledge Acquisition

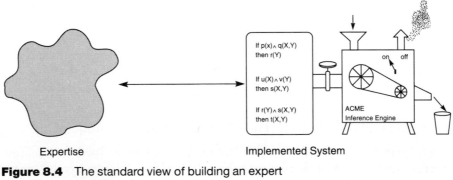

Expertise   Implemented System

Figure 8.4 The standard view of building an expert system.

Consequently, knowledge engineering is difficult and should be viewed as spanning the life cycle of any expert system. To simplify this task, it is useful to have, as in Figure 8.5, a *conceptual* or *mental* model that lies between the human expertise and the implemented program. By conceptual model, we mean the knowledge engineer's evolving conception of the domain knowledge. Although this is undoubtedly different from the domain expert's, it is this model that actually underlies the construction of the formal knowledge base.

Because of the complexity and multiple sources of ambiguity in the problem, we should not take this intermediate stage for granted. Knowledge engineers should document and make public their assumptions about the domain through common software engineering methodologies. An expert system should include a requirements document; however, because of the constraints of exploratory programming, expert system requirements should be treated as co-evolving with the prototype. Data dictionaries, graphic representations of state spaces, and comments in the code itself are all part of this model. By publicizing these design decisions, we reduce errors in both the implementation and the maintenance of the knowledge base.

Knowledge engineers should save recordings of interviews with domain experts. Often, as the knowledge engineer's understanding of the domain grows, she may form a new interpretation or discover new information in one of these sessions. The recordings, along with documentation of the interpretation given them, play a valuable role in reviewing design decisions and testing prototypes.

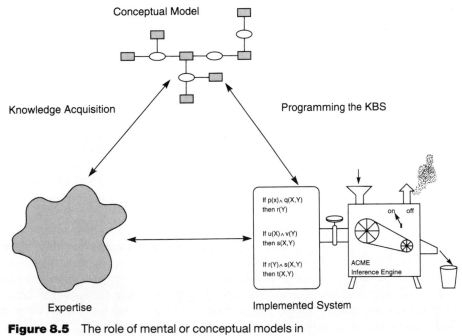

Figure 8.5 The role of mental or conceptual models in problem solving.

Finally, this model serves an intermediate role in the formalization of knowledge. The choice of a representation language exerts a strong influence on a knowledge engineer's model of the domain. The model is usually based on one of the AI representation languages, either the predicate calculus, as in Chapter 2, or frames, objects, or hybrid designs (Chapters 9, 13, 14, and 15).

The conceptual model is not formal or directly executable on a computer. It is an intermediate design construct, a template to begin to constrain and codify human skill. It can, if the knowledge engineer uses a predicate calculus model, begin as a number of simple networks representing the expert's states of reasoning through typical problem-solving situations. Only after further refinement does this network become explicit if . . . then . . . rules.

Questions often worked through in the context of a conceptual model include: Is the problem solving deterministic or search based? Is it data-driven, perhaps with a generate-and-test flavor? Is problem solving goal-driven, based on a small set of hypotheses about situations? Are there stages of reasoning? Is it exact or fuzzy (Section 8.3)? Is it nonmonotonic, with the need of a truth maintenance system (Section 8.3)?

The eventual users' needs should also be addressed in the context of the conceptual model: What are their expectations of the eventual program? Where is their level of expertise: novice, intermediate, or expert? What levels of explanation are appropriate? What interface best serves their needs?

The production system, first presented in Chapter 5 and used as a framework for representing and applying human knowledge in the next section, is often used as the basis for a conceptual model in rule-based expert system problem solving.

8.2 A Framework for Organizing and Applying Human Knowledge

8.2.1 Production Systems, Rules, and the Expert System Architecture

The architecture of rule-based expert systems may be understood in terms of the production system model for problem solving presented in Part II. In fact, the parallel between the two entities is more than a simple analogy: the production system was the intellectual precursor of modern expert system architecture. This is not surprising; when Newell and Simon began developing the production system model, their goal was to find a way to model human problem solving.

If we regard the expert system architecture in Figure 8.1 as a production system, the knowledge base is the set of production rules. The expertise of the problem area is represented by the productions. In a rule-based system, these condition-action pairs are represented as rules, with the premises of the rules (the if portion) corresponding to the condition and the conclusion (the then portion) corresponding to the action. Case-specific data are kept in the working memory. Finally, the inference engine is the recognize-act cycle of the production system. This control may be either data driven or goal driven.

Many problem domains seem to lend themselves more naturally to forward search. In an interpretation problem, for example, most of the data for the problem are initially given and it is often difficult to formulate a hypotheses (goal). This suggests a forward reasoning process in which the facts are placed in working memory and the system searches for an interpretation in a forward fashion. These issues were first discussed in Chapter 3.

In a goal-driven expert system, the goal expression is initially placed in working memory. The system matches rule conclusions with the goal, selecting one rule and placing its *premises* in the working memory. This corresponds to a decomposition of the problem into simpler subgoals. The process continues, with these premises becoming the new goals to match against rule conclusions. The system thus works back from the original goal until all the subgoals in working memory are known to be true, indicating that the hypothesis has been verified. Thus, backward search in an expert system corresponds roughly to the process of hypothesis testing in human problem solving.

In an expert system, subgoals are often solved by asking the user for information. Some expert system shells allow the system designer to specify which subgoals may be solved by asking the user. Other inference engines simply ask about all subgoals that fail to match with the conclusion of some rule in the knowledge base; i.e., if the program cannot infer the truth of a subgoal, it asks the user.

As a more detailed example of goal driven problem solving, we create a small expert system for diagnosing automotive problems:

Rule 1: if

the engine is getting gas, and

the engine will turn over,

then
the problem is spark plugs.

Rule 2: if
the engine does not turn over, and
the lights do not come on
then
the problem is battery or cables.

Rule 3: if
the engine does not turn over, and
the lights do come on
then
the problem is the starter motor.

Rule 4: if
there is gas in the fuel tank, and
there is gas in the carburetor
then
the engine is getting gas.

To run this knowledge base under a goal-directed control regime, place the top-level goal, the problem is X, in working memory as in Figure 8.6. X is a variable that can match with any phrase; it will become bound to the solution when the problem is solved.

Three rules match with the expression in working memory: rule 1, rule 2, and rule 3. If we resolve conflicts in favor of the lowest-numbered rule, then rule 1 will fire. This causes X to be bound to the value spark plugs and the premises of rule 1 to be placed in the working memory as in Figure 8.7. The system has thus chosen to explore the possible hypothesis that the spark plugs are bad. Another way to look at this is that the system has selected an or branch in an and/or graph (Chapter 3).

Note that there are two premises to rule 1, both of which must be satisfied to prove the conclusion true. These are and branches of the search graph representing a decomposition of the problem (finding whether the spark plugs are bad) into two subproblems (finding whether the engine is getting gas and whether the engine is turning over). We may then fire rule 4, whose conclusion matches with "engine is getting gas," causing its premises to be placed in working memory as in Figure 8.8.

At this point, there are three entries in working memory that do not match with any rule conclusions. Our expert system will query the user directly about these subgoals. If the

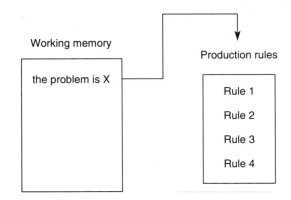

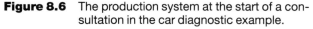

Figure 8.6 The production system at the start of a consultation in the car diagnostic example.

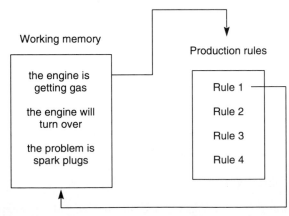

Figure 8.7 The production system after Rule 1 has fired.

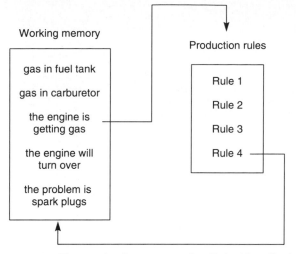

Working memory

gas in fuel tank

gas in carburetor

the engine is
getting gas

the engine will
turn over

the problem is
spark plugs

Production rules

Rule 1

Rule 2

Rule 3

Rule 4

Figure 8.8   The production system after Rule 4 has fired.

user confirms all three of these as true, the expert system will have successfully determined that the car will not start because the spark plugs are bad. In finding this solution, the system has searched the **and/or** graph presented in Figure 8.9.

This is, of course, a very simple example. Not only is its automotive knowledge limited at best, but also a number of important aspects of real implementations are ignored. The rules are phrased in English, rather than a formal language. On finding a solution, a real expert system will tell the user its diagnosis (our model simply stops). Also, we should maintain enough of a trace of the reasoning to allow backtracking if necessary; in our example, had we failed to determine that the spark plugs were bad, we would have needed to back up to the top level and try rule 2 instead. Notice that this information is implicit in the ordering of subgoals in working memory of Figure 8.8 and in the graph of Figure 8.9. This example of expert systems underscores their foundation in the production system and **and/or** graph search models of earlier chapters.

At the beginning of this chapter, we emphasized that an expert system needed to be open to inspection, easily modified, and heuristic in nature. The production system architecture is an important factor in each of these requirements. Ease of modification, for example, is made possible by the syntactic independence of production rules: each rule is a chunk of knowledge that can be independently modified. The heuristic nature of these rules is in the knowledge obtained from the domain expert and, as seen in Section 8.3, from use of confidence measures. The next section discusses the way in which this architecture supports explanations and inspection of the reasoning process.

8.2.2   Explanation and Transparency

The production system implements a graph search; the explanation routines of Figure 8.1 keep track of the graph search and use a trace of the search to answer user queries. The production rules themselves document each step of the reasoning process.

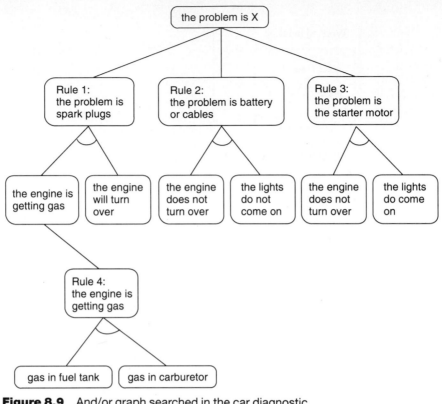

Figure 8.9 And/or graph searched in the car diagnostic example.

In general, the two questions supported by rule-based expert systems are why? and how? In a why query, the user has been asked for information by the program and responds with why, meaning "why did you ask that?" The answer is the current rule that the production system is attempting to fire. The answer to "how did you get that result?" is the sequence of rules that were used to conclude a goal.

Suppose our automotive expert system has an explanation facility, and assume that the consultation has reached the stage represented by the working memory configuration in Figure 8.8. The following dialogue begins with the computer asking the user about the goals present in working memory. User responses are in bold type.

gas in fuel tank?
yes

gas in carburetor?
yes

engine will turn over?
why

Here the user enters a why query, i.e., why do you want to know that?

It has been established that:

1. engine is getting gas,

therefore if

2. engine will turn over,

then the problem is spark plugs.

Because the user answered yes to the first two questions, rule 4 was able to fire, verifying the first premise of rule 1. When the why query was made, the system was trying to solve the second premise of rule 1. Note that the explanation is just a restatement of the current rule, but it provides an adequate explanation for why the program wants to know whether the engine will turn over. Continuing with the dialogue:

how engine is getting gas

Here the user asks how the program knew that the engine is getting gas. The response is a trace of the reasoning that led to this conclusion, working back from the goal along the rules that support it to the user responses:

This follows from rule 4:

if

gas in fuel tank, and

gas in carburetor

then

engine is getting gas.

gas in fuel tank was given by the user

gas in carburetor was given by the user

This simple example illustrates the explanations that expert systems provide the user. Why queries are answered by showing the current rule that the system is attempting to fire. How queries are answered by giving a trace of the reasoning that led to a goal. We implement this explanation methodology with rule stacks and proof trees in Section 13.2.2. Although the mechanisms are conceptually simple, they can exhibit remarkable explanatory power if the knowledge base is organized in a logical fashion.

The production system architecture provides an essential basis for these explanations. Each cycle of the control loop selects and fires another rule. The program may be stopped after each cycle and inspected. Because each rule represents a complete chunk of problem-solving knowledge, the current rule provides a context for the explanation. Contrast this with more traditional program architectures: if we stop a Pascal or FORTRAN program in mid execution, it is doubtful that the current statement will have much meaning.

If explanations are to behave logically, it is important not only that the knowledge base get the correct answer but also that each rule correspond to a single logical step in the problem-solving process. If a knowledge base combines several steps into a single rule or if it breaks up the rules in an arbitrary fashion, it may get correct answers but seem arbitrary and illogical in responding to how and why queries. This not only undermines the user's faith in the system but also makes the program much more difficult for its builders to understand and modify.

8.2.3 Heuristics and Control in Expert Systems

Because of the separation of the knowledge base and the inference engine and the fixed control regimes provided by the inference engine, the only way a programmer can control the search is through the structure of the rules in the knowledge base. This is an advantage, as the control strategies required for expert-level problem solving tend to be domain specific and knowledge intensive. Although a rule of the form if p, q, and r then s resembles a logical expression, it may also be interpreted as a series of procedures for solving a problem: to do s, first do p, then do q, then do r. This dual semantics of rules was already discussed in the introductory PROLOG chapter.

This procedural interpretation allows us to control search through the structure of the rules. For example, we may order the premises of a rule so the premise that is most likely to fail or is easiest to confirm will be tried first. This gives the opportunity of eliminating a rule (and hence a portion of the search space) as early in the search as possible. Rule 1 in the automotive example tries to determine whether the engine is getting gas before it asks if the engine turns over. This is inefficient, in that trying to determine whether the engine is getting gas invokes another rule and eventually asks the user two questions. By reversing the order of the premises, a negative response to the query "engine will turn over?" eliminates this rule from consideration before the more involved condition is examined.

Also, from another point of view, it makes more sense to determine whether the engine is turning over before checking to see whether it is getting gas; if the engine won't turn over it doesn't matter whether it is getting gas. Rule 4 asks the user to check for gas in the fuel tank before asking that the user open up the carburetor and look there. It is performing the easier check first.

In addition to the ordering of a rule's premises, the content of a rule itself may be fundamentally heuristic in nature. In the automotive example, all the rules are heuristic; consequently, the system may obtain erroneous results. For example, if the engine is getting gas and turning over, the problem may be a bad distributor rather than bad spark plugs.

Although the procedural interpretation of rules reduces many of the advantages of "purely" declarative representation, it is an essential component of practical knowledge engineering and often reflects the human expert's solution strategy. In the next section, we examine this problem and some ways of dealing with it.

8.3 Managing Uncertainty in Expert Systems

8.3.1 Introduction

Until Section 8.2, our inference procedures followed the model presented with the predicate calculus: from correct premises, sound inference rules produce new, guaranteed correct, conclusions. In expert systems, we must often attempt to draw correct conclusions from poorly formed and uncertain evidence using unsound inference rules.

This is not an impossible task; we do it successfully in almost every aspect of our daily survival. We deliver correct medical treatment for ambiguous symptoms; we mine natural resources with little or no guarantee of success before we start; we comprehend language statements that are often ambiguous or incomplete; and so on.

The reasons for this ambiguity may be better understood by referring once again to our automotive expert system example. Consider rule 2:

if

the engine does not turn over, and

the lights do not come on

then

the problem is battery or cables.

This rule is heuristic in nature; it is possible (although less likely) that the battery and cables are fine but that the car simply has a bad starter motor and burned-out headlights. This rule seems to resemble a logical implication, but it is not: failure of the engine to turn over and the lights to come on does not necessarily imply that the battery and cables are bad. What is interesting to note, however, is that the *converse* of the rule is a true implication:

if

the problem is battery or cables

then

the engine does not turn over, and

the lights do not come on.

Barring the supernatural, a car with a dead battery will not light its headlamps or turn the starter motor.

This is an example of *abductive* reasoning. Formally, abduction states that from $P \rightarrow Q$ and Q it is possible to infer P. Abduction is an *unsound* rule of inference, meaning that the conclusion is not necessarily true for every interpretation in which the premises are true. For example, if someone says "If it rains then I will not go running at 3:00" and you do not see that person on the track at 3:00, does it necessarily follow that it is raining? It is possible that the individual decided not to go running because of an injury, that he needed to work late, etc.

Although abduction is unsound, it is often essential to solving problems. The "correct" version of the battery rule is not particularly useful in diagnosing car troubles because its premise (bad battery) is our goal and its conclusions are the observable symptoms we must work with. Modus ponens cannot be applied and the rule must be used in an abductive fashion. This is generally true of diagnostic (and other) expert systems. Faults or diseases cause (imply) symptoms, not the other way around, but diagnosis must work from the symptoms back to the cause.

Uncertainty results from the use of abductive inference as well as from attempts to reason with missing or unreliable data. To get around this problem, we can attach some measure of confidence to the conclusions. For example, although battery failure does not always accompany the failure of a car's lights and starters, it almost always does, and confidence in this rule is justifiably high.

Note that some problems do not require certainty measures. When configuring a computer, for instance, the components either go together or they do not. The idea that "a particular disk drive and bus go together with certainty 0.75" does not even make sense. Similarly, if MACSYMA is attempting to find the integral of a function, a confidence of "0.6" that a result is correct is not useful. These programs may be either data driven (Digital's XCON) or goal driven (MIT's MACSYMA), but because they do not require abductive rules of inference or do not deal with unreliable data they do not require the use of confidence measures.

In this section we discuss several ways of managing the uncertainty that results from heuristic rules: first, the Bayesian approach (Section 8.3.2) and, second, the Stanford certainty theory (Section 8.3.3). Finally, we briefly consider Zadeh's *fuzzy set theory*, the Dempster/Shafer theory of evidential reasoning, and nonmonotonic reasoning.

8.3.2   Bayesian Probability Theory

The Bayesian approach to uncertainty is based in formal probability theory and has shown up in several areas of AI research, including pattern recognition and classification problems. The PROSPECTOR expert system, built at Stanford and SRI International and employed in mineral exploration (copper, molybdenum, and others), also uses a form of the Bayesian statistical model.

Assuming random distribution of events, probability theory allows the calculation of more complex probabilities from previously known results. In simple probability calculations we are able to conclude, for example, how cards might be distributed to a number of players.

Suppose that I am one person of a four-person card game where all the cards are equally distributed. If I do not have the queen of spades I can conclude that each of the other players has it with probability 1/3. Similarly, I can conclude that each player has the ace of hearts with probability 1/3 and that any one player has both cards at 1/3 * 1/3, or 1/9.

In the mathematical theory of probability, individual probability instances are worked out by sampling and combinations of probabilities are worked out as above, using a rule such as:

probability(A and B) = probability(A) * probability(B)

given that A and B are independent events.

One of the most important results of probability theory is Bayes' theorem. Bayes' results provide a way of computing the probability of a hypothesis following from a particular piece of evidence, given only the probabilities with which the evidence follows from actual causes (hypotheses).

Bayes' theorem states:

$$p(H_i \mid E) = \frac{P(E \mid H_i) * P(H_i)}{\sum\limits_{k=1}^{n} (P(E \mid H_k) * P(H_k))}$$

where:

$P(H_i \mid E)$ is the probability that H_i is true given evidence E.

$P(H_i)$ is the probability that H_i is true overall.

$P(E \mid H_i)$ is the probability of observing evidence E when H_i is true.

n is the number of possible hypotheses.

Suppose we desire to examine the geological evidence at some location to see whether the location is suited to finding copper. We must know in advance the probability of finding each of a set of minerals and the probability of certain evidence being present when each particular mineral is found. Then we can use Bayes' theorem to determine the likelihood that copper will be present using the evidence we collect at the location. This is the approach taken in the PROSPECTOR program, which has found commercially significant mineral deposits (Duda et al. 1979a) at several sites.

There are two major assumptions for the use of Bayes' theorem: first that all the statistical data on the relationships of the evidence with the various hypotheses are known; second, and more difficult to establish, that all relationships between evidence and hypotheses, or $P(E \mid H_k)$, are independent. Actually, this assumption of independence can be a quite tricky matter, especially when many assumptions of independence are needed to establish the validity of this approach across many rule applications. This represents the entire collected probabilities on the evidence given various hypothesis relationships in the denominator of Bayes' theorem. In general, and especially in areas such as medicine, this assumption of independence cannot be justified.

A final problem, which makes keeping the statistics of the "evidence given hypotheses" relationships virtually intractable, is the need to rebuild all probability relationships when any new relationship of hypothesis to evidence is discovered. In many active research areas (again, such as medicine) this is happening continuously. Bayesian reasoning requires complete and up-to-date probabilities if its conclusions are to be correct. In many domains, such extensive data collection and verification are not possible.

Where these assumptions are met, Bayesian approaches offer the benefit of a mathematically well-founded and statistically correct handling of uncertainty. Most expert system domains do not meet these requirements and must rely on more heuristic approaches. It is also felt that the human expert does not use the Bayesian model in successful problem solving. In the next section we describe certainty theory, a heuristic approach to the management of uncertainty.

8.3.3 The Stanford Certainty Factor Algebra

Several early expert system projects (besides PROSPECTOR) attempted to adapt Bayes' theorem to their problem-solving needs. The independence assumptions, continuous updates of statistical data, and other problems mentioned in Section 8.3.2 gradually led these researchers to search for other measures of "confidence." Probably the most important alternative approach was used at Stanford in developing the MYCIN program (Buchanan and Shortliff 1984).

Certainty theory is based on a number of observations. The first is that in traditional probability theory the sum of confidence for a relationship and confidence against the same relationship must add to 1. However, it is often the case that an expert might have confidence 0.7 (say) that some relationship is true and have no feeling about it being not true.

Another assumption that underpins certainty theory is that the knowledge content of the rules is much more important than the algebra of confidences that holds the system together. Confidence measures correspond to the informal evaluations that human experts attach to their conclusions, such as "it is probably true" or "it is highly unlikely."

Certainty theory makes some simple assumptions for creating confidence measures and has some equally simple rules for combining these confidences as the program moves toward its conclusion. The first assumption is to split "confidence for" from "confidence against" a relationship:

Call MB(H|E) the measure of belief of a hypothesis H given evidence E.

Call MD(H|E) the measure of disbelief of a hypothesis H given evidence E.

Now either:

$$1 > MB(H|E) > 0 \text{ while } MD(H|E) = 0, \quad \text{or}$$
$$1 > MD(H|E) > 0 \text{ while } MB(H|E) = 0.$$

The two measures constrain each other in that a given piece of evidence is either for or against a particular hypothesis. This is an important difference between certainty theory and probability theory. Once the link between measures of belief and disbelief has been established, they may be tied together again with the certainty factor calculation:

$$CF(H \mid E) = MB(H \mid E) - MD(H \mid E).$$

As the certainty factor (CF) approaches 1 the evidence is stronger for a hypothesis; as CF approaches -1 the confidence against the hypothesis gets stronger; and a CF around 0 indicates that little evidence exists either for or against the hypothesis.

When experts put together the rule base they must agree on a CF to go with each rule. This CF reflects their confidence in the rule's reliability. Certainty measures may be adjusted to tune the system's performance, although slight variations in this confidence measure tend to have little effect on the overall running of the system (again, "the knowledge gives the power").

The premises for each rule are formed of the and and or of a number of facts. When a production rule is used, the certainty factors associated with each condition of the premise are combined to produce a certainty measure for the overall premise in the following manner.

For P1 and P2, premises of the rule,

$$CF(P1 \text{ and } P2) = MIN(CF(P1), CF(P2)), \quad \text{and}$$
$$CF(P1 \text{ or } P2) = MAX(CF(P1), CF(P2)).$$

The combined CF of the premises, using the above combining rules, is then multiplied by the CF of the rule to get the CF for the conclusions of the rule.

For example, consider the rule in a knowledge base:

$$(P1 \text{ and } P2) \text{ or } P3 \rightarrow R1 (.7) \text{ and } R2 (.3)$$

where P1, P2, and P3 are premises and R1 and R2 are the conclusions of the rule having CFs 0.7 and 0.3, respectively. These numbers are added to the rule when it is designed and represent the expert's confidence in the conclusion if all the premises are known with complete certainty. If the running program has produced P1, P2, and P3 with CFs of 0.6, 0.4, and 0.2, respectively, then R1 and R2 may be added to the collected case-specific results with CFs 0.28 and 0.12, respectively.

Here are the calculations for this example:

CF(P1(.6) and P2(.4)) = MIN(.6,.4) = .4.

CF((.4) or P3(.2)) = MAX(.4,.2) = .4.

The CF for R1 is .7 in the rule, so R1 is added to the set of true facts with the associated CF of (.7) * (.4) = .28.

The CF for R2 is .3 in the rule, so R2 is added to the set of true facts with the associated CF of (.3) * (.4) = .12.

One further measure is required: how to combine multiple CFs when two or more rules support the same result R. This is the certainty theory analog of the probability theory procedure of multiplying the probability measures to combine independent evidence. By using this rule repeatedly one can combine the results of any number of rules that are used for determining result R. Suppose CF(R1) is the present certainty factor associated with result R and a previously unused rule produces result R (again) with CF(R2); then the new CF of R is calculated by:

CF(R1) + CF(R2) − (CF(R1) * CF(R2))   when CF(R1) and CF(R2) are positive

CF(R1) + CF(R2) + (CF(R1) * CF(R2))   when CF(R1) and CF(R2) are negative

$$\frac{CF(R1) + CF(R2)}{1 - MIN(|CF(R1)|, |CF(R2)|)}$$ otherwise

where |X| is the absolute value of X.

Besides being easy to compute, these equations have other desirable properties. First, the CFs that result from applying this rule are always between 1 and −1, as are the other CFs. Second, the result of combining contradictory CFs is that they cancel each other out, as would be desired. Finally, the combined CF measure is a monotonically increasing (decreasing) function in the manner one would expect for combining evidence.

Certainty theory may be criticized as being excessively ad hoc. Although it is defined in a formal algebra, the meaning of the certainty measures is not as rigorously founded as in formal probability theory. However, certainty theory does not attempt to produce an algebra for "correct" reasoning. Rather it is the "lubrication" that lets the expert system combine confidences as it moves along through the problem at hand. Its measures are ad hoc in the same sense that a human expert's confidence in his or her results is approximate, heuristic, and informal. In Section 8.4, when MYCIN is considered, the CFs are used in the heuristic search to give a priority for goals to be attempted and a cutoff point when a goal need not be considered further. But even though the CF is used to keep the program running and collecting information, the power of the program is in the content of the rules themselves. This is the justification for the weakness of the certainty algebra.

8.3.4 Nonmonotonic Logic and Reasoning with Beliefs

All of the methods we have examined can be criticized for using quantitative approximations of uncertainty. It is unlikely that humans use any of these techniques for reasoning with uncertainty, and many applications seem to require a more qualitative approach to the problem. For example, numeric approaches do not support adequate explanations of the causes of uncertainty. If we ask human experts why their conclusions are uncertain, they can answer in terms of the qualitative relationships between features of the problem instance. In a numeric model of uncertainty, this information is replaced by numeric measures. Similarly, numeric approaches do not address the problem of changing data. What should the system do if a piece of uncertain information is later found to be true or false?

Certainty factor algebra, like the reasoning strategies that we have examined so far in the text, is patterned after mathematical logic. Traditional mathematical logic is *monotonic*: it begins with a set of axioms, assumed to be true, and infers their consequences. If we add a new axiom or fact to such a system, it may cause the set of true statements to increase; however, adding knowledge will never make the set of true statements decrease.

This leads to problems if we are attempting to model reasoning based on beliefs and assumptions. In reasoning with uncertainty, humans will draw conclusions based on their current set of beliefs; however, unlike mathematical axioms, these beliefs may change as more information becomes available. *Nonmonotonic reasoning* addresses the problem of changing beliefs. A nonmonotonic reasoning system handles uncertainty by making the most reasonable assumptions in light of uncertain information. It proceeds with its reasoning as if these assumptions were true. At a later time, a belief may change, necessitating a reexamination of conclusions derived from that belief.

In implementing nonmonotonic reasoning, we may extend our logic with the operator unless. unless allows us to draw inferences based on the belief that its argument is not true. Suppose we have the following set of sentences:

```
p unless q -> r
p
r -> s
```

The first rule means that we may infer r if p is true and we do not believe q to be true. Because these conditions are met, we infer r and, using r, infer s. Subsequently, if we change our belief, or find that q is true, r and also s must be retracted. Note that unless deals with matters of belief rather than truth. Consequently, changing the value of its argument from "either unknown or believed false" to "believed or known to be true" can cause us to retract all inferences that depend upon these beliefs. By extending our logic to reason with beliefs, we introduce nonmonotonicity.

The reasoning scheme just described can also be used to encode default rules (Reiter 1980). If we replace p unless q -> r with p unless ab p -> r, where ab p represents abnormal p, we state that unless we have an abnormal instance of p, such as a bird with a broken wing, we can make the inference that if X is a bird then X can fly. Other representations for exception handling are presented with frame and object systems in Chapters 9 and 15.

Nonmonotonicity is an important feature of human problem solving and commonsense reasoning. When we drive to work, for example, we make numerous assumptions about the roads and traffic. If we find that one of these assumptions is violated, perhaps by construction or an accident on our usual route, we change our plans and devise an alternative route to work.

One of the problems facing nonmonotonic reasoning systems is in efficiently revising the conclusions of the reasoner in light of changing belief. In our example, we used r to infer s. Retracting r removed the support for s; unless there is an independent set of inferences supporting s, it must also be retracted. Implementing this process is complex, requiring in the worst case that we recompute all the conclusions of the knowledge base each time a belief changes. *Truth maintenance systems* attempt to reduce this complexity by storing the justifications for each inference. For example, on inferring r, a truth maintenance system would also record the justification for all subsequent inferences using r. On changing our belief in q and retracting r, the truth maintenance system would not have to recompute all conclusions; it would use these records to examine only the affected sentences.

For more information on nonmonotonic reasoning and truth maintenance, see Doyle 1979; Reiter 1980; de Kleer 1986; Davis 1990.

8.3.5 Fuzzy Logic, Dempster/Shafer, and Other Approaches to Uncertainty

Because of the importance of uncertain reasoning to expert-level problem solving and the limitations of certainty theory, work continues in this important area. In concluding this subsection, we mention briefly two other approaches to modeling uncertainty: Zadeh's *fuzzy set theory* and the Dempster/Shafer *theory of evidence*.

Zadeh's main contention (Zadeh 1983) is that, although probability theory is appropriate for measuring randomness of information, it is inappropriate for measuring the *meaning* of information. Indeed, much of the confusion surrounding the use of English words and phrases is related to lack of clarity (vagueness) rather than randomness. This is a crucial point for analyzing language structures and can also be important in creating a measure of confidence in production rules. Zadeh proposes *possibility theory* as a measure of vagueness, just as probability theory measures randomness.

Zadeh's theory expresses lack of precision in a quantitative fashion by introducing a set membership function that can take on real values between 0 and 1. This is the notion of a *fuzzy set* and can be described as follows: let S be a set and s a member of that set. A fuzzy subset F of S is defined by a membership function mF(s) that measures the "degree" to which s belongs to F.

A standard example of the fuzzy set is for S to be the set of positive integers and F to be the fuzzy subset of S called "small integers." Now various integer values can have a "possibility" distribution defining their "fuzzy membership" in the set of small integers: mF(1) = 1, mF(2) = 1, mF(3) = 0.9, mF(4) = 0.8, . . . , mF(50) = 0.001, etc. For the statement that positive integer X is a "small integer," mF creates a possibility distribution across all the positive integers (S).

Fuzzy set theory is not concerned with how these possibility distributions are created, but rather with the rules for computing the combined possibilities over expressions that each contain fuzzy variables. Thus it includes rules for combining possibility measures for expressions containing fuzzy variables. The laws for the or, and, and not of these expressions are similar to those just presented for certainty factors. In fact, the approach at Stanford was modeled on some of the combination rules described by Zadeh (Buchanan and Shortliffe 1984).

Dempster and Shafer approach the problem of measuring certainty by asking us to make a fundamental distinction between uncertainty and ignorance. In probability theory we are *forced* to express the extent of our knowledge about a belief X in a single number, P(X). The problem with this (say Dempster and Shafer) is that we simply cannot always know the values of prior probabilities, and thus any particular choice of P(X) may not be justified.

The Dempster/Shafer approach recognizes the distinction between uncertainty and ignorance by creating "belief functions." These belief functions satisfy axioms that are weaker than those of probability theory. Thus probability theory is seen as a subclass of belief functions, and the theory of evidence can reduce to probability theory when all the probabilities are obtainable. Belief functions therefore allow us to use our knowledge to bound the assignment of probabilities to events without having to come up with exact probabilities, when these may be unavailable.

Even though the Dempster/Shafer approach gives us methods of computing these various belief parameters, their greater complexity adds to the computational cost as well. Besides, any theory that has probability theory as a special case is plagued by the assumptions that have made probability theory already quite difficult to use. Conclusions using beliefs, even though they avoid commitment to a stronger and often unjustified assignment of probability, produce conclusions that are necessarily weaker. But, as the Dempster/Shafer model points out quite correctly, the stronger conclusion may not be justified.

In the next section, we examine the MYCIN expert system, illustrating the application of such techniques as rule-based reasoning, certainty factor algebra, how and why explanations, and knowledge-base validation. MYCIN addresses the difficult problem of assisting a medical doctor in diagnosing meningitis and bacteremia.

8.4 MYCIN: A Case Study

8.4.1 Introduction

Although our small automotive diagnostic example is useful in presenting some of the concepts of expert system design, it is a toy system and ignores much of the complexity encountered in building large knowledge-based programs. For this reason, we end this chapter with a case study of an expert system for a complex application.

The MYCIN project was a cooperative venture by the Department of Computer Science and the Medical School at Stanford University. The main work on the project was done during the middle and late 1970s, and about 50 person-years were expended in the effort. MYCIN was written in INTERLISP, a dialect of the LISP programming language. One of the earliest expert systems to be proposed and designed, it has become an important classic in the field. Indeed, it is often presented as the archetype for the rule-based program. One of the main reasons for the influence of the MYCIN program is the extensive documentation of the project by the Stanford research teams (Buchanan and Shortliffe 1984).

MYCIN was designed to solve the problem of diagnosing and recommending treatment for meningitis and bacteremia (blood infections). This particular domain was chosen largely because the program architects wanted to explore the way in which human experts reason with missing and incomplete information. Although there are diagnostic tools that can unambiguously determine the identity of the infecting organisms in a case of meningitis, these tools require on the order of 48 hours (chiefly to grow a culture of the infecting organisms) to return a diagnosis. Meningitis patients, however, are very sick, and some treatment must begin immediately. Because of this need, doctors have developed considerable expertise, based on initial symptoms and test results, for forming a diagnosis that *covers* (i.e., includes as a subset) the actual infecting organisms. Treatment begins with this diagnosis and is refined when more conclusive information becomes available. Thus, the domain of meningitis diagnosis provided a natural focus for studying how humans solve problems using incomplete or unreliable information.

Another goal of the MYCIN design team was to pattern the behavior of the program after the way in which human physicians interact in actual consultations. This was seen as an important factor in system acceptability, particularly because medical consultations tend to follow a standard set of protocols.

In the next subsections we examine the composition of the MYCIN rule and fact descriptions, including the syntax of MYCIN rules. Next, we present a trace of a MYCIN consultation, along with explanatory comments and a discussion of the design and structure of the dialogue. We then discuss the problem of evaluating expert systems and, finally, demonstrate the use of an experimental knowledge base editor, *Teiresias*. Editors such as Teiresias assist the domain experts (in this case the doctors) in correcting the MYCIN knowledge base without the need for the computer language expert. Although such tools are still mainly experimental, this is an important area of research and a potential key to increasing the range of applicability of expert system technology.

8.4.2 Representation of Rules and Facts

Facts in MYCIN are represented as *attribute-object-value triples*. The first element of this structure is an attribute of an object in the problem domain. For example, we may wish to describe the identity of a disease organism or its sensitivity to certain drugs. The name of the object and the value of the attribute follow. As information in this domain may be uncertain, a certainty factor is associated with MYCIN facts. Recall from Section 8.3.3 that this certainty factor will be between 1 and -1, with 1 being certain, -1 indicating certainty that the attribute is not true, and values about 0 indicating that nothing is known.

For example, MYCIN facts may be represented in English by:

There is evidence (.25) that the identity of the organism is Klebsiella.

and

It is known that the organism is not sensitive to penicillin.

These may be translated into the LISP s-expressions:

```
(ident organism_1 klebsiella .25)
```

and

(sensitive organism_1 penicillin −1.0)

We next present an example MYCIN rule both in English and in its formal equivalent. This sample rule is a condition-action pair in which the premise (condition) is the conjunction of three facts (attribute-object-value triples) and the action adds a new fact to the set of things known about the patient, the identity of a particular organism that is added to the "cover set" of possible infecting organisms. Because this is an abductive rule of inference (inferring the cause from the evidence), it has an attached certainty factor.
In the English version of the rule:

if (a) the infection is primary-bacteremia, and
   (b) the site of the culture is one of the sterile sites, and
   (c) the suspected portal of entry is the gastrointestinal tract

then there is suggestive evidence (.7) that infection is bacteroid

is rendered for MYCIN:

IF: (AND (same_context infection primary_bacteremia)
        (membf_context site sterilesite)
        (same_context portal GI))

THEN: (conclude context_ident bacteroid tally .7).

Syntactically, attribute-object-value (A-O-V) triples are essentially a restriction of predicate calculus expressions to binary predicates. This restriction is not particularly limiting, as algorithms exist for translating predicates of any arity into a set of binary predicates.

There is a deeper difference between predicate calculus and the A-O-V triples used in MYCIN: predicates may be either true or false. Predicate calculus uses sound rules of inference to determine the truth value of conclusions. In MYCIN, a fact has an attached confidence rather than a truth value. When the system is deriving new facts, it fails to fire any rule whose premise has a certainty value of less than 0.2. This contrasts with logic, which causes a rule to fail only if its premise is found to be false.

This comparison of attribute-object-value triples and predicate calculus expressions is included here to emphasize both the similarities and the trade-offs involved in different knowledge representations. At the highest conceptual level, the characteristics that define a rule-based expert system are independent of any commitment to a particular representational format. These characteristics have been discussed in the comparison of rule-based expert systems and the production system model of problem solving. At the level of an implementation, however, the selection of a particular representational formalism does involve a number of important trade-offs. These issues include the clarity of the representation, expressiveness (what knowledge can the formalism effectively capture?), naturalness of expression, and ease of implementing and verifying the system.

The action of a MYCIN rule can perform a number of tasks once the rule is satisfied. It may add new information about a particular patient to the working memory. It may also write information to the terminal (or other output device), change the value of an attribute or its certainty measure, look up information in a table (where this representation is more efficient), or execute any piece of LISP code.

Although the ability to execute arbitrary LISP code gives unlimited added power, it should be used judiciously, as excessive use of escapes to the underlying language can lose many of the benefits of the production system formalism. (As an absurd example of this, imagine an expert system with only one rule, whose action is to call a large and poorly structured LISP program that attempts to solve the problem!)

MYCIN rule and fact descriptions, like all knowledge representations, are a formal language and have a formal syntactic definition. This formal syntax is essential to the definition of well-behaved inference procedures. Furthermore, the formal syntax of rules can help a knowledge base editor, such as Teiresias, determine when the domain expert has produced an incorrectly formed rule and prevent that rule from entering the knowledge base. Teiresias can detect syntactic errors in a rule and, to an impressive degree, automatically remedy the situation (see Section 8.4.5). This is possible only when the entire program is built on a set of formal specifications.

8.4.3 MYCIN Diagnosing an Illness

MYCIN is a goal-driven expert system. Its main action is to try to determine whether a particular organism may be present in the meningitis infection in the patient. A possible infecting organism forms a goal that is either confirmed or eliminated. It is interesting to note that the decision to make MYCIN a goal-driven system was not based exclusively on the effectiveness of the strategy in pruning the search space. Early in the design of the system, the MYCIN architects considered the use of forward search. This was rejected because the questions the system asked the user seemed random and unconnected. Goal-driven search, because it is attempting to either confirm or eliminate a particular hypothesis, causes the reasoning to seem more focused and logical. This builds the user's understanding and confidence in the system's actions. An expert system needs to do more than obtain a correct answer; it must also do so in an intelligent and understandable fashion. This criterion influences the choice of search strategies as well as the structure and order of rules.

In keeping with this goal of making the program behave like a doctor, MYCIN's designers noted that doctors ask routine questions at the beginning of a consultation (e.g., "how old are you?" and "have you had any childhood diseases?") and ask more specific questions when they are needed. Collecting the general information at the beginning makes the session seem more focused in that it is not continually interrupted by trivial questions such as the name, age, sex, and race of the patient. Certain other questions are asked at other well-defined stages of a consultation (such as when beginning to consider a new hypothesis).

Eventually the questions get more specific (questions 16 and 17 in the trace below) and related to possible meningitis. When positive responses are given to these questions, MYCIN determines that the infection is meningitis, goes into full goal-driven mode, and tries to determine the actual infecting organisms. It does this by considering each infecting organism that it knows about and attempting to eliminate or confirm each hypothesis in turn. Because a patient may have more than one infecting organism, MYCIN searches exhaustively, continuing until all possible hypotheses have been considered.

MYCIN controls its search in a number of ways that have not yet been discussed. The knowledge base includes rules that restrict the hypotheses to be tested. For example, MYCIN concludes that it should test for meningitis when the patient has had headaches and other abnormal neurological signs.

Another feature of MYCIN's inference engine is the order in which it tries the backward chaining rules. After determining the general category of the infection (meningitis, bacteremia, etc.), each candidate diagnosis is examined exhaustively in a depth-first fashion.

To make the search behave more intelligently, MYCIN first examines all the premises of a rule to determine whether any of them are already known to be false. This prevents the program from trying to solve several of the premises, only to discover that the rule could have been eliminated immediately by one of the later premises.

MYCIN also attempts to find a *unity path*. In trying to prove a goal, it looks for rules that can conclude that goal with a certainty of 1. If one of these rules succeeds, the system does not have to try other rules; the goal is known to be true. This increases both the efficiency and rationality of the search procedure.

When the confidence measures for a rule premise get below a certain value, the depth-first search is terminated. As mentioned above, the certainty measure for each patient's data is combined with the measures resident in the rules to give the certainty of the new conclusions for the patient. When these get below 0.2, MYCIN abandons the search and goes back up the graph to try another branch of the search space.

When the user wants MYCIN to justify its request for some information, he or she can ask why. Initially, this is answered by the phrase "because I need the information as a necessary attribute of each patient." Once MYCIN begins its backward search for the causes of the patient's problems, however, the why question is answered by printing the rule that MYCIN is currently considering.

As was also mentioned earlier in this chapter, the "Englishlike" interaction that the computer offers the user is not a full English-language understanding program. Appropriate forms for English-language comments and questions are attached to each rule when it is created so that the proper query can be presented to the user when information is needed for use of the rule or so that a rule can be printed in response to a user query.

The following dialogue is a simulated run of the MYCIN program adapted from transcripts of actual MYCIN consultations. It is not necessary to understand either the medical terminology or the medical reasoning to appreciate MYCIN's problem solving.

Our comments on the MYCIN trace are reproduced in italics throughout the interaction. The MYCIN questions and answers are numbered, with the user's responses in this type.

@ mycin

MYCIN 26-March. . . .

Instructions? (Y or N)

N

26-March 10:42

-----PATIENT-1-----

Mycin has created an object (PATIENT-1) in its dynamic knowledge base or working memory. Certain attributes are immediately requested and are necessary for every patient. These make up the first four questions. . . .

(1) Patient's name:

Alan Apt

(2) Age?

34

(3) Sex

Why

MYCIN restates the question before answering. . . .

[i.e., Why is it important to determine the sex of PATIENT-1?]

[1.0] The sex of the patient is one of the four standard parameters that identify a patient. This may be useful later. . . .

[back to question 3 . . .]

Male

(4) Race?

Caucasian

(5) Are there any cultures for Alan Apt that may be related to the present illness, and from which organisms have been grown successfully in the lab?

No

MYCIN is a program to analyze and treat infectious diseases, so before it gets into close questioning of the patient's present condition it asks about any present or pending data (cultures) that are available. . . .

(6) Are there any pending cultures for Alan Apt?

Yes

-----CULTURE-1-----

Another object (CULTURE-1) is created and linked to PATIENT-1. . . .

(7) From what site was the specimen for CULTURE-1 taken?

CSF

(8) Please give the date and time when the pending CSF culture was obtained?

26-March-7:00

(9) Was a smear examined at the time the specimen was obtained?

Yes

(10) Were any cultures seen on the smear of the specimen?

No

Indentation indicates that MYCIN's attention has returned from consideration of the new object (CULTURE-1) back to the original object (PATIENT-1).

(11) Are there any other pending cultures?

No

.

.

.

(16) Has Alan Apt recently had symptoms of persistent headache or other abnormal neurologic symptoms (dizziness, lethargy, etc.)?

Yes

(17) Has Alan Apt recently had objective evidence of abnormal neurologic signs (nuchal rigidity, coma, seizures, etc.) documented by a physician?

Yes

With the answers of these last two questions in the affirmative, MYCIN decides to consider meningitis infections and goes into a full back chaining search to try to identify the organisms that might be causing the meningitis.

The CSF cultures will be considered to be associated with MENINGITIS.

(18) Please give the date on which clinical evidence (symptoms, signs, or laboratory tests) of the meningitis first appeared.

25 March 10:00

.

.

.

(36) Has Alan Apt had neurosurgery?

Why

[i.e., Why is it important to determine whether PATIENT-1 has had neurosurgery?]

[6.0] This will aid in determining the organisms (other than those seen on cultures or smears) that might be causing the infection.

    It has already been established that

        [6.1] the culture that requires therapy is meningitis, and

        [6.2] organisms were not seen on the stain of the pending csf culture

            (CULTURE-1), and

        [6.3] the type of infection is bacterial

    Therefore, if

        [6.4] Alan Apt has had neurosurgery, and

[6.5] the time since the neurosurgical operation is less than two
months, and

[6.5] the type of neurosurgery is not ventricular-urethral-shunt
then
there is evidence that the organisms that might be causing the
infection are staphylococcus-coag-pos (.75), staphylococcus-coag-neg (.5)
e.coli (.4), klebsiella. . . .

Author: Yu
[RULE511]
[back to question 36. . .]

How [6.3]

*The physician is concerned how MYCIN arrived at the conclusion that the
infection is bacterial. MYCIN responds, after restating its interpretation of
the question the doctor is asking, with the rules it used to determine that
the infection was indeed bacterial. This answering uses the rule-based
technique called the rule stack (Section 13.2.2). The answer to how is
given by the rules used, as well as their (positive and negative) certainty
factors, for determining this result. The how response is generated by
producing a proof tree (Section 13.2.2).*

[i.e., How was it established that the type of infection is bacterial?]

The following rules concluded about: the likelihood that the type of infection is
bacterial

Rule	Yes	No
[6.7] 500	(.4)	
[6.8] 501		(.17)
[6.9] 502	(.1)	
[6.10] 524	(.42)	
[6.11] 504	(.28)	

Thus it has been established that the type of infection might be bacterial.

[back to question 36. . .]

No

   .

   .

   .

(42) Is Alan Apt a burn patient?

Yes

I have found evidence (RULE507) that treatment should cover for
Diplococcus pneumoniae causing meningitis.

I have found evidence (RULE545) that treatment should cover for e.coli
causing meningitis.

I have found evidence (RULE545 RULE578) that the treatment should cover for Pseudomonas aeruginosa causing meningitis.

MYCIN now attempts to prescribe appropriate therapies for these infections. First, it must be determined whether the patient has any allergies to antibody therapies. The height and weight of the patient are also requested to determine proper dosages . . .

(43) Does Alan Apt have focal neurological signs?

No

[Determining which dosages are desirable for use against the e.coli . . .]
[Determining which drugs are desirable for use . . .]

INFECTION-1 is MENINGITIS
+ <ITEM-1> DIPLOCOCCUS-PNEUMONIAE (from clinical evidence only)
+ <ITEM-2> E.COLI (from clinical evidence only)
+ <ITEM-3> PSEUD. . . . .

.
.
.

[REC-1] My preferred therapy recommendation is as follows:
In order to cover for items <1 2 3>:
Give the following in combination:
1) AMPICILLIN
Dose: 3.85g (30.8ml) q4h IV

2) GENTAMICIN
Dose: 131mg (3.2ml) q8h IV

Comments: Monitor serum concentrations
Since high concentrations of penicillins can inactivate aminoglycosides, do not mix these antibiotics in the same IV bottle.

Do you wish to see the next choice therapy?

No

If the physician did not like the recommended treatment he or she could have asked for another, eliminating one of the drugs (ampicillin, for instance). MYCIN would then have attempted to find another treatment. . . .

8.4.4 Evaluation of Expert Systems

One of the difficult issues faced by expert system design teams is to determine when the program is ready for actual use. This problem is all the more difficult when the program, like MYCIN, deals with life-threatening situations; here, mistakes, such as overlooking an infecting agent, can be catastrophic. Many expert systems, including MYCIN (Buchanan and Shortliffe 1984), have been evaluated by using a form of the Turing test.

Ten randomly selected case histories of meningitis were rediagnosed by MYCIN and eight practitioners at the Stanford Medical School. These included five faculty members, one research fellow in infectious diseases, one resident physician, and one medical student. The actual therapy given by the original doctors on the case was also included, for a total of ten diagnoses.

These ten diagnoses were evaluated by eight infectious-disease experts away from Stanford. The diagnoses were "blind" in that they were uniformly coded so that the experts did not know whether they were looking at the computer's diagnosis or that of the humans. The evaluators rated each diagnosis as acceptable or unacceptable, with a practitioner being given one point for each acceptable rating. Thus, a perfect score would be 80 points. The results of this evaluation are given in Table 8.1:

Table 8.2 presents the results of asking another important question in this "life and death" analysis: in how many cases did the recommended therapy fail to cover for a treatable infection? The results in both tables indicate that MYCIN performed at least as well

TABLE 8.1 EXPERTS EVALUATE MYCIN AND NINE OTHER PRESCRIBERS

PRESCRIBER	SCORE	PERCENT
MYCIN	55	69
Faculty-5	54	68
Fellow	53	66
Faculty-3	51	64
Faculty-2	49	61
Faculty-4	47	59
Actual RX	47	59
Faculty-1	45	56
Resident	39	49
Student	28	35

TABLE 8.2 NUMBER OF CASES IN WHICH THERAPY MISSED A TREATABLE PATHOGEN

PRESCRIBER	NUMBER
MYCIN	0
Faculty-5	1
Fellow	1
Faculty-3	1
Faculty-2	0
Faculty-4	0
Actual RX	0
Faculty-1	0
Resident	1
Student	3

Note: On the average MYCIN gave fewer drugs than the human experts.

as the Stanford experts. This is an exciting result, but it should not surprise us as the MYCIN knowledge base represents the combined expertise of some of the best medical minds available. Finally, MYCIN gave fewer drugs than the human experts and thus did not overprescribe for the infections.

Another noteworthy aspect of this evaluation is how little agreement there was among human experts concerning the correctness of diagnoses. Even the best of the diagnosticians failed to receive a unanimous endorsement from the evaluators. This observation underscores the extent to which human expertise is still largely heuristic in nature.

These positive evaluation results do not mean that MYCIN is now ready to set up a medical practice and take on patients. In fact, MYCIN is not used for delivering medical care. There are several important reasons. First, and most important, the rules (approximately 600 of them) did not give a speedy response in the doctor-computer interaction. Each session with the computer lasted about one-half hour and required, as can be seen from the trace presented above, a good amount of typing.

Second, the program was "locked into" the particular part of its graph search for response to questions. It was not able to extrapolate to other situations or previous patients but remained strictly within the nodes and links of the graph it was evaluating.

Third, MYCIN's explanations were limited: when the doctor expected a deep medical justification for some particular result—a physiological or antibacterial justification, say—MYCIN simply returned the "condition action plus certainty factor" relationship contained in its rule base. It is difficult for an expert system to relate its heuristic knowledge to any deeper understanding of the problem domain. MYCIN, for example, does not really understand human physiology; it simply applies rules to case-specific data. Folklore has it that an early version of MYCIN, before recommending a particular drug, asked whether the patient was pregnant, in spite of the fact that MYCIN had been told that the patient was male! Whether this actually happened or not, it does indicate the limitations of current expert system technology. Attempting to give expert systems the flexibility and deeper understanding demonstrated by human beings is an important and open area of research.

Finally, unlike humans, who are extremely flexible in the way they apply knowledge, expert systems do not "degrade gracefully" when confronted with situations that do not fit the knowledge in their rule base. That is, whereas a human can shift to reasoning from first principles or to intelligent guesses when confronted with a new situation, expert systems simply fail to get any answer at all.

All of these issues have meant that MYCIN does not enjoy common use in the medical field. Nonetheless, it does serve as an archetype of this class of expert system, and many of its descendants, such as PUFF, an expert system to assist in pulmonary function testing, are being used in clinical situations.

8.4.5 Knowledge Acquisition and the Teiresias Knowledge-Base Editor

Another long-term goal of expert systems research is to design software that will allow the human expert to interact directly with the knowledge base to correct and improve it. This is seen as a potential remedy for what has been called the *knowledge engineering bottleneck*. This bottleneck is caused by the fact that building an expert system generally requires a substantial commitment of time by both the domain expert and the knowledge engineer.

This contributes to the expense and complexity of building expert systems. Both of these individuals tend to be highly paid professionals, and the loss in productivity caused by taking the domain expert away from other work during system development can add to the cost of the project. Additional cost and complexity come from the effort needed to communicate the domain expert's knowledge to the knowledge engineer, the logistics of getting these two people together, and the complexity of the programming required for an expert system.

The obvious solution to this problem is to automate as much of the process as possible. This has been done to a great extent through the development of expert system shells and environments that reduce the amount of programming required by the knowledge engineer. However, these shells still require that the programmer understand the methodologies of knowledge representation and search. A more ambitious goal is to eliminate the need for a knowledge engineer entirely. One way to accomplish this is to provide knowledge-base editors that allow the domain expert to develop the program, interacting with the knowledge base in terms that come from the problem domain and letting the software handle the details of representation and knowledge organization. This approach has been explored in an experimental program called *Teiresias* (Davis 1982), a knowledge-base editor developed at Stanford University as part of the MYCIN project. We discuss the Teiresias project in this section.

Another approach to the problem is to develop programs that can learn on their own by refining their problem-solving efforts in response to feedback from the outside. These approaches have been explored with varying degrees of success by the machine learning community. These issues are introduced in Chapter 12 and continue to be a promising and exciting area of artificial intelligence research.

With the assistance of a knowledge-base editor, the domain expert can analyze the performance of a knowledge base, find missing or erroneous rules, and correct the problem in a language appropriate to the expert's way of thinking about the domain. The knowledge-base editor designed for MYCIN is called Teiresias after the blind seer of the Greek tragedian Euripides. The name is altogether appropriate, as Teiresias was able to see and describe the relations of the world without the (literal) gift of sight; similarly, this software is able to understand relations in a knowledge base without (literally) understanding the referents of these relations.

Teiresias allows a doctor to step through MYCIN's treatment of a patient and locate problems with its performance. Teiresias also translates the doctor's corrections into the appropriate internal representations for the knowledge base. Thus Teiresias is able to maintain the syntactic consistency of the knowledge base by updating all appropriate program structures when new information is to be integrated into the knowledge base.

For example, MYCIN stores considerable knowledge in the form of tables. Certain rules include LISP code that retrieves information from these tables, such as characteristics of disease organisms. This improves the efficiency of the knowledge base, because a single table can capture information that would require numerous rules to encode. However, if a new object (for example, a disease organism) is added to the knowledge base, then all tables that contain information about disease organisms must be updated to reflect this.

Semantic consistency is a more difficult problem, requiring knowledge of how well the knowledge base actually reflects the problem domain. Although Teiresias cannot be said to truly maintain semantic consistency, it does make an effort to ensure that rules appear consistent with one another. It does this by maintaining *rule models*, or statistical profiles of all the rules. If a new rule is added to the knowledge base, Teiresias compares this new rule with the rule model for all existing rules that draw the same conclusion. The assumption is that rules that draw similar conclusions should examine similar conditions in their premises. This enables Teiresias to detect potential inconsistencies in a new rule and prompt the user for corrections.

To illustrate Teiresias, we analyze its interaction with the doctor after MYCIN has given its recommendations. The doctor disagrees with MYCIN's result, and with Teiresias' help, analyzes MYCIN's solution. The trace is a simulation taken from a session by Stanford researchers, where the analysis is in italics, Teiresias' questions are in regular type, and the doctor's responses are in bold type.

When a conclusion is given with which the doctor disagrees, the rule that drew this conclusion is not necessarily wrong. A number of things could have happened, as Teiresias correctly shows: a fact of the rule could have been improperly concluded; the rule might, in fact, be wrong; or another rule might be missing from the knowledge base. Finding the cause of an error is a difficult problem that potentially requires examination of the entire line of reasoning. Teiresias assists the physician in determining the problem by maintaining an **and/or** graph of the solution process and working systematically through this trace.

All rules are translated into an English-language syntax that assists the physician in understanding the trace. Once a problem is located, Teiresias lets the user add the missing rule in the same simplified syntax, translating the rule into an internal representation and checking the new rule for consistency with similar rules in the knowledge base.

MYCIN has reached a set of infections that it feels should be treated (as in the dialogue of Section 8.4.3). These are presented to the physician, who disagrees with MYCIN's analysis:

My therapy recommendation will be based on the following probable
infections and potential causative organisms:

INFECTION-1 is PRIMARY BACTEREMIA
    <item-1> E.COLI
    <item-2> PSEUDOMONAS-AERUGINOSA

Now Teiresias steps in:

Are all these identities correct?

No

Are there any identities missing?

Yes

Which ones?

KLEBSIELLA_PNEUMONIAE, PROTEUS-NON-MIRABILIS

Are there any identities which shouldn't have appeared?

Yes

Which ones?

PSEUDOMONAS-AERUGINOSA

Do you want to
    1) track down the problem yourself, or
    2) allow me to guide the debugging, or
    3) ignore it for now and fix it another time
Type 1, 2 or 3
    2

If the doctor had typed 1, he or she could have tried to sort out the problems with the traditional WHY and HOW queries on the preceding solution. Note that Teiresias has already begun to categorize the errors that appeared in the conclusions. It should also be noted that the three problems could well be related (perhaps to one missing rule). Teiresias starts by trying to find out why the wrong organism appeared for treatment. . . .

We'll start with PSEUDOMONAS-AERUGINOSA first:
The following rules were used in deducing that the identity of ORGANISM-1 is PSEUDOMONAS-AERUGINOSA.
RULE 184
    Since
    [1.1] The category of ORGANISM-1 is not known
    [1.2] The gram stain of ORGANISM-1 is gram negative
    [1.3] The morphology of ORGANISM-1 is rod
    [1.4] The aerobicity of ORGANISM-1 is facultative
    There is weakly suggestive evidence (.3) that the identity of
    ORGANISM-1 is PSEUDOMONAS-AERUGINOSA.
Is this rule correct?

Yes

Should its premise have failed in this case?

Yes

Which clause of the premise should have failed?

Clause 1

The expert feels the program should have been able to establish a category and that Rule 184 should not have fired.

Should it have been possible to conclude a category?

Yes

Which one?

ENTEROBACTERIACEAE

There were no rules successfully called in the attempt to deduce this category.
The following (potentially applicable) rules were NOT executed because the marked [++] clause failed:
RULE 116
    If
    1) the identity of ORGANISM-1 is not known
++ 2) the gram stain of ORGANISM-1 is not known

---

3) the morphology of ORGANISM-1 is not known

4) the site of CULTURE-1 is CSF

5) the infection is meningitis

6) the age of the patient is less than or equal to 2 months

Then there is weakly suggestive evidence (.33) that the category of ORGANISM-1 is ENTEROBACTERIACEAE

RULE 050

If

1) the morphology of ORGANISM-1 is rod

2) the gram stain of ORGANISM-1 is gramneg

3) the aerobicity of ORGANISM-1 is facultative

++ 4) infection ORGANISM-1 was acquired while the patient was hospitalized

Then there is suggestive evidence (.7) that the category of ORGANISM-1 is ENTEROBACTERIACEAE

Are all these rules correct?

Yes

Should any of them have been successfully invoked?

No

Is there a rule missing?

Yes

Would you like to give me such a rule now?

Yes

Good . . .

If

1 ** THE PATIENT'S INFECTION IS PRIMARY-BACTEREMIA

2 ** THE SITE IS ONE OF THE STERILE SITES

Then:

**** THERE IS SUGGESTIVE EVIDENCE (.8) THAT THE CATEGORY IS ENTEROBACTERIACEAE**

Teiresias parses this rule into its internal representation and then translates it back into English so the expert can check it. After the expert agrees on the parse, Teiresias attempts to integrate the new rule into the knowledge base. . . .

I hate to criticize, Dr Davis, but did you know that most rules about what the category of an organism might be that mention:

the site of a culture, and

the infection

also mention:

the portal of entry of the organism?

Shall I try to write a clause to account for this?

Yes

How about:

the portal of entry is gastrointestinal. OK?

Yes

Teiresias is itself a knowledge-based program with rules for reasoning about rules and objects in a MYCIN knowledge base. As the above trace illustrates, the program systematically searches back along the trace of the reasoning to find the source of the problem. Once this is done, it helps the user add to or correct the knowledge base. Using the rule models discussed at the beginning of this section, Teiresias is able to check the rule for consistency and correct the missing premise.

To help the user add new information, Teiresias keeps a model of each class of object that appears in the system. The model for a MYCIN object is called a *schema*. Each schema describes how to create new instances of a class of objects such as a new disease organism, drug, or test. The schema for a class of objects also describes how information is to be obtained for rules of that class—for example, to compute it from existing data, look it up, or ask the user.

Schemata record the interrelationships of all classes of objects in the MYCIN rule base. For example, if the addition of a new disease requires that a table of diseases and their sensitivities to various drugs also be updated, this is recorded in the disease schema. Schemata also include pointers to all current instances of each schema. This is very important if it is decided to change the form of the schema throughout the program.

Teiresias organizes its schemata into a hierarchy: a schema for describing bacterial infections may be a specification of a general class schema, which in turn is a specification of a general schema for MYCIN facts. Each schema includes pointers to its parents and children in this hierarchy. (See also the topics of frames, objects, and object-oriented programming in Chapters 9 and 15.)

Schemata also contain bookkeeping information. This includes the author and date of creation and addition of each instance to the program. It includes a description of the schema used to create it. Documentation of who created rules when is critical for discussion and analysis of the knowledge base; when rules are primarily condition-action pairs representing important aspects of an application domain and not full explications of these relationships, it is important to be able to trace the rules back to their authors for more complete discussion of the factors underlying their creation.

The top-level structure in the hierarchy of Teiresias' knowledge is the *schema-schema*. This structure is a schema for creating new schemata, when, for instance, the domain expert might wish to create a new category of objects. The schema-schema allows Teiresias to reason about its own knowledge structures, including creating new ones when appropriate. A schema-schema has the same basic structure as a schema itself and provides all the bookkeeping information to reconstitute the entire knowledge base.

Although the development of commercial programs to help with knowledge acquisition is still in the future, Teiresias has shown how **and/or** graph search and knowledge representation techniques provide a basis for automating knowledge base refinement.

8.5   Epilogue and References

The model for the rule-based expert system is the production system. Whether the final product is data driven or goal driven, the model for the software is production system-generated graph search. This material was presented in Chapters 3, 4, and 5.

We implement simple expert system shells in PROLOG and LISP in Chapters 13 and 14, respectively. These shells, and some sample rules presented with them, are able to create a goal-driven search much like MYCIN's. The rules can include certainty measures in a limited form for designing a heuristically based search. The student is encouraged to add rules to fill out the knowledge base either along the lines of the analysis of a car that won't start, as in the beginning of this chapter, or to implement some other application.

A number of references complement the material presented in this chapter; especially recommended is a collection of the original MYCIN publications from Stanford entitled *Rule-Based Expert Systems* by Buchanan and Shortliffe (1984).

Other important books on general knowledge engineering include *Building Expert Systems* by Hayes-Roth et al. (1984), *A Guide to Expert Systems* by Waterman (1986), *Expert Systems: Concepts and Examples* by Alty and Coombs (1984), *Expert Systems Technology: A Guide* by Johnson and Keravnou (1985), *Expert Systems: Tools and Applications* by Harmon et al. (1988), and *Expert Systems and Fuzzy Systems* by Negoita (1985). See also *Introduction to Expert Systems* by Ignizio (1991) and *An Introduction to Expert Systems* by Mockler and Dologite (1992).

Because of the domain specificity of expert system solutions, case studies are an important source of knowledge in the area. Books in this category include *Expert Systems: Techniques, Tools and Applications* by Klahr and Waterman (1986), *Competent Expert Systems: A Case Study in Fault Diagnosis* by Keravnou and Johnson (1986), *The CRI Directory of Expert Systems* by Smart and Langeland-Knudsen (1986), *Developments in Expert Systems* by Coombs (1984), and *Development and Management of Expert Systems* by Prerau (1990).

A number of techniques for knowledge acquisition have been developed. For more information on specific methodologies see *Knowledge Acquisition: Principles and Guidelines* by McGraw and Harbison-Briggs (1989) and *Knowledge Engineering* by Chorfas (1990), as well as *An Introduction to Expert Systems* by Mockler and Dologite (1992) and other books on expert systems.

There is a rich literature on nonmonotonic reasoning, belief logics, and truth maintenance; besides the original papers in the area (Doyle 1979; Reiter 1985; deKleer 1986) a useful introduction to this literature includes *Probabilistic Reasoning in Intelligent Systems* by Pearl (1988), *Readings in Uncertain Reasoning* by Shafer and Pearl (1990), *Representations of Commonsense Knowledge* by Davis (1990), and numerous articles in recent AAAI and IJCAI conference proceedings.

8.6 Exercises

1. In Section 8.2 we introduced a set of rules for diagnosing automobile problems. Identify possible knowledge engineers, domain experts, and potential end users for such an application. Discuss the expectations, abilities, and needs of each of these groups.

2. Take Exercise 1 above. Create in English or pseudocode 15 if-then rules (other than those prescribed in Section 8.2) to describe relations within this domain. Create a graph to represent the relationships within these 15 rules.

3. Consider the graph of Exercise 2 above. Do you recommend data-driven or goal-driven search? breadth-first or depth-first search? In what ways could heuristics assist the search? Justify your answers to these questions.

4. Pick another area of interest for designing an expert system. Answer Exercises 1–3 for this application.

5. Implement an expert system using a commercial shell program. These are widely available for personal computers as well as larger machines.

6. Critique the shell you used to do Exercise 5. What are its strengths and weaknesses? What would you do to improve it? Was it appropriate to your problem? What problems are best suited to that tool?

9 KNOWLEDGE REPRESENTATION

When you notice a cat in profound meditation,
The reason, I tell you, is always the same:
His Mind is engaged in a rapt contemplation of the
Thought, of the thought, of the thought of his name.

—T. S. ELIOT, *Old Possum's Book of Practical Cats*

We have always two universes of discourse—call them "physical" and "phenomenal," or
what you will—one dealing with questions of quantitative and formal structure, the other
with those qualities that constitute a "world." All of us have our own distinctive mental
worlds, our own inner journeyings and landscapes, and these, for most of us, require no
clear neurological "correlate."

—OLIVER SACKS, "The Man Who Mistook His Wife for a Hat"

9.0 Knowledge Representation Languages

In building a knowledge base, a programmer must select the significant objects and relations in the domain and map these into a formal language. The resulting program must contain sufficient knowledge to solve problems in the domain, it must make correct inferences from this knowledge, and it must do so efficiently.

We can think of a knowledge base in terms of a mapping between the objects and relations in a problem domain and the computational objects and relations in a program (Bobrow 1975). The results of inferences on the knowledge base should correspond to the results of actions or observations in the world. The computational objects, relations, and inferences available to programmers are determined by the knowledge representation language they select. The proper language can help the programmer acquire, organize, and debug the knowledge base.

There are general principles of knowledge organization that apply across a variety of domains and can be directly supported by a representation language. For example, class hierarchies are found in both scientific and commonsense classification systems. How may we provide a general mechanism for representing them? How may we represent definitions? What is the relation between a rule and its exceptions? When should a knowledge-based system make default assumptions about missing information and how should it adjust its reasoning if these assumptions prove wrong? How may we best represent time? Causality? Uncertainty? Progress in knowledge-based systems depends on discovering the principles of knowledge organization and supporting them in higher-level representational tools.

It is useful to distinguish between a representational *scheme* and the *medium* of its implementation (Hayes 1974). This is similar to the distinction between data structures and programming languages. Programming languages are the *medium* of implementation; the data structure is the *scheme*. Generally, knowledge representation languages are more constrained than predicate calculus or programming languages such as LISP and PROLOG. The constraints take the form of explicit structures for representing categories of knowledge. The medium in which they are implemented might be PROLOG, LISP, or a conventional language such as C, C^{++}, or ADA.

Over the past 25 years, numerous representational schemes have been proposed and implemented, each of them having its own strengths and weaknesses. Mylopoulos and Levesque (1984) have classified these into four categories:

1. **Logical representation schemes.** This class of representations uses expressions in formal logic to represent a knowledge base. Inference rules and proof procedures apply this knowledge to problem instances. First-order predicate calculus is the most widely used logical representation scheme, but it is only one of a number of logical representations (Turner 1984). PROLOG is an ideal programming language for implementing logical representation schemes.

2. **Procedural representation schemes.** Procedural schemes represent knowledge as a set of instructions for solving a problem. This contrasts with the declarative representations provided by logic and semantic networks. In a rule-based system, for example, an if . . . then . . . rule may be interpreted as a procedure for solving a goal in a problem domain, by solving the premises in order. A production system may be seen as an example of a procedural representation scheme.

3. **Network representation schemes.** Network representations capture knowledge as a graph in which the nodes represent objects or concepts in the problem domain and the arcs represent relations or associations between them. Examples of network representations include *semantic networks*, *conceptual dependencies*, and *conceptual graphs*.

4. **Structured representation schemes.** Structured representation languages extend networks by allowing each node to be a complex data structure consisting of named slots with attached values. These values may be simple numeric or symbolic data, pointers to other frames, or even procedures for performing a particular

task. Examples of structured representations include *scripts*, *frames*, and *objects* (Chapter 15).

Logical representations are discussed in Chapters 2 and 11; procedural approaches are discussed throughout the text, particularly in Chapters 8 and 14 and in the discussion of production systems in Section 5.3. This chapter introduces network and structured representation schemes.

9.1 Issues in Knowledge Representation

A number of important issues have dominated research in knowledge representation. In this section we introduce these issues and the difficulties they present to designers and users of knowledge representation schemes. Much of this work is motivated by the effort to program a computer to understand human languages such as English. Because of the breadth and complexity of the knowledge required for understanding natural language (Chapter 10), this application has motivated much of the research in representation.

In a pivotal paper, Woods criticized the tendency to base representation languages on intuitive responses to specific domains (Woods 1985). Generally speaking, Woods argued that it was not sufficient to examine the semantics of *natural* language and implement structures that seemed to capture these features, but that more attention should be paid to the semantics of the representation formalism itself. This representation language is the basis for all inferences that will be made by the system and therefore determines what can be known and ultimately expressed. A number of questions must be asked in designing a representation language.

Exactly what "things" can be represented by the objects and relations in the language? For example, if a predicate relates an object to a value, such as hascolor(car, red), how can that predicate be used to represent "John's car is redder than Mary's"? Here, the second argument is not a value at all but a comparison to the color of Mary's car; how should we capture this in our notation?

A related question concerns the granularity of the representation. In predicate calculus and semantic networks we can denote objects in the domain only by using simple symbols. Other representations, such as frames and objects, let us define complex structures by encapsulating multiple features and attributes to indicate a single object in the domain. For example, a person is a single entity that requires many properties for its description. This has the advantage of placing all the information about an object in one place, making it easier to access, update, or delete.

How can representations distinguish between *intensional* and *extensional* knowledge? Briefly, the *extension* of a concept is the set of all things denoted by a given concept; for example, "ball" has as its extension the set of all balls. The *intension* determines what a concept means in the abstract, such as the definition of a ball in terms of its roundness, its ability to roll, bounce, and be thrown, or its use in games. Though these two different definitions characterize the same set of objects, their role in understanding is very different. This issue is important if we are linking an expert system and a data base. The data base enumerates objects and relations of a domain (its extension), whereas the expert system includes the intensional knowledge used to reason about these objects.

How can we best represent *meta-knowledge*, or knowledge about the objects and structures of the representation language itself? This is important if we wish to reason about knowledge, as in describing the sentence "George believes that Tom knows that Mary's car is red." Teiresias (Chapter 8) used meta-knowledge to reason about knowledge and proofs in MYCIN.

Another important feature of knowledge is its organization into class hierarchies. The ability to represent the relationship between an object and its class or between a class and its superclass has proved so useful that many representation languages include mechanisms that define these relationships. *Inheritance* is a relation by which an individual assumes the properties of its class and by which properties of a class are passed on to its subclass.

For example, if chimpanzee is a subclass of primate and Bonzo is a chimpanzee, we may assume that Bonzo has all the properties of chimpanzees and primates. Inheritance provides a natural tool for representing taxonomically structured knowledge, as well as an economical means of expressing properties common to a class of objects. It provides benefits such as guaranteeing that all members of a class inherit the appropriate properties, ensuring consistency with the class definition. It reduces the size of the knowledge base, as properties are defined once for the most general type that shares these properties rather than for all subclasses or individuals. For example, the property of having flexible hands would be defined for primates and inherited by chimps, gorillas, humans, etc. Properties such as being small and highly intelligent, which are not common to all primates, would be specified for the appropriate class, such as chimpanzee. The property of having a spine would be defined at a higher level of abstraction, the type vertebrate, and inherited by all subtypes, including primate and chimpanzee.

Inheritance is also used to implement *default values* and *exceptions*. For example, we may state that all chimpanzees live in the jungle, except Bonzo, who lives in the circus. Default values are simply inherited from the appropriate superclass. We can represent exceptions to these defaults by redefining the property at a lower level in the hierarchy, such as for Bonzo (Section 9.5).

Type hierarchies may assume a number of different forms, including *trees*, *lattices*, or arbitrary graphs. In a tree hierarchy, each type has only one supertype. This is a simple and well-behaved model, but it is not as expressive as hierarchies that allow multiple parent types. Most natural classification systems allow individuals to belong to multiple types and let types have multiple supertypes. For example, Bonzo belongs not only to the type chimpanzee but also to the type circus performer. Although multiple inheritance hierarchies can introduce difficulties in the definition of representation languages, their benefits are great enough to offset these disadvantages. The lattice is a common form for multiple inheritance.

Finally, it is often helpful to attach procedures to object descriptions. These procedures, sometimes referred to as *demons*, are executed when an object is changed or created and provide a vehicle for implementing graphics I/O, consistency checks, and interactions between objects.

This discussion illustrates the subtlety and complexity of the knowledge representation problem. In the next section we show how some of these issues are addressed in the context of a specific network representation scheme.

9.2　A Survey of Network Representations

9.2.1　Associationist Theories of Meaning

Logical representations grew out of the efforts of philosophers and mathematicians to characterize the principles of correct reasoning. The major concern of this work is the development of formal representation languages with sound and complete inference rules. Consequently, the semantics of predicate calculus emphasizes *truth-preserving* operations on well-formed expressions. An alternative line of research has grown out of the efforts of psychologists and linguists to characterize the nature of human understanding. This work is less concerned with establishing a science of correct reasoning than with describing the way in which humans actually acquire and use knowledge of their world. As a result, this work has proved particularly useful to the AI application areas of natural language understanding and commonsense reasoning.

The problems that arise in mapping commonsense reasoning into formal logic can be illustrated through an example. It is common to think of the operators $\vee$ and $\rightarrow$ as corresponding to the English "or" and "if . . . then . . ." However, these operators are concerned solely with truth values and ignore the fact that the English "if . . . then . . ." suggests a specific relationship (generally causal) between its premises and its conclusion. For example, the English sentence "If a bird is a cardinal, then it is red" may be written in predicate calculus as

$\forall$ X (cardinal(X) $\rightarrow$ red(X)).

This may be changed, through a series of truth-preserving operations, into the logically equivalent expression

$\forall$ X ($\neg$ red(X) $\rightarrow$ $\neg$ cardinal(X)).

These two expressions are logically equivalent; that is, the second is true if and only if the first is true. However, truth value equivalence overlooks the more subtle connotations of the original English sentence. If we were to look for physical evidence of the truth of these statements, the fact that this sheet of paper is not red and also not a cardinal is evidence for the truth of the second expression. Because the two expressions are logically equivalent, it follows that it is also evidence for the truth of the first statement. This leads to the conclusion that the whiteness of the sheet of paper is evidence that cardinals are red.

Though logically sound, this line of reasoning strikes us as meaningless and rather silly. The reason for this incongruity is that logical implication only expresses a relationship between the truth values of its operands, while the original English sentence implies a causal relationship between membership in a class and the possession of properties of that class. The fact of being a cardinal causes a bird to be red. This relationship is lost in the second version of the expression. Although the fact that the paper is not red is consistent with the truth of both sentences, it is simply irrelevant to the color of birds.

To take another example, consider the logical expression

(2 + 2 = 5) $\rightarrow$ color(elephants,green).

Because $2 + 2 = 5$ is false and elephants are not green we have an expression that evaluates to false $\rightarrow$ false; this has a value of true. On the other hand, our commonsense response to this expression is that it is meaningless. Again, this anomaly is a result of predicate calculus's concern with truth value assignments rather than the semantic relationships between components of a world.

One answer to these problems is to be more careful in establishing conventions for mapping knowledge into predicate calculus or to extend the language with special operators that correspond to specific categories of knowledge.

The limitations of predicate calculus are largely a result of Tarskian semantics: the assignment of a truth value to logical expressions based on an interpretation in some possible world. It is not always enough to know that a statement such as "snow is white" is true; the meaning of the atomic symbols must also be addressed (Woods 1975). The representation should be able to answer questions about these objects such as: "What is snow made of?" "What temperature is Frosty the Snowman?" "If snow is white then what color is a snowman?" This requires that the representation not only preserve truth values when combining expressions but also have some means of making truth assignments based on knowledge of a *particular* world.

Associationist theories define the meaning of an object in terms of a network of associations with other objects in a mind or a knowledge base. Although symbols denote objects in a world, this denotation is mediated by our store of knowledge. When we perceive and reason about an object, that perception is first mapped into a concept in our minds. This concept is part of our entire knowledge of the world and is connected through appropriate relationships to other concepts. These relationships form an understanding of the properties and behavior of objects such as snow. For example, through experience we associate the concept snow with other concepts such as cold, white, snowman, slippery, and ice. Our understanding of snow and the truth of statements such as "snow is white" manifests itself out of this network of associations.

There is psychological evidence that in addition to their ability to associate concepts, humans also organize their knowledge hierarchically, with information kept at the highest appropriate levels of the taxonomy. Collins and Quillian (1969) modeled human information storage and management using a semantic network (Fig. 9.1). The structure of this hierarchy was derived from laboratory testing of human subjects. The subjects were asked questions about different properties of birds, such as, "Is a canary a bird?" or "Can a canary sing?" or "Can a canary fly?"

As obvious as the answers to these questions may seem, reaction time studies indicated that it took longer for subjects to answer "Can a canary fly?" than it did to answer "Can a canary sing?" Collins and Quillian explain this difference in response time by arguing that people store information at its most abstract level. Instead of trying to recall that canaries fly, and robins fly, and swallows fly (all stored with the individual bird), humans remember that canaries are birds and that birds have (usually) the property of flying. Even more general properties such as eating, breathing, and moving are stored at the "animal" level, and so trying to recall whether a canary can breathe should take longer than recalling whether a canary can fly. This is, of course, because the human must travel further up the hierarchy of memory structures to get the answer.

The fastest recall was for the traits specific to the bird, say, that it can sing or is yellow. Exception handling also seemed to be done at the most specific level. When subjects were

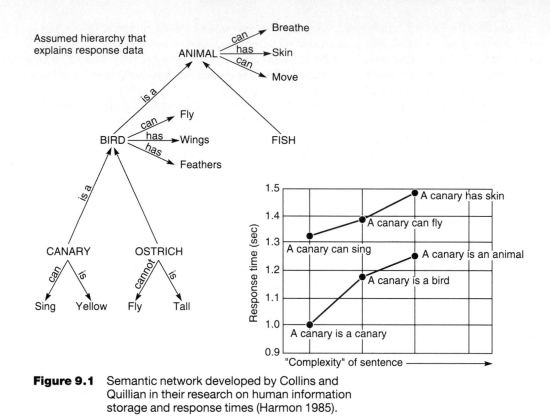

Figure 9.1 Semantic network developed by Collins and Quillian in their research on human information storage and response times (Harmon 1985).

asked whether an ostrich could fly, the answer was produced faster than when they were asked whether an ostrich could breathe. Thus the hierarchy ostrich → bird → animal seems not to be traversed to get the exception information: it is stored directly with ostrich. This approach to knowledge organization has been formalized in inheritance systems.

Inheritance systems allow us to store information at the highest level of abstraction, which reduces the size of knowledge bases and helps prevent update inconsistencies. For example, if we are building a knowledge base about birds, we can define the traits common to all birds, such as flying or having feathers, for the general class bird and allow a particular species of bird to inherit these properties. This reduces the size of the knowledge base by requiring us to define these essential traits only once, rather than requiring their assertion for every individual. Inheritance also helps us to maintain the consistency of the knowledge base when adding new classes and individuals. Assume that we are adding the species robin to an existing knowledge base of birds. When we assert that robin is a subclass of songbird; robin automatically inherits all of the common properties of both songbirds and birds. It is not up to the programmer to remember (or possibly forget) to add this information.

Graphs, by providing a means of explicitly representing relations using arcs and nodes, have proved to be an ideal vehicle for formalizing associationist theories of knowledge. A *semantic network* represents knowledge as a graph, with the nodes corresponding to facts or concepts and the arcs to relations or associations between concepts. Both nodes and links are generally labeled. For example, a semantic network that defines the properties of snow appears in Figure 9.2. This network could be used (with appropriate inference rules) to answer a range of questions about snow, ice, and snowmen. These inferences are made by following the appropriate links to related concepts. Semantic networks also implement inheritance; for example, frosty inherits all the properties of snowmen.

The term "semantic network" encompasses a family of graph-based representations. These representations differ chiefly in the names that are allowed for nodes and links and the inferences that may be performed on these structures. However, a common set of assumptions and concerns is shared by all network representation languages; these are illustrated by a discussion of the history of network representations. In Section 9.4 we examine *conceptual graphs* (Sowa 1984), a modern network representation language that integrates many of these ideas.

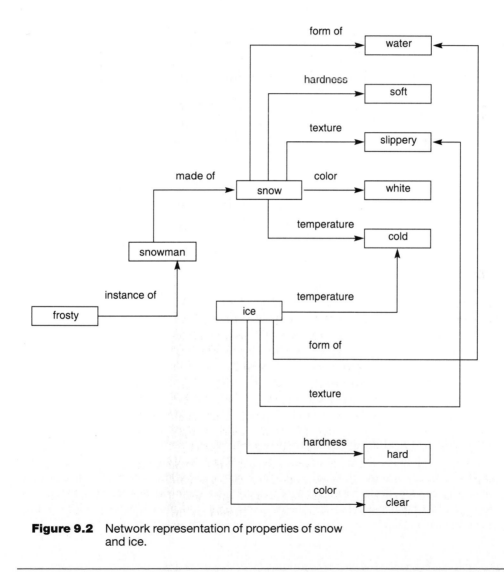

Figure 9.2 Network representation of properties of snow and ice.

9.2.2 Early Work in Semantic Nets

Network representations have almost as long a history as logic; Frege, for example, developed a tree notation for logical expressions. Perhaps the earliest work to have a direct influence on contemporary semantic nets was Charles S. Pierce's system of existential graphs, developed in the nineteenth century (Roberts 1973). Pierce's theory had all the expressive power of first-order predicate calculus, with an axiomatic basis and formal rules of inference.

Graphs have long been used in psychology to represent structures of concepts and associations. Selz (1913, 1922) pioneered this work, using graphs to represent concept hierarchies and the inheritance of properties. He also developed a theory of schematic anticipation that influenced AI work in frames and schemata. Anderson, Norman, Rumelhart, and others have used networks to model human memory and intellectual performance (Anderson and Bower 1973; Norman et al. 1975).

Much of the research in network representations has been done in the arena of natural language understanding. In the general case, natural language understanding requires far more knowledge than the specialized domains of expert systems. It includes an understanding of common sense, the ways in which physical objects behave, the interactions that occur between humans, and the way in which human institutions are organized. A natural language program must understand intentions, beliefs, hypothetical reasoning, plans, and goals. Because it requires such large amounts of broad-based knowledge, natural language understanding has always been a driving force for research in knowledge representation.

The first computer implementations of semantic networks were developed in the early 1960s for use in machine translation. Masterman (1961) defined a set of 100 primitive concept types and used them to define a dictionary of 15,000 concepts. Wilks (1972) continued to build on Masterman's work in semantic network-based natural language systems. Other early AI workers who explored network representations include Ceccato (1961), Raphael (1968), Reitman (1965), and Simmons (1966).

An influential program that illustrates many of the features of early semantic networks was written by Quillian in the late 1960s (Quillian 1967). This program defined English words in much the same way that a dictionary does: a word is defined in terms of other words, and the components of the definition are defined in the same fashion. Rather than formally defining words in terms of basic axioms, each definition simply leads to other definitions in an unstructured, possibly circular, fashion. In looking up a word, we traverse this "network" until we are satisfied that we understand the original word.

Each node in Quillian's network corresponded to a *word concept*, with associative links to other word concepts that formed its definition. The knowledge base was organized into *planes*, where each plane was a graph that defined a single word. Figure 9.3, taken from a paper by Quillian (1967), illustrates three planes that capture three different definitions of the word "plant": a living organism (plant 1), a place where people work (plant 2), and the act of putting a seed in the ground (plant 3).

The program used this knowledge base to find relationships between pairs of English words. Given two words, it would search the graphs outward from each word in a breadth-first fashion, searching for a common concept or *intersection node*. The paths to this node represented a relationship between the two word concepts. For example, Figure 9.4, from the same paper, shows the *intersection paths* between cry and comfort.

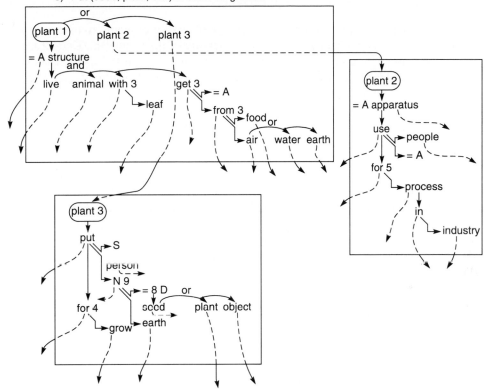

Plant:1) Living structure that is not an animal, frequently with leaves, getting its food from air, water, earth.
2) Apparatus used for any process in industry.
3) Put (seed, plant, etc.) in earth for growth.

Figure 9.3 Three planes representing three definitions of the word "plant" (Quillian 1967).

Using this intersection path, the program was able to conclude:

cry 2 is among other things to make a sad sound. To comfort 3 can be to make 2 something less sad (Quillian 1967).

The numbers in the response indicate that the program has selected from among different meanings of the words.

Quillian suggested that this approach to semantics might provide a natural language understanding system with the ability to:

1. Determine the meaning of a body of English text by building up collections of these intersection nodes.

2. Choose between multiple meanings of words by finding the meanings with the shortest intersection path to other words in the sentence. For example, it could

select a meaning for "plant" in "Tom went home to water his new plant" based on the intersection of the word concepts "water" and "plant."

3. Answer a flexible range of queries based on associations between word concepts in the queries and concepts in the system.

Although this and other early work established the power of graphs to model associative meaning, it was limited by the extreme generality of the formalism. Knowledge is generally structured in terms of specific relationships such as object/property, class/subclass, and agent/verb/object. Research in network representations has often focused on the specification of these relationships.

9.2.3 Standardization of Network Relationships

In itself, a graph notation of relationships has little advantage over predicate calculus; it is just another notation for relationships between objects. The power of network representations comes from the definition of links and associated inference rules that define a specific inference such as inheritance.

Though Quillian's early work established most of the significant features of the semantic network formalism, such as labeled arcs and links, hierarchical inheritance, and inferences along associational links, it proved limited in its ability to deal with the complexities of many domains. One of the main reasons for this failure was the poverty of relationships (links) that captured the deeper semantic aspects of knowledge. Most of the

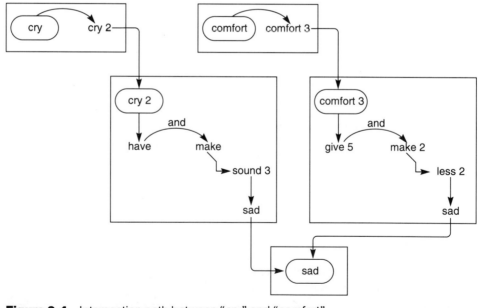

Figure 9.4   Intersection path between "cry" and "comfort" (Quillian 1967).

links represented extremely general associations between nodes and provided no real basis for the structuring of semantic relationships. The same problem is encountered in efforts to use pure predicate calculus to capture semantic meaning: although the formalism is highly expressive and can represent literally any kind of knowledge, it is too unconstrained and places the full burden of constructing appropriate sets of facts and rules on the programmer.

Much of the work in network representations that followed Quillian's focused on defining a richer set of link labels (relationships) that would more fully model the semantics of natural language. By implementing the fundamental semantic relationships of natural language as part of the *formalism*, rather than as part of the *domain knowledge* added by the system builder, knowledge bases require less handcrafting and achieve greater generality and consistency.

Brachman (1979) has stated:

> The key issue here is the isolation of the *primitives* for semantic network languages. The primitives of a network language are those things that the interpreter is programmed in advance to understand, and that are not usually represented in the network language itself.

Simmons (1973) addressed this need for standard relationships by focusing on the *case structure* of English verbs. In this verb-oriented approach, based on work by Fillmore (1968), links define the roles played by nouns and noun phrases in the action of the sentence. Case relationships include *agent, object, instrument, location,* and *time.* A sentence is represented as a verb node, with various case links to nodes representing other participants in the action. This structure is called a *case frame.* In parsing a sentence, the program finds the verb and retrieves the case frame for that verb from its knowledge base. It then binds the values of the agent, object, etc., to the appropriate nodes in the case frame. Using this approach, the sentence "Sarah fixed the chair with glue" might be represented by the network in Figure 9.5.

Thus, the representation language itself captures much of the deep structure of natural language, such as the relationship between a verb and its subject (the agent relation) or that between a verb and its object. Knowledge of the case structure of the English language is part of the network formalism itself. When the individual sentence is parsed, these built-in relationships indicate that Sarah is the person doing the fixing and that glue is used to put the chair together. Note that *these linguistic relationships are stored in a fashion that is independent of the actual sentence or even the language in which the sentence was*

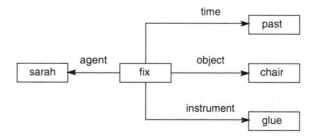

Figure 9.5 Case frame representation of the sentence "Sarah fixed the chair with glue."

expressed. A similar approach is also taken in network languages proposed by Norman (1972) and Rumelhart et al. (1972, 1973).

A number of major research endeavors attempted to standardize link names even further (Masterman 1961; Wilks 1972; Schank and Colby 1973; Schank and Nash-Webber 1975). Each effort worked to establish a complete set of primitives that could be used to represent the semantic structure of natural language expressions in a uniform fashion. These were intended to assist in reasoning with language constructs and to be independent of the idiosyncrasies of individual languages or phrasing.

Perhaps the most ambitious attempt to model formally the deep semantic structure of natural language is Roger Schank's conceptual dependency theory (Schank and Rieger 1974). Conceptual dependency theory offers a set of four primitive conceptualizations from which the world of meaning is built. These are equal and independent. They are:

ACTs   actions
PPs   objects (picture producers)
AAs   modifiers of actions (action aiders)
PAs   modifiers of objects (picture aiders)

For example, all actions are assumed to reduce to one or more of the primitive ACTs. These primitives, listed below, are taken as the basic components of action, with more specific verbs being formed through their modification and combination.

ATRANS   transfer a relationship (give)
PTRANS   transfer physical location of an object (go)
PROPEL   apply physical force to an object (push)
MOVE   move body part by owner (kick)
GRASP   grab an object by an actor (grasp)
INGEST   ingest an object by an animal (eat)
EXPEL   expel from an animal's body (cry)
MTRANS   transfer mental information (tell)
MBUILD   mentally make new information (decide)
CONC   conceptualize or think about an idea (think)
SPEAK   produce sound (say)
ATTEND   focus sense organ (listen)

These primitives are used to define *conceptual dependency relationships* that describe meaning structures such as case relations or the association of objects and values. Conceptual dependency relationships are *conceptual syntax rules* and constitute a grammar of meaningful semantic relationships. These relationships can be used to construct an internal representation of an English sentence. A list of basic conceptual dependencies (Schank and Rieger 1974) appears in Figure 9.6. These capture the fundamental semantic structures of natural language.

For example, the first conceptual dependency in Figure 9.6 describes the relationship between a subject and its verb, and the third describes the verb-object relation. These can be combined to represent a simple transitive sentence such as "John throws the ball" (Fig. 9.7).

Finally, tense and mode information must be added to the conceptualizations. Schank supplies a list of attachments or modifiers to the relationships. A partial list of these is:

p	past
f	future
t	transition
k	continuing
t_s	start transition
?	interrogative
t_f	finish transition
c	conditional
/	negative
nil	present
delta?	timeless

These relations are the first-level constructs of the theory, the simplest semantic relationships out of which more complex structures can be built. Further examples of how these

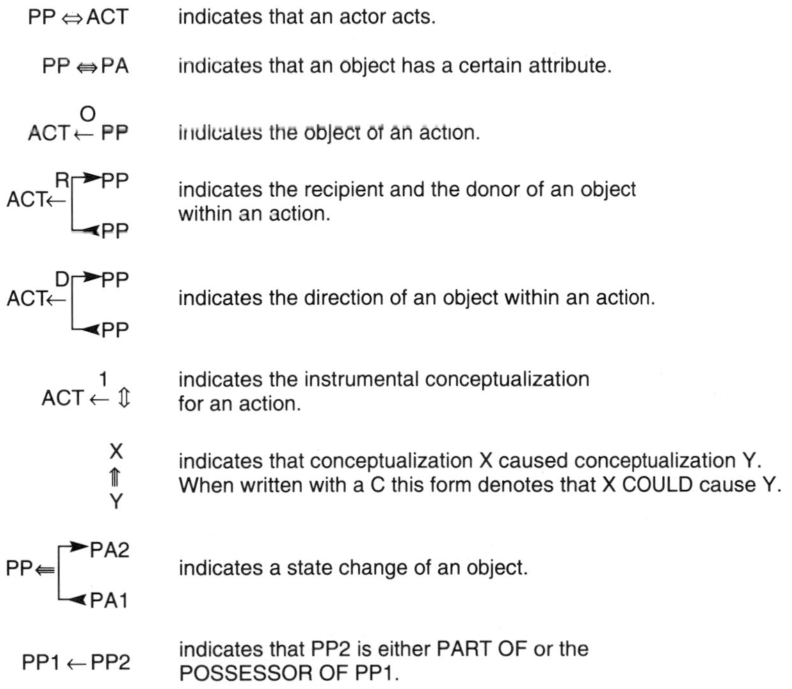

PP $\Leftrightarrow$ ACT   indicates that an actor acts.

PP $\Leftrightarrow$ PA   indicates that an object has a certain attribute.

ACT $\overset{O}{\leftarrow}$ PP   indicates the object of an action.

ACT $\overset{R}{\leftarrow} \begin{bmatrix} \rightarrow \text{PP} \\ \leftarrow \text{PP} \end{bmatrix}$ indicates the recipient and the donor of an object within an action.

ACT $\overset{D}{\leftarrow} \begin{bmatrix} \rightarrow \text{PP} \\ \leftarrow \text{PP} \end{bmatrix}$ indicates the direction of an object within an action.

ACT $\overset{1}{\leftarrow} \updownarrow$ indicates the instrumental conceptualization for an action.

$\begin{matrix} X \\ \Uparrow \\ Y \end{matrix}$ indicates that conceptualization X caused conceptualization Y. When written with a C this form denotes that X COULD cause Y.

PP $\Leftarrow \begin{bmatrix} \rightarrow \text{PA2} \\ \leftarrow \text{PA1} \end{bmatrix}$ indicates a state change of an object.

PP1 $\leftarrow$ PP2   indicates that PP2 is either PART OF or the POSSESSOR OF PP1.

Figure 9.6   Basic conceptual dependency relations (Schank 1974).

John $\Longleftrightarrow$ *PROPEL* $\overset{O}{\longleftarrow}$ Ball

Figure 9.7   Conceptual dependency representation of the sentence "John throws the ball."

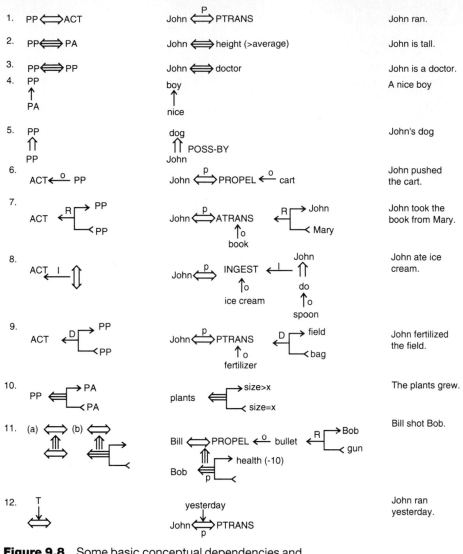

Figure 9.8 Some basic conceptual dependencies and their use in representing more complex English sentences (Rich 1983).

basic conceptual dependencies can be composed to represent the meaning of simple English sentences appear in Figure 9.8.

Based on these primitives, the English sentence "John ate the egg" is represented as shown in Figure 9.9. In Figure 9.9 the symbols have the following meanings:

←	indicates the direction of dependency
⇔	indicates the agent-verb relationship

p	indicates past tense
INGEST	is a primitive act of the theory
O	object relation
D	indicates the direction of the object in the action

A more complex example of the structures that can be built with conceptual dependencies is the representation of "John prevented Mary from giving a book to Bill" (Fig. 9.10). This particular example is interesting as a demonstration of how causality may be represented.

Conceptual dependency theory gives a number of important benefits. By providing a formal theory of natural language semantics, it reduces problems of ambiguity. Second, the representation itself directly captures much of natural language semantics.

Conceptual dependency attempts to provide a *canonical form* for the meaning of sentences. That is, all sentences that have the same meaning will be represented internally by *syntactically identical*, not just semantically equivalent, graphs. This is an effort to simplify the inferences required for understanding. For example, we can demonstrate that two sentences mean the same thing with a simple match of conceptual dependency graphs; a representation that did not provide a canonical form might require extensive operations on differently structured graphs.

Unfortunately, it is questionable whether a program may be written to reliably reduce sentences to canonical form. As Woods (1975) and others have pointed out, reduction to a canonical form is provably uncomputable for monoids, a type of algebraic group that is far simpler than natural language. Furthermore, there is no evidence that humans store their knowledge in any sort of canonical form.

Other criticisms of this point of view object to the computational price paid in reducing everything to such low-level primitives. Also, the primitives are not adequate to capture

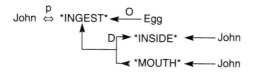
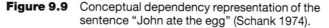

Figure 9.9 Conceptual dependency representation of the sentence "John ate the egg" (Schank 1974).

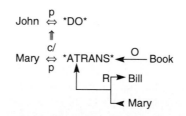
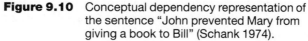

Figure 9.10 Conceptual dependency representation of the sentence "John prevented Mary from giving a book to Bill" (Schank 1974).

many of the more subtle concepts that are important in natural language. For example, the representation of "tall" in the second sentence of Figure 9.8 does not address the ambiguity of this term as carefully as is done in systems such as fuzzy logic (Zadeh 1983).

However, no one can say that the conceptual dependency model has not been fully automated and tested. More than a decade of research guided by Schank has focused on refining and extending the model. Important extensions of conceptual dependencies include research in "scripts" and "memory organization packets," or MOPs. This work examines the organization of knowledge in memory and the role this organization plays in reasoning. This is discussed in Section 9.4.2. Conceptual dependency theory is a fully developed model of natural language semantics with consistency of purpose and wide applicability.

9.3   Conceptual Graphs: A Network Representation Language

A number of network languages have been developed to model the semantics of natural language and other domains. In this section, we examine a particular language in detail, to show how the problems of representing meaning have been addressed. J. F. Sowa's *conceptual graphs* (Sowa 1984) is an example of a modern network representation language. We define the rules for forming and manipulating conceptual graphs and the conventions for representing classes, individuals, and relationships. In Chapter 10 we continue developing this formalism and show how it may be used to represent meaning in natural language understanding.

9.3.1   Introduction to Conceptual Graphs

A conceptual graph is a finite, connected, bipartite graph. The nodes of the graph are either *concepts* or *conceptual relations*. Conceptual graphs do not use labeled arcs; instead the conceptual relation nodes represent relations between concepts. Because conceptual graphs are bipartite, concepts can only have arcs to conceptual relations, and vice versa. In Figure 9.11 dog and brown are concept nodes and color is a conceptual relation. To distinguish these types of nodes, we represent concepts as boxes and conceptual relations as ellipses.

In conceptual graphs, concept nodes represent either concrete or abstract objects in the world of discourse. Concrete concepts, such as a cat, telephone, or restaurant, are characterized by our ability to form an image of them in our minds. Note that concrete concepts include generic concepts such as cat or restaurant along with concepts of specific cats and restaurants. We can still form an image of a generic cat. Abstract concepts include things such as love, beauty, and loyalty that do not correspond to images in our minds.

Conceptual relation nodes indicate a relation involving one or more concepts. One advantage of formulating conceptual graphs as bipartite graphs rather than using labeled arcs is that it simplifies the representation of relations of any arity. A relation of arity n is represented by a conceptual relation node having n arcs. Figure 9.11 illustrates conceptual relations of different arities.

Each conceptual graph represents a single proposition. A typical knowledge base will contain a number of such graphs. Graphs may be arbitrarily complex but must be finite. For example, one graph in Figure 9.11 represents the proposition "A dog has a color of brown." Figure 9.12 is a graph of somewhat greater complexity that represents the sentence "Mary gave John the book." This graph uses conceptual relations to represent the cases of the verb "to give" and indicates the way in which conceptual graphs are used to model the semantics of natural language.

9.3.2 Types, Individuals, and Names

Many early designers of semantic networks were careless in defining class/member and class/subclass relationships, with resulting semantic confusion. For example, the relation between an individual and its class is different from the relation between a class (such as dog) and its superclass (carnivore). Similarly, certain properties belong to individuals, and

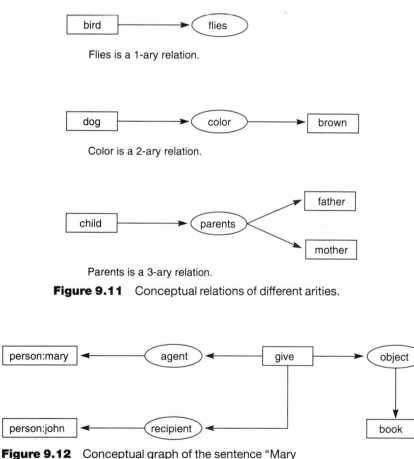

Figure 9.11 Conceptual relations of different arities.

Figure 9.12 Conceptual graph of the sentence "Mary gave John the book."

others belong to the class itself; the representation should provide a vehicle for making this distinction. The properties of having fur and liking bones belong to individual dogs; the class "dog" does not have fur or eat anything. Properties that are appropriate to the class include its name and membership in a zoological taxonomy.

In conceptual graphs, every concept is a unique individual of a particular type. Each concept box is labeled with a *type* label, which indicates the class or type of individual represented by that node. Thus, a node labeled dog represents some individual of that type. Types are organized into a hierarchy. The type dog is a subtype of carnivore, which is a subtype of mammal, etc. Boxes with the same type label represent concepts of the same type; however, these boxes may or may not represent the same individual concept.

Each concept box is labeled with the names of the type and the individual. The type and individual labels are separated by a colon, :. The graph of Figure 9.13 indicates that the dog "Emma" is brown. The graph of Figure 9.11 asserts that some unspecified entity of type dog has a color of brown. If the individual is not indicated, the concept represents an unspecified individual of that type.

Conceptual graphs also let us indicate specific but unnamed individuals. A unique token called a *marker* indicates each individual in the world of discourse. This marker is written as a number preceded by a #. Markers are different from names in that they are unique: individuals may have one name, many names, or no name at all, but they have exactly one marker. Similarly, different individuals may have the same name but may not have the same marker. This distinction gives us a basis for dealing with the semantic ambiguities that arise when we give objects names. The graph of Figure 9.14 asserts that a particular dog, #1352, is brown.

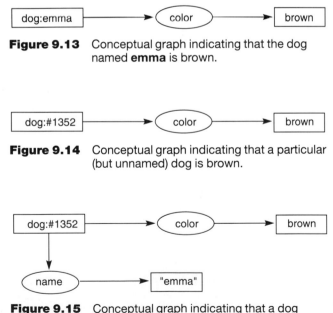

Figure 9.13 Conceptual graph indicating that the dog named **emma** is brown.

Figure 9.14 Conceptual graph indicating that a particular (but unnamed) dog is brown.

Figure 9.15 Conceptual graph indicating that a dog named **emma** is brown.

Markers allow us to separate an individual from its name. If dog #1352 is named "Emma," we can use a conceptual relation called name to add this to the graph. The result is the graph of Figure 9.15. The name is enclosed in double quotes to indicate that it is a string. Where there is no danger of ambiguity, we may simplify the graph and refer to the individual directly by name. Under this convention, the graph of Figure 9.15 is equivalent to the graph of Figure 9.13.

Although we frequently ignore it, both in casual conversation and in formal representations, this distinction between an individual and its name is an important one that should be supported by a representation language. For example, if we say that "John" is a common name among males, we are asserting a property of the name itself rather than of any individual named "John." This allows us to represent such English sentences as " 'Chimpanzee' is the name of a species of primates." Similarly, we may want to represent the fact that an individual has several different names. The graph of Figure 9.16 represents the situation described in the song lyric: "Her name was McGill and she called herself Lil, but everyone knew her as Nancy" (Lennon and McCartney 1968).

In addition to indicating an individual by its marker or name, we can use the generic marker * to indicate an unspecified individual. By convention, this is often omitted from concept labels; a node given just a type label, dog, is equivalent to a node labeled dog:*. In addition to the generic marker, conceptual graphs allow the use of named variables. These are represented by an asterisk followed by the variable name (e.g., *X or *foo). This is useful if two separate nodes are to indicate the same, but unspecified, individual. The graph of Figure 9.17 represents the assertion "The dog scratches its ear with its paw." Although we do not know which dog is scratching its ear, the variable *X indicates that the paw and the ear belong to the same dog that is doing the scratching.

To summarize, each concept node indicates an individual of a specified type. This individual is the *referent* of the concept and is indicated by either an individual marker or the generic marker. If it is an individual marker, the concept is an *individual* concept. If the referent is the generic marker, then the concept is a *generic concept*.

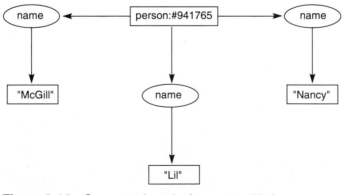

Figure 9.16 Conceptual graph of a person with three names.

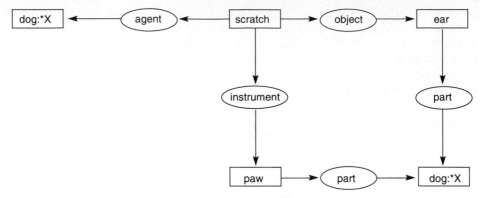

Figure 9.17 Conceptual graph of the sentence "The dog scratches its ear with its paw."

9.3.3 The Type Hierarchy

The type hierarchy, as illustrated by Figure 9.18, is a partial ordering on the set of types, indicated by the symbol $\leq$. If s and t are types and $t \leq s$, then t is said to be a *subtype* of s and s is said to be a *supertype* of t. Because it is a partial ordering, a type may have more than one supertype and more than one subtype. If s, t, and u are types, with $t \leq s$ and $t \leq u$, then t is said to be a *common subtype* of s and u. Similarly, if $s \leq v$ and $u \leq v$ then v is a *common supertype* of s and u.

The type hierarchy of conceptual graphs is a lattice, a common form of multiple inheritance system. In a lattice, types may have multiple parents and children. However, every pair of types must have a *minimal common supertype* and a *maximal common subtype*. For types s and u, v is a minimal common supertype if $s \leq v$, $u \leq v$, and for any w, a common supertype of s and u, $v \leq w$. Maximal common subtype has a corresponding definition. The minimal common supertype of a collection of types is the appropriate place to define properties common only to those types. Because many types, such as emotion and rock, have no obvious common supertypes or subtypes, it is necessary to add types that fill these roles. To make the type hierarchy a true lattice, conceptual graphs include two special types. The *universal type*, indicated by $\top$, is a supertype of all types. The *absurd type*, indicated by $\perp$, is a subtype of all types.

9.3.4 Generalization and Specialization

The theory of conceptual graphs includes a number of operations that allow us to form new graphs from existing graphs. These allow us to create a new graph by either *specializing* or *generalizing* an existing graph. This is done through four operations called *copy*, *restrict*, *join*, and *simplify* (Fig. 9.19). Assume that g_1 and g_2 are conceptual graphs. Then:

The *copy* rule allows us to form a new graph, g, that is the exact copy of g_1.

Restriction allows concept nodes in a graph to be replaced by a node representing their specialization. There are two cases:

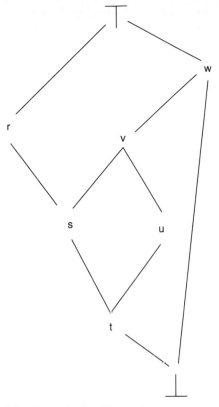

Figure 9.18 A type lattice illustrating subtypes, supertypes, the universal type and the absurd
type. Arcs represent the relationship.

1. If a concept is labeled with a generic marker, the generic marker may be replaced by an individual marker.

2. A type label on a concept may be replaced by one of its subtypes, as long as this is consistent with the referent of the concept. In Figure 9.19 we can replace animal with dog because Emma is a dog.

The *join* rule lets us combine two graphs into a single graph. If there is a concept node c_1 in the graph s_1 that is identical to a concept node c_2 in s_2, then we can form a new graph by deleting c_2 and linking all of the relations incident on c_2 to c_1. Join is a restriction rule, because the resulting graph is less general than either of its components.

If a graph contains two duplicate relations, then one of them may be deleted, along with all its arcs. This is the *simplify* rule. Duplicate relations often occur as the result of a join operation, as in graph g_4 of Figure 9.19.

One use of restriction rules is to make two concepts match so that a join can be performed. Together, join and restrict allow the implementation of inheritance. For example, the replacement of a generic marker by an individual implements the inheritance of the

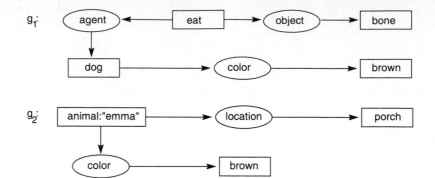

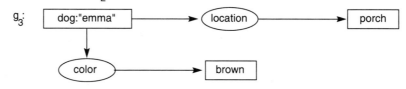

The restriction of g_2:

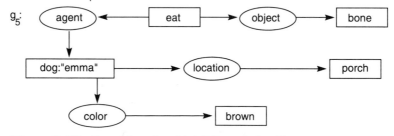

The join of g_1 and g_3:

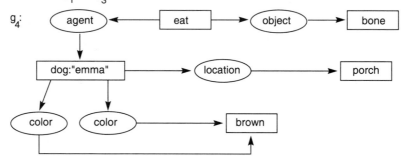

The simplify of g_4:

Figure 9.19 Examples of restrict, join, and simplify operations.

properties of a type by an individual. The replacement of a type label by a subtype label defines inheritance between a class and a superclass. By joining one graph to another and restricting certain concept nodes, we can implement inheritance of a variety of properties. Figure 9.20 shows how chimpanzees inherit the property of having a hand from the class **primates** by replacing a type label with its subtype. It also shows how the individual, **Bonzo**, inherits this property by instantiating a generic concept.

Similarly, we can use joins and restrictions to implement the plausible assumptions that play a role in common language understanding. If we are told that "Mary and Tom went out for pizza together," we automatically make a number of assumptions: they ate a round Italian bread covered with cheese and tomato sauce. They ate it in a restaurant and must have some way of paying for it. This reasoning can be done using joins and restrictions (Chapter 10). We form a conceptual graph of the sentence and join it with the conceptual graphs (from our knowledge base) for pizzas and restaurants. The resulting graph lets us assume that they ate tomato sauce and paid their bill.

Join and restrict are specialization rules. They define a partial ordering on the set of derivable graphs. If a graph g_1 is a specialization of g_2, then we may say that g_2 is a *generalization* of g_1. Generalization hierarchies are important in knowledge representation. Besides providing the basis for inheritance and other commonsense reasoning schemes, generalization hierarchies are used in many learning methods, allowing us, for instance, to construct a generalized assertion from a particular training instance.

These rules are not rules of inference. They do not guarantee that true graphs will be derived from true graphs. For example, in the restriction of the graph of Figure 9.19, the result may not be true; Emma may be a cat. Similarly, the join example of Figure 9.19 is not truth-preserving either: the dog on the porch and the dog that eats bones may be different animals. These operations are *canonical formation rules*, and although they do not preserve truth, they have the subtle but important property of preserving "meaningfulness." This is an important guarantee when we use conceptual graphs to implement natural language understanding. Consider the three sentences:

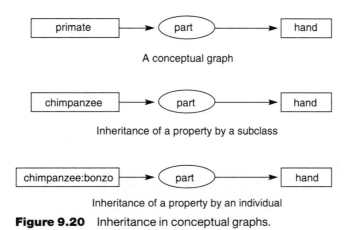

A conceptual graph

Inheritance of a property by a subclass

Inheritance of a property by an individual

Figure 9.20   Inheritance in conceptual graphs.

Albert Einstein formulated the theory of relativity.

Albert Einstein plays center for the Los Angeles Lakers.

Conceptual graphs are yellow flying popsicles.

The first of these sentences is true, and the second is false. The third sentence, however, is meaningless; though grammatically correct, it makes no sense. The second sentence, although false, is meaningful. I can imagine Albert Einstein on a basketball court. The canonical formation rules enforce constraints on meaningfulness; they do not allow us to form nonsensical graphs from meaningful ones. Although they are not sound inference rules, canonical formation rules form a basis for much of the plausible reasoning done in natural language understanding and commonsense reasoning.

9.3.5 Propositional Nodes

In addition to using graphs to define relations between objects in the world, we may also want to define relations between propositions. Consider, for example, the statement "Tom believes that Jane likes pizza." "Believes" is a relation that takes a proposition as its argument.

Conceptual graphs include a concept type, *proposition*, that takes a set of conceptual graphs as its referent and allows us to define relations involving propositions. Propositional concepts are indicated as a box that contains another conceptual graph. These proposition concepts may be used with appropriate relations to represent knowledge about propositions. Figure 9.21 shows the conceptual graph for the above assertion about Jane, Tom, and pizza. The experiencer relation is loosely analogous to the agent relation in that it links a subject and the verb. The experiencer link is used with belief states based on the notion that they are something one experiences rather than does.

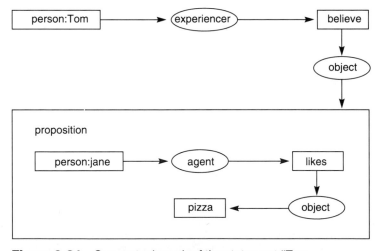

Figure 9.21 Conceptual graph of the statement "Tom thinks that Jane likes pizza," showing the use of a propositional concept.

Figure 9.21 shows how conceptual graphs with propositional nodes may be used to express the *modal* concepts of knowledge and belief. *Modal logics* are concerned with the various ways propositions are entertained: believed, asserted as possible, probably or necessarily true, intended as a result of an action, or counterfactual (Turner 1984).

9.3.6   Conceptual Graphs and Logic

Using conceptual graphs, we can easily represent conjunctive concepts such as "The dog is big and hungry," but we have not established any way of representing negation or disjunction. Nor have we addressed the issue of variable quantification.

We may implement negation using propositional concepts and a unary operation called **neg**. **neg** takes as argument a proposition concept and asserts that concept as false. The graph of Figure 9.22 uses **neg** to represent the statement "There are no pink dogs."

Using negation and conjunction, we may form graphs that represent disjunctive assertions according to the rules of logic. To simplify this, we may also define a relation **or**, which takes two propositions and represents their disjunction.

In conceptual graphs, generic concepts are assumed to be existentially quantified. For example, the generic concept **dog** in the graph of Figure 9.11 actually represents an existentially quantified variable. This graph corresponds to the logical expression:

$$\exists\, X\, \exists\, Y\, (dog(X) \wedge color(X,Y) \wedge brown(Y)).$$

Using negation and existential quantification, we can also represent universal quantification. For example, the graph of Figure 9.22 could be thought of as representing the logical assertion:

$$\forall\, X\, \forall\, Y\, (\neg\, (dog(X) \wedge color(X,Y) \wedge pink(Y))).$$

Conceptual graphs are equivalent to predicate calculus in their expressive power. As these examples suggest, there is a straightforward mapping from conceptual graphs into

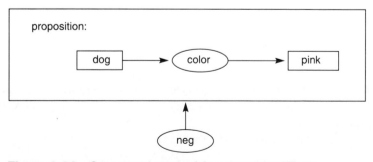

Figure 9.22   Conceptual graph of the proposition "There are no pink dogs."

predicate calculus notation. The algorithm for changing a conceptual graph, g, into a predicate calculus expression is:

1. Assign a unique variable, $x_1, x_2, \ldots, x_n$, to each of the n generic concepts in g.

2. Assign a unique constant to each individual concept in g. This constant may simply be the name or marker used to indicate the referent of the concept.

3. Represent each concept node by a unary predicate whose name is the same as the type of that node and whose argument is the variable or constant assigned to that node.

4. Represent each n-ary conceptual relation in g as an n-ary predicate whose name is the same as the name of the relation. Let each argument of the predicate be the variable or constant assigned to the corresponding concept node linked to that relation.

5. Take the conjunction of all atomic sentences formed under 3 and 4. This is the body of the predicate calculus expression. All the variables in the expression are existentially quantified.

For example, the graph of Figure 9.13 is given by the predicate calculus expression

$$\exists X_1 \, (dog(emma) \wedge color(emma, X_1) \wedge brown(X_1))$$

Although we can reformulate conceptual graphs into predicate calculus syntax, conceptual graphs support a number of special-purpose inferencing mechanisms, such as join and restrict, not normally part of the predicate calculus.

We have presented the syntax of conceptual graphs and defined the *restriction* operation as a means of implementing inheritance. We have not yet examined the full range of operations and inferences that may be performed on these graphs, nor have we addressed the problem of defining the concepts and relations needed for domains such as natural language. We address these issues in Chapter 10 and use the resulting language to implement a knowledge base for a simple natural language understanding program.

9.4　Structured Representations

9.4.1　Frames

Using network representations, we view knowledge as organized using explicit links or associations between objects in the knowledge base. Alternatively, we can organize knowledge into more complex units that represent situations or objects in the domain. These units are called *frames* or *schemas.*

In a 1975 paper, Minsky describes a frame:

> Here is the essence of the frame theory: When one encounters a new situation (or makes a substantial change in one's view of a problem) one selects from memory a structure called a

"frame." This is a remembered framework to be adapted to fit reality by changing details as necessary (Minsky, 1975).

According to Minsky, a frame may be viewed as a static data structure used to represent well-understood, stereotyped situations. Framelike structures seem to organize our own knowledge of the world. We adjust to ever new situations by calling up information structured by past experiences. We then specially fashion or revise the details of these past experiences to represent the individual differences for the new situation.

Anyone who has stayed in one or two hotel rooms has no trouble with entirely new hotels and their rooms. One expects to see a bed, a bathroom, a place to open a suitcase, a telephone, price and emergency evacuation information on the back of the door, and so on. The details of each room can be supplied when needed: color of the curtains, location and use of light switches, etc. There is also default information supplied with the hotel room frame: no sheets: call housekeeping; need ice: look down the hall; and so on. We do not need to build up our understanding for each new hotel room we enter. All of the pieces of a generic hotel room are organized into a conceptual structure that we access when checking into a hotel; the particulars of an individual room are supplied as needed.

We could represent these higher-level structures directly in a semantic network by organizing it as a collection of separate networks, each of which represents some stereotypic situation. Frames, as well as *object oriented systems*, provide us with a vehicle for this organization, representing knowledge as structured objects consisting of named slots with attached values. The notion of a frame or schema as a single complex entity is thus reinforced by the notation.

Figure 9.23 shows how a hotel bed may be represented using both conceptual graph and frame approaches. A hotel bed is a specialization of the general bed object. Many of the values in both versions are default assumptions about hotel beds. These include the size and firmness relations. Specific instances of hotel beds may or may not inherit these values. See Section 9.5 for a more detailed discussion of the inheritance and default knowledge. The slot names in the frame loosely correspond to the relations in the conceptual graph. The slot values may be values; pointers to other frames, as in the case of the mattress, or even attached procedures for performing some function, such as getting the bed made.

The components of a hotel room can be described by a number of individual frames. In addition to the bed, a frame could represent a chair: expected height is 20 to 40 cm, number of legs is 4, a default value, has design for sitting. A further frame represents the hotel telephone: this is a specialization of a regular phone except that billing is through the room, there is a special hotel operator (default), and a person can use the hotel phone to get meals served in the room. Figure 9.24 gives a frame representing the hotel room.

Each individual frame may be seen as a data structure, similar in many respects to the traditional "record," that contains information relevant to stereotyped entities. The slots in the frame contain information such as:

1. *Frame identification information.*

2. *Relationship of this frame to other frames.* The "hotel phone" might be a special instance of "phone," which in turn might be an instance of a "communication device."

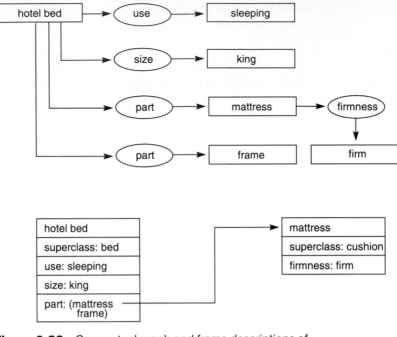

Figure 9.23 Conceptual graph and frame descriptions of a hotel bed.

3. *Descriptors of requirements for frame match.* A chair, for instance, has its seat between 20 and 40 cm from the floor, its back higher than 60 cm, etc. These requirements may be used to determine when new objects fit the stereotype defined by the frame.

4. *Procedural information on use of the structure described.* An important feature of frames is the ability to attach procedural code to a slot.

5. *Frame default information.* These are slot values that are taken to be true when no evidence to the contrary has been found. For instance, chairs have four legs, telephones are pushbutton, or hotel beds are made by the staff.

6. *New instance information.* Many frame slots may be left unspecified until given a value for a particular instance or needed for problem solving. For example, the color of the bedspread may be left unspecified in the definition of bed.

The presence, absence, or amount of detail in the six slots above depend on the particular problem-solving situation addressed.

Frames extend semantic networks in a number of important ways. Although the frame and network descriptions of hotel beds in Figure 9.23 are equivalent, the frame version makes it much clearer that we are describing a bed with its various attributes. In the network version, there is simply a collection of nodes and we depend more on our interpretation of the structure to see the hotel bed as the primary object being described. This ability to organize our knowledge into such structures is an important attribute of a knowledge base.

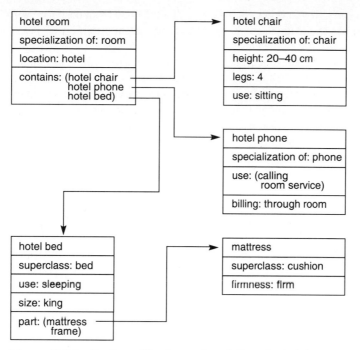

Figure 9.24 Portion of the frame description of a hotel room.

Frames make it easier to organize our knowledge hierarchically. In a network, every concept is represented by nodes and links at the same level of specification. Very often, however, we may like to think of an object as a single entity for some purposes and only consider details of its internal structure for other purposes. For example, we usually are not aware of the mechanical organization of a car until something breaks down; only then do we pull up our "car engine schema" and try to find the problem.

Procedural attachment is a particularly important feature of frames because certain knowledge does not adapt well to declarative representations. For example, we may want to include the ability to generate graphic images in a knowledge base. A graphics language is more appropriate for this than a network language. We use procedural attachment to create *demons*. A demon is a procedure that is invoked as a side effect of some other action in the knowledge base. For example, we may wish the system to perform type checks or to run consistency tests whenever a certain slot value is changed. We discuss procedural attachment and demons in greater detail in Chapter 15.

Frame systems support class inheritance. The slots and default values of a class frame are inherited across the class/subclass and class/member hierarchy. For instance, a hotel phone could be a subclass of a regular phone except that (1) all out-of-building dialing goes through the hotel switchboard (for billing) and (2) hotel services may be dialed directly. Default values are assigned to selected slots to be used only if other information is not available: assume that hotel rooms have beds and are, therefore, appropriate places to go if you want to sleep; if you don't know how to dial the hotel front desk try "zero"; the phone may be assumed (no evidence to the contrary) to be pushbutton.

When an instance of the class frame is created, the system will attempt to fill its slots, either by querying the user, accepting the default value from the class frame, or executing some procedure or demon to obtain the instance value. As with semantic nets, slots and default values are inherited across a class/subclass hierarchy. Of course, default information can cause the data description of the problem to be nonmonotonic, letting us make assumptions about default values that may not always prove correct.

Minsky's own work on vision provides an example of frames and their use in default reasoning: the problem of recognizing that different views of an object actually represent the same object. For example, the three perspectives of the one cube of Figure 9.25 actually look quite different. Minsky (1975) proposed a frame system that recognizes these as views of a single object by inferring the hidden sides as default assumptions.

The frame system of Figure 9.25 represents four of the faces of a cube. The broken lines indicate that a particular face is out of view from that perspective. The links between the frames indicate the relations between the views represented by the frames. The nodes, of course, could be more complex if there were colors or patterns that the faces contained. Indeed, each slot in one frame could be a pointer to another entire frame. Also, because given information can fill a number of different slots, face E in Figure 9.25, there need be no redundancy in the information that is stored.

Frames add to the power of semantic nets by allowing complex objects to be represented as a single frame, rather than as a large network structure. This also provides a natural way to represent stereotypic entities, classes, inheritance, and default values. Although frames, like logical and network representations, are a powerful tool, many of the problems of acquiring and organizing a complicated knowledge base must still be solved by the programmer's skill and intuition (Section 9.5). Nonetheless, because of their power and generality, frames have emerged as an important representation in AI.

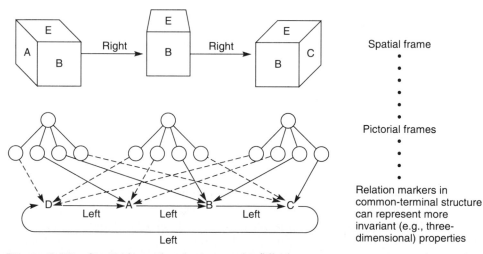

Figure 9.25 Spatial frame for viewing a cube (Minsky 1975).

9.4.2 Scripts

A natural language understanding program must use a large amount of background knowledge to understand even the simplest conversation. There is evidence that humans organize this knowledge into structures corresponding to typical situations (Bartlett 1932). If we are reading a story about restaurants, baseball, or politics, we resolve any ambiguities in the text in a way consistent with restaurants, baseball, or politics. If the subject of a story changes abruptly, there is evidence that people pause briefly in their reading, presumably to change knowledge structures. It is hard to understand a poorly organized or structured story, possibly because we cannot easily fit it into any of our existing knowledge structures. There is also a tendency for errors in understanding when the subject of a conversation changes abruptly, presumably because we are confused over which context or schema to use in resolving pronoun references and other ambiguities.

A *script* is a structured representation describing a stereotyped sequence of events in a particular context. The *script* was originally designed by Schank and his research group (Schank and Abelson 1977) as a means of organizing *conceptual dependency* structures into descriptions of typical situations. Scripts are used in natural language understanding systems to organize a knowledge base in terms of the situations that the system is to understand.

Most adults are quite comfortable (i.e., they know what to expect and how to act) in a restaurant. They are met at the entrance (or by a sign indicating that they should continue in) and directed to a seat. Either a menu is available at the table or presented by the waiter or the customer asks for it. We understand the routines for ordering food, eating, paying, and leaving.

In fact, the restaurant script is quite different from other eating scripts such as the "fast-food" model or the "formal family meal." In the fast-food model the customer enters, gets in line to order, pays for the meal (before eating), waits about for a tray with the food, takes the tray and tries to find a clean table, and so on. These are two different stereotyped sequences of events, and each has a potential script.

The components of a script are:

Entry conditions or descriptors of the world that must be true for the script to be called. In a restaurant script, these include a restaurant that is open and a customer who is hungry.

Results or facts that are true once the script has terminated; for example, the customer is full and poorer, the restaurant owner has more money.

Props or the "things" that make up the content of the script. These might include tables, waiters, and menus. This allows reasonable default assumptions about the situation: a restaurant is assumed to have tables and chairs unless stated otherwise.

Roles are the actions that the individual participants perform. The waiter takes orders, delivers food, and presents the bill. The customer orders, eats, and pays.

Scenes. Schank breaks the script into a sequence of scenes each of which presents a temporal aspect of the script. In the restaurant there is entering, ordering, eating, etc.

The elements of the script, the basic "pieces" of semantic meaning, are represented using conceptual dependency relationships. Placed together in a framelike structure, they

---

represent a sequence of meanings, or an event sequence. The restaurant script taken from this research is presented in Figure 9.26.

The program reads a small story about restaurants and parses it into an internal conceptual dependency representation. Because the key concepts in this internal description match with the entry conditions of the script, the program binds the people and things mentioned in the story to the roles and props mentioned in the script. The result is an expanded representation of the story contents, using the script to fill in any missing information and default assumptions. The program then answers questions about the story by referring to the script. The script allows the reasonable default assumptions that are essential to natural language understanding. For example:

EXAMPLE 9.4.1

John went to a restaurant last night. He ordered steak. When he paid he noticed he was running out of money. He hurried home since it had started to rain.

Using the script, the system can correctly answer questions such as: Did John eat dinner last night? Did John use cash or a credit card? How could John get a menu? What did John buy?

EXAMPLE 9.4.2

Sue went out to lunch. She sat at a table and called a waitress, who brought her a menu. She ordered a sandwich.

Questions that might reasonably be asked of this story include: Why did the waitress bring Sue a menu? Was Sue in a restaurant? Who paid? Who was the "she" who ordered the sandwich? This last question is difficult. The most recently named female is the waitress, an incorrect conclusion. Script *roles* help to resolve pronoun references and other ambiguities.

Scripts can also be used to interpret unexpected results or breaks in the scripted activity. Thus, in scene 2 of Figure 9.26 there is the choice point of "food" or "no food" delivered to the customer. This allows the following example to be understood.

EXAMPLE 9.4.3

Kate went to a restaurant. She was shown to a table and ordered steak from the waitress. She sat there and waited for a long time. Finally, she got mad and left.

Questions that can be answered from this story using the restaurant script include: Who is the "she" who sat and waited? Why did she wait? Who was the "she" who got mad and left? Why did she get mad? Note that there are other questions that the script cannot answer, such as why do people get mad when the waiter does not come promptly? Like any knowledge-based system, scripts require the knowledge engineer to correctly anticipate the knowledge required.

Scripts, like frames and other structured representations, are subject to certain problems, including the script *match* problem and the *between-the-lines* problem. Consider Example 9.4.4, which could call either the *restaurant* or *concert* scripts. The choice is critical because "bill" can refer to either the restaurant check or the playbill of the concert.

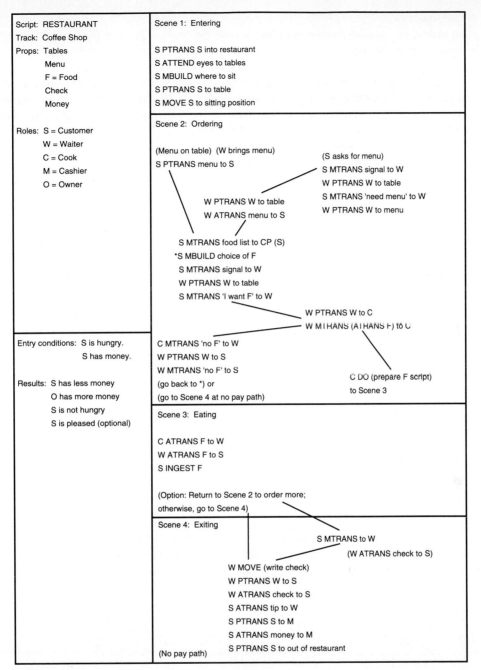

Script: RESTAURANT
Track: Coffee Shop
Props: Tables
     Menu
     F = Food
     Check
     Money

Roles: S = Customer
     W = Waiter
     C = Cook
     M = Cashier
     O = Owner

Entry conditions: S is hungry.
                 S has money.

Results: S has less money
     O has more money
     S is not hungry
     S is pleased (optional)

Scene 1: Entering

S PTRANS S into restaurant
S ATTEND eyes to tables
S MBUILD where to sit
S PTRANS S to table
S MOVE S to sitting position

Scene 2: Ordering

(Menu on table) (W brings menu)
S PTRANS menu to S

                             (S asks for menu)
                             S MTRANS signal to W
                             W PTRANS W to table
                             S MTRANS 'need menu' to W
          W PTRANS W to table   W PTRANS W to menu
          W ATRANS menu to S

       S MTRANS food list to CP (S)
     *S MBUILD choice of F
      S MTRANS signal to W
      W PTRANS W to table
      S MTRANS 'I want F' to W

                        W PTRANS W to C
                        W MTRANS (ATRANS F) to C

C MTRANS 'no F' to W
W PTRANS W to S
W MTRANS 'no F' to S   C DO (prepare F script)
(go back to *) or   to Scene 3
(go to Scene 4 at no pay path)

Scene 3: Eating

C ATRANS F to W
W ATRANS F to S
S INGEST F

(Option: Return to Scene 2 to order more;
otherwise, go to Scene 4)

Scene 4: Exiting

                         S MTRANS to W
                            (W ATRANS check to S)
          W MOVE (write check)
          W PTRANS W to S
          W ATRANS check to S
          S ATRANS tip to W
          S PTRANS S to M
          S ATRANS money to M
(No pay path)   S PTRANS S to out of restaurant

Figure 9.26   A restaurant script (Schank 1977).

EXAMPLE 9.4.4

John visited his favorite restaurant on the way to the concert. He was pleased by the bill because he liked Mozart.

It is often difficult to determine which of two or more potential scripts should be used. The script match problem is "deep" in the sense that no algorithm exists for guaranteeing correct choices. It requires heuristic knowledge about the organization of the world, and scripts assist only in the organization of that knowledge.

The between-the-lines problem is equally difficult: it is not possible to know ahead of time the possible occurrences that can break a script. For instance:

EXAMPLE 9.4.5

John was eating dinner at his favorite restaurant when a large piece of plaster fell from the ceiling and landed on his date. . . .

Questions: Was John eating a date salad? What did John do next? Was John's date plastered? As this example illustrates, structured representations can be inflexible. Reasoning can be locked into a single script, even though this may not be appropriate.

Memory organization packets (MOPs) address the problem of script inflexibility by representing knowledge as smaller components (MOPs) along with rules for dynamically combining them to form a schema that is appropriate to the current situation (Schank 1982). The organization of knowledge in memory is particularly important to implementations of case-based reasoning, in which the problem solver must efficiently retrieve a relevant prior problem solution from memory (Kolodner 1988a).

The problems of organizing and retrieving knowledge are difficult and inherent to the modeling of semantic meaning. Eugene Charniak (1972) has illustrated the amount of knowledge required to understand even simple children's stories. Consider a statement about a birthday party: "Mary was given two kites for her birthday so she took one back to the store." We must know about the tradition of giving gifts at a party; we must know what a kite is and why Mary doesn't want two of them; we must know about stores and their exchange policies. In spite of these problems, programs using scripts and other semantic representations can understand natural language in limited domains. An example of this work is a program that interprets messages coming over the news wire services. Using scripts for natural disasters, coups, or other stereotypic stories, programs have shown remarkable success in this limited but realistic domain (Schank and Riesbeck 1981).

9.5 Type Hierarchies, Inheritance, and Exception Handling

Inheritance across class or type hierarchies is an important feature of almost all network and structured representation languages. Inheritance is implemented through relations such as the type hierarchy of conceptual graphs, as well as through various links including ISA,

AKO (A Kind Of), and SUPERC (SUPER Class). Figure 9.27 shows a frame-based representation of knowledge about birds with directed arcs indicating the inheritance hierarchy.

A common, although controversial, use of inheritance is to implement default values and exceptions. In the birds example, we have established a class flightless bird, which does not fly. If we assume that the inheritance algorithm searches the hierarchy in order, it would encounter the flightless bird frame before the bird frame and correctly infer that opus cannot fly. Here we have established flying as a default value for birds with the subclass flightless bird overriding that default value.

Several authors (Brachman 1985a; Touretzky 1986) have pointed out a number of anomalies that arise in inheritance, particularly in multiple inheritance hierarchies and in the use of inheritance to implement defaults.

The network of Figure 9.27 illustrates tree inheritance. Each node has only a single parent. Tree hierarchies are well behaved, because an algorithm need only search straight up the hierarchy until it encounters the desired property. If it reaches the top node and still has not found the property, it fails. There is no need for decisions in the inheritance search. The situation is complicated, however, if we allow multiple inheritance, such as in a lattice. Multiple inheritance is supported in many knowledge representation languages because

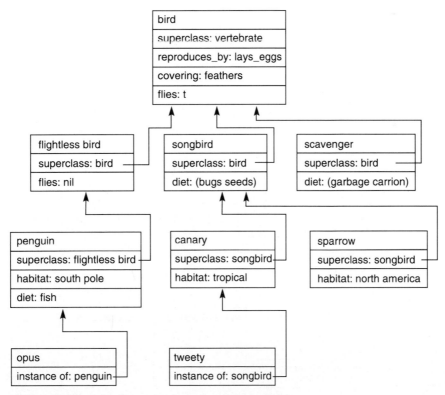

Figure 9.27   Inheritance system description of birds.

natural entities often belong to more than one class. In the network of Figure 9.28, we have added the class **cartoon character** and made **opus** an instance of this class as well as a penguin. **Cartoon characters** have a **habitat** of **funny papers**. It is no longer clear whether **opus** lives at the South Pole or in the funnies.

This problem may be solved in several ways. Most inheritance systems allow the programmer to specify the order with which parent nodes are searched; here we could require that **opus** inherit the properties of **cartoon character** before those of **penguin**. This solution has the undesirable property of violating the declarative semantics of the representation. We must rely on knowledge of the order of search to resolve any ambiguities.

Furthermore, this would not help us if there were two conflicts and we wished to resolve one in favor of **penguin** and the other in favor of **cartoon character**. For example, we may state that penguins eat herring and cartoon characters eat hamburgers. How could we represent the fact that **opus** lives in the funnies and eats fish? We could do this by defining a new class for **opus**, called **cartoon penguin**, that would be a subclass of both **penguin** and **cartoon character** and resolve these conflicts explicitly (Fig. 9.29). This resolves the problem, although in many cases, introduction of new classes seems artificial and can lead to further problems and restructuring of the network on later updates.

In addition, multiple problems occur when inheritance is used to implement defaults and exceptions. In the network of Figure 9.27, the class **flightless bird** is introduced to handle exceptions to the rule that birds fly. It seems reasonable to treat class membership as a transitive relation; from the fact that **penguin** is a subclass of **flightless bird** and **flightless bird** is a subclass of **bird**, we should be able to infer that **penguin** is a subclass of **bird**. Unfortunately, if we allow this intuitively appealing inference and add this link to the graph, we confuse the inheritance of the **flies** property (Fig. 9.30). We may prohibit these inferences, but that is no more appealing than the other remedies to multiple-inheritance anomalies.

There is a deeper problem in the use of inheritance to handle defaults and exceptions: it compromises the nature of definitions themselves (Brachman 1985*a*). It seems appropri-

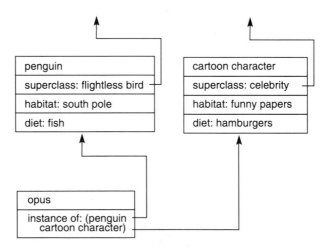

Figure 9.28 An ambiguous multiple inheritance situation.

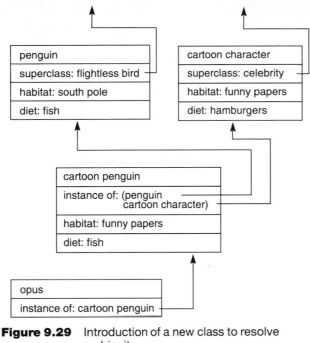

Figure 9.29 Introduction of a new class to resolve ambiguity.

ate to view a frame as a definition of a class. However, if we define a penguin as a bird that does not fly, what is to prevent us from asserting that a block of wood is a bird that does not fly, does not have feathers, and does not lay eggs? This careless use of inheritance to implement exception handling illustrates the subtleties that arise in knowledge representation. One solution would be to restrict the representation to a form that does not allow these problems, such as tree inheritance without exception handling. This also eliminates much of the power of inheritance. Another approach is to examine carefully and refine the semantics of the representation. Touretzky (1986) has resolved many of these ambiguities.

Unfortunately, most commercially available inheritance software does not provide a clean enough implementation of inheritance to avoid these problems. This is because many of these problems have not yet been solved or the solutions that are available are either too new or too inefficient to affect the design of current programs. The most effective approach to these problems still requires the programmer to be careful in structuring the knowledge base.

9.6 Further Problems in Knowledge Representation

In this text, we examine the major alternatives for knowledge representation, including the use of logic, rules, semantic networks, and frames. The results of careful study include an increased understanding of the advantages and limitations of each of these representations.

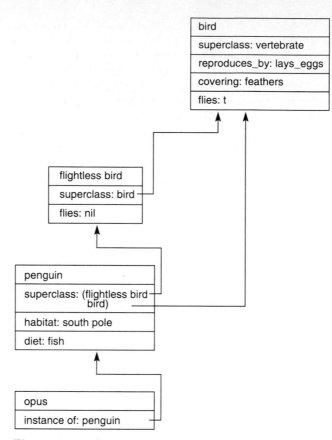

Figure 9.30 Introduction of an anomaly through the transitivity of the subclass relation.

Nonetheless, debate continues over the relative naturalness, efficiency, and appropriateness of each approach. Regardless of the representation language selected, a number of important problems remain in the area of knowledge representation.

The first of these is the *selection and granularity of atomic symbols* for the knowledge base. Objects in the world constitute the domain of the mapping; computational objects in the knowledge base are the range. The nature of the atomic elements in the language largely determines what can be described about the world. For example, if a "car" is the smallest atom of the representation, then the system cannot reason about engines, wheels, or any of the component parts of a car. However, if the atoms correspond to these parts, than a larger structure may be required to represent "car" as a single concept. This introduces a cost in efficiency (in manipulating this larger structure) and expressiveness (the larger structure may obscure the fact that a car is a single conceptual entity).

Another example of the trade-off in the choice of atomic symbols comes from work in natural language understanding. Programs that use single words as elements of meaning may have difficulty in representing complex concepts that do not have a one-word denotation. There is also difficulty in distinguishing between different meanings of the same word or different words with the same meaning. One approach to this problem is to use semantic primitives, language-independent conceptual units, as the basis for representing the meaning of natural language. Conceptual dependency theory takes this approach, and although it avoids the problems of using single words as units of meaning, it involves other trade-offs: many words require complex structures for their definitions; also, by relying on a small set of primitives, many subtle distinctions (e.g., push vs. shove, yell vs. scream) are difficult to express.

Exhaustiveness is a property of a knowledge base that is assisted by an appropriate representation. A mapping is *exhaustive* with respect to a property or class of objects if all occurrences correspond to an explicit element of the representation. Geographic maps are assumed to be exhaustive to some level of detail; a map with a missing city or river would not be well regarded as a navigational tool. Although most knowledge bases are not exhaustive, exhaustiveness with respect to certain properties or objects is a desirable goal. For example, the ability to assume that a representation is exhaustive may allow a planner to ignore possible effects of the *frame* problem.

When we describe problems as a state of the world that is changed by a series of actions or events, these actions or events generally change only a few components of the description; the program must be able to infer side effects and implicit changes in the world description. The problem of representing the side effects of actions is called the *frame problem*. For example, a robot stacking heavy boxes on a truck must compensate for the lowering of the truck bed due to the weight of the boxes. If a representation is exhaustive, there will be no unspecified side effects, and the frame problem effectively disappears. The difficulty of the frame problem results from the fact that it is impossible to build a completely exhaustive knowledge base for most domains. A representation language should assist the programmer in deciding what knowledge may safely be omitted and help deal with the consequences of this omission. (Section 5.1 discusses the frame problem in planning.)

Related to exhaustiveness is the *plasticity* or modifiability of the representation: the addition of knowledge in response to deficiencies is the primary solution to a lack of exhaustiveness. Because most knowledge bases are not exhaustive, it should be easy to modify or update them. In addition to the syntactic ease of adding knowledge, a representation should help to guarantee the consistency of a knowledge base as information is added or deleted. Inheritance, by allowing properties of a class to be inherited by new instances, is an example of how a knowledge representational scheme may help ensure consistency.

Another useful property of representations concerns the extent to which the mapping between the world and the knowledge base is *homomorphic*. Here, homomorphic implies a one-to-one correspondence between objects and actions in the world and the computational objects and operations of the language. In a homomorphic mapping the knowledge base reflects the perceived organization of the domain and can be organized in a more natural and intuitive fashion.

In addition to naturalness, directness, and ease of use, representational schemes may also be evaluated by their *computational efficiency*. Levesque and Brachman (1985) discuss the trade-off between expressiveness and efficiency. Logic, when used as a representational scheme, is highly expressive as a result of its completeness; however, systems based on unconstrained logic pay a considerable price in efficiency. We address this issue again in Chapter 11.

9.7 Epilogue and References

Knowledge representation is a large and difficult field that lies at the heart of modern artificial intelligence. In this chapter we introduced the major problems in representation and offered techniques for their solution. This chapter brings the reader through the early representational formalizing of AI. We continue our presentation of representational issues, including the connectionist or sub-symbolic, in the remaining chapters.

An important area that we have overlooked involves modifications and extensions to logic that enable it to address the problems of knowledge representation while retaining its well-defined semantics and inference strategies. Important alternatives to first-order predicate calculus include:

1. **Multiple-valued logics**. These extend logic by adding new truth values such as unknown to the standard values of true and false. This can, for example, provide a vehicle for distinguishing between assertions that are known to be false and those that are simply not known to be true.

2. **Modal logics**. Modal logic adds operators that enable it to deal with problems of knowledge and belief, necessity and possibility.

3. **Temporal logics**. Temporal logics enable us to quantify expressions with regard to time, indicating, for example, that an expression is *always* true or *will be true in the future*.

4. **Higher-order logics**. Many categories of knowledge correspond to higher-order logical concepts. Do we really need higher-order logics to deal with this knowledge, or can it all be done in first-order logic? If higher-order logics are needed, how may they best be formulated?

5. **Logical formulations of definitions, prototypes, and exceptions.** As we illustrated in the discussion of inheritance, exceptions are a necessary feature of a definitional system. However, careless use of exceptions undermines the semantics of a representation. Another issue is the difference between a definition and a prototype, or representation of a *typical* individual. What is the exact difference between the properties of a class and the properties of a typical member? How should prototypical individuals be represented? When is a prototype more appropriate than a definition?

Logical representation continues to be an important area of research (McCarthy 1968; Hayes 1979; Weyhrauch 1980; Moore 1982). *Logics for Artificial Intelligence* by Turner (1984) is an overview of work done in nonstandard logics.

Associationist theories have been studied as models of both computer and human memory and reasoning (Selz 1913, 1922; Anderson and Bower 1973; Sowa 1984; Collins and Quillian 1969).

Our overview of conceptual graphs owes a considerable debt to John Sowa's book *Conceptual Structures* (1984). The reader is referred to this book for details that we have omitted. In its full treatment, conceptual graphs combine the expressive power of predicate calculus, as well as modal and higher-order logic, with a rich set of built-in concepts and relations derived from epistemology, psychology, and linguistics.

Schema-based reasoning, in many ways similar to frames, was pursued by researchers at the AI Department of the University of Edinburgh (Bundy et al. 1979). Other important work in structured knowledge representation languages includes Bobrow and Winograd's representation language KRL (Bobrow and Winograd 1977) and Brachman's (1979) representation language KL-ONE, which pays particular attention to the semantic foundations of structured representations.

There are a number of other approaches of interest to the representation problem. For example, Brachman, Fikes, and Levesque have proposed representation that emphasizes *functional* specifications; that is, what can be asked of or told to a knowledge base (Brachman et al. 1985; Levesque 1984).

A number of books can help with an advanced study of these issues. *Readings in Knowledge Representation* by Brachman and Levesque (1985) is a compilation of important articles in this area. Many of the articles referred to in this chapter may be found there, although they were referenced in their original source. *Representation and Understanding* by Bobrow and Collins (1975), *Representations of Commonsense Knowledge* by Davis (1990), *Readings in Qualitative Reasoning about Physical Systems* by Weld and deKleer (1990), and the proceedings of any of the annual conferences on artificial intelligence in general or knowledge representation in particular, such as *Principles of Knowledge Representation and Reasoning* by Brachman et al. (1989), are helpful sources.

9.8 Exercises

1. Commonsense reasoning employs such notions as causality, analogy, and equivalence but uses them in a different way from formal languages. For example, if we say that "Inflation caused Jane to ask for a raise," we are suggesting a more complicated causal relationship than is generally found in simple physical laws. If we say "Use a knife or chisel to trim the wood," we are suggesting a different notion of equivalence than is found in most formal languages. Discuss the problems of translating these and other commonsense concepts into a formal language.

2. In Section 9.2.1 we presented some of the arguments against the use of logic for representing commonsense knowledge. Make an argument for the use of logic in representing this knowledge.

3. Translate each of the following sentences into predicate calculus, conceptual dependencies, and conceptual graphs:

    "Jane gave Tom an ice cream cone."
    "Basketball players are tall."
    "Paul cut down the tree with an axe."
    "Place all the ingredients in a bowl and mix thoroughly."

4. Read "What's in a Link" by Woods (1985). Section IV of this article lists a number of problems

in knowledge representation. Suggest a solution to each of these problems using logic, conceptual graphs, and frame notations.

5. Translate the conceptual graphs of Figure 9.31 into English sentences.

6. The operations join and restrict define a generalization ordering on conceptual graphs. Show that the generalization relation is transitive.

7. Specialization of conceptual graphs using join and restrict is not a truth-preserving operation. Give an example that demonstrates that the restriction of a true graph is not necessarily true. However, the generalization of a true graph is always true; prove this.

8. Define a specialized representation language to describe the activities of a public library. This language will be a set of concepts and relations using conceptual graphs. Do the same thing for a retail business. What concepts and relations would these two languages have in common? Which would exist in both languages but have a different meaning?

9. Translate the conceptual graphs of Figure 9.31 into predicate calculus.

10. Translate the financial advisor knowledge base (Chapter 2) into conceptual graph form.

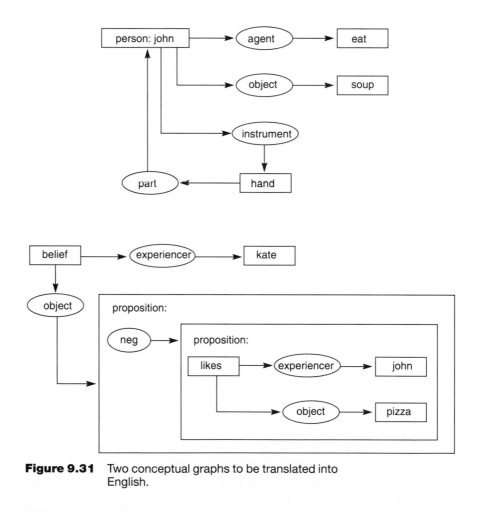

Figure 9.31   Two conceptual graphs to be translated into English.

11. Give evidence from your own experience that suggests a scriptlike or framelike organization of human memory.

12. Using conceptual dependencies, define a script for:
    a. A fast-food restaurant.
    b. Interacting with a used-car salesman.
    c. Going to the opera.

13. Construct a hierarchy of subtypes for the concept vehicle; for example, subtypes of vehicle might be land_vehicle or ocean-vehicle. These would have further subtypes. Is this best represented as a tree, lattice, or general graph? Do the same for the concept move; for the concept angry.

14. Construct a type hierarchy in which some types do not have a common supertype. Add types to make this a lattice. Could this hierarchy be expressed using tree inheritance? What problems would arise in doing so?

15. Each of the following sequences of characters is generated according to some general rule. Describe a representation that could be used to represent the rules for:
    a. 2,4,6,8, . . .
    b. 1,2,4,8,16, . . .
    c. 1,1,2,3,5,8, . . .
    d. 1,a,2,c,3,f,4, . . .
    e. o,t,t,f,f,s,s, . . .

    Define a representation that could be used to represent rules for sequences of numbers and letters.

16. Describe a representation that could be used in a program to solve analogy problems like that in Figure 9.32. This class of problems was addressed by T. G. Evans (1968). The representation must be capable of representing the essential features of size, shape, and relative position.

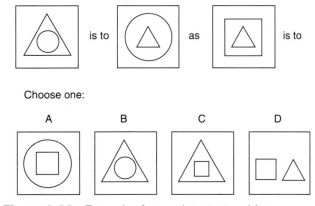

Choose one:

Figure 9.32 Example of an analogy test problem.

NATURAL LANGUAGE

Quid opus est verbis? (What need is there for words?)

—TERRENCE

I understand a fury in your words,
But not the words.

—WILLIAM SHAKESPEARE, *Othello*

They have been to a great feast of languages
And stolen the scraps.

—WILLIAM SHAKESPEARE, *Love's Labours Lost*

I wish someone would tell me what "Ditty wah ditty" means.

—ARTHUR BLAKE

10.0   Role of Knowledge in Language Understanding

Communicating with natural language, whether as text or as speech, depends heavily on knowledge of the domain of discourse. Understanding is not merely the transmission of words; it also requires inferences about the speaker's goals and assumptions and about the context of the interaction. Implementing a natural language understanding program requires that we represent large amounts of knowledge and reason effectively with it. We must consider such issues as nonmonotonicity, belief revision, metaphor, planning, learning, and the practical complexities of human interaction. These are the central problems of artificial intelligence.

Consider, for example, the following lines from Shakespeare's *Sonnett XVIII*:

Shall I compare thee to a summer's day?
Thou art more lovely and more temperate:

> Rough winds do shake the darling buds of May,
> And summer's lease hath all too short a date.

We cannot understand these lines through a simplistic, literal treatment of meaning. Instead, we must address such issues as:

1. What were Shakespeare's intentions in writing these lines? We must know a great deal about human love and the social conventions surrounding it to begin to understand these intensions.

2. Why did Shakespeare compare his beloved to a summer's day? Does he mean that she is 24 hours long and can cause sunburn or that she makes him feel the warmth and beauty of summer?

3. What inferences does the passage require? Shakespeare's intended meaning does not reside explicitly in the text; it must be inferred using metaphors, analogies, and background knowledge. For instance, how do we come to interpret the references to rough winds and the brevity of summer as lamenting the shortness of human life and love?

4. How does metaphor shape our understanding of these lines, as well as the semantics of human language in general? The words are not mere references to explicit objects such as blocks on a table; the heart of the poem's meaning is in the selective attribution of properties of a summer's day to the beloved.

5. What is the relationship between the syntactic structure of the lines and the knowledge and inferences involved in understanding the meaning and purpose of the poem?

We cannot merely chain together the dictionary meanings of Shakespeare's words and call the result understanding. Instead, we must employ a complex process of parsing the sentence to determine the parts of speech, constructing a representation of the semantic meaning, and interpreting this meaning in light of our prior understanding of the problem domain. This chapter provides a brief introduction to the problems of natural language understanding and the computational techniques developed for their solution. Throughout the chapter, we focus on the problems of understanding written text. Speech understanding systems must also solve these problems, as well as the additional difficulties associated with the recognition and disambiguation of words spoken in context.

Because of the knowledge required to understand unconstrained natural language, much progress in the area has come by restricting our focus to *microworlds*, limited applications that require little domain knowledge. This allows researchers to focus more directly on the problems of processing natural language itself. One of the earliest programs to take this approach was Terry Winograd's SHRDLU (Winograd 1972), which could converse about a *blocks world* consisting of differently shaped and colored blocks and a hand for moving them about (Fig. 10.1).

SHRDLU could respond to English-language queries and commands such as "What is sitting on the red block?" "What shape is the blue block on the table?" or "Place the green pyramid on the red brick." It could handle pronoun references such as "Is there a red block? Pick it up." It could even understand ellipses such as "What color is the block on the blue brick? Shape?" Because of the simplicity of the blocks world, it was possible to provide the system with complete knowledge of the world. Because the blocks world

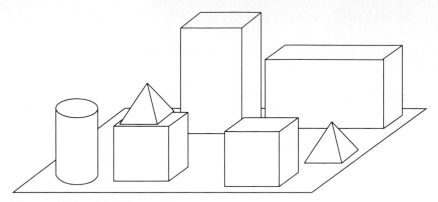

Figure 10.1 A blocks world.

did not involve the more difficult problems of commonsense reasoning such as understanding time, causality, possibilities, or beliefs, the techniques for representing this knowledge were relatively straightforward. In spite of its narrow subject matter, SHRDLU did provide a model for the integration of syntax and semantics and demonstrated that a program with sufficient knowledge of the domain of discourse could communicate meaningfully in natural language.

In Section 10.1 we introduce the commonly accepted levels of analysis of natural language. Section 10.2 presents a syntactic analysis; Section 10.3 combines syntax and semantics using augmented transition network parsing. In Section 10.4 we consider two applications where natural language understanding programs are useful: question answering and accessing information in data bases.

10.1   The Natural Language Problem

10.1.1   Introduction

Language is a complicated phenomenon, involving processes as varied as the recognition of sounds or printed letters, syntactic parsing, high-level semantic inferences, and even the communication of emotional content through rhythm and inflection. To manage this complexity, linguists have defined different levels of analysis for natural language:

1. *Prosody* deals with the rhythm and intonation of language. This level of analysis is difficult to formalize and often neglected; however, its importance is evident in the powerful effect of poetry or religious chants, as well as the role played by rhythm in children's wordplay and the babbling of infants.

2. *Phonology* examines the sounds that are combined to form language. This branch of linguistics is important to work in computerized speech recognition and generation.

3. *Morphology* is concerned with the components (morphemes) that make up words. These include the rules governing the formation of words, such as the effect of prefixes (un-, non-, anti-, etc.) and suffixes (-ing, -ly, etc.) that modify the meaning of root words. Morphological analysis is important in determining the role of a word in a sentence, including its tense, number, and part of speech.

4. *Syntax* studies the rules for combining words into legal phrases and sentences and the use of those rules to parse and generate sentences. This has been the best formalized and consequently the most successfully automated level of linguistic analysis.

5. *Semantics* considers the meaning of words, phrases, and sentences and the ways in which meaning is conveyed in natural language.

6. *Pragmatics* is the study of the ways in which language is used and its effects on the listener. For example, pragmatics would address the reasons that "Yes" is *usually* an inappropriate answer to the question "Do you know what time it is?"

7. *World knowledge* includes knowledge of the physical world, the world of human social interaction, and the role of goals and intentions in communication. This general background knowledge is essential to understand the full meaning of a text or conversation.

Although these levels of analysis seem natural and are supported by psychological evidence, they are, to some extent, artificial divisions that have been imposed on language. All of these interact extensively, with even low-level intonations and rhythmic variations having an effect on the meaning of an utterance, e.g., sarcasm. This interaction is evident in the relationship between syntax and semantics, and although some division along these lines seems essential, the exact boundary is difficult to characterize. For example, sentences such as "They are eating apples" have multiple parsings that can be resolved only by attention to meaning and context. Conversely, syntax affects semantics, as will be illustrated by the role of phrase structure in interpreting the meaning of a sentence. Although the exact nature of the distinction between syntax and semantics is often blurred and often debated, both the psychological evidence and its utility in managing the complexity of the problem argue for its retention. We address issues of language understanding and interpretation again in Chapter 16.

10.1.2 Stages of Language Analysis

Although the specific organization of natural language understanding programs varies with different philosophies and applications—e.g., a front end for a data base, an automatic translation system, a story understanding program—all of them must translate the original sentence into an internal representation of its meaning. Generally, natural language understanding follows the stages of Figure 10.2.

The first stage is *parsing*, which is analyzing the syntactic structure of sentences. Parsing not only verifies that sentences are syntactically well formed but also determines their linguistic structure. By identifying the major linguistic relations such as subject-verb, verb-object, and noun-modifier, the parser provides a framework for semantic interpretation.

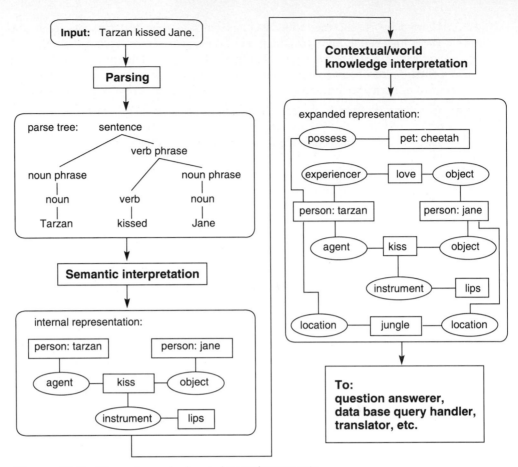

Figure 10.2 Stages in producing an internal representation of a sentence.

This is often represented as a *parse tree*. The parser employs knowledge of language syntax, morphology, and some semantics.

The second stage is *semantic interpretation*, which produces a representation of the meaning of the text. In Figure 10.2 this is shown as a conceptual graph. Other representations commonly used include conceptual dependencies, frames, and logic-based representations. Semantic interpretation uses knowledge about the meaning of words and linguistic structure, such as case roles of nouns or the transitivity of verbs. In the example of Figure 10.2, the program used knowledge of the meaning of kiss to add the default value of lips for the instrument of kissing. This stage also performs semantic consistency checks. For example, the definition of the verb kiss may include constraints that require the object to be a person if the agent is a person, i.e., Tarzan does not (normally) kiss Cheetah.

In the third stage, structures from the knowledge base are added to the internal representation of the sentence to produce an expanded representation of the sentence's meaning. This adds the necessary world knowledge required for complete understanding, such as the facts that Tarzan loves Jane, that Jane and Tarzan live in the jungle, and that Cheetah is Tarzan's pet. This resulting structure represents the meaning of the natural language text and is used by the system for further processing.

In a data base front end, for example, the extended structure would combine the representation of the query's meaning with knowledge about the organization of the data base. This could then be translated into an appropriate query in the data base language. In a story understanding program, this extended structure would represent the meaning of the story and be used to answer questions about it (see the discussion of scripts in Chapter 9).

These stages exist in all systems, although they may or may not correspond to distinct software modules. For example, many programs do not produce an explicit parse tree but generate the internal semantic representation directly. Nevertheless, the tree is implicit in the parse of the sentence. *Incremental parsing* (Allen 1987) is a commonly used technique in which a fragment of the internal representation is produced as soon as a significant part of the sentence is parsed. These fragments are combined into a complete structure as the parse proceeds. They are also used to resolve ambiguities and guide the parser.

10.2   Syntax

10.2.1   Specification and Parsing Using Context-Free Grammars

Chapters 4 and 6 introduced the use of *rewrite rules* to specify a grammar. The rules listed below define a grammar for simple transitive sentences such as "The man likes the dog." The rules are numbered for reference.

1. sentence ↔ noun_phrase verb_phrase
2. noun_phrase ↔ noun
3. noun_phrase ↔ article noun
4. verb_phrase ↔ verb
5. verb_phrase ↔ verb noun_phrase
6. article ↔ a
7. article ↔ the
8. noun ↔ man
9. noun ↔ dog
10. verb ↔ likes
11. verb ↔ bites

Rules 6 through 11 have English words on the right-hand side; these rules form a dictionary of words that may appear in sentences of the grammar. These words are the *terminals* of the grammar. Terms that describe higher-level linguistic concepts (sentence, noun_phrase, etc.) are called *nonterminals*. Nonterminals appear in this typeface. Note that terminals do not appear in the left-hand side of any rule.

A legal sentence is any string of terminals that can be *derived* using these rules. A derivation begins with the nonterminal symbol **sentence** and produces a string of terminals through a series of substitutions defined by the rules of the grammar. A legal substitution replaces a symbol that matches the left-hand side of a rule with the symbols on the right-hand side of that rule. At intermediate stages of the derivation, the string may contain both terminals and nonterminals and is called a *sentential form*. A derivation of the sentence "The man bites the dog" is given by:

STRING	APPLY RULE #
sentence	1
noun_phrase verb_phrase	3
article noun verb_phrase	7
The noun verb_phrase	8
The man verb_phrase	5
The man verb noun_phrase	11
The man bites noun_phrase	3
The man bites article noun	7
The man bites the noun	9
The man bites the dog	

This is an example of a *top-down* derivation: it begins with the **sentence** symbol and works down to a string of terminals. A bottom-up derivation starts with a string of terminals and replaces right-hand-side patterns with those from the left-hand side, terminating when all that remains is the **sentence** symbol.

A derivation may be represented as a tree structure, known as a *parse tree*, in which each node is a symbol of the grammar. The interior nodes of the tree are nonterminals; each node and its children correspond, respectively, to the left-hand side and right-hand side of a rule in the grammar. The leaf nodes are terminals and the **sentence** symbol is the root of the tree. The parse tree for "The man bites the dog" appears in Figure 10.3.

Not only does the existence of a derivation or parse tree prove that a sentence is legal in the grammar, but it also determines the structure of the sentence. The *phrase structure* of the grammar defines the deeper linguistic organization of the language. For example, the

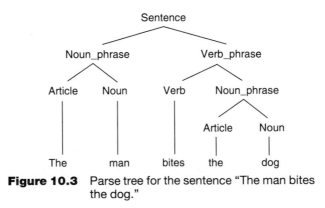

Figure 10.3 Parse tree for the sentence "The man bites the dog."

breakdown of a **sentence** into a **noun_phrase** and a **verb_phrase** specifies the relation between an action and its agent. This phrase structure plays an essential role in semantic interpretation by defining intermediate stages in a derivation at which semantic processing may take place.

Parsing is the problem of constructing a derivation or a parse tree for an input string from a formal definition of a grammar. Parsing algorithms fall into two classes: *top-down parsers*, which begin with the top-level **sentence** symbol and attempt to build a tree whose leaves match the target sentence, and *bottom-up parsers*, which start with the words in the sentence (the terminals) and attempt to find a series of reductions that yield the **sentence** symbol.

In parsing, the difficulty is in determining which of several potentially applicable rules should be used at each step of the derivation. If the wrong choice is made, the parser may fail to recognize a legal sentence. For example, in attempting to parse the sentence "The dog bites" in a bottom-up fashion, rules 7, 9, and 11 produce the string **article noun verb**. At this point, an erroneous application of rule 2 would produce **article noun_phrase verb**; this could not be reduced to the **sentence** symbol. The parser should use rule 3 instead. Similar problems can occur in a top-down parse.

The problem of selecting the correct rule at any stage of the parse is handled either by allowing the parser to backtrack if an incorrect choice is made (as in *recursive descent parsers*) or by using look-ahead to check the input string for features that will determine the proper rule to apply. With either approach, we must take care to control the complexity of execution while guaranteeing a correct parse.

The inverse problem is that of *generation*, or producing legal sentences from an internal semantic representation. Generation starts with a representation of some meaningful content (such as a semantic network or conceptual dependency graph) and constructs a grammatically correct sentence that communicates this meaning. However, generation is not merely the reverse of understanding; it encounters unique difficulties and requires separate methodologies.

Because parsing is particularly important in the processing of programming languages as well as natural language, researchers have developed a number of different parsing algorithms. These include both top-down and bottom-up strategies. Though a complete survey of parsing algorithms is beyond the scope of this chapter, we do consider *transition network* parsers in some detail. Although transition network parsers themselves are not sufficiently powerful for natural language, they form the basis for *augmented transition networks*, which have proved to be a powerful tool for natural language work.

10.2.2 Transition Network Parsers

A transition network parser represents a grammar as a set of finite-state machines or *transition networks*. Each network corresponds to a single nonterminal in the grammar. Arcs in the networks are labeled with either terminal or nonterminal symbols. Each path through the network, from the start state to the final state, corresponds to some rule for that nonterminal; the sequence of arc labels on the path is the sequence of symbols on the right-hand side of the rule. The grammar of Section 10.2.1 is represented by the transition networks of Figure 10.4. When there is more than one rule for a nonterminal, the corresponding

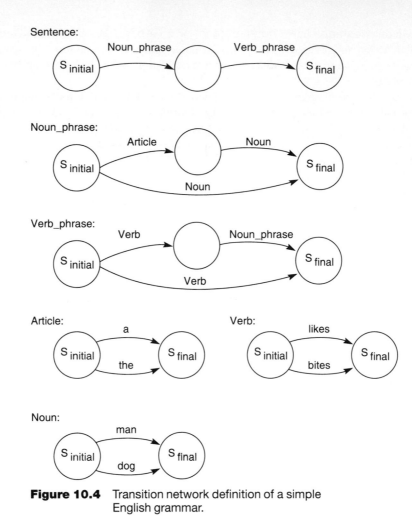

Figure 10.4 Transition network definition of a simple English grammar.

network has multiple paths from the start to the goal. For example, the rules noun_phrase ↔ noun and noun_phrase ↔ article noun are captured by alternative paths through the noun_phrase network of Figure 10.4.

Finding a successful transition through the network for a nonterminal corresponds to the replacement of that nonterminal by the right-hand side of a grammar rule. For example, to parse a sentence, a transition network parser must find a transition through the sentence network. It begins in the start state ($S_{initial}$) and takes the noun_phrase transition and then the verb_phrase transition to reach the final state (S_{final}). This is equivalent to replacing the sentence symbol by the string noun_phrase verb_phrase.

In order to cross an arc, the parser examines its label. If the label is a terminal symbol, the parser checks the input stream to see whether the next word matches the arc label. If it does not match, the transition cannot be taken. If the arc is labeled with a nonterminal symbol, the parser retrieves the network for that nonterminal and recursively attempts to find a path through it. If the parser fails to find a path through this network, the top-level arc cannot be traversed. This causes the parser to backtrack and attempt another path through the network. Thus, the parser tries to find a path through the **sentence** network; if it succeeds, the input string is a legal sentence in the grammar.

Consider the simple sentence "Dog bites." The first steps in parsing this sentence are illustrated in Figure 10.5:

1. The parser begins with the **sentence** network and tries to move along the arc labeled noun_phrase. To do so, it retrieves the network for noun_phrase.

2. In the noun_phrase network, the parser first tries the transition marked article. This causes it to branch to the network for article.

3. It fails to find a path to the finish node of the article network because the first word of the sentence, "Dog," matches neither of the arc labels. The parser fails and backtracks to the noun_phrase network.

4. The parser attempts to follow the arc labeled noun in the noun_phrase network and branches to the network for noun.

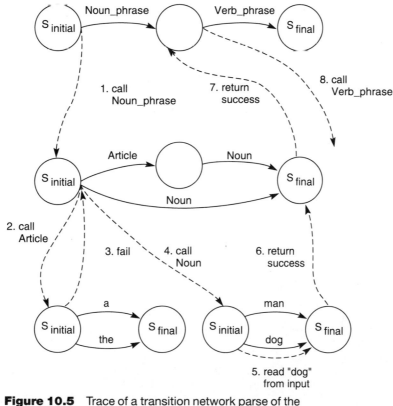

Figure 10.5   Trace of a transition network parse of the sentence "Dog bites."

5. The parser successfully crosses the arc labeled "dog," because this corresponds to the first word of the input stream.

6. The noun network returns success. This allows the arc labeled noun in the noun_phrase network to be crossed to the final state.

7. The noun_phrase network returns success to the top-level network, allowing the transition of the arc labeled noun_phrase.

8. Similar steps are followed in parsing the verb_phrase portion of the sentence.

Pseudocode for a transition network parser appears below. It is defined using two mutually recursive functions, parse and transition. Parse takes a grammar symbol as argument: if the symbol is a terminal, parse checks it against the next word in the input stream. If it is a nonterminal, parse retrieves the transition network associated with the symbol and calls transition to find a path through the network. Transition takes a state in a transition network as argument and tries to find a path through that network in a depth-first fashion. To parse a sentence, call parse(sentence).

```
function parse(grammar_symbol);

begin
  save pointer to current location in input stream;
  case

    grammar_symbol is a terminal:
      if grammar_symbol matches the next word in the input stream
        then return (success)
        else begin
          reset input stream;
          return (failure);
        end;

    grammar_symbol is a nonterminal:
      begin
        retrieve the transition network labeled by grammar symbol;
        state := start state of network;
        if transition(state) returns success
        then return (success)
        else begin
          reset input stream;
          return (failure);
        end;

    end;
end.
```

```
function  transition (current_state);

begin
  case

    current_state is a final state:
      return (success)

    current_state is not a final state:
      while there are unexamined transitions out of current_state
        do begin
          grammar_symbol := the label on the next unexamined transition;
          if parse(grammar_symbol) returns (success)
            then begin
              next_state := state at end of the transition;
              if transition(next_state) returns success
                  then return (success);
            end;
        end;

  end case;

  return (failure)
end.
```

Because the parser may make a mistake and have to backtrack, **parse** retains a pointer to the current location in the input stream. This allows the input stream to be **reset** to this location in the event the parser backtracks.

This transition network parser determines whether a sentence is grammatically correct, but it does not construct a parse tree. This may be accomplished by having the functions return a subtree of the parse tree instead of the symbol **success**. Modifications that would accomplish this are:

1. Each time the function **parse** is called with a terminal symbol as argument and that terminal matches the next symbol of input, it returns a tree consisting of a single leaf node labeled with that symbol.

2. When **parse** is called with a nonterminal, grammar_symbol, it calls **transition**. If **transition** succeeds, it returns an ordered set of subtrees (described below). **Parse** combines these into a tree whose root is grammar_symbol and whose children are the subtrees returned by **transition**.

3. In searching for a path through a network, **transition** calls **parse** on the label of each arc. On success, **parse** returns a tree representing a parse of that symbol. **Transition** saves these subtrees in an ordered set and, on finding a path through the network, returns the ordered set of parse trees corresponding to the sequence of arc labels on the path.

10.2.3 The Chomsky Hierarchy and Context-Sensitive Grammars

In Section 10.2.1, we defined a small subset of English using a *context-free grammar*. A context-free grammar allows rules to have only a single nonterminal on their left-hand side. Consequently, the rule may be applied to any occurrence of that symbol, regardless of its context. Though context-free grammars have proved to be a powerful tool for defining programming languages and other formalisms in computer science, there is reason to believe that they are not powerful enough, by themselves, to represent the rules of natural language syntax. For example, consider what happens if we add both singular and plural nouns and verbs to the grammar of Section 10.2.1:

noun ↔ men

noun ↔ dogs

verb ↔ bite

verb ↔ like

Although the resulting grammar will parse such sentences as "The dogs like the men," it will also accept ungrammatical sentences such as "A men likes a dogs." The parser will accept the erroneous sentence because the rules cannot use context to determine when the singular or plural forms must be used. For example, the rule defining a **sentence** as a **noun_phrase** followed by a **verb_phrase** cannot require that the subject and verb agree on number; the same problem occurs in trying to enforce article/noun agreement.

Languages defined by context-free grammars are only one in a hierarchy of classes of formal languages. This is the *Chomsky hierarchy* (Hopcroft and Ullman 1979; Chomsky 1965). At the bottom of the hierarchy is the class of *regular languages*. A regular language is one whose grammar may be defined using a finite-state machine. Although regular languages have many uses in computer science, they are not powerful enough to represent the syntax of most programming languages.

The *context-free languages* are above the regular languages in the Chomsky hierarchy. Context-free languages are defined using rewrite rules such as in Section 10.2.1; context-free rules may only have one nonterminal symbol on their left-hand side. Transition network parsers are able to parse the class of context-free languages. It is interesting to note that if we *do not* allow recursion in a transition network parser (i.e., arcs may be labeled only with terminal symbols, transitions may not "call" another network), then the class of languages that may be so defined corresponds to regular expressions. Thus, regular languages are a proper subset of the context-free languages.

The *context-sensitive* languages form a proper superset of the context-free languages. These are defined using *context-sensitive grammars* which allow more than one symbol on the left-hand side of a rule and make it possible to define a context in which that rule can be applied. This is used to ensure satisfaction of global constraints such as number agreement and other semantic checks. The only restriction on context-sensitive grammar rules is that the right-hand side be at least as long as the left-hand side of the rule (Hopcroft and Ullman 1979).

A fourth class, forming a superset of the context-sensitive languages, is the class of *recursively enumerable* languages. Recursively enumerable languages may be defined using unconstrained production rules; because these rules are less constrained than context-sensitive rules, the recursively enumerable languages are a proper superset of the context-sensitive languages. This class is not of interest in defining the syntax of natural language, although it is important in the theory of computer science. The remainder of this section focuses on English as a context-sensitive language.

A context-sensitive grammar for sentences of the form article noun verb that enforces number agreement both between article and noun and between subject and verb is given by:

sentence ↔ noun_phrase verb_phrase

noun_phrase ↔ article number noun

noun_phrase ↔ number noun

number ↔ singular

number ↔ plural

article singular ↔ a singular

article singular ↔ the singular

article plural ↔ some plural

article plural ↔ the plural

singular noun ↔ dog singular

singular noun ↔ man singular

plural noun ↔ men plural

plural noun ↔ dogs plural

singular verb_phrase ↔ singular verb

plural verb_phrase ↔ plural verb

singular verb ↔ bites

singular verb ↔ likes

plural verb ↔ bite

plural verb ↔ like

In this grammar, the nonterminals singular and plural provide a context to determine when different article, noun, and verb_phrase rules can be applied. This ensures number agreement. A derivation of the sentence "The dogs bite" using this grammar is given by:

sentence.

noun_phrase verb_phrase.

article plural noun verb_phrase.

The plural noun verb_phrase.

The dogs plural verb_phrase.

The dogs plural verb.

The dogs bite.

Similarly, we can use context-sensitive grammars to perform certain checks for semantic agreement. For example, we could disallow sentences such as "Man bites dog" by adding a nonterminal, act_of_biting, to the grammar. This nonterminal could be checked in the rules to prevent any sentence involving "bites" from having "man" as its subject.

Though context-sensitive grammars can define language structures that cannot be captured using context-free grammars, they have a number of disadvantages for the design of practical parsers:

1. Context-sensitive grammars increase drastically the number of rules and nonterminals in the grammar. Imagine the complexity of a context-sensitive grammar that would include number, person, and all the other forms of agreement required by English.

2. They obscure the phrase structure of the language that is so clearly represented in the context-free rules.

3. By attempting to handle more complicated checks for agreement and semantic consistency in the grammar itself, they lose many of the benefits of separating the syntactic and semantic components of language.

4. Context-sensitive grammars do not address the problem of building a semantic representation of the meaning of the text. A parser that simply accepts or rejects sentences is not sufficient; it must return a useful representation of the sentence's semantic meaning.

In the next section we examine *augmented transition networks* (ATNs), an extension of transition networks that can define context-sensitive languages but has several advantages over context-sensitive grammars in the design of parsers.

10.3   Combining Syntax and Semantics in ATN Parsers

An alternative to context-sensitive grammars is to retain the simpler structure of context-free grammar rules but augment these rules with attached procedures that perform the necessary contextual tests. These procedures are executed when a rule is invoked in parsing. Rather than using the grammar to describe such notions as number, tense, and person, we represent these as *features* attached to terminals and nonterminals of the grammar. The procedures attached to the rules of the grammar access these features to assign values and perform the necessary tests. Grammars that use augmentations of context-free grammars to implement context sensitivity include *augmented phrase structure grammars* (Heidorn 1975; Sowa 1984), *augmentations of logic grammars* (Allen 1987), and the *augmented transition network* (ATN).

In this section we present ATN parsing and outline the design of a simple ATN parser for sentences about the "dogs world" introduced in Section 10.2.1. We address the first two steps of Figure 10.2: creation of a parse tree and its use to construct a representation of the sentence's meaning. We use conceptual graphs in this example, although ATN parsers can also be used with script, frame, or logic representations.

10.3.1 Augmented Transition Network Parsers

Augmented transition networks extend transition networks by allowing procedures to be attached to the arcs of the networks. An ATN parser executes these attached procedures when it traverses the arcs. The procedures may assign values to grammatical features and perform tests, causing a transition to fail if certain conditions (such as number agreement) are not met. These procedures also construct a parse tree, which is used to generate an internal semantic representation of the sentence's meaning.

We represent both terminals and nonterminals as identifiers (e.g., verb, noun_phrase) with attached features. For example, a word is described using its morphological root, along with features for its part of speech, number, person, etc. Nonterminals in the grammar are similarly described. A noun phrase is described by its article, noun, number, and person. Both terminals and nonterminals can be represented using framelike structures with named slots and values. The values of these slots specify grammatical features or pointers to other structures. For example, the first slot of a sentence frame contains a pointer to a noun phrase definition. Figure 10.6 shows the frames for the sentence, noun_phrase, and verb_phrase nonterminals in our simple grammar.

Individual words are represented using similar structures. Each word in the dictionary is defined by a frame that specifies its part of speech (article, noun, etc.), its morphological root, and its significant grammatical features. In our example, we are only checking for number agreement and only record this feature. More sophisticated grammars indicate person and other features. These dictionary entries may also indicate the conceptual graph definition of the word's meaning for use in semantic interpretation. The complete dictionary for our grammar appears in Figure 10.7.

Figure 10.8 defines an ATN for our grammar, with pseudocode descriptions of the tests performed at each arc. Arcs are labeled with both nonterminals of the grammar (as in Fig. 10.4) and numbers; these numbers are used to indicate the procedure attached to each arc. The procedure is called after the arc is successfully traversed.

When the parser calls a network for a nonterminal, it creates a new frame for that nonterminal. For example, on entering the noun_phrase network it creates a new noun_phrase frame. The slots of the frame are filled by the procedures for that network. These slots may be assigned values of grammatical features or pointers to components of the syntactic structure (e.g., a verb_phrase consists of a verb and a noun phrase). When the final state is reached, the network returns this structure.

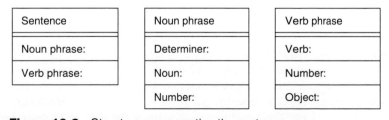

Figure 10.6 Structures representing the sentence, noun phrase, and verb phrase nonterminals of the grammar.

Word	Definition	Word	Definition

a	PART_OF_SPEECH: article	like	PART_OF_SPEECH: verb
	ROOT: a		ROOT: like
	NUMBER: singular		NUMBER: plural

bite	PART_OF_SPEECH: verb	likes	PART_OF_SPEECH: verb
	ROOT: bite		ROOT: like
	NUMBER: plural		NUMBER: singular

bites	PART_OF_SPEECH: verb	man	PART_OF_SPEECH: noun
	ROOT: bite		ROOT: man
	NUMBER: singular		NUMBER: singular

dog	PART_OF_SPEECH: noun	men	PART_OF_SPEECH: noun
	ROOT: dog		ROOT: man
	NUMBER: singular		NUMBER: plural

dogs	PART_OF_SPEECH: noun	the	PART_OF_SPEECH: article
	ROOT: dog		ROOT: the
	NUMBER: plural		NUMBER: plural or singular

Figure 10.7   Dictionary entries for a simple ATN.

When the network traverses arcs labeled noun, article, and verb, it reads the next word from the input stream and retrieves that word's definition from the dictionary. If the word is not the expected part of speech, the rule fails; otherwise the definition frame is returned.

In Figure 10.8 frames and slots are indicated using a Pascal-style record notation; e.g., the number slot of the verb frame is indicated by VERB.NUMBER.

As the parse proceeds, each procedure builds and returns a frame describing the associated syntactic structure. This structure includes pointers to structures returned by lower-level networks. The top-level sentence procedure returns a sentence structure representing the parse tree for the input. This structure is passed to the semantic interpreter. Figure 10.9 shows the parse tree that is returned for the sentence "The dog likes a man."

The next phase of natural language processing takes the parse tree (such as in Fig. 10.9) and builds a semantic representation of the meaning.

sentence:

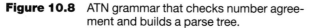

procedure sentence-1;
  begin
    NOUN_PHRASE := structure returned by
      noun_phrase network;

    SENTENCE.SUBJECT := NOUN_PHRASE;
  end.

procedure sentence-2;
  begin
    VERB_PHRASE := structure returned by
      verb_phrase network;

    if NOUN_PHRASE.NUMBER =
                VERB_PHRASE.NUMBER
      then begin
        SENTENCE.VERB_PHRASE := VERB_PHRASE;
        return SENTENCE
      end
      else fail
  end.

noun_phrase:

procedure noun_phrase-1;
  begin
    ARTICLE := definition frame for next word of input;

    if ARTICLE.PART_OF_SPEECH=article
      then NOUN_PHRASE.DETERMINER := ARTICLE
      else fail
  end.

procedure noun_phrase-2;
  begin
    NOUN := definition frame for next word of input;

    if NOUN.PART_OF_SPEECH=verb and
      NOUN.NUMBER agrees with
          NOUN_PHRASE.DETERMINER.NUMBER
      then begin
        NOUN_PHRASE.NOUN := NOUN;
        NOUN_PHRASE.NUMBER := NOUN.NUMBER
        return NOUN_PHRASE
      end
      else fail
  end.

Figure 10.8 ATN grammar that checks number agreement and builds a parse tree.

10.3.2 Combining Syntax and Semantics

The semantic interpreter constructs a representation of the input string's meaning by beginning at the root, or **sentence** node, and traversing the parse tree. At each node, it recursively interprets the children of that node and combines the results into a single conceptual graph; this graph is passed up the tree. For example, the semantic interpreter builds a rep-

```
procedure noun_phrase-3
  begin
    NOUN := definition frame for next word of input;

    if NOUN.PART_OF_SPEECH=noun
      then begin
        NOUN_PHRASE.DETERMINER := unspecified;
        NOUN_PHRASE.NOUN := NOUN
        NOUN_PHRASE.NUMBER := NOUN.NUMBER
      end
      else fail
  end.
```

verb_phrase:

```
procedure verb_phrase-1
  begin
    VERB := definition frame for next word of input;

    if VERB.PART_OF_SPEECH=verb
      then begin
        VERB_PHRASE.VERB := VERB;
        VERB_PHRASE.NUMBER := VERB.NUMBER;
      end;
  end.
```

```
procedure verb_phrase-2
  begin
    NOUN_PHRASE := structure returned by
                           noun_phrase network;

    VERB_PHRASE.OBJECT := NOUN_PHRASE;
    return VERB_PHRASE
  end.
```

```
procedure verb_phrase-3
  begin
    VERB := definition frame for next word of input;

    if VERB.PART_OF_SPEECH=verb
      then begin
        VERB_PHRASE.VERB := VERB;
        VERB_PHRASE.NUMBER := VERB.NUMBER;
        VERB_PHRASE.OBJECT := unspecified;
        return VERB_PHRASE;
      end;
  end.
```

Figure 10.8 cont'd   ATN grammar that checks number
agreement and builds a parse tree.

resentation of the verb_phrase by recursively building representations of the node's children, verb and noun_phrase, and joining these to form an interpretation of the verb phrase. This is passed to the sentence node and combined with the representation of the subject.

Recursion stops at the terminals of the parse tree. Some of these, such as nouns, verbs, and adjectives, cause concepts to be retrieved from the knowledge base. Others, such as

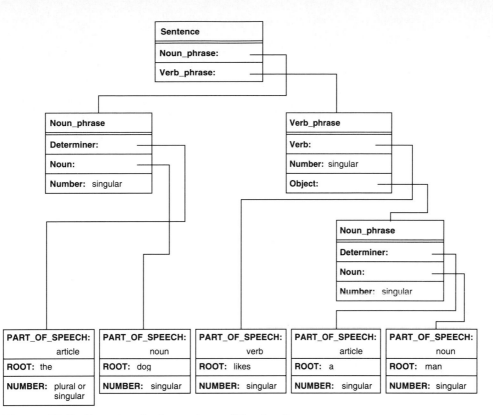

Figure 10.9 Parse tree for the sentence "The dog likes a man" returned by an ATN parser.

articles, do not directly correspond to concepts in the knowledge base but qualify other concepts in the graph.

The semantic interpreter in our example uses a knowledge base for the "dogs world." Concepts in the knowledge base include the objects dog and man and the actions like and bite. These concepts are described by the type hierarchy of Figure 10.10.

In addition to concepts, we must define the relations that will be used in our conceptual graphs. For this example, we use the following concepts:

agent links an act with a concept of type animate. agent defines the relation between an action and the animate object causing the action.

experiencer links a state with a concept of type animate. It defines the relation between a mental state and its experiencer.

instrument links an act with an entity and defines the instrument used to perform an action.

object links an event or state with an entity and represents the verb-object relation.

part links two concepts of type physobj and defines the relation between a whole and a part.

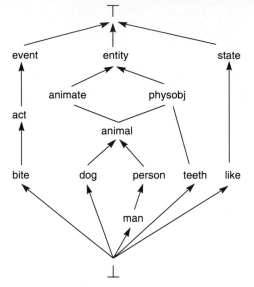

Figure 10.10 Type hierarchy used in "dogs world" example.

The verb plays a particularly important role in building an interpretation, as it defines the relationships between the subject, object, and other components of the sentence. We represent each verb using a *case frame* that specifies:

1. The linguistic relationships (agent, object, instrument, etc.) appropriate to that verb. Transitive verbs, for example, have an object; intransitive verbs do not.

2. Constraints on the values that may be assigned to any component of the case frame. For example, in the case frame for the verb "bites," we have asserted that the **agent** must be of the type **dog**. This causes "Man bites dog" to be rejected as semantically incorrect.

3. Default values on components of the case frame. In the "bites" frame, we have a default value of **teeth** for the concept linked to the **instrument** relation.

The case frames for the verbs **like** and **bite** appear in Figure 10.11.

We define the actions that build a semantic representation with rules or procedures for each potential node in the parse tree. Rules for our example are described as pseudocode procedures. In each procedure, if a specified join or other test fails, that interpretation is rejected as semantically incorrect:

```
procedure sentence;
  begin
    call noun_phrase to get a representation of the subject;
    call verb_phrase to get a representation of the verb_phrase;
    using join and restrict, bind the noun concept returned for the subject to
      the agent of the graph for the verb_phrase
  end.
```

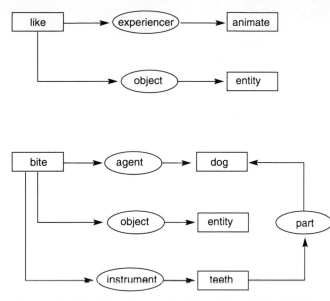

Figure 10.11   Case frames for the verbs "like" and "bite."

```
procedure noun_phrase;
  begin
    call noun to get a representation of the noun;
    case
      the article is indefinite and number singular:  the noun concept is generic;
      the article is definite and number singular: bind marker to noun concept;
      number is plural: indicate that the noun concept is plural
    end case
  end.


procedure verb_phrase;
  begin
    call verb to get a representation of the verb;
    if the verb has an object
      then begin
        call noun_phrase to get a representation of the object;
        using join and restrict, bind concept for object to object of the verb
      end
  end.


procedure verb;
  begin
    retrieve the case frame for the verb
  end.
```

```
procedure noun;
  begin
    retrieve the concept for the noun
  end.
```

Articles do not correspond to concepts in the knowledge base but determine whether their noun concept is generic or specific. We have not discussed the representation of plural concepts; refer to Sowa (1984) for their treatment in conceptual graphs.

Using these procedures, along with the concept hierarchy of Figure 10.10 and the case frames of Figure 10.11, we trace the actions of the semantic interpreter in building a semantic representation of the sentence "The dog likes a man" from the parse tree of Figure 10.9. This trace appears in Figure 10.12.

The actions taken in the trace are (numbers refer to Figure 10.12):

Beginning at the sentence node, call **sentence**.

sentence calls **noun_phrase**.

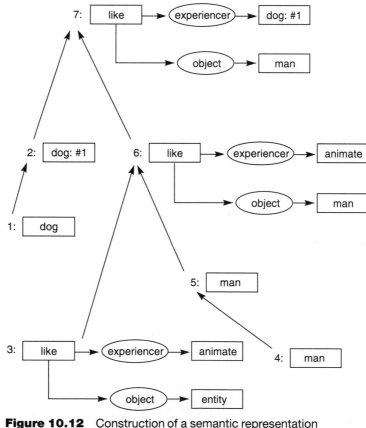

Figure 10.12 Construction of a semantic representation from the parse tree of Figure 10.9.

noun_phrase calls noun.

noun returns a concept for the noun dog (1 in Figure 10.12).

Because the article is definite, noun_phrase binds an individual marker to the concept (2) and returns this concept to sentence.

sentence calls verb_phrase.

verb_phrase calls verb, which retrieves the case frame for like (3).

verb_phrase calls noun_phrase, calls noun to retrieve the concept for man (4).

Because the article is indefinite, noun_phrase leaves this concept generic (5).

The verb_phrase procedure restricts the entity concept in the case frame and joins it with the concept for man (6). This structure is returned to sentence.

sentence joins the concept dog: #1 to the experiencer node of the case frame (7). This conceptual graph represents the meaning of the sentence.

Section 10.4 shows how a program can build an internal representation of natural language text. This representation is used by the program in a number of ways, depending on the particular application. Two such applications are discussed.

Language generation is a related problem addressed by natural language understanding programs. The generation of English sentences requires the construction of a semantically correct output from an internal representation of meaning. For example, the agent relation indicates a subject-verb relationship between two concepts. Simple approaches allow the appropriate words to be plugged into stored sentence *templates*. These templates are patterns for sentences and fragments, such as noun phrases and prepositional phrases. The output is constructed by walking the conceptual graph and combining these fragments. More sophisticated approaches use transformational grammars to map meaning into a range of possible sentences (Winograd 1972; Allen 1987).

10.4   Natural Language Applications

10.4.1   Story Understanding and Question Answering

An interesting test for natural language understanding technology is to write a program that can read a story or other piece of natural language text and answer questions about it. In Chapter 9 we discussed some of the representational issues involved in story understanding, including the importance of combining background knowledge with the explicit content of the text. As illustrated in Figure 10.2, a program can accomplish this by performing network joins between the semantic interpretation of the input and conceptual graph structures in a knowledge base. More sophisticated representations, such as scripts, can help to model more complex situations involving events occurring over time.

Once the program has built an expanded representation of the text, it can intelligently answer questions about what it has read. The program parses the question into an internal representation and matches that query against the expanded representation of the story.

Consider the example of Figure 10.2. The program has read the sentence "Tarzan kissed Jane" and built an expanded representation.

Assume that we ask the program "Who loves Jane?" In parsing the question, the interrogative (who, what, why, etc.) indicates the intention of the question. *Who* questions ask for the agent of the action; *what* questions ask for the object of the action; *how* questions ask for the means by which the action was performed; etc. The question "Who loves Jane?" produces the graph of Figure 10.13. The **agent** node of the graph is marked with a ? to indicate that it is the goal of the question.

This structure is then joined with the expanded representation of the original text. The concept that becomes bound to the **person: ?** concept in the query graph is the answer to the question: "Tarzan loves Jane."

10.4.2 A Data Base Front End

The major bottleneck in designing natural language understanding programs is the acquisition of sufficient knowledge about the domain of discourse. Current technology is limited to narrow domains with well-defined semantics. An application area that meets these criteria is the development of natural language front ends for data bases. Although data bases store enormous amounts of information, that information is highly regular and narrow in scope; furthermore, data base semantics are well defined. These features, along with the utility of a data base that can accept natural language queries, make data base front ends an important application of natural language understanding technology.

The task of a data base front end is to translate a question in natural language into a well-formed query in the data base language. For example, using the SQL data base language as a target (Ullman 1982), the natural language front end would translate the question "Who hired John Smith?" into the query:

```
SELECT MANAGER
FROM MANAGER_OF_HIRE
WHERE EMPLOYEE = 'John Smith'
```

In performing this translation, the program must do more than translate the original query; it must also decide where to look in the data base (the MANAGER_OF_HIRE relation), the name of the field to access (MANAGER), and the constraints on the query (EMPLOYEE = 'John Smith'). None of this information was in the original question; it

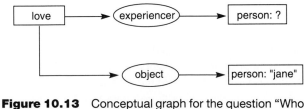

Figure 10.13 Conceptual graph for the question "Who loves Jane?"

was found in a knowledge base that knew about the organization of the data base and the meaning of potential questions.

A *relational data base* organizes data in relations across domains of entities. For example, suppose we are constructing a data base of employees and would like to access the salary of each employee and the manager who hired her. This data base would consist of three *domains*, or sets of entities: the set of managers, the set of employees, and the set of salaries. We could organize these data into two relations, employee_salary, which relates an employee and her salary, and manager_of_hire, which relates an employee and her manager. In a relational data base, relations are usually displayed as tables that enumerate the instances of the relation. The columns of the tables are often named; these names are called *attributes* of the relation. Figure 10.14 shows the tables for the employee_salary and the manager_of_hire relations. Manager_of_hire has two attributes, the employee and the manager. The values of the relation are the pairs of employees and managers.

If we assume that employees have a unique name, manager, and salary, then the employee name is a *key* for both salary and manager. An attribute is a key for another attribute if it uniquely determines the value of elements for the other attribute. A valid query indicates a target attribute and specifies a value or set of constraints; the data base returns the specified values of the target attribute. We can indicate the relationship between keys and other attributes graphically in a number of ways, including *entity-relationship diagrams* (Ullman 1982) and *data flow diagrams* (Sowa 1984). Both of these approaches display the mapping of keys onto attributes using directed graphs.

We can extend conceptual graphs to include diagrams of these relationships (Sowa 1984). The data base relation that defines the mapping is indicated by a rhombus, which is labeled with the name of the relation. The attributes of the relation are expressed as concepts in a conceptual graph and the direction of the arrows indicates the mapping of keys onto other attributes. Figure 10.15 shows the entity-relation graphs for the employee_salary and manager_of_hire relations.

In translating from English to a formal query, we must determine the record that contains the answer, the field of that record that must be returned, and the values of the keys that determine that field. Rather than translating directly from English into the data base language, we first translate into a more expressive language such as conceptual graphs. This is necessary because many English queries are ambiguous or require additional inter-

manager_of_hire:		employee_salary:	
employee	manager	employee	salary
John Smith	Jane Martinez	John Smith	$35,000.00
Alex Barrero	Ed Angel	Alex Barrero	$42,000.00
Don Morrison	Jane Martinez	Don Morrison	$50,000.00
Jan Claus	Ed Angel	Jan Claus	$40,000.00
Anne Cable	Bob Veroff	Anne Cable	$45,000.00

Figure 10.14   Two relations in an employee data base.

pretation to produce a well-formed data base query. The use of a more expressive representation language helps this process.

The natural language front end parses and interprets the query into a conceptual graph, as described earlier in this chapter. It then combines this graph with information in the knowledge base using join and restrict operations. In this example, we want to handle queries such as "Who hired John Smith?" or "How much does John Smith earn?" For each potential query, we store a graph that defines its verb, the case roles for that verb, and any relevant entity-relationship diagrams for the question. Figure 10.16 shows the knowledge base entry for the verb "hire."

The semantic interpreter produces a graph of the user's query and joins this graph with the appropriate knowledge base entry. If there is an attached entity relation graph that maps keys into the goal of the question, the program can use this entity relation graph to form a data base query. Figure 10.17 shows the query graph for the question "Who hired John Smith?" and the result of joining this with the knowledge base entry from Figure 10.16. It also shows the SQL query that is formed from this graph. Note that the name of the appro-

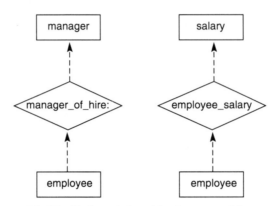

Figure 10.15 Entity-relationship diagrams of the manager_of_hire and employee_salary relations.

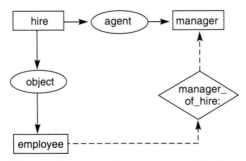

Figure 10.16 Knowledge base entry for "hire" queries.

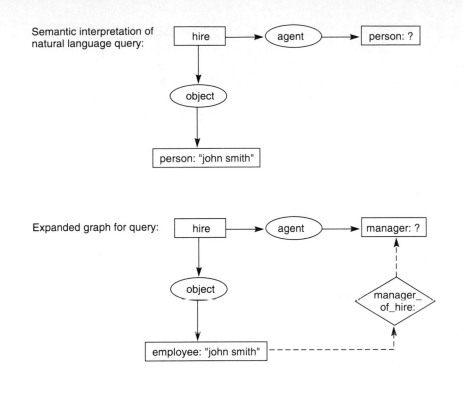

Semantic interpretation of natural language query:

Expanded graph for query:

Query in SQL data base language:

SELECT MANAGER
FROM MANAGER_OF_HIRE
WHERE EMPLOYEE = "john smith"

Figure 10.17 Development of a data base query from the graph of a natural language input.

priate record, the target field, and the key for the query were not specified in the natural language query. These were inferred by the knowledge base.

In Figure 10.17 the agent and object of the original query were known only to be of type person. To join these with the knowledge base entry for hire, they were first restricted to types manager and employee, respectively. The type hierarchy could thus be used to perform type checking on the original query. If john smith were not of type employee, the question would be invalid and the program could detect this.

Once the expanded query graph is built, the program examines the target concept, flagged with a ?, and determines that the manager_of_hire relation mapped a key onto this concept. Because the key is bound to a value of john smith, the question was valid and the program could form the proper data base query. Translation of the entity relationship graph into SQL or some other language is straightforward.

Although this example is simplified, it illustrates the use of a knowledge-based approach to building a natural language data base front end. The ideas in our example are expressed in conceptual graphs but could be mapped into other representations such as frames or logic-based languages.

10.5   Epilogue and References

As this chapter suggests, there are a number of approaches to defining grammars and parsing sentences in natural language. We have presented ATN parsers as a typical example of these approaches, although the serious student should be aware of other possibilities. These include *transformational grammars*, *semantic grammars*, *case grammars*, and *feature and function grammars* (Winograd 1983; Allen 1987).

Transformational grammars use context-free rules to represent the *deep structure*, or meaning, of the sentence. This deep structure may be represented as a parse tree that not only consists of terminals and nonterminals but also includes a set of symbols called *grammatical markers*. These grammatical markers represent such features as number, tense, and other context-sensitive aspects of linguistic structure. Next, a higher-level set of rules called transformational rules transform between this deep structure and a *surface structure*, which is closer to the actual form the sentence will have. For example, "Tom likes Jane" and "Jane is liked by Tom" will have the same deep structure but different surface structures.

Transformational rules act on parse trees themselves, performing the checks that require global context and produce a suitable surface structure. For example, a transformational rule may check that the number feature of the node representing the subject of a sentence is the same as the number feature of the verb node. Transformational rules may also map a single deep structure into alternative surface structures, such as changing active to passive voice or forming an assertion into a question. Although transformational grammars are not discussed in this text, they are an important alternative to augmented phrase structure grammars.

The various grammars presented here are not intended as models of the way in which human beings process natural language. This misconception was at the root of many of the criticisms aimed at Chomsky and other early workers in natural language by people who felt that the extreme formality of these approaches was not plausibly implemented in the human mind. Instead, as these linguists have emphasized, these models should be seen as mathematical abstractions that capture the knowledge of syntax that is used by people in the act of producing or understanding language. People may not have ATNs in their heads, but they do use equivalent knowledge of syntax and semantics in their everyday understanding. ATNs are a computationally feasible way of capturing this knowledge.

A comprehensive treatment of grammars and parsing techniques for natural language can be found in Terry Winograd's *Language as a Cognitive Process* (1983). This book offers a particularly thorough treatment of transformational grammars. *Natural Language Understanding* by James Allen (1987) provides an overview of the design and implementation of natural language understanding programs. *Introduction to Natural Language Processing* by Mary Dee Harris (1985) is another general text on natural language that expands on the issues raised in this chapter. Syntax is the most widely explored area of natural language understanding, and numerous books provide further discussion of this topic.

The semantic analysis of natural language involves a number of difficult issues that are addressed in the literature on knowledge representation (Chapter 9). In *Computational Semantics*, Charniak and Wilks (1976) have collected articles that address these issues in the context of natural language understanding.

Because of the difficulty in modeling the knowledge and social context required for natural language interaction, many authors have questioned the possibility of moving this technology beyond constrained domains. *Understanding Computers and Cognition* by Winograd and Flores (1986) and *Minds, Brains, and Programs* by John Searle (1980) address these issues.

Inside Computer Understanding by Schank and Riesbeck (1981) discusses natural language understanding using conceptual dependency technology. *Scripts, Plans, Goals and Understanding* by Schank and Abelson (1977) discusses the role of higher-level knowledge organization structures in natural language programs.

Speech Acts by John Searle (1969) discusses the role of pragmatics and contextual knowledge in modeling discourse. Fass and Wilks (1983) have proposed *semantic preference theory* as a vehicle for modeling natural language semantics. Semantic preference is a generalization of case grammars that allows transformations on case frames. This provides greater flexibility in representing semantics and allows the representation of such concepts as metaphor and analogy.

For a full discussion of the Chomsky hierarchy the reader may refer to any text on formal language theory (Hopcroft and Ullman 1979). We are indebted to John Sowa's *Conceptual Structures* (1984) for our treatment of conceptual graphs, including the discussion of modeling data base semantics.

10.6 Exercises

1. Classify each of the following sentences as either syntactically incorrect, syntactically correct but meaningless, meaningful but untrue, or true. Where in the understanding process is each of these problems detected?

   > Colorless green ideas sleep furiously.
   > Fruit flies like a banana.
   > Dogs the bite man a.
   > George Washington was the fifth president of the USA.
   > This exercise is easy.
   > I want to be under the sea in an octopus's garden in the shade.

2. Discuss the representational structures and knowledge necessary to understand the following sentences.

   > The brown dog ate the bone.
   > Attach the large wheel to the axle with the hex nut.
   > Mary watered the plants.
   > The spirit is willing but the flesh is weak.
   > My kingdom for a horse!

3. Parse each of these sentences using the "dogs world" grammar of Section 10.2.1. Which of these are illegal sentences? Why?

   > The dog bites the dog.
   > The big dog bites the man.

Emma likes the boy.
The man likes.
Bite the man.

4. Extend the dogs world grammar so it will include the illegal sentences in Exercise 3.

5. Parse each of these sentences using the context-sensitive grammar of Section 10.2.3.

The men like the dog.
The dog bites the man.

6. Produce a parse tree for each of the following sentences. You will have to extend our simple grammars with more complex linguistic constructs such as adverbs, adjectives, and prepositional phrases. If a sentence has more than one parsing, diagram all of them and explain the semantic information that would be used to choose a parsing.

Time flies like an arrow but fruit flies like a banana.
Tom gave the big, red book to Mary on Tuesday.
Reasoning is an art and not a science.
To err is human, to forgive divine.

7. Extend the dogs world grammar to include adjectives in noun phrases. Be sure to allow an indeterminate number of adjectives. Hint: use a recursive rule, adjective_list, that either is empty or contains an adjective followed by an adjective list. Map this grammar into transition networks.

8. Add the following context-free grammar rules to the dogs world grammar of Section 10.2.1. Map the resulting grammar into transition networks.

sentence ↔ noun_phrase verb_phrase prepositional_phrase
prepositional_phrase ↔ preposition noun_phrase
preposition ↔ with
preposition ↔ to
preposition ↔ on

9. Define an ATN parser for the dogs world grammar with adjectives (Exercise 7) and prepositional phrases (Exercise 8).

10. Define concepts and relations in conceptual graphs needed to represent the meaning of the grammar of Exercise 9. Define the procedures for building a semantic representation from the parse tree.

11. Extend the context-sensitive grammar of Section 10.2.3 to test for semantic agreement between the subject and verb. Specifically, men should not bite dogs, although dogs can either like or bite men. Perform a similar modification to the ATN grammar.

12. Expand the ATN grammar of Section 10.2.4 to include *who* and *what* questions.

13. Extend the data base front end example of Section 10.4.2 so that it will answer questions of the form "How much does Don Morrison earn?" You will need to extend the grammar, the representation language, and the knowledge base.

14. Assume that managers are listed in the employee_salary relation with other employees in the example of 10.4.2. Extend the example so that it will handle queries such as "Find any employee that earns more than his or her manager."

AUTOMATED REASONING

11

For how is it possible, says that acute man, that when a concept is given me, I can go beyond it and connect with it another which is not contained in it, in such a manner as if the latter necessarily *belonged to the former?*

—IMMANUEL KANT, "Prolegomena to a Future Metaphysics"

Any rational decision may be viewed as a conclusion reached from certain premises. . . . The behavior of a rational person can be controlled, therefore, if the value and factual premises upon which he bases his decisions are specified for him.

—SIMON, *Decision-Making and Administrative Organization,* 1944

Reasoning is an art and not a science. . . .

—WOS ET AL., *Automated Reasoning,* 1984

11.0 Introduction to Weak Methods in Theorem Proving

Wos et al. (1984) describe an *automated reasoning* program as one that "employs an unambiguous and exacting notation for representing information, precise inference rules for drawing conclusions, and carefully delineated strategies to control those inference rules". They add that applying strategies to inference rules to deduce new information is an art: "A good choice for representation includes a notation that increases the chance for solving a problem and includes information that, though not necessary, is helpful. A good choice of inference rules is one that meshes well with the chosen representation. A good choice for strategies is one that controls the inference rules in a manner that sharply increases the effectiveness of the reasoning program."

Automated reasoning, as just described, uses weak problem-solving methods. It uses a uniform representation such as the first-order predicate calculus (Chapter 2), the Horn clause calculus (Chapters 6 and 13), or the clause form used for resolution (Section 11.2). Its inference rules are sound and, whenever possible, complete. It uses general strategies such as breadth-first, depth-first, or best-first search and, as we see in this chapter, heuristics such as *set of support* and *unit preference* to combat the combinatorics of exhaustive search. The design of search strategies is very much an art; we cannot guarantee that they will find a useful solution to a problem using reasonable amounts of time and memory.

Weak method problem solving is an important tool in its own right as well as an essential basis for strong method problem solving. Production systems and rule-based expert system shells are both examples of weak method problem solvers. Even though the rules of the production system or rule-based expert system encode strong problem-solving heuristics, their application is supported by general (weak method) inference strategies.

Techniques for weak method problem solving have been the focus of AI research from its beginning. Quite often these techniques come under the heading of *theorem proving*, although we prefer the more generic title *automated reasoning*. We begin this chapter (Section 11.1) with an early example of automated reasoning, the *General Problem Solver*, and its use of *means-end analysis* and *difference tables* to control search. In Section 11.2 we present an important product of research in automated reasoning, the *resolution theorem prover*. We discuss the representation language, the resolution inference rule, the search strategies, and the answer extraction process used in resolution theorem proving. We conclude this chapter (Section 11.3) with some brief comments on *natural deduction*, equality handling, and more sophisticated inference rules.

11.1 The General Problem Solver and Difference Tables

The *General Problem Solver (GPS)* (Newell and Simon 1963*b*; Ernst and Newell 1969) came out of research by Allen Newell and Herbert Simon at Carnegie Mellon University, then Carnegie Institute of Technology. Its roots are in an earlier computer program called the *Logic Theorist (LT)* of Newell, Shaw, and Simon (Newell and Simon 1963*a*). The LT program proved many of the theorems in Russell and Whitehead's *Principia Mathematica* (Whitehead and Russell 1950).

As with all weak method problem solvers, the Logic Theorist employed a uniform representation medium and sound inference rules and adopted several strategies or heuristic methods to guide the solution process. The Logic Theorist used the propositional calculus (Section 2.1) as its representation medium. The inference rules were *substitution*, *replacement*, and *detachment*.

Substitution allows any expression to be substituted for every occurrence of a symbol in a proposition that is an axiom or theorem already known to be true. For instance, $(B \vee B) \rightarrow B$ may have the expression $\neg A$ substituted for B to produce $(\neg A \vee \neg A) \rightarrow \neg A$.

Replacement allows a connective to be replaced by its definition or an equivalent form. For example, the logical equivalence of $\neg A \vee B$ and $A \rightarrow B$ can lead to the replacement of $(\neg A \vee \neg A)$ with $(A \rightarrow \neg A)$.

Detachment is the inference rule we called modus ponens (Chapter 2).

The LT applies these inference rules in a breadth-first, goal-driven fashion to the theorem to be proved, attempting to find a series of operations that lead to axioms or theorems known to be true. The strategy of LT consists of four methods organized in an *executive routine*:

First, the substitution method is directly applied to the current goal, attempting to match it against all known axioms and theorems.

Second, if this fails to lead to a proof, all possible detachments and replacements are applied to the goal and each of these results is tested for success using substitution. If substitution fails to match any of these with the goal, then they are added to a *subproblem list*.

Third, the chaining method, employing the transitivity of implication, is used to find a new subproblem that, if solved, would provide a proof. Thus, if a → c is the problem and b → c is found, then a → b is set up as a new subproblem.

Fourth, if the first three methods fail on the original problem, go to the subproblem list and select the next untried subproblem.

The executive routine continues to apply these four methods until either the solution is found, no more problems remain on the subproblem list, or the memory and time allotted to finding the proof are exhausted. In this fashion, the logic theorist executes a goal-driven, breadth-first search of the problem space.

Part of the executive routine that enables the substitution, replacement, and detachment inference rules is the *matching process*. Suppose we wish to prove p → (q → p). The matching process first identifies one of the axioms, p → (q ∨ p), as more appropriate than the others—i.e., more nearly matching in terms of a domain-defined difference—because the main connective, here →, is the same in both expressions. Second, the matching process confirms that the expressions to the left of the main connective are identical. Finally, matching identifies the difference between expressions to the right of the main connective. This final difference, between → and ∨, suggests the obvious replacement for proving the theorem. The matching process helps control the (exhaustive) search that would be necessary for applying all substitutions, replacements, and detachments. In fact, the matching eliminated enough of the trial and error to make the LT into a successful problem solver.

A sample LT proof shows the power of the matching process. Theorem 2.02 of *Principia Mathematica* is p → (q → p). Matching immediately finds the axiom p → (q ∨ p) as appropriate for replacement. Substitution of ¬q for q proves the theorem. Matching, controlling substitution, and replacement rules proved this theorem directly without any search through other axioms or theorems.

In another example, suppose we wish LT to prove:

(p → ¬ p) → ¬ p.

1. (A ∨ A) → A	Matching identifies "best" axiom of five available.
2. (¬ A ∨ ¬ A) → ¬ A	Substitution of ¬ A for A in order to apply
3. (A → ¬ A) → ¬ A	replacement of → for ∧, and
4. (p → ¬ p) → ¬ p	substitution of p for A.
QED	

The original LT proved this theorem in about 10 seconds using five axioms. The actual proof took two steps and required no search. Matching selected the appropriate axiom for the first step because its form was much like the conclusion it was trying to establish: (expression) → proposition. Then ¬A was substituted for A. This allowed the replacement of the second and final step, which was itself motivated by the goal requiring a → rather than a ∨.

The Logic Theorist not only was the first example of an automated reasoning system but also demonstrated the importance of search strategies and heuristics in a reasoning program. In many instances LT found solutions in a few steps that exhaustive search might never find. Some theorems were not solvable by the LT, and Newell et al. pointed out improvements that might make their solution possible.

At about this time (1957) researchers at Carnegie and others at Yale (Moore and Anderson 1954) began to examine think-aloud protocols of human subjects solving logic problems. Although their primary goal was to identify human processes that could solve this class of problem, researchers began to compare human problem solving with computer programs, such as the Logic Theorist. This was to become the first instance of what is now referred to as *information processing psychology*, where an explanation of the observed behavior of an organism is provided by a program of primitive information processes that generates that behavior (Newell at el. 1958). We address this issue in more detail in Chapter 16.

Closer scrutiny of these first protocols showed many ways that LT's solutions differed from those of the human subjects. The human behavior showed strong evidence of a matching and difference reduction mechanism referred to as a *means-ends analysis.* In means-ends analysis the difference reduction methods (the *means*) were strongly linked to the specific differences to be reduced (the *ends*): the operators for difference reduction were indexed by the differences they could reduce.

In a very simple example, if the start statement was $p \rightarrow q$ and the goal was $\neg p \vee q$, the differences would include the → symbol in the start and ∨ in the goal (as well as the difference of p in the start and $\neg p$ in the goal). The difference table would contain the different ways that a → could be replaced by a ∨ and that ¬ could be removed. These transformations would be attempted one at a time until the differences were removed and the theorem was proven.

In most interesting problems the differences between start and goal could not be directly reduced. In this case an operator (from the table) was sought to partially reduce the difference. The entire procedure was applied recursively to these results until no differences existed. This might also require following different search paths, represented by different applications of reductions.

Figure 11.1 presents one of the proofs, from Newell and Simon (1963*a*), generated by a human subject. Before the proof, 12 rules are given for "reducing" expressions. The human subject, without experience in formal logic, is asked to change the expression $(R \supset \neg P) \bullet (\neg R \supset Q)$ to $\neg (\neg Q \bullet P)$. In the notation of this text ~ is ¬, • is ∧, and ⊃ is →. The → or ↔ of Figure 11.1 indicates a legal replacement. The difference reduction table (called the table of connections) for this problem is included as part of Figure 11.2.

Newell and Simon called the algorithm for applying means-ends analysis using difference reduction the *General Problem Solver.* The "methods" for GPS were described by Newell and Simon (1963*b*) using the flow diagram of Figure 11.2.

Objects are formed by building up expressions from letters (P, Q, R, ...) and connectives • (dot), $\vee$ (wedge), $\supset$ (horseshoe), and ~ (tilde). Examples are P, ~Q, P V Q, ~(R $\supset$ S) • ~P; ~~P is equivalent to P throughout.
Twelve rules exist for transforming expressions (where A, B, and C may be any expressions or subexpressions):

R 1.	$A \cdot B \rightarrow B \cdot A$ $A \vee B \rightarrow B \vee A$	R 8.	$A \cdot B \rightarrow A$ $A \cdot B \rightarrow B$	Applies to main expression only.
R 2.	$A \supset B \rightarrow \sim B \supset \sim A$	R 9.	$A \rightarrow A \vee X$	Applies to main expression only.
R 3.	$A \cdot A \leftrightarrow A$ $A \vee A \leftrightarrow A$	R 10.	$\left.\begin{matrix} A \\ B \end{matrix}\right\} \rightarrow A \cdot B$	A and B are two main expressions.
R 4.	$A \cdot (B \cdot C) \leftrightarrow (A \cdot B) \cdot C$ $A \vee (B \vee C) \leftrightarrow (A \vee B) \vee C$	R 11.	$\left.\begin{matrix} A \\ A \supset B \end{matrix}\right\} \rightarrow B \ldots C$	A and $A \supset B$ are two main expressions.
R 5.	$A \vee B \leftrightarrow \sim(\sim A \cdot \sim B)$	R 12.	$\left.\begin{matrix} A \supset B \\ B \supset C \end{matrix}\right\} \rightarrow A \supset C$	$A \supset B$ and $B \supset C$ are two main expressions.
R 6.	$A \supset B \leftrightarrow \sim A \vee B$			
R 7.	$A \cdot (B \vee C) \leftrightarrow (A \cdot B) \vee (A \cdot C)$ $A \vee (B \cdot C) \leftrightarrow (A \vee B) \cdot (A \vee C)$			

1.	$(R \supset \sim P) \cdot (\sim R \supset Q)$	$\sim(\sim Q \cdot P) \sim (\sim Q \cdot P)$
2.	$(\sim R \vee \sim P) \cdot (R \vee Q)$	Rule 6 applied to left and right of 1.
3.	$(\sim R \vee \sim P) \cdot (\sim R \supset Q)$	Rule 6 applied to left of 1.
4.	$R \supset \sim P$	Rule 8 applied to 1.
5.	$\sim R \vee \sim P$	Rule 6 applied to 4.
6.	$\sim R \supset Q$	Rule 8 applied to 1.
7.	$R \vee Q$	Rule 6 applied to 6.
8.	$(\sim R \vee \sim P) \cdot (R \vee Q)$	Rule 10 applied to 5 and 7.
9.	$P \supset \sim R$	Rule 2 applied to 4.
10.	$\sim Q \supset R$	Rule 2 applied to 6.
11.	$P \supset Q$	Rule 12 applied to 6 and 9.
12.	$\sim P \vee Q$	Rule 6 applied to 11.
13.	$\sim(P \cdot \sim Q)$	Rule 5 applied to 12.
14.	$\sim(\sim Q \cdot P)$	Rule 1 applied to 13. QED.

Figure 11.1 Transformation rules and trace of a GPS proof in the propositional calculus (Newell and Simon 1963*a*).

In Figure 11.2 the goal is to transform expression A into expression B. The first step is to locate a difference D between A and B. The subgoal, reduce D, is identified in the second box of the first line, and the reduction method is described in the second line of the diagram, where the operator Q is identified for reducing difference D. Actually, a list of

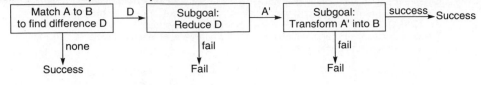

Goal: Transform object A into object B

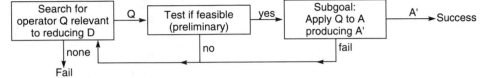

Goal: Reduce difference D between object A and object B

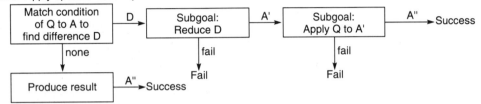

Goal: Apply operator Q to object A

For the logic task of the text:

Feasibility test (preliminary)
 Is the mean connective the same (e.g., A•B → B fails against P∨Q)?
 Is the operator too big (e.g., (A∨B)•(A∨C)→A∨(B•C) fails against P•Q)?
 Is the operator too easy (e.g., A→A•A applies to anything)?
 Are the side conditions satisfied (e.g., R8 applies only to main expressions)?

Table of connections

	R1	R2	R3	R4	R5	R6	R7	R8	R9	R10	R11	R12
Add terms			X				X		X	X	X	X
Delete terms			X				X	X			X	X
Change connective					X	X	X					
Change sign					X							
Change lower sign		X			X	X						
Change grouping				X			X					
Change position	X	X										

X means some variant of the rule is relevant. GPS will pick the appropriate variant.

Figure 11.2 Flowchart and difference reduction table for the General Problem Solver.

potential operators is identified from the table of connections. This list provides ordered alternatives for difference reduction should the chosen operator not be acceptable, for example, by not passing the *feasibility test* (Fig. 11.2). In the third line of Figure 11.2 the operator is applied and D is reduced.

The GPS model of problem solving requires two components. The first is a general procedure for comparing state descriptions and recognizing differences in them. This is similar to the matching process of the LT. The second component of the GPS model is the set of differences or *table of connections* appropriate to a particular application area. One table, like that in Figure 11.2, represents differences in propositional calculus expressions. Another could be for reducing differences between algebraic forms, and further tables could list the moves for tasks such as towers of Hanoi or more complex games such as chess. A number of the different application areas of the GPS technique are described by Ernst and Newell (1969).

The structuring of the difference reductions of a problem domain helps organize the search for that domain. A heuristic or priority order for reduction of different difference classes is implicit in the order of the transformations within the difference reduction table. This priority order might put the more generally applicable transformations before the specialized ones or give whatever order some domain expert might deem most appropriate.

A number of research directions evolved from work in the General Problem Solver. One of these is the use of AI techniques to analyze human problem-solving behavior. In particular, the production system replaced the means-ends methods of GPS as the preferred form for modeling human information processing (Chapter 16). The production rules in modern rule-based expert systems replaced the specific entries in GPS's table of differences.

In another interesting evolution of GPS, the difference table itself evolved in a further fashion, becoming the *operator table* for *planning* such as STRIPS and ABSTRIPS. Planning is important in robot problem solving. To accomplish a task, such as to go to the next room and bring back an object, the computer must develop a *plan*. This plan orchestrates the actions of the robot: put down anything it is now holding, go to the door of the present room, go through the door, find the required room, go through the door, go over to the object, and so on. Plan formation for STRIPS, the STanford Research Institute Problem Solver (Fikes and Nilsson 1971, 1972; Sacerdoti 1974) uses an operator table not unlike the GPS table of differences. Each operator (primitive act of the robot) in this table has an attached set of *preconditions* that are much like the feasibility tests of Figure 11.2. The operator table also contains *add* and *delete lists*, which update the model of the "world" once the operator is applied. We presented a predicate calculus–based planner in Chapters 5 and 6.

To summarize, the first models of automated reasoning in AI are found in the Logic Theorist and General Problem Solver developed at Carnegie Institute. Already these programs offered the full prerequisites for weak method problem solving: a uniform representation medium, a set of sound inference rules, and a set of methods or strategies for applying these rules. The same components make up the *resolution proof procedures*, a modern and more powerful basis for automated reasoning.

11.2 Resolution Theorem Proving

11.2.1 Introduction

Resolution is a technique for proving theorems in the propositional or predicate calculus that has been a part of AI problem-solving research from the mid-1960s (Bledsoe 1977; Robinson 1965; Kowalski 1979*b*). Resolution is a sound inference rule that, when used to produce a *refutation* (Section 11.2.3), is also complete. In an important practical application, resolution theorem proving, particularly the resolution refutation system, has made the current generation of PROLOG interpreters possible.

The resolution principle, introduced in an important paper by Robinson (1965), describes a way of finding contradictions in a data base of clauses with minimum use of substitution. Resolution refutation proves a theorem by negating the statement to be proved and adding this negated goal to the set of axioms that are known (have been assumed) to be true. It then uses the resolution rule of inference to show that this leads to a contradiction. Once the theorem prover shows that the negated goal is inconsistent with the given set of axioms, it follows that the original goal must be consistent. This proves the theorem.

Resolution refutation proofs involve the following steps:

1. Put the premises or axioms into *clause form* (11.2.2).

2. Add the negation of what is to be proved, in clause form, to the set of axioms.

3. *Resolve* these clauses together, producing new clauses that logically follow from them (11.2.3).

4. Produce a contradiction by generating the empty clause.

5. The substitutions used to produce the empty clause are those under which the opposite of the negated goal is true (11.2.4).

Resolution is a sound inference rule in the sense of Chapter 2. However, it is not complete. Resolution is *refutation complete*; that is, the empty or null clause can always be generated whenever a contradiction in the set of clauses exists. More is said on this topic when we present strategies for refutation in Section 11.2.4.

Resolution refutation proofs require that the axioms and the negation of the goal be placed in a normal form called *clause form*. Clause form represents the logical data base as a set of disjunctions of *literals*. A literal is an atomic expression or the negation of an atomic expression.

The most common form of resolution, called *binary resolution,* is applied to two clauses when one contains a literal and the other its negation. If these literals contain variables, the literals must be unified to make them equivalent. A new clause is then produced consisting of the disjuncts of all the predicates in the two clauses minus the literal and its negative instance (which are said to have been "resolved away"). The resulting clause receives the unification substitution under which the predicate and its negation are found as "equivalent."

Before this is all made more precise in the subsequent subsections, we take a simple example. Resolution produces a proof similar to one produced already with modus ponens. This is not intended to show that these inference rules are equivalent (resolution is actually more general than modus ponens) but to give the reader a feel for what is going on.

We wish to prove that "Fido will die" from the statements that "Fido is a dog" and "all dogs are animals" and "all animals will die." Changing these three premises to predicates and applying modus ponens gives:

1. All dogs are animals: $\forall(X) (dog (X) \rightarrow animal (X))$.
2. Fido is a dog: dog (fido).

3. Modus ponens and {fido/X} gives: animal (fido).
4. All animals will die: ∀(Y) (animal (Y) → die (Y)).
5. Modus ponens and {fido/Y} gives: die (fido).

Equivalent reasoning by resolution converts these predicates to clause form:

PREDICATE FORM   CLAUSE FORM

1. ∀(X) (dog (X) → animal (X))   ¬ dog (X) ∨ animal (X)
2. dog (fido)   dog (fido)
3. ∀(Y) (animal (Y) → die (Y))   ¬ animal (Y) ∨ die (Y)

Negate the conclusion that Fido will die:

4. ¬ die (fido)   ¬ die (fido)

Resolve clauses having opposite literals, producing new clauses by resolution (Fig. 11.3). This process is often called *clashing*.

The symbol ☐ in Figure 11.3 indicates that the empty clause is produced and the contradiction found. The ☐ symbolizes the clashing of a predicate and its negation: the situation where two mutually contradictory statements are present in the clause space. These are clashed to produce the empty clause. The sequence of substitutions (unifications) used to make predicates equivalent also gives us the value of variables under which a goal

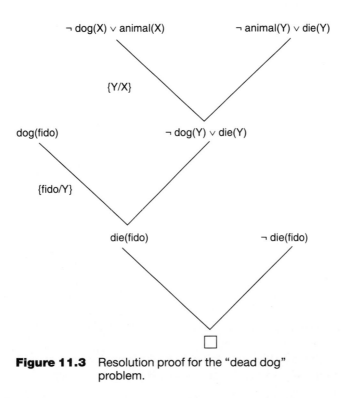

Figure 11.3   Resolution proof for the "dead dog" problem.

is true. For example, had we asked whether something would die, our negated goal would have been ¬ (∃ (Z) die(Z)), rather than ¬ die(fido). The substitution {fido/Z} in Figure 11.3 would determine that fido is an instance of an animal that will die. The issues implicit in this example are made clear in the remainder of Section 11.2.

11.2.2 Producing the Clause Form for Resolution Refutations

The resolution proof procedure requires all statements in the data base describing a situation to be converted to a standard form called *clause form*. This is motivated by the fact that resolution is an operator on pairs of disjuncts to produce new disjuncts. The form the data base takes is referred to as a *conjunction of disjuncts*. It is a *conjunction* because all the clauses that make up the data base are assumed to be true at the same time. It is a *disjunction* in that each of the individual clauses is expressed with disjunction (or ∨) as the connective. Thus the entire data base of Figure 11.3 may be represented in clause form as:

(¬ dog (X) ∨ animal (X)) ∧ (animal (Y) ∨ die (Y)) ∧ (dog (fido)).

To this expression we add (by conjunction) the negation of what we wish to prove: ¬ die(fido). Generally, the data base is written as a set of disjunctions and the ∧ operators are omitted.

We now present an algorithm, consisting of a sequence of transformations, for reducing any set of predicate calculus statements to clause form. It has been shown (Chang and Lee 1973) that these transformations may be used to reduce any set of predicate calculus expressions to a set of clauses that are inconsistent if and only if the original set of expressions is inconsistent. The clause form will not be strictly equivalent to the original set of predicate calculus expressions in that certain interpretations may be lost. This occurs because skolemization restricts the possible substitutions for existentially quantified variables (Chang and Lee 1973). It will, however, preserve unsatisfiability. That is, if there was a contradiction (a refutation) within the original set of predicate calculus expressions, a contradiction exists in the clause form: the transformations do not sacrifice completeness for refutation proofs.

We demonstrate this process of conjunctive normal form reduction through an example and give a brief description rationalizing each step. These are not intended to be proofs of the equivalence of these transformations across all predicate calculus expressions.

In the following expression, according to the conventions of Chapter 2, uppercase letters indicate variables (W, X, Y, and Z); lowercase letters in the middle of the alphabet indicate constants or bound variables (l, m, and n); and early alphabetic lowercase letters indicate the predicate names (a, b, c, d, and e). To improve readability of the expressions, we use two types of brackets: ( ) and [ ]. Where possible in the derivation, we remove redundant brackets: The expression we will reduce to clause form is:

(i) (∀X)([a(X) ∧ b(X)] → [c(X,l) ∧ (∃Y)((∃Z)[c(Y,Z) → d(X,Y)])]) ∨ (∀X)(e(X))

1. First we eliminate the → by using the equivalent form (proved in Chapter 2) a → b ≡ ¬ a ∨ b. This transformation reduces the expression in (i) above:

(ii) $(\forall X)(\neg\,[a(X) \wedge b(X)] \vee [c(X,I) \wedge (\exists Y)(\neg\,(\exists Z)[c(Y,Z) \vee d(X,Y)])] \vee (\forall X)(e(X))$

2. Next we reduce the scope of negation. This may be accomplished using a number of the transformations of Chapter 2. These include:

$\neg\,(\neg\,a) \equiv a$
$\neg\,(\exists X)\,a(X) \equiv (\forall X)\,\neg\,a\,(X)$
$\neg\,(\forall X)\,b(X) \equiv (\exists X)\,\neg\,b\,(X)$
$\neg\,(a \wedge b) \equiv \neg\,a \vee \neg\,b$
$\neg\,(a \vee b) \equiv \neg\,a \wedge \neg\,b$

Using the second and fourth equivalences (ii) becomes:

(iii) $(\forall X)([\neg\,a(X) \vee \neg\,b(X)] \vee [c(X,I) \wedge (\exists Y)((\forall Z)[\neg\,c(Y,Z) \vee d(X,Y))]) \vee (\forall X)(e(X))$

3. Next we standardize by renaming all variables so that variables bound by different quantifiers have unique names. As indicated in Chapter 2, because variable names are "dummies" or "place holders," the particular name chosen for a variable does not affect either the truth value or the generality of the clause. Transformations used at this step are of the form:

$((\forall X)a(X) \vee (\forall X)b(X)) = (\forall X)a(X) \vee (\forall Y)b(Y)$

Because (iii) has two instances of the variable X, we rename:

(iv) $(\forall X)([\neg\,a(X) \vee \neg\,b(X)] \vee [c(X,I) \wedge (\exists Y)((\forall Z)\,[\neg\,c(Y,Z) \vee d(X,Y))]) \vee (\forall W)(e(W))$

4. Move all quantifiers to the left without changing their order. This is possible because step 3 has removed the possibility of any conflict between variable names. (iv) now becomes:

(v) $(\forall X)(\exists Y)(\forall Z)(\forall W)([\neg\,a(X) \vee \neg\,b(X)] \vee [c(X,I) \wedge (\neg\,c\,(Y,Z) \vee d(X,Y))] \vee e(W))$

After step 4 the clause is said to be in *prenex normal* form, because all the quantifiers are in front as a *prefix* and the expression or *matrix* follows after.

5. At this point all existential quantifiers are eliminated by a process called *skolemization*. Expression (v) has an existential quantifier for Y. When an expression contains an existentially quantified variable, for example, $(\exists Z)(foo(\dots,Z,\dots))$, it may be concluded that there is an assignment to Z under which foo is true. Skolemization identifies such a value. Skolemization does not necessarily show *how* to produce such a value; it is only a method for giving a name to an assignment that *must* exist. If k represents that assignment, then we have $foo(\dots,k,\dots)$. Thus:

$(\exists X)(dog\,(X))$ may be replaced by dog(fido)

where the name fido is picked from the domain of definition of X to represent that individual X. fido is called a *skolem constant*. If the predicate has more than one argument and the existentially quantified variable is within the scope of universally quantified variables, the existential variable must be a function of those other variables. This is represented in the skolemization process:

$$(\forall X)\,(\exists Y)\,(mother\,(X,Y))$$

This expression indicates that every person has a mother. Every person is the X and the existing mother will be a function of the particular person X that is picked. Thus skolemization gives:

$$(\forall X)mother\,(X, m(X))$$

which indicates that each X has a mother (the m of that X). In another example:

$$(\forall X)(\forall Y)(\exists Z)(\forall W)(foo(X,Y,Z,W))$$

is skolemized to:

$$(\forall X)(\forall Y)(\forall W)(foo(X,Y,f(X,Y),W)).$$

We note that the existentially quantified Z was within the scope (to the right of) universally quantified X and Y. Thus the skolem assignment is a function of X and Y but not of W. With skolemization (v) becomes:

$$(vi)\ (\forall X)(\forall Z)(\forall W)([\neg\,a(X) \vee \neg\,b(X)] \vee [c(X,I) \wedge (\neg\,c(f(X),Z) \vee d(X,f(X)))]) \vee e(W))$$

where f is the skolem function of X that replaces the existential Y. Once the skolemization has occurred, step 6 can take place, which simply drops the prefix.

6. Drop all universal quantification. By this point only universally quantified variables exist (step 5) with no variable conflicts (step 3). Thus all quantifiers can be dropped, and any proof procedure employed assumes all variables are universally quantified. Formula (vi) now becomes:

$$(vii)\ [\neg\,a\,(X) \vee \neg\,b(X)] \vee [c(X,I) \wedge (\neg\,c(f(X),Z) \vee d(X,f(X)))] \vee e(W)$$

7. Next we convert the expression to the conjunct of disjuncts form. This requires using the associative and distributive properties of $\wedge$ and $\vee$. Recall from Chapter 2 that

$$a \vee (b \vee c) = (a \vee b) \vee c$$
$$a \wedge (b \wedge c) = (a \wedge b) \wedge c$$

which indicates that $\wedge$ or $\vee$ may be grouped in any desired fashion. The distributive property of Chapter 2 is also used, when necessary. Because

$$a \wedge (b \vee c)$$

is already in clause form, $\wedge$ is not distributed. However, $\vee$ must be distributed across $\wedge$ using:

$$a \vee (b \wedge c) = (a \vee b) \wedge (a \vee c)$$

The final form of (vii) is:

(viii) $[\neg a(X) \vee \neg b(X) \vee c(X,l) \vee e(W)] \wedge$
$\qquad [\neg a(X) \vee \neg b(X) \vee \neg c(f(X),Z) \vee d(X,f(X)) \vee e(W)]$

8. Now call each conjunct a separate clause. In the example (viii) above there are two clauses:

(ixa) $\neg a(X) \vee \neg b(X) \vee c(X,l) \vee e(W)$
(ixb) $\neg a(X) \vee \neg b(X) \vee \neg c(f(X),Z) \vee d(X,f(X)) \vee e(W)$

9. The final step is to *standardize the variables apart* again. This requires giving the variable in each clause generated by step 8 different names. This procedure arises from the equivalence established in Chapter 2 that

$$(\forall X) (a(X) \wedge b(X)) \equiv (\forall X) a(X) \wedge (\forall Y) b(Y)$$

which follows from the nature of variable names as place holders. (ixa) and (ixb) now become, using new variable names U and V:

(xa) $\neg a(X) \vee \neg b(X) \vee c(X,l) \vee e(W)$
(xb) $\neg a(U) \vee \neg b(U) \vee \neg c(f(U),Z) \vee d(U,f(U)) \vee e(V)$

The importance of this final standardization becomes apparent only as we present the unification steps of resolution. We find the most general unification to make two predicates within two clauses equivalent, and then this substitution is made across all the variables of the same name within each clause. Thus, if some variables (needlessly) share names with others, these may be renamed by the unification process with a subsequent (possible) loss of generality in the solution.

This nine-step process is used to change any data base of predicate calculus expressions to clause form. The completeness property of resolution refutations is not lost. Next we demonstrate the resolution procedure for generating proofs from these clauses.

11.2.3 The Binary Resolution Proof Procedure

The *resolution refutation* proof procedure answers a query or deduces a new result by reducing the set of clauses to a contradiction, represented by the *null* clause ($\square$). The contradiction is produced by resolving pairs of clauses from the data base. If a resolution does not produce a contradiction directly, then the clause produced by the resolution, the *resolvent*, is added to the data base of clauses and the process continues.

Before we show how the resolution process works in the predicate calculus, we give an example from the propositional or variable-free calculus. Consider two *parent* clauses p1 and p2 from the propositional calculus:

p1: $a_1 \vee a_2 \vee \cdots \vee a_n$
p2: $b_1 \vee b_2 \vee \cdots \vee b_m$

having two literals a_i and b_j, where $1 < i \le n$ and $1 \le j \le m$, such that $\neg a_i = b_j$. Binary resolution produces the clause:

$a_1 \vee \cdots \vee a_{i-1} \vee a_{i+1} \vee \cdots \vee a_n \vee b_1 \vee \cdots \vee b_{j-1} \vee b_{j+1} \vee \cdots \vee b_m.$

The notation above indicates that the resolvent is made up of the disjunction of all the literals of the two parent clauses except the literals a_i and b_j.

A simple argument can give the intuition behind the resolution principle. Suppose

$a \vee \neg b$ and $b \vee c$

are both true statements. Observe that one of b and $\neg$b must always be true and one always false ($b \vee \neg b$ is a tautology). Therefore, one of

$a \vee c$

must always be true. $a \vee c$ is the resolvent of the two parent clauses $a \vee \neg b$ and $b \vee c$.

Consider now an example from the propositional calculus, where we want to prove a from the following axioms:

$a \leftarrow b \wedge c$
b
$c \leftarrow d \wedge e$
$e \vee f$
$d \wedge \neg f$

We reduce the first axiom to clause form:

$a \leftarrow b \wedge c$
$a \vee \neg (b \wedge c)$ by $l \rightarrow m \equiv \neg l \vee m$
$a \vee \neg b \vee \neg c$ by de Morgan's law

The remaining axioms are reduced, and we have the following clauses:

a ∨ ¬ b ∨ ¬ c
b
c ∨ ¬ d ∨ ¬ e
e ∨ f
d
¬ f

The resolution proof is found in Figure 11.4. First, the goal to be proved, a, is negated and added to the clause set. The derivation of □ indicates that the data base of clauses is inconsistent.

To use binary resolution in the predicate calculus, where each literal may contain variables, there must be a process under which two literals with different variable names, or one with a constant value, can be seen as equivalent. Unification was defined in Chapter 2 as the process for determining consistent and most general substitutions for making two predicates equivalent.

The algorithm for resolution on the predicate calculus is very much like that on the propositional calculus except that:

1. A literal and its negation in parent clauses produce a resolvent only if they unify under some substitution σ. σ is then applied to the resolvent before adding it to the clause set.

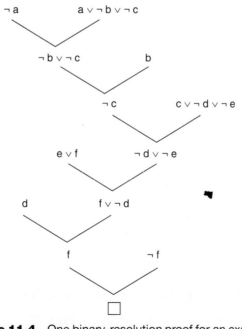

Figure 11.4 One binary-resolution proof for an example from the propositional calculus.

2. The unification substitutions used to find the contradiction offer variable bindings under which the original query is true. We explain this process, called *answer extraction,* shortly.

Occasionally, two or more literals in one clause have a unifying substitution. When this occurs there may not exist a refutation for a set of clauses containing that clause, even though the set may be contradictory. For instance, consider the clauses:

p(X) ∨ p(f(Y))
¬ p(W) ∨ ¬ p(f(Z))

The reader should note that with simple resolution these clauses can be reduced only to a tautological form and not to a contradiction.

This situation may be handled by *factoring* such clauses. If a subset of the literals in a clause has a most general unifier (Section 2.3.2), then the clause is replaced by a new clause, called a *factor* of that clause. The factor is the original clause with the most general unifier substitution applied and then redundant literals removed. For example, the two literals of the clause p(X) ∨ p(f(Y)) will unify under the substitution {X/f(Y)}. We make the substitution in both literals to obtain the clause p(X) ∨ p(X) and then replace this clause with its factor: p(X). Any resolution refutation system that includes factoring is refutation complete. Standardizing variables apart (Section 11.2.2 step 3) can be interpreted as a trivial application of factoring. Factoring may also be handled as part of the inference process in *hyperresolution* (Section 11.3.2).

We now present an example of a resolution refutation for the predicate calculus. Consider the following story of the "lucky student":

> Anyone passing his history exams and winning the lottery is happy. But anyone who studies or is lucky can pass all his exams. John did not study but he is lucky. Anyone who is lucky wins the lottery. Is John happy?

First change the sentences to predicate form:

> Anyone passing his history exams and winning the lottery is happy.
>
> ∀ X (pass (X,history) ∧ win (X,lottery) → happy (X))
>
> Anyone who studies or is lucky can pass all his exams.
>
> ∀ X ∀ Y (studies (X) ∨ lucky (X) → pass (X,Y))
>
> John did not study but he is lucky.
>
> ¬ study (john) ∧ lucky (john)
>
> Anyone who is lucky wins the lottery.
>
> ∀ X (lucky (X) → win (X,lottery))

These four predicate statements are now changed to clause form (Section 11.2.2):

1. ¬ pass (X, history) ∨ ¬ win (X, lottery) ∨ happy (X)
2. ¬ study (Y) ∨ pass (Y, Z)

3. ¬ lucky (W) ∨ pass (W, V)
4. ¬ study (john)
5. lucky (john)
6. ¬ lucky (U) ∨ win (U, lottery)

Into these clauses is entered, in clause form, the negation of the conclusion:

7. ¬ happy (john)

The resolution refutation graph of Figure 11.5 shows a derivation of the contradiction and, consequently, proves that John is happy.

As a final example for this subsection, suppose:

All people who are not poor and are smart are happy. Those people who read are not stupid. John can read and is wealthy. Happy people have exciting lives. Can anyone be found with an exciting life?

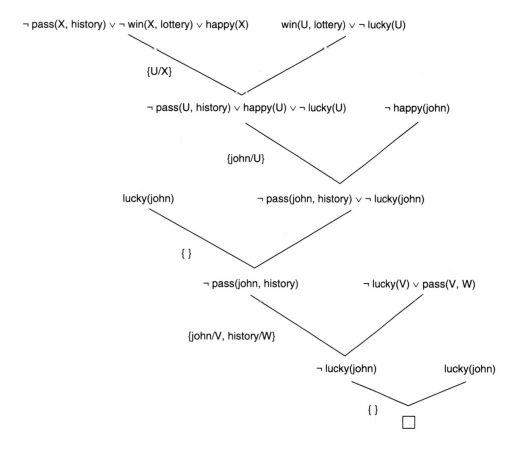

Figure 11.5 One resolution refutation for the "happy student" problem.

We translate the story into the predicate calculus expressions:

$\forall X (\neg \, poor \, (X) \land smart \, (X) \rightarrow happy \, (X))$
$\forall Y (read \, (Y) \rightarrow smart \, (Y))$
$read \, (john) \land wealthy \, (john)$
$\forall Z (happy \, (Z) \rightarrow exciting \, (Z))$

The negation of the conclusion is:

$\neg \, \exists \, W \, (exciting \, (W))$

These predicate calculus expressions are transformed into the following clauses:

$poor \, (X) \lor \neg \, smart \, (X) \lor happy \, (X)$
$\neg \, read \, (Y) \lor smart \, (Y)$
$read \, (john)$
$\neg \, poor \, (john)$
$\neg \, happy \, (Z) \lor exciting \, (Z)$
$\neg \, exciting \, (W)$

The resolution refutation for this example is found in Figure 11.6.

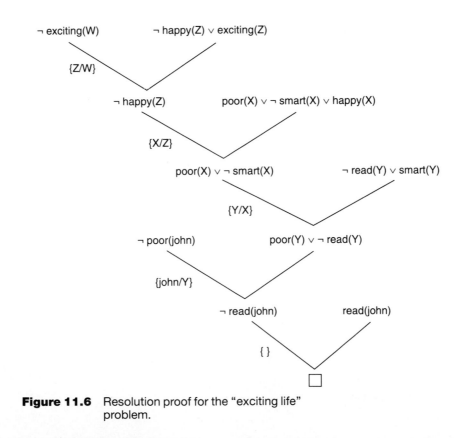

Figure 11.6 Resolution proof for the "exciting life" problem.

11.2.4 Strategies and Simplification Techniques for Resolution

A different proof tree within the search space for the problem of Figure 11.6 appears in Figure 11.7. There are some similarities in these proofs; for example, they both took five resolution steps. Also, the associative application of the unification substitutions found that John was the instance of the person with the exciting life in both proofs.

However, even these two similarities need not have occurred. When the resolution proof system was defined (Section 11.2.3) no order of clause combinations was implied. This is a critical issue: when there are N clauses in the clause space, there are N^2 ways of combining them or checking to see whether they can be combined at just the first level! The resulting set of clauses from this comparison is also large; if even 20% of them produce new clauses, the next round of possible resolutions will contain even more combinations than the first round. In a large problem this exponential growth will quickly get out of hand.

For this reason search heuristics are very important in resolution proof procedures, as they are in all weak method problem solving. As with the heuristics we considered in Chapter 4, there is no science that can determine the best strategy for any particular problem. Nonetheless, some general strategies can help us survive exponential combinatorics.

Before we describe our strategies, we need to make several clarifications. First, based on the definition of unsatisfiability of an expression in Chapter 2, a *set of clauses is unsatisfiable* if no interpretation exists that establishes the set as satisfiable. Second, an inference

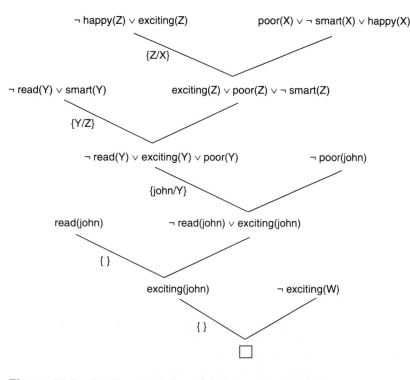

Figure 11.7 Another resolution refutation for the example of Figure 11.6.

rule is *refutation complete* if, given an unsatisfiable set of clauses, the unsatisfiability can be established by use of this inference rule alone. Resolution with factoring has this property (Chang and Lee 1973). Finally, a *strategy is complete* if by its use with a refutation-complete inference rule we can guarantee finding a refutation whenever a set of clauses is unsatisfiable. *Breadth first* is an example of a complete strategy.

The *Breadth-First* Strategy   The complexity analysis of exhaustive clause comparison just described was based on breadth-first search. Each clause in the clause space is compared for resolution with every clause in the clause space on the first round. The clauses at the second level of the search space are generated by resolving the clauses produced at the first level with all the original clauses. We generate the clauses at the nth level by resolving all clauses at level $n - 1$ against the elements of the original clause set and all clauses previously produced.

This strategy can quickly get out of hand for large problems. It does have an interesting property, however. Like any breadth-first search, it guarantees finding the shortest path solution, because it generates every search state for each level before going any deeper. It also is a complete strategy in that, if it is continued long enough, it is guaranteed to find a refutation if one exists. Thus, when the problem is small, as are the ones we have presented as examples, the breadth-first strategy can be a good one. Figure 11.8 applies the breadth-first strategy to the "exciting life" problem.

The *Set of Support* Strategy   An excellent strategy for large clause spaces is called the set of support (Wos and Robinson 1968). For a set of input clauses, S, we can specify a subset, T of S, called the set of support. The strategy requires that one of the resolvents in each resolution have an ancestor in the set of support. It can be proved that if S is unsatisfiable and S − T is satisfiable, then the set of support strategy is refutation complete (Wos et al. 1984).

If the original set of clauses is consistent, then any set of support that includes the negation of the original query meets these requirements. This strategy is based on the

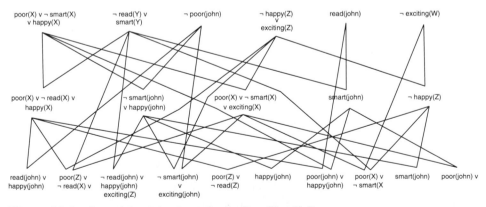

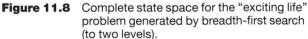

Figure 11.8   Complete state space for the "exciting life" problem generated by breadth-first search (to two levels).

insight that the negation of what we want to prove true is going to be responsible for causing the clause space to be contradictory. The set of support forces resolutions between clauses of which at least one is either the negated goal clause or a clause produced by resolutions on the negated goal.

Figure 11.6 is an example of the set of support strategy applied to the exciting life problem. Because a set of support refutation exists whenever any refutation exists, the set of support can be made the basis of a complete strategy. One way to do this is to perform a breadth-first search for all possible set of support refutations. This, of course, will be much more efficient than breadth-first search of all clauses. One need only be sure that all resolvents of the negated goal clause are examined, along with all their descendants.

The *Unit Preference* Strategy   Observe that in the resolution examples seen so far, the derivation of the contradiction is indicated by the clause with no literals. Thus, every time we produce a resultant clause that has fewer literals than the clauses that are resolved to create it, we are closer to producing the clause of no literals. In particular, resolving with a clause of one literal, called a *unit* clause, will guarantee that the resolvent is smaller than the largest parent clause. The unit preference strategy uses units for resolving whenever they are available.

Figure 11.9 uses the unit preference strategy on the exciting life problem. The unit preference strategy along with the set of support can produce a more efficient complete strategy.

Unit resolution is a related strategy that requires that one of the resolvents always be a unit clause. This is a stronger requirement than the unit preference strategy. We can show that unit resolution is not complete using the same example that shows the incompleteness of linear input form.

The *Linear Input Form* Strategy   The linear input form strategy is a direct use of the negated goal and the original axioms: take the negated goal and resolve it with one of the axioms to get a new clause. This result is then resolved with one of the axioms to get another new clause, which is again resolved with one of the axioms. This process continues until the empty clause is produced.

At each stage we resolve the clause most recently obtained with an original axiom. We never use a previously derived clause, nor do we resolve two of the axioms together. Linear input form is not a complete strategy, as can be seen by applying it to the following set of clauses (which are obviously unsatisfiable). Regardless of which clause is taken as the negation of the goal, linear input strategy cannot produce a contradiction:

$$\neg a \vee \neg b$$
$$a \vee \neg b$$
$$\neg a \vee b$$
$$a \vee b$$

Other Strategies and Simplification Techniques   We have not attempted to present an exhaustive set of strategies or even the most sophisticated techniques for proving theorems using resolution inference. These are available in the literature, such as Wos et al. (1984). Our goal is rather to introduce the basic tools for this research area and to describe how

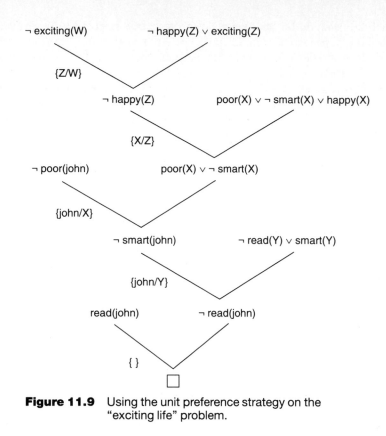

Figure 11.9 Using the unit preference strategy on the
"exciting life" problem.

these tools may be used in problem solving. The resolution proof procedure is but another
weak method problem-solving technique.

In this sense, resolution is an inference engine for the predicate calculus, but one that
requires much analysis and careful application of strategies before success. Randomly
clashing expressions together with resolution is as hopeless as striking random terminal
keys and hoping a quality paper will result. The number of combinations is that large!

The examples used in this chapter are trivially small and have all the clauses necessary
(and only those necessary) for the solution. This is seldom true of interesting problems. We
have given several simple strategies for combating these complexities, and we conclude
this subsection by describing a few more important considerations in resolution-based
problem solving. Later we show (in Section 13.3) how resolution refutations, with an interesting combination of strategies, define a "semantics" for logic programming, especially
the design of PROLOG interpreters.

A combination of strategies can be quite effective in controlling search—for instance,
the use of set of support plus unit preference. Search heuristics may also be built into the
design of rules (by creating a left-to-right ordering of literals for resolving). This order can
be most effective for pruning the search space. This implicit use of strategy is important in
PROLOG programming (Section 13.3).

The generality of conclusions can be a criterion for designing a solution strategy. On one side it might be important to keep intermediate solutions as general as possible, as this allows them to be used more freely in resolution. Thus the introduction of any resolution with clauses that require specialization by binding variables, such as {john/X}, should be put off as long as possible. If, on the other side, a solution requires specific variable bindings, such as an analysis of whether John has a staph infection, the {john/Person} and {staph/Infection} substitutions may restrict the search space and increase the probability and speed of finding a solution.

An important issue in selecting a strategy is the notion of completeness. It might be very important in some applications to know that a solution will be found (if one exists). This can be guaranteed by using only complete strategies.

We can also increase efficiency by speeding up the matching process. We can eliminate needless (and costly) unifications between clauses that cannot possibly produce new resolvents by indexing each clause with the literals it contains and whether they are positive or negative. This allows us directly to find potential resolvents for any clause. Also, we should eliminate certain clauses as soon as they are produced. First, any tautological clause need never be considered; these can never be falsified and so are of no use in a solution attempt.

Another type of clause that gives no new information is one that can be *subsumed,* that is, when a new clause has a more general instance already in the clause space. For example, if p(john) is deduced for a space that already contains $\forall$ X(p(X)), then p(john) may be dropped with no loss; in fact, there is a saving because there are fewer clauses in the clause space. Similarly, p(X) subsumes the clause p(X) $\vee$ q(X). Less general information does not add anything to more general information when both are in the clause space.

Finally, *procedural attachment* evaluates or otherwise processes without further search any clause that can yield new information. It does arithmetic, makes comparisons, or "runs" any other deterministic procedure that can add concrete information to the problem solving or in any manner constrain the solution process. For example, we may use a procedure to compute a binding for a variable when enough information is present to do so. This restricts possible resolutions and prunes the space.

In the next section we show how answers may be extracted from the resolution refutation process.

11.2.5   Answer Extraction from Resolution Refutations

The instances under which an hypothesis is true are exactly the substitutions with which the refutation is found. Therefore, retaining information on the unification substitutions made in the resolution refutation gives information for the correct answer. In this subsection we give three examples of this and introduce a bookkeeping method for extracting answers from a resolution refutation.

The answer recording method is simple: retain the original conclusion that was to be proved and, into that conclusion, introduce each unification that is made in the resolution process. Thus the original conclusion is the "bookkeeper" of all unifications that are made as part of the refutation. In the computational search for resolution refutations, this might require extra pointers, such as when more than one possible choice exists in the search for a refutation. A control mechanism such as backtracking may be necessary to produce alternative solution paths. But still, with a bit of care, this added information may be retained.

Let us see some examples of this process. In Figure 11.6, where a proof was found for the existence of a person with an exciting life, the unifications of Figure 11.10 were made. If we retain the original goal and apply all the substitutions of the refutation to this clause, we find the answer of which person it is who has an exciting life.

Figure 11.10 shows how a resolution refutation not only can show that "no one leads an exciting life" is false but also, in the process of that demonstration, can produce a happy person, John. This is a completely general result, where the unifications that produce a refutation are the same ones that produce the instances under which the original query is true.

A second example is the simple story:

Fido the dog goes wherever John, his master, goes. John is at the library. Where is Fido?

First we represent this story in predicate calculus expressions and then reduce these expressions to clause form. The predicates:

at (john,X) → at (fido,X)
at (john,library)

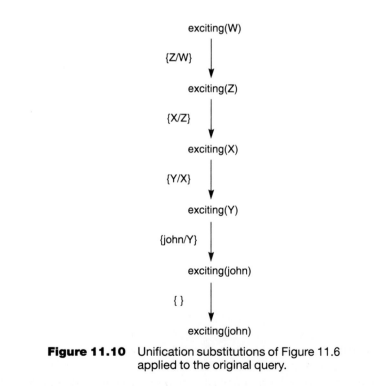

Figure 11.10   Unification substitutions of Figure 11.6
applied to the original query.

The clauses:

    ¬ at (john,Y) ∨ at (fido,Y)
    at (john,library)

The conclusion negated:

    ¬ at (fido,Z)

(Fido is nowhere!)

    Figure 11.11 gives the answer extraction process. The literal keeping track of unifications is the original question (where is Fido?):

    at (fido,Z)

Once again, the unifications under which the contradiction is found tell how the original query is true: Fido is at the library.

    The final example shows how the skolemization process can give the instance under which the answer may be extracted. Consider the following situation:

> Everyone has a parent. The parent of a parent is a grandparent. Given the person John, prove that John has a grandparent.

The following sentences represent the facts and relationships in the situation above:

Everyone has a parent.

    (∀ X)(∃ Y) p(X,Y)

A parent of a parent is a grandparent.

    (∀ X)(∀ Y)(∀ Z) p(X,Y) ∨ p(Y,Z) → gp(X,Z)

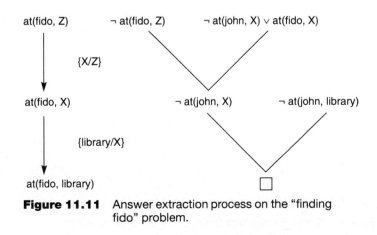

Figure 11.11   Answer extraction process on the "finding fido" problem.

The goal is to find a W such that gp(john,W) or ∃ (W)(gp(john,W)). The negation of the goal is ¬ ∃ (W)(gp(john,W)) or:

¬ gp(john,W)

In the process of putting the predicates above in clause form for the resolution refutation, the existential quantifier in the first predicate (everyone has a parent) requires a skolem function. This skolem function would be the obvious function: take the given X and find the parent of X. Let's call this the pa(X) for "find a parental ancestor for X." For John this would be either his father or his mother. The clause form for the predicates of this problem is:

p(X,pa(X))

¬ p(W,Y) ∨ ¬ p(Y,Z) ∨ gp(W,Z)

¬ gp(john,V)

The resolution refutation and answer extraction process for this problem are presented in Figure 11.12. Note that the unification substitutions in the answer are

gp(john,pa(pa(john)))

The answer to the question of whether John has a grandparent is to "find the parental ancestor of John's parental ancestor." The skolemized function allows us to compute this result.

The general process for answer extraction just described may be used in all resolution refutations, whether they be with the general unifications as in Figures 11.10 and 11.11 or

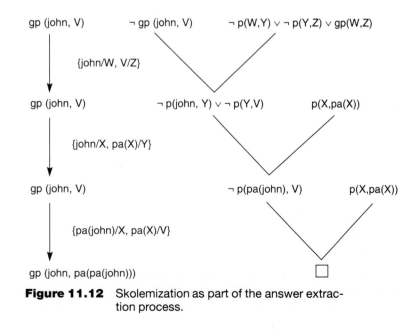

Figure 11.12 Skolemization as part of the answer extraction process.

from evaluating the skolem function as in Figure 11.12. The process will yield an answer. The method is really quite simple: the instances (unifications) under which the contradiction is found are exactly those under which the opposite of the negated conclusion (the original query) is true. Although this subsection has not demonstrated how this is true in every instance, it has shown several examples of how the process works; further discussion can be found in the literature (Nilsson 1980; Wos et al. 1984).

11.3 Further Issues in the Design of Automated Reasoning Programs

We described weak method problem solvers as using (a) a *uniform representation medium* for (b) *sound inference rules* that focus on syntactic features of the representation and are guided by (c) *methods or strategies* for combating the combinatorics of exhaustive search. We conclude this chapter with further comments on each of these aspects of the weak method solution process.

11.3.1 Uniform Representations for Weak Method Solutions

The resolution proof procedure requires us to place all our axioms in clause form. This uniform representation then allows us to resolve clauses and simplifies the design of problem-solving heuristics. One major disadvantage of this approach is that much valuable heuristic information can be lost in this uniform encoding.

The **if . . . then** format of a rule often conveys more information for use of modus ponens or production system search than one of its syntactic variants. It also offers us an efficient way to use the rule. For instance, **If the engine does not turn over and the lights do not come on then the battery may be dead** tells us exactly how to check the battery.

The disjunctive form of the same rule obscures this heuristic information about how the rule should be applied. If we express this rule in predicate calculus $\neg$ turns_over $\wedge$ $\neg$ lights $\rightarrow$ battery, the clause form of this rule is this: turns_over $\vee$ lights $\vee$ battery. This clause can have a number of equivalent forms, and each of these represents a different implication.

$$(\neg \text{ turns\_over } \vee \neg \text{ lights}) \rightarrow \text{battery}$$
$$(\neg \text{ turns\_over } \rightarrow (\text{battery } \vee \text{ lights}))$$
$$(\neg \text{ battery } \wedge \neg \text{ lights}) \vee \text{ turns\_over}$$
$$(\neg \text{ battery } \rightarrow (\text{turns\_over } \vee \text{ lights}))$$

and so on.

To retain heuristic information in the automated reasoning process several researchers, including Nilsson (1980), advocate reasoning methods that encode heuristics by forming rules according to the way in which the human expert might design the rule relationships. We have proposed this approach already in our **and/or** graph reasoning in Section 3.3. Rule-based expert systems also allow the programmer to control search through the structure of rules. We develop the idea further with the next two examples, one data driven and the second goal driven. Both of these retain the form of implications and use this information to guide search through an **and/or** graph.

Consider, for data-driven reasoning, the following facts, rules (axioms), and goal:

Fact:

$(a \vee (b \wedge c))$

Rules (or axioms):

$(a \rightarrow (d \wedge e))$

$(b \rightarrow f)$

$(c \rightarrow (g \vee h))$

Goal:

$e \vee f$

The proof of $e \vee f$ is found in the **and/or** graph of Figure 11.13. Note the use of **and** connectors on $\vee$ relations and the **or** connectors on $\wedge$ relations in the data-driven search space. If we are given that either **a** or **b** $\wedge$ **c** is true, then we must reason with both disjuncts to guarantee that our argument is truth preserving; hence these two paths are conjoined. When **b** and **c** are true, on the other hand, we can continue to explore either of these conjuncts. Rule matching takes any intermediate state, such as **c**, and replaces it with the

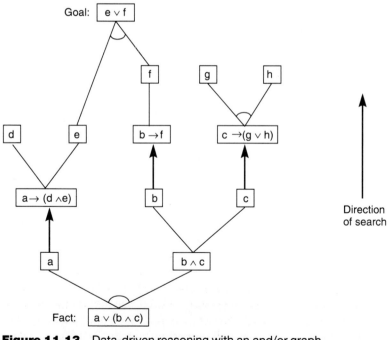

Figure 11.13 Data-driven reasoning with an and/or graph in the propositional calculus.

conclusion of a rule, such as (g ∨ h), whose premise matches that state. The discovery of both states e and f in Figure 11.13 indicates that the goal (e ∨ f) is established.

In a similar fashion we use matching of rules on and/or graphs for goal-driven reasoning. When a goal description includes a ∨, as in the example of Figure 11.14, then either alternative can be explored independently to establish the goal. If the goal is a conjunction, then, of course, both conjuncts must be established.

Goal:

(a ∨ (b ∧ c))

Rules (or axioms):

(f ∧ d) → a

(e → (b ∧ c))

(g → d)

Fact:

f ∧ g

Although these examples are taken from the propositional calculus, a similar search is generated using predicate calculus facts and rules. Unification makes literals compatible

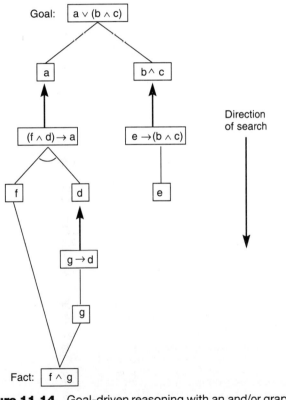

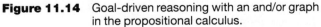

Figure 11.14   Goal-driven reasoning with an and/or graph in the propositional calculus.

for applying inference rules across different branches of the search space. Of course, unifications must be consistent (that is, unifiable) across different branches of and connectors.

This subsection has suggested a way to preserve heuristic information in the representational medium for weak method problem solving. This is essentially the way the inference engines of expert systems allow the programmer to specify control and heuristic information in a rule. For example, the rule $p \land q \land r \rightarrow s$ tells us that to solve s, try p, q, and r in order. Expert systems rely on the rule form for control of search rather than on general weak problem-solving methods. What is lost in this strong method approach is the ability to apply uniform proof procedures, such as resolution, across the representations. As can be noted in the examples of Figures 11.13 and 11.14, modus ponens may still be used. Strategies for inferencing must also be addressed, and a production system control (Chapter 5) using either depth-first, breadth-first, or best-first search offers one alternative control regime.

11.3.2 Alternative Inference Rules

Resolution is the most general sound inference rule we have presented so far. Several more sophisticated inference rules have been created in an attempt to make resolution more efficient. We briefly consider two of these: *hyperresolution* and *paramodulation*.

Resolution, as we have presented it, is actually a special variant called *binary resolution*: exactly two parent clauses are clashed. A successful application of hyperresolution replaces a sequence of binary resolutions to produce one clause. Hyperresolution clashes, in a single step, a clause with some negative literals, referred to as the *nucleus,* and a number of clauses with all positive literals, called the *satellites.* These satellites must have one positive literal that will match with a negative literal of the nucleus. There must also be one satellite for each negative literal of the nucleus. Thus the result of an application of hyperresolution is a clause with all positive literals.

An advantage of hyperresolution is that a clause of all positive literals is produced from each hyperresolution inference, and the clause space itself is kept smaller because no intermediate results are produced. Unifications across all clauses in the inference step must be consistent.

As an example of an inference using hyperresolution, consider the following clause set:

$\neg$ married(X,Y) $\lor$ $\neg$ mother(X,Z) $\lor$ father(Y,Z)
married(kate,george) $\lor$ likes(george,kate)
mother(kate,sarah)

We draw a conclusion in one step using hyperresolution:

father(george,sarah) $\lor$ likes(george,kate)

The first clause in the example is the nucleus; the second two are satellites. The satellites are all positive, and there is one for each negative literal in the nucleus. Note how the nucleus is just the clause form for the implication:

likes(X,Y) ∧ mother(X,Z) → father(Y,Z)

The conclusion of this rule is part of the final result. Note that there are no intermediate results, such as:

¬ mother(kate,Z) ∨ father(george,Z) ∨ married(george,kate)

which we would find in any binary resolution proof applied to the same clause space.

Hyperresolution is sound and complete when used by itself. When combined with other strategies, such as set of support, completeness may be comprised (Wos et al. 1984). It does require special search strategies to organize the satellite and nucleus clauses, although in most environments where hyperresolution is used, the clauses are often indexed by the name and positive or negative property of each literal. This makes it efficient to prepare the nucleus and satellite clauses for the hyperresolution inference.

Perhaps the most difficult issue in the design of theorem-proving mechanisms is the control of equality. Especially difficult are application areas, such as mathematics, where most facts and relationships have multiple representations, such as can be obtained by applying the associative and commutative properties to expressions. To convince yourself of this with a very simple example, consider the multiple ways the arithmetic expression 3 + (4 + 5) can be represented, including 3 + ((4 + 0) + 5). This is a difficult issue in that expressions need to be substituted for, unified with, and checked for equality with other expressions within automated mathematical problem solving.

Demodulation is the process of rephrasing or rewriting expressions so they automatically take on a chosen canonical form. The unit clauses used to produce this canonical form are *demodulators*. Demodulators specify the equality of different expressions, allowing us to replace an expression with its canonical form. With proper use of demodulators all newly produced information is reduced to a specified form before it is placed in the clause space. For example, we might have a demodulator:

equal(father(father(X)),grandfather(X))

and the new clause:

age(father(father(sarah))),78).

Before adding this new clause to the clause space, we apply the demodulator and add instead:

age(grandfather(sarah),78).

The equality problem here is one of naming. Do we wish to classify a person as father(father(X)) or grandfather(X)? Similarly, we can pick out canonical names for all family relations: a brother(father(Y)) is uncle(Y), etc. Once we pick the canonical names to store information under, we then design demodulators such as the equal clause to reduce all new information to this determined form. Note that demodulators are always unit clauses.

Paramodulation is a generalization of equality substitution at the term level. For example, given the expression:

older(mother(Y),Y)

and the equality relationship:

equal(mother(sarah),kate)

we can conclude with paramodulation:

older(kate,sarah)

Note the term-level matching and replacement of {sarah/Y} and mother(sarah) for kate. A vital difference between demodulation and paramodulation is that the latter allows a nontrivial replacement of variables in both the arguments of the equality predicate and the predicate into which the substitution is made. Demodulation does replacement based on the demodulator. Multiple demodulators may be used to get an expression into its final form; paramodulation is usually used only once in any situation.

We have given simple examples of these powerful inference mechanisms. They should be seen as more general techniques for use in a resolution clause space. Like all the other inference rules we have seen, these are tightly linked to the chosen representation and must be controlled by appropriate strategies.

11.3.3   Search Strategies and Their Use

Sometimes the domain of application puts special demands on the inference rules and heuristics for guiding their use. We have already seen the use of demodulators for assistance in equality substitution. Bledsoe, in his *natural deduction system*, identifies two important strategies for preparing theorems for resolution proof. He calls these strategies *split* and *reduce* (Bledsoe 1971).

Bledsoe designed his strategies for use in mathematics and, in particular, for application to *set theory*. The effect of these strategies is to break a theorem into parts to make it easier to prove by conventional methods such as resolution. Split takes various mathematical forms and splits them to appropriate pieces. The proof of $A \land B$ is equivalent to the proof of A and the proof of B. Similarly, the proof of $A \leftrightarrow B$ is the proof of $A \rightarrow B$ and the proof of $A \leftarrow B$.

The heuristic reduce also attempts to break down large proofs to their components. For example, the proof of $s \in A \cap B$ may be decomposed into the proofs of $s \in A$ and $s \in B$. Another example might be to prove some property true of $\neg (A \cup B)$ by proving the property for $\neg A$ or $\neg B$. By breaking up larger proofs into smaller pieces, Bledsoe hopes to contain the search space. His heuristics also include a limited use of equality substitution.

As mentioned throughout this book, the appropriate use of heuristics is very much an art that takes into account the application area as well as the representation and inference rules used. We close this chapter by citing some general proverbs, all of which are sometimes false but which can, with careful use, be very effective. These proverbs sum up thoughts taken from researchers in the area (Bledsoe 1983; Nilsson 1980; Wos et al. 1984; Wos 1988) as well as our own reflections on weak method problem solvers. We state them without further comment.

Use, whenever possible, clauses with fewer literals.

Break the task into subtasks before employing general inferencing.

Use equality predicates whenever this is appropriate.

Use demodulators to create canonical forms.

Use paramodulation when inferencing with equality predicates.

Use strategies that preserve "completeness."

Use set of support strategies, for these contain the potential contradiction.

Use units within resolution, as these shorten the resulting clause.

Perform subsumption checks with new clauses.

Use an ordering mechanism on clauses and literals within the clauses that reflect your intuitions and problem-solving expertise.

11.4   Epilogue and References

Automated reasoning programs and other weak method problem solvers are very important in artificial intelligence. They are used both to design general search strategies in game playing and theorem proving and to support much of our knowledge-based reasoning. Thus we see them in the design of "shells" for expert systems and inference mechanisms for network representations.

Weak method solvers require choosing a representational medium, inference mechanisms, and search strategies. These three choices are intricately interwoven and cannot be made in isolation from each other. The application domain also affects the choice of representation, inference rules, and strategies. The "proverbs" at the end of the previous section should be considered in making these choices.

Resolution is the process of constraining possible interpretations until it is seen that the clause space with the inclusion of the negated goal is inconsistent. This text does not go into the soundness of resolution or the completeness of resolution refutations. The arguments for these important issues are based on Herbrand's theorem (Chang and Lee 1973) and the notion of possible interpretations of the clause set. The interested reader is encouraged to go to the references for these proofs.

A number of other references are appropriate: Chang and Lee (1973) is a very readable introductory text. *Automated Theorem Proving: A Logical Basis* offers a formal approach (Loveland 1978). A number of classic early papers in the field are collected in a series *The Automation of Reasoning: Collected Papers, 1957 to 1970* (Siekmann 1983a, 1983b). Nilsson (1980), Genesereth and Nilsson (1987), Kowalski (1979b), Wos et al. (1984), and Wos (1988) offer valuable summaries of important concepts in automated reasoning. Robinson

(1965) and Bledsoe (1977) have made fundamental contributions to the field. An important theorem-proving research contribution is made by Boyer and Moore (1979). The early theorem-proving work by Newell and Simon and their colleagues at Carnegie Institute of Technology is reported in *Computers and Thought* (Feigenbaum and Feldman 1963) and *Human Problem Solving* (Newell and Simon 1972).

11.5   Exercises

1. Take the logic-based financial advisor of Section 2.4, put the predicates describing the problem into clause form, and use resolution refutations to answer queries such as whether a particular investor should make an investment(combination).

2. Use resolution to prove Wirth's statement in Exercise 13, Chapter 2.

3. Use resolution to answer the query in Example 3.3.4.

4. In Chapter 5 we presented a simplified form of the knight's tour. Take the path3 rule, put it in clause form, and use resolution to answer queries such as path3(3,6). Next, use the recursive path call, in clause form, to answer queries.

5. How might you use resolution to implement a "production system" search?

6. How would you do data-driven reasoning with resolution? Use this to address the search space of Exercise 1. What problems might arise in a large problem space?

7. Use resolution to answer queries in the farmer, wolf, goat, and cabbage problem of Chapter 6.

8. Use resolution to solve the following puzzle problem from Wos et al. (1984). There are four people: Roberta, Thelma, Steve, and Pete. The four hold eight different jobs. Each person has exactly two jobs. The jobs are, without sex bias, chef, guard, nurse, telephonist, police officer, teacher, actor, and boxer. The nurse is a male. The husband of the chef is the telephonist. Roberta is not a boxer. Pete has no education past the ninth grade. Roberta, the chef, and the police officer went golfing together. Who holds which jobs? Show how the addition of a sex bias changes the problem.

9. Work out two examples for hyperresolution where the nucleus has at least four literals.

10. Write a demodulator for sum that would cause clauses of the form equal(ans, sum(5, sum(6, minus(6)))) to be reduced to equal(ans, sum(5, 0)). Write a further demodulator to reduce this last result to equal(ans, 5).

11. Pick a "canonical set" of six family relations. Write demodulators to reduce alternative forms of relations to the set. For example, your "mother's brother" is "uncle."

12. Take the happy student problem of Figure 11.5 and apply three of the refutation strategies of Section 11.2.4 to its solution.

13. Put the following predicate calculus expression in clause form:

$$\forall (X)(p(X) \rightarrow \{\forall (Y)[p(Y) \rightarrow p(f(X,Y))] \wedge \neg \forall (Y)[q(X,Y) \rightarrow p(Y)]\})$$

14. Create the and/or graph for the following data-driven predicate calculus deduction.
    Fact: $\neg$ d(f) $\vee$ [b(f) $\wedge$ c(f)].
    Rules: $\neg$ d(X) $\rightarrow$ $\neg$ a(X) and b(Y) $\rightarrow$ e(Y) and g(W) $\leftarrow$ c(W).
    Prove: $\neg$ a(Z) $\vee$ e(Z).

15. Prove the linear input form strategy is not refutation complete.

16. Create the and/or graph for the following problem. Why is it impossible to conclude the goal:
$r(Z) \vee s(Z)$?
Fact: $p(X) \vee q(X)$.
Rules: $p(a) \rightarrow r(a)$ and $q(b) \rightarrow s(b)$.

17. Use factoring and resolution to produce a refutation for the following clauses: $p(X) \vee p(f(Y))$ and $\neg p(W) \vee \neg p(f(Z))$. Try to produce a refutation without factoring.

18. Derive a resolution proof of the theorem of Figure 11.1.

MACHINE LEARNING

12.0 Introduction

The ability to learn must be part of any system that would claim to possess general intelligence. Indeed, in our world of symbols and interpretation, the very notion of an unchanging intellect is a contradiction in terms. Intelligent agents must be able to change through the course of their interactions with the world, as well as through the experience of their own internal states and processes.

Learning is also important for practical applications of artificial intelligence. Feigenbaum and McCorduck (1983) have called the "knowledge engineering bottleneck" the major obstacle to the widespread use of expert systems. This "bottleneck" is the cost and difficulty of building expert systems using traditional knowledge acquisition techniques. One solution to this problem would be for programs to begin with a minimal amount of knowledge and learn from examples, high-level advice, or their own explorations of the domain.

Herbert Simon defines learning as

> any change in a system that allows it to perform better the second time on repetition of the same task or on another task drawn from the same population (Simon, 1983).

This definition, although brief, suggests many of the issues involved in developing programs that learn.

Learning involves changes in the learner; this is obvious. However, the exact nature of those changes and the best way to represent them are far from obvious. One approach models learning as the acquisition of explicitly represented domain knowledge. Based on its experience, the learner constructs or modifies expressions in a formal language, such as logic, and retains this knowledge for future use. This model, characterized by the algorithms of Sections 12.2 through 12.6, builds on the assumptions of knowledge-based systems: the primary influence on the program's behavior is its base of explicitly represented domain knowledge.

Neural networks, in contrast, do not learn by acquiring sentences in a symbolic language. Like an animal brain, which consists of a large number of interconnected nerve cells, neural networks are systems of interconnected, artificial neurons. The program's knowledge is implicit in the organization and interaction of these neurons. Unlike symbolic learning algorithms, neural nets do not learn by adding representations to their knowledge base; they learn by modifying their overall structure. In this chapter, we examine both approaches, contrasting their strengths and limitations.

Another challenge implicit in Simon's definition is the underconstrained nature of empirical learning. Learning involves generalization from experience: performance should improve not only on the "repetition of the same task," but also on similar tasks in the domain. Because interesting domains tend to be large, a learner may only examine a fraction of all possible examples; from this limited experience, the learner must acquire knowledge that will generalize correctly to unseen instances of the domain. This is the problem of *induction*, and it is central to learning. In most learning problems, the available training data are not sufficient to guarantee optimal generalization, no matter what algorithm the learner uses. Learning algorithms must generalize heuristically; they must select those aspects of their experience that are most likely to prove effective in the future. Such selection criteria are known as *inductive biases*.

Finally, Simon's definition describes learning as allowing the learner to "perform better the second time." As the previous paragraph indicates, selecting the possible changes to a system that will allow it to improve is a difficult task. Learning research must address the possibility that changes may actually degrade performance. Preventing and detecting such problems is another problem for a learning algorithm.

Machine learning has proven to be a fruitful area of research, spawning a number of different problems and algorithms for their solution. These algorithms vary in their goals, in the available training data, and in the learning strategies and knowledge representation languages they employ. However, all of these algorithms learn by searching through a space of possible concepts to find an acceptable generalization. In Section 12.1, we outline a framework for machine learning that emphasizes the common assumptions behind all of this work.

Although Section 12.1 outlines a variety of learning tasks, this chapter focuses primarily on *inductive learning*. Induction, which is learning a generalization from a set of examples, is one of the most fundamental learning tasks. *Concept learning* is a typical inductive learning problem: given examples of some concept, such as "cat," "soybean disease," or "good stock investment," infer a definition that will allow the learner to correctly recognize future instances of that concept. Sections 12.2 and 12.3 examine two algorithms used for concept induction, *version space search* and *ID3*.

Section 12.4 considers the role of *inductive bias* in learning. The search spaces encountered in learning tend to be extremely large, even by the standards of search-based problem solving. These complexity problems are exacerbated by the problem of choosing among the different generalizations supported by any given training data. Inductive bias refers to any method a learning program uses to constrain the space of possible generalizations.

The algorithms of Sections 12.2 and 12.3 are data driven. They use no prior knowledge of the learning domain but rely on large numbers of examples to define the essential properties of a general concept. Algorithms that generalize on the basis of patterns in training data are referred to as *similarity based*. In contrast to similarity-based methods, a learner may use prior knowledge of the domain to guide generalization. For example, humans, particularly as they move out of infancy, do not require large numbers of examples to learn effectively. Often, a single example, analogy, or high-level bit of advice is sufficient to communicate a general concept. Humans are able to learn in this fashion because we draw on our existing knowledge of the domain. The effective use of such knowledge can help an agent to learn more efficiently, and with less likelihood of error. Section 12.5 examines *explanation-based learning*, learning by analogy and other techniques that utilize prior knowledge to learn from a limited amount of training data.

The algorithms presented in Sections 12.2 through 12.5, though they differ in search strategies, representation languages, and the amount of prior knowledge used, all assume that the training data are classified by a teacher or some other means. The learner is told whether an instance is a positive or negative example of a target concept. A positive example belongs to the target concept; a negative example does not. This reliance on training instances of known classification defines the task of *supervised learning*. Section 12.6 continues the study of induction by examining *unsupervised learning*, which addresses how an intelligent agent can acquire useful knowledge in the absence of correctly classified training data. This important area of investigation underlies tasks as diverse as scientific discovery, learning in autonomous robots, and modelling human cognition. *Category formation*, or *conceptual clustering*, is a fundamental problem in unsupervised learning. Given a set of objects exhibiting various properties, how may an agent divide the objects into useful categories? How do we know whether a category is useful? What is the best way to represent those categories? In this section, we examine CLUSTER/2 and COBWEB, two approaches to the problem of category formation.

Parallel distributed processing (PDP) refers to a family of learning models, including neural networks, that examine the way in which intelligent behavior can arise from the interactions of large numbers of small, individually simple elements. Though neural networks (Section 12.7) are the best known example of PDP, the approach includes models that are not influenced by the architecture of the human brain. Genetic algorithms (Section 12.8), for example, model learning as an evolutionary process operating on a population of competing, candidate solutions.

All of the approaches in this chapter have one thing in common: they model learning as a variety of state space search. In the next section, we outline a general, search-based framework for research in machine learning.

12.1 A Framework for Learning

Learning algorithms may be characterized along several dimensions (Fig. 12.1):

1. *The data and goals of the learning task.* One of the primary ways in which we characterize learning problems is according to the goals of the learner and the data it is given. The concept learning algorithms of Sections 12.2 and 12.3, for example, begin with a collection of positive (and usually negative) examples of a target class; the goal is to infer a general definition that will allow the learner to recognize future instances of the class. In contrast to the data intensive approach taken by these algorithms, *explanation-based learning* (Section 12.5) attempts to infer a general concept from a single training example and a prior base of domain-specific knowledge. The conceptual clustering algorithms discussed in Section 12.6 illustrate another variation on the induction problem: instead of a set of training instances of known categorization, these algorithms begin with a set of unclassified

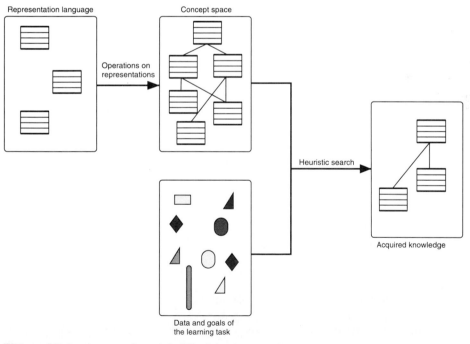

Figure 12.1 A general model of the learning process.

instances. Their task is discovering categorizations that may have some utility to the learner.

Examples are not the only source of training data. Humans, for instance, often learn from high-level advice. In teaching programming, professors generally tell their students that all loops must achieve a terminating condition. This advice, though correct, is not directly useful; it must be translated into specific rules for manipulating loop counters or logical conditions in a programming language. Analogies (Section 12.5.4) are another type of training data that must be correctly interpreted before they can be of use. If a teacher tells a student that electricity is like water, the student must infer the correct intent of the analogy: as water flows through a pipe, electricity flows through a wire. As with flowing water, we may measure the amount of electricity (amperage) and the pressure behind the flow (voltage). Unlike water, however, electricity does not make things wet or help us wash our hands. The interpretation of analogies involves finding the meaningful similarities and avoiding false or meaningless inferences.

We may also characterize a learning algorithm by the goal, or *target*, of the learner. The goal of many learning algorithms is a *concept*, or a general description of a class of objects. Learning algorithms may also acquire plans, problem-solving heuristics, or other forms of procedural knowledge.

The properties and quality of the training data itself are another dimension along which we classify learning tasks. The data may come from a teacher from the outside environment, or it may be generated by the program itself. Data may be reliable or may contain noise. It can be presented in a well-structured fashion or consist of unorganized instances. It may include both positive and negative examples or only positive examples. Data may be readily available or the program may have to construct experiments or perform some other form of data acquisition.

2. *The representation of learned knowledge.* Machine learning programs have made use of all the representation languages discussed in this text. For example, programs that learn to classify objects may represent these concepts as expressions in predicate calculus or they may use a structured representation such as frames or objects. Plans may be described as a sequence of operations or a triangle table. Heuristics may be represented as problem-solving rules.

A simple formulation of the concept learning problem represents instances of a concept as conjunctive sentences containing variables. For example, instances of the concept "ball" may be represented by:

size(obj1, small) ∧ color(obj1, red) ∧ shape(obj1, round)
size(obj2, large) ∧ color(obj2, red) ∧ shape(obj2, round)

and the general concept "ball" would be defined by:

size(X, Y) ∧ color(X, Z) ∧ shape(X, round)

Any sentence that unifies with this general definition represents a ball.

3. *A set of operations.* Given a set of training instances, the learner must construct a generalization, heuristic rule, or plan that satisfies its goals. This requires the abil-

ity to manipulate representations. Typical operations include generalizing or specializing symbolic expressions, adjusting the weights in a neural network, or otherwise modifying the program's representations.

In the concept learning example just introduced, a learner may generalize a concept definition by replacing constants with variables. If we begin with the concept:

size(obj1, small) ∧ color(obj1, red) ∧ shape(obj1, round)

replacing a single constant with a variable produces the generalizations:

size(obj1, X) ∧ color(obj1, red) ∧ shape(obj1, round)
size(obj1, small) ∧ color(obj1, X) ∧ shape(obj1, round)
size(obj1, small) ∧ color(obj1, red) ∧ shape(obj1, X)
size(X, small) ∧ color(X, red) ∧ shape(X, round)

4. *The concept space.* The representation language, together with the operations described above, defines a space of potential concept definitions. The learner must search this space to find the desired concept. The complexity of this concept space is a primary measure of the difficulty of a learning problem.

5. *Heuristic search.* Learning programs must commit to a direction and order of search, as well as to the use of available training data and heuristics to search efficiently. In our example of learning the concept "ball," a plausible algorithm may take the first example as a *candidate concept* and generalize it to include subsequent examples. For instance, on being given the training example

size(obj1, small) ∧ color(obj1, red) ∧ shape(obj1, round)

the learner will make that example a candidate concept; this concept correctly classifies the only positive instance seen.

If the algorithm is given the positive instance

size(obj2, large) ∧ color(obj2, red) ∧ shape(obj2, round)

the learner may generalize the candidate concept by replacing constants with variables as needed to form a concept that matches both instances. The result is a more general candidate concept that is closer to our target concept of "ball."

size(X, Y) ∧ color(X, red) ∧ shape(X, round)

Patrick Winston's work (1975) on learning concepts from positive and negative examples illustrates these components. His program learns general definitions of structural concepts, such as "arch," in a blocks world. The training data is a series of positive and negative examples of the concept: examples of blocks world structures that fit in the category, along with *near misses*. The latter are instances that almost belong to the category but fail on one property or relation. The near misses enable the program to single out features that can be used to exclude negative instances from the target concept. Figure 12.2 shows positive examples and near misses for the concept "arch."

The program represents concepts as semantic networks (Fig. 12.3). It learns by refining a candidate description of the target concept as training instances are presented. Winston's program refines candidate descriptions through generalization and specialization. Generalization changes the graph to let it accommodate new examples of the concept. Figure 12.3.a shows an arch built of three bricks and a graph that describes it. The next training example (Figure 12.3.b) is an arch with a pyramid rather than a brick on top. This example does not match the candidate description. The program matches these graphs, attempting to find a partial isomorphism between them. The graph matcher uses the node names to guide the matching process. Once the program matches the graphs, it may detect differences between them. In Figure 12.3, the graphs match on all components except that the top element in the first graph is brick and the corresponding node of the second example is pyramid. Part of the program's background knowledge is a generalization hierarchy of these concepts (Fig. 12.3.c). The program generalizes the graph by replacing this node with the least common supertype of brick and pyramid; in this example, it is polygon. The result is the concept of Figure 12.3.d.

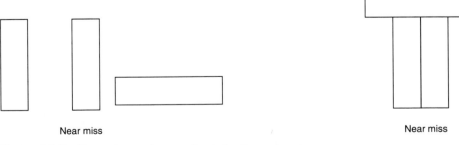

Arch

Arch

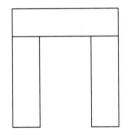

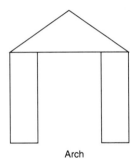

Near miss

Near miss

Figure 12.2   Examples and near misses for the concept
                 "arch."

a. An example of an arch and its network description.

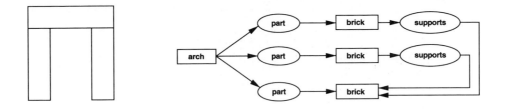

b. An example of another arch and its network description.

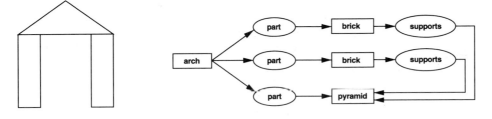

c. Given background knowledge that bricks and pyramids are both types of polygons.

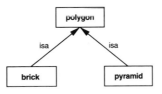

d. Generalization that includes both examples.

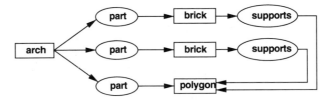

Figure 12.3 Generalization of descriptions to include multiple examples.

When presented with a near miss, an example that differs from the target concept in a single property, the program specializes the candidate description to exclude the example. Figure 12.4.a is a candidate description. It differs from the near miss of Figure 12.4.b in the touch relations of the near-miss example. The program specializes the graph by adding

a. Candidate description of an arch.

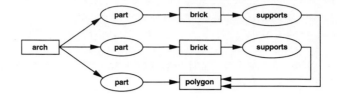

b. A near miss and its description.

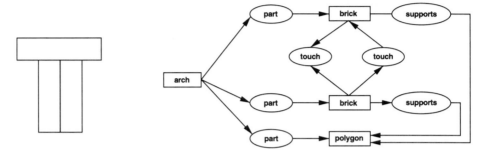

c. Arch description specialized to exclude the near miss..

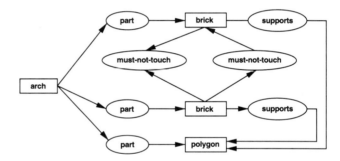

Figure 12.4 Specialization of a description to exclude a near miss.

must-not-touch links to exclude the near miss (Figure 12.4.c). Note that the algorithm depends heavily upon the closeness of the negative examples to the target concept. By differing from the goal in only a single property, a near miss helps the algorithm to determine exactly how to specialize the candidate concept.

These operations—specializing a network by adding links and generalizing it by replacing node or link names with a more general concept—define a space of possible concept definitions. Winston's program performs a hill climbing search (Chapter 4) on the concept space guided by the training data. Because the program does not backtrack, its performance is highly sensitive to the order of the training examples; a bad ordering can lead the program to dead ends in the search space. Training instances must be presented to the program in an order that assists learning of the desired concept, much as a teacher organizes lessons to help a student learn. The quality and order of the training examples are also important to the program's graph matching algorithm; efficient matching requires that the graphs not be too dissimilar.

Although an early example of inductive learning, Winston's program illustrates the features and problems shared by the majority of machine learning techniques: the use of generalization and specialization operations to define a concept space, the use of data to guide search through that space, and the sensitivity of the learning algorithm to the quality of the training data. The next sections examine these problems and the techniques that machine learning has developed for their solution.

12.2 Version Space Search

Version space search (Mitchell 1982) illustrates the implementation of inductive learning as search through a concept space. Version space search takes advantage of the fact that generalization operations impose an ordering on the concepts in a space, and then uses this ordering to guide the search.

12.2.1 Generalization Operators and the Concept Space

Generalization and specialization are the most common types of operations for defining a concept space. The primary generalization operations used in machine learning are:

1. Replacing constants with variables. For example,

    color(ball, red)

    generalizes to

    color(X, red)

2. Dropping conditions from a conjunctive expression.

    shape(X, round) ∧ size(X, small) ∧ color(X, red)

    generalizes to

    shape(X, round) ∧ color(X, red)

3. Adding a disjunct to an expression.

    shape(X, round) ∧ size(X, small) ∧ color(X, red)

generalizes to

shape(X, round) ∧ size(X, small) ∧ (color(X, red) ∨ color(X, blue))

4. Replacing a property with its parent in a class hierarchy. If we know that primary_color is a superclass of red, then

color(X, red)

generalizes to

color(X, primary_color)

We may think of generalization in set theoretic terms: let P and Q be the sets of sentences matching the predicate calculus expressions p and q, respectively. Expression p is more general than q iff P ⊇ Q. In the above examples, the set of sentences that match color(X, red) contains the set of elements that match color(ball, red). Similarly, in example 2, we may think of the set of round, red things as a superset of the set of small, red, round things. Note that the "more general than" relationship defines a partial ordering on the space of logical sentences. We express this using the "≥" symbol, where p ≥ q means that p is more general than q. This ordering is a powerful source of constraints on the search performed by a learning algorithm.

We formalize this relationship through the notion of *covering*. If concept p is more general than concept q, we say that *p covers q*. We define the covers relation: let p(x) and q(x) be descriptions that classify objects as being positive examples of a concept. In other words, for an object x, p(x) → positive(x) and q(x) → positive(x). p covers q iff q(x) → positive(x) is a logical consequence of p(x) → positive(x).

For example, the concept color(X, Y) covers color(ball, Z), which in turn covers color(ball, red).

As a simple example, consider a domain of objects that have properties and values:

size = {large, small}
colors = {red, white, blue}
shape = {ball, brick, cube}

These objects can be represented using the predicate obj(Size, Color, Shape). The generalization operation of replacing constants with variables defines the space of Figure 12.5. We may view inductive learning as searching this space for a concept that is consistent with all the training examples.

12.2.2   The Candidate Elimination Algorithm

This section presents three algorithms (Mitchell 1982) for searching the concept space. These algorithms rely upon the notion of a *version space,* which is the set of all concept descriptions consistent with the training examples. These algorithms work by reducing the

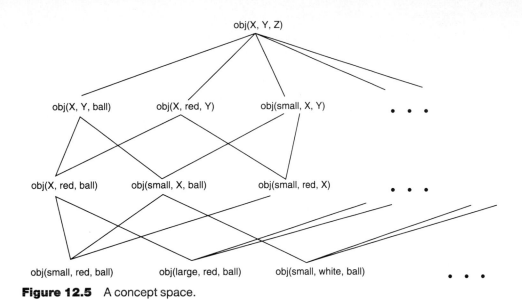

Figure 12.5 A concept space.

size of the version space as more examples become available. The first two algorithms reduce the version space in a specific to general direction and a general to specific direction, respectively. The third algorithm, called *candidate elimination,* combines these approaches into a bi-directional search. In this section we describe and evaluate these algorithms; Chapter 13 demonstrates their implementation in the PROLOG language.

These algorithms are data driven; they generalize based on regularities found in the training data. Also, in using training data of known classification, these algorithms perform a variety of *supervised learning*.

As with Winston's program for learning structural descriptions, version space search uses both positive and negative examples of the target concept. Although it is possible to generalize from positive examples only, negative examples are important in preventing the algorithm from overgeneralizing. Not only must the learned concept be general enough to cover all positive examples; it also must be specific enough to exclude all negative examples. In the space of Figure 12.5, one concept that would cover all sets of exclusively positive instances would simply be obj(X, Y, Z). However, this concept is probably too general, because it implies that all instances belong to the target concept. One way to avoid overgeneralization is to generalize as little as possible to cover positive examples; another is to use negative instances to eliminate overly general concepts. As Figure 12.6 illustrates, negative instances prevent overgeneralization by forcing the learner to specialize concepts in order to exclude negative instances. The algorithms of this section use both of these techniques.

Specific to general search maintains a set, S, of *hypotheses*, or candidate concept definitions. To avoid overgeneralization, these candidate definitions are the *maximally specific generalizations* from the training data. A concept, c, is maximally specific if it covers all positive examples, none of the negative examples, and for any other concept, c′, that covers the positive examples, c ≤ c′. We define specific to general search as:

```
Begin
Initialize S to the first positive training instance;
N is the set of all negative instances seen so far;


For each positive instance p
    Begin
    For every s ∈ S, if s does not match p, replace s with its most specific
        generalizations that match p;
    Delete from S all hypotheses more general than some other hypothesis in S;
    Delete from S all hypotheses that match a previously observed negative
        instance in N;
    End;


For every negative instance n
    Begin
    Delete all members of S that match n;
    Add n to N to check future hypotheses for overgeneralization;
    End;
End
```

Figure 12.7 shows an example of applying this algorithm to the version space of Figure 12.5.

We may also search in a general to specific direction. This algorithm maintains a set, G, of *maximally general concepts* that cover all of the positive and none of the negative instances. A concept, c, is maximally general if it covers none of the negative training instances, and for any other concept, c′, that covers no negative training instance, c ≥ c′. In this algorithm, negative instances lead to the specialization of candidate concepts; the algorithm uses positive instances to eliminate overly specialized concepts.

```
Begin
Initialize G to contain the most general concept in the space;
P contains all positive examples seen so far;


For each negative instance n
    Begin
    For each g ∈ G that matches n, replace g with its most general specializations
        that do not match n;
    Delete from G all hypotheses more specific than some other hypothesis in G;
    Delete from G all hypotheses that fail to match some positive example in P;
    End;


For each positive instance p
    Begin
    Delete from G all hypotheses that fail to match p;
    Add p to P;
    End;
End
```

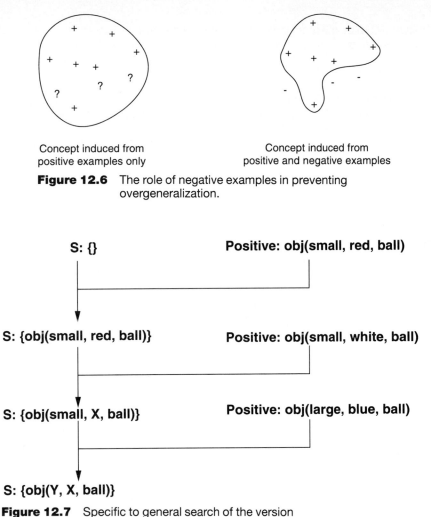

Concept induced from
positive examples only

Concept induced from
positive and negative examples

Figure 12.6 The role of negative examples in preventing
overgeneralization.

S: {}   Positive: obj(small, red, ball)

S: {obj(small, red, ball)}   Positive: obj(small, white, ball)

S: {obj(small, X, ball)}   Positive: obj(large, blue, ball)

S: {obj(Y, X, ball)}

Figure 12.7 Specific to general search of the version
space learning the concept "ball."

Figure 12.8 shows an example of applying this algorithm to the version space of Figure 12.5. In this example, the algorithm uses background knowledge that size may have values {large, small}, color may have values {red, white, blue}, and shape may have values {ball, brick, cube}. This knowledge is essential if the algorithm is to specialize concepts by substituting constants for variables.

The *candidate elimination algorithm* combines these approaches into a bi-directional search of the version space. As we shall see, this bi-directional approach has a number of benefits for the learner. The algorithm maintains two sets of candidate concepts: G is the set of maximally general candidate concepts, and S is the set of maximally specific candidates. The algorithm specializes G and generalizes S until they converge on the target concept. The algorithm is defined:

Begin
Initialize G to be the most general concept in the space;
Initialize S to the first positive training instance;

For each new positive instance p
    Begin
    Delete all members of G that fail to match p;
    For every s ∈ S, if s does not match p, replace s with its most specific
        generalizations that match p;
    Delete from S any hypothesis more general than some other hypothesis in S;
    Delete from S any hypothesis not more specific than some hypothesis in G;
    End;

For each new negative instance n
    Begin
    Delete all members of S that match n;
    For each g ∈ G that matches n, replace g with its most general specializations
        that do not match n;
    Delete from G any hypothesis more specific than some other hypothesis in G;
    Delete from G any hypothesis more specific than some hypothesis in S;
    End;

If G = S and both are singletons, then the algorithm has found a single concept that
    is consistent with all the data and the algorithm halts;
If G and S become empty, then there is no concept that covers all positive instances
    and none of the negative instances;
End

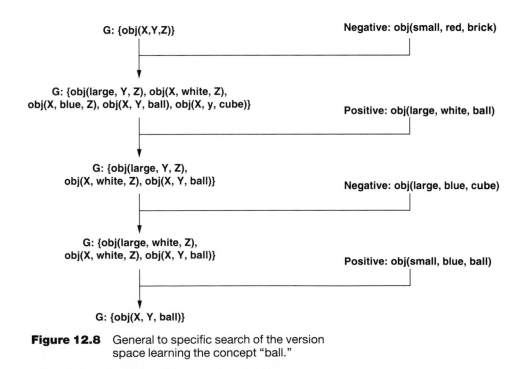

Figure 12.8   General to specific search of the version
space learning the concept "ball."

Figure 12.9 illustrates the behavior of the candidate elimination algorithm in searching the version space of Figure 12.5. Note that the figure does not show those concepts that were produced through generalization or specialization but eliminated as overly general or specific. We leave the elaboration of this part of the algorithm as an exercise.

Combining the two directions of search into a single algorithm has several benefits. The G and S sets summarize the information in the negative and positive training instances respectively, eliminating the need to save these instances. For example, after generalizing S to cover a positive instance, the algorithm uses G to eliminate concepts in S that do not cover any negative instances. Because G is the set of *maximally general* concepts that do not match any negative training instances, any member of S that is more general than any

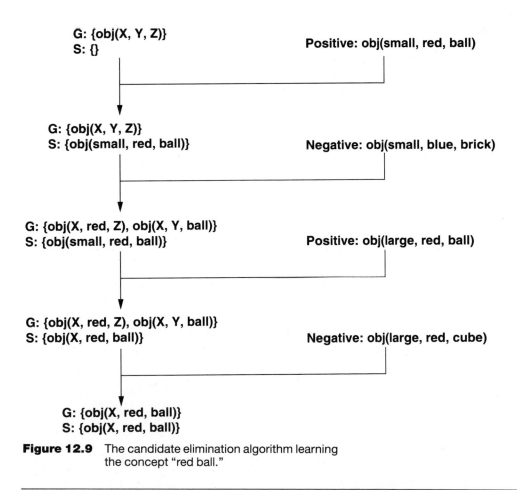

Figure 12.9 The candidate elimination algorithm learning the concept "red ball."

member of G must match some negative instance. Similarly, because S is the set of *maximally specific* generalizations that cover all positive instances, any new member of G that is more specific than a member of S must fail to cover some positive instance and may also be eliminated.

Figure 12.10 gives an abstract description of the candidate elimination algorithm. The "+" signs represent positive training instances; "−" signs indicate negative instances. The innermost circle encloses the set of known positive instances covered by the concepts in S. The outermost circle encloses the instances covered by G; any instance outside this circle is negative. The shaded portion of the graphic contains the target concept, along with concepts that may be overly general or specific (the ?'s). The search "shrinks" the outermost concept as necessary to exclude negative instances; it "expands" the innermost concept to include new positive instances. Eventually, the two sets converge on the target concept. In this fashion, candidate elimination can detect when it has found a single, consistent target concept. When both G and S converge to the same concept the algorithm may halt. If G and S become empty, then there is no concept that will cover all positive instances and none of the negative instances. This may occur if the training data is inconsistent or if the goal concept may not be expressed in the representation language (Section 12.2.4).

An interesting aspect of candidate elimination is its incremental nature. An incremental learning algorithm accepts training instances one at a time, forming a usable, although possibly incomplete, generalization after each example. This contrasts with batch algorithms (ID3, Section 12.3) that require all training examples to be present before they may begin learning. Even before the candidate elimination algorithm converges on a single concept, the G and S sets provide usable constraints on that concept: if c is the goal concept, then for all $g \in G$ and $s \in S$, $s \leq c \leq g$. Any concept that is more general than some concept in G will cover negative instances; any concept that is more specific than some concept in S will fail to cover some positive instances. This suggests that instances that

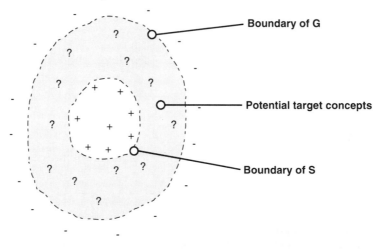

Figure 12.10 Converging boundaries of the G and S sets in the candidate elimination algorithm.

have a "good fit" with the concepts bounded by G and S are at least plausible instances of the concept.

In the next section, we clarify this intuition with an example of a program that uses candidate elimination to learn search heuristics. LEX (Mitchell et al. 1983) learns heuristics for solving symbolic integration problems. Not only does this work demonstrate the use of G and S to define partial concepts; it also illustrates such additional issues as the complexities of learning multistep tasks, credit/blame assignment, and the relationship between the learning and problem-solving components of a complex system.

12.2.3 LEX: Inducing Search Heuristics

LEX learns heuristics for solving symbolic integration problems. LEX integrates algebraic expressions through heuristic search, begining with the expression to be integrated and searching for its goal: an expression that contains no integral signs. The learning component of the system uses data from the problem solver to induce heuristics that improve the problem solver's performance.

LEX searches a space defined by operations on algebraic expressions. Its operators are the typical transformations used in performing integration. They include:

OP1: $\int r\, f(x)\, dx \to r \int f(x)\, dx$
OP2: $\int u\, dv \to uv - \int v\, du$
OP3: $1 \cdot f(x) \to f(x)$
OP4: $\int (f_1(x) + f_2(x))\, dx \to \int f_1(x)\, dx + \int f_2(x)\, dx$

Operators are rules, whose left-hand side defines when they may be applied. Although the left-hand side defines the circumstances under which the operator may be used, it does not include heuristics for when the operator *should* be used. LEX must learn usable heuristics through its own experience. Heuristics are expressions of the form:

If the current problem state matches P then apply operator O with bindings B.

For example, a typical heuristic that LEX might learn is:

If a problem state matches $\int x$ transcendental(x) dx,
    then apply op2 with bindings
            u = x
            dv = transcendental(x) dx

Here, the heuristic suggests applying integration by parts to solve the integral of x times some transcendental function (e.g., a trigonometric function) in x.

LEX's language for representing concepts consists of the symbols described in Figure 12.11. Note that the symbols exist in a generalization hierarchy, with any symbol matching any of its descendants in the hierarchy. LEX generalizes expressions by replacing a symbol with its ancestor in this hierarchy.

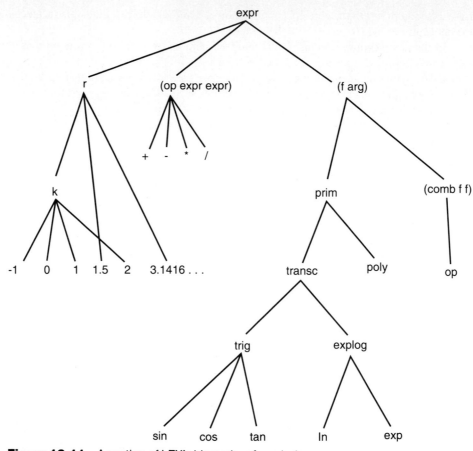

Figure 12.11　A portion of LEX's hierarchy of symbols.

For example, given the expression:

∫ 3x cos(x) dx

LEX may replace cos with trig. This yields the expression:

∫ 3x trig(x) dx

Alternatively, it may replace 3 with the symbol k, which represents any integer:

∫ kx cos(x) dx

Figure 12.12 shows a version space for OP2 as defined by these generalizations. The overall architecture of LEX consists of four components:

1. a *generalizer* that uses candidate elimination to find heuristics
2. a *problem solver* that produces traces of problem solutions

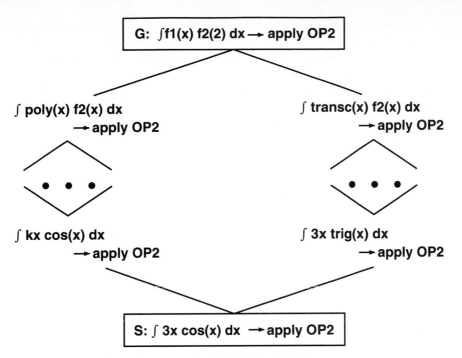

Figure 12.12 A version space for OP2 (Mitchell 1983).

3. a *critic* that produces positive and negative instances from a problem trace

4. a *problem generator* that produces new candidate problems

LEX maintains a set of version spaces. Each version space is associated with an operator and represents a partially learned heuristic for that operator. The generalizer updates these version spaces using positive and negative examples of the operator's application, as generated by the critic. On receiving a positive instance, LEX determines whether a version space associated with that operator includes the instance. A version space includes a positive instance if the instance is covered by some of the concepts in G. LEX then uses the positive instance to update that heuristic. If no existing heuristic matches the instance, LEX creates a new version space, using that instance as the first positive example. Note that this can lead to the creation of multiple version spaces for the same operator.

LEX's problem solver builds a tree of the space searched in solving an integration problem. LEX limits the CPU time the problem solver may use to solve a problem. LEX performs best-first search, using its own developing heuristics. An interesting aspect of LEX's performance is its use of G and S as partial definitions of a heuristic. If more than one operator may apply to a given state, LEX chooses the one that exhibits the highest degree of partial match to the problem state. Degree of partial match is defined as the percentage of all the concepts included between G and S that match the current state. Because the computational expense of testing the state against all such candidate concepts would be prohibitive, LEX estimates the degree of match as the percentage of entries actually in G and S that match the state. Note that performance should improve steadily as LEX improves its heuristics. Empirical results have confirmed this conjecture.

LEX obtains positive and negative examples of operator applications from the solution trace generated by the problem solver. In the absence of a teacher, LEX must classify operator applications as positive or negative; this is an example of the *credit assignment* problem. When learning is undertaken in the context of multistep problem solving, it is often unclear which action in a sequence should be given responsibility for the result. If a problem solver arrives at a wrong answer, how do we know which of several steps actually caused the error? LEX's critic approaches this problem by assuming that the solution trace returned by the problem solver represents a shortest path to a goal. LEX classifies applications of operators along this (assumed) shortest path as positive instances; operator applications that diverge from this path are treated as negative instances.

However, in treating the problem solver's trace as a shortest path solution, the critic must address the fact that LEX's evolving heuristics are not guaranteed to be admissible (Chapter 4). The solution path found by the problem solver may not actually be a shortest path solution. To ensure that it has not erroneously classified an operator application as negative, LEX first extends the paths begun by such operators to make sure they do not lead to a better solution. Usually, a problem solution produces 2 to 20 training instances. LEX passes these positive and negative instances on to the generalizer, which uses them to update the version spaces for the associated operators.

The problem generator is the least developed part of the program. Although various strategies were used to automate problem selection, most of the work involved hand-chosen instances. However, a problem generator was constructed that explored a variety of strategies. One approach generates instances that were covered by the partial heuristics for two different operators, in order to make LEX learn to discriminate between them.

Empirical tests show that LEX is effective in learning useful heuristics. In one test, LEX was given 5 test problems and 12 training problems. Before training, it solved the 5 test problems in an average of 200 steps; these solutions used no heuristics to guide the search. After developing heuristics from the 12 training problems, it solved these same test problems in an average of 20 steps.

LEX addresses a number of issues in learning, including such problems as credit assignment, the selection of training instances, and the relationship between the problem solving and generalization components of a learning algorithm. LEX also underscores the importance of an appropriate representation for concepts. Much of LEX's effectiveness stems from the hierarchical organization of concepts. This hierarchy is small enough to constrain the space of potential heuristics and to allow efficient search, while being rich enough to represent effective heuristics.

12.2.4 Evaluating Candidate Elimination

The candidate elimination algorithm demonstrates the way in which knowledge representation and state space search can be applied to the problem of machine learning. However, as with most important research, the algorithm should not be evaluated in terms of its successes alone. It raises problems that continue to form a sizeable portion of machine learning's research agenda.

Search-based learning, like all search problems, must deal with the combinatorics of problem spaces. Because the candidate elimination algorithm performs breadth-first search, it can be inefficient. If an application is such that G and S grow excessively, it may be useful to develop heuristics for pruning states from G and S, implementing a *beam search* (see Chapter 4) of the space.

Another approach to this problem, discussed in Section 12.4, involves using an *inductive bias* to reduce the size of the concept space. Such biases constrain the language used to represent concepts. LEX imposed a bias through the choice of concepts in its generalization hierarchy. Though not complete, LEX's concept language was strong enough to capture many effective heuristics; of equal importance, it reduced the size of the concept space to manageable proportions. Biased languages are essential in reducing the complexity of the concept space, but they may leave the learner incapable of representing the concept it is trying to learn. In this case, candidate elimination would fail to converge on the target concept, leaving G and S empty. This trade-off between expressiveness and efficiency is an essential issue in learning.

Failure of the algorithm to converge may also be due to some noise or inconsistency in the training data. The problem of learning from noisy data is particularly important in realistic applications, where data cannot be guaranteed to be complete or consistent. Candidate elimination is not particularly noise resistant. Even a single misclassified training instance can prevent the algorithm from converging on a consistent concept. One solution to this problem maintains multiple G and S sets. In addition to the version space derived from all training instances, it maintains additional spaces based on all but 1 of the training instances, all but 2 of the training instances, etc. If G and S fail to converge, the algorithm can examine these alternatives to find those that remain consistent. Unfortunately, this approach leads to a proliferation of candidate sets and is too inefficient to be practical in most cases.

Another issue raised by this research is the role of prior knowledge in learning. LEX's concept hierarchy summarized a great deal of knowledge about algebra; this knowledge was essential to the algorithm's performance. Can greater amounts of domain knowledge make learning even more effective? Section 12.5 examines this problem.

An important contribution of this work is its explication of the relationship between knowledge representation, generalization, and search in inductive learning. Although candidate elimination is only one of many learning algorithms, it raises general questions concerning complexity, expressiveness, and the use of knowledge and data to guide generalization. These problems are central to all machine learning algorithms; we continue to address them throughout this chapter.

12.3 The ID3 Decision Tree Induction Algorithm

ID3 (Quinlan 1986a), like candidate elimination, induces concepts from examples. It is particularly interesting for its representation of learned knowledge, its approach to the management of complexity, its heuristic for selecting candidate concepts, and its potential for handling noisy data. ID3 represents concepts as *decision trees*, a representation that allows us to determine the classification of an object by testing its values for certain properties.

For example, consider the problem of estimating an individual's credit risk on the basis of such properties as credit history, current debt, collateral, and income. Table 12.1 lists a sample of individuals with known credit risks. The decision tree of Figure 12.13 represents the classifications in Table 12.1, in that this tree can correctly classify all the objects in the table. In a decision tree, each internal node represents a test on some property, such as credit history or debt; each possible value of that property corresponds to a branch of the tree. Leaf nodes represent classifications, such as low or moderate risk. An individual of unknown type may be classified by traversing this tree: at each internal node, test the individual's value for that property and take the appropriate branch. This continues until reaching a leaf node and the object's classification.

Note that in classifying any given instance, this tree does not use all the properties present in Table 12.1. For instance, if a person has a good credit history and low debt, we may, according to the tree, ignore her collateral and income and classify her as a low risk. In spite of omitting certain tests, this tree correctly classifies all the examples in the table.

In general, the size of the tree necessary to classify a given set of examples varies according to the order with which properties are tested. Figure 12.14 shows a tree that is considerably simpler than that of Figure 12.13 but that also classifies the examples in Table 12.1.

Given a set of training instances and a number of different decision trees that correctly classify them, we may ask which tree has the greatest likelihood of correctly classifying

TABLE 12.1   DATA FROM CREDIT HISTORY OF LOAN APPLICATIONS

NO.	RISK	CREDIT HISTORY	DEBT	COLLATERAL	INCOME
1.	high	bad	high	none	$0 to $15k
2.	high	unknown	high	none	$15 to $35k
3.	moderate	unknown	low	none	$15 to $35k
4.	high	unknown	low	none	$0 to $15k
5.	low	unknown	low	none	over $35k
6.	low	unknown	low	adequate	over $35k
7.	high	bad	low	none	$0 to $15k
8.	moderate	bad	low	adequate	over $35k
9.	low	good	low	none	over $35k
10.	low	good	high	adequate	over $35k
11.	high	good	high	none	$0 to $15k
12.	moderate	good	high	none	$15 to $35k
13.	low	good	high	none	over $35k
14.	high	bad	high	none	$15 to $35k

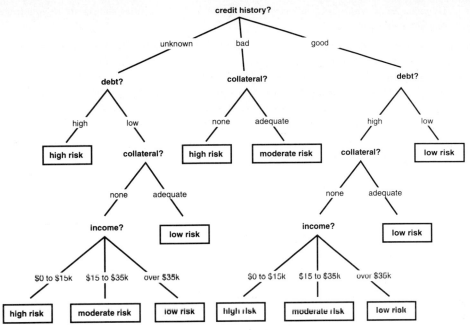

Figure 12.13 A decision tree for credit risk assessment.

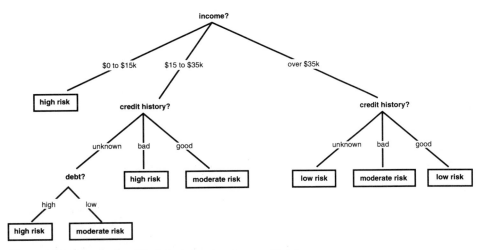

Figure 12.14 A simplified decision tree for credit risk assessment.

unseen instances of the population. The ID3 algorithm assumes that this is the simplest decision tree that covers all the training examples. The rationale for this assumption is the time-honored heuristic of preferring simplicity and avoiding unnecessary assumptions. This principle, known as *Occam's Razor*, was first articulated by the medieval logician William of Occam in 1324:

It is vain to do with more what can be done with less. . . . Entities should not be multiplied beyond necessity.

A more contemporary version of Occam's Razor argues that we should always accept the simplest answer that correctly fits our data. In this case, it is the smallest decision tree that correctly classifies all given examples.

Although Occam's Razor has proven itself as a general heuristic for all manner of intellectual activity, its use here has a more specific justification. If we assume that the given examples are sufficient to construct a valid generalization, then our problem becomes one of distinguishing the necessary properties from the extraneous ones. The simplest decision tree that covers all the examples should be the least likely to include unnecessary constraints. Although this idea is intuitively appealing, it is an assumption that must be empirically tested; Section 12.3.3 presents some of these empirical results. Before examining these results, however, we present the ID3 algorithm for inducing decision trees from examples.

12.3.1 Top-Down Decision Tree Induction

ID3 constructs decision trees in a top-down fashion. Note that for any property, we may partition the set of training examples into disjoint subsets, where all the examples in a partition have a common value for that property. ID3 selects a property to test at the current node of the tree and uses this test to partition the set of examples; the algorithm then recursively constructs a subtree for each partition. This continues until all members of the partition are in the same class; that class becomes a leaf node of the tree. Because the order of tests is critical to constructing a simple decision tree, ID3 relies heavily on its criteria for selecting the test at the root of each subtree. To simplify our discussion, this section describes the algorithm for constructing decision trees, assuming an appropriate test selection function. In Section 12.3.2, we present the selection heuristic used by the ID3 algorithm.

The decision tree induction algorithm begins with a sample of correctly classified members of the target categories. ID3 constructs a decision tree according to the algorithm:

```
function induce_tree (example_set, Properties)

begin
if all entries in example_set are in the same class
    then return a leaf node labeled with that class
    else if Properties is empty
      then return leaf node labeled with disjunction of all classes in example_set
      else begin
        select a property, P, to test on and make it the root of the current tree;
        delete P from Properties;
          for each value, V, of P,
            begin
                create a branch of the tree labeled with V
                let partition_v be elements of example_set with V for property P;
                call induce_tree(partition_v, Properties), attach result to branch V
            end;
      end;
end
```

For example, consider the way in which ID3 constructs the tree of Figure 12.14 from Table 12.1. Beginning with the full table of examples, ID3 selects income as the root property using the selection function described in Section 12.3.2. This partitions the example set as shown in Figure 12.15, with the elements of each partition being listed by their number in the table.

ID3 applies the induce_tree function recursively to each partition. The partition {1, 4, 7, 11} consists entirely of high-risk individuals; ID3 creates a leaf node accordingly. ID3 selects the credit history property as the root of the subtree for the partition {2, 3, 12, 14}. In Figure 12.16, credit history further divides this partition into {2,3}, {14}, and {12}.

Continuing to select tests and construct subtrees in this fashion, ID3 eventually produces the tree of Figure 12.14. We let the reader work through the remaining stages of this construction.

Before presenting ID3's test selection heuristic, it is worth examining the relationship between the tree construction algorithm and our view of learning as search through a concept space. We may think of the set of all possible decision trees as defining a space. Our operations for moving through this space consist of adding tests to a tree. ID3 implements a form of hill climbing in the space of all possible trees: it adds a subtree to the current tree and continues its search; it does not backtrack. This makes the algorithm highly efficient; it also makes it highly dependent upon the criteria for selecting properties to test.

12.3.2   Information Theoretic Test Selection

We may think of each property of an instance as contributing a certain amount of information to its classification. For example, if our goal is to determine the species of an animal, the discovery that it lays eggs contributes a certain amount of information to that goal. ID3 measures the information gained by making each property the root of the current subtree. It then picks the property that provides the greatest information gain.

Information theory (Shannon 1948) provides a mathematical basis for measuring the information content of a message. We may think of a message as an instance in a universe of possible messages; the act of transmitting a message is the same as selecting one of these possible messages. From this point of view, it is reasonable to define the information content of a message as depending upon both the size of this universe and the frequency with which each possible message occurs.

The importance of the number of possible messages is evident in an example from gambling: compare a message correctly predicting the outcome of a spin of the roulette wheel with one predicting the outcome of a toss of an honest coin. Because roulette can

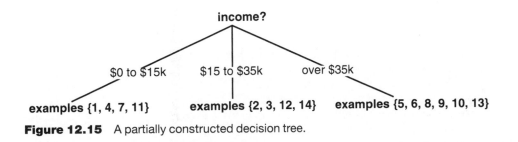

Figure 12.15   A partially constructed decision tree.

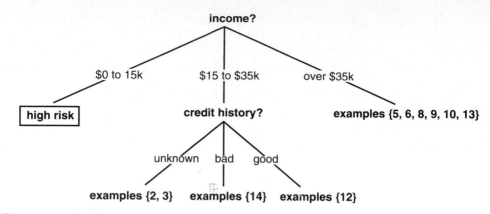

Figure 12.16 Another partially constructed decision tree.

have more outcomes than a coin toss, a message concerning its outcome is of more value to us. Winning at roulette also pays better than winning at a coin toss; consequently, we should regard this message as conveying more information.

The influence of the probability of each message on the amount of information is evident in another gambling example. Assume that I have rigged a coin so that it will come up heads ¾ of the time. Because I already know enough about the coin to wager correctly ¾ of the time, a message telling me the outcome of a given toss is worth less to me than it would be for an honest coin.

Shannon formalized these intuitions by defining the amount of information in a message as a function of the probability of occurrence of each possible message. Given a universe of messages, $M = \{m_1, m_2, \ldots m_n\}$ and a probability, $p(m_i)$, for the occurrence of each message, the information content of a message in M is given by:

$$I(M) = \sum_{i=1}^{n} - p(m_i) \log_2 (p(m_i))$$

The information in a message is measured in bits. For example, the information content of a message telling the outcome of the flip of an honest coin is:

$$I(\text{Coin toss}) = -p(\text{heads}) \log_2 (p(\text{heads})) - p(\text{tails}) \log_2 (p(\text{tails}))$$
$$= -\frac{1}{2} \log_2 \left(\frac{1}{2}\right) - \frac{1}{2} \log_2 \left(\frac{1}{2}\right)$$
$$= 1 \text{ bit}$$

However, if the coin has been rigged to come up heads 75 percent of the time, then the information content of a message is:

$$I(\text{Coin toss}) = -\frac{3}{4} \log_2 \left(\frac{3}{4}\right) - \frac{1}{4} \log_2 \left(\frac{1}{4}\right)$$
$$= -\frac{3}{4} * (-0.415) - \frac{1}{4} * (-2)$$
$$= 0.811 \text{ bits}$$

This definition formalizes many of our intuitions about the information content of messages. Information theory is widely used in computer science and telecommunications, including such applications as determining the information-carrying capacity of communications channels, developing data compression algorithms, and developing noise-resistant communication strategies. ID3 uses information theory to select the test that gives the greatest information gain in classifying the training examples.

We may think of a decision tree as conveying information about the classification of examples in the decision table; the information content of the tree is computed from the probabilities of the different classifications. For example, if we assume that all the examples in Table 12.1 occur with equal probability, then

p(risk is high) = $^6/_{14}$
p(risk is moderate) = $^3/_{14}$
p(risk is low) = $^5/_{14}$

It follows that the information in the table, and, consequently, any tree that covers those examples, is

$$I(\text{Table } 12.1) = -\frac{6}{14}\log_2\left(\frac{6}{14}\right) - \frac{3}{14}\log_2\left(\frac{3}{14}\right) - \frac{5}{14}\log_2\left(\frac{5}{14}\right)$$

$$= -\frac{6}{14} * (-1.222) - \frac{3}{14} * (-2.222) - \frac{5}{14} * (-1.485)$$

$$= 1.531 \text{ bits}$$

For a given test, the information gain provided by making that test at the root of the current tree is equal to the total information in the tree minus the amount of information needed to complete the classification after performing the test. The amount of information needed to complete the tree is defined as the weighted average of the information in all its subtrees. We compute the weighted average by multiplying the information content of each subtree by the percentage of the examples present in that subtree and summing these products.

Assume a set of training instances, C. If we make property P, with n values, the root of the current tree, this will partition C into subsets, $\{C_1, C_2, \ldots C_n\}$. The expected information needed to complete the tree after making P the root is:

$$E(P) = \sum_{i=1}^{n} \frac{|C_i|}{|C|} I(C_i)$$

The gain from property P is computed by subtracting the expected information to complete the tree from the total information content of the tree:

gain(P) = I(C) − E(P)

In the example of Table 12.1, if we make income the property tested at the root of the tree, this partitions the table of examples into the partitions $C_1 = \{1,4,7,11\}$, $C_2 = \{2,3,12,14\}$, and $C_3 = \{5,6,8,9,10,13\}$. The expected information needed to complete the tree is:

$$E(\text{income}) = \frac{4}{14} * I(C_1) + \frac{4}{14} * I(C_2) + \frac{6}{14} * I(C_3)$$
$$= \frac{4}{14} * 0.0 + \frac{4}{14} * 1.0 + \frac{6}{14} * 0.650$$
$$= 0.564 \text{ bits}$$

The information gain is:

$$\text{gain}(\text{income}) = I(\text{table } 12.1) - E(\text{income})$$
$$= 1.531 - 0.564$$
$$= 0.967 \text{ bits}$$

Similarly, we may show that

$$\text{gain}(\text{credit history}) = 0.266$$
$$\text{gain}(\text{debt}) = 0.581$$
$$\text{gain}(\text{collateral}) = 0.756$$

Because income provides the greatest information gain, ID3 will select it as the root of the tree. The algorithm continues to apply this analysis recursively to each subtree until it has completed the tree. Chapter 14 presents a LISP implementation of this algorithm.

12.3.3 Evaluating ID3

Although the ID3 algorithm produces simple decision trees, it is not obvious that such trees will be effective in predicting the classification of unknown examples. ID3 has been evaluated in both controlled tests and applications and has proven to work well in practice.

Quinlan, for example, has evaluated ID3's performance on the problem of learning to classify boards in a chess endgame (Quinlan 1983). The endgame involved white, playing with a king and a rook, against black, playing with a king and a knight. ID3's goal was to learn to recognize boards that led to a loss for black within 3 moves. The attributes were different high-level properties of boards, such as "an inability to move the king safely." The test used 23 such attributes.

Once board symmetries were taken into account, the entire problem domain consisted of 1.4 million different boards, of which 474,000 were a loss for black in 3 moves. ID3 was tested by giving it a randomly selected training set and then testing it on 10,000 different boards, also randomly selected. Quinlan's tests gave the results found in Table 12.2. The predicted maximum errors were derived from a statistical model of ID3's behavior in the domain. For details see Quinlan (1983).

These impressive results are supported by further empirical studies and by anecdotal results from further applications. Variations of ID3 have been developed to deal with such problems as noise and excessively large training sets. For more details, see Quinlan (1986a; 1986b).

12.4 Inductive Bias and Learnability

So far, our discussion has emphasized the use of empirical data to guide generalization. However, successful induction also depends upon prior knowledge and assumptions about the nature of the concepts being learned. *Inductive bias* refers to any criteria a learner uses

TABLE 12.2 THE EVALUATION OF ID3

SIZE OF TRAINING SET	PERCENTAGE OF WHOLE UNIVERSE	ERRORS IN 10,000 TRIALS	PREDICTED MAXI-MUM ERRORS
200	0.01	199	728
1,000	0.07	33	146
5,000	0.36	8	29
25,000	1.79	6	7
125,000	8.93	2	1

to constrain the concept space or to select concepts within that space. In the next section, we examine the need for bias and the types of biases that learning programs typically employ. Section 12.4.2 introduces theoretical results in quantifying the effectiveness of inductive biases.

12.4.1 Inductive Bias

Learning spaces tend to be large; without some way of pruning them, search-based learning would be a practical impossibility. For example, consider the problem of learning a classification of bit strings (strings of 0s and 1s) from positive and negative examples. Because a classification is simply a subset of the set of all possible strings, the total number of possible classifications is equal to the power set, or set of all subsets, of the entire population. If there are m instances, then there are 2^m possible classifications. But for strings of n bits, there are 2^n different strings. Thus, there are 2^{2^n} different classifications of bit strings of length n. Without some heuristic constraints, it would be impossible for a learner to effectively search such spaces in all but the most trivial domains.

Another reason for the necessity of bias is the nature of inductive generalization itself. Generalization is not truth preserving. For example, if we encounter an honest politician, are we justified in assuming that all politicians are honest? How many honest politicians must we encounter before we are justified in making this assumption? Hume discussed this problem, known as the problem of induction, several hundred years ago:

> You say that the one proposition is an inference from the other; but you must confess that the inference is not intuitive, neither is it demonstrative. Of what nature is it then? To say it is experimental is begging the question. For all inferences from experience suppose, as their foundation, that the future will resemble the past and that similar powers will be conjoined with similar sensible qualities (Hume 1748).

In induction, the training data are only a subset of all instances in the domain; consequently, any training set may support many different generalizations. In our example of a bit string classifier, assume that the learner has been given the strings {1100, 1010} as positive examples of some class of strings. Many generalizations are consistent with these examples: the set of all strings beginning with "1" and ending with "0," the set of all strings beginning with "1," the set of all strings of even parity, or any other subset of the entire population that includes {1100, 1010}. What criteria can the learner use to choose one of these generalizations? The data alone are not sufficient; all of these choices are consistent with that data. The learner must make additional assumptions about the nature of likely concepts.

In learning, these assumptions often take the form of heuristics for choosing a branch of the search space. The information theoretic test selection function used by ID3 (Section 12.3.2) is an example of such a heuristic. ID3 performs a hill-climbing search through the space of possible decision trees. At each stage of the search, it examines all the tests that could be used to extend the tree and chooses the test that gains the most information. This is a "greedy" heuristic: it favors branches of the search space that seem to move the greatest distance toward a goal state.

This heuristic allows ID3 to efficiently search the space of decision trees, and it also addresses the problem of choosing plausible generalizations from limited data. ID3 assumes that the smallest tree that correctly classifies all the given examples will be the most likely to classify future training instances correctly. The rationale for this assumption is that small trees are less likely to make assumptions not supported by the data. If the training set is large enough and truly representative of the population, such trees should include all and only the essential tests for determining class membership. As discussed in Section 12.3.3, empirical evaluations have shown this assumption to be quite justified. This preference for simple concept definitions is used in a number of learning algorithms, such as the CLUSTER/2 algorithm of Section 12.6.2.

Another form of inductive bias consists of syntactic constraints on the representation of learned concepts. Such biases are not heuristics for selecting a branch of the concept space. Instead, they limit the size of the space itself by requiring that learned concepts be expressed in a constrained representation language. Decision trees, for example, are a much more constrained language than full predicate calculus. The corresponding reduction in the size of the concept space is essential to ID3's efficiency.

An example of a syntactic bias that might prove effective in classifying bit strings would limit concept descriptions to patterns of symbols from the set {0, 1, #}. A pattern defines the class of all matching strings, where matching is determined according to the following rules:

If the pattern has a "0" in a certain position, then the target string must have a "0" in the corresponding position.

If the pattern has a "1" in a certain position, then the target string must have a "1" in the corresponding position.

A "#" in a given position can match either a "1" or a "0".

For example, the pattern, "1##0" defines the set of strings {1110, 1100, 1010, 1000}.

Considering only those classes that could be represented as a single such pattern reduces the size of the concept space considerably. For strings of length n, we may define 3^n different patterns. This is considerably smaller than the 2^{2^n} possible concepts in the unconstrained space. This bias also allows a straightforward implementation of version space search, where generalization involves replacing a 1 or a 0 in a candidate pattern with a #. However, the cost we incur for this bias is the inability to represent (and consequently learn) certain concepts. For example, a single pattern of this type cannot represent the class of all strings of even parity.

This trade-off between expressiveness and efficiency is typical. LEX, for example, does not distinguish between odd or even integers in its taxonomy of symbols. Consequently, it cannot learn any heuristic that depends upon this distinction. Although work has been done in programs that can change their bias in response to data (Utgoff 1986), most learning programs assume a fixed inductive bias.

Machine learning has explored a number of representational biases:

Conjunctive biases restrict learned knowledge to conjunctions of literals. This is particularly common because the use of disjunction in concept descriptions creates problems for generalization. For example, assume that we allow arbitrary use of disjuncts in the representation of concepts in the candidate elimination algorithm. Because the maximally specific generalization of a set of positive instances is simply the disjunction of all the instances, the learner will not generalize at all. It will add disjuncts ad infinitum, implementing a form of rote learning.

Limitations on the number of disjuncts. Purely conjunctive biases are too limited for many applications. One approach that increases the expressiveness of a representation while addressing the problems of disjunction is to allow a small, bounded number of disjuncts.

Feature vectors are a representation that describes objects as a set of features whose values differ from object to object. The objects in Table 12.1 are represented as sets of features.

Decision trees are a concept representation that has proven effective in the ID3 algorithm.

Horn clauses (Chapter 13) are a restriction on the form of implications that has been used by a number of programs for learning rules from examples.

In addition to the syntactic biases discussed in this section, a number of programs use domain specific knowledge to consider the known or assumed semantics of the domain. Such knowledge can provide an extremely effective bias. Section 12.5 examines these knowledge-based approaches. However, before considering the role of knowledge in learning, we briefly examine theoretical results quantifying inductive bias.

12.4.2 The Theory of Learnability

The goal of inductive bias is to restrict the set of target concepts in such a way that we may both search the set efficiently and find high-quality concept definitions. An interesting body of theoretical work addresses the problem of quantifying the effectiveness of an inductive bias.

We define the quality of concepts in terms of their ability to correctly classify objects that were not included in the set of training instances. It is not hard to write a learning algorithm that produces concepts that will correctly classify all the examples that it has seen; rote learning would suffice for this. However, due to the large number of instances in most domains, algorithms can only afford to examine a portion of the possible examples. Thus, the performance of a learned concept on new instances is critically important. In testing learning algorithms, we generally divide the set of all instances into nonintersecting sets of training instances and test instances. After training a program on the training set, we test it on the test set.

It is useful to think of efficiency and correctness as properties of the language for expressing concepts (i.e., the inductive bias) rather than a particular learning algorithm. Learning algorithms search a space of concepts; if this space is of manageable complexity and contains high-quality concept definitions, any reasonable learning algorithm should find these definitions; if the space is not, no algorithm will succeed. An extreme example may clarify this point.

The concept of "ball" is obviously learnable, given a suitable language for describing the properties of objects. After seeing a relatively small number of balls, a person will be able to define them concisely: balls are round. Contrast this with a concept that is obviously not learnable: suppose a team of people runs around the planet and selects a set of several million objects entirely at random, calling the resulting class "bunch_of_stuff." Not only would a concept induced from any sample of bunch_of_stuff require an extremely complex representation, but it also is highly unlikely that this concept would correctly classify unseen members of the set.

These observations make no assumption about the learning algorithms used, other than that they search in a reasonable fashion. "Ball" is learnable because we can define it in terms of a few features: the concept can be expressed in a biased language. Attempting to describe the concept "bunch_of_stuff" would require a concept definition at least as long as a list of all the properties of all the objects in the class. The space of all expressions in such a language would not allow efficient learning, regardless of the algorithm used.

Thus, rather than defining learnability in terms of specific algorithms, we define it in terms of the language used to represent concepts. Also, to achieve generality, we do not define learnability over specific problem domains, such as learning "bunch_of_stuff." Instead we define it in terms of the syntactic properties of the concept definition language.

In defining learnability, we must not only take efficiency into account; we must also deal with the fact that induction is not sound. No learning algorithm is guaranteed to produce a correct concept from an incomplete sample of training instances. Consequently, the correctness of a concept is the probability, over the entire population of instances, that it will correctly classify an instance.

We still have not solved all our problems. In addition to the correctness of learned concepts, we must also consider the likelihood with which an algorithm may find such concepts. We may think of a concept as defining a distribution of instances (the positive instances) in the entire population of instances. A set of training examples is a sample of this population. A particular distribution of positive instances, or a particular training set selected from these instances, may or may not be sufficient to select a high-quality concept. We must therefore be concerned with the probability that the algorithm will find a quality concept.

To summarize, learnability is a property of concept spaces and is determined by the language required to represent concepts. In evaluating these spaces, we must take into account both the probability that an algorithm will find a quality concept and the probability with which the resulting concept will correctly classify instances. Valiant has formalized these intuitions in the theory of Probably Approximately Correct (PAC) learning (1984).

A class of concepts is *learnable* if an algorithm exists that executes efficiently and has a high probability of finding an "approximately correct" concept. By approximately correct, we mean that the concept correctly classifies a high percentage of all possible instances.

Formally, Valiant defines learnability as follows. Let C be a set of concepts and I a set of instances. The concepts may be algorithms, patterns, or some other means of dividing I into positive and negative instances. Assume that an algorithm may query the set of instances, obtaining as many positive examples of a concept as it needs; the only restriction is that the algorithm must run in polynomial time. Note that this prevents exhaustive search of the example set, as doing so would require exponential time.

C is learnable if there exists an algorithm with the following properties:

1. The execution time for the algorithm is polynomial in the size of the concept learned, the number of properties examined, and adjustable parameters, $\in$ and σ.

2. For all distributions of positive examples, the program will, with probability of at least $(1-\sigma)$, produce a concept $c \in C$ such that c fails to correctly classify instances in I with probability of less than $\in$.

Note that we do not expect the algorithm to find an optimal concept definition; this is not possible given the inherent limitations of induction. We only expect it to find, with a high probability, a concept that is very likely to be correct. An interesting aspect of this definition is that it does not depend upon the distribution of positive examples in the instance space. It only depends upon the nature of the concept language (i.e., the bias) and the desired degree of correctness.

Using this definition of PAC learnability, researchers have shown the tractability of several inductive biases. For example, Valiant (1984) proves that the class of k-CNF expressions is learnable. k-CNF expressions are sentences in conjunctive normal form with a bound on the number of disjuncts; expressions are the conjunction of clauses, $c_1 \wedge c_2 \wedge \ldots c_n$, where each c_i is the disjunction of no more than k literals. This theoretical result supports the common restriction of concepts to conjunctive form used in many learning algorithms. We do not duplicate the proof here but refer the reader to Valiant's paper, where he proves this result, along with the learnability of other biases. For additional results in learnability and inductive bias, see Haussler (1988).

12.5   Knowledge and Learning

ID3 and the candidate elimination algorithm generalize on the basis of regularities in training data. Such algorithms are often referred to as *similarity based*, in that generalization is primarily a function of similarities across training examples. The biases employed by these algorithms are limited to syntactic constraints on the form of learned knowledge; they make no strong assumptions about the semantics of the domains. In this section, we examine algorithms, such as *explanation-based learning*, that use prior domain knowledge to guide generalization.

Initially, the idea that prior knowledge is necessary for learning seems contradictory. However, researchers have made a case for exactly that notion, arguing that the most effective learning occurs when the learner already has considerable knowledge of the domain. One argument for the importance of knowledge in learning is the reliance of similarity-based learning techniques on relatively large amounts of training data. Humans, in contrast, can form reliable generalizations from as few as a single training instance, and many practical applications require that a learning program do the same.

Another argument for the importance of prior knowledge recognizes that any set of training examples can support an unlimited number of generalizations, most of which are either irrelevant or nonsensical. Inductive bias is one means of making this distinction. In this section, we examine algorithms that go beyond purely syntactic biases to consider the role of strong domain knowledge in learning.

12.5.1 Meta-DENDRAL

Meta-DENDRAL (Buchanan and Mitchell 1978) is one of the earliest and still one of the best examples of the use of knowledge in inductive learning. Meta-DENDRAL acquires rules to be used by the DENDRAL program for analyzing mass spectrographic data. DENDRAL, introduced in Chapter 1, infers the structure of organic molecules from their chemical formula and mass spectrographic data.

A mass spectrograph bombards molecules with electrons, causing some of the chemical bonds to break. Chemists measure the weight of the resulting pieces and interpret these results to gain insight into the structure of the compound. DENDRAL employs such knowledge in the form of rules for interpreting mass spectrographic data. The premise of a DENDRAL rule is a graph of some portion of a molecular structure. The conclusion of the rule is that graph with the location of the cleavage indicated.

Meta-DENDRAL infers these rules from spectrographic results on molecules of known structure. Meta-DENDRAL is given the structure of a known compound, along with the mass and relative abundance of the fragments produced by spectrography. It interprets these, constructing an account of where the breaks occurred. These explanations of breaks in specific molecules are used as examples for constructing general rules.

In determining the site of a cleavage in a training run, DENDRAL uses a "half-order theory" of organic chemistry. This theory, though not powerful enough to support the direct construction of DENDRAL rules, does support the interpretation of cleavages in known molecules. The half-order theory consists of such constraints and heuristics as:

> Double and triple bonds do not break.
> Only fragments larger than two carbon atoms show up in the data.

Using the half-order theory, meta-DENDRAL constructs explanations of the cleavage. These explanations indicate the likely sites of cleavages along with possible migrations of atoms across the break.

These explanations become the set of positive instances for a rule induction program. This component induces the constraints in the premises of DENDRAL rules through a general to specific search. It begins with a totally general description of a cleavage: $X_1 * X_2$. This pattern means that a cleavage, indicated by the asterisk, can occur between any two atoms. It specializes the pattern by:

adding atoms: $X_1{}^*X_2 \rightarrow X_3{-}X_1{}^*X_2$

where the "$-$" operator indicates a chemical bond, or

instantiating atoms or attributes of atoms: $X_1{}^*X_2 \rightarrow C^*X_2$

Meta-DENDRAL learns from positive examples only and performs a hill-climbing search of the concept space. It prevents overgeneralization by limiting candidate rules to cover only about half of the training instances. Subsequent components of the program evaluate and refine these rules, looking for redundant rules or modifying rules that may be overly general or specific.

The strength of meta-DENDRAL is in its use of domain knowledge to change raw data into a more usable form. This gives the program noise resistance, through the use of its theory to eliminate extraneous or potentially erroneous data, and the ability to learn from relatively few training instances. The insight that training data must be so interpreted to be fully useful is the basis of explanation-based learning.

12.5.2   Explanation-Based Learning

Explanation-based learning uses an explicitly represented domain theory to construct an explanation of a training example, usually a proof that the example logically follows from the theory. By generalizing from the explanation of the instance, rather than from the instance itself, explanation-based learning filters noise, selects relevant aspects of experience, and organizes training data into a systematic and coherent structure.

There are several alternative formulations of this idea. For example, the STRIPS program for learning general operators for planning (Chapter 5) has exerted a powerful influence on this research (Fikes et al. 1972). Meta-DENDRAL, as we have just discussed, established the power of theory-based interpretation of training instances. More recently, a number of authors (DeJong and Mooney 1986; Minton 1988) have proposed alternative formulations of this idea. The *Explanation-Based Generalization* algorithm of Mitchell et al. (1986) is also typical of the genre. In this section, we examine a variation of the explanation-based learning (EBL) algorithm developed by DeJong and Mooney (1986).

EBL begins with:

1. *A target concept.* The learner's task is to determine an effective definition of this concept. Depending upon the specific application, the target concept may be a classification, a theorem to be proven, a plan for achieving a goal, or a heuristic for a problem solver.

2. *A training example,* an instance of the target.

3. *A domain theory,* a set of rules and facts that are used to explain how the training example is an instance of the goal concept.

4. *Operationality criteria,* some means of describing the form that concept definitions may take.

To illustrate EBL, we present an example of learning about when an object is a cup. This is a variation of a problem explored by Winston et al. (1983) and adapted to explanation-based learning by Mitchell et al. (1986). The target concept is a rule that may be used to infer whether an object is a cup:

premise(X) → cup(X)

where premise is a conjunctive expression containing the variable X.

Assume a domain theory that includes the following rules about cups:

liftable(X) ∧ holds_liquid(X) → cup(X)
part(Z, W) ∧ concave(W) ∧ points_up(W) → holds_liquid(Z)
light(Y) ∧ part(Y, handle) → liftable(Y)
small(A) → light(A)
made_of(A, feathers) → light(A)

The training example is an instance of the goal concept. That is, we are given:

cup(obj1)
small(obj1)
part(obj1, handle)
owns(bob, obj1)
part(obj1, bottom)
part(obj1, bowl)
points_up(bowl)
concave(bowl)
color(obj1, red)

Finally, assume the operationality criteria require that target concepts be defined in terms of observable, structural properties of objects, such as part and points_up. We may provide domain rules that enable the learner to infer whether a description is operational, or we may simply list operational predicates.

Using this theory, a theorem prover may construct an explanation of why the example is indeed an instance of the training concept: a proof that the target concept logically follows from the example, as in the first tree in Figure 12.17. Note that this explanation eliminates such irrelevant concepts as color(obj1, red) from the training data and captures those aspects of the example known to be relevant to the goal.

The next stage of explanation-based learning generalizes the explanation to produce a concept definition that may be used to recognize other cups. EBL accomplishes this by substituting variables for those constants in the proof tree that depend solely on the particular training instance, as in Figure 12.17. Based on the generalized tree, EBL defines a new rule whose conclusion is the root of the tree and whose premise is the conjunction of the leaves:

small(X) ∧ part(X, handle) ∧ part(X, W) ∧ concave(W) ∧ points_up(W) → cup(X).

In constructing a generalized proof tree, our goal is to substitute variables for those constants that are part of the training instance while retaining those constants and constraints that are part of the domain theory. In this example, the constant handle originated

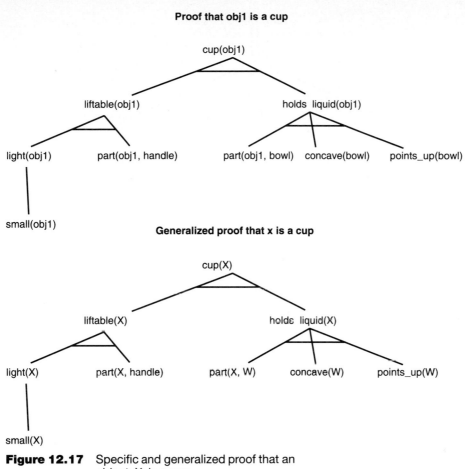

Figure 12.17 Specific and generalized proof that an object, X, is a cup.

in the domain theory rather than the training instance. We have retained it as an essential constraint in the acquired rule.

We may construct a generalized proof tree in a number of ways using a training instance as a guide. Mitchell et al. (1986) accomplish this by first constructing a proof tree that is specific to the training example and subsequently generalizing the proof through a process called *goal regression*. Goal regression matches the generalized goal (in our example, cup(X)) with the root of the proof tree, replacing constants with variables as required for the match. The algorithm applies these substitutions recursively through the tree until all appropriate constants have been generalized. See Mitchell et al. (1986) for a detailed description of this process.

DeJong and Mooney (1986) propose an alternative approach that essentially builds the generalized and the specific trees in parallel. This is accomplished by maintaining a variation of the proof tree consisting of the rules used in proving the goal distinct from the variable substitutions used in the actual proof. This is called an *explanation structure* (Fig.

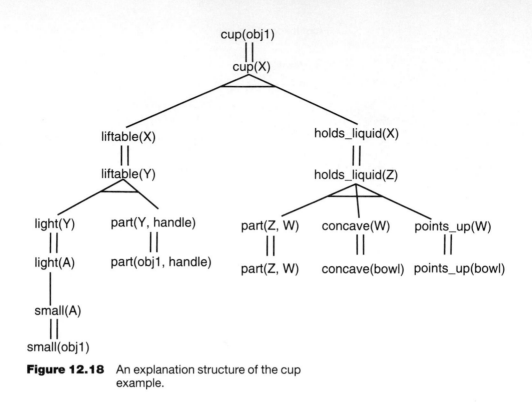

Figure 12.18 An explanation structure of the cup example.

12.18) and represents the abstract structure of the proof. The learner maintains two distinct substitution lists for the explanation structure: a list of the specific substitutions required to explain the training example and a list of general substitutions required to explain the generalized goal. It constructs these substitution lists as it builds the explanation structure.

We construct the lists of general and specific substitutions as follows: let s_s and s_g be the lists of specific and general substitutions, respectively. For every match between expressions e_1 and e_2 in the explanation structure, update s_s and s_g according to the following rule:

```
if e₁ is in the premise of a domain rule and e₂ is the conclusion of a domain rule
then begin
    Tₛ := the most general unifier of e₁sₛ and e₂sₛ          % unify e₁ and e₂ under sₛ
    sₛ := sₛTₛ                                               % update sₛ by composing it with Tₛ
    Tₘ := the most general unifier of e₁sₘ and e₂sₘ          % unify e₁ and e₂ under sₘ
    sₘ := sₘTₘ                                               % update sₘ by composing it with Tₘ
end
if e₁ is in the premise of a domain rule and e₂ is a fact in the training instance
then begin                                                  % only update sₛ
    Tₛ := the most general unifier of e₁sₛ and e₂sₛ          % unify e₁ and e₂ under sₛ
    sₛ := sₛTₛ                                               % update sₛ by composing it with Tₛ
end
```

In the example of Figure 12.18,

s_s = {obj1/X, obj1/Y, obj1/A, obj1/Z, bowl/W}
s_g = {X/Y, X/A, X/Z}

Applying these substitutions to the explanation structure of Figure 12.18 gives us the specific and general proof trees of Figure 12.17. See Chapter 13 for an implementation of EBL.

Explanation-based learning offers a number of benefits:

1. Training examples often contain irrelevant information, such as the color of the cup in the preceding example. The domain theory allows the learner to select the relevant aspects of the training instance.

2. A given example may allow numerous possible generalizations, most of which are either useless, meaningless, or wrong. EBL forms generalizations that are known to be relevant to specific goals and that are guaranteed to be logically consistent with the domain theory.

3. By using domain knowledge EBL allows learning from a single training instance.

4. Construction of an explanation allows the learner to hypothesize unstated relationships between its goals and its experience, such as deducing a definition of a cup based on its structural properties.

EBL has been applied to a number of learning problems. For instance, Mitchell et al. (1983) discuss the addition of EBL to the LEX algorithm. Suppose that the first positive example of the use of OP1 is in solving the instance $\int 7\, x^2\, dx$. LEX will make this instance a member of S, the set of maximally specific generalizations. However, a human would immediately recognize that the techniques used in solving this instance do not depend upon the specific values of the coefficient and exponent but will work for any real values, so long as the exponent is not equal to -1. The learner is justified in inferring that OP1 should be applied to any instance of the form $\int r_1\, x^{(r_2 \neq -1)}\, dx$, where r_1 and r_2 are any real numbers. LEX has been extended to use its knowledge of algebra with explanation-based learning to make this type of generalization.

12.5.3   EBL and Knowledge-Level Learning

Although an elegant formulation of the role of knowledge in learning, EBL raises a number of important questions. One of the more obvious ones concerns the issue of what an explanation-based learner actually learns. Pure EBL can only learn rules that are within the *deductive closure* of its existing theory. This means the learned rules could have been inferred from the knowledge base without using the training instance at all. The sole function of the training instance is to focus the theorem prover on relevant aspects of the problem domain. Consequently, EBL is often viewed as a form of *speed up learning* or knowledge base reformulation; EBL can make a learner work faster, because it does not have to reconstruct the proof tree underlying the new rule. However, because it could always have reconstructed the proof, EBL cannot make the learner do anything new. This distinction has been formalized by Dietterich in his discussion of *knowledge-level learning* (1986).

There are three responses to this objection. The first is to question its importance. For example, consider the game of chess: a minimal knowledge of the rules of chess, when coupled with an ability to perform unlimited look-ahead on board states, would allow a computer to play extremely well. Unfortunately, chess is too complex for this approach. An explanation-based learner that could master chess strategies would indeed learn something that was, for all practical purposes, new.

A second approach is to abandon the requirement that the learner have a complete and correct theory of the domain and focus on techniques for refining incomplete theories within the context of EBL. Here, the learner constructs a partial solution tree. Those branches of the proof that cannot be completed indicate deficiencies in the theory. A number of interesting questions remain to be examined in this area. These include the development of heuristics for reasoning with imperfect theories, credit assignment methodologies, and choosing which of several failed proofs should be repaired.

The third approach to this problem is to focus on integrating explanation-based learning and similarity-based approaches. Again, a number of basic schemes suggest themselves, such as using EBL to refine training data where the theory applies and then passing this partially generalized data on to a similarity-based learner for further generalization. Alternatively, we could use failed explanations as a means of targeting deficiencies in a theory, thereby guiding data collection for a similarity-based learner.

Other issues in EBL research include techniques for reasoning with unsound theories, alternatives to theorem proving as a means of constructing explanations, methods of dealing with noisy or missing training data, and methods of determining which generated rules to save.

12.5.4 Analogical Reasoning

Whereas "pure" EBL is limited to deductive learning, analogies offer a more flexible method of using existing knowledge. Analogical reasoning assumes that if two situations are known to be similar in some respects, it is likely that they will be similar in others. For example, if two houses have similar locations, construction, and condition, then they probably have the same sales value. Unlike the proofs used in EBL, analogy is not logically sound. In this sense it is like induction. As Russell (1989) and others have observed, analogy is a species of single instance induction. In our house example, we are inducing properties of one house from what is known about another.

Analogy allows great flexibility in applying existing knowledge to new situations. For example, assume that a student is trying to learn about the behavior of electricity, and assume that the teacher tells her that electricity is analogous to water, with voltage corresponding to pressure, amperage to the amount of flow, and resistance to the capacity of a pipe. Using analogical reasoning, the student may more easily grasp such concepts as Ohm's law.

The standard computational model of analogy defines the *source* of an analogy to be a problem solution, example, or theory that is relatively well understood. The *target* is not completely understood. Analogy constructs a *mapping* between corresponding elements of the target and source. Analogical inferences extend this mapping to new elements of the target domain. Continuing with the "electricity is like water" analogy, if we know that this analogy maps switches onto valves, amperage onto quantity of flow, and voltage onto water pressure, we may reasonably infer that there should be some analog to the capacity (i.e., the cross-sectional area) of a water pipe; this could lead to an understanding of electrical resistance.

A number of authors have proposed a unifying framework for computational models of analogical reasoning (Hall 1989; Kedar-Cabelli 1988; Wolstencroft 1989). A typical framework consists of the following stages:

1. *Retrieval.* Given a target problem, it is necessary to select a potential source analog. Problems in analogical retrieval include selecting those features of the target and source that increase the likelihood of retrieving a useful source analog and indexing knowledge according to those features. Generally, retrieval establishes the initial elements of an analogical mapping.

2. *Elaboration.* Once the source has been retrieved, it is often necessary to derive additional features and relations of the source. For example, it may be necessary to develop a specific problem-solving trace (or explanation) in the source domain as a basis for analogy with the target.

3. *Mapping and inference.* This stage involves developing the mapping of source attributes into the target domain. This involves both known similarities and analogical inferences.

4. *Justification.* Here we determine that the mapping is indeed valid. This stage may require modification of the mapping.

5. *Learning.* In this stage the acquired knowledge is stored in a form that will be useful in the future.

These stages have been developed in a number of computational models of analogical reasoning. For example, *structure mapping theory* (Falkenhainer 1990; Falkenhainer et al. 1989; Gentner 1983) not only addresses the problem of constructing useful analogies but also provides a plausible model of how humans understand analogies. A central question in the use of analogy is how we may distinguish expressive, deep analogies from more superficial comparisons. Gentner argues that true analogies should emphasize systematic, structural features of a domain over more superficial similarities. For example, the analogy, "the atom is like the solar system" is deeper than "the sunflower is like the sun," because the former captures a whole system of causal relations between orbiting bodies whereas the latter describes superficial similarities such as the fact that both sunflowers and the sun are round and yellow. This property of analogical mapping is called *systematicity.*

Structure mapping formalizes this intuition. Consider the example of the atom/solar system analogy (Fig. 12.19) as explicated by Gentner (1983). The source domain includes the predicates:

```
yellow(sun)
blue(earth)
hotter-than(sun, earth)
causes(more-massive(sun, earth), attract(sun, earth))
causes(attract(sun, earth), revolves-around(earth, sun))
```

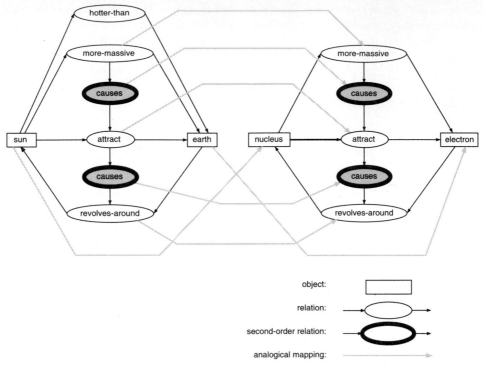

object: ▭

relation: ⟶⬭⟶

second-order relation: ⟶⬭⟶

analogical mapping: ⟶

Figure 12.19 An analogical mapping.

The target domain that the analogy is intended to explain includes

more-massive(nucleus, electron)
revolves-around(electron, nucleus)

Structure mapping attempts to transfer the causal structure of the source to the target. The mapping is constrained by the following rules:

1. Properties are dropped from the source. Because analogy favors systems of relations, the first stage is to eliminate those predicates that describe superficial properties of the source. Structure mapping formalizes this by eliminating predicates of a single argument (unary predicates) from the source. The rationale for this is that predicates of higher arity, by virtue of describing a relationship between two or more entities, are more likely to capture the systematic relations intended by the analogy. In our example, this eliminates such assertions as yellow(sun) and blue(earth). Note that the source may still contain assertions, such as hotter-than(sun, earth), that are not relevant to the analogy.

2. Relations map unchanged from the source to the target; the arguments to the relations may differ. In our example, such relations as revolves-around and more-massive are the same in both the source and the target. This constraint is used by

many theories of analogy and greatly reduces the number of possible mappings. It is also consistent with the heuristic of giving relations preference in the mapping.

3. In constructing the mapping, higher-order relations are preferred as a focus of the mapping. In our example, causes is a higher-order relation, because it takes other relations as its arguments. This is called the *systematicity principle*.

These constraints lead to the mapping:

sun → nucleus
earth → electron

Extending the mapping leads to the inference:

causes(more-massive(nucleus, electron), attract(nucleus, electron))
causes(attract(nucleus, electron), revolves-around(electron, nucleus))

Structure mapping theory has been implemented and tested in a number of domains. Though it remains far from a complete theory of analogy, failing to address such problems as source analog retrieval, it has proven both computationally practical and able to explain many aspects of human analogical reasoning. Before concluding our discussion of analogy, it is useful to comment on *case-based reasoning*.

12.5.5 Case-Based Reasoning

Case-based reasoning, unlike the learning and problem-solving methods discussed in the text so far, de-emphasizes the use of general rules. Instead, it stores solutions to problems in their original or slightly modified form. On addressing a new problem, a case-based reasoner retrieves a case it deems sufficiently similar and uses that case as a basis for solving the new problem. This involves a number of interesting problems.

Given a new problem and a set of solutions to previous problems, a case-based problem solver must:

1. Retrieve an appropriate case from its memory. This means that the memory of cases must be organized to aid such retrieval. Typically, case-based problem solvers index cases by their significant features, retrieving those cases that have the most features in common with the current problem. The selection of these features is highly problem dependent.

2. Modify the retrieved case so that it will apply to the current problem. Typically, a case is a sequence (or a tree) of operations that transform a starting state into a goal state. Case-based reasoners modify cases by deleting, adding, and reordering operations.

3. Apply the transformed case to the new problem. Step 2 modifies a case so that it may be applied to the new problem; however, this does not guarantee that the case will produce a correct solution. In applying the case to the current problem, the

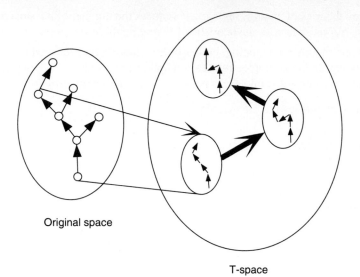

Original space

T-space

Figure 12.20   Transformational analogy (Carbonell 1983).

problem solver must test to make sure the results are correct. This may require
further modifications to the solution.

4. Save the new solution for future use.

Transformational analogy (Carbonell 1983) is an example of a case-based approach
to problem solving. It solves new problems by modifying existing solutions until they may
be applied to the new instance. Operators that modify complete problem solutions define a
higher-level space in which states are problem solutions and operators transform these solutions (Fig. 12.20). The goal is to transform a source solution into a solution to the target
problem. Operators modify solutions in ways such as inserting or deleting steps in a solution path, reordering steps in a solution, splicing new solutions into a portion of an old
solution, or changing the bindings of parameters in the current solution.

Transformational analogy typifies the approach used by case-based problem solving.
Later work has refined the approach, considering such issues as the representation of cases,
strategies for organizing a memory of prior cases, retrieval of relevant prior cases, and the
use of cases in solving new problems. For further information on case-based reasoning, see
Hammond (1989) and Kolodner (1988b).

12.6   Unsupervised Learning

The learning algorithms discussed so far implement forms of *supervised learning*. They
assume the existence of a teacher, fitness function, or some other external method of classifying training instances. *Unsupervised learning* eliminates the teacher and requires that
the learner form and evaluate concepts on its own. Science is perhaps the best example of

unsupervised learning in humans. Scientists do not have the benefit of a teacher. Instead, they propose hypotheses to explain observations; evaluate their hypotheses using such criteria as simplicity, generality, and elegance; and test hypotheses through experiments of their own design.

12.6.1 Discovery and Unsupervised Learning

AM (Davis and Lenat 1982; Lenat and Brown 1984) is one of the earliest and most successful discovery programs, deriving a number of interesting, even if not original, concepts in mathematics. AM began with the concepts of set theory, operations for creating new knowledge by modifying and combining existing concepts, and a set of heuristics for detecting "interesting" concepts. By searching this space of mathematical concepts, AM discovered the natural numbers along with several important concepts of number theory, such as the existence of prime numbers.

For example, AM discovered the natural numbers by modifying its notion of "bags." A bag is a generalization of a set that allows multiple occurrences of the same element. For example, {a, a, b, c, c} is a bag. By specializing the definition of bag to allow only a single type of element, AM discovered an analogy of the natural numbers. For example, the bag {1, 1, 1, 1} corresponds to the number 4. Union of bags led to the notion of addition: {1,1} $\cup$ {1,1} = {1,1,1,1}, or 2 + 2 = 4. Exploring further modifications of these concepts, AM discovered multiplication as a series of additions. Using a heuristic that defines new operators by inverting existing operators, AM discovered integer division. It found the concept of prime numbers by noting that certain numbers had exactly two divisors (themselves and 1).

On creating a new concept, AM evaluates it according to a number of heuristics, keeping those concepts that prove "interesting." AM determined that prime numbers were interesting based on the frequency with which they occur. In evaluating concepts using this heuristic, AM generates instances of the concept, testing each to see whether the concept holds. If a concept is true of all instances it is a tautology, and AM gives it a low evaluation. Similarly, AM rejects concepts that are true of no instances. If a concept is true of a significant portion of the examples (as is the case with prime numbers), AM evaluates it as interesting and selects it for further modification.

Although AM discovered prime numbers and several other interesting concepts, it failed to progress much beyond elementary number theory. In a later analysis of this work, Lenat and Brown (1984) examine the reasons for the program's success and its limitations. Although Lenat originally believed that AM's heuristics were the prime source of its power, this later evaluation attributed much of the program's success to the language used to represent mathematical concepts. AM represented concepts as recursive structures in a variation of the LISP programming language. Because of its basis in a well-designed programming language, this representation defined a space that contained a high density of interesting concepts. This was particularly true in the early stages of the search. As exploration continued, the space grew combinatorially, and the percentage of interesting concepts "thinned out." This observation further underscores the relationship between representation and search.

Another reason AM failed to continue the impressive pace of its early discoveries is its inability to "learn to learn." It did not acquire new heuristics as it gained mathematical knowledge; consequently, the quality of its search degraded as its mathematics grew more complex. In this sense, AM never developed a deep understanding of mathematics. Lenat has addressed this problem in later work on a program called EURISKO, which attempts to learn new heuristics (Lenat 1983).

A number of other programs have continued to explore the problems of automatic discovery. IL (Sims 1987) applies a variety of learning techniques to mathematical discovery, including analytical methods such as theorem proving and explanation-based learning (Section 12.5). BACON (Langley et al. 1987) has developed computational models of the formation of quantitative scientific laws. For example, using data on the distance of the planets from the sun and the period of their orbits, BACON "re-discovered" Kepler's laws of planetary motion. By providing a plausible computational model of how humans may have achieved discovery in a variety of domains, BACON has provided a useful tool and methodology for examining the process of human scientific discovery. Shrager and Langley (1990) describe a number of other discovery systems.

Although scientific discovery is an important research area, progress to date has been slight. A more basic, and perhaps more fruitful, problem in unsupervised learning concerns the discovery of categories. Lakoff (1987) suggests that categorization is fundamental to human cognition: higher-level theoretical knowledge depends upon the ability to organize the particulars of our experience into coherent taxonomies. Most of our knowledge is about categories of objects, such as cows, rather than about specific individuals, such as Blossom or Ferdinand. Nordhausen and Langley have emphasized the formation of categories as the basis for a unified theory of scientific discovery (Nordhausen and Langley 1990). In developing explanations of why chemicals react in the ways they do, chemistry built on prior work in classifying compounds into categories such as "acid" and "alkaline." In the next section, we examine *conceptual clustering*, which is the problem of discovering useful categories in unclassified data.

12.6.2 Conceptual Clustering

The *clustering problem* begins with a collection of unclassified objects and some means of measuring the similarity of objects. Its goal is organizing the objects into a hierarchy of classes that meet some standard of quality, such as maximizing the similarity of objects in the same class.

Numeric taxonomy is one of the oldest approaches to the clustering problem. Numeric methods rely upon the representation of objects as a collection of features, each of which may have some numeric value. A reasonable similarity metric treats each object (a vector of n feature values) as a point in n-dimensional space. The similarity of two objects is the euclidean distance between them in this space.

Using this similarity metric, a common clustering algorithm builds clusters in a bottom-up fashion. This approach, often called an *agglomerative clustering* strategy, forms categories by:

1. Examining all pairs of objects, selecting the pair with the highest degree of similarity, and making that pair a cluster.

2. Defining the features of the cluster as some function, such as average, of the features of the component members and then replacing the component objects with this cluster definition.

3. Repeating this process on the collection of objects until all objects have been reduced to a single cluster.

The result of this algorithm is a binary tree whose leaf nodes are instances and whose internal nodes are clusters of increasing size.

We may extend this algorithm to objects represented as sets of symbolic, rather than numeric, features. The only problem is in measuring the similarity of objects defined using symbolic rather than numeric values. A reasonable approach defines the similarity of two objects as the proportion of features that they have in common. Given the objects

```
object1 = {small, red, rubber, ball}
object2 = {small, blue, rubber, ball}
object3 = {large, black, wooden, ball}
```

this metric would compute the similarity values:

```
similarity(object1, object2) = ¾
similarity(object1, object3) = similarity(object2, object3) = ¼
```

However, similarity-based clustering algorithms do not adequately capture the underlying role of semantic knowledge in cluster formation. For example, humans did not define constellations of stars on the basis of their closeness in the sky. Instead, these definitions were formed on the basis of existing human concepts, such as "the big dipper." In defining categories, we cannot give all features equal weight. In any given context, certain of an object's features are more important than others; simple similarity metrics treat all features equally. Human categories depend upon the goals of the categorization and prior knowledge of the domain much more than on surface similarity. Consider, for example, the classification of whales as mammals instead of fish. Surface similarities cannot account for this classification, which depends upon the wider goals of biological classification and extensive physiological and evolutionary evidence.

Traditional clustering algorithms not only fail to take goals and background knowledge into account, but they also fail to produce meaningful semantic explanations of the resulting categories. These algorithms represent clusters *extensionally*, which means by enumerating all of their members. The algorithms produce no *intensional* definition, or no general rule that defines the semantics of the category and that may be used to classify both known and future members of the category. For example, an extensional definition of the set of people who have served as secretary-general of the United Nations would simply list those individuals. An intensional definition, such as:

```
{X | X has been elected secretary-general of the United Nations}
```

would have the added benefits of defining the class semantically and allowing us to recognize future members of the category.

Conceptual clustering addresses these problems by using machine learning techniques to produce general concept definitions and apply background knowledge to the formation of categories. CLUSTER/2 (Michalski and Stepp 1983) is a good example of this approach. It uses background knowledge in the form of biases on the language used to represent categories.

CLUSTER/2 forms k categories by constructing individuals around k *seed* objects. k is a parameter that may be adjusted by the user. CLUSTER/2 evaluates the resulting clusters, selecting new seeds and repeating the process until its quality criteria are met. The algorithm is defined:

1. Select k seeds from the set of observed objects. This may be done randomly or according to some selection function.

2. For each seed, using that seed as a positive instance and all other seeds as negative instances, produce a maximally general definition that covers all of the positive and none of the negative instances. Note that this may lead to multiple classifications of other, nonseed, objects.

3. Classify all objects in the sample according to these descriptions. Replace each maximally general description with a maximally specific description that covers all objects in the category. This decreases likelihood that classes overlap on unseen objects.

4. Classes may still overlap on given objects. CLUSTER/2 includes an algorithm for adjusting overlapping definitions.

5. Using a distance metric, select an element closest to the center of each class. The distance metric could be similar to the similarity metric discussed above.

6. Using these central elements as new seeds, repeat steps 1–5. Stop when clusters are satisfactory. A typical quality metric is the complexity of the general descriptions of classes. For instance, a variation of Occam's Razor might prefer clusters that yield syntactically simple definitions, such as those with a small number of conjuncts.

7. If clusters are unsatisfactory and no improvement occurs over several iterations, select the new seeds closest to the edge of the cluster, rather than those at the center.

Figure 12.21 shows the stages of a CLUSTER/2 execution.

12.6.3 COBWEB and the Structure of Taxonomic Knowledge

Many clustering algorithms, as well as many supervised learning algorithms such as ID3, define categories in terms of necessary and sufficient conditions for membership. These conditions are a set of properties possessed by all members of a category and only by members of the category. Though many categories, such as the set of all United Nations delegates, may be so defined, human categories do not always fit this model. Indeed, human categorization is characterized by greater flexibility and a much richer structure than we have so far examined.

For example, if human categories were indeed defined by necessary and sufficient conditions for membership, we could not distinguish degrees of category membership.

After selecting seeds (step 1).

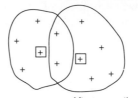

After generating general descriptions (step 3). Note that the categories overlap.

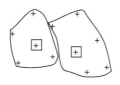

After specializing concept descriptions (step 4). There are still intersecting elements.

After eliminating duplicate elements (step 5).

Figure 12.21 The steps of a CLUSTER/2 run.

However, psychologists have noted a strong sense of prototypicality in human categorization (Rosch 1978). For instance, we generally think of a robin as a better example of a bird than a chicken; an oak is a more typical example of a tree than a palm (at least in northern latitudes).

Family resemblance theory (Wittgenstein 1953) supports these notions of prototypicality by arguing that categories are defined by complex systems of similarities between members, rather than by necessary and sufficient conditions for membership. Such categories may not have any properties shared by all of their members. Wittgenstein cites the example of games: not all games require two or more players, such as solitaire; not all games are fun for the players, such as pro football; not all games have well-articulated rules, such as children's games of make believe; and not all games involve competition, such as jumping rope. Nonetheless, we consider the category to be well-defined and unambiguous.

Human categories also differ from most formal inheritance hierarchies (Chapter 9) in that not all levels of human taxonomies are equally important. Psychologists (Rosch 1978) have demonstrated the existence of *base-level* categories. The base-level category is the classification most commonly used in describing objects, the terminology first learned by children, and the level that in some sense captures the most fundamental classification of an object. For example, the category "chair" is more basic than either its generalizations, such as "furniture," or its specializations, such as "office chair." "Car" is more basic than either "sedan" or "vehicle."

Common methods of representing class membership and hierarchies, such as logic, inheritance systems, feature vectors, or decision trees, do not account for these effects. Yet doing so is not only important to cognitive scientists, whose goal is the understanding of human intelligence; it is also valuable to the engineering of useful AI applications. Users evaluate a program in terms of its flexibility, its robustness, and its ability to behave in ways that seem reasonable by human standards. Although we do not require that AI algorithms parallel the architecture of the human mind, any algorithm that proposes to discover categories must meet user expectations as to the structure and behavior of those categories.

COBWEB (Fisher 1987) addresses these issues. Although it is not intended as a model of human cognition, it does account for base-level categorization and degrees of category membership. In addition, COBWEB learns incrementally: it does not require that all instances be present before it begins learning. In many applications, the learner acquires data over time. In these situations, it must construct usable concept descriptions from an initial collection of data and update those descriptions as more data become available. COBWEB also addresses the problem of determining the correct number of clusters. CLUSTER/2 produced a prespecified number of categories. Although the user could vary this number or the algorithm could try different values in an effort to improve categorization, such approaches are not particularly flexible. COBWEB uses global quality metrics to determine the number of clusters, the depth of the hierarchy, and the category membership of new instances.

Unlike the algorithms we have seen so far, COBWEB represents categories probabilistically. Instead of defining category membership as a set of values that must be present for each feature of an object, COBWEB represents the probability with which each feature value is present. $p(f_i = v_{ij} | c_k)$ is the conditional probability with which feature f_i will have value v_{ij}, given that an object is in category c_k.

Figure 12.22 illustrates a COBWEB taxonomy taken from Gennari et al. (1989). In this example, the algorithm has formed a categorization of the four single-cell animals at the bottom of the figure. Each animal is defined by its value for the features: number of tails, color, and number of nuclei. The members of category C3, for example, have a 1.0 probability of having 2 tails, a 0.5 probability of having light color, and a 1.0 probability of having 2 nuclei.

As the figure illustrates, each category in the hierarchy includes probabilities of occurrence for all values of all features. This is essential to both categorizing new instances and modifying the category structure to better fit new instances. Indeed, as an incremental algorithm, COBWEB does not separate these actions. When given a new instance, COBWEB considers the overall quality of either placing the instance in an existing category or modifying the hierarchy to accommodate the instance. The criterion COBWEB uses for evaluating the quality of a classification is called *category utility* (Gluck and Corter 1985). Category utility was developed in research on human categorization. It accounts for base-level effects and other aspects of human category structure.

Category utility attempts to maximize both the probability that two objects in the same category have values in common and the probability that objects in different categories will have different property values. Category utility is defined:

$$\sum_k \sum_i \sum_j p(f_i = v_{ij}) \, p(f_i = v_{ij} | c_k) \, p(c_k | f_i = v_{ij})$$

This sum is taken across all categories, c_k, all features, f_i, and all feature values, v_{ij}. $p(f_i = v_{ij} | c_k)$, called *predictability*, is the probability that an object has value v_{ij} for feature

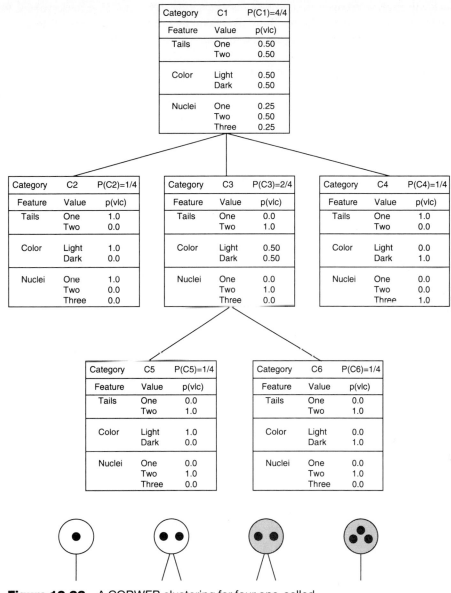

Figure 12.22 A COBWEB clustering for four one-celled organisms (Gennari 1989).

f_i given that the object belongs to category c_k. The higher this probability, the more likely two objects in a category share the same feature values. $p(c_k \mid f_i = v_{ij})$, called *predictiveness,* is the probability with which an object belongs to category c_k given that it has value v_{ij} for feature f_i. The greater this probability, the less likely objects not in the category will have those feature values. $p(f_i = v_{ij})$ serves as a weight, assuring that frequently occurring feature values will exert a stronger influence on the evaluation. By combining these values, high category utility measures indicate a high likelihood that objects in the same category will share properties, while decreasing the likelihood of objects in different categories having properties in common.

The COBWEB algorithm is defined:

```
cobweb(Node, Instance)
begin
  if Node is a leaf
    then begin
      create two children of Node, L₁ and L₂;
      set the probabilities of L₁ to those of Node;
      initialize the probabilities for L₂ to those of Instance;
      add Instance to Node, updating Node's probabilities;
    end
    else begin
      add Instance to Node, updating Node's probabilities;
      for each child, C, of Node, compute the category utility of the clustering
          achieved by placing Instance in C;
      let S₁ be the score for the best categorization, C₁;
      let S₂ be the score for the second best categorization, C₂;
      let S₃ be the score for placing instance in a new category;
      let S₄ be the score for merging C₁ and C₂ into one category;
      let S₅ be the score for splitting C₁ (replacing it with its child categories)
    end
  If S₁ is the best score
    then cobweb(C₁, Instance)                              % place the instance in C₁
      else if S₃ is the best score
        then initialize the new category's probabilities to those of Instance
        else if S₄ is the best score
          then begin
            let Cₘ be the result of merging C₁ and C₂;
            cobweb(Cₘ, Instance)
          end
          else if S₅ is the best score
            then begin
              split C₁;
              cobweb(Node, Instance)
            end;
end
```

COBWEB performs a hill-climbing search of the space of possible taxonomies using category utility to evaluate and select possible categorizations. It initializes the taxonomy to a single category whose features are those of the first instance. For each subsequent instance, the algorithm begins with the root category and moves through the tree. At each level it uses category utility to evaluate the taxonomies resulting from:

1. Placing the instance in the best existing category.

2. Adding a new category containing only the instance.

3. Merging two existing categories into one and adding the instance to that category.

4. Splitting an existing category and placing the instance in the best category in the resulting taxonomy.

Figure 12.23 illustrates the processes of merging and splitting nodes. To merge two nodes, the algorithm creates a new node and makes the existing nodes children of that node. It computes the probabilities for the new node by combining the probabilities for the children. Splitting replaces a node with its children.

This algorithm is efficient and produces taxonomies with a reasonable number of classes. Because it allows probabilistic membership, its categories are flexible and robust. In addition, it has demonstrated base-level category effects and, through its notion of partial category matching, supports notions of prototypicality and degree of membership.

Instead of relying on two-valued logic to achieve soundness and completeness in reasoning, COBWEB, like fuzzy logic, views the often frustrating vagueness of human cognition as a necessary component for learning and reasoning in a flexible and intelligent fashion. This point of view is partly motivated by the brittleness (Section 12.7.1) that plagues symbolic approaches to AI. Systems including COBWEB, fuzzy reasoning, and certainty theory (Chapter 8) attempt to solve these problems in a symbolic context. The remainder of this chapter examines *subsymbolic* models of intelligence and their success in solving such problems.

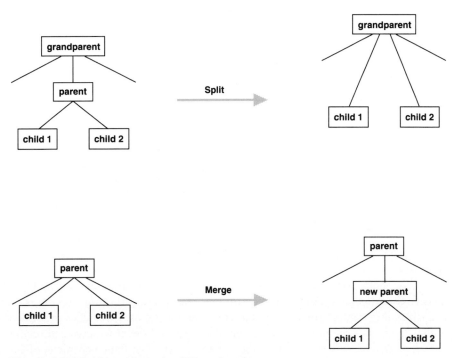

Figure 12.23   Merging and splitting of nodes.

12.7 Parallel Distributed Processing

Throughout this chapter, as well as the majority of this text, we emphasize a symbol-based approach to artificial intelligence. The algorithms and representations considered reflect the physical symbol system hypothesis, as discussed in Chapter 16: intelligence can be achieved through formal operations on symbol structures. A central aspect of this hypothesis is the use of symbols to refer to objects and relations in a domain of interpretation. In this section, we introduce *subsymbolic* approaches. Subsymbolic models, also known as *parallel distributed processing (PDP),* de-emphasize the use of symbols to denote objects and relations. Instead, they view intelligence as arising from the collective behavior of large numbers of simple, interacting components.

Biological brains provide a paradigm for this architecture. Brains consist of an extremely large number of interconnected neurons (Figure 1.2). Relative to an entire brain, a biological neuron is not capable of very much. However, the brain, with its billions of neurons and trillions of connections between them, is capable of a great deal. *Neural networks*, a family of computational architectures inspired by biological brains, are a typical example of parallel distributed processing. However, PDP also encompasses a variety of approaches including cellular automata, genetic algorithms, and models based on the thermodynamic behavior of physical materials.

Much of the motivation for parallel distributed models stems from the shortcomings of symbol-based AI. Most symbolic AI programs suffer from the problem of *brittleness.* Though brittleness is difficult to define succinctly, it encompasses a number of phenomena that stem from the all or nothing nature of two-valued logic. In humans, performance degrades steadily as problems get harder; an expert system, in contrast, will perform perfectly until it fails to perform at all. A human expert will never simply fail to come up with an answer to a problem; instead she will propose a reasonable response to even the most difficult problems.

Connectionist approaches, such as neural networks, contrast with more traditional architectures in relying upon large numbers of simple computational units instead of on a single, powerful processor, although most implementations model this parallelism on a sequential machine. This approach undermines the distinction between data and process inherent in traditional von Neumann computing. Computation is not constrained to the sequential operations on data; the units of computation, like biological neurons, function independently. Unlike symbol-based AI, PDP assumes no correspondence between the units of computation and objects or relations in the world. There is no unit of computation, no symbol, that corresponds to a concept such as "dog," "purple," or "justice." Instead of representing knowledge explicitly and manipulating it through an inference engine, connectionist programs represent knowledge implicitly in patterns of interactions between components.

Both symbolic and neural computing have addressed this problem. Fuzzy logic has seen success in this area: instead of requiring the truth of all of a rule's premises, fuzzy logic enables the problem solver to find the rule that most closely matches the data. PDP algorithms address these problems by de-emphasizing high-level features and relying on an overall pattern of activation of its artificial neurons. The distributed character of knowledge in a neural network allows reasonable performance with incomplete or noisy data. For similar reasons, *connectionist approaches* tend to demonstrate graceful degradation when faced with unusual problems.

Figure 12.24 illustrates a simple type of neural network, called a *perceptron network*, as it might be used to recognize shapes in a vision system. The inputs to the network are the values of pixels in the image, having a value of 0 or 1, depending on whether the pixel is on or off. Each input passes its value to one or more perceptron units along weighted arcs. Each unit computes a function of the weighted input values and outputs a 0 or 1 in turn. A user, or some other external process, interprets the output values as a classification of the shape.

Unlike traditional programs or expert systems, neural networks are trained rather than programmed. The weights on the arcs change in response to the network's experience in classifying a set of training examples. We next examine the perceptron learning algorithm in detail.

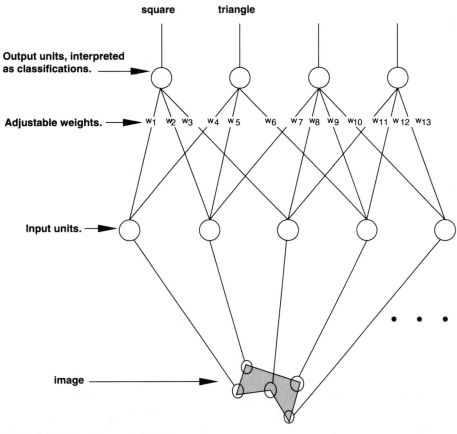

Figure 12.24 A perceptron network.

12.7.1 Foundations of Neural Networks

Although neural nets are often thought of as a recent development, we may trace their origins to early work in computer science, psychology, and philosophy. John von Neumann, for example, was fascinated by both cellular automata and neurally inspired approaches to computation. Early work in neural learning was influenced by psychological theories of animal learning. In this section, we outline the basic components of neural network learning and present some of the historically important early work in the field.

The basis of neural networks is the artificial neuron (Fig. 12.25). An artificial neuron consists of:

Input values, x_i. This data may come from the environment or the activation of other neurons. Different implementations vary in the possible values of the inputs; typically they are either discrete values from the set $\{0,1\}$ or $\{-1, 1\}$ or real valued numbers.

A set of real valued weights, w_i.

A set of activation values. The neuron computes its activation value from its weights and inputs. This value may become the input to other cells or contribute to the results of the system as a whole.

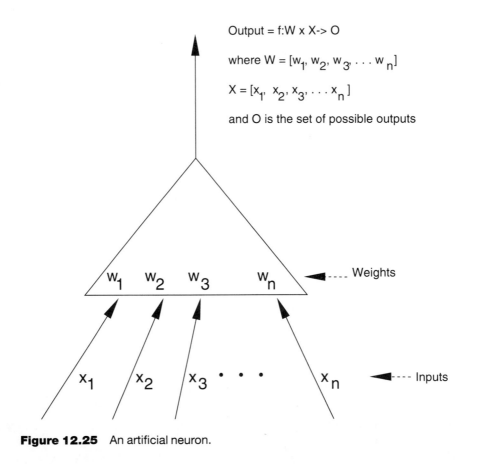

Output = f:W x X-> O

where W = [w_1, w_2, w_3, ... w_n]

X = [x_1, x_2, x_3, ... x_n]

and O is the set of possible outputs

Figure 12.25 An artificial neuron.

An activation function, **F**, that computes the neuron's activation value as a function of its weights and input data.

In addition to these properties of individual neurons, a neural network is also characterized by global properties such as

The network topology, or the pattern of connections between the individual neurons.

The topology of a network is the primary source of its inductive bias.

The learning algorithm used.

The environment. This includes the interpretation placed on the data to the network and results of processing.

The earliest example of neural computing is the McCulloch-Pitts neuron (McCulloch and Pitts, 1943). The inputs to a McCulloch-Pitts neuron are either excitatory (+1) or inhibitory (0). The activation function multiplies each input by its corresponding weight and sums the results; if the sum is greater than or equal to 0, the neuron returns 1; otherwise, it returns to 0. McCulloch and Pitts showed how these neurons could be constructed to compute any logical function, demonstrating that systems of these neurons provide a complete computational model.

Figure 12.26 shows the McCulloch-Pitts neurons for computing the basic logical functions. The and neuron has three inputs: X and Y are the values to be conjoined, and the third input has a constant value of +1. The inputs have weights of +1, +1, and −2, respectively. For any values of X and Y, the neuron computes the value of X + Y − 2: if this value is less than 0, it outputs 0; otherwise it outputs 1. As Table 12.3 illustrates, the neuron computes the logical and of X and Y. Similarly, the weighted sum of inputs to the or neuron is greater than or equal to 0 unless both X and Y equal 0.

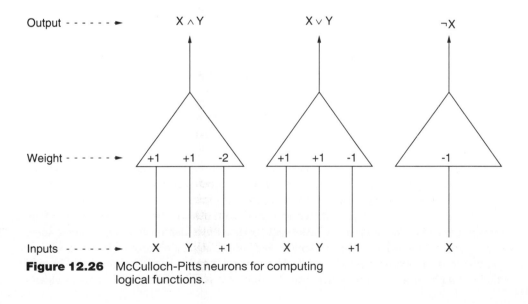

Figure 12.26 McCulloch-Pitts neurons for computing logical functions.

TABLE 12.3

X	Y	X+Y−2	OUTPUT
1	1	0	1
1	0	−1	0
0	1	−1	0
0	0	−2	0

McCulloch and Pitts demonstrated the power of neural computation, and interest in the approach flourished with the development of practical learning algorithms for neural networks. Learning in neural computers drew heavily on the work of the psychologist D. O. Hebb, who theorized that learning occurred in brains through the modification of synapses (Hebb 1949). Hebb theorized that repeated firings across a synapse increase its sensitivity and the future likelihood of its firing. If a particular stimulus repeatedly caused activity in a group of cells, those cells would come to be strongly associated. In the future, similar stimuli would tend to excite the same pathways through these cells, resulting in recognition of the stimuli.

In the late 1950s, Frank Rosenblatt devised a learning algorithm for a type of single-layer neural network called a *perceptron* (Rosenblatt 1958). In a single-layer network, there is only one set of weighted arcs between the input and output units. The inputs and activation levels of the perceptron are either 0 or 1; weights are real valued. Perceptrons implement a simple linear thresholding function; given inputs x_i, weights w_i, and a threshold, t, the perceptron computes its activation as:

1 if $\Sigma \, x_i w_i > t$
0 otherwise

The perceptron implements a simple form of supervised learning. After it attempts to solve a problem instance, a teacher gives it the correct results. The perceptron then changes its weights according to the following rules. Let d be a constant whose size determines the learning rate:

If the activation of the unit is correct, do nothing.

If the activation is 0 and should be 1, increment the weights on the active lines (lines whose input is 1) by d.

If the activation is 1 and should be 0, decrement the weights on the active lines by d.

This procedure has the effect of moving the weights closer to the desired output. The perceptron learning procedure has been shown to converge to a correct assignment of weights if such an assignment exists (Minsky and Papert 1969).

Perceptrons were initially greeted with great enthusiasm. However, Minsky and Papert, in their book *Perceptrons* (Minsky and Papert 1969), demonstrated that single-layer perceptron networks have inherent limitations. For example, a perceptron is not capable of representing the **exclusive-or** function. To learn this function, a perceptron would have to find a weight assignment that satisfied the inequalities of Figure 12.27. This is clearly impossible. Unfortunately, though multiple-layer networks can represent exclusive-or, the perceptron learning algorithm only works for single-layer networks. This is a severe problem, as it means that single-layer networks are not computationally complete.

The problem with exclusive-or is a special case of a much more general restriction on single-layer networks: they can only learn classes that are *linearly separable*. We may think of the set of possible data for a network as defining a space. Each input corresponds to one dimension, with each possible set of input values defining a point. The problem of learning a binary classification of training instances reduces to that of separating these points into two groups. For a space of n dimensions, a classification is linearly separable if these groups could be separated with a single, n-1 dimensional hyperplane. Figure 12.28

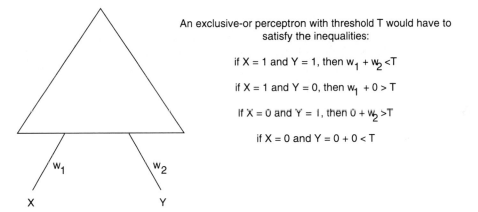

An exclusive-or perceptron with threshold T would have to satisfy the inequalities:

if $X = 1$ and $Y = 1$, then $w_1 + w_2 < T$

if $X = 1$ and $Y = 0$, then $w_1 + 0 > T$

If $X = 0$ and $Y = 1$, then $0 + w_2 > T$

if $X = 0$ and $Y = 0 + 0 < T$

Figure 12.27   The impossibility of computing exclusive-or in a single-layer perceptron.

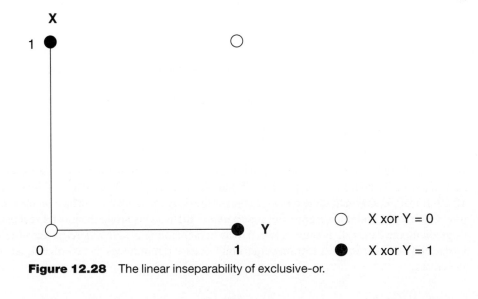

Figure 12.28   The linear inseparability of exclusive-or.

shows the linear inseparability of exclusive-or; there is no way to draw a single straight line that separates the black dots from the white dots.

As a result of these limitations, research emphasis shifted toward symbol-based AI, slowing progress in neural networks. However, subsequent work has shown these problems to be solvable. In Section 12.7.3, we discuss *backpropagation*, a learning procedure that works for multilayered networks and overcomes the limitations of one-layer perceptrons. Before examining backpropagation, however, we define the *delta rule*, a generalization of the perceptron learning algorithm that is used in many neural network implementations, including backpropagation.

12.7.2 The Delta Rule

Perceptron learning, though it converges on a correct set of weights for all linearly separable classifications, does not take into account the amount of the error in the network. If we modify the neurons to have real-valued activation functions, we may more accurately measure the amount of error. A simple linear activation function can be obtained by subtracting the threshold, $+$, from the weighted sum of the inputs and returning this result. The output, O, of a unit is computed by

$$O = \Sigma\ x_i w_i - t$$

If the result must be a discrete value, such as 0 or 1, the application may simply round the result to the closest of the desired values or apply a thresholding function to each output.

Given this activation function, we may define the amount of error as the difference between the actual output and the desired output. The delta rule adjusts the weights as a function of this error. Let O_a be the actual output of a neuron and O_c be the correct output. As with perceptrons, d is a constant determining learning rate and x_i is the input on the line. For each weight w_i, the new value is computed by:

$$w_i(new) = w_i(old) + d(O_c - O_a)\ x_i$$

The delta rule is highly efficient in minimizing the overall error of the neuron. We define the overall error of a unit as a function of its errors over all possible input values. A common error measure is given by the sum of squares of the error over all outputs, or

$$Error = \Sigma\ (O_c - O_a)^2$$

If we plot the amount of error against the possible sets of weights, the result is a curved surface, with its bottom corresponding to the optimal weight assignment, as in Figure 12.29. It may be shown that the delta rule moves the weights along this surface on the most direct path to the optimal weights. Because it moves the weights along the most direct path, or gradient, the delta rule is often referred to as implementing *gradient descent learning*. It is also called a *least squares* learning algorithm because it minimizes the average square of the errors.

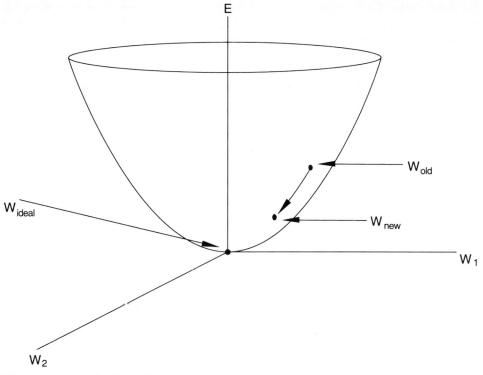

Figure 12.29 Gradient descent learning.

The learning constant, d, exerts an important influence on the performance of the delta rule, as further contemplation of Figure 12.29 illustrates. The value of d determines how much the weight values move in a single learning episode. The larger the value of d, the more quickly the weights move toward an optimal value. However, if d is too large, the algorithm may overshoot the bottom and end up oscillating around the optimal weights. Smaller values of d are less prone to this problem but do not allow the system to learn as quickly. The optimal value of the learning rate is a parameter that is often adjusted through experiment.

Although the delta rule does not in itself overcome the limitations of single-layer networks, it is central to the functioning of backpropagation, an algorithm for implementing learning in a multilayer network.

12.7.3 Backpropagation

As we mentioned in Section 12.7.1, all single-layer neural networks are severely limited as to the relationships that they can represent. Though multilayered networks are computationally complete, early researchers had not solved the problem of learning for any but single-layer networks. If we examine the delta rule, we see that all the information needed to update the weights on a neuron is local to that neuron, except for the amount of error.

For output units, this is easily computed as the difference between the correct and actual outputs. How can a neural network determine the error committed by an internal neuron that has contributed to the errors of several other units?

Backpropagation is an algorithm for apportioning the error responsibility through a multilayered network. The neurons in a backpropagation network are connected in layers, with units in layer k passing their activations only to neurons in layer k+1. In solving a problem, activation passes from the input units, through one or more internal layers of neurons, called *hidden units*, and ultimately passes to the output layer and the environment.

Given the correct results, the network may calculate the error in the output units just as it did for a single-layer network. The error for a neuron in the layer directly below the output layer is a function of the errors on all the units that use its output. In general, the error for a neuron at layer n is a function of the errors of all the neurons at layer n+1 that use its output. In a backpropagation network, activation moves forward through the net in a layer by layer fashion. Error propagation moves backward in a similar fashion (Fig. 12.30).

Unlike the networks that we have already examined, backpropagation nets do not compute a linear thresholding function on their inputs. Instead, they use a *sigmoidal* activation function. Sigmoidal functions are so called because their graph is an "S"-shaped curve (see Fig. 12.31). A common activation function used in backpropagation is:

$$O = 1/(1 + e^{-S})$$
$$\text{where } S = \Sigma\, x_i w_i - t$$

As with the previously defined functions, x_i is the input on line i, w_i is the weight on line i, and t is the threshold.

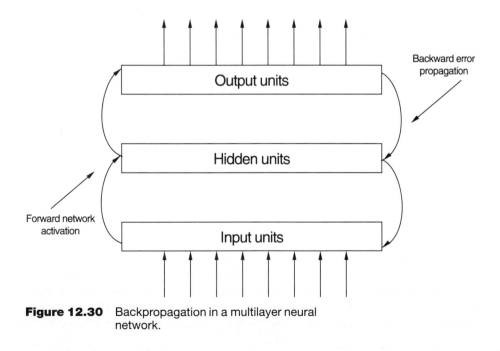

Figure 12.30 Backpropagation in a multilayer neural network.

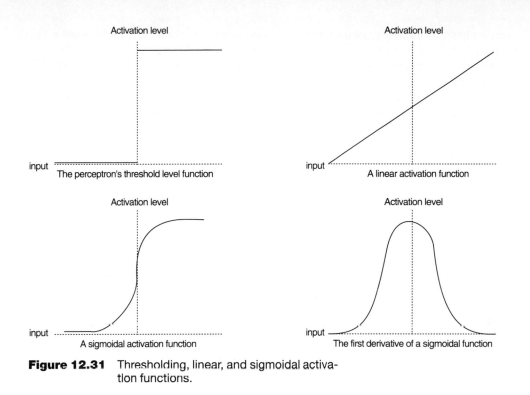

Figure 12.31 Thresholding, linear, and sigmoidal activation functions.

Figure 12.31 shows the graph of this function, along with the linear activation function of the previous section and the threshold function used by the perceptron. These graphs plot the inputs, the horizontal axis, against the activation or output of the neuron, the vertical axis. The sigmoidal activation function is continuous, which allows a meaningful measure of the error on a unit. However, it behaves more like the threshold function, with a rapid transition between low and high values. In a sense, it approximates a thresholding behavior while providing a continuous output function. More important, however, is its role in determining the error assignment for each neuron.

Intuitively, the error assigned to a hidden unit should depend upon the errors of the neurons that use its output and the state of the unit's own activation. For hidden unit n, the total error is the weighted sum of the errors of all units that use n's output. The activation of unit n is accounted for by multiplying the total error by the first derivative of the activation function, applied to n's inputs. Let E_j be the error on the jth unit, let w_{nj} be the weight on the line from unit n to unit j, and let I be the input to unit n. The error for unit n is computed by:

$$E_n = f'(I) \, \Sigma \, w_{nj} \, E_j$$

The derivative of the activation function is central to the functioning of backpropagation. As the graph of the derivative in Figure 12.31 shows, $f'(I)$ is highest for middle values of the inputs. This means that those neurons whose activation level was somewhere in the middle range will assume more responsibility for the overall error of the system. This has an intuitive appeal in that we could regard these neurons as "less certain." Neurons whose activation levels were more pronounced will change less. Thus, the learning algorithm tends to stabilize as neurons converge to activation values that are close to 1 or 0.

The derivative of our activation function is easy to compute, with $f'(x) = f(x) (1 - f(x))$. Because $f(x)$ is just the neuron's prior output, the error computation for hidden units becomes:

$$E_n = O (1 - O) \Sigma (w_{nj} E_j)$$

Once backpropagation has computed the error for each neuron in the network, the individual units may learn by applying the delta rule.

Though it provides a solution to the problem of learning in multilayer networks, backpropagation is not without its own difficulties. Unlike perceptron learning, backpropagation is not guaranteed to converge to a stable configuration of weights. As with hill climbing, it may converge to local minima. Finally, backpropagation can be computationally expensive in practice, often proving slow to converge.

12.7.4 NETtalk

NETtalk is an interesting example of a neural net solution to a difficult learning problem (Sejnowski and Rosenberg 1987). NETtalk learned to pronounce English text. This is difficult for a rule-based approach because English pronunciation is highly irregular. Although rule-based programs have been written for this task, they are complex and do not perform perfectly.

NETtalk learned to read a string of text and return a phoneme and an associated stress for each letter in the string. A phoneme is the basic unit of sound in a language; the stress is the relative loudness of that sound. Because the pronunciation of a single letter depends upon the letters around it, NETtalk was given a 7-character window. As the text moves through this window, NETtalk returns a phoneme/stress pair for each letter.

Figure 12.32 shows the architecture of NETtalk. The network consists of three layers of units. The input units correspond to the 7-character window on the text. Each position in the window is represented by 29 input units: 1 for each letter of the alphabet and 3 for punctuation and spaces. The letter in each position activates the corresponding unit. The output units encode phonemes using 21 different features of human articulation. The remaining 5 units encode stress and syllable boundaries. NETtalk has 80 hidden units, 26 outputs, and 18,629 connections. NETtalk is trained by giving it a 7-character window and letting it attempt to pronounce the middle character. Comparing its attempted pronunciation to the correct pronunciation, it adjusts its weights using backpropagation.

The program illustrates a number of interesting properties of neural networks, many of which reflect the nature of human learning. For example, learning, when measured as a percentage of correct responses, proceeds rapidly at first and slows as the percent correct increases. As with humans, the more words the network learns to pronounce, the better it is at correctly pronouncing new words. Experiments in which some of the weights in a fully trained network were randomly altered showed the network to be damage resistant,

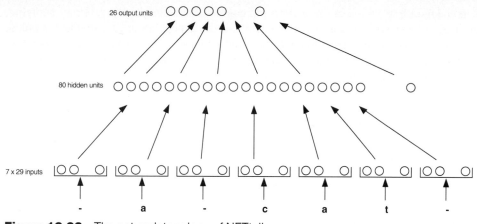

Figure 12.32 The network topology of NETtalk.

degrading gracefully as weights were altered. Researchers also found that relearning in a damaged network was highly efficient.

Another interesting aspect of multilayered networks is the role of the hidden layers. Any learning algorithm must learn generalizations that apply to unseen instances in the problem domain. The hidden layers play an important role in allowing a neural network to generalize. NETtalk, like many backpropagation networks, has fewer neurons in the hidden layer than in the input layer. This forces the network to encode patterns of similar inputs in the hidden units, as opposed to merely learning a one-to-one mapping of inputs onto outputs. These patterns of similarity serve the function of generalization.

NETtalk learns effectively, although it requires a large number of training instances as well as repeated passes through the training data. In a series of empirical tests comparing backpropagation and ID3 on this problem, Shavlik et al. (1991) found that the algorithms performed comparably. This research evaluated the algorithms by dividing the total set of examples into separate training sets and test sets. Both ID3 and NETtalk were able to correctly pronounce about 60 percent of the test data after training on 500 examples. However, where ID3 required only a single pass through the training data, NETtalk required many repetitions of the training set. In this research, NETtalk was allowed 100 passes through the training data.

As this research demonstrates, the relationship between parallel distributed processing and symbolic AI is more complicated than it might seem at first. In Chapter 16, we contrast these two approaches, considering their relative strengths and weaknesses and the contributions that each can make to the other.

12.8 Genetic Algorithms

Genetic algorithms (Holland 1986; Holland et al. 1986) are another approach to learning that exploits parallelism and subsymbolic representation. Like neural networks, genetic algorithms are based on a biological metaphor; however, instead of the biological brain, genetic algorithms view learning in terms of competition among a population of evolving, alternative concepts. A genetic algorithm maintains a population of candidate problem solutions. Based on their performance, the fittest of these solutions not only survive, but, through an analogy with sexual reproduction, exchange information with other candidates to form new solutions.

12.8.1 The Genetic Algorithm

Let $P(t)$ define a population of candidate solutions at time t:

$$P(t) = \{x_1^t, x_2^t, \ldots x_n^t\}$$

The genetic algorithm is defined

```
procedure genetic algorithm;
  begin
  t := 0;
  initialize P(t);
  while termination condition not met do
    begin
        evaluate P(t);
        select pairs of solutions according to the quality of their evaluation;
        produce the offspring of these pairs using genetic operators;
        replace the weakest candidates with the offspring;
        t := t+1;
    end;
  end
```

For example, suppose we want a genetic algorithm to learn to classify strings of 1s and 0s. We can represent a class of bit strings as a pattern of 1s, 0s, and #s, where # may match with either 0 or 1. For example, the pattern 1##00##1 represents all strings of eight bits that begin and end with 1 and have two 0s in the middle. We first discussed this representation, along with its strengths and weaknesses, in Section 12.4.1. The algorithm initializes $P(0)$ to a population of candidate patterns. Typically, initial populations are selected randomly.

Evaluation of candidate solutions assumes a fitness function, $f(x_i^t)$, that returns a measure of the candidate's fitness at time t. A common measure of a candidate's fitness is to test each candidate on a set of training instances and return the percentage of correct classifications. Using such a fitness function, a typical evaluation assigns each candidate solution the value:

$$\frac{f(x_i^t)}{m(P,t)}$$

where $m(P,t)$ is the average fitness over all members of the population.

After evaluating each candidate, the algorithm selects pairs for recombination. Recombination uses *genetic operators* to produce new solutions that combine components of their parents. As with natural evolution, the fitness of a candidate determines the extent to which it reproduces, with those candidates having the highest evaluations being given a greater probability of reproducing. Note that selection is probabilistic; weaker candidates are given a smaller likelihood of reproducing but are not eliminated outright. This is important because a seemingly bad candidate may still include some essential component of a solution, and reproduction may extract this component.

A number of genetic operators produce offspring having features of their parents; the most common of these is *crossover*. Crossover takes two candidate solutions and divides them, swapping components to produce two new candidates. Figure 12.33 illustrates crossover on bit string patterns of length 8. The operator splits them in the middle and forms two children whose initial segment comes from one parent and whose tail comes from the other.

For example, suppose the target class is the set of all strings beginning and ending with a 1. Both parent strings in Figure 12.33 would have performed relatively well on this task. However, the offspring at the top of the figure would be much better than either parent: it would not have any false positives and would fail to recognize fewer strings that were actually in the class. Note also that its sibling is worse than either parent and will probably be eliminated over the next few generations.

Mutation is another important genetic operator. Mutation takes a single candidate and randomly changes some aspect of it. In our example, mutation may randomly select an element of a pattern and change it, switching a 1 to a 0 or #, and so forth. Mutation is important in that the initial population may have excluded some essential component of a solution. In our example, if no member of the initial population has a 1 in the first position, then crossover alone will not produce any solution that does. The genetic algorithm continues until some termination requirement is met, such as having one or more candidate solutions whose fitness exceeds some threshold.

12.8.2 Evaluating the Genetic Algorithm

The power of genetic algorithms is in the parallel nature of their search. Genetic algorithms implement a powerful form of hill climbing that maintains multiple solutions, eliminates unpromising solutions, and improves good solutions. Figure 12.34, adapted from Holland (1986), shows multiple solutions converging toward optimal points in a search space. In

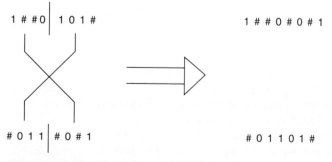

Figure 12.33 Crossover on bit strings.

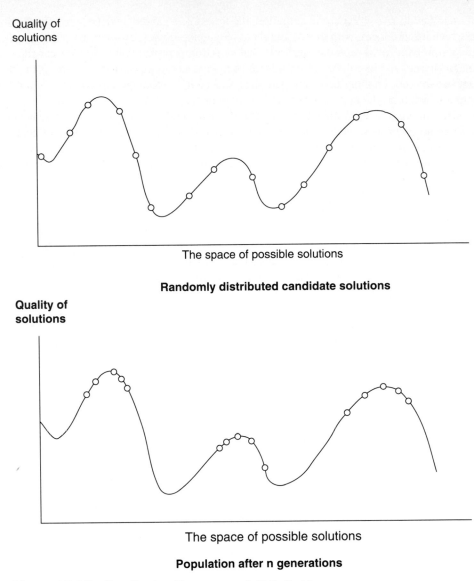

Quality of
solutions

The space of possible solutions

Randomly distributed candidate solutions

Quality of
solutions

The space of possible solutions

Population after n generations

Figure 12.34   Genetic algorithms as parallel hill climbing.

this figure, the horizontal axis represents the possible points in a solution space, the vertical axis measures the quality of those solutions. The dots on the curve are members of the genetic algorithm's current population of candidate solutions. Initially, the solutions are randomly scattered through the space of possible solutions. After several generations, they tend to cluster around areas of high solution quality.

Note that genetic algorithms, unlike sequential forms of hill climbing, do not immediately discard unpromising solutions. Through genetic operators, even weak solutions may continue to contribute to the makeup of future candidate solutions.

Another source of the algorithm's power is the *implicit parallelism* inherent in the evolutionary metaphor. By restricting the reproduction of weak candidates, genetic algorithms eliminate not only that solution but also all of its descendants. This tends to make the algorithm likely to converge toward high-quality solutions in fewer generations. For example, the string 101#0##1, if broken at its midpoint, can parent a whole family of strings of the form 101#____. If the parent string is found to be unfit, its elimination also eliminates all of these potential descendants.

The genetic operators used are important to the success of this search. All genetic algorithms require some form of recombination, as this allows the creation of new solutions that have, by virtue of their parents' success, a high probability of exhibiting good performance. In practice, crossover is the most important of the genetic operators, whereas mutation is used much less frequently. Although crossover attempts to preserve the beneficial aspects of candidate solutions and to eliminate undesirable components, the random nature of mutation probably is more likely to degrade a strong candidate solution than it is to improve it.

By representing solutions as bit strings, we may apply crossover with a great deal of flexibility. This flexibility is important, giving genetic algorithms many of the advantages of other subsymbolic approaches. An important issue in genetic algorithm research is the extension of this methodology to different representations (Koza 1991).

This problem has been approached in a number of ways. One is to define analogs of crossover that may apply to higher-level representations such as rules. However, it is difficult to define such operators that honor the syntactic constraints of logic. Alternatively, we may translate the logical rules into bit strings and use the standard crossover operator. Here the problem is that under many approaches to translation, most bit strings do not correspond to meaningful logical sentences. Perhaps the most promising way of applying genetic algorithms is to avoid the issues of logical representation altogether by finding ways of translating problems into bit strings or similar representations.

Research continues on this and other problems. Holland, for example, has developed a problem-solving architecture called classifier systems that implements genetic learning in the context of a parallel production system (Holland 1986). Classifier systems increase the expressiveness of the representation by allowing multiple-step problem-solving processes.

12.9 Epilogue and References

Machine learning is one of the most exciting subfields in artificial intelligence, addressing a problem that is central to intelligent behavior and raising a number of important questions about knowledge representation, search, and even the basic assumptions of AI itself. In particular, it has focused attention on some of the weaknesses of purely symbolic approaches and led to the development of alternative metaphors for intelligent architectures.

One of the best surveys of work in the field is found in *Machine Learning: An Artificial Intelligence Approach* (Kodratoff and Michalski 1990; Michalski et al. 1983; Michalski et al. 1986). This series consists of three volumes (to date) and includes both introductory material, surveys, and papers on specific research. *Readings in Machine Learning*

(Shavlik and Dietterich 1990) collects a number of important papers in the field, going back as far as 1958. By placing all this research in a single volume, the editors have provided a valuable service to both researchers and those seeking an introduction to the field. *Production System Models of Learning and Development* (Klahr et al. 1987) collects a number of papers in machine learning, including some work that reflects a more cognitive approach.

Computer Systems That Learn (Weiss and Kulikowski 1991) is an introductory survey of the whole field, including treatments of neural networks, statistical methods, and machine learning techniques. It is particularly strong in its treatment of the evaluation of learning systems.

Readers interested in a deeper discussion of analogical reasoning should examine Carbonell (1983; 1986), Holyoak (1985), Kedar-Cabelli (1988), and Thagard (1988).

Readers interested in discovery and theory formation may want to examine *Scientific Discovery: Computational Explorations of the Creative Processes* (Langley et al. 1987) and *Computational Models of Scientific Discovery and Theory Formation* (Shrager and Langley 1990).

Concept Formation: Knowledge and Experience in Unsupervised Learning (Fisher et al. 1991) presents a number of papers on clustering, concept formation, and other forms of unsupervised learning.

The two volumes of *Parallel Distributed Processing* (Rumelhart et al. 1986) give a thorough introduction to neural networks. *Neural Networks and Natural Intelligence* (Grossberg 1988) is another thorough treatment of the subject. Genetic algorithms are discussed in Michalski et al. (1986) as well as in Holland et al. (1986).

Machine Learning is the primary journal of the field. Other sources of current research include the yearly proceedings of the International Conference on Machine Learning, as well as the proceedings of the American Association of Artificial Intelligence Conference and the International Joint Conference on Artificial Intelligence.

12.10 Exercises

1. Consider the behavior of Winston's concept learning program when learning the concept "step," where a step consists of a short box and a tall box placed in contact with each other (Fig. 12.35). Create semantic net representations of three or four examples and near misses and show the development of the concept.

2. The run of the candidate elimination algorithm shown in Figure 12.9 does not show candidate concepts that were produced but eliminated because they were either overly general, overly spe-

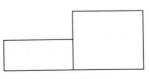

Figure 12.35 A step.

cific, or subsumed by some other concept. Re-do the execution trace, showing these concepts and the reasons each was eliminated.

3. Using the information theoretic selection function of Section 12.4.3, show in detail how ID3 constructs the tree of Figure 12.14 from examples in Table 12.1. Be sure to show the calculations used in computing the information gain for each test and the resulting test selections.

4. Using Shannon's formula, show that a message about the outcome of a spin of a roulette wheel has more information than one about the outcome of a coin toss.

5. Develop a simple table of examples in some domain, such as classifying animals by species, and trace the construction of a decision tree by the ID3 algorithm.

6. Implement ID3 in a language of your choice and run it on the credit history example from the text.

7. Develop a domain theory in some problem area of your choice. Trace the behavior of an explanation-based learner in applying this theory to several training instances.

8. Construct a multilayer perceptron network that represents the exclusive-or function.

9. Show that if outputs are restricted to 0 and 1, the delta rule of Section 12.7.2 reduces to the perceptron learning algorithm.

ADVANCED AI PROGRAMMING TECHNIQUES

"Come, we shall have some fun now!" thought Alice. "I'm glad they've begun asking riddles—I believe I can guess that," she added aloud.

"Do you mean that you think you can find out the answer to it?" said the March Hare.

"Exactly so," said Alice.

"Then you should say what you mean," the March Hare went on.

"I do," Alice hastily replied; "at least—at least I mean what I say—that's the same thing, you know."

"Not the same thing a bit!" said the Hatter. "Why you might just as well say that 'I see what I eat' is the same thing as 'I eat what I see'!"

"You might just as well say," added the March Hare, "that 'I like what I get' is the same thing as 'I get what I like'!"

"You might just as well say," added the Dormouse, who seemed to be talking in his sleep, "that 'I breathe when I sleep' is the same thing as 'I sleep when I breathe'!"

"It is the same thing with you," said the Hatter. . . .

—Lewis Carroll, "A Mad Tea Party," *Alice's Adventures in Wonderland*

AI Languages and Meta-Interpreters

In Part V we implement the representations and algorithms introduced in the previous section. In particular, we build interpreters for production rules, design and build semantic network and frame systems, and implement several machine learning algorithms. An important feature of LISP and PROLOG is their support for designing *meta-interpreters*. A meta-interpreter processes statements written in the language's syntax, allowing us to tailor the semantics of the language to our problem-solving needs. We use this methodology to build the programs in this section.

Chapter 13 presents these programs in PROLOG, Chapter 14 in LISP. Our goals are to give the student an appreciation of the *semantics* or mathematical foundations of each of these programming paradigms and to show the ease with which these languages support the construction of meta-interpreters for AI representations.

Before we continue with the advanced PROLOG and LISP chapters, we introduce a third approach to AI problem solving, *object-oriented programming*. We also discuss an important by-product of object-oriented programming, the *hybrid AI environment*. Chapter 15 presents advanced knowledge representation within the object-oriented paradigm and designs for object-oriented interpreters in LISP and PROLOG.

Object-Oriented Programming

Object-oriented programming, unlike LISP and PROLOG, has its roots in software engineering and simulation rather than in abstract mathematics. Smalltalk, the first "object-oriented" language, was developed in the early 1970s at Xerox Palo Alto Research Center under the direction of Alan Kay. Building on ideas from Simula, the Norwegian simulation language developed in the 1960s, and Seymour Papert's work in using LOGO to teach children programming, "Small" talk was intended to be simple enough for children to learn. Smalltalk later influenced work on the Dynabook, a portable computer the size of a loose-leaf binder, intended to be a general tool for the non–computer scientist.

Because of this target user, the operating system and applications software needed to be nontechnical and easily understood. Their solution to this problem was a graphics interface based on the "desktop" metaphor: multiple process windows, like papers scattered on a desk; use of menus, graphic icons, and pointing devices; a mouse or a touch screen for selecting options; and a rich set of programs for editing, graphics, and communications. The user interface design of the Dynabook has influenced the design of user interfaces for a range of computers, including personal computer operating systems such as the Apple Macintosh, Microsoft Windows, and IBM OS/2; workstation environments such as X-windows; and the numerous specialized LISP computers available for AI program development.

In a Smalltalk program, everything is represented as an *object*, an active computational structure of arbitrary complexity. Objects include not only the data types needed to define a computational entity but also the *methods* (executable code) necessary to compute the object's state. The values of an object are represented as *slots* as in frames. Objects may be class objects, describing all instances of a type, or instances, representing a single member. When instances of a data type are defined as objects, these instance objects inherit (Chapter 9) both the type definitions and the associated methods from their class. For example, the number 3 is a member of the class **integers** and inherits the integer operators ($+$, $-$, $*$, 1, MOD) from the class. To perform an operation on an object, a message is sent to the object invoking the appropriate method. For example, to add 3 and 4, the message $+4$ is sent to the object 3; 3 responds with the answer 7.

By providing a means for combining data types and the operations on them into a single entity, called the object, Smalltalk supports the development of modular code and applies strong typing to both data elements and the code for their manipulation. Because

Smalltalk objects are organized into a network of classes, with more specialized objects inheriting part or all of the methods of the more general, it is simple to create new program structures that incorporate the functionality of existing program objects. Thus, any program can readily incorporate the full power of the underlying system, including graphics, editing, and communications. In addition, important software development techniques such as information hiding, operator overloading, code reuse through class inheritance, online documentation, and embedded languages are supported in a natural fashion.

Object-oriented programming languages incorporate many of the features found in frame-based knowledge representations, including class inheritance and the ability to represent structured knowledge. For these reasons, object-oriented languages have become widely used in AI programming.

Commercial systems that support the object-oriented approach to knowledge engineering are available for a range of hardware, from personal computers to Unix workstations to large time-sharing systems. *CLOS,* the *Common Lisp Object System,* is widely used in artificial intelligence and is supported by most general-purpose workstations. Other important object-oriented languages include C++ and Objective C. Hybrid object-oriented/rule-based knowledge engineering languages such as KAPPA, NEXPERT Object, and Level5 Object apply these techniques to the problems of representing knowledge in an expert system.

Most important, Smalltalk defined the methodology of object-oriented programming. Object-oriented programming techniques are being adopted in software engineering, data base design, and the teaching of programming and data structures. The methodology has emerged as an important AI programming technique, especially in development of hybrid AI environments. Object-oriented design is presented in detail in Chapter 15.

Hybrid Environments

The demands of knowledge-based programming have led to the development of a number of programming and representation techniques, including production systems, rules, and frame/object-based representations. A hybrid system combines multiple representation paradigms into a single integrated programming environment. Although hybrid environments differ, they generally include the following features:

1. **Frame or object-oriented representations of domain objects**. Such systems support inheritance of class properties and often include a message-passing mechanism for object interactions.

2. **Rules for representing heuristic knowledge**. Although frames and objects are the preferred means of describing taxonomies of objects, rules remain the most natural means of describing heuristic problem-solving knowledge. The if . . . then . . . syntax fits the way human experts describe their decision-making process. Rules are able to access information in objects, either through use of a language that directly reads and writes to slots in an object or by using message passing to query an object indirectly.

3. **Support for a variety of search strategies**. Most systems support both forward and backward search. Generally, presentation of a goal query initiates a backward-chaining search. Addition of a new fact to working memory may initiate forward reasoning from rules enabled by this new fact.

4. **Definition of demons to implement interactions and side effects**. A *demon* is a procedure that is invoked as a side effect of some other action. A conventional example of the use of demons is a controller in a time-sharing system that is invoked periodically to monitor a printer or other device. Demons are not called directly but are invoked by a clock. AI environments extend this idea, allowing the creation of demons that are invoked, for example, whenever an object or slot is created or modified. Such demons are used to update a display in response to a changed slot value, to perform consistency checks when the modification of one entity requires a change in a different object, or to implement the interactions between objects in a simulation. Typical demons include *if changed* demons that run whenever the value of a variable is changed, *read* demons that run whenever a variable value is read in, *when created* demons that run when an instance is created, *timed* demons that refresh the value of time-sensitive data, and *active values* or *active images* that link a graphic with the value of a variable.

5. **Rich graphics-based interfaces**. These include a range of trace facilities that allow both continuous and stepwise monitoring of executions. For example, graphic displays can describe the rule structure of a knowledge base as a tree structure. An important feature of hybrid environments is the ability to attach, using demons, a graphic display to a slot in an object. This allows a gauge, for example, or other graphic to display its value in real time. Similarly, most environments provide high-level support for graphics input devices such as buttons or sliders that may be set using a mouse or other pointing device.

6. **Escapes to an underlying language**. Methods are represented in a special language defined by the environment or, more often, in LISP, PROLOG, or even a conventional language such as C or Pascal. Not only does this allow a natural description of procedural knowledge, but it also allows a knowledge-based program to call more conventional languages to perform arithmetic, array manipulation, sensor monitoring, or other actions that are better implemented using conventional algorithmic techniques.

7. **The ability to compile a knowledge base for faster execution or delivery on a smaller machine**. Once a knowledge-based program is completed, the rich interpreted development environment is often an overhead that slows down execution. Most modern AI environments allow applications to be compiled and run under a faster, simpler, often also smaller and cheaper delivery machine.

A Hybrid Example

A good many problems are naturally thought of in terms of objects, relationships, and the interactions between them. In Figure V.1 we present a battery connected with a switch to a lightbulb. The bulb, battery, and switch may each be represented by classes that describe

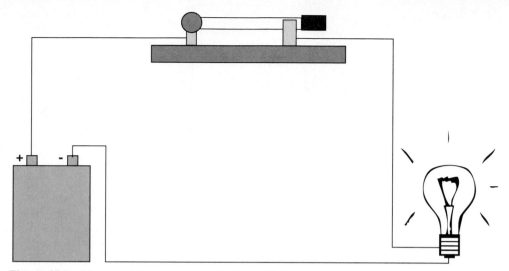

Figure V.1 Many problems are naturally thought of in terms of objects and relations.

properties of batteries, switches, and bulbs in general. The electronic components of Figure V.1 may then be represented as particular instances of these general classes. Note that instances take on particular *instance values* of their class object. The controls slot of each component is appropriately linked to simulate the system. For example, if the state of switch1 is changed to off, the controls slot indicates that light1 is affected. We show part of a class/instance hierarchy in Figure V.2.

A rule may also be created to reason about these components:

IF the light won't come on AND the switch is closed AND the battery is okay
THEN look for a broken connection

In the hybrid representation, the rules access properties, or more properly, the instance values of the classes and objects. As can be noted in Figure V.2, the condition information for this rule is checked by accessing the appropriate slot values of the object instances in the domain. The rule may be seen as part of a back-chaining rule system attempting to debug this circuit, or it may be demon driven, asking for a check of the state of a switch's control's state value whenever the state of the switch is changed. In Chapter 15 we build object systems and continue our discussion of hybrid design.

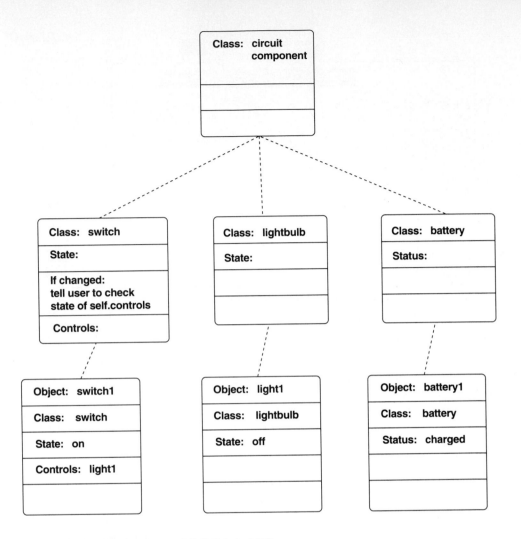

IF **X** is an instance of **lightblub AND**
   X. state is **off AND**
   Y is an instance of **switch AND**
   Y. state is **on AND**
   Z is an instance of **battery AND**
   Z. status is charged
THEN check for **broken connection**

Figure V.2   In a hybrid system, rules access the slots of
               classes and objects.

ADVANCED REPRESENTATION IN PROLOG

The task of mathematics consists in the organization of a series of aids to the imagination in the process of reasoning.

—A. N. WHITEHEAD

O body swayed to music, O brightening glance,
How can we know the dancer from the dance?

—W. B. YATES, "Among School Children"

13.0   Introduction

This chapter presents a number of AI programming techniques using PROLOG. Section 13.1 introduces *meta-predicates*, predicates whose domain of interpretation consists of PROLOG expressions themselves. For example, atom(X) succeeds if X is bound to an atom; it affirms a property of a PROLOG expression. As an example of the use of meta-reasoning, we discuss the implementation of *types* in PROLOG and the use of unification in equality testing and structure creation.

Section 13.2 explores the design of *meta-interpreters.* Meta-interpreters are PROLOG programs that process PROLOG expressions. Meta-interpreters enable us to redefine the semantics of PROLOG and are a useful vehicle for creating expert system shells, frame systems, and other representations using PROLOG as a basis. We create meta-interpreters for rule-based expert systems in Sections 13.2.1 and 13.2.2 and for inheritance evaluation in semantic nets and frames in Sections 13.2.3 and 13.2.4. Along the way, we show how rule, frame, and semantic net representations may be cast in PROLOG. Finally, in Section 13.3 we construct a recursive descent parser for sentences in English. This parser constructs a representation of the meaning of a sentence by joining frame structures representing word and phrase meaning.

In Section 13.4 we implement version space search and in Section 13.5 explanation-based learning, two machine learning algorithms discussed in Chapter 12. These sections not only provide implementations of learning algorithms; they also illustrate a number of interesting programming techniques.

Finally, in Section 13.6, we emphasize the power that a clean and precise semantics offers AI programmers. We define the semantics of PROLOG as a resolution refutation theorem prover with certain proof strategies. We also present Flat Concurrent PROLOG (Shapiro 1987a) as an alternative model for logic programming. Flat Concurrent PROLOG will be important for the design of an interpreter for objects, messages, and inheritance in Chapter 15.

13.1   PROLOG Tools: Meta-Predicates, Types, and Unification

13.1.1   Meta-Logical Predicates

Meta-logical constructs extend the expressive power of any programming environment. We refer to these predicates as *meta* because they query and manipulate other predicates rather than the terms or objects these other predicates denote. We need meta-predicates in PRO-LOG for (at least) five reasons:

1. To determine the "type" of an expression.
2. To add "type" restrictions to logic programming.
3. To build, take apart, and evaluate PROLOG structures.
4. To compare values of expressions.
5. To convert predicates passed as data to executable code.

We have already described how global structures, which are those that can be accessed by the entire clause set, are entered into a PROLOG program. The command assert(C) adds the clause C to the current set of clauses.

There are dangers associated with programming with assert and retract. Because they create and remove global structures, these commands introduce side effects and may cause other problems associated with poorly structured programs. We discussed this issue when designing a loop check for graph search in Chapter 6. Yet, it is sometimes necessary to use global structures. We do this when creating *semantic nets* and *frames* in a PROLOG environment. We may also use global structures to describe new results as they are found with our rule-based shell. We want this information to be global so that other predicates (rules) may access it when appropriate (Section 13.2).

Other meta-predicates that are useful for manipulating representations include:

var(X) succeeds only when X is an unbound variable.

nonvar(X) succeeds only when X is bound to a nonvariable term.

=.. creates a list from a predicate term.

For example, foo(a,b,c) =.. Y unifies Y with [foo,a,b,c]. The head of the list Y is the function name, and its tail is the function's arguments. =.. also can be used "backward," of course. Thus, if X =.. [foo,a,b,c] succeeds, then X has the value foo(a,b,c).

functor(A, B, C) succeeds with A a term whose principal functor has name B and arity C.

For example, functor(foo(a,b),X,Y) will succeed with X = foo and Y = 2. functor(A,B,C) can also be used with any of its arguments bound in order to produce the others, such as all the terms with a certain name and/or arity.

clause(A,B) unifies B with the body of a clause whose head unifies with A.

If p(X) :- q(X) exists in the data base, then clause(p(a),Y) will succeed with Y = q(a). This is useful for controlling rule chaining in an interpreter.

any_predicate(...,X,...) :- X executes predicate X, the argument of an arbitrary predicate.

Thus a predicate, here X, may be passed as a parameter and executed at any desired time in the computation.

call(X), where X is a clause, also succeeds with the execution of predicate X.

This short list of meta-logical predicates will be very important in building and interpreting the AI data structures of the preceding chapters. Because PROLOG can manipulate its own structures in a straightforward fashion, it is easy to implement interpreters that modify the PROLOG semantics. For example, in building a meta-interpreter for production rules (Section 13.2), it is important to be able to distinguish a rule (clause) from a fact (true) and to be able to create new predicates or relationships as needed.

13.1.2 Types in PROLOG

For a number of problem-solving applications, the unconstrained use of unification can introduce unintended error. PROLOG is an untyped language; unification simply matches patterns, without restricting them according to type. For example, append(nil,6,6) is deducible from the definition of append. Strongly typed languages such as Pascal have shown how type checking can help the programmer avoid these problems. A number of researchers have proposed the introduction of *types* to PROLOG (Neves et al. 1986; Mycroft 1984).

Typed data are particularly appropriate in a relational date base (Neves et al. 1986; Malpas 1987). The rules of logic can be used as constraints on the data and the data can be typed to enforce consistent and meaningful interpretation of the queries.

Suppose that there is a department store data base of inventory, suppliers, supplier_inventory, and other appropriate relations. We define the data base as relations with named fields; these can be thought of as sets of data tuples. For example, inventory might consist of a set of 4-tuples, where:

$< $ Pname, Pnumber, Supplier, Weight $ > \in$ inventory

only when Supplier is the supplier name of an inventory item numbered Pnumber that is called Pname and has weight Weight. Suppose also

$$< \text{Supplier, Snumber, Status, Location} > \in \text{suppliers}$$

only when Supplier is the name of a supplier numbered Snumber who has status Status and lives in city Location, and

$$< \text{Supplier, Pnumber, Cost, Department} > \in \text{supplier\_inventory}$$

only if Supplier is the name of a supplier of part number Pnumber in the amount of Cost to department Department.

We may define PROLOG rules that implement various queries and perform type checking in these relations. For instance, the query "are there suppliers of part number 1 that live in London?" is given in PROLOG as:

```
?- getsuppliers (Supplier,1,london).
```

The rule:

```
getsuppliers (Supplier, Pnumber, City) :-
            cktype (City, suppliers, city),
            suppliers (Supplier,_,_,City),
            cktype (Pnumber, inventory, number),
            supplier_inventory (Supplier,Pnumber,_,_),
            cktype (Supplier, inventory, name).
```

implements this query and also enforces the appropriate constraints across the tuples of the data base. First the variables Pnumber and City are bound when the query unifies with the head of the rule; our predicate cktype tests that Supplier is an element of the set of suppliers, that 1 is a legitimate inventory number, and that london is a suppliers city.

We define cktype to take three arguments—a value, a relation name, and a field name—and to check that each value is of the appropriate type for that relation. For example, we may define lists of legal values for Supplier, Pnumber, and City and enforce data typing by requiring member checks of candidate values across these lists. Alternatively, we may define logical constraints on possible values of a type; for example, we may require that inventory numbers be less than 1000.

We should note the differences in type checking between standard languages such as Pascal and PROLOG. We might define a Pascal data type for suppliers as:

```
type supplier = record
            sname: string;
            snumber: integer;
            status: boolean;
            location: string
    end
```

The Pascal programmer defines new types, here supplier, in terms of already defined types, such as boolean or integer. When the programmer uses variables of this type, the compiler automatically enforces type constraints on their values.

In PROLOG, we could represent the supplier relation as instances of the form:

```
supplier(sname(Supplier),
         snumber(Snumber),
         status(Status),
         location(Location)).
```

We would implement type checking on these instances using rules such as getsuppliers and cktype.

The distinction between Pascal and PROLOG type checking is clear and important: the Pascal type declaration tells the compiler the form for both the entire structure (record) and the individual components (boolean, integer, string) of the data type. In Pascal we declare variables to be of a particular type (record) and then create procedures to access these typed structures.

```
procedure changestatus (X: supplier);
    begin
        if X.status then. . . .
```

Because it is nonprocedural, PROLOG does not separate the declaration from the use of data types, and any type checking must be done as the program is executing. Consider the rule:

```
supplier_name(supplier(sname(Supplier),
                       snumber(Snumber),
                       status(true),
                       location (london))) :-
          integer(Snumber), write(Supplier).
```

supplier_name takes as argument an instance of the supplier predicate and writes the name of the supplier. However, this rule will succeed only if the supplier's number is an integer, the status is active (true), and the supplier lives in London. An important part of the type check is handled by the unification algorithm (true, london) and the rest is the built-in system predicate integer. Further constraints could restrict values to be from a particular list; for example, Snumber could be constrained to be from a list of supplier numbers. We define constraints on data base queries using rules such as cktype and supplier_name to implement type checking when the program is executed.

So far, we have seen three ways that data may be typed in PROLOG. First, and most powerful, is the use of unification to constrain variable assignment. Second, PROLOG itself provides predicates to do limited type checking. We saw this with meta-predicates such as var(X), clause(X,Y), and integer(X). The third limited use of typing occurred in the inventory example where rules checked lists of legitimate suppliers, pnumbers, and cities to enforce type constraints.

A fourth, and more radical, approach is the complete predicate and data type check proposed by Mycroft and O'Keefe (1984). Here all predicate names are typed and given a fixed arity. Furthermore, all variable names are themselves typed. A strength of this approach is that the constraints on the constituent predicates and variables of the PROLOG program are themselves enforced by a (meta) PROLOG program. Even though the result may be slower program execution, the security gained through total type enforcement may justify this cost.

Rather than providing built-in type checking as a default, PROLOG allows run time type checking under complete programmer control. This approach offers a number of benefits for AI programmers, including the following:

1. The programmer is not forced to adhere to strong type checking at all times. This allows us to write predicates that work across any type of object. For example, the **member** predicate performs general member checking, regardless of the type of elements in the list.

2. Flexibility in typing helps exploratory programming. Programmers can relax type checking in the early stages of program development and introduce it to detect errors as they come to better understand the problem.

3. AI representations seldom conform to the built-in data types of languages such as Pascal. PROLOG allows types to be defined using the full power of predicate calculus. The data base example showed the advantages of this flexibility.

4. Because type checking is done at run time rather than compile time, the programmer determines when the program should perform a check. This allows programmers to delay type checking until it is necessary or until certain variables have become bound.

5. Programmer control of type checking at run time also lets us write programs that create and enforce new types during execution. This could be of use in a learning program, for example.

13.1.3 Unification, the Engine for Predicate Matching and Evaluation

An important feature of PROLOG programming is the interpreter's behavior as a resolution-based theorem prover, presented in Section 13.6. As a theorem prover PROLOG performs a series of resolutions on data base entries, rather than sequentially evaluating statements and expressions like a traditional language. This has an important result: variables are bound (assigned values, instantiated, . . .) by unification and *not* by evaluation unless, of course, an evaluation is explicitly requested. This programming paradigm has several implications.

The first and perhaps most important result is the relaxation of the requirement to specify variables as input or output. We already saw some of the power of this in the **append** predicate, which could either join lists together, test whether two lists are correctly appended, or break a list into parts consistent with the definition of **append**. We also saw unification as a matcher and constraint handler for parsing and generating sentences (Chapter 6).

Unification is a powerful technique for rule-based and frame-based expert systems, where it matches case-specific data to the rules that best meet these specifications. All production systems require a form of this matching, and it is often necessary to write a unification algorithm in languages that don't provide it (see Chapter 7 for a LISP implementation of unification).

An important difference between unification-based computing and the use of more traditional languages is that unification performs syntactic matches (with appropriate parameter substitutions) on structures. It does *not* evaluate expressions. Suppose, for example, we wished to create a successor predicate that succeeds if its second argument is the arithmetic successor of its first. Not understanding unification, one might be tempted to define successor:

successor (X, Y) :- Y = X + 1.

This will fail because the = operator does not evaluate its arguments but only attempts to unify the expressions on either side. This predicate succeeds if Y unifies with the structure X + 1. Because 4 does not unify with 3 + 1, the call successor(3, 4) fails! On the other hand, = can test for equivalence, as defined by unification, of *any* two expressions.

To correctly define successor and other arithmetic predicates, we need to evaluate arithmetic expressions. PROLOG provides an operator, is, that performs arithmetic evaluation.

is evaluates the expression on its right-hand side and attempts to unify the result with the object on its left. Thus,

X is Y + Z

unifies X with the value of Y added to Z. Because it performs arithmetic evaluation:

1. If Y and Z do not have values (are not bound at execution time) evaluation of the is causes a run-time error. Thus

2. X is Y + Z cannot (as one might think with a declarative programming language) give a value to Y when X and Z are bound.

3. Programs must use is to evaluate expressions containing arithmetic operators, +, -, *, /, and mod.

Finally, as in the predicate calculus, variables in PROLOG may have one and only one binding. Once given a value, through local assignment or unification, they can never take on a new value, except through a backtrack in the and/or search space of the current interpretation (Section 13.6). Thus, is does not function like a traditional assignment operator; an expression such as X is X + 1 will always fail.

Using is, we can now properly define successor(X, Y) as:

successor (X, Y) :- Y is X + 1.

This will have the correct behavior as long as X is bound to a numeric value. It can be used either to compute Y, given X, or to test values of X and Y:

```
?- successor (3,X).
X = 4
yes
?- successor (3,4).
yes
?- successor (4,2).
no
?- successor (Y,4).
failure, error in arithmetic expression
```

As this discussion illustrates, PROLOG does not evaluate expressions as a default as in traditional languages. The programmer must explicitly indicate evaluation using is. Though this feature would be problematic in a language such as FORTRAN, which is used chiefly for arithmetic computing, it is extremely useful for symbolic computing. Explicit control of evaluation makes it easy to treat expressions as data, passing them as parameters and creating or modifying them in the program. We do not evaluate the expression until the appropriate time.

This feature, like the ability to manipulate predicate calculus expressions as data and execute them using call, greatly simplifies the development of different interpreters, such as the expert system shell of the next section.

We close this discussion of the power of unification-based computing with an example that does string catenation through the use of *difference lists*. As an alternative to the standard PROLOG list notation, we can represent a list as the difference of two lists. For example, [a, b] is equivalent to [a,b| []] - [] or [a,b,c] - [c]. This representation has certain expressive advantages over the traditional list syntax. When the list [a,b] is represented as the difference [a, b | Y] - Y, it actually describes the potentially infinite class of all lists that have a and b as their first two elements. Now this representation has an interesting property, namely addition:

$$X - Z = X - Y + Y - Z$$

We can use this property to define the following single-clause logic program where X - Y is the first list, Y - Z is the second list, and X - Z is the result of catenating them:

catenate(X - Y, Y - Z, X - Z).

This operation joins two lists of any length in constant time by unification on the list structures, rather than by repeated assignment based on the length of the lists (as with append). Thus the call:

?- catenate ([a,b|Y] - Y, [1,2,3] - [],W).

gives:

```
Y = [1,2,3]
W = [a,b,1,2,3] - []
```

As noted in Figure 13.1, the (subtree) value of Y in the second parameter is unified with *both* occurrences of Y in the first parameter of catenate. This demonstrates the power of unification, not simply for substituting values for variables but also for matching general structures: all occurrences of Y take the value of the entire subtree. The example also illustrates the advantages of an appropriate representation. This algorithm is made possible by the ability of difference lists to represent a whole class of lists, including the desired catenation.

In this section we have discussed a number of idiosyncrasies and advantages of PROLOG's unification-based approach to computing. Unification is at the heart of PROLOG's declarative semantics.

Addition of difference lists:

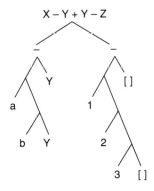

After binding Y to [1, 2, 3], binding Z to [ ], and performing the addition:

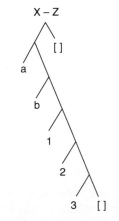

Figure 13.1 Tree diagrams of catenation using difference lists.

13.2 Meta-Interpreters in PROLOG

13.2.1 An Introduction to Meta-Interpreters: PROLOG in PROLOG

In both LISP and PROLOG, it is easy to write programs that manipulate expressions written in the language syntax. We call such programs *meta-interpreters*. For example, an expert system shell interprets a set of rules and facts that describe a particular problem. Although the rules are written in the syntax of the underlying language, the meta-interpreter redefines their semantics.

As an example of a meta-interpreter, we define the semantics of pure PROLOG using PROLOG itself. solve takes as its argument a PROLOG goal and processes it according to the semantics of PROLOG:

```
solve(true) :-!.
solve(not A) :- not(solve(A)).
solve((A,B)) :- !, solve(A), solve(B).
solve(A) :- clause(A,B), solve(B).
```

If we assume the following simple set of assertions,

```
p(X, Y) :- q(X), r(Y).
q(X) :- s(X).
r(X) :- t(X).
s(a).
t(b).
t(c).
```

solve has the behavior we expect of PROLOG:

```
?- solve(p(a, b)).
  yes
?- solve(p(X, Y)).
  X = a, Y = b;
  X = a, Y = c;
  no
?- solve(p(f, g)).
  no
```

solve implements the same left-to-right, depth-first, goal-directed search as the built-in PROLOG interpreter.

The ability to easily write meta-interpreters for a language has certain theoretical advantages. For example, McCarthy wrote a simple LISP meta-interpreter as part of a proof that the language is Turing complete (McCarthy 1960). From a more practical standpoint, we can use meta-interpreters to extend or modify the semantics of the underlying language to better fit our application. This is the programming methodology of *meta-linguistic abstraction*, the creation of a high-level language that is designed to help solve a specific problem.

For example, we may wish to modify the standard PROLOG semantics so that it will ask the user about the truth value of any goal that does not succeed in the knowledge base. We can do so by adding the following clause at the end of the previous definitions of solve:

```
solve(A) :- askuser(A).
```

We define askuser as:

```
askuser(A) :- write(A),
          write('? Enter true if the goal is true, false otherwise'),nl,
          read(true).
```

Because we add this definition to the end of the other solve rules, it is called only if all of these fail. solve invokes askuser to query the user for the truth value of the goal A. askuser prints the goal and instructions for answering. read(true) attempts to unify the user's input with the term true, failing if the user enters false (or anything that will not unify with true). In this way we have changed the semantics of solve and extended the behavior of PROLOG. An example, using the simple knowledge base defined above, illustrates the behavior of the augmented solve predicate:

```
?- solve(p(f, g)).
s(f)? Enter true if the goal is true, false otherwise
true.
t(g)? Enter true if the goal is true, false otherwise
true.
   yes
```

Another extension to the meta-interpreter allows it to respond to "why" queries. When the interpreter asks the user a question, the user can respond with why; the appropriate response to this query is the current rule that the program is trying to solve. We implement this by storing the stack of rules in the current line of reasoning as the second parameter to solve. Whenever solve calls clause to backward chain on a goal, it places the selected rule on the stack. Thus, the rule stack records the chain of rules from the top-level goal to the current subgoal.

Because the user may now enter two valid responses to a query, askuser calls respond, which either succeeds if the user enters true (as before) or prints the top rule on the stack if the user enters why. respond and askuser are mutually recursive, so that after printing the answer to a why query, respond calls askuser to query the user about the goal again. Note, however, that it calls askuser with the tail of the rule stack. Thus, a series of why queries will simply chain back up the rule stack until the stack is exhausted, letting the user trace the entire line of reasoning.

```
solve(true,_) :-!.
solve(not(A),Rules) :- not(solve(A,Rules)).
solve((A,B),Rules) :- !, solve(A,Rules), solve(B,Rules).
solve(A,Rules) :- clause(A,B), solve(B,[(A :- B)|Rules]).
solve(A,Rules) :- askuser(A,Rules).

askuser(A,Rules) :- write(A),
        write('? Enter true if goal is true, false otherwise'),nl,
        read(Answer), respond(Answer,A,Rules).

respond(true,_,_).
respond(why,A,[Rule|Rules]) :- write(Rule),nl,
        askuser(A,Rules).
respond(why,A,[ ]) :- askuser(A,[ ]).
```

For example, we may run this version of **solve** on the simple database introduced earlier in the section. Note how successive why queries trace back up the line of reasoning.

```
?- solve(p(f, g), []).
s(f)? Enter true if goal is true, false otherwise
why.
q(f) :- s(f)
s(f)? Enter true if goal is true, false otherwise
why.
p(f,g) :- (q(f),r(g))
s(f)? Enter true if goal is true, false otherwise
true.
t(g)? Enter true if goal is true, false otherwise
true.
    yes
```

Another useful extension to the **solve** predicate constructs a proof tree for any successful goal. The ability to build proof trees provides expert system shells with the means of responding to "how" queries; it is also important to any algorithm, such as explanation-based learning (Section 13.5), that reasons about the results of a problem solver.

We may modify the pure PROLOG interpreter to recursively build a proof tree for a goal as it solves that goal. In the definition that follows, the proof is returned as the second parameter of the **solve** predicate. The proof of the atom true is that atom; this halts the recursion. In solving a goal A using a rule A :- B, we construct the proof of B and return the structure (A :-ProofB). In solving a conjunction of goals, A and B, we simply conjoin the proof trees for each goal: (ProofA,ProofB).

The definition of a meta-interpreter that constructs proof trees is:

```
solve(true, true) :-!.
solve(not(A), not ProofA) :- not (solve(A, ProofA)).
solve((A,B),(ProofA,ProofB)) :- solve(A,ProofA), solve(B,ProofB).
solve(A,(A :- ProofB)) :- clause(A,B), solve(B,ProofB).
solve(A,(A:-given)) :- askuser(A).
```

```
askuser(A,Proof) :- write(A),
        write('enter true if goal is true, false otherwise'),
        read(true).
```

Running this on our simple data base gives the results:

```
?- solve(p(a, b), Proof).
   Proof = p(a,b) :-
              ((q(a) :-
                (s(a) :-
                   true)),
              (r(b) :-
                (t(b) :-
                   true)))
```

In the next section, we use these techniques to implement an expert system shell. exshell uses a knowledge base in the form of rules to solve problems. It asks the user for needed information, keeps a record of case-specific data, responds to how and why queries, and implements the certainty factor algebra of Chapter 8. Although this program, exshell, is much more complex than the PROLOG meta-interpreters discussed above, it is just an extension of this methodology. Its heart is a solve predicate that implements a back-chaining search of rules and facts.

13.2.2 Shell for a Rule-Based Expert System

In this section we present the key predicates used in the design of an interpreter for a goal-driven, rule-based expert system. At the end of this section, we demonstrate the performance of exshell using an automotive diagnostic knowledge base. If the reader would prefer to read through this trace before examining exshell's key predicates, we encourage looking ahead.

An exshell knowledge base consists of rules and specifications of queries that can be made to the user. Rules are represented using a two-parameter rule predicate of the form rule(R, CF). The first parameter is an assertion to the knowledge base, written using standard PROLOG syntax. Assertions may be PROLOG rules, of the form (G :- P), where G is the head of the rule and P is the conjunctive pattern under which G is true. The first argument to the rule predicate may also be a PROLOG fact. CF is the confidence the designer has in the rule's conclusions. exshell implements the certainty algebra of MYCIN, presented in Chapter 8. CFs range from 100, a fact that is true, to −100, something that is known to be false. If the CF is around 0, the truth value is unknown. Typical rules from a knowledge base for diagnosing automotive failures are:

```
rule((bad_component(starter) :- (bad_system(starter_system),
        lights(come_on))), 50).

rule(fix(starter, 'replace starter'),100).
```

The first rule states that if the bad system is shown to be the starter system and the lights come on, then conclude that the bad component is the starter, with a certainty of 50. The second asserts the fact that we may fix a broken starter by replacing it, with a certainty of 100. exshell uses the rule predicate to retrieve those rules that conclude about a given goal, just as the simpler versions of solve used the built-in clause predicate to retrieve rules from the global PROLOG database.

exshell supports user queries for unknown data; however, because we do not want the interpreter to ask for every unsolved goal, we allow the programmer to specify exactly what information may be so obtained. We do this with the askable predicate; the argument to askable is the goal under consideration. For example:

```
askable(car_starts).
```

specifies that the interpreter may ask the user for the truth of the car_starts goal when nothing is known or can be concluded about that goal.

In addition to the programmer-defined knowledge base of rules and askables, exshell maintains its own record of case-specific data. Because the shell asks the user for information, it needs to remember what it has been told; this prevents the program from asking the same question twice during a consultation (decidedly non-expert behavior!).

The heart of the exshell meta-interpreter is a predicate of four arguments called, surprisingly, solve. The first of these arguments is the goal to be solved. On successfully solving the goal, exshell binds the second argument to the confidence in the goal as computed from the knowledge base. The third argument is the rule stack, used in responding to why queries, and the fourth is the cutoff threshold for the certainty factor algebra. This allows pruning of the search space if the confidence falls below the threshold.

In attempting to satisfy a goal, G, solve/4 first tries to match G with any facts that it already has obtained from the user. We represent known facts using the two-parameter known(A,CF) predicate. For example, known(car_starts, 85) indicates that the user has already told us that the car starts, with a confidence of 85. If the goal is unknown, solve/4 attempts to solve the goal using its knowledge base. It handles the negation of a goal by solving the goal and multiplying the confidence in that goal by -1. It solves conjunctive goals in left-to-right order. If G is a positive literal, solve/4 tries any rules whose head matches G. If this fails, solve queries the user. On obtaining the user's confidence in a goal, solve/4 asserts this information to the data base using a known/2 predicate.

```
% Case 1: truth value of goal is already known
solve(Goal, CF, _, Threshold) :-
    known(Goal, CF),!,
    above_threshold(CF, Threshold).                 % Test confidence threshold


% Case 2: negated goal
solve(not(Goal), CF, Rules, Threshold) :- !,
    invert_threshold(Threshold, New_threshold),
    solve(Goal, CF_goal, Rules, New_threshold),
    negate_cf(CF_goal, CF).
```

```
% Case 3: conjunctive goals
solve((Goal_1,Goal_2), CF, Rules, Threshold) :- !,
    solve(Goal_1, CF_1, Rules, Threshold),
    above_threshold(CF_1, Threshold),
    solve(Goal_2, CF_2, Rules, Threshold),
    above_threshold(CF_2, Threshold),
    and_cf(CF_1, CF_2, CF).                          % Compute CF for and

% Case 4: back chain on a rule in knowledge base
solve(Goal, CF, Rules, Threshold) :-
    rule((Goal :- (Premise)), CF_rule),
    solve(Premise, CF_premise, [rule((Goal :- Premise), CF_rule)|Rules], Threshold),
    rule_cf(CF_rule, CF_premise, CF),
    above_threshold(CF, Threshold).

% Case 5: fact assertion in knowledge base
solve(Goal, CF, _, Threshold) :-
    rule(Goal, CF),
    above_threshold(CF, Threshold).

% Case 6: ask user
solve(Goal, CF, Rules, Threshold) :-
    askable(Goal),
    askuser(Goal, CF, Rules), !,
    assert(known(Goal, CF)),
    above_threshold(CF, Threshold).
```

We start a consultation using a two-argument version of solve. The first argument is the top-level goal in the knowledge base, and the second is a variable that will be bound to the confidence in the goal's truth as inferred from the knowledge base. solve/2 prints a set of instructions to the user, calls retractall(known(_,_)) to clean up any residual information saved in the previous use of exshell, and calls solve/4 with appropriate values for its arguments.

```
solve(Goal,CF) :-
    print_instructions,
    retractall(known(_,_)),
    solve(Goal,CF,[],20).                            % A threshold of 20
```

print_instructions tells the user the allowable responses to an exshell query:

```
print_instructions :-
    nl,  write('Response must be either:'),
    nl,  write('   A confidence in the truth of the query.'),
    nl,  write('    This is a number between -100 and 100.'),
    nl,  write('   why.'),
    nl,  write('   how(X), where X is a goal'), nl.
```

The next set of predicates compute certainty factors: the certainty factor of the **and** of two goals is the minimum of the certainty factors of the individual goals; the certainty factor of the negation of a fact is -1 times the certainty of that fact. Confidence in a fact concluded using a rule equals the certainty of the premise times the certainty factor in the rule. **above_threshold** determines whether the value of a certainty factor is too low given a particular threshold. **exshell** uses the threshold value to prune a goal if its certainty gets too low. Note that we define **above_threshold** separately for negative and positive values of the threshold. A positive threshold enables us to prune if the goal's confidence is less than the threshold. However, a negative threshold indicates that we are trying to prove a goal false; we can only prune if the value of the goal's confidence is greater than the threshold. **invert_threshold** is called when a goal is negated and multiplies a threshold by -1. This material is all discussed in Section 8.3.3.

```
and_cf(A,B,A) :-
    A =< B.

and_cf(A,B,B) :-
    B < A.

negate_cf(CF,Negated_CF) :-
    Negated_CF is -1 * CF.

rule_cf(CF_rule,CF_premise,CF) :-
    CF is round(CF_rule * CF_premise/100).

above_threshold(CF,T) :-
    T >= 0, CF >= T.

above_threshold(CF,T) :-
    T < 0, CF =< T.

invert_threshold(Threshold,New_threshold) :-
    New_threshold is -1 * Threshold.
```

askuser writes out a query and reads the user's answer; the **respond** predicates take the appropriate action for each user input.

```
askuser(Goal,CF,Rules) :-                          % Ask user for answer to goal
    nl, write('User query:'),
    write(Goal), nl, write('? '),
    read(Answer),
    respond(Answer,Goal,CF,Rules).                 % Processes answer
```

The user can respond to the query with a **CF** between 100 and -100, indicating his confidence in the goal's truth, **why** to ask why the question was asked, or **how(X)** to inquire how result **X** was established.

The response to a why query is the rule currently on top of the rule stack. As with our previous implementation, successive why queries will chain back up the rule stack, enabling the user to reconstruct the entire line of reasoning. If the user answer matches how(X), respond calls build_proof to build a proof tree for X and write_proof to print that proof in a readable form. There is also a "catchall" respond for unrecognized input values.

```
% Case 1: user enters a valid confidence factor
respond(CF, _, CF, _) :-
    number(CF),
    CF =< 100, CF >= -100.

% Case 2: user enters a why query
respond(why, Goal, CF, [Rule|Rules]) :-
    write_rule(Rule),
    askuser(Goal, CF, Rules).

respond(why, Goal, CF, []) :-
    write('Back to top of rule stack.'),
    askuser(Goal, CF, []).

% Case 3: user enters a how query. Build and print a proof
respond(how(X), Goal, CF, Rules) :-
    build_proof(X, CF_X, Proof),!,
    write(X), write(' was concluded with certainty '), write(CF_X), nl, nl,
    write('The proof is '),nl, nl,
    write_proof(Proof, 0), nl, nl,
    askuser(Goal, CF, Rules).

% User enters how query, could not build proof
respond(how(X), Goal, CF, Rules) :-
    write('The truth of '), write(X), nl,
    write('is not yet known.'), nl,
    askuser(Goal, CF, Rules).

% Case 4: unrecognized input
respond(_, Goal, CF, Rules) :-
    write('Unrecognized response.'), nl,
    askuser(Goal, CF, Rules).
```

The definition of build_proof is almost completely parallel to that of solve/4. However, build_proof does not ask the user for unknown facts, as these have already been saved as case-specific data. build_proof constructs a proof tree as it proves the goal.

```
build_proof(Goal,CF,(Goal,CF :- given)) :-
    known(Goal,CF), !.

build_proof(not Goal,CF,not Proof) :-
    !, build_proof(Goal,CF_goal,Proof), negate_cf(CF_goal,CF).
```

```
build_proof((Goal_1, Goal_2),CF, (Proof_1, Proof_2)) :-
    !, build_proof(Goal_1,CF_1,Proof_1),
    build_proof(Goal_2,CF_2,Proof_2), and_cf(CF_1,CF_2,CF).

build_proof(Goal,CF,(Goal,CF :- Proof)) :-
    rule((Goal :- Premise),CF_rule),
    build_proof(Premise,CF_premise,Proof),
    rule_cf(CF_rule,CF_premise,CF).

build_proof(Goal,CF,(Goal,CF :- fact)) :-
    rule(Goal,CF).
```

The final predicates create a simple user interface. As is so often true, the interface requires the bulk of the code! First, we define a predicate to write out a rule in a readable format:

```
write_rule(rule((Goal :- (Premise)), CF)) :-
    write(Goal), write(':-'), nl,
    write_premise(Premise), nl,
    write('CF = '), write(CF), nl.
write_rule(rule(Goal, CF)) :-
    write(Goal), nl,
    write('CF = '), write(CF), nl.
```

write_premise writes the conjuncts of a rule premise:

```
write_premise((Premise_1, Premise_2)) :-
    !, write_premise(Premise_1),
    write_premise(Premise_2).
write_premise(not Premise) :-
    !, write('   '), write(not), write(' '), write(Premise), nl.
write_premise(Premise) :-
    write('   '), write(Premise), nl.
```

write_proof prints out a proof, using indentation to show the structure of the tree:

```
write_proof((Goal, CF :- given), Level) :-                    % Prints proof tree, with
    indent(Level), write(Goal),                               % indentation for levels of tree
    write(' CF= '), write(CF),
    write(' was given by the user'), nl, !.

write_proof((Goal, CF :- fact), Level) :-
    indent(Level), write(Goal), write(' CF= '), write(CF),
    write(' was a fact in the knowledge base'), nl, !.

write_proof((Goal, CF :- Proof), Level) :-
    indent(Level), write(Goal), write(' CF= '), write(CF), write(' :-'),
    nl, New_level is Level + 1, write_proof(Proof,New_level), !.
```

```
write_proof(not Proof, Level) :-
   indent(Level), write((not)), nl,
   New_level is Level + 1, write_proof(Proof,New_level), !.


write_proof((Proof_1, Proof_2),Level) :-
   write_proof(Proof_1,Level), write_proof(Proof_2,Level), !.


indent(0).
indent(I) :-
   write('   '), I_new is I - 1, indent(I_new).
```

As an illustration of the behavior of exshell, consider the following sample knowledge base for diagnosing car problems. The top-level goal is fix/1. The knowledge base decomposes the problem solution into finding the bad system, finding the bad component within that system, and finally linking the diagnosis to the advice for its solution. Note that the knowledge base is incomplete; there are sets of symptoms that it cannot diagnose. In this case, exshell simply fails. Extending the knowledge base to some of these cases and adding a rule that succeeds if all others fail are left as exercises.

```
rule((fix(Advice) :-                                        % Top-level query
      (bad_component(X), fix(X,Advice))),100).


rule((bad_component(starter) :-
         (bad_system(starter_system), lights(come_on))), 50).
rule((bad_component(battery) :-
         (bad_system(starter_system), not lights(come_on))), 90).
rule((bad_component(timing) :-
         (bad_system(ignition_system), not tuned_recently)), 80).
rule((bad_component(plugs) :-
         (bad_system(ignition_system), plugs(dirty))), 90).
rule((bad_component(ignition_wires) :-
         (bad_system(ignition_system), not plugs(dirty), tuned_recently)), 80).


rule((bad_system(starter_system) :-
         (not car_starts, not turns_over)), 90).
rule((bad_system(ignition_system) :-
         (not car_starts, turns_over, gas_in_carb)), 80).
rule((bad_system(ignition_system) :-
         (runs(rough), gas_in_carb)), 80).
rule((bad_system(ignition_system) :-
         (car_starts, runs(dies), gas_in_carb)), 60).


rule(fix(starter,'replace starter'), 100).              % Advice for problems
rule(fix(battery,'replace or recharge battery'), 100).
rule(fix(timing,'get the timing adjusted'), 100).
rule(fix(plugs,'replace spark plugs'), 100).
rule(fix(ignition_wires,'check ignition wires'), 100).
```

```
askable(car_starts).                                    % May ask user about goal
askable(turns_over).
askable(lights(_)).
askable(runs(_)).
askable(gas_in_carb).
askable(tuned_recently).
askable(plugs(_)).
```

The following consultation shows a run of **exshell** using this knowledge base; there are no how or why queries. Figure 13.2 illustrates the space searched in the consultation. In Figure 13.2, the solid lines indicate branches searched, bold lines indicate the successful solution, and dotted lines indicate branches not searched.

```
?- solve(fix(X), CF).

Response must be either:
   A confidence in the truth of the query.
     This is a number between -100 and 100.
   why.
   how(X), where X is a goal

User query:car_starts
? -100.

User query:turns_over
? 85.

User query:gas_in_carb
? 75.

User query:tuned_recently
? -90.
     X = 'get the timing adjusted', CF = 48.0
```

We now run the same problem situation with how and why queries. Compare the responses with the corresponding subtrees and paths in Figure 13.2:

```
?- solve(fix(X), CF).

Response must be either:
   A confidence in the truth of the query.
     This is a number between -100 and 100.
   why.
   how(X), where X is a goal

User query:car_starts
? -100.
```

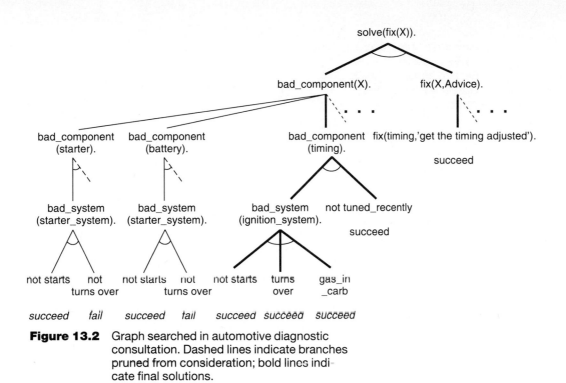

Figure 13.2 Graph searched in automotive diagnostic
consultation. Dashed lines indicate branches
pruned from consideration; bold lines indicate final solutions.

```
User query:turns_over
? why.
bad_system(starter_system):-
  not car_starts
  not turns_over

CF = 90

User query:turns_over
? why.
bad_component(starter):-
  bad_system(starter_system)
  lights(come_on)

CF = 50

User query:turns_over
? why.
fix(_0):-
  bad_component(starter)
  fix(starter,_0)
```

```
CF = 100

User query:turns_over
? why.
Back to top of rule stack.
User query:turns_over
? 85.

User query:gas_in_carb
? 75.

User query:tuned_recently
? why.
bad_component(timing):-
   bad_system(ignition_system)
   not tuned_recently

CF = 80

User query:tuned_recently
? how(bad_system(ignition_system)).
bad_system(ignition_system) was concluded with certainty 60.0

The proof is

bad_system(ignition_system) CF= 60.0 :-
   not
      car_starts CF= -100 was given by the user
   turns_over CF 85 was given by the user
   gas_in_carb CF= 75 was given by the user

User query:tuned_recently
? -90.
   X = 'get the timing adjusted', CF = 48.0
```

13.2.3   Semantic Nets in PROLOG

In this section, we discuss the implementation of inheritance for a simple semantic network language (Chapter 9). Our language lacks the full power and generality of a language such as conceptual graphs; in particular, we ignore the important distinction between classes and instances (see also Chapter 15). This restricted language simplifies the implementation.

In the semantic net of Figure 13.3, nodes represent individuals such as the canary tweety and classes such as ostrich, crow, robin, bird, and vertebrate. isa links represent the class hierarchy relationship.

For representational clarity and consistency as well as for ease in building search procedures, we adopt canonical forms for the data relationships within the net. We use an isa(Type, Parent) predicate to indicate that Type is a member of Parent and a has-

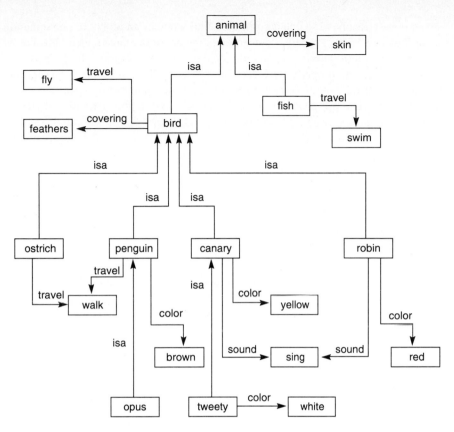

Figure 13.3 Portion of a semantic network describing birds and other animals.

prop(Object, Property, Value) predicate to represent property relations. hasprop indicates that Object has Property with Value. Object and Value are nodes in the network, and Property is the name of the link that joins them.

A partial list of the predicates necessary to describe the semantic network of Figure 13.3 is:

isa (canary, bird).   isa (robin, bird).
isa (ostrich, bird).   isa (penguin, bird).
isa (bird, animal).   isa (fish, animal).
isa (opus, penguin).   isa (tweety, canary).
hasprop (tweety, color, white).   hasprop (robin, color, red).
hasprop (canary, color, yellow). hasprop (penguin, color, brown).
hasprop (bird, travel, fly).   hasprop (fish, travel, swim).
hasprop (ostrich, travel, walk). hasprop (penguin, travel, walk).
hasprop (robin, sound, sing).   hasprop (canary, sound, sing).
hasprop (bird, cover, feathers). hasprop (animal, cover, skin).

We create a recursive search algorithm to find whether an object in our semantic net has a particular property. Properties are stored in the net at the most general level at which they are true. Through inheritance, an individual or subclass acquires the properties of its superclasses. Thus the property fly holds for bird and all its subclasses. Exceptions are located at the specific level of the exception. Thus, ostrich and penguin travel by walking instead of flying. The hasproperty predicate begins search at a particular object. If the information is not directly attached to that object, hasproperty follows isa links to superclasses. If no more superclasses exist and hasproperty has not located the property, it fails.

```
hasproperty(Object, Property, Value) :-
        hasprop(Object, Property, Value).

hasproperty(Object, Property, Value) :-
        isa(Object, Parent),
        hasproperty(Parent, Property, Value).
```

hasproperty searches the inheritance hierarchy in a depth-first fashion. In the next section, we show how inheritance can be applied to a frame-based representation and implement both tree and multiple-inheritance relations.

13.2.4 Frames and Schemata in PROLOG

Semantic nets can be partitioned, with additional information added to node descriptions, to give them a frame structure. We redefine the bird example of the previous subsection using frames, where each frame represents a collection of relationships of the semantic net and the isa slots of the frame define the frame hierarchy (Fig. 13.4).

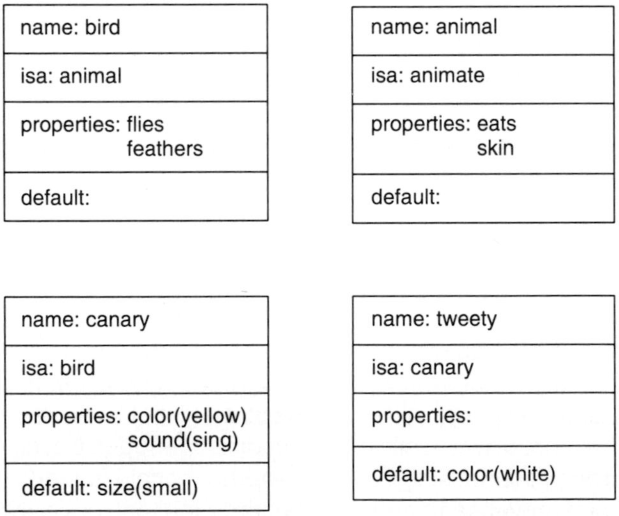

Figure 13.4 Frames from a knowledge base of birds.

The first slot of each frame names the node, such as name(tweety) or name(vertebrate). The second slot gives the inheritance links between the node and its parents. Because our example has a tree structure, each node has only one link, the isa predicate with one argument. The third slot in the node's frame is a list of features that describe that node. In this list we use any PROLOG predicate such as flies, feathers, or color(brown). The final slot in the frame is the list of exceptions and default values for the node, again either a single word or predicate indicating a property.

In our frame language, each frame organizes its slot names into lists of properties and default values. This allows us to distinguish these different types of knowledge and give them different behaviors in the inheritance hierarchy. Although our implementation allows subclasses to inherit properties from both lists, other representations are possible and may be useful in certain applications. We may wish to specify that only default values are inherited. Or we may wish to build a third list containing the properties of the class itself rather than the members, sometimes called *class values*. For example, we may wish to state that the class canary names a species of songbird. This should not be inherited by subclasses or instances: tweety does not name a species of songbird. Students are asked to define and build different frame representations and inheritance schemes in the exercises.

We now represent the relationships in Figure 13.4 with the PROLOG fact predicate frame with four arguments. We may use the methods suggested in Section 13.1.2 to check the parameters of the frame predicate for appropriate type, for instance, to ensure that the third frame slot is a list that contains only values from a fixed list of properties.

```
frame(name(bird),
      isa(animal),
      [travel(flies), feathers],
      []).

frame(name(penguin),
      isa(bird),
      [color(brown)],
      [travel(walks)]).

frame(name(canary),
      isa(bird),
      [color(yellow), call(sing)],
      [size(small)]).

frame(name(tweety),
      isa(canary),
      [],
      [color(white)]).
```

Once the full set of descriptions and inheritance relationships are defined for the frame of Figure 13.4, we create procedures to infer properties from this representation:

```
get(Prop, Object) :-
       frame(name(Object), _, List_of_properties, _),
       member(Prop, List_of_properties).
```

```
get(Prop, Object) :-
        frame(name(Object), _, _, List_of_defaults),
        member(Prop, List_of_defaults).

get(Prop, Object) :-
        frame(name(Object), isa(Parent), _, _),
        get(Prop, Parent).
```

If the frame structure allows multiple inheritance of properties (Section 9.5), we make this change both in our representation and in our search strategy. First, in the frame representation we make the argument of the isa predicate the list of superclasses of the Object. Thus, each superclass in the list is a parent of the entity named in the first argument of frame. If opus is a penguin and a cartoon_char (Fig. 9.27), we can represent this by:

```
frame(name(opus),
        isa([penguin, cartoon_char]),
        [color(black)],
        []).
```

Now, we test for properties of opus by recurring up the isa hierarchy for both penguin and cartoon_char. We add the additional solve definition between the third and fourth get predicates of the previous example.

```
get(Prop, Object) :-
        frame(name(Object), isa(List), _, _),
        get_multiple(Prop, List).
```

We define get_multiple by:

```
get_multiple(Prop, [Parent|_]) :-
        get(Prop, Parent).

get_multiple(Prop, [ _|Rest]) :-
        get_multiple(Prop, Rest).
```

With this inheritance preference, properties of penguin and its superclasses will be examined before those of cartoon_char.

Finally, any PROLOG procedure may be attached to a frame slot. As we have built the frame representation in our examples, this would entail adding a PROLOG rule, or list of PROLOG rules, as a parameter of frame. This is accomplished by enclosing the entire rule in parentheses, as we did for rules in exshell, and making this structure an argument of the frame predicate. For example, we could design a list of response rules for opus, giving him different responses for different questions.

This list of rules, each rule in parentheses, would then become a parameter of the frame and, depending on the value of X passed to the opus frame, would define the appropriate response. More complex examples could be rules describing the control of a thermostat or creating a graphic image appropriate to a set of values. These examples are presented in Chapter 15, where attached procedures, often called *methods*, play an important role in object-oriented representations.

13.3 Natural Language Understanding in PROLOG

13.3.1 Introduction

Because of its built-in search and pattern matching, PROLOG easily accommodates natural language processing. We can write natural language grammars directly in PROLOG, as we saw with both the context-free and context-sensitive grammars of Section 6.3. Semantic representations are also easy to create in PROLOG. Semantic relationships can be built either directly using the first-order predicate calculus or by constructing a meta-interpreter for another representation language, as suggested by the frame system of the previous section. Finally, semantic inference, such as join, restrict, and inheritance in conceptual graphs, can be done directly in PROLOG or with inference procedures built on top of PROLOG.

Conceptual graphs are an example of such an approach. As we saw in Chapter 9, conceptual graphs can be translated directly into predicate calculus and hence into PROLOG. The conceptual relation nodes become the predicate name, and the arity of the relation is the number of arguments of the predicate. Each PROLOG predicate, as with each conceptual graph, represents a single proposition.

The conceptual graphs of Figure 9.11 may be rendered in PROLOG as:

bird(X), flies(X).

dog(X), color(X,Y), brown(Y).

child(X), parents(X,Y, Z), father(Y), mother(Z).

where X, Y, and Z are bound to the appropriate individuals. Type information can be added to parameters as indicated in Section 13.1.2. We can also define the type hierarchy through a variation of **isa** predicates.

Case frames (Chapter 10) are also easily defined in PROLOG. Each verb may be paired with a list of the semantic relations assumed to be part of the verb. These may include agents, instruments, and objects. For example, we could define an instance of the verb **give** that requires a subject, object, and indirect object using the case frame:

verb(give,
      [human (Subject),
        agent (Subject, give),
        act_of_giving (give),
        object (Object, give),
        inanimate (Object),
        recipient (Ind_obj, give),
        human (Ind_obj)]).

The second argument defines the constraints on the verb give, such as the requirement that the agent and recipient be human. In the English sentence "John gives Mary the book," this structure takes on the obvious assignments.

We could define defaults in a case frame by binding the appropriate values. For example, we could give bite a default instrument of teeth by

```
verb(bite,
        [animate (Subject),
        agent (Subject, Action),
        act_of_biting (Action),
        object (Object, Action),
        animate (Object),
        instrument (teeth, Action),
        part_of (teeth, Subject)]).
```

Again, type constraints (Section 13.1.2) may be used to enforce appropriate variable binding.

Logic programming offers a powerful medium for building grammars as well as representations for semantic meanings. The reader is encouraged to build some of the structures, such as context-sensitive grammars and conceptual graphs, presented in Chapters 9 and 10. We present a final example, a recursive descent semantic net parser, in the next section.

13.3.2 A Recursive Descent Semantic Net Parser

This parser is an extension of the context-free and context-sensitive parsers built in the final section of Chapter 6. In these earlier examples we saw that when the parse descended to the leaves of the parse tree it matched on dictionary entries. In the context-free example these were simple word matches, such as noun(man) or verb(like). When we reached the leaves of the context sensitive parse tree, we matched structures such as noun(man, singular) and verb(like, plural). With this context sensitivity, we were able to enforce noun-verb agreement in the sentence.

We now extend this set of context-sensitive constraints to include semantic consistency. We do this by matching case frames for the verbs of sentences to semantic descriptions of subjects and objects. After we make each match and return up the tree with our potential parse, we constrain these semantic net graphs to be consistent with each other. We do this by performing graph operations, such as join and restrict, to each piece of the graph as it is returned up the parse tree.

We first present the grammar rules. Notice that the top-level predicate utterance returns not just a Sentence but also a Sentence_graph. Each component of the grammar relationships, such as nounphrase and verbphrase, call join to merge together the constraints of their respective graphs.

```
utterance(X, Sentence_graph) :-
        sentence(X, [], Sentence_graph).
```

```
sentence((Start, End, Sentence_graph) :-
        nounphrase(Start, Rest, Subject_graph),
        verbphrase(Rest, End, Predicate_graph).
        join([agent(Subject_graph)], Predicate_graph, Sentence_graph)).

nounphrase([Noun | End], End, Noun_phrase_graph) :-
        noun(Noun, Noun_phrase_graph).

nounphrase([Article, Noun | End], End, Noun_phrase_graph) :-
        article(Article),
        noun(Noun, Noun_phrase_graph).

verbphrase([Verb | End], End, Verb_phrase_graph) :-
        verb(Verb, Verb_phrase_graph).

verbphrase([Verb | Rest], End, Verb_phrase_graph) :-
        verb(Verb, Verb_graph),
        nounphrase(Rest, End, Noun_phrase_graph),
        join([object(Noun_phrase_graph)], Verb_graph, Verb_phrase_graph).
```

We next present predicates for the graph join operation. These are meta-predicates because their domain is other PROLOG structures. These operators may be seen as utilities that propagate constraints across the pieces of semantic nets they merge together. join takes three arguments: the first two are semantic graphs, and the third argument is the result of joining these graphs on matching properties. join examines the cases of joining two frames, joining a slot to a frame, and joining two slots.

```
join(X, X, X).
join(A, B, C) :-
        isframe(A), isframe(B), !,
        join_frames(A, B, C, not_joined).
join(A, B, C) :-
        isframe(A), is_slot(B), !,
        join_slot_to_frame(B, A, C).
join(A, B, C) :-
        isframe(B), is_slot(A), !,
        join_slot_to_frame(A, B, C).
join(A, B, C) :-
        is_slot(A), is_slot(B), !,
        join_slots(A, B, C).
```

join_frames recursively matches each slot (property) of the first frame to matching slots of the second.

```
join_frames([A | B], C, D, OK) :-
        join_slot_to_frame(A, C, E) , !,
        join_frames(B, E, D, ok).
```

```
join_frames([ A | B], C, [A | D], OK) :-
        join_frames(B, C, D, OK).
join_frames([], A, A, ok).
```

join_slot_to_frame takes a slot and a frame and searches the frame for matching slots.

```
join_slot_to_frame(A, [B | C], [D | C]) :-
        join_slots(A, B, D).
join_slot_to_frame(A, [B | C], [B | D]) :-
        join_slot_to_frame(A, C, D).
```

join_slots matches two slots, taking the type hierarchy into account. match_with_inheritance specializes properties as needed to achieve a match.

```
join_slots(A, B, D) :-
        functor(A, FA, _), functor(B, FB, _),
        match_with_inheritance(FA, FB, FN),
        arg(1, A, Value_a), arg(1, B, Value_b),
        join(Value_a, Value_b, New_value),
        D =.. [FN | [New_value]].
```

```
isframe([ _ | _ ]).
isframe([]).
```

```
is_slot(A) :- functor(A, _, 1).
```

Finally, we create the dictionary entries, the inheritance hierarchy, and the case frames for the verbs. In this example, we use a simple hierarchy that lists all valid specializations; the third argument to match_with_inheritance is the common specialization of the first two. A more realistic implementation would maintain a graph of the hierarchies and search it for common specializations, as in Section 13.2.2. Implementation of this is left as an exercise.

```
match_with_inheritance(X, X, X).
match_with_inheritance(dog, animate, dog).
match_with_inheritance(animate, dog, dog).
match_with_inheritance(man, animate, man).
match_with_inheritance(animate, man, man).
```

```
article(a).
article(the).
```

```
noun(fido, [dog(fido)]).
noun(man, [man(X)]).
noun(dog, [dog(X)]).
```

```
verb(likes, [action([liking(X)]), agent([animate(X)]), object([animate(Y)])]).
verb(bites, [action([biting(Y)]), agent([dog(X)]), object([animate(Z)])]).
```

We now parse several sentences and print out the Sentence_graph. The first sentence states that some man, with name unknown, likes an unnamed dog.

```
?- utterance([the, man, likes, the, dog], X).
X = [action([liking(_54)]), agent([man(_23)]), object([dog(_52)])].
?- utterance([fido, likes, the, man], X).
X = [action([liking(_62)]), agent([dog(fido)]), object([man(_70)])].
?- utterance([the, man, bites, fido], Z).
no
```

The last sentence, although it was syntactically correct, did not meet the semantic constraints, where a dog had to be the agent of the verb bites. In the second sentence, a particular dog, Fido, likes an unnamed man. In the final example we see whether Fido can bite an unnamed man:

```
?- utterance([fido, bites, the, man], X).
X = [action([biting(_12)]), agent([dog(fido)]), object([man(_17)])].
```

This parser may be extended in many interesting directions, such as by adding adjectives, adverbs, and prepositional phrases or by allowing compound sentences. The within-sentence additions should all have their semantic representations. These are first matched and then constrained as they are merged into the sentence graph. Each dictionary item may also have multiple meanings that are only accepted as they meet the general requirements of the sentence.

13.4 Version Space Search in PROLOG

In Chapter 12, we presented a number of machine learning algorithms. In this section and the next, we implement two of them: version space search and explanation-based learning. PROLOG is widely used in machine learning research because, as these implementations illustrate, its meta-level reasoning capabilities simplify the construction and manipulation of new representations. Because we do not discuss the algorithms in the present chapter, the reader should feel comfortable with the associated material in Chapter 12 before proceeding.

In Section 12.2.2 we presented three different algorithms for searching a concept space:

1. Searching in a specific to general direction.

2. Searching in a general to specific direction.

3. A bi-directional search, the candidate elimination algorithm.

In this section we implement the specific to general search and give hints on how the reader may construct a general to specific version space search. Finally, we present the full, bi-directional candidate elimination algorithm.

13.4.1 The Feature Vector Representation of Concepts and Instances

These algorithms are independent of the representation used for concepts, as long as it supports appropriate generalization and specialization operations. To simplify this presentation, we use a representation of objects as lists of features. For example, we describe a small, red, ball as the list:

[small, red, ball]

Similarly, we represent the concept of all small, red things by including a variable in the list:

[small, red, X]

This representation, called a *feature vector,* is less expressive than full logic. For example, it cannot represent the class "all red or green balls." However, this representation simplifies generalization and provides a strong inductive bias (Section 12.4). We generalize a feature vector by substituting a variable for a constant. For example, the most specific common generalization of [small, red, ball] and [small, green, ball] is [small, X, ball]. This vector covers both of the specializations and is the most specific vector to do so.

We define a feature vector as covering another if the first is either identical to or more general than the second. Note that unlike unification, covers is asymmetrical: values exist for which X covers Y but Y does not cover X. For example, [X, red, ball] covers [large, red, ball], but the reverse is not true. We define covers for feature vectors as:

```
covers([],[]).
covers([H1|T1], [H2|T2]) :-                    % variables cover each other
    var(H1), var(H2),
    covers(T1, T2).
covers([H1|T1], [H2|T2]) :-                    % variable covers a constant
    var(H1), atom(H2),
    covers(T1, T2).
covers([H1|T1], [H2|T2]) :-                       % matching constants
    atom(H1), atom(H2), H1 = H2,
    covers(T1, T2).
```

In the algorithm, we need to determine whether one feature vector is strictly more general than another, that is the vectors are not identical. We define the more_general/2 predicate as:

```
more_general(X, Y) :- not(covers(Y, X)), covers(X, Y).
```

We implement generalization of feature vectors as a predicate, generalize/3, where the first argument is a feature vector representing a hypothesis (this vector may contain variables) and the second argument is an instance, containing no variables. generalize/3 binds its third argument to the most specific generalization of the hypothesis that covers the instance. generalize/3 recursively scans the feature vectors, comparing corresponding elements. If two elements match, the result contains the value of the hypothesis vector in that position; if two elements do not match, it places a variable in the corresponding position of the generalized feature vector. Note the use of the expression not(Feature \= Inst_prop) in the second definition of generalize; this double negative enables us to test whether two atoms will unify without actually performing the unification and forming any unwanted variable bindings. We define generalize:

```
generalize([],[],[]).
generalize([Feature|Rest], [Inst_prop|Rest_inst], [Feature|Rest_gen]) :-
   not(Feature \= Inst_prop),
   generalize(Rest, Rest_inst, Rest_gen).
generalize([Feature|Rest], [Inst_prop|Rest_inst], [_|Rest_gen]) :-
   Feature \= Inst_prop,
   generalize(Rest, Rest_inst, Rest_gen).
```

These predicates define the essential operations on feature vector representations. The remainder of the implementations in Sections 13.4.2 and 13.4.3 are independent of any specific representation and may be adapted to a variety of representations and generalization operators (Section 12.2.1).

13.4.2 Specific to General Search

As discussed in Chapter 12, we may search a concept space in a specific to general direction by maintaining a list, H, of candidate hypotheses. The hypotheses in H are the most specific concepts that cover all the positive examples and none of the negative examples seen so far.

The heart of the algorithm is process/5. The first argument to process is a training instance, positive(X) or negative(X), indicating that X is a positive or negative example. The second and third arguments are the current list of hypotheses and the list of negative instances. On completion, process binds its fourth and fifth arguments to the updated lists of hypotheses and negative examples, respectively.

The first clause in the definition initializes an empty hypothesis set to the first positive instance. The second handles positive training instances by generalizing candidate hypotheses to cover the instance. It then deletes all-over generalizations by removing those that are more general than some other hypothesis and eliminating any hypothesis that covers some negative instance. The third clause in the definition handles negative examples by deleting any hypothesis that covers those instances.

```
process(positive(Instance), [], N, [Instance], N).
process(positive(Instance), H, N, Updated_H, N) :-
    generalize_set(H, Gen_H, Instance),
    delete(X, Gen_H, (member(Y, Gen_H), more_general(X, Y)), Pruned_H),
    delete(X, Pruned_H, (member(Y, N), covers(X, Y)), Updated_H).

process(negative(Instance), H, N, Updated_H, [Instance|N]) :-
            delete(X, H, covers(X, Instance), Updated_H).

process(Input, H, N, H, N) :-                          % Catches mistyped input
    Input \= positive(_),
    Input \= negative(_),
    write("Enter either positive(Instance) or negative(Instance) "), nl.
```

An interesting aspect of this implementation is the delete predicate, a generalization of the usual process of deleting all matches of an element from a list. One of the arguments to delete is a test that determines which elements to remove from the list. Using bagof, delete matches its first argument (usually a variable) with each element of its second argument (this must be a list). For each such binding, it then executes the test specified in argument three; this test is any sequence of PROLOG goals. If a list element causes this test to fail, delete includes that element in the resulting list and returns the result in its final argument. The delete predicate is an excellent example of the power of meta-reasoning in PROLOG: by letting us pass in a specification of the elements we want to delete from a list, delete gives us a general tool for implementing a range of list operations. Thus, delete lets us define the various filters used in process/5 in an extremely compact fashion. We define delete:

```
delete(X, L, Goal, New_L) :-
    (bagof(X, (member(X, L), not(Goal)), New_L); New_L = []).
```

generalize_set is a straightforward predicate that recursively scans a list of hypotheses and generalizes each one against a training instance. Note that this assumes that we may have multiple candidate generalizations at one time. In fact, the feature vector representation of Section 13.4.1 only allows a single most specific generalization. However, this is not true in general, and we have defined the algorithm for the general case.

```
generalize_set([], [], _).

generalize_set([Hypothesis|Rest],Updated_H,Instance):-
    not(covers(Hypothesis, Instance)),
    (bagof(X, generalize(Hypothesis, Instance, X), Updated_head);
        Updated_head = []),
    generalize_set(Rest,Updated_rest, Instance),
    append(Updated_head, Updated_rest, Updated_H).

generalize_set([Hypothesis|Rest],[Hypothesis|Updated_rest],Instance):-
    covers(Hypothesis, Instance),
    generalize_set(Rest,Updated_rest, Instance).
```

specific_to_general implements a straightforward loop that reads and processes training instances.

```
specific_to_general(H, N) :-
   write("H = "), write(H), nl,
   write("N = "), write(N), nl,
   write("Enter Instance "),
   read(Instance),
   process(Instance, H, N, Updated_H, Updated_N),
   specific_to_general(Updated_H, Updated_N).
```

The following transcript illustrates the execution of the algorithm.

```
?- specific_to_general([], []).
"H = "[]
"N = "[]
"Enter Instance "positive([small, red, ball]).
"H = "[[small,red,ball]]
"N = "[]
"Enter Instance "negative([large, green, cube]).
"H = "[[small,red,ball]]
"N = "[[large,green,cube]]
"Enter Instance "negative([small, blue, brick]).
"H = "[[small,red,ball]]
"N = "[[small,blue,brick],[large,green,cube]]
"Enter Instance "positive([small, green, ball]).
"H = "[[small,_66,ball]]
"N = "[[small,blue,brick],[large,green,cube]]
"Enter Instance "positive([large, blue, ball]).
"H = "[[_116,_66,ball]]
"N = "[[small,blue,brick],[large,green,cube]]
```

The second version of the algorithm searches in a general to specific direction (Section 12.2.2). In this version, the set of candidate hypotheses are initialized to the most general possible concept. In the case of the feature vector representation, this is a list of variables. It specializes candidate concepts to prevent them from covering negative instances. In the feature vector representation, this involves replacing variables with constants. When given a new positive instance, it eliminates any candidate hypothesis that fails to cover the instance. For a more detailed description of the algorithm, refer to Section 12.2.2.

We may implement this algorithm in a way that closely parallels the specific to general search described above, including the use of the general delete predicate to define the various filters of the list of candidate concepts. Each predicate in the specific to general search has its counterpart in the general to specific version.

In defining a general to specific search, process takes six arguments. The first five reflect the specific to general version: the first is a training instance (of the form positive(Instance) or negative(Instance)); the second is a list of candidate hypotheses that are the most general hypotheses that cover no negative instances. The third argument is the list of positive examples; the algorithm uses this argument to delete any overly specialized candidate hypothesis. The fourth and fifth arguments are the updated lists of hypotheses and positive examples, respectively.

The sixth argument is a list of allowable variable substitutions for specializing concepts. Specialization by substituting a constant for a variable requires the algorithm to know the allowable constant values for each field of the feature vector. These values will have to be passed in as the sixth argument to process. In our example of [Size, Color, Shape] vectors, a sample list of types might be [[small, medium, large], [red, white, blue], [ball, brick, cube]]. Note that the position of each sublist determines the position in a feature vector where those values may be used. For example, the first sublist defines allowable values for the first position of a feature vector.

We leave construction of this algorithm to the reader (Exercise 28). For further guidance to the reader, we include a run of our implementation of the algorithm:

```
?- general_to_specific([[_,_,_]], [],
[[small, medium, large], [red, blue, green], [ball, brick, cube]]).
"H = "[[_0,_1,_2]]
"P = "[]
"Enter Instance "positive([small, red, ball]).
"H = "[[_0,_1,_2]]
"P = "[[small,red,ball]]
"Enter Instance "negative([large, green,cube]).
"H = "[[small,_89,_90],[_79,red,_80],[_69,_70,ball]]
"P = "[[small,red,ball]]
"Enter Instance "negative([small, blue, brick]).
"H = "[[_79,red,_80],[_69,_70,ball]]
"P = "[[small,red,ball]]
"Enter Instance "positive([small, green, ball]).
"H = "[[_69,_70,ball]]
"P = "[[small,green,ball],[small,red,ball]]
```

13.4.3 Candidate Elimination

The full candidate elimination algorithm, as defined in Chapter 12, is a combination of the two single direction searches. As before, the heart of the algorithm is the definition of process/6. Also as before, the first argument to process is a training instance. Arguments two and three are G and S, the sets of maximally general and maximally specific hypotheses, respectively. The fourth and fifth arguments are bound to the updated versions of these sets. The sixth argument lists allowable variable substitutions for specializing feature vectors.

On positive instances, process generalizes S, the set of most specific generalizations, to cover the training instance. It then eliminates any elements of S that have been overgeneralized. It also eliminates any elements of G that fail to cover the training instance. It is interesting to note that an element of S is overly general if there is no element of G that covers it; this is true because G contains those candidate hypotheses that are both maximally general and cover no negative instances. process uses delete to eliminate these hypotheses.

On a negative training instance, **process** specializes all hypotheses in G to exclude that instance. It also eliminates any candidates in S that cover the negative instance. As discussed above, specialization of feature vectors requires replacing variables with constants. This requires that we pass a list of allowable substitutions as the sixth argument to **process**. We define **process**:

```
process(negative(Instance), G, S, Updated_G, Updated_S, Types) :-
    delete(X, S, covers(X, Instance), Updated_S),
    specialize_set(G, Spec_G, Instance, Types),
    delete(X, Spec_G, (member(Y, Spec_G), more_general(Y, X)), Pruned_G),
    delete(X, Pruned_G, (member(Y, Updated_S), not(covers(X, Y))), Updated_G).

process(positive(Instance), G, [], Updated_G, [Instance],_) :-        % Initialize S
    delete(X, G, not(covers(X, Instance)), Updated_G).

process(positive(Instance), G, S, Updated_G, Updated_S,_) :-
    delete(X, G, not(covers(X, Instance)), Updated_G),
    generalize_set(S, Gen_S, Instance),
    delete(X, Gen_S, (member(Y, Gen_S), more_general(X, Y)), Pruned_S),
    delete(X, Pruned_S, not((member(Y, Updated_G), covers(Y, X))), Updated_S).

process(Input, G, P, G, P,_) :-
    Input \= positive(_),
    Input \= negative(_),
    write("Enter either positive(Instance) or negative(Instance)"), nl.
```

generalize_set generalizes all members of a set of candidate hypotheses to cover a training instance. It is identical to the version defined for the specific to general search. **specialize_set** takes a set of candidate hypotheses and computes all maximally general specializations of those hypotheses that exclude (do not cover) a training instance. Note the use of **bagof** to get all specializations.

```
specialize_set([], [], _, _).

specialize_set([Hypothesis|Rest], Updated_H, Instance, Types) :-
    covers(Hypothesis, Instance),
    (bagof(Hypothesis, specialize(Hypothesis, Instance, Types), Updated_head);
      Updated_head = []),
    specialize_set(Rest, Updated_rest, Instance, Types),
    append(Updated_head, Updated_rest, Updated_H).

specialize_set([Hypothesis|Rest], [Hypothesis|Updated_rest], Instance, Types) :-
    not(covers(Hypothesis, Instance)),
    specialize_set(Rest, Updated_rest, Instance, Types).
```

specialize finds an element of a feature vector that is a variable. It binds that variable to a constant value that it selects from the list of allowable values and that does not match the training instance. Recall that **specialize_set** called **specialize** with **bagof** to get all specializations. If we call specialize once, it will only substitute a constant into the first variable; the use of bagof causes it to produce all specializations.

```
specialize([Prop|_], [Inst_prop|_], [Instance_values|_]) :-
  var(Prop),
  member(Prop, Instance_values),
  Prop \= Inst_prop.
specialize([_|Tail], [_|Inst_tail], [_|Types]) :-
  specialize(Tail, Inst_tail, Types).
```

The definitions of generalize/3, more_general/2, covers/2, and delete/4 are identical to the definitions in the specific to general algorithm defined above.

candidate_elim/3 implements a top-level read-process loop. It prints out the current G set and the S set and calls process on the input.

```
candidate_elim([G],[S],_) :-
    covers(G,S),covers(S,G),
    write("target concept is "), write(G),nl.

candidate_elim(G, S, Types) :-
    write("G= "), write(G),nl,
    write("S= "), write(S),nl,
    write("Enter Instance "),
    read(Instance),
    process(Instance, G, S, Updated_G, Updated_S, Types),
    candidate_elim(Updated_G, Updated_S, Types).
```

To conclude this section we present a trace of candidate elimination algorithm. Note the initializations of G, S, and the list of allowable substitutions:

```
?- candidate_elim([[_,_,_]], [],
[[small, medium, large], [red, blue, green], [ball, brick, cube]]).
"G= "[[_0,_1,_2]]
"S= "[]
"Enter Instance "positive([small, red, ball]).
"G= "[[_0,_1,_2]]
"S= "[[small,red,ball]]
"Enter Instance "negative([large, green, cube]).
"G= "[[small,_96,_97],[_86,red,_87],[_76,_77,ball]]
"S= "[[small,red,ball]]
"Enter Instance "negative([small, blue, brick]).
"G= "[[_86,red,_87],[_76,_77,ball]]
"S= "[[small,red,ball]]
"Enter Instance "positive([small, green, ball]).
"G= "[[_76,_77,ball]]
"S= "[[small,_351,ball]]
"Enter Instance "positive([large, red, ball]).
"target concept is "[_76,_77,ball]
  yes
```

13.5 Explanation-Based Learning in PROLOG

In this section, we present a PROLOG implementation of the explanation-based learning algorithm of Section 12.4.2. Our implementation is based upon Kedar-Cabelli and McCarty's elegant formulation (Kedar-Cabelli and McCarty 1987), called prolog_ebg, and illustrates the power of unification in PROLOG. Indeed, though it would be difficult to implement explanation-based learning in most languages, the PROLOG version is actually quite simple.

Instead of building an explanation structure and maintaining separate sets of specific and general substitutions (as discussed in Chapter 12), this algorithm builds both the proof of the training instance and the generalized proof tree concurrently.

In this example, we represent proof trees as we did in exshell (Section 13.2.2). When prolog_ebg discovers a fact, it returns this fact as the leaf of a proof tree. The proof of conjunctive goals is the conjunction of the proof of the conjuncts. The proof of a goal that requires rule chaining is represented as (Goal :- Proof), where Proof becomes bound to the proof tree for the rule premise.

The heart of the algorithm is prolog_ebg. This predicate takes four arguments: the first is the goal being proved in the training example, and the second is the generalization of that goal. If the domain theory enables a proof of the specific goal, it binds the third and fourth arguments to a proof tree for the goal and the generalization of that proof. For instance, implementing the cup example from Chapter 12, we would call prolog_ebg with the arguments:

```
prolog_ebg(cup(obj1), cup(X), Proof, Gen_proof).
```

If we assume that PROLOG also has the domain theory and training instance of Section 12.4.2, this will succeed with Proof and Gen_proof bound to the proof trees of Figure 12.16.

prolog_ebg is a straightforward variation of the basic meta-interpreter of Section 13.2. The primary difference is in solving the goal and the generalized goal in parallel. An interesting aspect of the algorithm is the use of the predicate duplicate to create two versions of each rule: the first version is the rule as it appears in the domain theory and the second binds variables in the rule to the values in the training instance. We define prolog_ebg:

```
prolog_ebg(A, GenA, A, GenA) :- clause(A, true).

prolog_ebg((A, B), (GenA,GenB), (AProof, BProof), (GenAProof,GenBProof)) :- !,
    prolog_ebg(A, GenA, AProof, GenAProof),
    prolog_ebg(B, GenB, BProof, GenBProof).

prolog_ebg(A, GenA, (A :- Proof), (GenA :- GenProof)) :-
    clause(GenA, GenB),
    duplicate((GenA :- GenB), (A :- B)),
    prolog_ebg(B, GenB, Proof, GenProof).
```

Duplicate relies upon the behavior of **assert** and **retract** to create a copy of a PRO-LOG expression with all new variables.

```
duplicate(Old, New) :- assert('$marker'(Old)),
                       retract('$marker'(New)).
```

extract_support returns the sequence of the highest level operational nodes, as defined by the predicate **operational**. The predicate implements a recursive tree walk, terminating the recursion when it finds a node in the proof tree that qualifies as operational.

```
extract_support(Proof, Proof) :- operational(Proof).

extract_support((A :- _), A) :- operational(A).

extract_support((AProof, BProof), (A,B)) :-
   extract_support(AProof, A),
   extract_support(BProof, B).

extract_support((_ :- Proof), B) :- extract_support(Proof, B).
```

The final component of the algorithm constructs the learned rule, using **prolog_ebg** and **extract_support**:

```
ebg(Goal, Gen_goal, (Gen_goal :- Premise)) :-
   prolog_ebg(Goal, Gen_goal, _, Gen_proof),
   extract_support(Gen_proof, Premise).
```

We illustrate the execution of these predicates with the example of learning structural definitions of cups (Mitchell 1986). The learner begins with a domain theory that allows it to reason about cups and other physical objects. The theory includes the rules:

```
cup(X) :- liftable(X), holds_liquid(X).
holds_liquid(Z) :- part(Z, W), concave(W), points_up(W).
liftable(Y) :- light(Y), part(Y, handle).
light(A) :- small(A).
light(A) :- made_of(A, feathers).
```

The learner is also given the following example, in which **obj1** is known to be a cup:

```
small(obj1).
part(obj1, handle).
owns(bob, obj1).
part(obj1, bottom).
part(obj1, bowl).
points_up(bowl).
concave(bowl).
color(obj1, red).
```

The operationality criteria define those predicates that may be used in a rule:

```
operational(small(_)).
operational(part(_,_)).
operational(owns(_, _)).
operational(points_up(_)).
operational(concave(_)).
```

A run of the algorithm on the cup example illustrates the behavior of these predicates. First, we call **prolog_ebg** to demonstrate the construction of proof trees:

```
?- prolog_ebg(cup(obj1), cup(X), Proof, Gen_proof).
  X = _0,
  Proof = cup(obj1) :-
          ((liftable(obj1) :-
              ((light(obj1) :-
                  small(obj1)), part(obj1,handle))),
          (holds_liquid(obj1) :-
              (part(obj1,bowl),
                concave(bowl), points_up(bowl))))),
  Gen_proof = cup(_0) :-
          ((liftable(_0) :-
              ((light(_0) :-
                small(_0)),
                part(_0,handle))),
          (holds_liquid(_0) :-
              (part(_0,_106),
              concave(_106),
              points_up(_106))))
```

When we give **extract_support** the generalized proof from the previous execution of **prolog_ebg**, it returns the operational nodes of the proof, in left-to-right order:

```
?- extract_support((cup(_0) :-
          ((liftable(_0) :-
              ((light(_0) :-
                small(_0)),
              part(_0,handle))),
          (holds_liquid(_0) :-
              (part(_0,_106),
                concave(_106),
                points_up(_106))))), Premise).
  _0 = _0, _106 = _1,
  Premise =  (small(_0), part(_0,handle)),
          part(_0,_1),
        concave(_1), points_up(_1)
```

Finally, **ebg** uses these predicates to construct a new rule from the example.

```
?- ebg(cup(obj1), cup(X), Rule).
   X = _0,
   Rule = cup(_0) :-
        ((small(_0), part(_0,handle)),
         part(_0,_110),
           concave(_110), points_up(_110))
```

13.6   PROLOG and Programming with Logic

13.6.1   Introduction

Only by understanding the implementation of a computer language can we properly guide its use, control its side effects, and have confidence in its results. In this section we describe the semantics of PROLOG. We offer two semantic models for logic programming: the usual PROLOG interpreter (Section 13.6.2) and Flat Concurrent PROLOG (Section 13.6.3).

A serious criticism of the resolution proof procedure (Section 11.2) is that it requires a totally homogeneous data base to represent the problem. When predicate calculus descriptors are reduced or transformed to clause form, important problem-solving information is left out. The omitted information is not the truth or fallacy of any part of the problem but rather the control hints or procedural descriptions on how to *use* the information. For example, a negated goal clause in a resolution format might be of the form:

$$a \vee \neg b \vee c \vee \neg d$$

where a, b, c, and d are literals. The resolution inference mechanism applies a search strategy to deduce the empty clause. All literals are open to the strategy and the one used depends on the particular strategy selected. The strategies used to guide resolution theorem proving are weak heuristics; they do not incorporate deep knowledge of a specific problem domain.

For example, the negated goal clause in the resolution example above might be a transformation of the predicate calculus statement:

$$a \leftarrow b \wedge \neg c \wedge d$$

This can be understood as "to see whether a is true go out and see whether b is true and c is false and d is true." The rule was intended as a procedure for solving a and implements heuristic information specific to this use. Indeed, the subgoal b might offer the easiest way to falsify the entire predicate, so the order "try b then see whether c is false then test d" could save much problem-solving time. The implicit heuristic says "test the easiest way to falsify the problem first, then if this is passed go ahead and generate the remaining (perhaps much more difficult) part of the solution." Human experts design procedures and relationships that not only are true but also contain information critical for *using* this truth. In most interesting problem-solving situations we cannot afford to ignore these heuristics (Kowalski 1979*b*).

In the next section we present Horn clauses and use their procedural interpretation as an explicit strategy that preserves this heuristic information. We then present the PROLOG interpreter as an instance of the answer extraction process on resolution refutations with Horn clauses. In the final section of this chapter, we show Flat Concurrent PROLOG as an alternative semantic model for logic programming. In Chapter 15 we use Concurrent PROLOG to create objects, methods, and messages in PROLOG.

13.6.2   Logic Programming and PROLOG

To understand the mathematical foundations of PROLOG, we first define *logic programming*. Once we have made this definition, we will add an explicit search strategy to logic programming to approximate the search strategy, sometimes referred to as the *procedural semantics*, of PROLOG. To get full PROLOG, we also discuss the use of not and the *closed world assumption*.

Consider the data base of clauses prepared for resolution refutation (Section 11.2). If we restrict this set to clauses that have at most one positive literal (zero or more negative literals), we have a clause space with some interesting properties. First, problems describable with this set of clauses preserve unsatisfiability for resolution refutations, or are refutation complete (Section 11.2). Second, an important benefit of restricting our representation to this subclass of all clauses is a very efficient search strategy for refutations: a linear input form, unit preference based, left-to-right and depth-first goal reduction (Section 11.2). With well-founded recursion (recursive calls that eventually terminate) and occurs checking, this strategy guarantees finding refutations if the clause space is unsatisfiable (van Emden and Kowalski 1976). A Horn clause contains at most one positive literal, which means it is of the form

$$a \vee \neg b_1 \vee \neg b_2 \vee \cdots \vee \neg b_n$$

where a and all the b_is are positive literals. To emphasize the key role of the one positive literal in resolutions, we generally write Horn clauses as implications with the positive literal as the conclusion:

$$a \leftarrow b_1 \wedge b_2 \wedge \cdots \wedge b_n$$

Before we discuss further the search strategy, we formally define this subset of clauses, called *Horn clauses*. These, together with a *nondeterministic* goal reduction strategy, are said to constitute a *logic program*.

DEFINITION

LOGIC PROGRAM

A *logic program* is a set of universally quantified expressions in first-order predicate calculus of the form:

$$a \leftarrow b_1 \wedge b_2 \wedge b_3 \wedge \cdots \wedge b_n$$

The a and b$_i$ are all positive literals, sometimes referred to as atomic goals. The a is the clause *head*, the conjunction of b$_i$, the *body*.

These expressions are the *Horn clauses* of the first-order predicate calculus. They come in three forms: first, when the original clause has no positive literals; second, when it has no negative literals; and third, when it has one positive and one or more negative literals. These cases are 1, 2, and 3, respectively:

1. $\leftarrow b_1 \wedge b_2 \wedge \cdots \wedge b_n$
   called a *headless* clause or *goals* to be tried: b$_1$ and b$_2$ and . . . and b$_n$.

2. $a_1 \leftarrow$
   $a_2 \leftarrow$
   .
   .
   .
   $a_n \leftarrow$
   called the *facts*.

3. $a \leftarrow b_1 \wedge \cdots \wedge b_n$
   called a *rule* relation.

Horn clause calculus allows only the forms just presented; there may be only one literal to the left of $\leftarrow$ and this literal must be positive. All literals to the right of $\leftarrow$ are also positive.

The reduction of clauses that have at most one positive literal into Horn form requires three steps. First, select the positive literal in the clause, if there is a positive literal, and move this literal to the very left (using the commutative property of $\vee$). This single positive literal becomes the *head* of the Horn clause, as just defined. Second, change the entire clause to Horn form by the rule:

$$a \vee \neg b_1 \vee \neg b_2 \vee \cdots \vee \neg b_n \equiv a \leftarrow \neg (\neg b_1 \vee \neg b_2 \vee \cdots \vee \neg b_n)$$

Finally, use de Morgan's law to change this specification to:

$$a \leftarrow b_1 \wedge b_2 \cdots \wedge b_n$$

where the commutative property of $\wedge$ can be used to order the b$_i$ subgoals.

It should be noted that it may not be possible to transform clauses from an arbitrary clause space to Horn form. Some clauses, such as $\neg p \vee \neg q$, have no Horn form. To create a Horn clause, there can be at most one positive literal in the original clause. If this criterion is not met it may be necessary to rethink the original predicate calculus specification for the problem. The payoff for Horn form representation is a very efficient refutation strategy, as we see shortly.

The computation algorithm for logic programs proceeds by nondeterministic goal reduction. At each step of the computation where there is a goal of the form:

$$\leftarrow a_1 \wedge a_2 \wedge \cdots \wedge a_n$$

the interpreter *arbitrarily* chooses some a_i for $1 \leq i \leq n$. It then *nondeterministically* chooses a clause:

$$a^1 \leftarrow b_1 \wedge b_2 \wedge \cdots \wedge b_n$$

such that the a^1 unifies with a_i with substitution ς and uses this clause to reduce the goal. The new goal then becomes:

$$(a_1 \wedge \cdots \wedge a_{i-1}, b_1 \wedge b_2 \wedge \cdots \wedge b_n \wedge a_{i+1} \wedge \cdots \wedge a_n)\varsigma$$

This process continues until the computation terminates with the goal set empty.

If we eliminate the nondeterminism by imposing an order on the reduction of subgoals, we do not change the result of the computation. All results that can be found nondeterministically can be found through an exhaustive ordered search. However, by reducing the amount of nondeterminism, we can define strategies that prune unnecessary branches from the space. Thus, a major concern of practical logic programming languages is to provide the programmer with facilities to control and, when possible, reduce the amount of nondeterminism. These facilities allow the programmer to influence both the order in which the goals are reduced and the set of clauses that are used to reduce each goal.

The abstract specification of a logic program has a very clean semantics, that of the resolution refutation system. It can be shown (van Emden and Kowalski 1976) that the smallest interpretation on which a logic program is true is *the* interpretation of the program. The price paid by practical programming languages (such as PROLOG) for control is that programs executed by these interpreters may compute only a subset of their associated interpretations (Shapiro 1987).

Sequential PROLOG is an approximation to an interpreter for the logic programming model, designed for efficient execution on von Neumann computers. This is the interpreter that we have used so far in this text. Sequential PROLOG uses both the order of goals in a clause and the order of clauses in the program to control the search for a proof. When a number of goals are available, PROLOG always pursues them left to right. In the search for a unifiable clause on a goal, the possible clauses are checked in the order they are presented by the programmer. When each selection is made, a backtracking pointer is placed with the recorded unification that allows other clauses to be used (again, in the programmer's order) should the original selection of a unifiable clause fail. If this attempt fails across all possible clauses in the clause space, then the computation fails.

More formally, given a goal:

$$\leftarrow a_1 \wedge a_2 \wedge a_3 \cdots \wedge a_n$$

and a program P, the PROLOG interpreter sequentially searches for the first clause in P whose head unifies with a_1. This clause is then used to reduce the goals. If:

$$a^1 \leftarrow b_1 \wedge b_2 \wedge \cdots \wedge b_n$$

is the reducing clause with ξ the unification, the goal clause then becomes:

$$(b_1 \wedge b_2 \wedge \cdots \wedge b_n \wedge a_2 \wedge a_3 \wedge \cdots \wedge a_n)\xi$$

The PROLOG interpreter then continues by trying to reduce the leftmost goal, b_1 in this example, using the first clause in the program P that unifies with b_1. Suppose it is:

$$b^1 \leftarrow c_1 \wedge c_2 \wedge \cdots \wedge c_p$$

under unification ϕ. The goal then becomes:

$$(c_1 \wedge c_2 \wedge \cdots \wedge c_p \wedge b_2 \wedge \cdots \wedge b_n \wedge a_2 \wedge a_3 \wedge \cdots \wedge a_n)\xi\,\phi$$

Note that the goal list is treated as a **stack** enforcing depth-first search. If the PROLOG interpreter ever fails to find a unification that solves a goal it then backtracks to its most recent unification choice point, restores all bindings made since that choice point, and chooses the next clause that will unify (by the order in P). In this way, PROLOG implements its left-to-right, depth-first search of the clause space.

If the goal is reduced to the null clause ($\square$) then the composition of unifications that made the reductions:

$$(\square)\xi\,\phi \cdots \omega$$

(here $\xi\,\phi \cdots \omega$), provides an interpretation under which the original goal clause was true.

Besides backtracking on the order of clauses in a program, sequential PROLOG allows the *cut* or "!." As described in Chapter 6, a cut may be placed in a clause as a goal itself. The interpreter, when encountering the cut, is committed to the current execution path and in particular to that subset of unifications made since the choice of the clause containing the cut. It also commits the interpreter to the choice of that clause itself as the only method for reducing the goal. Should failure be encountered within the clause after the cut, the entire clause fails.

Procedurally, the cut makes it unnecessary to retain backtrack pointers for the reducing clause and all its components *before* the cut. Thus, cut can mean that only some of the possible interpretations of the model are ever computed.

We summarize our discussion of sequential PROLOG by comparing it to the resolution refutation model of Section 11.2.

1. The resolution clause space is a superset of the set of Horn clause expressions in logic programming. Each clause must have at most one positive literal to be in Horn form.
2. The following structures represent the problem in Horn form:
   a. The facts,

$$a_2 \leftarrow$$
.
.
$$a_n \leftarrow$$

are each separate clauses for resolution.

b. The goals

$$\leftarrow a_1 \wedge a_2 \wedge \cdots \wedge a_n$$

are a list of clause statements that make up the goals to be tested by resolution refutation. Each a_i is in turn negated, unified with, and reduced until the empty clause is found (if this is possible). Finally,

c. The Horn clause rules or axioms,

$$a \leftarrow b_1 \wedge b_2 \wedge \cdots \wedge b_n$$

allow us to reduce matching subgoals.

3. With a *unit preference, linear input form* strategy (always preferring fact clauses and using the negated goal and its descendant resolvents; see Section 11.2) and a left-to-right, depth-first (with backtracking) order for selecting clauses for resolutions, the resolution theorem prover is acting as a PROLOG interpreter. Because this strategy is complete, it guarantees that the solution will be found (provided that part of the interpretation was not pruned away by using cut).

4. Finally, the composition of unifications in the proof provides the answer (interpretation) for which the goal is true. This is exactly equivalent to the answer extraction process of Section 11.2.4. Recording the composition of unifications in the goal literal produces each answer interpretation.

An important issue with current PROLOG interpreters is the *closed world* assumption implicit in their implementation. In predicate calculus, the proof of $\neg p(X)$ is exactly the proof that $p(X)$ is logically false. That is, $p(X)$ is false under every interpretation that makes the axiom set true. The PROLOG interpreter, based on the unification algorithm of Chapter 2, offers a more restricted result than the general resolution refutation of Section 11.2. Rather than trying all interpretations, it examines only those explicit in the data base. We now axiomatize these constraints to see exactly the restrictions implicit in PROLOG.

For every predicate p, and every variable X belonging to p, suppose $a_1, a_2, \ldots, a_n$ make up the domain of X. The PROLOG interpreter, using unification, enforces:

1. The *unique name* axiom. For all atoms of the domain $a_i \not\equiv a_j$ unless they are identical. This implies that atoms with distinct names are distinct.

2. The *closed world* axiom.

$$p(X) \rightarrow p(a_1) \vee p(a_2) \vee \cdots \vee p(a_n).$$

This means the only possible instances of a relation are those implied by the clauses present in the problem specification.

3. The *domain closure* axiom.

$$(X = a_1) \vee (X = a_2) \vee \cdots \vee (X = a_n).$$

This guarantees that the atoms occurring in the problem specification constitute all and the only atoms.

These three axioms are implicit in the action of the PROLOG interpreter. They may be seen as added to the set of Horn clauses making up a problem description and thus as constraining the set of possible interpretations to a PROLOG query.

Intuitively, this means that PROLOG assumes as false all goals that it cannot prove to be true. This can introduce anomalies: if a goal's truth value is actually unknown to the current data base, PROLOG will assume it to be false.

Other limitations are implicit in PROLOG, as there seem to be in all computing languages. The most important of these, besides the problem of negation as failure, represent violations of the semantic model for logic programming. In particular, there are the lack of an occurs check (see Chapters 2 and 6; this allows a clause to unify with a subset of itself) and the use of cut. The current generation of PROLOG interpreters should be looked at pragmatically. Some problems arise because "no efficient way is currently known" to get around the issue (the occurs check); others arise from attempts to optimize use of the depth-first with backtrack search (the cut).

Many of the anomalies of PROLOG are a result of trying to implement the nondeterministic semantics of pure logic programming on a sequential computer. This includes the problems introduced by the cut. In the next section we present another model for logic programming, concurrent PROLOG. Because it defines goal reduction in terms of multiple concurrent processes, the semantics of concurrent PROLOG are closer to the nondeterministic model of pure logic programming.

13.6.3 Parallel PROLOG and an Alternative Semantics

The abstract computation model for logic programs (Section 12.6.2) suggests that they are open to parallel execution. A logic program, as we have seen, is the construction of a proof of a goal statement from axioms that describe the problem. The search space for such a program may be described as an and/or graph where the and nodes correspond to the conjunction of a number of goals that may indeed be checked in parallel and the or node corresponds to the different ways to reduce a goal using the axioms (the disjunctive possibilities) of the program, which may also be tested in parallel.

As we have seen, the nondeterministic model of a logic program interpreter is assumed to make the correct and/or selections on the search graph and can thus prune the tree in arbitrary order. The sequential PROLOG interpreter traces and/or trees in depth-first, left-to-right order: the ands of several alternatives are evaluated in program order (depth first) with backtracking. However, other strategies are possible for this search. Concurrent PROLOG assumes that an independent process is assigned to solve each branch of the and/or graph.

Two forms of execution occur in traversing this and/or graph in parallel: and parallelism, where the conjunction of goal reductions is done in parallel, and or parallelism, where the alternatives for each goal reduction are attempted in parallel. In and parallelism, variables may be shared by several children of an and node; the processes attempting to reduce these goals are not independent and thus may interfere with each other by producing solutions that are not compatible. Noncompatible solutions are two or more solutions (instantiations) of a single variable that are not unifiable. Thus, there is a need to coordinate the computations of and parallel processes. Process synchronization is accomplished through the shared variable with the *read-only* commitment.

Logic programming provides both a declarative and a procedural interpretation of clauses. For the Horn clause

$$a \leftarrow b_1 \wedge b_2 \wedge \cdots \wedge b_m$$

the declarative reading says a is true if b_1 and b_2 and ... and b_m are true. The procedural reading says a can be accomplished by doing b_1 and then b_2 and then ... b_m. The concurrent PROLOG model proposes a third or *behavioral interpretation* of clause reduction: a process a can replace itself by the system of processes that contain b_1 and b_2 and ... b_m. A process terminates by replacing itself with the empty clause. Thus, each of the b_j is an object. State is shown by the variable bindings of each of these predicates (Shapiro 1987).

In the procedural reading of logic clauses, unification provides the mechanism for parameter passing, variable binding, and data access. In the behavioral analysis, unification is the mechanism for sending, receiving, and coordinating the actions of different messages.

To synchronize this process communication, we introduce *read-only* variables. When variables are created as read only, the process suspends until that variable, and every reduction using it, is presented with a bound (nonvariable) value. The variable X is annotated read only in our examples by X?. In the behavioral analysis of the logic clause, as a clause reduces itself to other clauses, variables shared with other clauses (processes) may be instantiated by the unification of that process with the head of the reducing process and thus achieve the effect of process communication.

The second addition of concurrent PROLOG is the *guarded clause* or *commit* operator used to synchronize or parallel execution. A concurrent PROLOG program is made up of a set of guarded clauses or universally quantified axioms of the form:

$$a \leftarrow g_1 \wedge g_2 \wedge \cdots \wedge g_n : b_1 \wedge b_2 \wedge \cdots \wedge b_m \quad m,n > = 0$$

The b_i and the g_i are atomic formulas. a is the clause head, the conjunction of the g_i is the guard, and the b_j make up the clause body. The symbol : is the commit operator; when $n = 0$ (for g_n), this operator may be omitted. This model for logic programming is called *flat* because none of the g_i are allowed to be recursive (Shapiro 1987).

The semantics of the : (guard) goal in reducing a process A using clause a above is to unify A with a, reduce the g_i to the empty clause, commit to that clause, and reduce a to the conjunction of the b_j. Each step is taken only if the previous step succeeds; the reduction of clause a may suspend or fail during any of these steps. The unification of the process against the head of the clause suspends if it requires the binding of (unbound) read-only variables in a; it also fails if A and a are not unifiable. The computation of the guard suspends if any of its processes suspend and fails if any of them fail.

Besides allowing the possibility of the or parallel execution of all clauses whose head is a, the guard clause is an attempt to clean up the semantics of the cut. Like the cut, it means that only some of the possible semantic interpretations of the logic programming model are ever computed. Once the guard is satisfied, the unification interpretation is committed to that of the particular clause. The partial results by the first two steps of the reduction, the unification substitution with a and solving the constraints of the guard, are not accessible to the other processes for A's reduction. After the commit, all the other or parallel attempts to reduce A using other clauses are abandoned.

The reduction of all processes in the logic specification is attempted in parallel, as well as the search for clauses to reduce a process. There are still restrictions, however, to complete parallelism. For or parallelism, only the guards are executed in parallel. Once a guard evaluation fails, the computation of other or parallel guards is halted. For and parallelism, read-only restrictions enforce severe constraints on the order and speed of process reduction.

A final construct, the otherwise command, is also added to the concurrent PROLOG semantics by Shapiro. otherwise is described in Chapter 14 to implement default assignments for objects. An otherwise clause is a guard clause that succeeds only when all other or parallel guards fail.

We conclude this section with a simple example of a counter. This example is written in concurrent PROLOG and taken from a similar example in Shapiro (1987). counter processes streams, implemented in this example as a list of arbitrary length. The stream is made up of four symbols: clear, up, down, and show. The object counter has two arguments; one is an input stream, the other its internal State. When it encounters a clear message in the stream, it resets its State to 0. When it receives an up or down message, it increments or decrements its State by 1. show writes out the current state and the empty message terminates the process. plus(X, Y, Z) suspends until two of its arguments are bound, at which time it returns the third.

counter uses several read-only variables and calls plus, which uses the guard to overcome the variable binding constraint imposed by is. This example implements both and parallel and or parallel processes.

```
counter([clear|S], State) :- counter(S?,0).

counter([up|S], State) :-
    plus(State, 1, Newstate), counter(S?, Newstate?).

counter([down|S], State) :-
    plus(Newstate, 1, State), counter(S?, Newstate?).

counter([show|S], State) :-
    wait_write(State), counter(S?, State).

counter([], State) :- call((write('All done.'), nl)).

plus(X, Y, Z) :- integer(X?), integer(Y?) : Z is X + Y.

plus(X, Y, Z) :- integer(X?), integer(Z?) : Y is Z - X.

plus(X, Y, Z) :- integer(Y?), integer(Z?) : X is Z - Y.
```

If we call counter with the message stream

counter([clear,up,up,up,show,down,down,up,show,show,up,show],_).

We get the following trace:

3 2 2 3 3 All done.

This simple example illustrates the behavior of concurrent PROLOG and shows how its concurrent semantics simplify the implementation of streams and objects. In Chapter 14 we refer to the set of procedures counter as an object, because it can be seen as a nonterminating process (taking data from the stream), includes procedures or methods that describe its state at any time, and can communicate with other objects.

Flat concurrent PROLOG is a model for commitment of multiple co-routining processes to the parallel reduction of a set of logic specifications. An interpreter for concurrent PROLOG, built as a meta-interpreter in Edinburgh PROLOG by E. Shapiro (1987), is available with the software for this book (Benjamin/Cummings, 390 Bridge Parkway, Redwood City, CA 94065) or in Shapiro (1987).

13.7   Epilogue and References

The comments and references at the end of the first PROLOG chapter are also appropriate here. The foundations of PROLOG in theorem-proving research also make the material on resolution theorem proving presented in Chapter 11 relevant. The semantics of logic programming and declarative specifications is addressed by a number of authors. Especially recommended are Maarten van Emden and Robert Kowalski (van Emden 1976; Kowalski 1979*b*). The closed world axioms and unique naming assumptions are also important in data base research, and discussions may be found in Reiter (1978), Levesque (1984), and Gallaire (1986). The two-volume *Concurrent Prolog: Collected Papers* edited by Ehud Shapiro (1987a) offers a valuable introduction and set of example applications in concurrent execution of logic specifications.

Most PROLOG texts (Sterling and Shapiro 1986; Walker et al. 1987) treat the metapredicates, type constraints, and difference lists as presented in Section 13.1. A more complete discussion of types, as well as suggestions for building a type checker, is presented in *A Polymorphic Type System for Prolog* by Alan Mycroft and Richard O'Keefe (1984). The use of rule stacks and proof trees in the design of meta-interpreters for rule-based expert systems was suggested by Leon Sterling and Ehud Shapiro (1986).

Building AI representations such as semantic nets, frames, and objects is discussed in a number of books, especially *Knowledge Systems and Prolog* by Adrian Walker, Michael McCord, John Sowa, and Walter Wilson (1987) and *PROLOG: A Relational Language and Its Applications* by John Malpas (1987).

The PROLOG representation medium is so applicable for natural language understanding that many projects use PROLOG to model language. The first PROLOG interpreter was designed to analyze French using *metamorphosis grammars* (Colmerauer 1975).

Fernando Pereira and David Warren (1980) created *definite clause grammars*. Veronica Dahl (1977, 1983), Michael McCord (1982, 1986), and John Sowa (Sowa 1984; Walker et al. 1987) have all contributed to this research.

13.8 Exercises

1. Create a type check that prevents the append(nil,6,6) anomaly.

2. Is the difference list append really a linear time append? Explain.

3. Create the "inventory supply" data base of Section 13.1.2. Build type checks for a set of six useful queries on these data tuples.

4. Create and design a type check mechanism for the data base of Section 10.4.

5. Extend the simple definition of PROLOG in PROLOG (Section 13.2) to include or and to include cut.

6. Fill out the rules used with the exshell cars example in the text. You might add new subsystems such as the transmission or brakes.

7. Create a knowledge base in a new domain for exshell.

8. How would you design a data-driven shell in PROLOG? Describe your design and create the top-level solve predicates.

9. Create another example semantic network and design a hasproperty-like inference mechanism to test whether entities in the net have properties.

10. Determine two expert system application areas where tree inheritance is sufficient for simulation and property inheritance. Determine two other application areas where multiple inheritance would seem more appropriate.

11. Take the conceptual graphs used to describe the "dogs world" of Section 9.3. Translate each of the graphs used into PROLOG notation. Design PROLOG rules to the restrict, join, and simplify operations. Hint: one way to see the problem is to create a list of the propositions whose conjunction make up a graph. Then operations on the graphs become manipulations of the lists.

12. Implement a frame system with inheritance that allows us to define three kinds of slots: properties of a class that may be inherited by subclasses, properties that are inherited by instances of the class but not by subclasses, and properties of the class and its subclasses that are not inherited by instances (class properties). Discuss the benefits, uses, and problems with this distinction.

13. Build in PROLOG the ATN parser of Section 10.2.4. Add who and what questions.

14. Build in PROLOG the relational data base and the English-language query mechanisms described in Section 10.4.2.

15. Expand your program for Exercise 14 so it will answer questions of the form "How much does Don Morrison earn?" and "List all employees who earn more than their managers."

16. Write an object/process specification in concurrent PROLOG that counts and prints out all odd integers from a stream of integers.

17. Use concurrent PROLOG to create a stack process. For instance, let stack have two arguments: the first the input stream and the second the stack. pop would be: stack([pop(X)|S], [X|Xs]) :- stack(S?, Xs).

18. Implement **counter** in sequential PROLOG. Compare it to the concurrent PROLOG version in the text.

19. Currently, if **exshell** cannot solve a goal using the rule base, it simply fails. Extend the algorithm so that if it cannot prove a goal using the rules, and if the goal is not askable, it will call that goal as a general PROLOG query. This lets us include built-in PROLOG predicates such as arithmetic and write predicates in rules. Note that adding this option requires modifications to both **solve/4** and **build_proof/3**.

20. Currently **exshell** will respond to how queries by printing a proof tree for the goal. Extend **solve/2** so that it will automatically print the proof tree for the top-level query. Hint: this is straightforward if we think of it as executing an internal how query on the top-level goal.

21. **exshell** allows the user to respond to queries by entering their confidence in the query's truth, a why query or a how query. Extend the definition of **respond** to allow the user to answer questions with:

   a. y if the query is true; n if it is false. This corresponds to certainty factors of 100 and -100.
   b. A pattern that matches the query; **exshell** will unify this with the query. This is useful if the user needs to enter variable bindings.
   c. rule(Goal). **exshell** responds to this query by printing all rules that conclude about Goal. This particular feature is useful in extending and debugging the rule base, and it mirrors similar features in commercial tools.
   d. **help**. This causes **exshell** to print a list of allowable responses.
   e. **quit**. To quit a consultation.

22. The cars knowledge base presented in Section 13.2.2 is incomplete, failing in a number of different situations. Using the incremental refinement methodology of Chapter 8, find and repair these deficiencies.

23. Using **exshell**, develop an expert system for a domain of your choice.

24. Implement the domain theory for the float example of Chapter 12, and run it with **prolog_ebg**.

25. Extend the definition of **ebg** so that after it constructs a new rule it asserts that rule to the logic data base, where it may be used in future queries. Test the performance of the resulting system using a theory for a suitably rich domain. You might do this by constructing a theory for a domain of your choice or by extending the theory from the cup example to allow it to explain different types of cups such as Styrofoam cups, cups without handles, etc.

26. Rework the semantic net parser of Section 13.3.2 to allow a richer representation of class hierarchies. Specifically, rewrite the definition of **match_with_inheritance** so that instead of enumerating the common specializations of two items, it computes this by searching a type hierarchy.

27. Chapter 14 presents a LISP implementation of the ID3 algorithm from Chapter 12. Using this implementation as a reference, implement ID3 in PROLOG. Do not think of this as simply translating the LISP code to PROLOG. The languages are different and, like different natural languages, require different idioms to say the same thing. Make your PROLOG implementation follow what you feel is a lucid and pleasing PROLOG style.

28. Implement a general to specific search of the version space using the feature vector representation of Section 13.4.1. We specialize feature vectors by replacing variables with constants; because this requires telling the algorithm of allowable values for each field of the feature vector, we must pass this in as an extra argument. The following definition of **run_general**, the top-

level goal, illustrates the necessary initializations for the example used in the text: objects may be small, medium, or large; their color may be red, blue, or green; and their shape may be ball, brick, or cube.

```
run_general :-
general_to_specific([[_,_,_]], [],
[[small, medium, large], [red, blue, green], [ball, brick, cube]]).
```

ADVANCED LISP PROGRAMMING TECHNIQUES FOR ARTIFICIAL INTELLIGENCE

All our knowledge is symbolic.

—GOETHE, *Table Talk*

See simplicity in the complicated.

—LAO TZU

Order and simplification are the first steps toward the mastery of a subject . . .

—THOMAS MANN, *The Magic Mountain*

14.0   Introduction: Abstraction and Complexity

In discussing AI programming in LISP, we have emphasized list-based data structures and a functional programming style. A goal of this chapter is to discuss general techniques for managing the complexity of large programs, particularly large AI programs. Abstraction, the organization of a program into increasingly general, higher-level conceptual structures, is the basis of all of these techniques. Abstraction allows the programmer to organize a program in terms appropriate to the problem being solved, rather than at the level of programming language or machine-specific detail.

We continue to use the techniques of procedural and data abstraction introduced in Chapter 7 and introduce three other approaches to program design: *meta-linguistic abstraction, stream processing,* and *object-oriented programming.*

Meta-linguistic abstraction uses the underlying programming language, in this case, LISP, to implement a specialized, high-level language that may be more effective for solving a particular class of problems. The term "meta-linguistic abstraction" refers to our use of the base language to implement this other programming language, rather than to directly solve the problem. The implementation of exshell in Chapter 13 illustrated this technique in PROLOG. LISP also supports this technique because it is easy to write LISP programs that process expressions written in LISP syntax. As an example of meta-linguistic abstraction, we implement a PROLOG-like logic programming language that reasons with rules and facts written in s-expression syntax (Section 14.1). Building on the simple logic programming interpreter, we define an expert system shell supporting both uncertain reasoning and user queries for missing information (Section 14.3) and an inheritance algorithm for a semantic network representation (Section 14.4).

Many problems may naturally be thought of in terms of the flow of data through a series of operations and filters. We can formalize this data-oriented view of program organization using structures called *streams*. A stream is a sequence of data elements; the program acts on data streams using maps and filters to produce a stream of solutions. Both the simple logic programming implementation and the more complex expert system shell are based on a stream-oriented approach. In Section 14.2 we examine the implementation of streams using *delayed evaluation*. This technique postpones the computation of stream elements until they are actually needed by the program; in doing so, it enables us to greatly increase the power and efficiency of the resulting programs.

Though many problems lend themselves to a stream processing point of view, others are naturally thought of as collections of distinct objects and relations. We introduce this approach in the implementation of a semantic network interpreter with inheritance (Section 14.4) and use it, in Section 14.5, to construct the ID3 learning algorithm of Chapter 12. Our implementation uses LISP's *structure* facility to organize our program in terms of *objects,* data structures that include both the data and functions needed to describe some object in the problem domain. However, this example only hints at the power of object-oriented programming, particularly as represented in LISP. In Chapter 15, we introduce CLOS, the Common LISP Object System, an object-oriented extension to the Common LISP programming language.

14.1 Logic Programming in LISP

As an example of metalinguistic abstraction, we develop a LISP-based logic programming interpreter, using the unification algorithm from Chapter 7. As in PROLOG, our logic programs consist of a data base of facts and rules in the predicate calculus. The interpreter processes queries (or goals) by unifying them against entries in the logic data base. If a goal unifies with a simple fact, it succeeds; the solution is the set of bindings generated in the match. If it matches the head of a rule, the interpreter recursively attempts to satisfy the rule premise in a depth-first fashion, using the bindings generated in matching the head. On success, the interpreter prints the original goal, with variables replaced by the solution bindings.

This interpreter supports conjunctive goals and implications; or and not are not defined. Features such as arithmetic, I/O, or the usual PROLOG built-in predicates are not supported. Although we do not implement full PROLOG, and the exhaustive nature of the search and absence of the *cut* prevent the proper treatment of recursive predicates, the shell captures the basic behavior of logic programming languages. The addition of such features to the interpreter is an interesting and valuable exercise.

14.1.1 A Simple Logic Programming Language

Our logic programming interpreter supports Horn clauses (Section 13.6), a subset of full predicate calculus. Well-formed formulas consist of terms, conjunctive expressions, and rules written in a LISP-oriented syntax. For simplicity's sake, we do not include negation or disjunction; readers may add these as exercises.

A compound term is a list in which the first element is a predicate name and the remaining elements are the arguments. Arguments may be either constants, variables, or other compound terms. As in the discussion of unify, we represent variables as lists of two elements, the word var followed by the name of the variable. Examples include:

```
(likes bill music)
(on block (var x))
(friend bill (father robert))
```

A conjunctive expression is a list whose first element is and and whose subsequent arguments are either propositions or conjunctive expressions:

```
(and (smaller david sarah) (smaller peter david))
(and (likes (var x) (var y)) (likes (var z) (var y)))
(and (hand-empty) (and (on block-1 block-2) (on block-2 table)))
```

Implications are expressed in a syntactically sweetened form that simplifies both their writing and recognition. Rules have the form:

```
(rule if <premise> then <conclusion>)
```

where *<premise>* is either a simple or conjunctive proposition and *<conclusion>* is always a simple proposition. Examples of rules include:

```
(rule if (and (likes (var x) (var z))
              (likes (var y) (var z)))
        then (friend (var x) (var y)))
```

```
(rule if (and (size (var x) small)
              (color (var x) red)
              (smell (var x) fragrant))
        then (kind (var x) rose))
```

The logical data base is a list of facts and rules bound to a global variable, *assertions*. We can define an example knowledge base by a call to setq.:

```
(setq *assertions*
  '((likes george beer)
    (likes george kate)
    (likes george kids)
```

```
            (likes bill kids)
            (likes bill music)
            (likes bill pizza)
            (likes bill wine)

            (rule
               if (and (likes (var x) (var z))
                       (likes (var y) (var z)))
               then (friend (var x) (var y)))))
```

The top level of the interpreter is a function, logic-shell, that reads goals and attempts to satisfy them against the logic data base bound to *assertions*. Given the above data base, logic-shell will have the following behavior (comments are added in italics):

```
> (logic-shell)                                     logic-shell prompts with a ?
?(likes bill (var x))               successful queries are printed with substitutions
(likes bill kids)
(likes bill music)
(likes bill pizza)
(likes bill wine)

?(likes george kate)
(likes george kate)

?(likes george taxes)                              failed query returns nothing

?(friend bill george)
(friend bill george)                      from (and(likes bill kids)(likes george kids))

?(friend bill roy)                  roy does not exist in knowledge base, query fails

?(friend bill (var x))
(friend bill george)                      from (and(likes bill kids)(likes george kids))
(friend bill bill)                          from (and(likes bill kids)(likes bill kids))
(friend bill bill)                        from (and(likes bill music)(likes bill music))
(friend bill bill)                        from (and(likes bill pizza)(likes bill pizza))
(friend bill bill)                          from (and(likes bill wine)(likes bill wine))

?quit
bye
>
```

Before discussing the implementation of the logic programming interpreter, we introduce the *stream* data type.

14.1.2 Streams and Stream Processing

As the preceding example suggests, even a small knowledge base can produce complex behaviors. It is necessary not only to determine the truth or falsity of a goal but also to determine the variable substitutions that make that goal true in the knowledge base. A single goal can match with different facts, producing different substitution sets; conjunctions of goals require that all conjuncts succeed and also that the variable bindings be consistent throughout. Similarly, rules require that the substitutions formed in matching a goal with a rule conclusion be made in the rule premise when it is solved. The management of these multiple substitution sets is the major source of complexity in the interpreter. Streams help us to address this complexity by focusing on the movement of a sequence of candidate variable substitutions through the constraints defined by the logic data base.

A *stream* is a sequence of data objects. Perhaps the most common example of stream processing is a typical interactive program. The data from the keyboard are viewed as an endless sequence of characters, and the program is organized around reading and processing the *current* character from the input stream. Stream processing is a generalization of this idea: streams need not be produced by the user; they may also be generated and modified by functions. A *generator* is a function that produces a stream of data objects. A *map* applies some function to each of the elements of a stream. A *filter* eliminates selected elements of a stream according to the constraints of some predicate.

The solutions returned by an inference engine may be represented as a stream of different variable substitutions under which a goal follows from a knowledge base. The constraints defined by the knowledge base are used to modify and filter a stream of candidate substitutions, producing the result.

Consider the conjunctive goal

```
(and (likes bill (var z))
     (likes george (var z)))
```

using the logic data base from the preceding section. The stream-oriented view regards each of the conjuncts in the expression as a *filter* for a stream of substitution sets. Each set of variable substitutions in the stream is applied to the conjunct and the result is matched against the knowledge base. If the match fails, that set of substitutions is eliminated from the stream; if it succeeds, the match may create new sets of substitutions by adding new bindings to the original substitution set.

Figure 14.1 illustrates the stream of substitutions passing through this conjunctive goal. It begins with a stream of candidate substitutions containing only the empty substitution set and grows after the first proposition matches against multiple entries in the data base. It then shrinks to a single substitution set as the second conjunct eliminates substitutions that do not allow (likes george (var z)) to succeed. The resulting stream, ((((var z) . kids))), contains the only variable substitution that allows both subgoals in the conjunction to succeed in the knowledge base.

As this example illustrates, a goal and a single set of substitutions may generate several new substitution sets, one for each match in the knowledge base. Alternatively, a goal will eliminate a substitution set from the stream if no match is found. The stream of substitution sets may grow and shrink as it passes through a series of conjuncts.

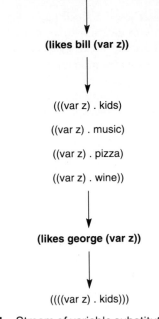

((()))

(likes bill (var z))

(((var z) . kids)
((var z) . music)
((var z) . pizza)
((var z) . wine))

(likes george (var z))

((((var z) . kids)))

Figure 14.1 Stream of variable substitutions filtered through conjunctive subgoals.

The basis of stream processing is a set of functions to create, augment, and access the elements of a stream. We can define a simple set of stream functions using lists and the standard list manipulators. The functions that constitute a list-based implementation of the stream data type are:

```
; Cons-stream adds a new first element to a stream
(defun cons-stream (element stream) (cons element stream))

; head-stream returns the first element of the stream
(defun head-stream (stream) (car stream))

; tail-stream returns the stream with its first element deleted.
(defun tail-stream (stream) (cdr stream))

; empty-stream-p is true if the stream is empty
(defun empty-stream-p (stream) (null stream))

; make-empty-stream creates an empty stream
(defun make-empty-stream () nil)

; combine-stream appends two streams.
(defun combine-streams (stream1 stream2)
   (cond ((empty-stream-p stream1) stream2)
         (t (cons-stream (head-stream stream1)
               (combine-streams
                     (tail-stream stream1)
                     (stream2)))))
```

Although the implementation of streams as lists does not allow the full power of stream-based abstraction, the definition of a stream data type helps us to view the program from a data flow point of view. In Section 14.2 we discuss some limitations of this list-based implementation of streams and present an alternative approach.

14.1.3 A Stream-Based Logic Programming Interpreter

We invoke the interpreter through a function called logic-shell, a straightforward variation of the read-eval-print loop discussed in Chapter 7. After printing a prompt, "?," it reads the next s-expression entered by the user and binds it to the symbol goal. If goal is equal to quit, the function halts; otherwise, it calls solve to generate a stream of substitution sets that satisfy the goal. This stream is passed to print-solutions, which prints the goal with each of these different substitutions. The function then recurs. logic-shell is defined by:

```
(defun logic-shell ()
  (print '? )
  (let ((goal (read)))
    (cond ((equal goal 'quit) 'bye)
          (t (print solutions goal (solve goal nil))
             (terpri)
             (logic-shell)))))
```

solve is the heart of the interpreter. solve takes a goal and a set of substitutions and finds all solutions that are consistent with the knowledge base. These solutions are returned as a stream of substitution sets; if there are no matches, solve returns the empty stream. From the stream processing point of view, solve is a *source*, or *generator*, for a stream of solutions. solve is defined by:

```
(defun solve (goal substitutions)
  (declare (special *assertions*))
  (if (conjunctive-goal-p goal)
    (filter-through-conj-goals (body goal)
          (cons-stream substitutions (make-empty-stream)))
    (infer goal substitutions *assertions*)))
```

The declaration at the beginning of this definition tells the LISP compiler that *assertions* is a *special*, or global, variable and should be bound dynamically in the environment in which solve is called.

solve first tests whether the goal is a conjunction; if it is, solve calls filter-through-conj-goals to perform the filtering described in Section 14.1.2. If goal is not a conjunction, solve assumes it is a simple goal and calls infer to solve it against the knowledge base.

solve calls filter-through-conj-goals with the body of the conjunction (i.e., the sequence of conjuncts with the and operator removed) and a stream that contains only the initial substitution set. The result is a stream of substitutions representing all of the solutions for this goal. We define filter-through-conj-goals by:

```
(defun filter-through-conj-goals (goals substitution-stream)
  (if (null goals)
      substitution-stream
      (filter-through-conj-goals (cdr goals)
        (filter-through-goal (car goals) substitution-stream))))
```

If the list of goals is empty, the function halts, returning substitution stream unchanged. Otherwise, it calls filter-through-goal to filter substitution-stream through the first goal on the list. It passes this result on to a recursive call to filter-through-conj-goals with the remainder of the goal list. Thus, the stream is passed through the goals in left-to-right order, growing or shrinking as it passes through each goal.

filter-through-goal takes a single goal and uses it as a filter to the stream of substitutions. This filtering is done by calling solve with the goal and the first set of substitutions in the substitution stream. The result of this call to solve is a stream of substitutions resulting from matches of the goal against the knowledge base. This stream will be empty if the goal does not succeed under any of the substitutions contained in the stream, or it may contain multiple substitution sets representing alternative bindings. This stream is combined with the result of filtering the tail of the input stream through the same goal:

```
(defun filter-through-goal (goal substitution-stream)
  (if (empty-stream-p substitution-stream)
      (make-empty-stream)
      (combine-streams
        (solve goal (head-stream substitution-stream))
        (filter-through-goal goal (tail-stream substitution-stream)))))
```

To summarize, filter-through-conj-goals passes the stream through a sequence of goals, and filter-through-goal filters the substitution stream through a single goal. A recursive call to solve solves the goal under each substitution set.

Whereas solve handles conjunctive goals by calling filter-through-conj-goals, simple goals are handled by the function infer, which takes a goal and a substitution set and finds all solutions in the knowledge base. infer's third parameter, kb, is a data base of logical expressions. When solve first calls infer, it passes the knowledge base contained in the global variable *assertions*. infer searches kb sequentially, trying the goal against each fact or rule conclusion.

The recursive implementation of infer builds the backward-chaining search typical of PROLOG and most expert system shells. infer takes a goal, a set of substitutions, and a knowledge base. It first checks whether kb is empty, returning an empty stream if it is. Otherwise, it binds the first item in kb to the symbol assertion using a let* block. let* is like let except it is guaranteed to evaluate the initializations of its local variables in order. It also defines the variable match: if assertion is a rule, let initializes match to the substitutions required to unify the goal with the conclusion of the rule; if assertion is a fact, let binds match to those substitutions required to unify assertion with the goal. After attempting to unify the goal with the first element of the knowledge base, infer tests whether the unification succeeded. If it failed to match, infer recurs, attempting to solve the goal using the remainder of the knowledge base. If the unification succeeded and assertion is a rule, infer calls solve on the premise of the rule using the augmented set of substitutions bound to match. combine-stream joins the resulting stream of solutions to that constructed by calling infer on the rest of the knowledge base. If assertion is not a rule, it is a fact; infer adds the solution bound to match to those provided by the rest of the knowledge base. Note that once the goal unifies with a fact, it is solved; this terminates the search. We define infer:

```
(defun infer (goal substitutions kb)
  (if (null kb)
      (make-empty-stream)
      (let* ((assertion (rename-variables (car kb)))
             (match (if (rulep assertion)
                        (unify goal (conclusion assertion) substitutions)
                        (unify goal assertion substitutions))))
        (if (equal match 'failed)
            (infer goal substitutions (cdr kb))
            (if (rulep assertion)
                (combine-streams
                  (solve (premise assertion) match)
                  (infer goal substitutions (cdr kb)))
                (cons-stream match (infer goal substitutions (cdr kb)))))))))
```

Before the first element of kb is bound to assertion, it is passed to rename-variables to give each variable a unique name. This prevents name conflicts between the variables in the goal and those in the knowledge base entry; e.g., if (var x) appears in a goal, it must be treated as a different variable than a (var x) that appears in the rule or fact. The simplest way to handle this is by renaming all variables in the assertion with unique names. We define rename-variables at the end of this section.

This completes the implementation of the core of the logic programming interpreter. Like PROLOG, our logic programming interpreter takes a goal and finds all variable bindings that make it true against a given knowledge base. solve is the top-level function and generates a stream of substitution sets that represent solutions to the goal using the knowledge base. filter-through-conj-goals solves conjunctive goals in a left-to-right order, using each goal as a filter on a stream of candidate solutions: if a goal cannot be proven true against the knowledge base using a substitution set in the stream, filter-through-conj-goals eliminates those substitutions from the stream. If the goal is a simple literal, solve calls infer to generate a stream of all substitutions that make the goal succeed against the knowledge base. All that remain are a number of straightforward functions for accessing components of knowledge base entries, managing variable substitutions, and printing solutions.

print-solutions takes as arguments a goal and a stream of substitutions. For each set of substitutions in the stream, it prints the goal with variables replaced by their bindings in the substitution set.

```
(defun print-solutions (goal substitution-stream)
  (cond ((empty-stream-p substitution-stream) nil)
        (t (print (apply-substitutions goal (head-stream substitution-stream)))
           (terpri)
           (print-solutions goal (tail-stream substitution-stream)))))
```

The replacement of variables with their values under a substitution set is done by apply-substitutions, which does a car-cdr recursive tree walk on a pattern. If the pattern is a constant, it is returned unchanged. If it is a variable, apply-substitutions tests if it is bound. If it is unbound, the variable is returned; if it is bound, apply-substitutions calls itself recursively on the value of this binding. Note that the binding value may be either a constant, another variable, or a pattern of arbitrary complexity.

```
(defun apply-substitutions (pattern substitution-list)
    (cond ((is-constant-p pattern) pattern)
        ((varp pattern)
            (let ((binding (get-binding pattern substitution-list)))
                (cond (binding (apply-substitutions (binding-value binding)
                                                    substitution-list))
                    (t pattern))))
        (t (cons (apply-substitutions (car pattern) substitution-list)
                 (apply-substitutions (cdr pattern) substitution-list)))))
```

infer renamed the variables in each knowledge base entry before matching it with a goal. This is necessary to prevent undesired name collisions in matches. For example, the goal (p a (var x)) should match with the knowledge base entry (p (var x) b), because the scope of each (var x) is restricted to a single expression. As unification is defined, however, this match will not occur. Name collisions are prevented by giving each variable in an expression a unique name. The basis of our renaming scheme is a Common LISP built-in function called gensym that takes no arguments; each time it is called, it returns a unique symbol consisting of a number preceded by #:G. For example:

```
> (gensym)
#:G4
> (gensym)
#:G5
> (gensym)
#:G6
>
```

Our renaming scheme replaces each variable name in an expression with the result of a call to gensym. rename-variables performs certain initializations (described below) and calls rename-rec to make substitutions recursively in the pattern. When a variable is encountered, the function rename is called to return a new name. To allow multiple occurrences of a variable in a pattern to be given consistent names, each time a variable is renamed, the new name is placed in an association list bound to the *special* variable *name-list*. The special declaration makes all references to the variable dynamic and shared among these functions. Thus, each access of *name-list* in rename will access the instance of *name-list* declared in rename-variables. rename-variables initializes *name-list* to nil when it is first called. These functions are defined:

```
(defun rename-variables (assertion)
  (declare (special *name-list*))
  (setq *name-list* nil)
  (rename-rec assertion))

(defun rename-rec (exp)
    (declare (special *name-list*))
    (cond ((is-constant-p exp) exp)
          ((varp exp) (rename exp))
          (t (cons (rename-rec (car exp))(rename-rec (cdr exp))))))

(defun rename (var)
  (declare (special *name-list*))
  (list 'var (or (cdr (assoc var *name-list* :test #'equal))
            (let ((name (gensym)))
                  (setq *name-list* (acons var name *name-list*))name))))
```

The remaining functions required for the implementation are concerned with accessing components of rules and goals and are self-explanatory:

```
(defun premise (rule) (nth 2 rule))

(defun conclusion (rule) (nth 4 rule))

(defun rulep (pattern)
  (and (listp pattern)
    (equal (nth 0 pattern) 'rule)))

(defun conjunctive-goal-p (goal)
  (and (listp goal)
    (equal (car goal) 'and)))

(defun body (goal) (cdr goal))
```

14.2 Streams and Delayed Evaluation

As we demonstrated in the implementation of logic-shell, a stream-oriented view can help
with the organization of a complex program. However, our implementation of streams as
lists did not provide the full benefit of stream processing. In particular, this implementation
suffers from inefficiency and an inability to handle infinitely long data streams.

In the list implementation of streams, all of the elements must be computed before
that stream (list) can be passed on to the next function. In logic-shell this leads to an
exhaustive search of the knowledge base for each intermediate goal in the solution process.
In order to produce the first solution to the top-level goal, the program must produce a list
of all solutions. If we want only the first solution on this list, the program must still search
the entire space. It would be preferable if the program produced the first solution by search-

ing only that portion of the space needed to produce that goal and delayed finding the rest of the solutions until they were needed.

A second problem is the inability to process infinitely long streams. Although this problem does not arise in logic-shell, it occurs naturally in the stream-based solution to many problems. Assume, for example, that we would like to write a function that returns a stream of the first n odd Fibonacci numbers. A straightforward implementation would use a generator to produce a stream of Fibonacci numbers, a filter to eliminate even-valued numbers from the stream, and an accumulator to gather these into a solution list of n elements (Fig. 14.2). Unfortunately, the stream of Fibonacci numbers is infinite in length and we cannot decide in advance how long a list will be needed to produce the first n odd numbers.

Instead, we would like the generator to produce the stream of Fibonacci numbers one at a time and pass each number through the filter until the accumulator has gathered n values. This behavior more closely fits our intuitive notion of a stream than does the list-based implementation. We may accomplish this through the use of *delayed evaluation*.

Instead of letting the generator run to completion to produce the entire stream of results, we let the function produce the first element of the stream and then freeze or delay its execution until the next element is needed. When the program needs the next element of the stream, it causes the function to resume execution and produce only that element and again delay evaluation of the rest of the stream. Thus, instead of containing the entire list of numbers, the stream consists of just two components, its first element and the frozen computation of the rest of the stream (Fig. 14.3).

We use *function closures* to create the delayed portion of the stream illustrated in Figure 14.3. A closure consists of a function, along with all its variable bindings in the

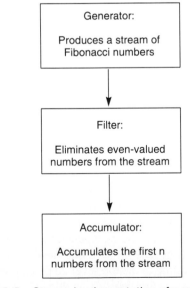

Figure 14.2 Stream implementation of a program to find the first **n** odd Fibonacci numbers.

A list-based stream containing an indeterminate number of elements:

$$(e_1 \quad e_2 \quad e_3 \quad e_4 \quad \dots)$$

A stream with delayed evaluation of its tail containing only two elements but capable of producing any number of elements:

$$(e_1 \quad . \quad \text{<delayed evaluation of remainder of stream>})$$

Figure 14.3 List-based versus delayed evaluation implementations of streams.

current environment; we may bind a closure to a variable, or pass it as a parameter, and evaluate it using funcall. Essentially, a closure "freezes" a function application until a later time. We can create closures using the LISP form function. For example, consider the following LISP transcript:

```
> (setq v 10)
10
> (+ v 10)
20
> (let ((v 20)) (setq f_closure (function (lambda () (+ v 10)))))
#<COMPILED-LEXICAL-CLOSURE #x28641E>
> (funcall f_closure)
30
> (+ v 10)
20
```

The initial setq binds v to 10 in the global environment. The subsequent addition of 10 and v gives the expected result. In the let block, we create a local binding of v to 20 and create a closure of a function that adds this v to 10. It is interesting to note that this binding of v does not disappear when we exit the let block, because it is retained in the function closure that is bound to f_closure. It is a lexical binding, however, so it doesn't shadow the global binding of v. If we subsequently evaluate this closure, it returns 30, the result of adding 10 to the local binding of v, even though the global v is still bound to 10.

The heart of this implementation of streams is a pair of functions, delay and force. delay takes an expression as argument and does not evaluate it; instead it takes the unevaluated argument and returns a closure. force takes a function closure as argument and uses funcall to force its application. These functions are defined:

```
(defmacro delay (exp) '(function (lambda () ,exp)))

(defun force (function-closure) (funcall function-closure))
```

delay is an example of a LISP form called a *macro*. We cannot define delay using defun because all functions so defined evaluate their arguments before executing the body. Macros give us complete control over the evaluation of their arguments. We define macros using the defmacro form. When a macro is executed, it does not evaluate its arguments. Instead, it binds the unevaluated s-expressions in the call to the formal parameters and evaluates its body *twice*. The first evaluation is called a *macro-expansion*; the second evaluates the resulting form.

To define the delay macro, we introduce another LISP form, the *backquote*. Backquote prevents evaluation just like a quote, except that it allows us to evaluate selectively elements of the backquoted expression. Any element of a backquoted s-expression preceded by a comma is evaluated and its value inserted into the resulting expression.

For example, assume the call (delay (+ 2 3)). The expression (+ 2 3) is not evaluated; instead it is bound to the formal parameter, exp. When the body of the macro is evaluated the first time, it returns the backquoted expression with the formal parameter, exp, replaced by its value, the unevaluated s-expression (+ 2 3). This produces the expression (function (lambda () (+ 2 3))). This is evaluated again, returning a function closure.

If we later pass this closure to force, it will evaluate the expression (lambda () (+ 2 3)). This is a function that takes no arguments and whose body evaluates to 5. Using force and delay, we can implement streams with delayed evaluation. We rewrite cons-stream as a macro that takes two arguments and conses the value of the first onto the delayed evaluation of the second. Thus, the second argument may be a function that will return a stream of any length; it is not evaluated. We define tail-stream so that it forces the evaluation of the tail of a stream. These are defined:

```
(defmacro cons-stream (exp stream) '(cons ,exp (delay ,stream)))
```

```
(defun tail-stream (stream) (force (cdr stream)))
```

We also redefine combine-streams as a macro that takes two streams but does not evaluate them. Instead, it uses delay to create a closure for the second stream and passes this and the first stream to the function comb-f. comb-f is similar to our earlier definition of combine-streams, except that in the event that the first stream is empty, it forces evaluation of the second stream. If the first stream is not empty, the recursive call to comb-f is done using our delayed version of cons-stream. This freezes the recursive call in a closure for later evaluation.

```
(defmacro combine-streams (stream1 stream2)
  '(comb-f ,stream1 (delay ,stream2)))
```

```
(defun comb-f (stream1 stream2)
  (if (empty-stream-p stream1)
    (force stream2)
    (cons-stream (head-stream stream1)
          (comb-f (tail-stream stream1) stream2))))
```

If we add these definitions to the versions of head-stream, make-empty-stream, and empty-stream-p from Section 14.1.2, we have a complete stream implementation with delayed evaluation.

We can use these functions to solve our problem of producing the first n odd Fibonacci numbers. fibonacci-stream returns a stream of all the Fibonacci numbers; note that fibonacci-stream is a nonterminating recursive function. Delayed evaluation prevents it from looping forever; it produces the next element only when needed. filter-odds takes a stream of integers and eliminates the even elements. accumulate takes a stream and a number n and returns a *list* of the first n elements of the stream.

```
(defun fibonacci-stream (fibonacci-1 fibonacci-2)
   (cons-stream (+ fibonacci-1 fibonacci-2)
                (fibonacci-stream fibonacci-2 (+ fibonacci-1 fibonacci-2))))


(defun filter-odds (stream)
   (cond ((evenp (head-stream stream)) (filter-odds (tail-stream stream)))
         (t (cons-stream (head-stream stream) (filter-odds (tail-stream stream))))))


(defun accumulate-into-list (n stream)
  (cond ((zerop n) nil)
        (t (cons (head-stream stream) (accumulate-into-list (- n 1) (tail-stream stream))))))
```

To obtain a list of the first 25 odd Fibonacci numbers, we simply evaluate:

```
(accumulate-into-list 25 (filter-odds (fibonacci-stream 0 1)))
```

We may use these stream functions in the definition of the logic programming interpreter of Section 14.1 to improve its efficiency under certain circumstances. Assume that we would like to modify print-solutions so that instead of printing all solutions to a goal, it prints the first and waits for the user to ask for the additional solutions. Using our implementation of lists as streams, the algorithm would still search for all solutions before it could print out the first. Using delayed evaluation, this is not necessary: the first solution will be the head of a stream, and the function evaluations necessary to find the additional solutions will be frozen in the tail of the stream.

In the next section we modify this logic programming interpreter to implement a LISP-based expert system shell. Before presenting the expert system shell, however, we mention two additional stream functions that are used in its implementation. In Chapter 7 we presented a general mapping function and a general filter for lists. These functions, map-simple and filter, can be straightforwardly modified to function on streams. We use filter-stream and map-stream in the next section. We leave their implementation as an exercise.

14.3   An Expert System Shell in LISP

The expert system shell developed in this section is an extension of the backward-chaining engine of Section 14.2. The major modifications include the use of certainty factors to manage uncertain reasoning, the ability to ask the user for unknown facts, and the use of a working memory to save user responses. This expert system shell is called lisp-shell.

14.3.1   Implementing Certainty Factors

The logic programming interpreter returned a stream of the substitution sets under which a goal logically followed from a data base of logical assertions. Bindings that did not allow the goal to be satisfied using the knowledge base were either filtered from the stream or not generated in the first place. In implementing reasoning with certainty factors, however, simple truth values are replaced by a numeric value between -1 and 1, as described in Chapter 8.

This requires that the stream of solutions to a goal not only contain the variable bindings that allow the goal to be satisfied; they must also include measures of the confidence under which each solution follows from the knowledge base. Consequently, instead of processing streams of substitution sets, lisp-shell processes streams of pairs: a set of substitutions and a number representing the confidence in the truth of the goal under those variable substitutions.

We implement stream elements as an abstract data type: the functions for manipulating the substitution and certainty factor pairs are subst-record, which constructs a pair from a set of substitutions and a certainty factor; subst-list, which returns the set of bindings from a pair; and subst-cf, which returns the certainty factor. Internally, records are represented as dotted pairs, of the form (*<substitution list>* . *<cf>*). The functions that handle these pairs are:

```
; Returns the list of variable bindings from a substitution/certainty factor pair.
(defun subst-list (substitutions)
    (car substitutions))


; Returns the certainty factor from a substitution/certainty factor pair.
(defun subst-cf (substitutions)
    (cdr substitutions))


; Forms a substitution set/certainty factor pair.
(defun subst-record (substitutions cf)
    (cons substitutions cf))
```

Similarly, rules and facts are stored in the knowledge base with an attached certainty factor. Facts are represented as dotted pairs, (*<assertion>* . *<cf>*), where *<assertion>* is a positive literal and *<cf>* is its certainty measure. Rules are in the format (rule if *<premise>* then *<conclusion>* *<cf>*), where *<cf>* is the certainty factor. A sample rule is

```
(rule
   if (and (rose (var x)) (color (var x) red))
   then (kind (var x) american-beauty) 1)
```

The functions for handling rules and facts are:

```
; Returns the premise of a rule.
(defun premise (rule)
   (nth 2 rule))

; Returns the conclusion of a rule.
(defun conclusion (rule)
   (nth 4 rule))

; Returns the cf of a rule.
(defun rule-cf (rule)
   (nth 5 rule))

; Tests whether a given pattern is a rule.
(defun rulep (pattern)
   (and (listp pattern)
      (equal (nth 0 pattern) 'rule)))

; Returns the pattern part of a fact.
(defun fact-pattern (fact)
   (car fact))

; Returns the cf of a fact.
(defun fact-cf (fact)
   (cdr fact))
```

Using these functions, we implement the balance of the rule interpreter through a series of modifications to the logic programming interpreter (Section 14.2).

14.3.2   Architecture of lisp-shell

solve is the heart of lisp-shell. solve does not return a solution stream directly but first passes it through a filter that eliminates any substitutions whose certainty factor is less than 0.2. This prunes results that lack sufficient confidence.

```
(defun solve (goal substitutions)
   (filter-stream
    (if (conjunctive-goal-p goal)
        (filter-through-conj-goals
           (cdr (body goal))
           (solve (car (body goal)) substitutions))
        (solve-simple-goal goal substitutions))
    #'(lambda (x) (< 0.2 (subst-cf x))))))
```

This has changed only slightly from the definition of solve in logic-shell. It is still a conditional statement that distinguishes between conjunctive goals and simple goals. One difference is the use of the general filter filter-stream to prune all solutions whose certainty factor falls below a certain value. This test is passed as a lambda expression that checks whether or not the certainty factor of a substitution set /cf pair is less than 0.2. The other major difference is the use of solve-simple-goal in place of infer. The treatment of simple goals is complicated by the ability to ask the user for information. We define solve-simple-goal as:

```
(defun solve-simple-goal (goal substitutions)
    (declare (special *assertions*))
    (declare (special *case-specific-data*))
    (or (told goal substitutions *case-specific-data*)
        (infer goal substitutions *assertions*)
        (ask-for goal substitutions)))
```

solve-simple-goal uses an or form to try three different solution strategies in order. First it calls told to check whether the goal has already been solved by the user in response to a previous query. User responses are bound to the global variable *case-specific-data*; told searches this list to try to find a match for the goal. This keeps lisp-shell from asking for the same piece of information twice. If this fails, solve-simple-goal attempts to infer the goal using the rules in *assertions*. Finally, if these fail, it calls ask-for to query the user for the information. These functions are defined below.

The top-level read-solve-print loop has changed little, except for the inclusion of a statement initializing *case-specific-data* to nil before solving a new goal. Note that when solve is called initially, it is not just passed the empty substitution set, but a pair consisting of the empty substitution set and a cf of 0. This certainty value has no real meaning: it is included for syntactic reasons until a meaningful substitution set and certainty factor pair is generated by user input or a fact in the knowledge base.

```
(defun lisp-shell ()
  (declare (special *case-specific-data*))
  (setq *case-specific-data* ())
  (prin1 'lisp-shell> )
  (let ((goal (read)))
    (terpri)
    (cond ((equal goal 'quit) 'bye)
      (t (print-solutions goal (solve goal (subst-record nil 0)))
        (terpri)
        (lisp-shell)))))
```

filter-through-conj-goals is not changed, but filter-through-goal must compute the certainty factor for a conjunctive expression as the minimum of the certainties of the conjuncts. To do so, it binds the first element of substitution-stream to the symbol subs in a let block. It then calls solve on the goal and this substitution set; the result is passed through the general mapping function, map-stream, which takes the stream of substitution pairs returned by solve and recomputes their certainty factors as the minimum of the certainty factor of the result and the certainty factor of the initial substitution set, subs. These functions are defined:

```
(defun filter-through conj-goals (goals substitution-stream)
  (if (null goals)
      substitution-stream
      (filter-through-conj-goals
          (cdr goals)
          (filter-through-goal (car goals) substitution-stream))))

(defun filter-through-goal (goal substitution-stream)
  (if (empty-stream-p substitution-stream)
      (make-empty-stream)
      (let ((subs (head-stream substitution-stream)))
          (combine-streams
              (map-stream (solve goal subs)
                  #'(lambda (x) (subst-record (subst-list x)(min (subst-cf x) (subst-cf subs)))))
              (filter-through-goal goal (tail-stream substitution-stream))))))
```

The definition of infer has been changed to take certainty factors into account. Although its overall structure reflects the version of infer written for the logic programming interpreter, we must now compute the certainty factor for solutions to the goal from the certainty factors of the rule and the certainties of solutions to the rule premise. solve-rule calls solve to find all solutions to the premise and uses map-stream to compute the resulting certainties for the rule conclusion.

```
(defun infer (goal substitutions kb)
  (if (null kb)
    (make-empty-stream)
    (let* ((assertion (rename-variables (car kb)))
           (match (if (rulep assertion)
                      (unify goal conclusion assertion) (subst-list substitutions))
                      (unify goal assertion (subst-list substitutions)))))
      (if (equal match 'failed)
        (infer goal substitutions (cdr kb))
        (if (rulep assertion)
          (combine-streams
              (solve-rule assertion (subst-record match (subst-cf substitutions)))
              (infer goal substitutions (cdr kb)))
          (cons-stream (subst-record match (fact-cf assertion))
              (infer goal substitutions (cdr kb))))))))

(defun solve-rule (rule substitutions)
  (map-stream (solve (premise rule) substitutions)
              #'(lambda (x) (subst-record
                  (subst-list x)
                  (* (subst-cf x) (rule-cf rule))))))
```

Finally, print-solutions is modified to take certainty factors into account:

```
(defun print-solutions (goal substitution-stream)
  (cond ((empty-stream-p substitution-stream) nil)
        (t (print (apply-substitutions goal (subst-list (head-stream substitution-stream))))
           (write-string "cf =")
           (prin1 (subst-cf (head-stream substitution-stream)))
           (terpri)
           (print-solutions goal (tail-stream substitution-stream)))))
```

The remaining functions, such as **apply-substitutions** and functions for accessing components of rules and goals, are unchanged from their definition in Section 14.1.

14.3.3   User Queries and Working Memory

The remainder of **lisp-shell** consists of the functions **ask-for** and **told**, which handle user interactions. These are straightforward, although the reader should note that we have made some simplifying assumptions. In particular, the only response allowed to queries is either "**y**" or "**n**." This causes the binding set passed to **ask-for** to be returned with a cf of either 1 or −1, respectively; the user may not give an uncertain response directly to a query. **ask-rec** prints a query and reads the answer, repeating until the answer is either y or n. The reader may expand **ask-rec** to take on any uncertain value within the −1 to 1 range.

askable verifies whether the user may be asked for a particular goal. Any goal asked of the user must exist as a pattern in the global list *askables*; the architect of an expert system may in this way determine which goals may be asked and which may only be inferred from the knowledge base. **told** searches through the entries in the global *case-specific-data* to find whether the user has already answered a query. It is similar to **infer** except it assumes that everything in *case-specific-data* is stored as a fact. We define these functions:

```
(defun ask-for (goal substitutions)
  (declare (special *askables*))
  (declare (special *case-specific-data*))
  (if (askable goal *askables*)
    (let* ((query (apply-substitutions goal (subst-list substitutions)))
           (result (ask-rec query)))
      (setq *case-specific-data* (cons (subst-record query result) *case-specific-data*))
      (cons-stream (subst-record (subst-list substitutions) result) (make-empty-stream)))))

(defun ask-rec (query)
  (prin1 query)
  (write-string " >")
  (let ((answer (read)))
    (cond ((equal answer 'y) 1)
```

```
              ((equal answer 'n) −1)
               (t (print "answer must be y or n")
                  (terpri)
                  (ask-rec query)))))

    (defun askable (goal askables)
       (cond ((null askables) nil)
          ((not (equal (unify goal (car askables) ()) 'failed)) t)
          (t (askable goal (cdr askables)))))

    (defun told (goal substitutions case-specific-data)
       (cond ((null case-specific-data) (make-empty-stream))
         (t (combine-streams
             (use-fact goal (car case-specific-data) substitutions)
             (told goal substitutions (cdr case-specific-data))))))
```

This completes the implementation of our LISP-based expert system shell. In the next section we use lisp-shell to build a simple classification expert system.

14.3.4 Classification Using lisp-shell

We now present a small expert system for classifying trees and bushes. Although it is far from botanically complete, it illustrates the use and behavior of the tool. The knowledge base resides in two global variables: *assertions*, which contains the rules and facts of the knowledge base, and *askables*, which lists the goals that may be asked of the user. The knowledge base used in this example is constructed by two calls to setq:

```
    (setq *assertions* '(

     (rule
       if (and (size (var x) tall) (woody (var x)))
       then (tree (var x)) .9)

     (rule
       if (and (size (var x) small) (woody (var x)))
       then (bush (var x)) .9)

     (rule
       if (and (tree (var x)) (evergreen (var x))(color (var x) blue))
       then (kind (var x) spruce) .8)

     (rule
       if (and (tree (var x)) (evergreen (var x))(color (var x) green))
       then (kind (var x) pine) .9)

     (rule
       if (and (tree (var x)) (deciduous (var x)) (bears (var x) fruit))
       then (fruit-tree (var x)) 1)
```

```
(rule
  if (and (fruit-tree (var x)) (color fruit red) (taste fruit sweet))
  then (kind (var x) apple-tree) .9)

(rule
  if (and (fruit-tree (var x)) (color fruit yellow) (taste fruit sour))
  then (kind (var x) lemon-tree) .8)

(rule
  if (and (bush (var x)) (flowering (var x)) (thorny (var x)))
  then (rose (var x)) 1)

(rule
  if (and (rose (var x)) (color (var x) red))
  then (kind (var x) american-beauty) 1)))

(setq *askables* '(
  (size (var x) (var y))
  (woody (var x))
  (soft (var x))
  (color (var x) (var y))
  (evergreen (var x))
  (thorny (var x))
  (deciduous (var x))
  (bears (var x) (var y))
  (taste (var x) (var y))
  (flowering (var x))))
```

A sample run of the trees knowledge base appears below. The reader is encouraged to trace through the rule base to observe the order in which rules are tried, the propagation of certainty factors, and the way in which possibilities are pruned when found to be false:

```
> (lisp-shell)
lisp-shell>(kind tree-1 (var x))
(size tree-1 tall) >y
(woody tree-1) >y
(evergreen tree-1) >y
(color tree-1 blue) >n
(color tree-1 green) >y

(kind tree-1 pine) cf = 0.81

(deciduous tree-1) >n
(size tree-1 small) >n

lisp-shell>(kind bush-2 (var x))
(size bush-2 tall) >n
(size bush-2 small) >y
(woody bush-2) >y
```

```
(flowering bush-2) >y
(thorny bush-2) >y
(color bush-2 red) >y

(kind bush-2 american-beauty) cf = 0.9

lisp-shell>(kind tree-3 (var x))
(size tree-3 tall) >y
(woody tree-3) >y
(evergreen tree-3) >n
(deciduous tree-3) >y
(bears tree-3 fruit) >y
(color fruit red) >n
(color fruit yellow) >y
(taste fruit sour) >y

(kind tree-3 lemon-tree) cf = 0.7200000000000001

(size tree-3 small) >n

lisp-shell>quit

bye
?
```

In this example, several anomalies may be noted. For example, the shell occasionally asks whether a tree is small even though it was told the tree is tall, or it asks whether the tree is deciduous even though the tree is an evergreen. This is typical of the behavior of expert systems. The knowledge base does not know anything about the relationship between tall and small or evergreen and deciduous: they are just patterns to be matched. Because the search is exhaustive, all rules are tried. If a system is to exhibit deeper knowledge than this, the relationships must be coded in the knowledge base. For example, a rule may be written that states that small implies not tall. In this example, lisp-shell is not capable of representing these relationships because we have not implemented the not operator. This extension is left as an exercise.

14.4 Network Representations and Inheritance

This section introduces the implementation of semantic networks in LISP. As a family of representations, semantic networks provide a basis for a large variety of inferences, some of which were described in Chapter 9. We do not discuss all of these, but focus on a basic approach to constructing network representations using *property lists*. After these are discussed and used to define a simple semantic network, we define a function for class inheritance. The ideas illustrated in this section are important precursors of the object-oriented programming techniques of Chapter 15.

14.4.1 Representing Semantic Nets in LISP

LISP is a convenient language for representing any graph structure, including semantic nets. Lists provide the ability to create computational objects of arbitrary complexity and these objects may be bound to names, allowing for easy reference and the definition of relationships between them. Indeed, all LISP data structures are based on an internal implementation as chains of pointers, a natural isomorph to graph structures.

For example, labeled graphs may be represented using association lists: each node is an entry in an association list with all the arcs out of that node stored in the datum of the node as a second association list. Arcs are described by an association list entry that has the arc name as its key and the arc destination as its datum. Using this representation, the built-in association list functions are used to find the destination of a particular arc from a given node. For example, the labeled, directed graph of Figure 14.4 is represented by the association list:

```
((a (1 . b))
 (b (2 . c))
 (c (2 . b) (3 . a)))
```

This approach is the basis of many network implementations. Another way to implement semantic networks is through the use of *property lists*.

Essentially, property lists are a built-in feature of LISP that allow named relationships to be attached to symbols. Rather than using setq to bind an association list to a symbol, with property lists we can program the direct attachment of named attributes to objects in the global environment. These are bound to the symbol not as a value but as an additional component called the property list.

Functions for managing property lists are get, setf, remprop, and symbol-plist. get, which has the syntax

```
(get <symbol> <property-name>)
```

retrieves a property from *<symbol>* by its *<property-name>*. For example, if the symbol rose has a color property of red and a smell property of sweet, then get would have the behavior:

```
(get 'rose 'color)
red
(get 'rose 'smell)
sweet
(get 'rose 'party-affiliation)
nil
```

As the last of these calls to get illustrates, if an attempt is made to retrieve a nonexistent property, one that is not on the property list, get returns a value of nil.

Figure 14.4 A simple labeled directed graph

Properties are attached to objects using the setf function, which has the syntax:

(setf *<form>* *<value>*)

setf is a generalization of setq. The first argument to setf is taken from a large but specific list of forms that evaluate to a memory location. This list includes such forms as car and cdr. setf places the value of its second argument in that location. For example, we may use setf along with list functions to modify lists in the global environment, as the following transcript shows:

```
? (setq l '(a b c d e))
(a b c d e)
? (setf (nth 2 l) 3)
3
? l
(a b 3 d e)
```

We use setf, along with get, to change the value of properties. For instance, we may define the properties of a rose by:

```
> (setf (get 'rose 'color) 'red)
red
> (setf (get 'rose 'smell) 'sweet)
sweet
```

remprop takes as arguments a symbol and a property name and causes a named property to be deleted. For example:

```
> (get 'rose 'color)
red
> (remprop 'rose 'color)
color
> (get 'rose 'color)
nil
```

symbol-plist takes as argument a symbol and returns its property list. For example:

```
> (setf (get 'rose 'color) 'red)
red
> (setf (get 'rose 'smell) 'sweet)
```

```
sweet
> (plist 'rose)
(smell sweet color red)
```

Using property lists, it is straightforward to implement a semantic network. For example, the following calls to setf implement the semantic network description of species of birds from Figure 13.3. The isa relations define inheritance links.

```
(setf (get 'animal 'covering) 'skin)
(setf (get 'bird 'covering) 'feathers)
(setf (get 'bird 'travel) 'flies)
(setf (get 'bird 'isa) animal)
(setf (get 'fish 'isa) animal)
(setf (get 'fish 'travel) 'swim)
(setf (get 'ostrich 'isa) 'bird)
(setf (get 'ostrich 'travel) 'walk)
(setf (get 'penguin 'isa) 'bird)
(setf (get 'penguin 'travel) 'walk)
(setf (get 'penguin 'color) 'brown)
(setf (get 'opus 'isa) 'penguin)
(setf (get 'canary 'isa) 'bird)
(setf (get 'canary 'color) 'yellow)
(setf (get 'canary 'sound) 'sing)
(setf (get 'tweety 'isa) 'canary)
(setf (get 'tweety 'color) 'white)
(setf (get 'robin 'isa) 'bird)
(setf (get 'robin 'sound) 'sings)
(setf (get 'robin 'color) 'red)
```

14.4.2   Implementing Inheritance

Using this representation of semantic nets, we now define hierarchical inheritance. This is simply a search along superclass links until a parent is found with the desired property. The difficult part, as described in Chapter 9, is deciding the type of search to use, the order in which parent links are tried, and the handling of defaults and multiple inheritance. Here we take a simple approach: the parents are searched in a depth-first fashion, and search stops when an instance of the property is found. This is typical of the inheritance algorithms provided by many commercial systems. Variations on this approach include the use of breadth-first search as a search strategy.

inherit-get is a variation of get that first tries to retrieve a property from a symbol; if this fails, inherit-get calls get-from-parents to implement the search. get-from-parents takes as its first argument either a single parent or a list of parents; the second argument is a property name. If the parameter parents is nil, the search halts with failure. If parents is an atom, it calls inherit-get on the parent to either retrieve the property from the parent itself or continue the search. If parents is a list, get-from-parents calls itself recursively on the car and cdr of the list of parents. These functions are defined:

```
(defun inherit-get (object property)
  (or (get object property)
      (get-from-parents (get object 'isa) property)))

(defun get-from-parents (parents property)
  (cond ((null parents) nil)
        ((atom parents) (inherit-get parents property))
        (t (or (get-from-parents (car parents) property)
               (get-from-parents (cdr parents) property)))))
```

In Chapter 15 we present a LISP implementation of object-oriented programming that builds on many of the ideas presented in this section. In particular, we use an inheritance algorithm much like the one just defined to let objects inherit properties and methods from superclasses.

14.5   The ID3 Induction Algorithm

In this section, we implement the ID3 induction algorithm described in Chapter 12. ID3 infers decision trees from a set of training examples. A decision tree enables us to classify an object on the basis of its properties. Each internal node tests one of the properties of a candidate object and uses the resulting value to select a branch of the tree. It continues through the nodes of the tree, testing various properties, until it reaches a leaf. Each leaf node names a classification. Using a decision tree, we may classify objects through a simple tree walk. ID3 uses an information theoretic test selection function to order tests so as to construct an optimal (or nearly optimal) decision tree.

As with the other demonstrations of this text, our purpose is not just to provide a working version of the algorithm; we also want to examine general programming techniques that comprise a LISP programming style. In building the logic programming language and the expert system shell, we emphasized the use of streams to organize programs around the flow of data through a system of maps and filters. In implementing ID3, we have organized our code around a set of data type definitions using the LISP form defstruct.

Although the ID3 algorithm is conceptually elegant, its implementation requires that we manage a number of complex data structures, including objects, properties, sets, and decision trees. The heart of our implementation is a set of *structure definitions,* which are aggregate data types similar to records in Pascal or structures in C. With defstruct, Common LISP allows us to define types as collections of named *slots*; defstruct also constructs the functions needed to create and manipulate objects of that type.

Along with the use of structures to define data types, we continue to exploit higher-order functions such as mapcar. As the stream-based approach to our expert system shell demonstrated, the use of maps and filters to apply functions to lists of objects can often capture the intuition behind an algorithm with greater clarity than less expressive programming styles. The ability to treat functions as data, to bind function closures to symbols, and process them using other functions is a cornerstone of LISP programming style. As we will see in Chapter 15, it is also the basis of *object-oriented programming.*

14.5.1 Defining Structures Using defstruct

Many applications require that we represent objects as aggregates of heterogeneous components. For instance, an employee record might consist of a name, address, serial number, department, and salary. These fields might be represented as a list, a string, an integer, a symbol, and a floating point number, respectively. We could represent each employee record as a list:

((Doe Jane) "1234 Main, Randolph, Vt" 98765 Sales 4500.00)

However, this leaves implicit such essential constraints as the fact that all records have exactly five elements. Also, the use of expressions such as (nth 3 record) to access fields of the record tells us little about their meaning in terms of the problem domain.

A solution to this problem, of course, is to implement the necessary operations as a set of appropriately named functions, defining employee records as an abstract data type. Common LISP simplifies this through the use of defstruct.

Using defstruct, we could define a data type, employee, by evaluating the form:

```
(defstruct employee
  name
  address
  serial-number
  department
  salary)
```

Here, employee is the name of the defined type; name, address, serial-number, department, and salary are the names of its *slots*. Evaluation of this defstruct does not create any instances of an employee record; instead, it defines the type as well as the functions needed to create and manipulate objects of this type.

defstruct takes as its arguments a symbol, which will become the name of a new type, and a number of *slot specifiers*. Here, we have defined five slots by name. Slot specifiers also allow us to define different properties of slots, including type and initialization information (see Steele 1990).

Evaluating the form

```
(defstruct <type name>
  <slot name 1>
  <slot name 2>
  ...
  <slot name n>)
```

has a number of effects:

1. It defines a function, named according to the scheme make-<type name>, that lets us create instances of this type. For example, after defining the structure employee we may bind new-employee to an object of this type by evaluating:

```
(setq new-employee (make-employee))
```

We can also use slot names as keyword arguments to the make function, giving the instance initial values. For example:

```
(setq new-employee
      (make-employee
       :name '(Doe Jane)
       :address "1234 Main, Randolph, Vt"
       :serial-number 98765
       :department 'Sales
       :salary 4500.00))
```

2. It makes <type name> the name of a data type. We may use this name with typep to test whether an object is of that type. For example:

```
> (typep new-employee 'employee)
T
```

3. It defines a function, <type-name>-p, that we may also use to test whether an object is of the defined type. For instance:

```
> (employee-p new-employee)
T
> (employee-p '(Doe Jane))
nil
```

4. It defines an accessor for each slot of the structure. These accessors are named according to the scheme:

```
<type name>-<slot name>
```

In our example, we may access the values of various slots of new-employee using these accessors:

```
> (employee-name new-employee)
(Doe Jane)
> (employee-address new-employee)
"1234 Main, Randolph, Vt"
> (employee-department new-employee)
Sales
>
```

We may also use these accessors in conjunction with setf to change the slot values of an instance. For example:

```
> (employee-salary new-employee)
4500.0
> (setf (employee-salary new-employee) 5000.00)
5000.0
> (employee-salary new-employee)
5000.0
>
```

Using structures, we can define predicates and accessors of a data type in a single LISP form. These definitions are central to our implementation of the ID3 algorithm.

14.5.2   Representing Objects and Properties

When given a set of examples of known classification, ID3 induces a tree that will correctly classify all the training instances and has a high probability of correctly classifying unseen objects. In the discussion of ID3 in Chapter 12, we described training instances in a tabular form, explicitly listing the properties and their values for each instance. For example, Table 12.1 lists a set of instances for learning to predict an individual's credit risk. Throughout this section, we continue to refer to this problem.

Tables are only one way of representing examples; it is more general to think of them as objects that may be tested for various properties. Our implementation makes few assumptions about the representation of objects. For each property, it requires a function of one argument that may be applied to an object to return a value of that property. For example, if **credit-profile-1** is bound to the first example in Table 12.1 and history is a function that returns the value of an object's credit history, then:

```
> (history credit-profile-1)
bad
```

Similarly, we would require functions for the other properties of a credit profile:

```
> (debt credit-profile-1)
high
> (collateral credit-profile-1)
none
> (income credit-profile-1)
0-to-15K
> (risk credit-profile-1)
high
```

Beyond these requirements, our implementation is independent of any particular object representation.

Because we would like to illustrate our program on a specific example, we will implement a representation for the credit assignment example. Choosing a simple approach, we represent objects as association lists in which the keys are property names and the data are property values. For instance, the first example of Table 12.1 would be represented by the association list:

```
((risk . high) (history . bad) (debt . high) (collateral . none) (income . 0-to-15k))
```

We represent the set of training instances as a list of association lists. We bind this list to the symbol examples:

```
(setq examples
    '(((risk . high) (history . bad) (debt . high) (collateral . none) (income . 0-to-15k))
      ((risk . high) (history . unknown) (debt . high) (collateral . none) (income . 15k-to-35k))
      ((risk . moderate) (history . unknown) (debt . low) (collateral . none) (income . 15k-to-35k))
      ((risk . high) (history . unknown) (debt . low) (collateral . none) (income . 0-to-15k))
      ((risk . low) (history . unknown) (debt . low) (collateral . none) (income . over-35k))
      ((risk . low) (history . unknown) (debt . low) (collateral . adequate) (income . over-35k))
      ((risk . high) (history . bad) (debt . low) (collateral . none) (income . 0-to-15k))
      ((risk . moderate) (history . bad) (debt . low) (collateral . adequate) (income . over-35k))
      ((risk . low) (history . good) (debt . low) (collateral . none) (income . over-35k))
      ((risk . low) (history . good) (debt . high) (collateral . adequate) (income . over-35k))
      ((risk . high) (history . good) (debt . high) (collateral . none) (income . 0-to-15k))
      ((risk . moderate) (history . good) (debt . high) (collateral . none) (income . 15k-to-35k))
      ((risk . low) (history . good) (debt . high) (collateral . none) (income . over-35k))
      ((risk . high) (history . bad) (debt . high) (collateral . none) (income . 15k-to-35k))))
```

Because the purpose of a decision tree is the determination of risk for a new individual, test instances will include all properties except risk:

```
(setq test-instance
    '((history . good) (debt . low) (collateral . none) (income . 15k-to-35k)))
```

Given this representation of objects, we define properties as the following set of functions:

```
(defun history (object)
  (cdr (assoc 'history object :test #'equal)))

(defun debt (object)
  (cdr (assoc 'debt object :test #'equal)))

(defun collateral (object)
  (cdr (assoc 'collateral object :test #'equal)))

(defun income (object)
  (cdr (assoc 'income object :test #'equal)))

(defun risk (object)
  (cdr (assoc 'risk object :test #'equal)))
```

Before continuing, it is important to stress that the implementation that follows does not assume this or any other specific representation of objects and properties. For instance, we could represent examples as structures using **defstruct**. It only assumes that the appropriate functions are defined. This separation of the implementation and the behavior of objects is a cornerstone of object-oriented programming.

14.5.3   Data Structures in ID3

We define decision trees using the following structures:

```
(defstruct decision-tree
  test-name
  test
  branches)

(defstruct leaf
  value)
```

A tree is either an instance of **decision-tree** or an instance of **leaf**. **leaf** has one slot, a value corresponding to a classification. Instances of type **decision-tree** represent internal nodes of the tree and consist of a **test**, a **test-name**, and a set of branches. **test** is a function of one argument that takes an object and returns the value of a property. In classifying an object, we will apply **test** to it using **funcall** and use the returned value to select a branch of the tree. **test-name** is the name of the property. We include it to make it easier for the user to inspect decision trees; it plays no real role in the program's execution. **branches** is an association list of subtrees: the keys are the possible values returned by **test**; the data are subtrees.

For example, the tree of Figure 12.13 would correspond to the following set of nested structures. The "#S" is a convention of Common LISP I/O; it indicates that an s-expression represents a structure.

```
#S(decision-tree
      :test-name income
      :test #<Compiled-function income #x3525CE>
      :branches
        ((0-to-15k . #S(leaf :value high))
         (15k-to-35k.
         (rf#S(decision-tree
               :test-name history
               :test #<Compiled-function history #x3514D6>
               :branches
                 ((good . #S(leaf :value moderate))
                  (bad . #S(leaf :value high))
                  (unknown .
                    #S(decision-tree
                          :test-name debt
                          :test #<Compiled-function debt #x351A7E>
```

```
            :branches
               ((high . #S(leaf :value high))
                (low . #S(leaf :value moderate))))))))
        (over-35k .
          #S(decision-tree :test-name history
                :test #<Compiled-function history #x3514D6>
                :branches
                ((good . #S(leaf :value low))
                 (bad . #S(leaf :value moderate))
                 (unknown . #S(leaf :value low)))))))))
```

A property is a function on objects; we represent these functions as a slot in a structure that includes other useful information:

```
(defstruct property
   name
   test
   values)
```

The test slot of an instance of property is bound to a function that returns a property value. name is the name of the property and is included solely to help the user inspect definitions. values is a list of all the values that may be returned by test. Requiring that the values of each property be known in advance simplifies the implementation greatly and is not an unreasonable assumption.

Though a set of training examples is, conceptually, just a collection of objects, we will make it a part of a structure that includes slots for other information used by the algorithm. We define example-frame as:

```
(defstruct example-frame
   instances
   properties
   classifier
   size
   information)
```

instances is a list of structures of known classification; this is the training set used to construct a decision tree. properties is a list of structures of type property; these are the properties that may be used in the nodes of that tree. classifier is also an instance of property; it represents the classification that ID3 is attempting to learn. Because the examples are of known classification, we include it as another property. size is the number of examples in the instance slot; information is the information content of that set of examples. We compute size and information content from the examples; however, as these values take time to compute and will be used several times, we save them in these slots.

As you will recall from Chapter 12, ID3 constructs trees recursively. Given a set of examples, in our implementation, an instance of example-frame, it selects a property and uses it to partition the set of training instances into non-intersecting subsets. Each subset contains all the instances that have the same value for that property. The property selected becomes the test at the current node of the tree. For each subset in the partition, ID3 recursively constructs a subtree using the remaining properties. The algorithm halts when a set of examples all belong to the same class, at which point it creates a leaf.

Our final structure definition is a partition, a division of an example set into subproblems using a particular property. We define the type partition:

```
(defstruct partition
  test-name
  test
  components
  info-gain)
```

In an instance of partition, the test slot is bound to the property used to create the partition. test-name is the name of the test, included for readability. components will be bound to the subproblems of the partition. In our implementation, components is an association list: the keys are the different values of the selected test; each datum is an instance of example-frame. info-gain is the information gain that results from using test as the node of the tree. As with size and information in the example-frame structure, this slot caches a value that is costly to compute and is used several times in the algorithm.

These structure definitions are complex, but ID3 is a complex algorithm. By organizing our program around these data types, we hope to make our implementation more clearly reflect the structure of the algorithm.

14.5.4   Implementing ID3

The heart of our implementation is the function build-tree, which takes an instance of example-frame and recursively constructs a decision tree.

```
(defun build-tree (training-frame)
  (cond
    ;Case 1: empty example set
    ((null (example-frame-instances training-frame))
        (make-leaf :value "unable to classify: no examples"))


    ;Case 2: all tests have been used
    ((null (example-frame-properties training-frame))
        (make-leaf :value (list-classes training-frame)))


    ;Case 3: all examples in same class
    ((zerop (example-frame-information training-frame))
        (make-leaf :value (funcall
                    (property-tested (example-frame-classifier training-frame))
                    (car (example-frame-instances training-frame)))))
```

```
;Case 4: select test and recur
(t (let ((part (choose-partition (gen-partitions training-frame))))
     (make-decision-tree
        :test-name (partition-test-name part)
        :test (partition-test part)
        :branches (mapcar #'(lambda (x) (cons (car x) (build-tree (cdr x))))
                            (partition-components part)))))))
```

Using cond, build-tree analyzes four possible cases.

In case 1, the example frame does not contain any training instances. This might occur if ID3 is given an incomplete set of training examples, with no instances for a given value of a property. In this case it creates a leaf consisting of the message "unable to classify: no examples."

The second case occurs if the properties slot of training-frame is empty. In recursively building the decision tree, once the algorithm selects a property, it deletes it from the properties slot in the example frames for all subproblems. If the example set is inconsistent, the algorithm may exhaust all properties before arriving at an unambiguous classification of training instances. In this case, it creates a leaf whose value is a list of all classes remaining in the set of training instances.

The third case represents a successful termination of a branch of the tree. If training-frame has an information content of zero, then all of the examples belong to the same class (this follows from Shannon's definition of information; see Section 12.3). The algorithm halts, returning a leaf node in which the value is equal to this remaining class.

Whereas the first three cases terminate tree construction, the fourth case recursively calls build-tree to construct the subtrees of the current node. gen-partitions produces a list of all possible partitions of the example set, using each test in the properties slot of training-frame. choose-partition selects the test that gives the greatest information gain. After binding the resulting partition to the variable part in a let block, build-tree constructs a node of a decision tree in which the test is that used in the chosen partition, and the branches slot is bound to an association list of subtrees. Each key in branches is a value of the test and each datum is a decision tree constructed by a recursive call to build-tree. Because the components slot of part is already an association list in which the keys are property values and the data are instances of example-frame, we can easily implement the construction of subtrees using mapcar to apply build-tree to each datum in this association list.

gen-partitions takes one argument, training-frame, an object of type example-frame, and generates all partitions of its instances. Each partition is created using a different property from the properties slot. gen-partitions employs a function, partition, that takes an instance of an example-frame and an instance of a property; it partitions the examples using that property. Note the use of mapcar to generate a partition for each element of the properties slot of training-frame.

```
(defun gen-partitions (training-frame)
  (mapcar #'(lambda (x) (partition training-frame x))
          (example-frame-properties training-frame)))
```

choose-partition searches a list of candidate partitions and chooses the one with the highest information gain:

```
(defun choose-partition (candidates)
  (cond ((null candidates) nil)
        ((= (list-length candidates) 1) (car candidates))
        (t (let ((best (choose-partition (cdr candidates))))
             (if (> (partition-info-gain (car candidates)) (partition-info-gain best))
                 (car candidates)
                 best)))))
```

partition is the most complex function in the implementation. It takes as arguments an example frame and a property and returns an instance of a partition structure. We define partition as:

```
(defun partition (root-frame property)
  (let ((parts (mapcar #'(lambda (x) (cons x (make-example-frame)))
                       (property-values property))))
    (dolist (instance (example-frame-instances root-frame))
      (push instance (example-frame-instances
                       (cdr (assoc (funcall (property-test property) instance) parts)))))
    (mapcar #'(lambda (x)
                (let ((frame (cdr x)))
                  (setf (example-frame-properties frame)
                        (remove property (example-frame-properties root-frame)))
                  (setf (example-frame-classifier frame)
                        (example-frame-classifier root-frame))
                  (setf (example-frame-size frame)
                        (list-length (example-frame-instances frame)))
                  (setf (example-frame-information frame)
                        (compute-information
                          (example-frame-instances frame)
                          (example-frame-classifier root-frame)))))
            parts)

    (make-partition
      :test-name (property-name property)
      :test (property-test property)
      :components parts
      :info-gain (compute-info-gain root-frame parts))))
```

partition begins by defining a local variable, parts, using a let block. It initializes parts to an association list whose keys are the possible values of the test in property and whose data will be the subproblems of the partition. partition implements this using the dolist macro. dolist binds local variables to each element of a list and evaluates its body for each binding. At this point, they are "empty" instances of example-frame: the instance slots of each subproblem are bound to nil. Using a dolist form, partition pushes each element of the instances slot of root-frame onto the instances slot of the appropriate subproblem in parts.

push is a LISP macro that modifies a list by adding a new first element; unlike cons, push permanently adds a new element to the list. That is, push has the behavior:

```
> (setq l' (a b c))
(a b c)
> (push 1 l)
(1 a b c)
> l
(1 a b c)                                               ;push changes l
```

This section of the code accomplishes the actual partitioning of root-frame. After the dolist terminates, parts is bound to an association list in which each key is a value of property and each datum is an example frame whose instances share that value.

Using mapcar, the algorithm then completes the information required of each example-frame in parts, assigning appropriate values to the properties, classifier, size and information slots. It then constructs and returns an instance of partition, binding the components slot to parts.

list-classes is used in case 2 of build-tree to create a leaf node for an ambiguous classification. list-classes employs a do loop to enumerate the classes in a list of examples. The do loop initializes classes to all the values of the classifier in training-frame. list-classes adds each element of classes to classes-present if there is an element of the instances slot of training-frame that belongs to that class.

```
(defun list-classes (training-frame)
  (do
  ((classes (property-values (example-frame-classifier training-frame)) (cdr classes))
   (classifier (property-test (example-frame-classifier training-frame))) classes-present)
  ((null classes) classes-present)
  (if (member (car classes) (example-frame-instances training-frame)
        :test #'(lambda (x y) (equal x (funcall classifier y))))
  (push (car classes) classes-present))))
```

The remaining functions compute the information content of sets of examples and the information gain for a choice of a test.

compute-information determines the information content of a list of examples. Using a do loop, it counts the number of instances in each class and computes the proportion of the total training set belonging to each class. Assuming that this proportion equals the probability that an object belongs to a class, it computes the information content of examples using Shannon's definition.

```
(defun compute-information (examples classifier)
  (let ((class-count
        (mapcar #'(lambda (x) (cons x 0)) (property-values classifier)))
        (size 0))
```

```
; count number of instances in each class
(dolist (instance examples)
  (incf size)
  (incf (cdr (assoc (funcall (property-test classifier) instance)
                class-count))))


; compute information content of examples
(sum #'(lambda (x) (if (= (cdr x) 0) 0
              (* -1
                 (/ (cdr x) size)
                 (log (/ (cdr x) size) 2))))
     class-count))))
```

compute-info-gain computes the information gain of a partition by subtracting the weighted average of the information in its components from the information in the parent set of examples.

```
(defun compute-info-gain (root parts)
  (- (example-frame-information root)
     (sum #'(lambda (x) (* (example-frame-information (cdr x))
                 (/ (example-frame-size (cdr x))
                    (example-frame-size root))))
        parts)))
```

sum implements mathematical summation: it sums the values returned by applying f to all elements of list-of-numbers:

```
(defun sum (f list-of-numbers)
  (apply '+ (mapcar f list-of-numbers)))
```

This completes the implementation of build-tree. The remaining component of the ID3 algorithm is a function, classify, that takes as arguments a decision tree as constructed by build-tree and an object to be classified; it determines the classification of the object by recursively walking the tree. The definition of classify is straightforward: classify halts when it encounters a leaf; otherwise it applies the test from the current node to the instance and uses the result as the key to select a branch in a call to assoc.

```
(defun classify (instance tree)
  (if (leaf-p tree)
      (leaf-value tree)
      (classify instance
          (cdr (assoc (funcall (decision-tree-test tree) instance)
                (decision-tree-branches tree))))))
```

14.5.5   Learning Classifications Using build-tree

Using the object definitions of Section 14.5.2, we can execute build-tree on the credit example of Table 12.1. We bind **tests** to a list of property definitions for history, debt, collateral, and income. **classifier** tests the risk of an instance. Using these definitions, along with the definition of **examples** from Section 14.5.2, we bind **credit-examples** to an instance of **example-frame**.

```
(setq tests
    (list
      (make-property
       :name 'history
       :test #'history
       :values '(good bad unknown))
      (make-property
       :name 'debt
       :test #'debt
       :values '(high low))
      (make-property
       :name 'collateral
       :test #'collatoral
       :values '(none adequate))
      (make property
       :name 'incomc
       :test #'income
       :values '(0-to-15k 15k-to-35k over -35k))))

(setq classifier
    (make-property
     :name 'risk
     :test #'risk
     :values '(high moderate low)))

(setq credit-examples
    (make-example-frame
     :instances examples
     :properties tests
     :classifier classifier
     :size (list-length examples)
     :information (compute-information examples class)))
```

Using these definitions, we may induce decision trees and use them to classify instances according to their credit risk:

```
> (setq credit-tree (build-tree credit-examples))
#S(decision-tree
        :test-name income
        :test #<Compiled-function income #x3525CE>
```

```
:branches
  ((0-to-15k . #S(leaf :value high))
   (15k-to-35k .
      #S(decision-tree
              :test-name history
              :test #<Compiled-function history #x3514D6>
              :branches
  ((good . #S(leaf :value moderate))
   (bad . #S(leaf :value high))
   (unknown .
      #S(decision-tree
              :test-name debt
              :test #<Compiled-function debt #x351A7E>
              :branches
                ((high . #S(leaf :value high))
                 (low . #S(leaf :value moderate)))))))))
   (over-35k .
      #S(decision-tree :test-name history
                 :test #<Compiled-function history #x3514D6>
                 :branches
                   ((good. #S(leaf :value low))
                    (bad . #S(leaf :value moderate))
                    (unknown . #S(leaf :value low)))))))
> (classify '((history . good) (debt . low) (collateral . none) (income . 15k-to-35k))
       credit-tree)
moderate
```

14.5.6 The Object-Oriented Approach to Program Structure

Our implementation of ID3 illustrates a number of techniques that are commonly associated with *object-oriented programming*. Though we often think of object-oriented programming in association with so-called *object-oriented languages,* the phrase more aptly describes a language-independent design aesthetic, a set of criteria for correct, understandable, and maintainable programs. In our implementation of ID3, we attempted to meet these criteria using structures, higher-order functions, association lists, and other LISP techniques. Aspects of this style include:

1. *Information hiding.* A good program should be divided into separate modules that interact in explicitly defined ways. Structures give us another tool for modularizing our code.

2. *The separation of implementation and behavior.* One of the specific dimensions along which we hide information is the separation of what a component does from the way in which it does it. In our implementation of ID3, we require a set of training instances in which properties are functions applied to objects. As long as a property returns the value of an object, we do not care how it is implemented.

3. *The creation of structured data types.* Most programs manipulate data items that go together semantically, even though they are of different syntactic types. Our

employee record example of Section 14.5.2 was a good example of this. One of the reasons we rejected the list representation of employee records was that we find it more satisfying if the elements of a list are all of the same type. As is often the case in programming, aesthetic judgments promote sound programming methodologies. If we let lists be heterogeneous jumbles of data, then we lose a great deal of coherence along with the benefits of type checking. By using **defstruct** to integrate syntactically distinct but semantically linked data items, we overcome these problems.

4. *Integration of process and data.* As programmers, we have grown up with a strong distinction between programs and data. However, though this distinction seems necessary for traditional hardware, it is quite arbitrary to the design of programming languages. In creating structures, our goal is to create aggregates of semantically related data items. Why shouldn't we also include relevant functions in our object definitions? As our **property** type illustrated, combining functions and data in a single structure can greatly improve the organization of our code.

5. *Code reuse and the building block approach to programming.* One of the benefits of information hiding and a modular programming style is that we may often use our modules in different contexts. A good example of this in ID3 was the extensive use we made of association lists to handle data items of different types; as long as the task requires a key-datum type of data structure, association lists don't care about the types of the items. The ability to use such a powerful tool in a flexible fashion greatly simplified our implementation. Thus, by simplifying the reuse of code, we can think of programming as the combination of much higher-level, powerful components.

As we mentioned earlier, these techniques are simply good programming style. Recently, object-oriented design has integrated them into a unified methodology based on the definition of structured modules of data and program code called *objects.* Objects, along with their behaviors and organization into classes, are supported directly in object-oriented programming languages. We discuss the benefits of this approach, along with its natural fit with the LISP language, in Chapter 15.

14.6 Epilogue and References

In discussing LISP programming techniques for AI, we have followed LISP's historical development. Chapter 7 introduced LISP as a purely functional language. That is, the behavior of a function was determined solely by the values of its input parameters. As the discussion continued, we introduced **setq** and property lists, both of which allow the definition of functions with side effects.

Both PROLOG and LISP are based on formal mathematical models of computation: PROLOG on logic and theorem proving, LISP on the theory of recursive functions. This sets these languages apart from more traditional languages whose architecture is just a refinement of the architecture of the underlying computing hardware. By deriving their syntax and semantics from mathematical notations, LISP and PROLOG inherit both expressive power and clarity.

Although PROLOG, the newer of the two languages, has remained close to its theoretical roots, LISP has been extended until it is no longer a purely functional programming language. LISP is, above all, a practical programming language that has grown to support the full range of modern techniques. These include functional programming, data abstraction, stream processing, and object-oriented programming.

For example, in spite of the many advantages of functional programming, some problems are best conceptualized in terms of objects that have a state that changes over time. Simulation problems are typical of this kind of problem. Imagine trying to simulate the behavior of a steam heating system for a large building: the natural way to think of this is as a system of objects (rooms, thermostats, boilers, steam pipes, etc.) that interact to change the temperature and behavior of each other over time. This requires the ability to define objects that have a state that may be modified, a very different idea from functional programming. Chapter 15 discusses object-oriented programming as another programming model and presents a LISP implementation of object-oriented programming.

The strength of LISP, then, is that it has built up a range of modern programming techniques as extensions of its core model of functional programming. This, combined with the power of lists to create a variety of symbolic data structures, forms the basis of modern LISP programming. We hope these chapters have helped to illustrate that style.

In designing the algorithms of this chapter, we have been influenced by Abelson and Sussman's book *The Structure and Interpretation of Computer Programs* (1985). Steele (1990) is an essential guide to using Common LISP.

14.7 Exercises

1. Rewrite print-solutions in the logic programming interpreter so that it prints the first solution and waits for a user response (such as a carriage return) before printing the second solution.

2. Modify the logic programming interpreter to handle or and not. Disjunctive expressions should succeed if at least one of the disjuncts succeeds; in processing a disjunctive expression, the interpreter should return the union of all the solutions returned by the disjuncts.

    Negation is more difficult, since a negated goal can succeed only if the goal fails. Thus, it is not possible to return any variable bindings for a negated goal. This is a result of the closed world assumption and the negation as failure rules described in Chapter 13.

3. Implement the general map and filter functions, map-stream and filter-stream, described in Section 14.2.

4. Rewrite the solution to the first n odd Fibonacci numbers problem so that it uses the general stream filter, filter-stream, instead of filter-odds. Modify this to return the first n even Fibonacci numbers and to return the squares of the first n Fibonacci numbers.

5. Expand the logic programming interpreter to include LISP write statements. This will allow rules to print messages directly to the user. Hint: modify solve first to examine if a goal is a write statement. If it is, evaluate the write and return a stream containing the initial substitution set.

6. Expand the logic programming language to include arithmetic comparisons, =, <, and >. Hint:

as in Exercise 5, modify solve to detect these comparisons before calling infer. If an expression is a comparison, replace any variables with their values and evaluate it. If it returns nil, solve should return the empty stream; if it returns non-nil, solve should return a stream containing the initial substitution set. Assume that the expressions do not contain unbound variables.

For a more challenging exercise, define = so that it will function like the PROLOG is operator and assign a value to an unbound variable and simply do an equality test if all elements are bound.

7. Use the logic programming interpreter with arithmetic (Exercise 6) to solve the financial advisor problem of Chapter 2.

8. Select a problem such as automotive diagnosis or classifying different species of animals and solve it using lisp-shell.

9. Expand the expert system shell of Section 14.3 to allow the user responses other than y or n. For example, we may want the user to be able to provide bindings for a goal. This may be done by changing ask-for and the related functions to let the user also enter a pattern, which is matched against the goal. If the match succeeds, ask for a certainty factor.

10. Extend lisp-shell to include not. For an example of how to treat negation using uncertain reasoning, refer to Chapter 8 or the PROLOG-based expert system shell in Chapter 13.

11. Write an ATN parser for the subset of English discussed in Chapter 10.

12. Both logic-shell and lisp-shell implemented backward chaining on rules. Implement a forward-chaining production system engine using Common LISP. This should be simpler than the interpreters presented in this chapter, because each iteration will simply add a new fact to working memory. Thus the shell will not need to handle rule chaining or backtracking explicitly. In implementing the shell, be sure to include some conflict resolution strategies such as the *recency* rule (Chapter 5) to prevent the production system from looping on the same rule.

13. A major source of inefficiency in both lisp-shell and the logic programming interpreter is the use of linear search of the knowledge base to find facts or rule conclusions that match a goal. We may improve efficiency greatly by indexing the knowledge base using a *hash table*. Common LISP provides built-in hash-table functions for efficiently accessing components of a data base. Using these functions, modify the definition of infer to retrieve matching rules or facts by hashing on a goal. Use the Common LISP macro time to test the effect of the change.

14. The version of ID3 developed in this chapter depended upon a previously defined set of objects using rather complex data structures. From the user's point of view, a table-based input format may be preferable.

    a. Write a front end to the build-tree functions that takes tabular input and creates the required data structures.
    b. Write an interactive front end to classify. This front end should ask the user questions about properties. Hint: add a slot for a question to the definition of the property structure.

15. Pick a domain and test ID3's performance. Do this by generating a set of examples, training ID3 on a subset of the examples, and evaluating ID3's performance on the rest.

16. Build a frame-based representation language by extending the ideas in Section 14.4.1. Modify the ATN parser of Exercise 11 so that it returns a representation of the sentence's meaning in this language. For an example of a PROLOG program that does this, see Section 13.3.2.

OBJECTS, MESSAGES, AND HYBRID EXPERT SYSTEM DESIGN

The Medium is the Message . . .

—MARSHALL MCLUHAN

No ideas but in things.

—WILLIAM CARLOS WILLIAMS

15.0   Introduction

The techniques of object-oriented software development evolved from several different strains of computer science. Software engineering, programming language design, and artificial intelligence have all contributed to the methodologies of information hiding, structured representation, class inheritance, and data typing that constitute the object-oriented paradigm. A goal of these methodologies is to make programming efficient, reliable, and more intuitive by allowing programmers to use the same terminology in writing programs that they use in thinking about the problem domain. Another benefit of object-oriented programming is in code reuse and maintainability. By organizing a program into distinct modules with explicitly defined interfaces, we simplify the modification and construction of programs by reusing applicable modules.

Structured representation languages provide a tool for building *computational* objects that exhibit the structure and behavior of their counterparts in the problem domain. Using structures of slots and values, such as frames, we may represent different aspects of complex domain objects. Values bound to slots describe the state of an object; attached procedures, referred to as *methods* or *demons*, model their behavior and interactions. Procedural attachment adds considerable expressive power to these formalisms, allowing inherently procedural descriptions to be expressed in an appropriate language and integrated into the framework of a declarative representation.

We model relationships in the domain as relations between computational objects. Perhaps the most important relationships in an object-oriented program are class membership and the hierarchical organization of classes. Objects are organized into a hierarchy of classes, allowing the inheritance of properties and procedures. Not only are such taxonomies a common and intuitive tool for representing human information, but also class hierarchies add a dimension of abstraction.

Interactions between domain objects, such as causality, correspond to messages between computational objects. Message passing allows objects to interact in explicitly defined ways, preserving the benefits of information hiding in a large and complex program.

In an *object-oriented* language, everything is defined as an object or system of interacting objects. The diversity supported by this approach allows the programmer to select the appropriate tool for each situation: a rule base for heuristic or knowledge-oriented descriptions, a procedural language for algorithms.

In Section 15.1 we present objects, messages, and inheritance as a general programming technique and then as a vehicle for knowledge base construction. In Section 15.2 we build a simple object-oriented programming language as a meta-interpreter in LISP and use it to simulate a heater/room/thermostat system; Section 15.3 examines CLOS, the Common LISP Object System, an object-oriented extension to LISP. Section 15.4 considers the relationship of the object-oriented model to the logic-based paradigm and discusses PROLOG implementations of objects. Finally, in Section 15.5 we discuss both the role of object-oriented programming in knowledge engineering and the architecture of hybrid expert system environments.

15.1   Object-Oriented Knowledge Representation

15.1.1   Objects and Abstraction

The basis of object-oriented languages is the ability to define computational objects of complex internal structure, concealing the particulars of that structure from the rest of the program. *Information hiding* is an important goal of all forms of abstraction, allowing us to limit the interactions of system modules and separate the specifics of a module's implementation from its behavior. Procedures, packages, abstract data types, and other approaches to modularity all support some form of information hiding.

Unlike traditional approaches to program modularity, such as procedures or abstract data types, computational objects encapsulate both state and behavior. Objects bind procedures to the object itself, combining procedures with their associated data structures, rather than implementing them apart from the data they manipulate. These attached procedures, called *methods*, are invoked through messages sent to the object by the user or by other objects. We may think of methods as analogous to functions, with messages corresponding to the function call. On receiving a message, an object selects the method indicated by the message, executes it, and responds accordingly.

It is the active nature of objects that distinguishes them from other forms of structured representation. In an object-oriented language, objects execute their methods in response to a received message. Object-oriented programming thus reconsiders the traditional separation of data and procedure, providing another means of organizing programs and further emphasizing the view of computational objects as corresponding to objects in the world. One benefit of this view is an added dimension of abstraction. Because procedures are invoked by sending a message to an object, we have effectively separated the behavior and the implementation of both data structure and function. As long as an object responds appropriately to messages, we may change its implementation freely. This greatly simplifies program maintenance and modification.

The other major feature of object-oriented programming languages is the support of classes and inheritance. In a pure object-oriented system, all objects representing individuals, or instances, belong to classes. Classes are further organized into a hierarchy of classes and subclasses. Instances of a class inherit properties from their parent classes. This allows us to define the slot names (also called *instance variables*), values, and methods for an entire class of objects in a single definition. The class defines a common pattern for representing all of its instances. Instance objects bind slots to all the particular information, such as size and location, that distinguishes individuals from each other. The behavior of members of a class, or the set of all messages to which the class responds, is called the *protocol* of the class.

The remainder of this section illustrates these ideas through the example of an object-oriented graphics program. Although all graphics operations ultimately reduce to operations on pixel arrays, the object-oriented approach lets us organize the program in terms of more intuitive, higher-level conceptual objects, such as windows, icons, and pens. This example clearly shows the isomorphism between the components of an object-oriented program and the objects it is describing.

We represent objects in a notation similar to that used in Section 9.4 to describe frames. We define methods in pseudocode. We have assumed that our pseudocode language is augmented with the procedures message, make-object, and make-instance. message sends a message to an object, taking as arguments the name of the object, a message name, and any parameters to the message. make-object and make-instance define new classes and instances, respectively.

Suppose we wish to provide users with the ability to create and manipulate square boxes on the display screen. Figure 15.1 shows a definition of the class box. Instance variables for this class are location (the box location), tilt, size, color, and scribe. Instances of the class bind these variables to specific values. location is bound to the coordinates of the upper left-hand corner, size is the length of each side (the box is square), tilt gives the rotation (from the horizontal) of the box, and color is the color of the box. scribe is an instance of the class pens; pens are objects that allow us to draw lines on the screen. Through these variables, the class object provides a template for defining instances. Instance methods are procedures, attached to the class name, describing the behavior of instances when they receive appropriate messages. The object also includes class methods, which we describe shortly.

Suppose we have defined box1 as an instance of type box with the following instance variables: location = (200, 200); tilt = 0; size = 20; color = black. scribe is bound to an instance of class pen. box1 inherits methods from the box class. We have assumed that the class pen is already defined, with the methods move, up, down, forward, and rotate. set-value is a method that allows an object to change the value of one of its instance

```
┌─────────────────────────────────────────────────────┐
│ Class name: box                                     │
├─────────────────────────────────────────────────────┤
│ Superclass: display object                          │
├─────────────────────────────────────────────────────┤
│ Instance Variables                                  │
├─────────────────────────────────────────────────────┤
│   location:                                         │
│   tilt:                                             │
│   size:                                             │
│   color:                                            │
│   scribe:                                           │
├─────────────────────────────────────────────────────┤
│ Instance Methods                                    │
├─────────────────────────────────────────────────────┤
│   draw() : begin                                    │
│           message(scribe, up);                      │
│           message(scribe, move, location);          │
│           message(scribe, rotate, tilt);            │
│           message(scribe, down);                    │
│           for i := 1 to 4 do begin                  │
│               message(scribe, forward, size);       │
│               message(scribe, rotate, 90);          │
│             end                                     │
│         end.                                        │
├─────────────────────────────────────────────────────┤
│   show(): begin                                     │
│           message(scribe, set-value, ink, color);   │
│           message(self, draw);                      │
│         end.                                        │
├─────────────────────────────────────────────────────┤
│   erase(): begin                                    │
│           message(scribe, set-value, ink, background);│
│           message(self, draw);                      │
│         end.                                        │
├─────────────────────────────────────────────────────┤
│   grow(amount): begin                               │
│           message(self, erase);                     │
│           message(self, set-value, size, size*amount);│
│           message(self, show);                      │
│         end.                                        │
├─────────────────────────────────────────────────────┤
│ Class Methods                                       │
├─────────────────────────────────────────────────────┤
│         . . .                                       │
└─────────────────────────────────────────────────────┘
```

Figure 15.1 Definition of a **box** object.

variables. Both pen and box use the set-value method and inherit it from a common ancestor in the inheritance hierarchy (see Fig. 15.3).

To have box1 display itself on the screen, we send it the message:

message(box1, show)

On receiving this message, box1 retrieves the show method from the class definition and executes it using its own instance variables. All references to location in the method are interpreted as referring to the location of box1. This dynamic binding of variables in methods is important to the proper behavior of method inheritance. It lets us define methods generally in a class and guarantees that they will behave properly when applied to instances.

show first sends box1's scribe a message to set its color to ink. It then sends self a draw message. self is a special variable that is dynamically bound to the current instance, in this case, box1. The self variable gives us a general way of allowing an instance to refer to itself in a method.

box1 then inherits the draw method from its class. draw first sends scribe a message to pick itself up (so no mark will be made) and then sends it a message to move to location (200, 200). (We assume a screen or drawing surface representing the first quadrant of an X, Y coordinate system, X > 0 and Y > 0.) The pen then turns to 0-degree tilt, puts the drawing pen down to the surface, and repeats the process of going forward 20 units and turning 90 degrees four times. This displays box1 at the desired location.

Note that program execution is a sequence of messages sent between objects. This enables a strong form of information hiding that is central to object-oriented languages: we may understand the procedures for drawing lines on the screen purely in terms of the functionality of pen. Separating the behavior and the implementation of objects provides a number of benefits for code reuse and maintainability. Building a new program using existing classes is simplified by the fact that we do not need to understand the details of an object's implementation in order to use it. If we should later need to change the implementation of an object such as pen, perhaps to accommodate different hardware, we may do so more easily. As long as we change the implementation but not the behavior of pens, none of the methods using them will be affected.

Now, consider the method grow. The message

message(box1, grow, 30)

causes box1 to grow by 30 units. Note that grow takes a parameter to describe how an existing box should increase its size. In general, messages consist of a destination, a method name, and any required parameters. grow first erases itself, then increases its size, and finally shows itself.

draw, show, erase, and grow are instance methods; they are inherited and used by instances, as we have just shown. Classes also include *class methods*. Class methods are not inherited by instances, but rather define the functionality of the class itself. For example, suppose we would like to define a method for creating new instances at a selected location with default values for tilt, size, and color. This method should not be inherited by instances; it properly belongs to the class itself. Therefore, we define it as a class method, which can be passed from a class to a subclass but not to an instance. Figure 15.2 shows this method, new-box-at; the method creates an instance of pen for the new box and then creates an instance of box with default values for its instance variables. make-instance takes as arguments an instance name, a class, and the values for the instance variables.

For example:

message(box, new-box-at, box2, (300, 300))

causes the box class to construct a new box, box2, drawn in black, at location = (300, 300) with a tilt of 0 degrees and with a size of 100 units. box2, like box1, inherits all the functionality of the box class.

The instance/class hierarchy defined above is part of a much larger tree structure that defines the entire software system. Figure 15.3 illustrates a portion of this hierarchy, including the class box, the class window, and the class pen. The box class is itself a subclass of the class called displayObject.

Class name: box
Superclass: display object
Instance Variables
. . .
Instance Methods
. . .
Class Methods

new-box-at(name, loc):
   begin
      make-instance(new-pen, pen)
      make-instance(name, box, loc, 0,100, black, new-pen);
   end.

Figure 15.2   box object showing **Class Method.**

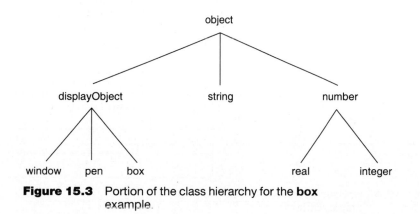

Figure 15.3   Portion of the class hierarchy for the **box** example.

The figure also shows the classes string and number as branches of the same hierarchy. This portion of the tree has object as its root. This is the most general class in the hierarchy and forms the root of the entire inheritance tree. set-value, because it is potentially used by all instances in the system, would be defined at the root of the hierarchy.

The superclass of box is displayObject. This class defines the functionality common to all of its subclasses, including the instance variables common to all displayed objects. We should, for example, have defined the location instance variable at this level of the hierarchy rather than in the class box, because it is used to indicate the location of any display item. General instance methods should also be attached to this more general class; for example, both show and erase could actually be defined at the displayObject level. These procedures are written in such a fashion that they will function correctly for any subclass of displayObject. Only the definition of draw must be unique to the subclass. This ensures that behaviors that are intuitively seen as common across several classes will indeed have common definitions. It also simplifies extension of the system. If we later want to define a display object, ellipse, we do not need to define these methods. We only need to implement an appropriate definition of draw and make ellipse a subclass of display-

Class name: displayObject
Superclass: object
Instance Variables
location: . . .
Instance Methods

move(new-location): begin
   message(self, erase);
   message(self, set-value, location, new-location);
   message(self, show, black);
end.
 	
show(): begin
   message(scribe, set-value, ink, color);
   message(self, draw);
end.
 	
erase(): begin
   message(scribe, set-value, ink, background);
   message(self, draw);
end.

Class Methods
. . .

Class name: box
Superclass: displayObject
Instance Variables
tilt: size: color: scribe:
Instance Methods

draw() : begin
   message(scribe, up);
   message(scribe move, location);
   message(scribe rotate, tilt);
   message(scribe down);
   for i := 1 to 4 do begin
     message(scribe forward, size);
     message(scribe rotate, 90);
   end
end.

grow(amount): begin
   message(self, erase);
   message(self, set-value, size, size*amount);
   message(self, show);
end.

Class Methods
. . .

Figure 15.4   Revised definitions of **box** and **displayObject**.

Object; it will inherit the other required methods. Figure 15.4 shows the revised displayObject and box objects.

These definitions also include a general method for moving display objects. The command:

message(box1, move, (400, 200))

tells box1 to move to a new location.

When box1 receives the message, it attempts to inherit the move method from its class. Because there is no instance method to handle move in the box definition, the inheritance algorithm examines the superclass, displayObject. displayObject has an instance method called move that erases the present instance and assigns the new location of (400, 200) to the variable location. Finally, move instructs the instance to show itself at the new location. When the move method is inherited, it executes in the environment defined by the instance. This flexibility for a method to be used on instances of different classes within the inheritance hierarchy, and to bind its constraining parameters at the time of execution, is referred to as *polymorphism*. This will provide appropriate bindings for all instance variables and methods. For example, the definition of draw used by show and erase would vary across subclasses of displayObject.

This example illustrates *tree* inheritance: every instance belongs to a single class; each class is a descendant of a single, more general class that defines the common properties of all its children. Any two classes have a single lowest common superclass above them. Thus, properties that are shared by several classes may be defined *once* in a parent class, ensuring consistency of the method. The root of the hierarchy is the most general class, called object, which defines the functionality common to the entire structure. Smalltalk is an example of a language with tree inheritance.

Many object-oriented languages, including CLOS and the language implemented in Section 15.2, allow objects to have more than one parent class; this is called *multiple inheritance*. The resulting structure is not a tree but a *directed acyclic graph,* or *DAG*. This is also known as the *tangled hierarchy* model. In realistic domains, objects are often thought of as belonging to several classes, inheriting properties from each. A group of people, for instance, can belong to either the male or female class, to the under-30 or 30-or-older class, and to other classes based on hometown, religion, income—to any appropriate class abstraction. Individuals may belong to many of these superclasses at once, inheriting properties (possibly incompatible; see Section 9.5) from each. Although this greatly complicates inheritance, it adds considerable expressive power to the language.

To demonstrate multiple inheritance, we add the label class to the displayObject example. label, which is a specialization of a string class, lets us label any of the objects created under displayObject in Figure 15.3. A label includes instance variables point for character size, font for a particular font, text, and label-location. However, only label-location must be directly attached to the label object; text, point, and font are inherited from the string superclass. The ability to draw and erase labels would also be inherited from string.

We can create new classes inheriting properties from both label and subclasses of displayObject. An example of this class would be the labeledBox of Figure 15.5. An instance of this class would be a box with some label at a particular location. labeledBox

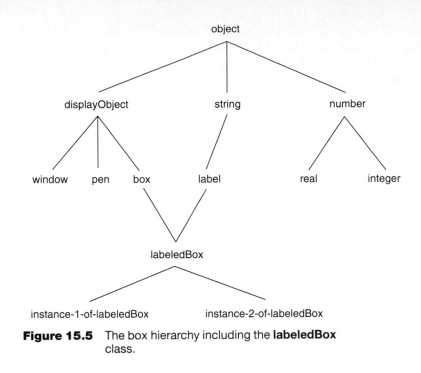

Figure 15.5 The box hierarchy including the **labeledBox** class.

inherits its size, shape, and scribe from box and its font, point, text, and label-location from label. A portion of the tangled hierarchy including these classes is presented in Figure 15.5.

15.1.2   Benefits of Object-Oriented Programming

There are numerous benefits of this approach to organizing software. By attaching the definition of an operator to an object (a class of operands), operators may be strongly typed without requiring global type checking. The type of the operand is implicitly defined by the object receiving the message. This approach to typing gives the application both the expressive power and integrity of typed languages while simplifying the addition of new types and operations.

Object-oriented programming is a powerful tool for creating software abstractions. Class objects organize the world into a hierarchy, defining instance variables and methods at the highest appropriate level of abstraction. These are inherited by *all* subclasses unless overridden by a definition lower in the hierarchy. This gives us abstraction of data types and control mechanisms: subclasses allow the behavior of classes to be modified for particular instances, where new variables and methods correctly specify the individuating differences. The properties that are common across all subclasses are inherited from the parent.

An issue that is closely related to strong typing and modularity in the object-message model is the *overloading of operators*. Many operators in traditional typed languages are overloaded, meaning that they accept operands of several different types. Most arithmetic operators, for example, are overloaded, applying to integers and floating point numbers alike. However, object-oriented languages make it easy for the programmer to overload operators. For example, assume that + is defined in the usual fashion for real and integer numbers and that a programmer would like to extend its meaning to include string concatenation. Because real numbers are an object class (with instances pi, e, etc.) and integers are another object class (with instances 1, 2, . . .), the appropriate definition of + is attached to each class. To overload the operator + to include strings, we simply attach the desired definition to the **string** class where all **string** instances may inherit it. This extends the operator's functionality:

Real number addition:

message(1.3, +, 1.5) returns 2.8.

Integer addition:

message(2, +, 3) returns 5.

String catenation:

message(COOK, +, BOOK) returns COOKBOOK.

All three messages use +, but in each instance + is interpreted differently, according to the method of the object it is sent to. This allows the programmer to use the operator without rewriting centralized global definitions, as would be the case with traditional languages. Overloading allows the creation of *generic operations* such as **erase** that have meaning for any object in the system, even though each class requires its own actual implementation of the method.

These techniques support reuse. In adding ellipses to our graphics example, we overloaded the **draw** operator. This allowed us to extend existing methods for showing, erasing, and moving objects to ellipses.

Object-oriented programming supports the abstraction of both data and procedures, simplifies the creation of procedures used by many classes of objects, allows the overloading of operators to create generic procedures, and makes it possible to organize code in a way that reflects the natural organization of the problem. In spite of its many benefits, there are limitations to this approach that should be kept in mind. First, there is no guarantee that different designers would build structures the same way to represent a given situation; the ultimate responsibility for organizing code in a clear fashion lies with the software designer. Second, much work still needs to be done in defining the semantics of object-oriented languages themselves. As discussed in Section 9.5, techniques such as inheritance and its use in defining and overriding default values can introduce severe anomalies into a program or knowledge base.

15.1.3   Object-Oriented Knowledge Bases

The properties of object-oriented programming that make it a natural way to organize large and complex software implementations are equally applicable in the design of knowledge bases. In addition to the benefits of class inheritance for representing taxonomic knowl edge, the message-passing aspect of object-oriented systems simplifies the representation of interacting components.

As a simple example, consider the task of modeling the behavior of a steam heater for a small office building. We may naturally view this problem in terms of interacting components. For example:

Each office has a thermostat that turns the heat in that office on and off; this functions independently of the thermostats in other offices.

The boiler for the heating plant turns itself on and off in response to the heat demands made by the offices.

When the demand on the boiler increases, there may be a time lag while more steam is generated.

Different offices place different demands on the system; for example, corner offices with large windows lose heat faster than inner offices. Inner offices may even gain heat from their neighbors.

The amount of steam that the system may route to a single office is affected by the total demand on the system.

These points are only a few of those that must be taken into account in modeling the behavior of such a system; the possible interactions are extremely complex. An object-oriented representation allows the programmer to focus on describing one class of objects at a time. We would represent thermostats, for example, by the temperature at which they call for heat, along with the speed with which they respond to changes in temperature.

The steam plant could be characterized in terms of the maximum amount of heat it can produce, the amount of fuel used as a function of heat produced, the amount of time it takes to respond to increased heat demand, and the rate at which it consumes water.

A room could be described in terms of its volume, the heat loss through its walls and windows, the heat gain from neighboring rooms, and the rate at which the radiator adds heat to the room.

The knowledge base is built up of class objects such as room and thermostat, which define the properties of the class, and instances such as room-322 and thermostat-211, which model individuals.

The interactions between components are described by messages between instances. For example, a change in room temperature would cause a message to be sent to an instance of the class thermostat. If this new temperature is low enough, the thermostat would switch after an appropriate delay. This would cause a message to be sent to the steam plant requesting more heat. This would cause the steam plant to consume more oil, or, if the plant is already operating at maximum capacity, to route some heat away from other rooms to respond to the new demand. This would cause other thermostats to trip, and so on.

Using this simulation, we can test the ability of the system to respond to external changes in temperature, measure the effect of heat loss, or determine whether the projected heating is adequate. We could use this simulation in a diagnostic program to verify that a hypothesized fault could indeed produce a particular set of symptoms. For example, if we have reason to believe that a heating problem is caused by a blocked steam pipe, we could introduce such a fault into the simulation and see whether it produces the observed symptoms. As we will discuss in Section 15.4, a rule base could send messages to the object-oriented simulation to perform these tests.

The significant thing about this example is the way in which an object-oriented approach allows knowledge engineers to deal with the complexity of the simulation. It enables them to build the model a piece at a time, focusing only on the behaviors of simple classes of objects. The full complexity of the system behavior emerges when we execute the model.

15.2 LISP and Object-Oriented Programming

There are a number of similarities between functional and object-oriented programming: function invocations, for example, may be viewed as a form of message passing, with a message (parameters) being passed to an object (function), which replies (returns a result). Both programming models cleanly exploit the *information-hiding* potential found in the ability to create computational entities (functions or objects) that may be treated in terms of their behavior rather than their internal structure. These similarities, along with the ease of writing meta-interpreters and manipulating code as data, make LISP a natural tool for implementing object-oriented programming.

Object-oriented programming differs from pure functional programming, however, in a number of important ways. Perhaps the most fundamental of these differences is that objects, unlike functions, have an internal state that persists and changes across time. Another important feature found in most object-oriented programming languages is the inheritance of variables and methods through class hierarchies.

In this section we build a small object-oriented language in LISP and demonstrate its use in simulating the behavior of a room, thermostat, and heater. We call the language OOPS, for Object-Oriented Programming System. Although much simpler than commercial object languages, OOPS contains mechanisms for object definition, method attachment, message passing, and inheritance. With OOPS we both explore the relationship between object-oriented and functional programming and illustrate some of the practical considerations in implementing an object-oriented language.

15.2.1 OOPS: A Simple Object-Oriented Programming Language

We now define three functions to do object-oriented programming in OOPS: def-object, def-method, and message. These functions allow the user to create and interact with objects in a hierarchy. For simplicity, we do not support a distinction between classes and instances. This extension is left as an exercise.

def-object is used to define a new object. It takes three arguments: the name of the new object, the name of its parent or a list of parents, and a list of instance variable/value pairs. For example, the rectangle object in a plane geometry knowledge base might be defined by the call:

```
(def-object 'rectangle 'object
    '((numsides 4) (description "four-sided figure, all angles equal 90°.")))
```

This defines an object, rectangle, that is a child of object. object is the root of the hierarchy and implements much of the functionality of the system in its methods. The third parameter attaches two instance variables, numsides and description, to the rectangle object; the initial values of these variables are defined by the second components of the pairs, 4, and the string that describes rectangles. def-object evaluates these initial values and binds them to their variables.

Other objects in a geometry knowledge base might include the class of squares, as well as instances of this class. Examples of these definitions include:

```
(def-object 'rectangle-1 'rectangle '((length 8) (width 4)))
```

```
(def-object 'square 'rectangle '((description "rectangle whose sides are equal")))
```

```
(def-object 'square-1 'square '((side 10)))
```

Whereas def-object creates objects in the inheritance hierarchy, def-method is used to bind methods to those objects. def-method takes three arguments: the name of the object, the name of the method, and the definition of the method. Generally, we represent methods as lambda expressions, although the name of a defined function may also be used. For example, a method for computing area is attached to the rectangle object by:

```
(def-method 'rectangle 'area '(lambda () (* length width)))
```

When the area method is evaluated, length and width will be bound to the values of a particular object's instance variables.

Other classes of objects will also require area methods. Although each area method performs the same function, each class of objects requires a different definition of how area is computed. For example, the class of squares would have an area method defined by:

```
(def-method 'square 'area '(lambda () (expt side 2)))
```

The above definitions create the hierarchy illustrated in Figure 15.6. rectangle-1 is a child of the rectangle object with width and length of 4 and 8 units, respectively; it inherits any variables and methods attached to its ancestors rectangle and object. square is a specialization of rectangle and will inherit any variables attached to rectangle and object, except the method area and the instance variable description, which have been redefined for squares.

This example also illustrates some of the limitations of this simple version of OOPS. Because it does not distinguish between classes and instances, we may not distinguish between class methods and instance methods. Furthermore, lacking this distinction, an instance cannot inherit slot names from its class; this prevents classes from functioning as templates for the creation of instances. These features may be added to the interpreter (Exercise 1).

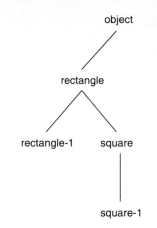

Figure 15.6 An **OOPS** object hierarchy.

Message passing between objects is effected by the function message. message takes two or more arguments: the first is the name of the object receiving the message; the second is the name of the method. Any arguments required by the method are passed as additional parameters. For example, rectangle-1 may be queried for its area by the call:

```
> (message 'rectangle-1 'area)
32
```

The object rectangle-1 will inherit the area method from its parent object. The method is evaluated in an environment in which the free variables, length and width, are bound to the instance variables of the object rectangle-1. Ensuring that such references to either directly attached or inherited instance variables are handled correctly is an important issue in the implementation of object-oriented languages and is discussed in the next section.

The object square-1 may be asked for its area through a similar call. Note that a different method is applied to the computation of the area:

```
> (message 'square-1 'area)
100
```

Much of the functionality of the system is defined in the methods of the root object, object. These are discussed in the next section and include functions for accessing and changing instance variables. Making object the root of any application is necessary to ensure that these methods are inherited throughout the system. One method defined for all objects is show-value, which takes as argument the name of an instance variable and returns its value. In the following message, square-1 is queried for the value of numsides, a variable inherited from the object rectangle:

```
> (message 'square-1 'show-value 'numsides)
4
```

This small example illustrates the behavior of OOPS, the definition of objects and methods, and the inheritance of both methods and instance variables. The next section discusses the implementation of these and other features.

15.2.2 Implementing OOPS in LISP

OOPS represents objects as symbols in the global LISP environment, using property lists to attach methods and instance variables. Each object is defined by three properties: isa, variables, and methods. The isa property names either a single parent object or a list of parents. The variables property is bound to a list of pairs; the first element is the name of an instance variable and the second is its value. The methods property is an association list of method names and lambda definitions.

def-object, which places an object and instance variables in the hierarchy, is straight-forwardly defined as:

```
(defun def-object (obj parent &optional vars)
  (setf (get obj 'isa) parent)
  (setf (get obj 'variables) (evaluate-bindings vars)))
```

evaluate-bindings takes the list of variable-binding pairs provided by the user and evaluates the bindings. This is needed to allow users to specify bindings that are the result of some calculation. It is implemented using mapcar to apply an evaluation function to each element of the variable list. This evaluation is done by a lambda expression that takes as its argument a list of two elements and returns the same list with the second element evaluated:

```
(defun evaluate-bindings (vars)
  (mapcar #'(lambda (x) (list (car x) (eval (cadr x)))) vars))
```

def-method adds a method to an object by updating the association list bound to its methods property. def-method calls replace-method to search the list recursively, replacing any definition of that method that is already present or adding the new method to the end of the list if it was not previously defined. These functions are defined:

```
(defun def-method (obj name definition)
  (setf (get obj 'methods) (replace-method name definition (get obj 'methods))))
```

```
(defun replace-method (name definition list-of-methods)
  (cond ((null list-of-methods) (acons name definition nil))
        ((equal name (caar list-of-methods)) (acons name definition (cdr list-of-methods)))
        (t (cons (car list-of-methods)
                 (replace-method name definition (cdr list-of-methods))))))
```

message is the function that implements message passing between objects. Its definition is complicated by the need to implement inheritance of both methods and instance variables. Method inheritance is done by inherit-method, which searches the inheritance hierarchy in a depth-first fashion. inherit-method is a slightly modified version of the general inheritance algorithm presented in Chapter 14, using get-method rather than the general get to retrieve a method from an object. Their definitions are:

```
(defun inherit-method (object method)
  (cond ((null object) nil)
        ((atom object)
          (or (get-method object method)
              (inherit-method (get object 'isa) method)))
        (t (or (inherit-method (car object) method)
               (inherit-method (cdr object) method)))))

(defun get-method (object name)
  (cdr (assoc name (get object 'methods))))
```

Essentially, message calls inherit-method to retrieve the appropriate method definition; if the method is found, it evaluates it using apply. An initial version of this function is:

```
(defun message (object method &rest method-parameters)
  (let ((meth (inherit-method object method))))
    (cond (meth (apply meth method-parameters))
          (t (print "unknown method") (print method)))))
```

This version of message uses a cond statement to check whether the method is defined for the object. If it is not, an error message is written; otherwise the method is applied to its arguments. Because the method is examined twice, once by the conditional test for its existence and a second time when it is actually applied to its parameters, a let block is used to bind the definition to the symbol meth. This saves the overhead of multiple searches of the inheritance hierarchy.

There is, however, a serious flaw in this definition. Recall, for example, the definition of the area method for rectangles presented in Section 15.2.

```
(def-method 'rectangle 'area '(lambda () (* length width)))
```

When an area message is sent to rectangle-1 (an instance of rectangle), the body of the method (the lambda expression) is inherited from the rectangle object and evaluated. It is intended that the free variables length and width refer to the so-named instance variables of rectangle-1. If, however, this message is evaluated by the version of message defined above, apply will bind all free variables in the *global LISP environment*, rather than searching the inheritance lattice for their values.

A straightforward way to allow a method to access the instance variables of the recipient object is to define message so that free variables in a method are given bindings as instance variables in the inheritance hierarchy if such bindings exist. Free variables should be given their bindings in the global environment only if they are not inherited as instance variables.

At first glance, an obvious way to do this is to construct a list of all inherited variables and their values by walking the inheritance hierarchy and retrieving all variable-binding pairs inherited by the object. We can use this as the list of variable-value pairs in a let block and evaluate the apply function within this environment. This will not work in Common LISP, however, because the language is *lexically scoped*. That is, references to LISP symbols are determined at compile time based on interpretation of the program text. In order to define local variables in a let block, these variables and the s-expressions that compute their values must be present explicitly in the text of the program. The variable list of a let block may not be computed as the program is run.

Instead, we must dynamically compute such a local environment. The bindings of instance variables cannot in principle be known from the program text (i.e., at compile time) because program execution may result in messages that add, delete, or change these variables. Interestingly, before Common LISP was developed, most dialects of LISP were dynamically scoped, which meant variable bindings were not computed until the program was run. The let block approach to this problem will work in FRANZ LISP and other dynamically scoped dialects of the language.

Fortunately, Common LISP provides a form that solves this problem. progv is a Common LISP function that defines a block containing local variables but, unlike let, allows these variables to be determined at run time. progv takes as arguments a list of symbols, a list of their corresponding values, and a sequence of LISP forms. These forms are evaluated in an environment that binds free variables whose names are in the list of symbols to the corresponding values in the list of values. This provides a means of implementing the needed scoping of free variables in the message function.

We modify the above definition of message so that before evaluating the method, it calls build-env to construct the list of variable-binding pairs. This list is bound to the local variable env. It then computes separate lists of variables and values for the progv block. In addition, it defines a special local variable, self, that refers to the recipient object; this allows a method to specify that the recipient object send itself a message. The final version of message appears below:

```
(defun message (object method &rest method-parameters)
  (let ((meth (inherit-method object method)) env)
    (cond (meth (setq env (build-env object))
                (progv (cons 'self (mapcar 'car env))
                       (cons object (mapcar 'cadr env))
                  (apply meth method-parameters))
          (t (print "unknown method")
             (print method)))))))
```

build-env constructs the environment in a fairly straightforward tree walk. The only tricky part is making sure that multiple definitions of an instance variable are treated correctly. If an instance variable is defined in more than one place in the hierarchy, the value inherited should be the first encountered in a left-to-right, depth-first search. build-env does not check for such multiple definitions, as it would be inefficient to do so. Instead, it places all variables in the hierarchy in its list in such a fashion that the desired occurrence of the instance variable is the *last* one in the list. progv is defined so that if there are multiple instances of symbol in its list, only the last one will be visible to the enclosed forms. Thus, build-env constructs the list of variable-binding pairs in a way that guarantees that the "leftmost closest" occurrence of an instance variable is the rightmost one in the list. build-env is defined:

```
(defun build-env (obj)
  (cond ((null obj) nil)
        ((listp obj) (append (build-env (cdr obj)) (build-env (car obj))))
        (t (append (build-env (get obj 'isa)) (get obj 'variables)))))
```

This completes the definition of the interpreter for OOPS. The remaining functionality of the language is defined in OOPS itself, as methods attached to the general root object named (appropriately) object. These are methods that enable an object to return information about itself, such as the values of specific instance variables or the list of its parents. All objects should have object as their farthest ancestor. object has neither parents nor instance variables and is defined:

```
(def-object 'object nil)
```

The method show causes an object to print its internal structure to the screen. This is everything that is *directly* attached to the object: parents, variables, and methods. show is useful for examining the debugging OOPS programs.

```
(def-method 'object 'show
  '(lambda ()
     (terpri)
     (prin1 self) (prin1 "has parents ") (terpri)
     (pprint (get self 'isa))
     (terpri)
     (prin1 self) (prin1 "has attached variables ") (terpri)
     (pprint (get self 'variables))
     (terpri)
     (prin1 self) (prin1 "has attached methods ")
     (pprint (get self 'methods))
     (terpri)))
```

show-parents and show-value return the parents of an object and the value of a named instance variable, respectively. show-parents simply returns the object's isa property. show-value takes the name of an instance variable and evaluates it in the proper environment.

```
(def-method 'object 'show-parents '(lambda () (get self 'isa)))
```

```
(def-method 'object 'show-value '(lambda (name) (eval name)))
```

show-env shows all variables visible to an object, both those directly attached to it and those it inherits. show-env calls build-env to list all instance variables inherited by the object and returns this result.

```
(def-method 'object 'show-env '(lambda () (build-env self)))
```

set-value sets the value of an existing variable or adds a new variable and its binding to an object. This is necessary because objects must be able to change the state of other objects. set-value uses the list function rplacd to modify the association list, variables, in place. That is, rplacd does not return a modified copy of its argument as do most LISP functions; instead, it goes into memory and modifies the original list.

```
(def-method 'object 'set-value
  '(lambda (variable value)
     (let ((pair (assoc variable (get self 'variables))))
       (cond (pair (rplacd pair (list value)))
             (t (setf (get self 'variables) (cons (list variable value) (get self 'variables))))))))
```

These functions define OOPS. The next section demonstrates its use in writing an object-oriented simulation of a simple system.

15.2.3 An Object-Oriented Simulation Using OOPS

A room with a heater and a thermostat provides an interesting domain for object-oriented simulation. In spite of its simplicity, it illustrates the interactions of messages between objects and the modularity of object-oriented programs. The simulation involves three classes of objects: rooms, heaters, and thermostats. Thermostats have a setting that is defined with a default value of 65 degrees. Rooms are given a default temperature of 65, heaters a default state of off. These classes are defined:

```
(def-object 'thermostat 'object '((setting 65)))
```

```
(def-object 'room 'object '((temperature 65)))
```

```
(def-object 'heater 'object '((state 'off)))
```

The simulation implemented here focuses on a single room and involves one instance of each of these classes. room-327 has an attached variable naming its thermostat; this allows room-327 to send messages to the thermostat when temperature changes occur. Similarly, thermostat-327 has instance variables that name its location and the heater it controls; heater-327 knows the room it heats.

```
(def-object 'room-327 'room '((thermostat 'thermostat-327)))
```

```
(def-object 'thermostat-327 'thermostat '((heater 'heater-327)(location 'room-327)))
```

```
(def-object 'heater-327 'heater '((location 'room-327)))
```

These definitions form the hierarchy illustrated in Figure 15.7.

room has a single method, change-temp, that defines what happens if the room's temperature changes. It takes a single parameter, the amount of the change, and computes the new temperature by adding this to the current temperature. It then sends itself a message changing the value of its temperature variable, prints a message to the screen, and sends its thermostat a message to check the temperature.

```
(def-method 'room 'change-temp
  '(lambda (amount-of-change)
    (let ((new-temp (+ amount-of-change temperature)))
      (message self 'set-value 'temperature new-temp)
      (terpri)
      (prin1 "temperature in ")
      (prin1 self)
      (prin1 " changes to ")
      (prin1 new-temp)
      (prin1 " degrees.")
      (terpri)
      (message thermostat 'check-temp))))
```

The thermostat method, check-temp, queries the location for its temperature and compares the reply with its own setting. If the room temperature is less than the setting, it sends the heater a turn-on message; otherwise it sends it a turn-off message.

```
(def-method 'thermostat 'check-temp
  '(lambda ()
    (cond ((< (message location 'show-value 'temperature) setting)
           (message heater 'turn-on))
      (t   (message heater 'turn-off)))))
```

The other method defined for thermostats is change-setting, which takes as its argument the new setting. It causes the thermostat object to send itself a message changing the

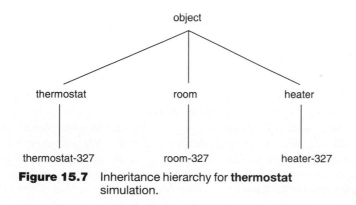

Figure 15.7 Inheritance hierarchy for **thermostat** simulation.

value of its setting and then print a message to the screen. Last, it sends itself a message to check the temperature.

```
(def-method 'thermostat 'change-setting
  '(lambda (temp)
     (message self 'set-value 'setting temp)
     (terpri)
     (prin1 "New setting of ")
     (prin1 self)
     (prin1 " is ")
     (prin1 temp)
     (prin1 "degrees.")
     (terpri)
     (message self 'check-temp)))
```

The heater class has two methods, **turn-on** and **turn-off**. These will cause the heater object to send itself a message changing the value of the instance variable, **state**, if necessary. In addition, the **turn-on** method sends its location a message to raise its temperature 1 degree.

```
(def-method 'heater 'turn-on
  '(lambda ()
     (cond ((equal state 'off)
            (terpri)
            (prin1 "Heater turns on in ")
            (prin1 location) (terpri)
            (message self 'set-value 'state 'on)))
     (message location 'change-temp 1)))
```

```
(def-method 'heater 'turn-off
  '(lambda ()
     (cond ((equal state 'on)
            (terpri)
            (prin1 "Heater turns off in ")
            (prin1 location) (terpri)
            (message self 'set-value 'state 'off )))))
```

After these definitions are evaluated, the simulation is run by sending a message to any object, changing its state. For example, the temperature of the room is changed or the thermostat setting reset. This causes messages to be sent to other objects, reflecting the actual sequence of events that occur in the physical world. We now present a transcript of two sample executions; one is started by changing the temperature of the room, the other by changing the thermostat setting. The reader is urged to trace through the sequence of messages that occurs in each run.

> (message 'room-327 'change-temp -5)
Temperature in room-327 changes to 60 degrees.

Heater turns on in room-327

Temperature in room-327 changes to 61 degrees.

Temperature in room-327 changes to 62 degrees.

Temperature in room-327 changes to 63 degrees.

Temperature in room-327 changes to 64 degrees.

Temperature in room-327 changes to 65 degrees.

Heater turns off in room-327

> (message 'thermostat-327 'change-setting 70)
New setting of thermostat-327 is 70 degrees.

Heater turns on in room-327

Temperature in room-327 changes to 66 degrees.

Temperature in room-327 changes to 67 degrees.

Temperature in room-327 changes to 68 degrees.

Temperature in room-327 changes to 69 degrees.

Temperature in room-327 changes to 70 degrees.

Heater turns off in room-327

As this example illustrates, we can use object-oriented representations to perform a *qualitative simulation* of a system of interacting components. We use such models to do hypothetical or "what if" reasoning with a simulation. For example, in the thermostat simulation, we can answer the question, "what happens if the thermostat fails to turn off the heater?" by disabling the turn-off message in the check-temp method and changing the room temperature.

This stands in sharp contrast to the reasoning usually provided by rule-based diagnostic expert systems. These systems typically have no knowledge of the structure and interactions of what they propose to understand. They are just collections of rules mapping symptoms onto faults. If none of the rules fit the given set of symptoms, then the program simply fails. Object-oriented simulations provide a means for reasoning about the deep structure of the domain.

For example, mechanics could use a simulation of a diesel engine to assist in fault diagnosis. If they suspect that the problem is in the fuel injectors, they may run the simulation with the fuel injectors disabled and see whether it produces the same symptoms as the actual engine fault. This may be simpler than replacing the fuel injectors to see whether the problem goes away. Similarly, a robot planner may use a qualitative model of its domain to verify the effects of planned actions before actually performing them.

Qualitative simulations can also play an important role in training technicians, allowing them to experiment with a model before working on an actual application.

For these reasons, object-oriented programming has emerged as a powerful tool for AI programming. Many hybrid knowledge engineering environments include object-oriented programming as a central part of their architecture. These are discussed in Section 15.5.

15.2.4 Evaluating OOPS

Although OOPS implements object-oriented programming, it is considerably simpler than commercially available systems. For example, OOPS does not distinguish between classes and instances, supporting only a single kind of object and a simple child-parent relationship; more elaborate software supports this distinction directly, providing a clearer and more robust semantics. Due partly to the inefficiency of dynamic inheritance (especially repeated calls to build-env), OOPS is less efficient than commercial software; because it is a tutorial system, we have chosen simplicity and clarity over speed in defining the interpreter. OOPS has far fewer system-defined options available for defining objects, providing more of a bare-bones architecture for object definition and message passing. OOPS simplifies the definition of objects by using property lists in the global environment; most commercial software accesses memory directly to both increase efficiency and avoid global side effects. However, the advantages of OOPS are precisely in this simplicity. It provides the user with an easily learned tool for exploring both the design and use of object-oriented languages. The reader is encouraged to experiment with extensions to this basic language.

15.3 The Common LISP Object System

Although OOPS illustrates many of the features of object-oriented programming languages, it does not provide the functionality needed for realistic software development. CLOS, the Common LISP Object System, extends Common LISP with features of object-oriented programming, including class and instance declarations, multiple inheritance, and the implementation of methods using generic functions. The designers of CLOS have made a particular effort to integrate these object-oriented features into the architecture of Common LISP.

An interesting aspect of CLOS is the way in which it combines object-oriented styles with the underlying functional programming model of Common LISP. Class definitions, for example, are integrated fully with the Common LISP type system; we may test whether an object is an instance of a class by using typep, just as we test the type of ordinary s-expressions. In addition, many Common LISP types also have class definitions. For example, the type array corresponds to the class array.

Instead of using message passing to invoke methods, CLOS provides *generic functions*. A generic function may be applied to various types of objects, with its behavior depending upon the type of its arguments. A generic function in CLOS contains a set of methods; each method is a function on arguments belonging to specific classes. We invoke generic functions using the same syntax as ordinary functions; however, the function selects and evaluates an appropriate method based on the types of its arguments. By using generic functions to implement methods, CLOS further integrates object-oriented programming with the underlying LISP architecture.

In this section, we examine the essential aspects of CLOS, including the definition of classes, instances, and methods using generic functions. Due to space limitations, we have simplified our discussion somewhat; for a more complete treatment of CLOS, see Steele (1990).

15.3.1 Defining Classes and Instances in CLOS

We define classes using the defclass macro. defclass has the syntax:

```
(defclass <class-name> (<superclass-name>*)
          (<slot-specifier>*))
```

<class-name> is a symbol. Following the class name is a list of direct superclasses; these are the class's immediate parents in the inheritance hierarchy. This list may be empty. Following the list of parent classes is a list of zero or more slot specifiers. A slot specifier is either the name of a slot or a list consisting of a slot name and zero or more slot options:

```
slot-specifier ::= slotname | (slot-name [slot-option])
```

For instance, we may define a class, rectangle, which has slots for length and width, by:

```
> (defclass rectangle ()
   (length width))
```

```
#<standard-class rectangle>
```

make-instance allows us to create instances of a class, taking as its argument a class name and returning an instance of that class. We may bind a symbol, rect, to an instance of rectangle using make-instance and setq:

```
> (setq rect (make-instance 'rectangle))
#<rectangle #x286AC1>
```

The slot options in a defclass define optional properties of slots. Slot options have the syntax (where "|" indicates alternative options):

```
slot-option ::= :reader <reader-function-name> |
                :writer <writer-function-name> |
                :accessor <reader-function-name> |
                :allocation <allocation-type> |
                :initarg <initarg-name> |
                :initform <form>
```

We declare slot options using keyword arguments. Keyword arguments are a form of optional parameter in a LISP function. The keyword, which always begins with a ":", precedes the value for that argument. Available slot options include those that provide accessors to a slot. The :reader option defines a function called reader-function-name that returns the value of a slot for an instance. The :writer option defines a function named writer-function-name that will write to the slot. :accessor defines a function that may read a slot value or may be used with setf to change its value. In the following transcript, we define rectangle to have slots for length and width, with slot accessors get-length and get-width, respectively. After binding rect to an instance of rectangle using make-instance, we use the accessor, get-length, with setf to bind the length slot to a value of 10. Finally, we use the accessor to read this value.

```
> (defclass rectangle ()
      ((length :accessor get-length)
       (width :accessor get-width)))
#<standard-class rectangle>
> (setq rect (make-instance 'rectangle))
#<rectangle #x289159>
> (setf (get-length rect) 10)
10
> (get-length rect)
10
```

In addition to defining accessors, we can access a slot using the primitive function slot-value. slot-value is defined for all slots; it takes as arguments an instance and a slot name and returns the value of that slot. We can use it with setf to change the slot value. For example, we could use slot-value to access the width slot of rect:

```
> (setf (slot-value rect 'width) 5)
5
> (slot-value rect 'width)
5
```

:allocation lets us specify the memory allocation for a slot. allocation-type may be either :instance or :class. If allocation type is :instance, then CLOS allocates a local slot for each instance of the type. If allocation type is :class, then all instances share a single location for this slot. In class allocation, all instances will share the same value of the slot; changes made to the slot by any instance will affect all other instances. If we omit the :allocation specifier, allocation defaults to :instance.

:initarg allows us to specify an argument that we can use with make-instance to specify an initial value for a slot. For example, we can modify our definition of rectangle to allow us to initialize the length and width slots of instances:

```
> (defclass rectangle ()
   ((length :accessor get-length :initarg init-length)
    (width :accessor get-width :initarg init-width)))
#<standard-class rectangle>
> (setq rect (make-instance 'rectangle 'init-length 100 'init-width 50))
#<rectangle #x28D081>
> (get-length rect)
100
> (get-width rect)
50
```

:initform lets us specify a form that CLOS evaluates on each call to make-instance to compute an initial value of the slot. For example, if we would like our program to ask the user for the values of each new instance of rectangle, we may define a function to do so and include it in an initform:

```
> (defun read-value (query) (print query)(read))
read-value
> (defclass rectangle ()
   ((length :accessor get-length :initform (read-value "enter length"))
    (width :accessor get-width :initform (read-value "enter width"))))
#<standard-class rectangle>
> (setq rect (make-instance 'rectangle))

"enter length" 100

"enter width" 50
#<rectangle #x290461>
> (get-length rect)
100
> (get-width rect)
50
```

15.3.2 Defining Generic Functions and Methods

Instead of binding methods directly to their associated class definition and invoking them with a message, as we discussed in Section 15.1 and implemented in OOPS, CLOS uses *generic functions*. A generic function is one whose behavior depends upon the type of its arguments. In CLOS, generic functions contain a set of *methods*, indexed by the type of their arguments. We call generic functions with a syntax like that of regular functions; the generic function retrieves and executes the method associated with the type of its parameters.

CLOS uses the structure of the class hierarchy in selecting a method in a generic function; if there is no method defined directly for an argument of a given class, it uses the method associated with the "closest" ancestor in the hierarchy. Generic functions provide most of the advantages of "purer" approaches of methods and message passing, including inheritance and overloading. However, they are much closer in spirit to the functional programming paradigm that forms the basis of LISP. For instance, we can use generic functions with mapcar, funcall, and other higher-order constructs in the LISP language, integrating object-oriented programming with most of the programming techniques discussed in Chapters 7 and 14.

We define generic functions using either defgeneric or defmethod. defgeneric lets us define a generic function and several methods using one form. defmethod enables us to define each method separately, although CLOS combines all of them into a single generic function.

defgeneric has the (simplified) syntax:

```
(defgeneric f-name lambda-list <method-description>*)
```

where

```
<method-description> ::= (:method specialized-lambda-list form)
```

defgeneric takes a name of the function, a lambda list of its arguments, and a series of zero or more method descriptions. In a method description, specialized-lambda-list is just like an ordinary lambda list in a function definition, except that a formal parameter may be replaced with a (symbol parameter-specializer) pair: symbol is the name of the parameter, and parameter-specializer is the class of the argument. If an argument in a method has no parameter specializer, its type defaults to t, which is the most general class in a CLOS hierarchy. Parameters of type t can bind to any object. The specialized lambda list of each method specifier must have the same number of arguments as the lambda list in the defgeneric. A defgeneric creates a generic function with the specified methods, replacing any existing generic functions.

As an example of a generic function, we may define classes for rectangles and circles and implement the appropriate methods for finding areas:

```
(defclass rectangle ()
  ((length :accessor get-length :initarg init-length)
   (width :accessor get-width :initarg init-width)))

(defclass circle ()
  ((radius :accessor get-radius :initarg init-radius)))

(defgeneric area (shape)
  (:method ((shape rectangle))
    (* (get-length shape)
       (get-width shape))))
```

```
(:method ((shape circle))
        (* (get-radius shape) (get-radius shape) pi)))

(setq rect (make-instance 'rectangle 'init-length 10 'init-width 5))

(setq circ (make-instance 'circle 'init-radius 7))
```

We can use the **area** function to compute the area of either shape:

```
> (area rect)
50
> (area circ)
153.93804002589985
```

We can also define methods using **defmethod**. Syntactically, **defmethod** is similar to **defun**, except it uses a specialized **lambda** list to declare the class to which its arguments belong. When we define a method using **defmethod**, if there is no generic function with that name, **defmethod** creates one; if a generic function of that name already exists, **defmethod** adds a new method to it. For example, we could add the class **square** to the above definitions by:

```
(defclass square ()
  ((side :accessor get-side :initarg init-side)))

(defmethod area ((shape square))
  (* (get-side shape)
     (get-side shape)))

(setq sqr (make-instance 'square 'init-side 6))
```

defmethod does not change the previous definitions of the area function; it simply adds a new method to the generic function:

```
> (area sqr)
36
> (area rect)
50
> (area circ)
153.93804002589985
```

15.3.3 Inheritance in CLOS

CLOS is a multiple-inheritance language. As we have discussed before, multiple inheritance introduces the potential for anomalies when inheriting slots and methods: if two ancestors have defined the same method, which one does an instance inherit? CLOS resolves potential ambiguities by defining a *class precedence* list, a total ordering on the class hierarchy.

Each defclass lists the direct parents of a class in left-to-right order. Using the order of direct parents for each class, CLOS computes a partial ordering of all the ancestors in the inheritance hierarchy. From this partial ordering, it derives the total ordering of the class precedence list through a topological sort.

The class precedence list follows two simple rules:

1. Any direct parent class precedes any more distant ancestor.
2. In the list of immediate parents in defclass, each class precedes those to the right of it.

CLOS computes the class precedence list for an object by topologically sorting its ancestor classes according to the following algorithm. Let C be the class for which we are defining the precedence list:

1. Let S_c be the set of C and all its superclasses.
2. For each class, c, in S_c, define the set of ordered pairs:

$$R_c = \{(c, c_1), (c_1, c_2), (c_2, c_3) ...(c_{n-1}, c_n)\}$$

   where c_1 through c_n are the direct parents of c in the order they are listed in defclass. Note that each R_c defines a total order.
3. Let R be the union of the R_cs for all elements of S_c. R may or may not define a partial ordering. If it does not define a partial ordering, then the hierarchy is inconsistent and the algorithm will detect this.
4. Topologically sort the elements of R by:

   4.1 Begin with an empty precedence list, P.
   4.2 Find a class in R having no predecessors. Add it to the end of P and remove the class from S_c and all pairs containing it from R. If there are several classes in S_c with no predecessor, select the one that has a direct subclass nearest the end in the current version of P.
   4.3 Repeat steps 4.1 and 4.2 until no element can be found that has no predecessor in R.
5. If S_c is not empty, then the hierarchy is inconsistent; it may contain ambiguities that cannot be resolved using this technique.

Because the resulting precedence list is a total ordering, it resolves any ambiguous orderings that may have existed in the class hierarchy. CLOS uses the class precedence list in the inheritance of slots and the selection of methods.

In selecting a method to apply to a given call of a generic function, CLOS first selects all applicable methods. A method is applicable to a generic function call if each parameter specializer in the method is consistent with the corresponding argument in the generic function call. A parameter specializer is consistent with an argument if the specializer either matches the class of the argument or the class of one of its ancestors.

CLOS then sorts all applicable methods using the precedence lists of the arguments. CLOS determines which of two methods should come first in this ordering by comparing their parameter specializers in a left-to-right fashion. If the first pair of corresponding parameter specializers are equal, CLOS compares the second, continuing in this fashion until it finds corresponding parameter specializers that are different. Of these two, it designates as more specific the method whose parameter specializer appears leftmost in the precedence list of the corresponding argument.

After ordering all applicable methods, the default method selection applies the most specific method to the arguments. For more details, see Steele (1990).

15.3.4   Advanced Features of CLOS

CLOS is an extremely complex language, and we have described only a few of its features. For instance, most of CLOS's functionality is defined in a set of objects called *meta-classes*. All classes belong to a meta-class. The behavior of classes, such as the inheritance algorithm described above, is defined in the meta-class. In CLOS, these meta-classes are open to the programmer, allowing bold individuals to modify the semantics of the language.

Another interesting feature of the language is the ability to combine methods. Whereas the default method inheritance simply uses the first method encountered in the precedence list, CLOS lets us specify method combinations. These allow us to select components of a method from different classes in the hierarchy and evaluate them in order. This technique augments the opportunities for abstraction provided by simple method inheritance; we can abstract out common portions of a method and place them high in the hierarchy, implementing more specialized aspects of a method lower in the inheritance hierarchy.

Though space limitations prevent us from discussing these and other features, we have presented the most important aspects of CLOS. These sections capture the heart of the language and are sufficient for most implementations.

15.3.5   Implementing a Thermostat Simulation

We conclude by demonstrating the implementation of the thermostat example of Section 15.2 using the Common LISP Object System. The basis of our implementation is a set of object definitions. Thermostats have a single slot called setting. The setting of each instance is initialized to 65 using initform. heater-thermostats are a subclass of thermostat for controlling heaters (as opposed to air conditioners); they have a single slot that will be bound to an instance of the heater class. Note that the heater slot has a class allocation; this captures the constraint that thermostats in different rooms of a building control the same heater.

```
(defclass thermostat ()
        ((setting :initform 65
                :accessor therm-setting)))

(defclass heater-thermostats (thermostat)
        ((heater :allocation :class
                :initarg heater-obj))))
```

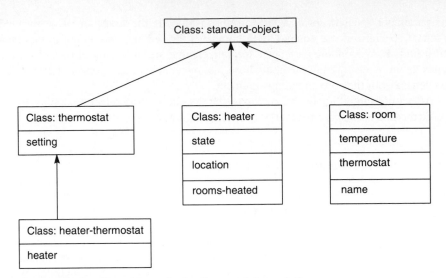

Figure 15.8 Class hierarchy for thermostat simulation.

A heater has a state (on or off) which is initialized to off, and a location. It also has a slot, rooms-heated, that will be bound to a list of objects of type room. Note that instances, like any other structure in LISP, may be elements of a list.

```
(defclass heater ()
        ((state :initform 'off
                :accessor heater-state)
         (location :initarg loc)
         (rooms-heated)))
```

room has slots for temperature, initialized to 65 degrees; thermostat, which will be bound to an instance of thermostat; and name, the name of the room.

```
(defclass room ()
        ((temperature :initform 65
                :accessor room-temp)
         (thermostat :initarg therm
                :accessor room-thermostat)
         (name :initarg name
                :accessor room-name)))
```

These class definitions define the hierarchy of Figure 15.8.

We represent our particular simulation as a set of instances of these classes. We will implement a simple system of one room, one heater, and one thermostat:

```
(setf office-heater (make-instance 'heater 'loc 'office))

(setf room-325 (make-instance 'room
                'therm (make-instance 'heater-thermostats
                          'heater-obj office-heater)
                'name 'room-325))

(setf (slot-value office-heater 'rooms-heated) (list room-325))
```

Figure 15.9 shows the definition of instances, the allocation of slots, and the bindings of slots to values.

We define the behavior of rooms through the methods change-temp, check-temp, and change-setting. change-temp sets the temperature of a room to a new value, prints a message to the user, and calls check-temp to determine whether the heater should come on. Similarly, change-setting changes the thermostat setting and calls check-temp. check-temp simulates the thermostat. If the temperature of the room is less than the setting of the thermostat, it sends the heater a message to turn on; otherwise it sends the heater an "off" message.

```
(defmethod change-temp ((place room) temp-change)
    (let ((new-temp (+ (room-temp place) temp-change)))
        (setf (room-temp place) new-temp)
        (terpri)
```

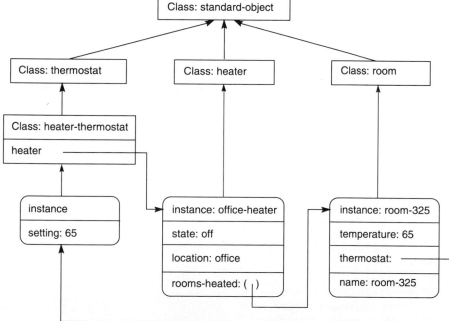

Figure 15.9 Thermostat simulation showing instances,
 initial values and slot allocation.

```
(prin1 "the temperature in ")
(prin1 (room-name place))
(prin1 " is now ")
(prin1 new-temp)
(terpri)
(check-temp place)))

(defmethod change-setting ((room room) new-setting)
        (let ((therm (room-thermostat room)))
                (setf (therm-setting therm) new-setting)
                (prin1 "changing setting of thermostat in ")
                (prin1 (room-name room))
                (prin1 " to ")
                (prin1 new-setting)
                (terpri)
                (check-temp room)))

(defmethod check-temp ((room room))
        (let* ((therm (room-thermostat room))
                (heater (slot-value therm 'heater)))
            (cond ((> (therm-setting therm) (room-temp room))
                        (send-heater heater 'on))
                (t (send-heater heater 'off)))))
```

The heater methods control the state of the heater and change the temperature of the rooms. send-heater takes as arguments an instance of heater and a message, new-state. If new-state is on it calls the turn-on method to start the heater; if new-state is off it shuts the heater down. After turning the heater on, send-heater calls heat-rooms to increase the temperature of each room by one degree.

```
(defmethod send-heater ((heater heater) new-state)
        (case new-state
                (on (if (equal (heater-state heater) 'off)
                        (turn-on heater))
                        (heat-rooms (slot-value heater 'rooms-heated) 1))
            (off (if (equal (heater-state heater) 'on)
                        (turn-off heater)))))

(defmethod turn-on ((heater heater))
        (setf (heater-state heater) 'on)
        (prin1 "turning on heater in ")
        (prin1 (slot-value heater 'location))
    (terpri))

(defmethod turn-off ((heater heater))
        (setf (heater-state heater) 'off)
        (prin1 "turning off heater in ")
        (prin1 (slot-value heater 'location))
    (terpri))
```

```
(defun heat-rooms (rooms amount)
     (cond ((null rooms) nil)
          (t (change-temp (car rooms) amount)
             (heat-rooms (cdr rooms) amount))))
```

The following transcript illustrates the behavior of the simulation.

```
> (change-temp room-325 -5)

"the temperature in "room-325" is now "60
"turning on heater in "office

"the temperature in "room-325" is now "61

"the temperature in "room-325" is now "62

"the temperature in "room-325" is now "63

"the temperature in "room-325" is now "64

"the temperature in "room-325" is now "65
"turning off heater in "office
nil

> (change-setting room-325 70)

"changing setting of thermostat in "room-325" to "70
"turning on heater in "office

"the temperature in "room-325" is now "66

"the temperature in "room-325" is now "67

"the temperature in "room-325" is now "68

"the temperature in "room-325" is now "69

"the temperature in "room-325" is now "70
"turning off heater in "office
nil
```

15.4   Object-Oriented Programming and Concurrency in PROLOG

15.4.1   Introduction

The use of declarative rather than procedural representations to describe objects, messages, and inheritance is a new and challenging area of research. In this section, we present one approach (Shapiro 1987) to this problem. We view objects as active processes that receive messages and perform actions on their internal states according to the content of those messages. During computation the object can send messages to other objects; these may thus be thought of as distinct but complete computational entities encapsulating both structure definition and process. To create a computer model that embodies this directly would require a highly parallel asynchronous computational environment, with a processor and memory being assigned to each object. This relationship between object-oriented programming and parallel architectures is a natural one, with object-oriented approaches forming the basis of several languages for parallel computation.

The view of objects as asynchronous parallel computational entities is a useful abstraction, even if their ultimate implementation is sequential. For example, in the room-thermostat-heater example of Section 15.2, no attention was paid to the order of execution of methods; each object was defined independently, with the interactions of messages determining the ultimate sequence of actions. This is a natural way to model physical systems, which are themselves highly parallel. Even when the language is not implemented in a physically parallel architecture, much insight and semantic clarity is gained by viewing it in these terms.

In implementing objects in PROLOG, we adhere to this multiparallel-process semantics. Like object-oriented programming, PROLOG exhibits strong potential for parallelism. The modularity of predicate definitions and the local scoping of variables suggest a model of evaluation that assigns a processor to each of a set of subgoals.

The standard semantics for PROLOG is based on sequential evaluation using a single processor. The sequential PROLOG interpreter implements *resolution refutation* with *linear input form* and *unit preference* strategies guiding sequential left-to-right and depth-first search of Horn clauses (Section 13.3).

In Section 13.3 we also presented an alternative semantics for PROLOG, designed by Ehud Shapiro, called *Concurrent PROLOG* (Shapiro 1987). This elegant semantics supports a parallel model of PROLOG interpretation and provides a basis for building objects as asynchronous parallel entities. Several new constructs are added to standard PROLOG, including *read-only* variables and the *commit* operator. These allow the programmer to coordinate parallel interpretation of subgoals.

Concurrent PROLOG itself may be implemented directly on either a parallel or sequential computer architecture, or as a meta-interpreter on top of standard PROLOG. Continuing our philosophy of building a language (interpreter) within an AI language, the following section describes a meta-interpreter that alters the procedural semantics of sequential PROLOG to define Concurrent PROLOG; the parallel constructs of this language are then used to define objects and messages.

15.4.2   Objects in Concurrent PROLOG

From our concurrent point of view, objects correspond to the processes assigned to goals. Concurrent PROLOG realizes objects by creating a perpetual process holding its internal state in unshared arguments. An object acts by reducing itself to other objects. That is, when clause

A:- ..., B,...

is called (A is reduced), then B is created. A perpetual object acts by reducing itself to itself, i.e., by calling itself tail recursively with different arguments. (Most interpreters optimize tail recursion, so this is done in constant space.)

Objects communicate with each other by instantiating shared variables. Parallel processes are created by and parallelism. That is, for clauses:

A :- B1, B2, B3.

when A is called, B1 and B2 and B3 are evaluated in parallel. They are activated when all their *read-only* variables are bound and they communicate through shared variables.

Message passing is performed by binding a shared variable to a message. Because a shared variable can be referred to by multiple processes, messages can be sent to multiple objects at once. Successive communication is possible by stream communication, which means by binding a *channel variable*, also possibly shared, to the binary term <message>.X, where <message> is the message to be sent and X is a new variable to be used in the next communication. In PROLOG this is accomplished by [<message>| X], the PROLOG equivalent of the dotted pair in LISP.

An object becomes active only when it receives a message; otherwise it is suspended. The synchronization mechanism forces a process to suspend (and save state) when it is unable to bind *read-only* variables.

When an object sends a message requiring a response, the response cannot be sent through the same shared variable, because variables in logic are able to have only a single assignment. Two techniques are available for responding to a message. One is to prepare another shared variable for the return communication. The second technique is *incomplete messages*: the sender sends a message that contains an unbound variable and then examines that variable in *read-only* mode. This causes the sender process to suspend until this variable gets bound to the response of the recipient of the message. For example, a sender asks a target object about its internal state with the message show(State), where the variable State is used as the communication channel that carries the response from the target back to the sender. The sender gets this response some time in the future after the message is received and processed. The sender must wait for the response variable to be bound if it needs to refer to the response.

The counter program is a simple example of an object (first presented, with a trace, in Section 13.6):

```
counter ([clear|S], State) :- counter (S?,0).
counter ([up|S], State) :- plus (State, 1, Newstate),
            counter (S?, Newstate?).
counter([down|S], State) :- plus (Newstate, 1, State),
            counter (S?, Newstate?).
counter ([show(State)|S], State) :- counter (S?, State).
counter ([], State).
```

The stream variable, the first argument of counter, is used recursively. At every reduction it is bound to a pair: the message and the new variable to be used in the next communication.

Object-instance creation is accomplished by parallel and. When a new goal is created, the bindings of its variables are the bindings of instance variables. For example, a new instance of the object counter may be created by executing the following code:

```
?- terminal(X), use_counter(X?,C1), counter (C1?,0).
```

terminal is an object that generates the stream of commands produced by a user at a terminal. The use_counter object receives commands from the terminal and passes these commands on to the object counter. When the message is show, use_counter passes it to counter, causes the object use_counter to wait for the response from the object counter, and then writes the response from counter to the screen. Note that the first argument of use_counter and the second argument of the object counter are treated as *read-only* variables, because they are used only when bound to message values received from the terminal.

```
use_counter([show(Val)|Input],[show(Val)|Command])  :-
  use_counter(Input?,Command), wait_write(Val).
use_counter([X|Input],[X|Command])  :-
  dif(X, show(Y)) : use_counter(Input?,Command).
use_counter([],[]).
```

wait_write(X) suspends if X is not instantiated and succeeds otherwise. dif(U, V) is a system predicate that succeeds if and when it can determine that U and V are not variables and are different. Note that the stream variable is used as an object-instance name. Message passing is performed against the stream variable and not against the target object itself, because there are no global names in Concurrent PROLOG, and the only information about an object that is accessible from outside is the communication channels to the object.

A new object-instance is created using a rule in the program. Object-instances created from the same definition are distinguished by the names of their communication channels. The next example demonstrates this. The object use_many_counters is similar to use_counter. It receives a command stream from the terminal. When it receives a create(Name) message, it creates a new object counter and saves its name and a communication channel to it in its internal state. Other messages must be of the form (Name,Command), where Name specifies the name of an object counter to which the message Command should be sent.

```
use_many_counters([create(Name)|Input],List_of_counters)  :-
  counter(Com?,0),
  use_many_counters(Input?,[(Name,Com)|List_of_counters]).
use_many_counters([(Name,show(Val))|Input],List_of_counters)  :-
  send(List_of_counters,Name,show(Val),NewList)  :
  use_many_counters(Input?,NewList), wait_write(Val).
use_many_counters([(Name,X)|Input],List_of_counters)  :-
  X \= create(Y),
  X \= show(Y),
  send(List_of_counters,Name,X,NewList)  :
  use_many_counters(Input?,NewList).
```

```
send([(Name,[Message|Y])|List],Name,Message,[(Name,Y)|List]).
send([C|List],Name,Message,[C|L1]) :- send(List,Name,Message,L1).
```

The object use_many_counters has two arguments. One is an input stream from the terminal and the other is a list of (Name, Channel), where Name is an identifier of the object counter given by the create command and Channel is the communication channel to that object. The object send takes four arguments. The first argument is the same as the second argument of use_many_counters. The second and the third arguments are an identifier of the object counter and a message to be sent, respectively. The fourth argument is the updated list of counters. We now show with a trace of Concurrent PROLOG using the counter code a situation in which three create commands are processed. Note that because there are no global variables in Concurrent PROLOG, an object must keep channel variables associated with other objects in order to send messages to them.

```
C-Prolog version 1.5
| ?- ['prolog.con',code].
prolog.con consulted 7600 bytes 2.35 sec.
code consulted 3012 bytes 0.95 sec.

yes
| ?- solve((terminal(In),use_many_counters(In?,[]))).
|: create(c1).
|: create(c2).
|: create(c3).
|: (c1,up).
|: (c2,down).
|: (c3,up).
|: (c3,up).
|: (c1,show(_)).
|: (c2,show(_)).
1
|: (c3,show(_)).
-1
|: end_of_file.
2
```

The next example demonstrates how Concurrent PROLOG can implement default programming, filters, and object hierarchies. The language does not have direct mechanisms to support object hierarchies. However, a programming technique called *filters*, together with a new Concurrent PROLOG construct, otherwise, achieves a similar effect.

Consider the following hierarchy of objects: a rectangular_area; a frame, which is a rectangular_area with four border lines; a window_with_label, which is a frame with a label at the bottom of the window. These can be defined by the class-superclass hierarchy of Figure 15.10.

In a language that supports such hierarchies directly, the functionality of a rectangular_area is inherited by the frame, and the functionality of a frame is inherited by a window with a label. Operationally, an object that receives a message checks whether it knows

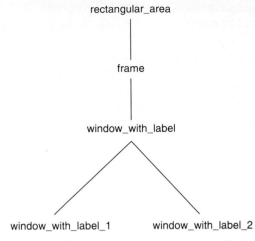

Figure 15.10   Class hierarchy for **window_with_label**.

how to respond to it. If it does not, it defaults to its parent in the hierarchy for a response. In this sense every object in the hierarchy functions like a filter on a stream of messages.

In Concurrent PROLOG, every object in a hierarchy must have at least one designated input stream and one designated output stream, except the topmost object, which has an input stream only. The hierarchical structure of the objects is reflected by the structure of the communication network that they form. An object A lower in the hierarchy has its output stream connected to the input stream of an object B next above it in the hierarchy. If A receives a message that it cannot respond to, it simply defaults to B by passing it the message.

The following Concurrent PROLOG implementation of the window hierarchy demonstrates this technique. First a rectangular_area is defined.

```
rectangular_area([clear|M], Parameters) :-
  clear_primitive (Parameters), rectangular_area(M?, Parameters).
rectangular_area([ask(Parameters)|M], Parameters) :-
  rectangular_area(M?, Parameters).
```

Parameters is a data structure consisting of four values, in this case the instance variables for rectangular_area: (Xpos, Ypos, Width, Height), where Xpos and Ypos are the coordinates of the upper left corner of the area and Width and Height are the dimensions of the area. clear_primitive is a system-defined predicate that clears the screen area specified in its arguments.

The frame object can be viewed as a filter on the input stream of a rectangular_area. It filters two types of message, for which it knows how to respond: draw and refresh.

```
create_frame(M, Parameters) :-
  rectangular_area(M1?, Parameters), frame(M, M1).
frame([draw|M], [ask(Parameters)|M1]) :-
  draw_lines(Parameters?), frame(M?, M1).
```

```
frame([refresh|M], [clear|M1]) :-
  frame([draw|M], M1).
frame([X|M], [X|M1]) :-
  X \= draw, X \= refresh : frame(M?, M1).
```

The first clause specifies the initialization procedure, which creates a rectangular_area object by passing the Parameters and an original frame object with the communication channel to the rectangular_area. The rest of the clauses specify the method for interpreting each message. On receiving a draw message, it asks the rectangular_area about the dimensional Parameters and then draws four border lines. On receiving a refresh message, it sends two messages, clear and draw, to the rectangular_area and self, respectively. On receiving other messages, it passes them to rectangular_area.

The last clause for frame may be replaced by:

```
frame([X|M], [X|M1) :-
  otherwise : frame(M?, M1).
```

An otherwise goal that occurs in a guard succeeds if and when all other or parallel guards fail. If all clauses for an object have empty guards, then otherwise can be implemented via a preprocessor that expands it to an appropriate sequence of calls such as X \= draw. If the guards are not empty, then otherwise may be implemented via a negation-as-failure primitive. In this sense otherwise does not increase the expressive power of Concurrent PROLOG more than the addition of negation as failure does. An efficient implementation of otherwise requires a modification to the Concurrent PROLOG interpreter.

Now, a window frame with a label is defined.

```
create_window_with_label(M, Label, Parameters) :-
  create_frame(M1?, Parameters),
  window_with_label(M?, Label, M1).
window_with_label([change(Label)|M], OldLabel, M1) :-
  window_with_label(M?, Label, M1).
window_with_label([show|M], Label, [ask(Parameters)|M1]) :-
  show_label_primitive(Label, Parameters?),
  window_with_label(M?,Label, M1).
window_with_label([refresh|M], Label, [refresh|M1]) :-
  window_with_label([show|M], Label, M1).
window_with_label([X|M], Label, [X|M1]) :-
  X \= show, X \= refresh, X \= change,:
  window_with_label(M?, Label, M1).
```

The first clause defines the initialization procedure that creates the object frame with the Parameters and a window_with_label with a communication channel to the object frame. The rest of the clauses define the methods for interpreting messages. On receiving a change message, it changes the Label. On receiving a show message, it asks the object frame about its Parameters and displays the Label in the appropriate position in the window, using the predefined predicate show_label_primitive. On receiving a refresh message, it sends two messages, refresh and show, to the frame and self, respectively. On receiving other messages, it passes them on to the frame.

In the class-superclass hierarchy, a message that cannot be processed by an object is passed to the superclasses of the object. In Concurrent PROLOG such a hierarchy is simulated by a network of objects connected via communication channels, through which messages are sent. Systems such as Flavors and Smalltalk-80 permit objects to access the instance variables of their superclasses. In Concurrent PROLOG, because a superclass of an object is also an object, such direct access to states of other objects is not possible. Instead, an object has to send a message asking about states to the objects that make up its superclasses.

Figure 15.11 shows the relation between objects and acceptable messages. For the object window_with_label, there are two types of methods: an *own* method and a *generic* method. Generic methods are invoked by sending messages up the class hierarchy.

In this cooperating object approach, there is no difference between the class-superclass hierarchy and the part-whole relation. In other words, the role of an object in a group of cooperating objects is not determined from a structural description (such as superclass or part declarations) but from a behavioral description in the form of a communication network. From this point of view, a rectangular_area can be seen both as a superclass of a frame and as a part of a frame.

We now present a script of the window_with_label code interpreted by Concurrent PROLOG. We have added a trace to indicate when messages are sent and received.

```
% This prints text as rectangular_area runs.
show_label_primitive(Label, Parameters) :-
    call(write('window_with_label show_label: Label = '), write(Label),
            write(' Parameters = '), write(Parameters), nl)).

draw_lines(Parameters) :-
    call((write('frame draw_lines: Parameters = '), write(Parameters), n1)).

clear_primitive(Parameters) :-
    call((write('rectangular_area clear'), n1)).


C-Prolog version 1.5
| ?- ['prolog.con',code].
prolog.con consulted 7600 bytes 2.3 sec.
code consulted 3336 bytes 1.15 sec.


yes
| ?- solve((terminal(X),create_window_with_label(X?,'Label 1',(0,0,10,20)))).
| : show.
| : draw.
window_with_label show_label: Label = Label 1? Parameters = (0,0,10,20)?
| : refresh.
| : clear.
frame draw_lines: Parameters = (0,0,10,20)?
| : change('Label 2').
window_with_label show_label: Label = Label 1? Parameters = _1741?
```

```
rectangular_area clear
frame draw_lines:  Parameters = (0,0,10,20)?
| : show.
| : draw.
rectangular_area clear
window_with_label show_label:  Label = Label 2? Parameters = (0,0,10,20)?
| : refresh.
| : clear.
frame draw_lines:  Parameters = (0,0,10,20)?
| : end_of_file.
window_with_label show_label:  Label = Label 2? Parameters = _4865?
rectangular_area clear
frame draw_lines:  Parameters = (0,0,10,20)?
rectangular_area clear
```

To summarize: first, the user can never directly access the internal state of an object. All a user can do is send a message that specifies the operation to be performed. Thus, the encapsulation of state is established. Second, component objects of a hierarchy are accessed from the outside, by using incomplete messages. Thus, the encapsulation of abstraction-based hierarchies is also established. With these properties, it is possible to construct complicated simulations of situations from simple objects in a modular fashion.

We designed a *meta-interpreter* in PROLOG called Concurrent PROLOG. This interpreter uses (optimized) recursive predicates to describe objects and a form of list-based parameters to encode messages. *Read-only* variables within and parallel goals as well as *guard* operators within or parallel goals allow multiple objects and messages to have a nondeterministic and pseudoparallel interpretation.

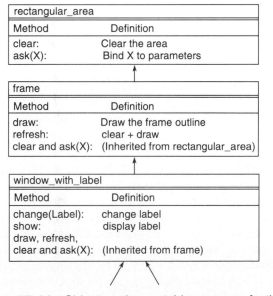

Figure 15.11 Objects and acceptable messages for the
window_with_label example.

15.5   Hybrid Expert System Tools

15.5.1   Hybrid Environments: Integrating Objects, Rules, and Procedures

As mentioned in Chapter 9 and in the introduction to Part V, most single representational formalisms have both advantages and disadvantages for representing domain knowledge. Rules are a natural formalism for representing heuristics and problem-solving knowledge. Inheritance provides the best means of representing taxonomic knowledge. Object-oriented systems, in addition to supporting inheritance, provide a convenient way of modeling the behavior of interacting objects.

Integration of these elements is surprisingly straightforward. For example, we may allow rules to execute arbitrary pieces of LISP code in their premises, with the premise succeeding if the LISP function returns non-nil. Similarly, rules could send messages to objects and test the responses in their premises.

Assume, for example, a hybrid program for reasoning about actions of a robot arm in a blocks world. We could use an object-oriented knowledge base to represent the properties of differently shaped blocks and a rule base to reason about them. A typical rule might state that it is okay to stack one block on top of another if the top block has a smaller volume than the bottom block. We could write this rule (using the syntax of the LISP shell in Section 14.3) as:

```
(rule
  if (< (message (var x) 'volume) (message (var y) 'volume))
  then (safe-to-stack (var x) (var y)))
```

This rule uses the volume method for the objects bound to (var x) and (var y) to compute their respective volumes and passes these results to the LISP function < to test them. If the test succeeds, then the conclusion that (var x) is safe to stack on (var y) also follows.

We can easily modify lisp-shell from Section 14.3 so that it will handle this type of query. We modify solve-simple-goal so that after it tries to solve a goal using the knowledge base, it tries to solve the goal through evaluation. This requires that it first verify that the goal is an evaluable LISP form and then replace variables with their values under the current substitution set and evaluate the goal using eval. In our safe-to-stack example, the attempt to evaluate the < test would first evaluate the function arguments, causing the messages to be sent to the designated objects. We leave the implementation of this extension as an exercise.

Similarly, an object may access the rule base as part of its methods. This is even easier to add to our lisp-shell/OOPS hybrid environment. Because methods are arbitrary pieces of LISP code, they can access the rule base through a call to the function solve.

This discussion suggests ways in which the OOPS language of this chapter and lisp-shell from Chapter 14 can be combined into a simple hybrid expert systems environment. However, this example does not illustrate a number of other features of commercial hybrid environments. We discuss these in this section.

15.5.2   Facets, Demons, and Graphics in Hybrid Environments

There are a number of commercially available expert system tools that support this hybrid approach to knowledge engineering. In addition to allowing rules and objects to interact as described above, most commercial hybrid environments include such useful features as demons, built-in type checking, and support for a graphics interface. One way in which these are provided is through an extension to the slot/value structure to subdivide each slot into multiple *facets*, or named subcomponents. These facets allow the programmer to attach several different components to a single slot, including its value, type specifications, and demons.

Figure 15.12 illustrates an object describing the class dog. dog is a subclass of three classes, pet, carnivore, and mammal, and inherits properties of each. The object shows three slots, name, breed, and owner, with multiple facets. These facets are built into the environment and are bound by the user when an object is created. The value facet of each slot represents the value of the slot.

```
Objoot: dog

Superclass: (pet, carnivore, mammal)

Slot: name
   value:
   minimum cardinality: 1
   maximum cardinality: 1
   type: string
   default value: fido
   execute-when-created: ask-user(name.value)
   execute-when-changed:
        message(owner.value, set-name, name.value)

Slot: breed
   value:
   minimum cardinality: 1
   type: (doberman poodle shorthair shepherd terrier)
   active-image: radio buttons

Slot: owner
   value:
   minimum cardinality: 1
   maximum cardinality: 1
   type: instance of person
```

Figure 15.12   Typical object showing the slot-facet-value architecture.

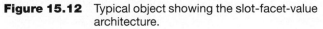

Other facets include minimum cardinality and maximum cardinality; these allow us to specify the number of values that can be attached to a slot. Both the name and owner slots must have exactly one value. The breed slot must have at least one value but no upper limit is specified; dogs may be mixed breed.

In addition to specifying the cardinality of the slot values, many systems define facets for declaring the type of the slot. In our example, this is the type facet. The name slot is of type string; the owner slot indicates another object, an instance of the class person. In this example, we also allow the programmer to declare enumerated types by attaching a list of allowable values to the type facet; this was done for the breed slot. Another common facet allows the specification of default values, such as a default of fido for the name slot.

Along with type-checking information, most hybrid environments provide facets that allow the attachment of demons to slots. Two common demons illustrated in Figure 15.12 are execute-when-created, which is evaluated when a new instance of the class is defined, and execute-when-changed, which is evaluated every time the slot value of an instance is changed.

In this example, we have used the execute-when-created facet of the name slot to specify how the system should obtain a binding for that slot when a new instance is created. This is a typical application of this type of demon.

name also has an execute-when-changed demon, which sends a message to the instance's owner whenever the dog's name is changed. This implements consistency checking in the knowledge base, making sure that the owner knows the name of her pet. Consistency checking is an important use of execute-when-changed demons; other uses include the implementation of side effects and causal relations for different objects in the knowledge base.

Active images are another kind of demon that many systems provide. They allow graphics images to be selected from a library and attached to a slot to display its value. Typical images include dials, gauges, and button devices. These images may respond to the mouse or other selection device, allowing the user to change the value of the slot by clicking on the image itself. For example, the breed slot of Figure 15.12 has a "radio button" image attached to it. This is a set of selectable labeled "buttons"; the user may select these buttons and change the value of the slot. Figure 15.13 shows the radio button image for the breed slot of an instance of the dog object as it would appear on the screen. In the figure, the user has selected the doberman and shorthair buttons, indicating that the dog is mixed breed.

This section presented a few of the features of hybrid knowledge engineering environments. These tools, which are becoming increasingly available, represent a synthesis of the techniques described in this text, techniques developed through the history of AI to simplify the implementation of intelligent systems.

15.5   Epilogue and References

A number of programming languages support object-oriented programming. The oldest of these is Smalltalk, which is documented by Goldberg and Robson (1983) and MacLennan (1987).

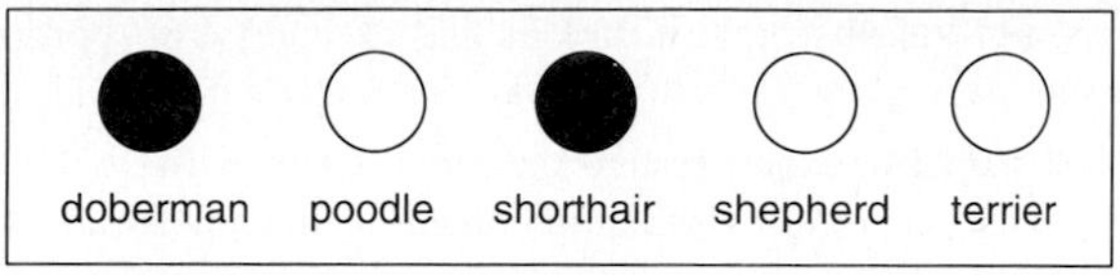

Figure 15.13 Radio button for the breed slot of an instance of the dog object in Figure 15.12.

CLOS is the *de facto* standard for object-oriented programming in LISP. For more details see Steel (1990) and Touretzky (1990).

A number of commercial expert system packages include object-oriented programming in the context of a hybrid environment. Some of the most notable of these hybrid environments are mentioned in Harmon et al. (1988).

The material for the subsection on implementing objects using concurrent PROLOG is based on work by Shapiro and Takeuchi (E. Shapiro 1987). The reader is referred to this resource for further examples and explanations.

15.6   Exercises

1. The implementation of OOPS does not distinguish between class and instance objects. Extend the language so it makes this distinction and properly handles inheritance for both instance methods and class methods as discussed in Section 15.1.

2. Extend the thermostat example of Section 15.2.3 to include an air conditioner that turns on if the room becomes too hot.

3. Use OOPS to implement a simulation of a steam engine, consisting of a boiler, water tank, fuel tank, engine, and throttle. The components of the engine should interact realistically. For example, increasing the speed of the engine should reflect an increased use of steam and an increased drain on the water and fuel tanks.

4. Use OOPS to implement a simulation of a computer network. Objects would be nodes in the network with certain message-handling capabilities. Classes of objects might include file servers, mainframes, and personal computers. Instances would include variables representing that node's message-handling capability and lists of neighboring nodes. Message queues would also be represented as instance variables. Use this simulation to test the effect of various faults, such as node or line failures, on the system as a whole.

5. OOPS implements objects by using the property lists of symbols in the global LISP environment. Along with always placing objects in the global environment, this does not allow us to create unnamed objects and pass them between functions.

    a. Discuss several reasons why this approach may not be desirable.

    b. Rewrite OOPS so that the function **def-object** returns unnamed objects that are then bound to global variables using **setq** or simply passed as parameters. Hint: represent an object as an association list rather than as properties of global symbols.

6. Extend OOPS so that it allows **execute-when-changed** demons. One way to do this is to add a list called **demons** to an object definition. This list would pair a variable name with the demon

definition. Rewrite set-value so that it inherits and executes any appropriate demon when a variable is changed.

7. Integrate lisp-shell, the LISP expert system shell from Chapter 14, with OOPS as described in Section 15.4.1. Use the resulting hybrid environment to implement an expert system in some appropriate domain.

8. We can use the concurrent PROLOG implementation of a perpetual process to create axiomatic definitions of abstract data types. For example, a *stack* may be defined:

```
stack(S) :- stack(S?, []).
stack([pop(X) | S], [X | Xs]) :- stack(S?, Xs).
stack([push(X) | S], Xs) :- stack(S?, [X | Xs]).
stack([], []).
```

Use concurrent PROLOG to give an axiomatic definition of a queue (E. Shapiro 1987).

9. Build the rectangle/square hierarchy of Section 15.2.2 in concurrent PROLOG.

10. Build the room/furnace/thermostat example of Section 15.2.3 in concurrent PROLOG.

11. The implementation of ID3 in Chapter 14 took an object-oriented approach using defstruct. Rewrite ID3 using CLOS.

12. Extend the simulation of Section 15.3.5 to implement a *discrete event simulation*:

    a. Use an agenda to implement a notion of time. To do this, instead of evaluating methods as they are called in the simulation, represent each method invocation as an *event*. Events are function closures that are given a time stamp to indicate when they should be evaluated and placed on the agenda. Items on the agenda are sorted by time stamp. A central control loop selects the next scheduled event from the agenda and evaluates it, causing the next step in the simulation. Note that you will have to rewrite methods so that instead of performing an action, the method computes how long it will take the action to occur and returns an agenda item with that time stamp. For instance, in heating a room, the method computes how long it will take to heat the room 1 degree, computes the time at which the temperature change will occur, and creates a heat-room event for that time. Similarly, the check-temp method will compute how long it takes the thermostat to respond to a temperature change and signal the heater.

    b. Use estimates of the heat loss of the room as a function of the outside temperature, and add methods to create events representing the cooling of rooms.

    c. Extend the timed simulation to include two or more rooms and a single heater.

PART VI

EPILOGUE

The potential of computer science, if fully explored and developed, will take us to a higher plane of knowledge about the world. Computer science will assist us in gaining a greater understanding of intellectual processes. It will enhance our knowledge of the learning process, the thinking process, and the reasoning process. Computer science will provide models and conceptual tools for the cognitive sciences. Just as the physical sciences have dominated humanity's intellectual endeavors during this century as researchers explored the nature of matter and the beginning of the universe, today we are beginning the exploration of the intellectual universe of ideas, knowledge structures, and language. I foresee significant advances continuing to be made that will greatly alter our lives. The work Tarjan and I started in the 1970s has led to an understanding of data structures and how to manipulate them. Looking ahead, I can foresee an understanding of how to organize and manipulate knowledge.

—J. HOPCROFT, ACM Turing Award Lecture, 1987

What's past is prologue.

—WILLIAM SHAKESPEARE, *The Tempest*

This text has focused on the engineering techniques used to build intelligent computer programs. In concluding, we take a few pages to consider the philosophical foundations of artificial intelligence, reexamine the possibility of a science of intelligence using AI techniques, and speculate on the future of progress in artificial intelligence. As we have noted throughout this text, research on human cognition and problem solving has made many important contributions to the design of AI programs and paradigms. In examining the foundations of AI, we consider several important issues such as the problem of falsifiability of models and the importance of the scientific method. Finally, we argue that AI and epistemology (the science of knowing) offer mutual constraints, the understanding of which adds power and maturity to both disciplines.

16 ARTIFICIAL INTELLIGENCE AS EMPIRICAL ENQUIRY

Computer science is an empirical discipline. We would have called it an experimental science, but like astronomy, economics, and geology, some of its unique forms of observation and experience do not fit a narrow stereotype of the experimental method. Nonetheless, they are experiments. Each new machine that is built is an experiment. Actually constructing the machine poses a question to nature; and we listen for the answer by observing the machine in operation and analyzing it by all analytical and measurement means available. Each new program that is built is an experiment. It poses a question to nature, and its behavior offers clues to an answer. Neither machines nor programs are black boxes; they are artifacts that have been designed, both hardware and software, and we can open them up and look inside. We can relate their structure to their behavior and draw many lessons from a single experiment.

—A. NEWELL AND H. A. SIMON, ACM Turing Award Lecture, 1976

Where is the knowledge we have lost in information?

—T. S. ELIOT, *Choruses from the Rock*

Do I dare to eat a peach?

—T. S. ELIOT, *The Love Song of J. Alfred Prufrock*

16.0   Introduction

Artificial intelligence, along with much of computer science, is an empirical discipline. Each AI program can be viewed as an experiment; it proposes a question to the natural world, and the results of that running program are nature's response. As Newell and Simon note, the structure of computers and their programs indicate their potential behavior: they may be examined, and their representations and search algorithms understood. Nature's response to our design commitments shapes our understanding of formalism, mechanism, and intelligence.

Much of the excitement of AI is a result of its potential for solving important problems previously thought to require human intelligence: delivering financial advice or medical care, configuring computers, troubleshooting hardware, and controlling processes in factories and spaceflights. Although the potential applications of AI seem unbounded, responsible engineering decisions depend upon an understanding of both the strengths and limitations of this technology.

In this final chapter we return to the questions asked in Chapter 1: what is intelligence? how can we understand its power? how can we build mechanisms that use it? We begin with a revised definition of artificial intelligence and show how much current work in AI is rooted in the physical symbol system hypothesis of Newell and Simon. In Section 16.2 we show how the tools of AI may be used to better understand intelligence. The discipline that uses AI tools to explore the nature of human intelligence is called *Cognitive Science*.

Finally, in Section 16.3 we discuss the future of AI by exploring the philosophical foundations of a symbol-based science of intelligence. There remain a number of fundamental limitations to our current understanding of intelligence, but as we will see, these are none other than the limitations of the empirical method itself. We show this methodology as our best and only tool for exploring the nature of intelligence.

16.1 Artificial Intelligence: A Revised Definition

Based on our experience of the last 15 chapters, we offer a revised definition of artificial intelligence:

> AI is the study of the mechanisms underlying intelligent behavior through the construction and evaluation of artifacts that enact those mechanisms.

This definition is a commitment to the scientific method of designing, running, and evaluating experiments with the goal of model refinement and further experiment. Besides describing current practice in the field of AI, this definition reflects our commitment to understanding the general principles underlying intelligent behavior.

Currently, the dominant approach to artificial intelligence involves the construction of representational formalisms and the corresponding search-based mechanisms. The guiding principle of this representational AI methodology is the *physical symbol system* hypothesis, first articulated by Newell and Simon (1976). This hypothesis states that:

> The necessary and sufficient condition for a physical system to exhibit general intelligent action is that it be a physical symbol system.
>
> *Sufficient* means that intelligence can be achieved by any appropriately organized physical symbol system.
>
> *Necessary* means that any agent that exhibits general intelligence must be an instance of a physical symbol system. The necessity of the physical symbol system hypothesis requires that any intelligent agent, whether human, space alien, or computer, achieve intelligence through the physical implementation of operations on symbol structures.

General intelligent action means the same scope of action seen in human action. Within physical limits, the system exhibits behavior appropriate to its ends and adaptive to the demands of its environment.

Both AI and cognitive science have explored the territory delineated by the physical symbol system hypothesis; both have supported its conjectures and clarified its scope. Newell and Simon have summarized the arguments for both the *necessity* and *sufficiency* of the hypothesis (Newell and Simon 1976; Newell 1981; Simon 1991).

The physical symbol system hypothesis leads us to four significant methodological commitments: (a) the use of symbols and systems of symbols (representations) to describe the world; (b) the design of search mechanisms, especially heuristic search, to explore the environment; (c) the disembodiment of cognitive architecture, by which we mean that an appropriately designed symbol system can provide a full causal account of intelligence, regardless of its medium of implementation; and (d) the empirical view of computer programs as experiments. As an empirical science, AI takes a constructive approach: we attempt to understand intelligence by building a working model of it.

Tokens in a formal language, referred to as *symbols*, can denote or reference something other than themselves. Like verbal tokens in a natural language, symbols can stand for or refer to other things in an intelligent agent's world of experience. Tarski demonstrated the possibility of a science of meaning in this object-referent relationship (Chapter 2).

AI's use of physical symbols goes beyond the questions addressed in Tarskian semantics, extending them to represent all forms of knowledge, skill, intention, and causality. However, all such constructive efforts rely on the fact that symbols, together with their semantics, can be embedded in formal systems. These define a *representation language*. This ability to formalize symbolic models of intelligence is essential to the implementation of these models as running computer programs. We studied several representations in detail: the predicate calculus, semantic networks, scripts, conceptual graphs, frames, and objects. The mathematics of formal systems allows us to argue such important issues as soundness, completeness, and the organization of knowledge.

The evolution of representational formalisms has allowed us to establish more complex (richer) semantic relationships. For example, inheritance systems constitute a semantic theory of taxonomic knowledge and its role in intelligence. By formally defining a model of class inheritance, such languages both simplify the construction of expert systems and provide testable models of the organization of categories in the human mind.

Closely bound to representational schemata and their use in reasoning is the notion of search. Search is the step-by-step examination of instances within the representational framework, looking for solutions, subproblem goals, problem symmetries, or whatever aspect of the problem is under consideration.

Representation and search are linked because a commitment to a particular representation determines a state space to be searched. Indeed, some problems can be made more difficult, or even impossible, through a poor choice of a representation language. The discussion of inductive bias in Chapter 12 illustrates this point.

A dramatic example of the interplay between search and representation and the difficulty of choosing an appropriate representation is the problem of placing dominos on a truncated chessboard. Assume that we have a chessboard and a set of dominos such that each domino will cover exactly two squares of the board, as in Figure 16.1. Also, assume

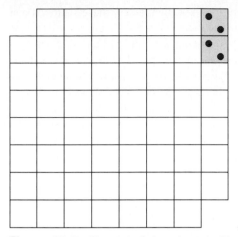

Figure 16.1 Truncated chessboard with two squares covered by a domino.

that the board has some missing squares; in Figure 16.1 the upper left-hand corner and lower right-hand corner have been truncated. This problem asks whether there is a way of placing dominos on the board so that each square is covered and each domino covers exactly two squares.

We can solve the problem by trying all placements of dominos on the board; this is the obvious search-based approach and is suggested by representing the board as a simple matrix, ignoring such seemingly irrelevant features as the color of squares. We could also start with a smaller board, such as 2×2 or 3×3, and attempt to reason to an answer for the 8×8 case.

A more sophisticated solution would note that every placement of a domino must cover both a black and a white square. This truncated board has 32 black squares but only 30 white squares; thus, the desired placement is not possible. How could we design a representation that allows a problem solver to access knowledge with this degree of flexibility and creativity? This remains a major continuing challenge for artificial intelligence.

The final issue that arises in search-based approaches to modeling intelligence is the use of heuristics. A heuristic is a mechanism for organizing search across the alternatives offered by a particular representation. Heuristics are designed to overcome the complexity of exhaustive search, the barrier to useful solutions for most classes of interesting problems. In computers, just as in humans, intelligence requires the informed choice of "what to do next."

Throughout the history of AI research, heuristics have taken many forms. The earliest problem-solving techniques, such as *hill climbing* in Samuel's checker-playing program (Chapter 4) or *means-ends analysis* in Newell, Shaw, and Simon's General Problem Solver (Chapter 11), came into AI from other disciplines, such as from the field of *operations research*, and gradually matured into general techniques for AI problem solving. Search properties, including *admissibility, monotonicity*, and *informedness,* are important results from the early studies. These techniques are often referred to as *weak methods.* Weak methods were general search strategies intended to be applicable across entire classes of problem domains (Newell and Simon 1972; Ernst and Newell 1969). We saw these methods and their properties in Chapters 3, 4, and 11.

We introduced *strong methods* for AI problem solving with the rule-based expert system. Strong methods focus on the information specific to each problem area, such as internal medicine or integral calculus, rather than on designing heuristic methods that generalize across these problem areas. Strong methods underlie expert systems and other knowledge-intensive approaches to problem solving. Strong methods emphasize such issues as the amount of knowledge needed for problem solving, learning and knowledge acquisition, the syntactic representation of knowledge, the management of uncertainty, and the quality of knowledge.

The amount of knowledge in a program represents problem-solving power. An essential feature of human expertise in areas such as medicine, mathematics, or configuring computers is the fact that these humans know a lot of things. It has been estimated that a grand master chess player has on the order of 50,000 patterns guiding his or her play.

The power of large rule sets is now available in many expert system application programs. The computer configuration expert at Digital Equipment Corporation contains over 6,000 rules (Soloway 1987). CYC (Lenat and Guha 1990) employs several hundred thousand rules in an attempt to represent commonsense knowledge of the world. CYC represents a valuable experiment on the possibility of symbolically representing commonsense knowledge. CYC has addressed a number of issues in knowledge representation, acquiring and integrating new knowledge, and the use of knowledge in continued learning.

The large amounts of knowledge required for such problems represent a departure from the "toy" domains or microworld applications found in much early AI research. Viable knowledge representation and problem-solving strategies must scale up in such large applications, effectively managing the problems of combinatorial growth.

A second source of heuristic power is the representation of individual rules and its effect on a program's behavior. We saw in Chapters 2 and 11 that there are often several equivalent expressions for any predicate calculus relationship. For instance:

$$(A \lor B) \to C = \neg A \land \neg B \lor C = \ldots.$$

With the equivalence of various forms of the same relationship, the way the rule is presented is important for using it within a reasoning scheme, such as back chaining. Often the human expert can assist us in structuring rules and guiding inferences. Perhaps the most important of the human expert's skills is the ability to pick the relevant issues from a myriad of possible alternatives and, focusing on the important details in data, use these to prune the search space and draw appropriate conclusions. We often try to mimic this skill in our rule- and object-based problem solving.

MYCIN offers an example of how heuristic methods, linked through a representation, contribute to intelligent problem solving in an application area. MYCIN (Chapter 8) closely modeled the performance of doctors delivering treatment to meningitis patients. In applying its medical knowledge to specific cases, MYCIN used a goal-driven, depth-first, exhaustive search, guided by a certainty factor algebra. Its performance was equal to or better than that of the human doctor. In MYCIN, the semantics of the computer model is an approximation of the goals, knowledge, and intention of the human doctor delivering treatment to meningitis patients.

A third aspect of heuristic search in knowledge-based programs is the management of the uncertainty introduced by heuristic reasoning. A certainty factor measures the confidence the expert has in the rule. The use of an algebra for combining and propagating certainty measures is a weak heuristic method, in that it is a general method applicable to a number of problem domains. The assignment of certainty measures to rules in a particular condition-action form is part of a strong method, in that it represents an explicit piece of knowledge.

Of course, our entire enterprise rests on the integrity of the information in our knowledge base. Eliciting problem-solving skill from human experts; dealing with subtly interconnected and sometimes misleading descriptions; creating and maintaining the knowledge base; and adding, without inconsistencies, new knowledge: these very human skills are still the most difficult part of producing a knowledge-based program. But when everything does come together, we are reminded again of Bacon's famous claim, *in knowledge is power!*

Perhaps the most significant challenge to the physical symbol system hypothesis is that brought by the neural net, or PDP, research community. Although the details of this problem-solving approach were presented in the machine learning chapter, Chapter 12, the philosophical underpinnings are addressed here. The PDP approach asserts that a physical symbol system is neither a necessary nor a sufficient characterization of intelligence.

We feel that neural networks and symbolic AI are simply different models of intelligence. Although both are fundamentally bounded by Church/Turing, in the context of a specific application it may be meaningful to ask whether one approach will work better than another. As theoreticians, we are concerned with generalized models of intelligent behavior and seeing what these models tell us about the nature of mind. In this context, these approaches are, at least for now, incommensurable.

By this we mean that each approach talks about intelligence in a different language; each approach asks different questions, proposes different models, and suggests and interprets different experiments to evaluate these models. Though researchers may someday show how symbols may be reduced to patterns in a network, or how symbol systems can indeed equal the behavior of neural nets, such reductions will not necessarily eliminate one model or the other. To take an example from another field, although chemistry may reduce to quantum mechanics, many of the questions asked by chemists are only formulated and answered at a chemical rather than a quantum mechanical level.

In machine learning, for example, an important question concerns the role of prior knowledge. Can effective learning occur on a *tabula rasa,* or "blank slate," starting with no initial knowledge and learning entirely from experience? Or must it start out with some prior inductive bias? What about the role of knowledge in more sophisticated forms of learning, such as scientific discovery?

Neural networks are not very good at answering these questions. Though the design of the network, the number of nodes at each layer, the patterns of connections, and so on, all constitute a form of bias, it is difficult to describe this bias as knowledge about the domain. Instead, neural network researchers characterize nets in terms of their statistical properties. No matter how developed a connectionist theory of learning may become, questions about the knowledge used by a learner may inherently require a symbolic answer.

For example, suppose we are developing a computational model of scientific discovery and want to theorize about how Copernicus shifted from a geocentric to heliocentric view of the universe. This requires that we represent both the Copernican and Ptolemaic views in a computer program. Although we could represent these views as patterns of activations in a neural network, our networks would tell us nothing about their behavior *as theories*. Instead, we prefer explanations such as "Copernicus was troubled by the complexity of the Ptolemaic system and preferred the simpler model of letting the planets revolve around the sun." Explanations such as this require symbols.

Similarly, neural nets can answer a number of questions that may be outside the expressive abilities of symbol based AI. An important class of such questions concerns perception. Nature is not so generous as to deliver our perceptions in the form of neat bundles of predicate calculus expressions. Neural networks are perhaps better at learning to recognize "meaningful" patterns in the chaos of sensory stimuli.

Currently, there is considerable interest in multi-agent or cooperative process problem solving, including the integration of network and symbol based approaches. Indeed, many neural networks do not completely escape the issues associated with symbolic representation. In many applications, the output units, and well as the input data, are given some sort of symbolic interpretation.

A theory of how symbols reduce to patterns in a network would be an extraordinary contribution to AI, allowing a number of developments, such as integrating network-based perceptual and knowledge-based reasoning facilities into a single agent. In the meantime, however, both approaches have considerable work to do. For researchers who may feel uncomfortable with two incommensurable models of intelligence, we point out that even physics functions quite comfortably with the seemingly contradictory notion that light is sometimes best understood as a wave and sometimes as a particle.

To summarize, the development of models of intelligence, based on the physical symbol system hypothesis—that is, by using explicit symbols, designed representations, and heuristic search—forms the primary subject matter of artificial intelligence. Our methodology is the use of machine and program to ask questions of nature: to implement and test our models. The results of our empirical queries indicate how well we understand the natural phenomena under scrutiny. In this sense our running programs offer a formal model of intelligent and purposeful human activity.

Artificial intelligence techniques may thus be used for two purposes. The first is simply to produce programs that use intelligence to solve practical problems. Expert systems and natural language understanding programs are examples of this approach. The second is to model and *understand* intelligence itself; research with this focus, referred to as *cognitive science,* is presented in the next section. In the final section we address theoretical limits of using the automated formal system as a model for intelligence.

16.2   Cognitive Science: An Overview

It is not a coincidence that a major subgroup of the artificial intelligence community has focused its research on understanding *human* intelligence. Humans provide the best example of intelligent activity, and AI engineers, even though they are usually *not* committed to "making their programs act like humans," seldom ignore the human's solution. Some applications, such as delivering medical care, are deliberately modeled on the solution processes of human experts working in the area. Most important, understanding human intelligence is a fascinating and open scientific challenge.

Modern cognitive science began with the advent of the digital computer, even though (Chapter 1) there were many intellectual forebears of this discipline, from Aristotle through Descartes to more modern theorists such as Turing, McCulloch, and Pitts, the founders of the *neural net* model, and John von Neumann. The study became a science, however, with the ability to design and run experiments based on these theoretical notions; that is, with the arrival of the computer.

16.2.1   The Analysis of Human Performance

Early research in cognitive science examined human solutions to logic problems, simple games, planning, and concept learning. At the beginning of Chapter 11 we described the Logic Theorist, a program by Newell, Shaw, and Simon, that proved many of the theorems in Russell and Whitehead's *Principia Mathematica*. Heuristic mechanisms, such as replacing a problem with a series of simpler subproblems, were used to manage the combinatorics involved in exhaustive search.

Coincident with their work on the Logic Theorist, Newell and Simon began to compare their computational heuristics with search strategies used by human subjects. Their data consisted of *think-aloud protocols*, descriptions by human subjects of their conscious thoughts during the process of devising a logic proof. Newell and Simon then compared these protocols with the behavior of the computer program solving the same problem. The researchers found remarkable similarities and interesting differences across both problems and subjects (Feigenbaum and Feldman 1963; Newell and Simon 1972; Simon 1989).

In the research that eventually led to the General Problem Solver (GPS), Newell and Simon proposed a theory of human problem solving and tested that theory with an implemented program. The difference reduction algorithm that compared two states of the problem and attempted to reduce the differences between them was called *means-ends analysis*. The link between the differences in the states of the problem was the *table of connections*, that is, the problem-specific information that linked states of the problem solution. The table of connections allowed the solution to progress from state to state (see Section 11.1 and Figure 11.2).

The GPS reduction algorithm of Figure 11.1 is an example of a *weak heuristic* method. As AI problem solving evolved toward expert systems, emphasis was placed more on the knowledge implicit in the table of connections for the problem and away from the weak general methods of recursively reducing differences.

Models for memory and concept learning also got attention early in the history of cognitive science. The work of Collins and Quillian on human associative memory, Section 9.2, is an important example of this. The semantic network representation that resulted from this research has had a far-reaching influence on AI data structures.

During the period 1956 to 1964, Edward Feigenbaum and Herbert Simon developed a program called EPAM, Elementary Perceiver And Memorizer. This program modeled human rote learning of nonsense syllables, an area of research called *verbal learning behavior*. The task involves the memorization of syllables consisting of two constants with a vowel between them, such as JUK, JIR, DAX. These syllables are designed to be free of any meaning that might affect their encoding by the human. A data structure called a *discrimination net* was created by Feigenbaum and Simon that modeled the learning behavior of human subjects on this task (Feigenbaum 1963).

These early projects established the methodology that cognitive science would employ during the following decades:

1. Based on data from humans solving particular classes of problems, design a representational scheme and related search strategy for solving the problem.

2. Run this computer-based model to produce a trace of its problem-solving behavior.

3. Observe human subjects working on these problems and keep track of measurable parameters of their solution process, such as think-aloud protocols, eye movements, written partial results, or whatever might aid the researchers in understanding the solution process.

4. Analyze and compare the human and computer solutions.

5. Revise the computer model for the next test and comparison.

This approach closely reflects the empirical methodologies described in Newell and Simon's Turing Award Lecture (excerpted at the beginning of this chapter); these are the methods that underlie science in general. An important aspect of cognitive science is the use of experiments to validate a problem-solving architecture, such as a production system. In addition to validating theories of human cognition, this methodology enables us to examine details of such models, fine-tuning them to more closely fit human performance. The production system, supported by decades of research in a number of diverse applications (Chapter 5; Newell and Simon 1972) is discussed in the next session.

16.2.2   The Production System and Human Cognition

In viewing the production system as a model of human problem solving, the *production memory* takes the role of the human's long-term memory or permanent store of problem-solving skills; these might range from generating moves in chess to delivering medical treatment. *Working memory* represents the human's short-term memory or attention. The *control mechanism*, matching the contents of working memory to the set of production rules, models the current focus of attention triggering one of the set of permanent skills. This, in turn, changes the locus of attention.

The production system offers an important link between strong and weak heuristic methods for problem solving. The division between the logic or knowledge and the control mechanism for using the knowledge allows focus either on the general (weak) heuristic methods as used in the control mechanism, or on the number and power of the production rules in the knowledge base (strong methods).

In recent years, a number of research projects have used the production system model to describe human problem-solving performance. Areas of research interest include:

Intelligent tutoring systems. If we conjecture that a person's problem-solving skills can be represented by a set of production rules, then errors in problem-solving efforts can be described by the absence, incorrectness, or misuse of one of these rules. Intelligent computer-aided instruction seeks to identify the missing or incorrect rule and then to teach the learner that skill or rule. This approach has been used in the areas of:

1. Teaching children subtraction skills (Brown and Burton 1978; Brown and vanLehn 1980).

2. Teaching skills in algebra problem solving (Sleeman and Smith 1981; Sleeman 1982).

3. Teaching concepts in debugging electronic circuits (Brown 1982).

4. Teaching computer programming skills (Soloway et al. 1983; Johnson and Keravnou 1985; Anderson 1989).

5. Teaching medical skills to doctors (Clancey 1983; Clancey and Shortliffe, 1984*a*).

Analysis of game-playing and problem-solving skills. A most thorough analysis of subjects solving cryptarithmetic problems, playing chess, and proving theorems in the propositional calculus is found in Newell and Simon (1972). This early work influenced the design of the General Problem Solver (Section 11.1), as well as in supporting the production system as a viable model of human problem-solving performance. Simon and his colleagues (Simon 1975) have also studied subjects in the process of acquiring problem-solving skills on the task of solving the four- and five-ring tower of Hanoi problem and its isomorphs (Simon 1975; Luger and Bauer 1978).

Analysis of problem-solving skills in applied mathematics. This problem area includes human performance on distance-rate-time problems, moment of inertia problems, and energy problems (Hinsley et al. 1977; deKleer 1975; Novak 1977). Research at the University of Edinburgh showed that search strategies responsible for generating systems of simultaneous equations to represent the relationships within these problems could be produced with goal-driven search on a set of production rules, each representing potential relationships within the problem (Bundy et al. 1979; Luger 1981). Other work at Carnegie Mellon University characterized the knowledge, referred to as problem related schemata, that high school students possessed for successfully solving algebra word problems. Several researchers constructed such schemata and tested them in computational models to determine their sufficiency for the problem-solving task (Hinsley et al. 1977; Luger 1981). Genesereth has created a consultation program for MACSYMA users (Genesereth 1982).

Comparisons of novices' and experts' problem-solving skills. These studies describe and compare skills within a particular problem area, such as the differences between the novice and expert problem solver in physics (Larkin et al. 1980) or in solving algebra word problems (Simon and Simon 1978). Studying these novice/expert differences can lead to better designs for rule bases or object specifications for expert systems, as well as offering suggestions for teaching these skills in the classroom.

Modelling the developmental skills. A related use of production rules or object representations is to describe the developmental stages of language or other skills. Piaget (1954, 1970), Anderson (1982), and others have shown how the human problem solver matures through distinct growth periods. Recognition, conservation, and use skills evolve through fixed invariant stages. These stages can be described at each level of development by precise algorithms, and then compared to better understand their evolution. These stages are studied for seriation tasks by Young (1976), for object permanence by Luger et al. (1983; 1985), and for language development (Luger and Johnson, in press).

The separation of knowledge and control and the modularity of the production rules make the production system ideally suited for experimentally modeling skilled problem-solving behavior, where altered results can be achieved by removing, adding, or simply changing the priority of the rules (Luger 1981; Neches et al. 1987). Alternatively, criticisms of this very simplicity, a number of which were mentioned in Chapters 9 and 10, have led to more advanced representations for AI problem solving. These have also played an important role in modeling human performance.

The organization of memory is an important feature of human intelligence that is not fully explained by the production system. Human memory does not appear to be an unstructured collection of productions. Instead, it is organized into thematically related structures called *schemata*, that enable a human to efficiently retrieve the knowledge that may be needed in a given context. Schemata also provide a reasonable source of default assumptions. There is also evidence that human memory exploits the organization of knowledge into class hierarchies. Such representations as semantic networks, frames, scripts and objects provide formal models of this organization.

We have already mentioned the Collins and Quillian model of associative memory. Research at Carnegie Mellon (Bhaskar and Simon 1977) used schema-based representation to account for problem solving in applied mathematics. Researchers at the University of Edinburgh examined subjects solving classes of pulley problems. The result of this research was to produce a running program that simulated much of the experts' problem-solving behavior and offered explicit information content for experts' knowledge schemata (Bundy et al. 1979; Luger 1981).

Research in English language understanding also used AI data structures to model human behavior. Simple tree hierarchies provided models for Linde's (1974) research on apartment descriptions and Grosz's (1977) work on task-based dialogues. Grosz's research is interesting in that she models performance in a complex task: working with an expert to build a pump. This interaction is modeled with a task-subtask hierarchy.

Cobweb (Section 12.6.3) addresses the problems of category formation and a family resemblance model of category structure. Though not intended as a model of human categorization, it provides a plausible account of such human characteristics as base level category effects and the distribution of properties throughout a taxonomy. Lakoff (1987) is an extensive survey of results on human category structure.

A number of researchers are attempting to model the full range of human perception, problem solving, and learning. This project offers an opportunity to integrate many of the issues that are too often addressed in a manner isolated from the rest of intellectual activity. This attempt at integrating models into a larger explanatory unit offers important constraints on its individual pieces as well as the total model.

ACT* (Anderson 1983b) is one of the first efforts to establish a complete theory of human cognition. ACT* combines declarative knowledge in the form of semantic nets with procedural knowledge in the form of production rules. ACT* learns through *knowledge compilation*, a process of forming new procedures through the combination of existing production rules.

SOAR (Rosenbloom and Newell 1986; Newell et al. 1989) attempts to model human cognition through an extension of the production system architecture. SOAR solves problems by defining and searching a *problem space*. An important issue in the SOAR architecture is the management of attention across different problem spaces. It models learning through a mechanism called *chunking*, which is related to explanation-based learning.

ACT* and SOAR are similar in attempting to provide a comprehensive account of intelligence in terms of a single, uniform architecture. Although different knowledge is used in different situations, a basic production system architecture underlies all performance. An alternative approach argues that a single architecture cannot account for all intelligent behavior. Instead, intelligence results from the cooperation of highly specialized agents. Minsky's (1985) *The Society of Mind* outlines such a model. In this model, mind consists of a collection of specialized agents; each agent contributes a particular ability to such tasks as understanding visual data, communicating in natural language, or high level problem solving. Intelligence results from the cooperation of groups of these agents. Other proponents of this cooperating multi agent view of mind include Selfridge (1959); Fodor (1983); Dennett (1991).

Even with the help of powerful representation techniques and some impressive early successes, cognitive science is a discipline yet to reach its promise. A number of the deep issues that both support its power as well as plague its continued progress are presented in the final section.

16.3 Representational Models for Intelligence: Issues and Directions

like the geometer who strives
  to square the circle and cannot find
  by thinking the principle needed,

was I at that new sight. . .

—DANTE, *Paradiso*

Although the use of AI techniques to solve practical problems has demonstrated its utility, the use of these techniques to found a general science of intelligence is a difficult and continuing problem. In this final section we address this issue.

The computational characterization of intelligence begins with the abstract specification of computational devices. Research through the nineteen-thirties, forties, and fifties began this task, with Turing, Post, Markov, and Church all contributing formalisms describing computation. The goal of this research was not just to specify what it meant to compute, but rather to specify limits on what could be computed. The Universal Turing Machine (Turing 1950), is the most commonly studied specification, although Post's rewrite rules, the basis for production system computing (Post 1943), is an important contribution. Church's model (1941), based on partially recursive functions, is also an important support for modern high-level functional languages, such as LISP, Scheme (Abelson and Sussman 1985), and Standard ML (Milner et al. 1990; Milner and Tofte 1991).

Theoreticians have proven that all of these formalisms have equivalent computational power in that any function computable by one is computable by the others. In fact, it is possible to show that the universal Turing machine is equivalent to any modern computational device. Based on these results, the Church-Turing thesis makes the even stronger argument that no model of computation can be defined which is more powerful than these known models. Once we establish equivalence of computational specifications, we have freed ourselves from the medium of mechanizing these specifications: we can implement our algorithms with vacuum tubes, silicone, protoplasm, or tinker toys. The automated design in one medium can be seen as equivalent to mechanisms in another. This makes the empirical enquiry method even more critical, as we experiment in one medium to test our understanding on mechanism implemented in another.

One of the possibilities we are exploring is that the universal machine of Turing and Post may be too general. Paradoxically, intelligence may require a less powerful computational mechanism with more focused control. Levesque and Brachman (1985) have suggested that human intelligence may require more computationally efficient (although less expressive) representations including the use of Horn clauses for reasoning, the restriction of factual knowledge to ground literals, and the use of computationally tractable truth maintenance systems.

Another philosophical point addressed by the formal equivalence of our models of mechanism is the duality issue and the mind-body problem. At least since Descartes (see Section 1.1), philosophers have asked the question of the interaction and integration of mind, consciousness, and a physical body. Philosophers have offered every possible response, from total materialism to the denial of material existence, even to the supporting intervention of a benign god. AI and cognitive science research reject Cartesian dualism in favor of a material model of mind based on the physical implementation or instantiation of symbols, the formal specification of computational mechanisms for manipulating those symbols, the equivalence of representational paradigms, and the mechanization of knowledge and skill in the automated formal system. The success of this research is an indication of the validity of this model (Johnson-Laird 1988; Dennett 1987; Luger and Johnson, in press).

Many consequential issues remain, however, within the epistemological foundations of intelligence in a physical system. We present several of these issues.

1. **Representational indeterminacy.** Anderson's representational indeterminacy conjecture (Anderson 1978) suggests that it may in principle be impossible to determine what representational scheme best approximates the human problem solver in the context of a particular act of skilled performance. This conjecture is founded on the fact that every representational scheme is inextricably linked to a larger computational architecture, as well as search strategies. In the detailed analysis of human skill, it may be impossible to control the process sufficiently so that we can determine the representation; or establish a representation to the point where a process might be uniquely determined. As with the uncertainty principle of physics, this is an important concern for constructing models of intelligence but need not limit their utility, as we show below.

2. **The assumptions of the physical symbol system hypothesis.** Newell and Simon hypothesized that the physical symbol system and its potential for search are necessary and sufficient explanations for intelligence (see 16.1). Many researchers in

cognitive science take this hypothesis literally. In what sense may it be demonstrated? Or is it simply a conjecture necessary to support much of the research in the area? Are the successes of the neural or subsymbolic models of intelligence refutations of the physical symbol hypothesis?

Even a weak interpretation of this hypothesis—that the physical symbol system is a *sufficient* model for intelligence—has produced many powerful and useful results in the modern field of cognitive psychology. What this argues is that we can implement physical symbol systems that will demonstrate intelligent behavior. Sufficiency allows creation and testing of symbol-based models for many aspects of human performance (Pylyshyn 1984; Posner 1989; Luger and Johnson, in press). But the strong interpretation—that the physical symbol system and search are *necessary* for explanation of intelligent activity—is open to question (Searle 1980; Weizenbaum 1976; Winograd and Flores 1986; Dreyfus and Dreyfus 1985).

3. **The necessity of designing computational models that are falsifiable.** Popper (1959) and others have argued that scientific theories must be falsifiable. This means that there must exist circumstances under which the model is not a successful approximation of the phenomenon. The obvious reason for this is that *any* number of confirming experimental instances is not sufficient for confirmation of a model. Much research is done in response to the failure of existing theories.

The general nature of the physical symbol system hypothesis may make it impossible to falsify and therefore of limited use as a model. The same criticism can also be made of the conjectures of the phenomenological tradition (see point 5 below). Some AI data structures, such as the semantic network, are so general that they can model almost anything describable, or as with the universal Turing machine, any computable function. When a cognitive scientist is asked under what conditions his or her model for intelligent activity does *not* work, the answer is often as difficult as determining the limitations of any scientific theory.

4. **Characterizing the nature of interpretation.** Most computational models in the representational tradition work with an already interpreted domain: that is, there is an implicit and *a priori* commitment of the system's designers to an interpretive context. Under this commitment there is little ability to shift contexts, goals, or representations as the problem solving evolves. Currently, there is also little effort at illuminating the process by which humans construct interpretations.

The Tarskian view of a semantic commitment as a mapping between symbols and objects is certainly too weak and doesn't explain, for example, the fact that one domain may have different interpretations in the light of different practical goals. Linguists generally try to remedy the limitations of Tarskian semantics by adding a theory of pragmatics (Austin 1962 and see Section 10.1). Research in discourse analysis, with its fundamental dependence on symbol use in context, has dealt with these issues extensively in recent years, although the problem is much broader in that it deals with the use and failure of referential tools in general (Lave 1988; Grosz et al. 1989).

The semiotic tradition started by C. S. Peirce (1955) and continued by Eco, Seboek, and others (Eco 1976; Seboek 1985) takes a more radical approach to language. It places symbolic expressions within the wider context of signs and sign interpretation. This suggests the meaning of a symbol can only be understood in the context of its role as interpretant, that is, in the context of an interpretation and interaction with the environment (Grice 1975; Stern and Luger 1992).

5. **The limitations of the scientific method.** A number of researchers (Winograd and Flores 1986; Weizenbaum 1976) claim that the most important aspects of intelligence are not and, in principle, cannot be modeled, and in particular not with a symbolic representation. These areas include learning, understanding natural language and the production of speech acts. Many of these issues have deep roots in philosophical tradition. Winograd and Flores's criticisms, for example, are based on issues raised in phenomenology (Husserl 1970; Heidegger 1962).

   Most of the assumptions of modern AI can trace their roots back from Carnap, Frege, and Leibniz through Hobbes, Locke, and Hume to Aristotle. This tradition argues that intelligent processes conform to universal laws and are, in principle, understandable.

   Heidegger and his followers represent an alternative approach to understanding intelligence. For Heidegger, reflective awareness is founded in a world of embodied experience (life-world). This position, shared by Winograd and Flores, Dreyfus, and others, argues that a person's understanding of things is rooted in the practical activity of coping with the everyday world. This world is essentially a context of socially organized roles and purposes. This context, and human functioning within it, is not something explained by propositions and understood by theorems. It is rather a flow that shapes and is itself continuously created. In a fundamental sense, human expertise is not knowing *that*, but rather, in a world of evolving social norms and implicit purposes, knowing *how*. We are inherently unable to place our knowledge and most of our intelligent behavior into language, either formal or natural.

   Let us consider this point of view. First, as a criticism of the *pure* rationalist tradition, it is correct. Rationalism asserts that all human activity, intelligence, and responsibility can, in principal at least, be represented, formalized, and understood. Most reflective people do not believe this to be the case, reserving important roles for emotion, self-affirmation and responsible commitment (at least!). Aristotle himself said, in his *Essay on Rational Action*, "Why is it that I don't feel compelled to perform that which is entailed?" There are many human activities outside the realms of the scientific method that play an essential role in responsible human interaction; these cannot be reproduced by or abrogated to machines.

   This being said, however, the scientific tradition of examining data, constructing models, running experiments, and examining results with model refinement for further experiments has brought an important level of understanding, explanation, and ability to predict to the human community. The scientific method is a powerful tool for increasing human understanding. Nonetheless, there remain a number of caveats to this approach that any scientist must understand.

   First, scientists must not confuse the model with the phenomenon being modeled. The model allows us to progressively approximate the phenomenon: there will, of necessity, always be a "residue" that is not empirically explained. In this sense also representational indeterminacy is *not* an issue. A model is used to explore, explain, and predict; and if it allows scientists to accomplish this it is successful (Kuhn 1962). Indeed, different models may successfully explain different aspects of a single phenomenon, for instance, the wave and particle theories of light.

Furthermore, when researchers claim that aspects of intelligent phenomena are outside the scope and methods of the scientific tradition, this statement itself can be verified only by using that very tradition. The scientific method is the only tool we have for explaining in what sense issues may still be outside our current understanding. Every viewpoint, even that from the phenomenological tradition, if it is to have any meaning, must relate to our current notions of explanation—even to give a coherent explanation of the sense in which phenomena cannot be explained.

Perhaps the most exciting aspect of work in AI is that to be coherent and contribute to the endeavor we must address these issues. To understand problem solving, learning, and language we must comprehend the philosophical level of representations and knowledge. In a humbling way we are asked to resolve Aristotle's tension between *theoria* and *praxis*, to fashion a union of understanding and practice, of the theoretical and practical, to live between science and art.

We are tool makers. Our representations, algorithms, and languages are tools for designing and building mechanisms that exhibit intelligent behavior. Through experiment we test both their computational adequacy for solving porblems as well as our own understanding of our environment.

Indeed, we have a tradition of this: Hobbes, Leibniz, Descartes, Babbage, Turing, and others whose contributions we presented in Chapter 1. Engineering and philosophy, the nature of ideas, knowledge, and skill, the power and limitations of formalism and mechanism; these are the limitations and tensions with which we must live and from which we continue our explorations.

16.4   Epilogue and References

We refer the reader to the references at the end of Chapter 1 and add *Computation and Cognition* (Pylyshyn 1984) and *Understanding Computers and Cognition* (Winograd and Flores 1986). For issues in cognitive science see Norman (1981), Newell and Simon (1972), Posner (1989), Luger and Johnson (in press).

Haugland (1981) and Dennett (1978) describe the philosophical foundations of cognitive science. Anderson's book on cognitive psychology offers valuable examples of information processing models (Anderson 1990). Pylyshyn (1984) and Anderson (1978) give detailed descriptions of many critical issues in cognitive science, including a discussion of representational indeterminacy. Dennett (1991) applies the methodology of cognitive science to an exploration of the structure of consciousness itself. We also recommend books on the philosophy of science (Popper 1959; Kuhn 1962; Bechtel 1988; Hempel 1965; Lakatos 1976; Quine 1953).

We leave the reader with address information on two important groups:

The American Association for Artificial Intelligence
445 Burgess Drive
Menlo Park, CA 94025

Computer Professionals for Social Responsibility
P.O. Box 717
Palo Alto, CA 94301

BIBLIOGRAPHY

Abelson, H., and Sussman, G. J. with Sussman, J. 1985. *Structure and Interpretation of Computer Programs*, Cambridge, MA: MIT Press.

Ackley, D. H., Hinton, G. E. and Sejnowski, T. J. 1985. A learning algorithm for Boltzmann machines. *Cognitive Science* 9.

Aho, A. V. and Ullman, J. D. 1977. *Principles of Compiler Design*. Reading, MA: Addison-Wesley.

Allen, J. 1987. *Natural Language Understanding*. Menlo Park, CA: Benjamin/Cummings.

Allen, J., Hendler, J. and Tate, A. 1990. *Readings in Planning*. Los Altos, CA: Morgan Kaufmann.

Alty, J. L. and Coombs, M. J. 1984. *Expert Systems: Concepts and Examples*. Manchester: NCC Publications.

Anderson, J. R. 1989. *Cognitive Psychology and its Implications,* 3rd edition, New York: W. H. Freeman.

Anderson, J. R. 1978. Arguments concerning representations for mental imagery. *Psychological Review* 85:249–277.

Anderson, J. R. 1982. Acquisition of cognitive skill. *Psychological Review* 89:369–406.

Anderson, J. R. 1983a. Acquisition of proof skills in geometry. In Michalski et al. (1983).

Anderson, J. R. 1983b. *The Architecture of Cognition*. Cambridge, MA: Harvard University Press.

Anderson, J. R. 1990. *Cognitive Psychology and its Implications*. New York: W. H. Freeman.

Anderson, J. and Bower, G. H. 1973. *Human Associative Memory*. Hillsdale, N.J.: Erlbaum.

Andrews, P. 1986. *An Introduction to Mathematical Logic and Type Theory: To Truth Through Proof*. New York: Academic Press.

anon. Digitalk. 1986. *Smalltalk/V: Tutorial and Programming Handbook*. Los Angeles: Digitalk.

Appelt, D. 1985. *Planning English Sentences*. London: Cambridge University Press.

Austin, J. L. 1962. *How to do Things with Words,* Cambridge, MA: Harvard University Press.

Bach, E. and Harms, R., eds. 1968. *Universals of Linguistic Theory*. New York: Holt Rinehart and Winston.

Bachant, J. and McDermott, J. 1984. R1 revisited: Four years in the trenches. *AI Magazine* 5(3).

Backus, J. 1978. Can programming be liberated from the Von Neumann style? A functional style and its algebra of programs, *Communications of the ACM*, 21(8), 613–641.

Balzer, R., Erman, L. D., London, P. E. and Williams, C. 1980. HEARSAY III: A domain independent framework for expert systems. *Proceedings AAAI 1980.*

Barr, A. and Feigenbaum, E., eds. 1981. *Handbook of Artificial Intelligence*, Volumes I and II. Los Altos, CA: William Kaufman.

Barker, V. E. & O'Connor, D. E., Expert Systems for configuration at DIGITAL: XCON and beyond, *Communications of the ACM,* vol 32, no. 3, p. 298–318, March 1989.

Bartlett, F. 1932. *Remembering.* London: Cambridge University Press.

Bateson, G. 1979. *Mind and Nature: A Necessary Unity.* New York: Dutton.

Bechtel, William. 1988. *Philosophy of Mind.* Hillsdale, NJ: Erlbaum.

Bhaskar, R. and Simon, H. A. 1977. Problem solving in semantically rich domains. *Cognitive Science* 1.

Bledsoe, W. W. 1971. Splitting and reduction heuristics in automatic theorem proving. *Artificial Intelligence* 2:55–77.

Bledsoe, W. W. 1977. Non-resolution theorem proving. *Artificial Intelligence* 9.

Bobrow, D. G. 1975. Dimensions of representation. In Bobrow and Collins (1975).

Bobrow, D. G. and Collins A., eds. 1975. *Representation and Understanding.* New York: Academic Press.

Bobrow, D. G. and Winograd, T. 1977. An overview of KRL, a knowledge representation language. *Cognitive Science* 1(1).

Boole, G. 1847. *The Mathematical Analysis of Logic.* Cambridge: MacMillan, Barclay & MacMillan.

Boole, G. 1854. *An Investigation of the Laws of Thought.* London: Walton & Maberly.

Boyer, R. S., and Moore, J. S. 1979. *A Computational Logic.* New York: Academic Press.

Brachman, R. J. 1979. On the epistemological status of semantic networks. In Brachman and Levesque (1985).

Brachman, R. J. 1985. I lied about the trees. *AI Magazine* 6(3).

Brachman, R. J. and Levesque, H. J. 1985. *Readings in Knowledge Representation.* Los Altos, CA: Morgan Kaufmann.

Brachman, R. J., Fikes, R. E., and Levesque, H. J. 1985. KRYPTON: A functional approach to knowledge representation. In Brachman and Levesque (1985).

Brachman, R. J., Levesque, H. J. and Reiter, R. eds. 1990. *Proceedings of the First International Conference on Principles of Knowledge Representation and Reasoning,* Los Altos, CA: Morgan Kaufmann.

Brodie, M. L., Mylopoulos, J. and Schmidt, J. W. 1984. *On Conceptual Modelling.* New York: Springer-Verlag.

Brown, J. S. and Burton, R. R. 1978. Diagnostic models for procedural bugs in basic mathematical skills. *Cognitive Science* 2.

Brown, J. S. and VanLehn, K. 1980. Repair theory: A generative theory of bugs in procedural skills. *Cognitive Science* 4:379–426.

Brown, J. S., Burton, R. R. and deKleer, J. 1982. Pedagogical, natural language and knowledge engineering techniques in SOPHIE. In Sleeman and Brown (1982).

Brownston, L., Farrell, R., Kant E., Martin, N. 1985. *Programming Expert Systems in OPS5: An Introduction to Rule-Based Programming.* Reading, MA: Addison-Wesley.

Buchanan, B. G. and T. M. Mitchell. 1978. Model-directed learning of production rules. In Waterman and Hayes-Roth (1978).

Buchanan, B. G. and Shortliff, E., H., eds. 1984. *Rule-Based Expert Systems: The MYCIN Experiments of the Stanford Heuristic Programming Project.* Reading, MA: Addison-Wesley.

Bundy, A. 1983. *Computer Modelling of Mathematical Reasoning.* New York: Academic Press.

Bundy, A., Byrd, L., Luger, G., Mellish, C., Milne, R. and Palmer, M. 1979. Solving mechanics problems using meta-level inference. *Proceedings of IJCAI-1979* 1017–1027.

Bundy, A. and Welham, R. 1981. Using meta-level inference for selective application of multiple rewrite rules in algebraic manipulation, *Artificial Intelligence* 16:189–212.

Burstall, R. M. and Darlington, J. A. 1977. A transformational system for developing recursive programs. *JACM* 24(January).

Burstein, M. 1986. Concept formation by incremental analogical reasoning and debugging. In Michalski et al. (1986).

Carbonell, J. G. 1983. Learning by analogy: Formulating and generalizing plans from past experience. In Michalski et al. (1983).

Carbonell, J. G. 1986. Derivational analogy: A theory of reconstructive problem solving and expertise acquisition. In Michalski et al. (1986).

Carbonell, J., Michalski, R. S. and Mitchell, T. M. 1983. An Overview of Machine Learning. In Michalski et al. (1983).

Carpenter, P. A. and Just, M. A. 1977. *Cognitive processes in Comprehension.* Hillsdale, N.J.: Erlbaum.

Ceccato, S. 1961. *Linguistic Analysis and Programming for Mechanical Translation.* New York: Gordon and Breach.

Chang, C. L. and Lee, R. C. T. 1973. *Symbolic Logic and Mechanical Theorem Proving.* New York: Academic Press.

Charniak, E. 1972. Toward a model of children's story comprehension. Rep No. TR- 266, AI Laboratory, MIT.

Charniak, E. and McDermott, D. 1985. *Introduction to Artificial Intelligence.* Reading, MA: Addison Wesley.

Charniak, E., Riesbeck, C. K., McDermott, D. V. and Meehan, J. R. 1987. *Artificial Intelligence Programming,* 2nd ed. Hillsdale, N. J: Erlbaum.

Charniak, E. and Wilks, Y. 1976. *Computational Semantics.* Amsterdam: North-Holland.

Chomsky, N. 1965. *Aspects of the Theory of Syntax.* Cambridge, MA: MIT Press.

Chorafas, Dimitris N. 1990. *Knowledge Engineering.* New York: Van Norstrand Reinhold. 1990.

Church, A. 1941. The calculi of lambda-conversion. *Annals of Mathematical Studies* Vol 6. Princeton: Princeton University Press.

Churchland, P. S. 1986. *Neurophilosophy: Toward a Unified Science of the Mind/Brain,* Cambridge MA: MIT Press.

Clancy, W. J. 1983. The advantages of abstract control knowledge in expert system design. *AAAI-3.*

Clancy, W. J. and Shortliffe, E. H. 1984a. Introduction: Medical artificial intelligence programs. In Clancy and Shortliffe (1984b).

Clancy, W. J. and Shortliffe, E. H., eds. 1984b. *Readings in Medical Artificial Intelligence: the First Decade.* Reading, MA: Addison Wesley.

Clocksin, W. F. and Mellish, C. S. 1984. *Programming in PROLOG*, 2nd edition. New York: Springer Verlag.

Cohen, P. R. and Feigenbaum, E. A. 1982. *The Handbook of Artificial Intelligence*, Volume 3. Los Altos, CA: William Kaufmann.

Cole, P. and Morgan, J. L. eds. 1975. *Studies in Syntax, Volume 3*. New York: Academic Press.

Collins A. and Quillian, M. R. 1969. Retrieval time from semantic memory. *Journal of Verbal Learning & Verbal Behavior* 8: 240–247.

Colmerauer, A. 1975. Les Grammaires de Metamorphose, Groupe Intelligence Artificielle, Universite Aix-Marseille II.

Colmerauer, A., Kanoui, H., Pasero, R., and Roussel, P. 1973. *Un Systeme de Communication Homme-machine en Francais*. Research Report, Groupe Intelligence Artificielle, Universite Aix-Marseille II, France.

Coombs, M. J., ed. 1984. *Developments in Expert Systems*. New York: Academic Press.

Corman, T. H., Leiserson, C. E. and Rivest, R. J. 1990. *Introduction to Algorithms.* Cambridge, Mass:MIT Press.

Crick, F. H. and Asanuma, C. 1986. Certain aspects of the anatomy and physiology of the cerebral cortex. In McClelland et al. (1986).

Dahl, V. 1977. Un Systeme Deductif d'Interrogation de Banques de Donnes en Espagnopl, PhD. Thesis. Universite Aix-Marseille.

Dahl, V. and McCord, M. C. 1983. Treating Coordination in Logic Grammars. *American Journal of Computational Linguistics* 9: 69–91.

Davis, Ernest. 1990. *Representations of Commonsense Knowledge*. Los Altos, CA: Morgan Kaufmann.

Davis, R. 1982. Applications of meta level knowledge to the construction, maintenance, and use of large knowledge bases. In Davis and Lenat (1982).

Davis, R. and D. B. Lenat. 1982. *Knowledge-based Systems in Artificial Intelligence*. New York: McGraw-Hill.

DeJong, G. and R. Mooney. 1986. Explanation-based learning: An alternative view. *Machine Learning* 1 (2): 145–176.

deKleer, J. 1975. Qualitative and quantitative knowledge of classical mechanics. Technical Report AI-TR-352, AI Laboratory, MIT.

deKleer, J. 1986. An assumption based truth maintenance system, *Artificial Intelligence*, 28.

Dennett, D. C. 1978. *Brainstorms: Philosophical Essays on Mind and Psychology*. Montgomery, AL: Bradford.

Dennett, D. C. 1984. *Elbow Room: The Varieties of Free Will Worth Wanting*. London: Cambridge University Press.

Dennett, Daniel. 1987. *The Intentional Stance*. Cambridge MA: MIT Press.

Dennett, Daniel. 1991. *Consciousness Explained*. Boston: Little, Brown.

Dietterich, T. G. 1986. Learning at the knowledge level. *Machine Learning* 1 (3): 287–316.

Dietterich, T. G. and Michalski, R. S. 1981. Inductive learning of structural descriptions: Evaluation criteria and comparative review of selected methods. *Proceedings IJCAI 6*.

Dietterich, T. G. and Michalski, R. S. 1986. Learning to predict sequences. In Michalski et al. (1986).

Doyle, J. 1979. A truth maintenance system. *Artificial Intelligence*, 12.

Dreyfus, H. L. and Dreyfus, S. E. 1985. *Mind Over Machine*. New York: Macmillan/The Free Press.

Duda, R. O., Gaschnig, J., Hart, P. E. 1979a. Model design in the PROSPECTOR consultant system for mineral exploration. In Michie (1979).

Duda, R. O., Hart, P. E., Konolige, K. and Reboh, R. 1979b. A computer-based consultant for mineral exploration. SRI International.

Eco, Umberto. 1976. *A Theory of Semiotics*. Bloomington, Indiana: University of Indiana Press.

Erman, L. D., Hayes-Roth, F., Lesser, V., and Reddy, D. 1980. The HEARSAY II speech understanding system: Integrating knowledge to resolve uncertainty. *Computing Surveys* 12(2): 213–253.

Erman, L. D., London, P. E. and Fickas, S. F. 1981. The design and an example use of HEARSAY III. In *Proceedings IJCAI 7*.

Ernst, G. W. and Newell, A. 1969. *GPS: A Case Study in Generality and Problem Solving*. New York: Academic Press.

Etherington, D. W. and Reiter, R. 1983. On inheritance hierarchies with exceptions. *Proceedings AAAI-83* 104–108.

Euler, L. 1735. The seven bridges of Konigsberg. In Newman (1956).

Evans, T. G. 1964. A heuristic program to solve geometric analogy problems. In Minsky (1968).

Falkenhainer, B., K. D. Forbus, and D. Gentner 1989 The structure mapping engine: Algorithm and examples. *Artificial Intelligence* 41 (1): 1–64.

Falkenhainer, B. 1990. Explanation and theory formation. In Shrager and Langley (1990).

Fass, D. and Wilks, Y 1983. Preference semantics with ill-formedness and metaphor. *American Journal of Computational Linguistics IX*, 178–187.

Feigenbaum, E. A. 1963. The simulation of verbal learning behavior. In Feigenbaum and Feldman (1963).

Feigenbaum, E. A., and Feldman, J., eds. 1963. *Computers and Thought*. New York: McGraw-Hill.

Feigenbaum, E. and McCorduck, P. 1983. *The Fifth Generation: Artificial Intelligence and Japan's Computer Challange to the World*. Reading, MA: Addison-Wesley.

Fikes, R. E. and Nilsson, N. J. 1971. STRIPS: A new approach to the application of theorem proving to artificial intelligence. *Artificial Intelligence* 1(2).

Fikes, R. E., P. E. Hart, and N. J. Nilsson. 1972. Learning and executing generalized robot plans. *Artificial Intelligence* 3 (4): 251–88.

Fillmore, C. J. 1968. The case for case. In Bach and Harms (1968).

Fisher, D. 1987. Knowledge acquisition via incremental conceptual clustering. *Machine Learning* 2 : 139–172.

Fisher, Douglas H. Jr., Michael J. Pazzani, and Pat Langley. 1991. *Concept Formation: Knowledge and Experience in Unsupervised Learning*. San Mateo, CA: Morgan Kaufmann Publishing.

Fodor, J. A. 1983.*The Modularity of Mind,* Cambridge, MA:MIT Press.

Frege, G. 1879. *Begriffsschrift, eine der arithmetischen nachgebildete Formelsprache des reinen Denkens*. Halle: L. Niebert.

Frege, G. 1884. *Die Grundlagen der Arithmetic*. Breslau: W. Koeber.

Gadamer, H. G. 1976. *Philisophical Hermeneutics.*, translated by Linge, D. E. Berkeley: University of California Press.

Gallier, J. H. 1986. *Logic for Computer Science: Foundations of Automatic Theorem Proving.* New York: Harper and Row.

Garey, M. and Johnson, D. 1979. *Computers and Intractability: A Guide to the Theory of NP-Completeness.* San Francisco: Freeman.

Genesereth, M. and Nilsson, N. 1987. *Logical Foundations of Artificial Intelligence.* Los Altos, CA: Morgan Kaufmann.

Genesereth, M. R. 1982. The role of plans in intelligent teaching systems. In Sleeman and Brown (1982).

Gennari, J. H., P. Langley, and D. Fisher. 1989. Models of incremental concept formation. *Artificial Intelligence* 40 (1-3): 11–62.

Gentner, Dedre. 1983. Structure-mapping: A theoretical framework for analogy. *Cognitive Science* 7 : 155–170.

Gluck, M. and J. Corter. 1985. Information, uncertainty and the utility of categories. *Seventh Annual Conference of the Cognitive Science Society in Irvine, Cal.*

Goldberg, A. and Robson, D. 1983. *Smalltalk 80: The Language and Its Implementation.* Reading, MA: Addison Wesley.

Goldstine, H. H. 1972. *The Computer from Pascal to Von Neumann.* Princeton, N.J.: Princeton University Press.

Goodman, Nelson. 1954. *Fact, Fiction and Forecast.* 4th ed., Cambridge, MA: Harvard University Press.

Grice, H. Paul. 1975. Logic and conversation. in Cole and Morgan (1975).

Grossberg, Stephen, ed. 1988. *Neural Networks and Natural Intelligence.* Cambridge, MA: MIT Press.

Grosz, B. 1977. The representation and use of focus in dialogue understanding. Ph.D. Thesis, University of California, Berkeley.

Grosz, B. J. & Sidner, C. L . 1990. Plans for discourse, 417–444, in Cohen, P. R., Morgan, J., and Pollack, M. E., eds. *Intentions in Communication,* Cambridge: MIT Press.

Hall, R.P. 1989. Computational approaches to analogical reasoning: A comparitive analysis. 39 (1): 39–120.

Hammond, K., ed. 1989. *Case Based Reasoning Workshop.* San Mateo, CA: Morgan Kaufmann.

Harmon, P. and King, D. 1985. *Expert Systems: Artificial Intelligence in Business.* New York: Wiley.

Harmon, P., Maus, R. and Morrissey, W. 1988. *Expert Systems: Tools and Applications.* New York: Wiley.

Harris, M. D. 1985. *Introduction to Natural Language Processing.* Reston, Va: Reston.

Haugheland, J., ed. 1981. *Mind Design: Philosophy, Psychology, Artificial Intelligence.* Cambridge, MA: MIT.

Haugheland, J. 1985. *Artificial Intelligence: the Very Idea.* Cambridge/Bradford, MA: MIT Press.

Haussler, D. 1988. Quantifying inductive bias: AI learning algorithms and Valiant's learning framework. *Artificial Intelligence* 36 : 177–222.

Hayes, P. J. 1974. Some problems and non-problems in representation theory. *Proc. AISB Summer Conference* 63-69. University of Sussex.

Hayes, P. J. 1977. In defense of logic. *Proceedings IJCAI-77,* 559–564. Cambridge, MA.

Hayes, P. J. 1979. The logic of frames. In Metzing (1979).

Hayes-Roth, F. and McDermott, J. 1983. An inference matching technique for inducing abstractions. *Communications of the ACM* 26:401–410.

Hayes-Roth, F., Waterman, D., and Lenat, D. 1984. *Building Expert Systems*. Reading, MA: Addison-Wesley.

Hebb, D. O. 1949. *The Organization of Behavior.* New York: Wiley.

Heidegger, Martin. 1962. *Being and Time.* translated by Masquarrie, J. and Robinson, E. New York: Harper and Row.

Heidorn, G. E. 1975. Augmented phrase structure grammar. In Schank and Nash-Webber (1975).

Helman, David H. 1988. *Analogical Reasoning: Perspective of Artificial Intelligence, Cognitive Science, and Philosophy,* Kauwer.

Helman, P. and Veroff, R. 1986. *Intermediate Problem Solving and Data Structures: Walls and Mirrors*, Menlo Park, CA: Benjamin/Cummings.

Hempel, Carl G. 1965. *Aspects of Scientific Explanation.* New York: The Free Press.

Henderson, Peter. 1980. *Functional programming: Application and Implementation.* Englewood Clifs N.J.: Prentice-Hall.

Hillis, D. W. 1985. *The Connection Machine.* Cambridge: MIT Press.

Hinsley, D., Hayes, J. and Simon, H. 1977. From words to equations: Meaning and representation in algebra word problems. In Carpenter and Just (1977).

Hinton, G. E. and Sejnowski, T. E. 1986. Learning and relearning in Boltzmann machines. In McClelland et al. (1986).

Hinton, G. E. and Sejnowski, T. J. 1987. Neural network architectures for AI. Tutorial, AAAI Conference.

Hodges, A. 1983. *Alan Turing: The Enigma.* New York: Simon and Schuster.

Holland, John. H. 1986. Escaping brittleness: The possibilities of general purpose learning algorithms applied to parallel rule-based systems. In Michalski, Carbonell, and Mitchell (1986).

Holland, John H., Kieth J. Holyoak, Richard E. Nisbett, and Paul R. Thagard. 1986. *Induction: Processes of Inference, Learning and Discovery.* Cambridge, MA: MIT Press.

Holyoak, K. J. 1985. The pragmatics of analogical transfer. *The Psychology of Learning and Motivation* 19 : 59–87.

Hopcroft, J. E. and Ullman, J. D. 1979. *Introduction to Automata Theory, Languages and Computation.* Reading, MA: Addison-Wesley.

Hopfield, J. J. 1982. Neural networks and physical systems with emergent collective computational abilities. *Proceedings of the National Academy of Sciences 79.*

Horowitz, E. and Sahni, S. 1978. *Fundamentals of Computer Algorithms.* Rockville, MD: Computer Science Press.

Hume, David. 1748. *An Inquiry Concerning Human Understanding.* New York: Bobbs-Merril.

Husserl, E. 1970.*The Crisis of European Sciences and Transcendental Phenomenology*, translated by David Carr, Evanston Ill.: Northwestern University Press.

Husserl, E. 1972. *Ideas: General Introduction to Pure Phenomenology.* New York: Collier.

Ignizio, James P. 1991 *Introduction to Expert Systems: The Development and Implementation of Rule-Based Expert Systems*, New York: McGraw-Hill.

Johnson, L. and Keravnou, E. T. 1985. *Expert Systems Technology: A Guide*. Cambridge, MA: Abacus Press.

Johnson, W. L. and Soloway, E. 1985. Proust. *Byte* (April).

Johnson-Laird, P. 1983. *Mental Models*. Cambridge, MA: Harvard University Press.

Johnson-Laird, P. 1988. *The Computer and the Mind*. Cambridge, MA: Harvard University Press.

Kedar-Cabelli, S. 1988. Analogy—From a unified perspective. In Helman (1988).

Kedar-Cabelli, S. T. and McCarty, L. T. 1987. Explanation based generalization as resolution theorem proving. *Proceedings of the Fourth International Workshop on Machine Learning*.

Keravnou, E. T. and Johnson, L. 1986. *Competent Expert Systems: A Case Study in Fault Diagnosis*. London: Kegan Paul.

Klahr, D., Langley, P. and Neches, R. ed. 1987. *Production System Models of Learning and Development*. Cambridge MA: MIT Press.

Klahr, P. and Waterman, D. A. 1986. *Expert Systems: Techniques, Tools and Applications*. Reading, MA: Addison-Wesley.

Kodratoff, Yves and Ryszard S. Michalski, ed. 1990. *Machine Learning: An Artificial Intellience Approach*. Vol. 3. Los Altos, CA: Morgan Kaufmann Publishing.

Kolodner, J. L. 1987. Extending problem solver capabilities through case based inference. *Proceedings of the Fourth International Workshop on Machine Learning*. Los Altos, CA: Morgan Kaufmann.

Kolodner, J. L. 1988a. Retrieving events from a case memory: A parallel implementation. *Proceedings of the Case Based Reasoning Workshop*. Los Altos, CA: Morgan Kaufmann.

Kolodner, J. L., ed. 1988b. *Case Based reasoning Workshop*. San Mateo, CA: Morgan Kaufmann.

Korf, R. E. 1987. Search. In Shapiro (1987b).

Kowalski, R. 1979a. Algorithm = Logic + Control. *Communications of the ACM* 22:424–436.

Kowalski, R. 1979b. *Logic for Problem Solving*. Amsterdam: North Holland.

Koza, John R. 1991. Genetic evolution and co-evolution of computer programs. In Langton et al. (1991).

Kuhn, T. S. 1962. *The Structure of Scientific Revolutions*. Chicago: Universtiy of Chicago Press.

Laird, J., Rosenbloom, P. and Newell, A. 1986a. Chunking in SOAR: The Anatomy of a General Learning Mechanism. *Machine Learning* 1(1).

Laird, J., Rosenbloom, P. and Newell, A. 1986b. *Universal Subgoaling and Chunking: The automatic Generation and Learning of Goal Hierarchies*. Dordrecht: Kluwer.

Lakoff, George. 1987. *Women, Fire and Dangerous Things*. Chicago: University of Chicago Press.

Lakatos, Imre. 1976. *Proofs and Refutations: The Logic of Mathematical Discovery*. Cambridge University Press.

Langley, P., Bradshaw, G. L., and Simon, H. A. 1981. Bacon 5: The discovery of conservation laws, in *Proceedings of the Seventh International Joint Conference on Artificial Intelligence*.

Langley, P., Simon, H. A., Bradshaw, G. L. and Zytkow, J. M. 1987. *Scientific Discovery: Computational Explorations of the Creative Processes*. Cambridge, MA: MIT Press.

Langley, P., Zytkow, J., Simon, H. A., and Bradshaw, G. L. 1986. The search for regularity: Four aspects of scientific discovery. in Michalski et al. (1986).

Langton, C. G., Taylor, C., Farmer, J. D., and Rasmussen, S. *Artificial Life II, SFI Studies in the Sciences of Complexity*. Vol. 10. Reading, MA: Addison-Wesley.

Larkin, J. H., McDermott, J., Simon, D.P. and Simon, H. A. 1980. Models of Competence in solving physics problems. *Cognitive Science* 4.

Lave, Jean. 1988. Cognition in Practice, Cambridge: Cambridge Univ. Press.

Leibniz, G. W. 1887. *Philosophische Schriften*. Berlin.

Lenat, D. B. 1977. On automated scientific theory formation: a case study using the AM program. *Machine Intelligence* 9:251–256.

Lenat, D. B. 1982. AM: an artificial intelligence approach to discovery in mathematics as heuristic search. In Davis and Lenat (1982).

Lenat, D. B. 1983. EURISKO: A program that learns new heuristics. *Artificial Intelligence* 21 (1 & 2): 61–98.

Lenat, D. B. and Brown, J. S. 1984. Why AM and Eurisko appear to work. *Artificial Intelligence* 23 (3):

Lenat, D. B. and Guha, R. V. 1990. *Building Large Knowledge Based Systems,* Reading MA: Addison Wesley.

Lennon, J. and McCartney, P. 1968. Rocky Raccoon. *The White Album*. Apple Records.

Lesser, V. R. and Corkill, D. D. 1983. The distributed vehicle monitoring testbed. *AI Magazine* 4(3).

Levesque, H. 1984. Foundations of a functional approach to knowledge representation. *Artificial Intelligence* 23(2).

Levesque, H. J. and Brachman, R. J. 1985. A fundamental tradeoff in knowledge representation and reasoning (Revised Version). In Brachman and Levesque (1985).

Linde, C. 1974. Information structures in discourse. Ph.D. Thesis, Columbia University.

Lindsay, R. K. Buchanan, B. G.. Feigenbaum, E. A., and Lederberg, J. 1980. *Applications of artificial intelligence for organic chemistry: the DENDRAL project*. New York: McGraw-Hill.

Lloyd, J. W. 1984. *Foundations of Logic Programming* . New York: Springer Verlag.

Lovelace, A. 1961. Notes upon L. F. Menabrea's sketch of the Analytical Engine invented by Charles Babbage. In Morrison (1961).

Loveland, D. W. 1978. *Automated Theorem Proving: a Logical Basis*. New York: North-Holland.

Luger, G. F. 1981. Mathematical model building in the solution of mechanics problems: human protocols and the MECHO trace. *Cognitive Science* 5:55–77.

Luger, G. F., Bower, T. G. R., & Wishart, J. G., 1983. A Model of the development of the early infant object concept. *Perception,* vol 12, p 21–34.

Luger, G. F., Wishart, J. G., and Bower, T. G. R. 1984. Modelling the stages of the identity theory of object-concept development in infancy. *Perception,* vol 13, p 97–115.

Luger, G. F. and Bauer, M. A. 1978. Transfer effects in isomorphic problem solving. *Acta Psychologia* 42.

Luger, G. F. 1978. Formal analysis of problem solving behavior. in *Cognitive Psychology: Learning and Problem Solving*, Open University Press, Walton Hall, Milton Keynes.

Luger, George. F. and Johnson, Peder. In press. *Cognitive Science: A Science of Intelligent Systems,* New York: Academic Press.

Machtey, M. and Young, P. 1979. *An Introduction to the General Theory of Algorithms*. Amsterdam: North Holland.

MacLennan, B. J. 1987. *Principles of Programming Languages: Design, Evaluation, and Implementation*, 2nd ed. New York: Holt, Rinehart & Winston.

Maier, D. and Warren, D. S. 1988. *Computing with Logic*. Menlo Park, CA: Benjamin Cummings.

Malpas, J. 1987. *PROLOG: A Relational Language and its Applications*. Englewood Cliffs, N.J.: Prentice Hall.

Manna, Z. and Waldinger, R. 1985. *The Logical Basis for Computer Programming*. Reading, MA: Addison-Wesley.

Markov, A. 1954. A theory of algorithms, *National Acadamy of Sciences*, USSR.

Masterman, M. 1961. Semantic message detection for machine translation, using Interlingua. *Proceedings of the 1961 International Conference on Machine Translation.*

McCarthy, J. 1960. Recursive functions of symbolic expressions and their computation by machine. *Communications of the ACM* 3(4).

McCarthy, J. 1968. Programs with common sense. In Minsky (1968), 403–418.

McCarthy, J. 1977. Epistemological problems in artificial intelligence. *Proceedings IJCAI-77,* 1038–1044.

McCarthy, J. 1980. Circumscription - A form of non-monotonic reasoning. *Artificial intelligence* 13.

McCarthy, J. and Hayes, P. J. 1969. Some philosophical problems from the standpoint of artificial intellience. In Meltzer and Michie (1969).

McClelland, J. L., Rumelhart, D. E. and The PDP Research Group. 1986. *Parallel Distributed Processing*, Volumes 1 and 2. Cambridge, MA: MIT Press.

McCord, M. C. 1982. Using slots and modifiers in logic grammars for natural language. *Artificial Intelligence* 18, 327–367.

McCord, M. C. 1986. Design of a PROLOG based machine translation system. *Proceedings of the Third International Logic Programming Conference*. London.

McCulloch, W. S. and W. Pitts. 1943. A logical calculus of the ideas immanent in nervous activity. *Bulletin of Mathematical Biophysics* 5 : 115–133.

McDermott, D. 1978. Planning and acting. *Cognitive Science 2*.

McDermott, J. 1981. R1, The formative years. *AI Magazine* (Summer).

McDermott, J. 1982. R1: A rule based configurer of computer systems. *Artificial Intelligence* 19.

McDermott, J. and Bachant, J. 1984. R1 revisited: Four years in the trenches. *AI Magazine*, 5 (3).

McGraw, Karen L. and Harbison-Briggs, Karen. 1989. *Knowledge Acquisition: Principles and Guidelines*, Englewood Cliffs, N. J.: Prentice-Hall.

Meltzer, B. and Michie, D. 1969. *Machine Intelligence 4*. Edinburgh: Edinburgh University Press.

Metzing, D., ed. 1979. *Frame Conceptions and Text Understanding*. Berlin: Walter de Gruyter and Co.

Michalski, Ryszard S., Jaime G. Carbonell, and Tom M. Mitchell, ed. 1983. *Machine Learning: An Artificial Intellience Approach*. Vol. 1. Palo Alto, CA: Tioga.

Michalski, Ryszard S., Jaime G. Carbonell, and Tom M. Mitchell, ed. 1986. *Machine Learning: An Artificial Intellience Approach*. Vol. 2. Los Altos, CA: Morgan Kaufmann.

Michalski, Ryszard, S. and Robert E. Stepp. 1983. Learning from observation: conceptual clustering. In Michalski, Carbonell, and Mitchell (1983).

Michie, D., ed. 1979. *Expert Systems in the Micro-electronic Age*. Edinburgh: Edinburgh University Press.

Milner, Robin, Tofte, Mads and Harper, Robert. 1990. *Definition of Standard ML,* Cambridge, MA: MIT Press, 1990.

Milner, Robin and Tofte, Mads. 1991. *Commentary on Standard ML,* Cambridge, MA: MIT Press.

Minsky, M. 1975. A framework for representing knowledge. In Brachman and Levesque (1985).

Minsky, M. 1985. *The Society of Mind,* New York: Simon and Schuster.

Minsky, M. and Papert, S. 1969. *Perceptrons: An Introduction to Computational Geometry.* Cambridge, MA: MIT Press.

Minsky, M. ed. 1968. *Semantic Information Processing.* Cambridge, MA: The MIT Press.

Minton, Steven. 1988. *Learning Search Control Knowledge.* Dordrecht: Kluwer Academic Publishers.

Mitchell, T. M. 1978. Version spaces: an approach to concept learning. Rep No. STAN-CS-78–711, Computer Science Dept., Stanford University.

Mitchell, T. M. 1979. An analysis of generalization as a search problem. *Proceedings IJCAI 6.*

Mitchell, T. M. 1982. Generalization as search. *Artificial Intelligence* 18 (2): 203–226.

Mitchell, T. M., Utgoff, Paul E. and Banarji, Ranan. 1983. Learning by experimentation: Acquiring and refining problem solving heuristics. In Michalski, Carbonell, and Mitchell (1983).

Mitchell, T. M., R. M. Keller, and S. T. Kedar-Cabelli. 1986. Explanation-based generalization: A unifying view. *Machine Learning* 1 (1): 47–80.

Mockler, Robert, J. and Dologite, D. G. 1992. *An Introduction to Expert Systems*, New York: Macmillan.

Moore, O. K. and Anderson, S. B. 1954. Modern logic and tasks for experiments on problem solving behavior. *Journal of Psychology.* 38:151–160.

Moore, R. C. 1982. The role of logic in knowledge representation and commonsense reasoning. *Proceedings AAAI-82.*

Moret, B. M. E. and Shaprio, H. D. 1991. *Algorithms from P to NP,* vol 1. Redwood City, CA: Benjamin Cummings.

Morrison, P. and Morrison, E., eds. 1961. *Charles Babbage and His Calculating Machines.* New York: Dover.

Mostow, D. J. 1983. Machine transformation of advice into a heuristic search procedure. In Michalski et al. (1983).

Mycroft, A. and O'Keefe, R. A. 1984. A polymorphic type system for PROLOG. *Artificial Intelligence* 23: 295–307.

Mylopoulos, J. and Levesque, H. J. 1984. An overview of knowledge representation in Brodie et al. (1984).

Nagel, E. and Newman, J. R. 1958. *Godel's Proof.* New York: New York University Press.

Neches, R., Langley, P. and Klahr, D. 1987. Learning, development and production systems. In Klahr et al. (1987).

Negoita, C. 1985. *Expert Systems and Fuzzy Systems.* Menlo Park, CA: Benjamin/Cummings.

Neves, J. C. F. M, Luger, G. F. and Carvalho, J. M. 1986. A Formalism for views in a logic data base. in *Proceedings of the ACM Computer Science Concerence, Cincinatti 1986.*

Newell, A. 1990. *Unified Theories of Cognition,* Cambridge: Harvard University Press.

Newell, A. 1981, Physical symbol systems, in Norman (1981).

Newell, A. 1982. The knowledge level. *Artificial Intelligence* 18(1): 87–127.

Newell, A. Rosenbloom, P. S. and Laird, J. E. 1989. Symbolic architectures for cognition, in Posner (1989).

Newell, A., Shaw, J. C. and Simon, H. A. 1958. Elements of a theory of human problem solving. *Psychological Review* 65: 151–166.

Newell, A. and Simon, H. 1956. The logic theory machine. *IRE Transactions of Information Theory* 2:61–79.

Newell, A. and Simon, H. 1963a. Empirical explorations with the Logic Theory Machine: a case study in heuristics. In Feigenbaum and Feldman (1963).

Newell, A. and Simon, H. 1963b. GPS: a program that simulates human thought. In Feigenbaum and Feldman (1963).

Newell, A. and Simon, H. 1972. *Human Problem Solving*. Engelwood Cliffs, N. J. : Prentice Hall.

Newell, A. and Simon, H. 1976. Computer science as empirical inquiry: symbols and search. *Communications of the ACM* 19:3:113–126.

Newman, J. R. 1956. *The World of Mathematics*. New York: Simon and Schuster.

Nii, H. P. 1986a. Blackboard systems: The blackboard model of problem solving and the evolution of blackboard architectures. *AI Magazine* 7(2).

Nii, H. P. 1986b. Blackboard systems: Blackboard application systems from a knowledge based perspective. *AI Magazine* 7(3).

Nii, H. P. and Aiello, N. 1979. AGE: A knowledge based program for building knowledge based programs. *Proceedings IJCAI 6*.

Nilsson, N. J. 1980. *Principles of Artificial Intelligence*. Palo Alto, CA: Tioga.

Nordhausen, B. and Langley, P. 1990. An integrated approach to empirical discovery. In Shrager and Langley (1990).

Norman, D. A. 1972. Memory, knowledge and the answering of questions. CHIP Technical Report 25, Center for Human Information Processing, University of California, San Diego.

Norman, D. A. 1981. *Perspectives on Cognitive Science*. Hillsdale, N.J.: Erlbaum.

Norman, D. A. and Rumelhart, D. E., and the LNR Research Group. 1975. *Explorations in Cognition*. San Francisco: Freeman.

Novak, G. S. 1977. Computer understanding of physics problems stated in natural language. *Proceedings IJCAI 5*.

O'Keefe, Richard. 1990. *The Craft of PROLOG*. Cambridge, MA: MIT Press.

Papert, S. 1980. *Mindstorms*. New York: Basic Books.

Pearl, J. 1984. *Heuristics: Intelligent Strategies for Computer Problem Solving*. Reading, MA: Addison-Wesley.

Pearl, J. 1988. *Probablistic Reasoning in Intelligent Systems: Networks of Plausible Inference*. Los Altos, CA: Morgan Kaufmann.

Peirce, C. S. 1955. T*he Philosophical Writings of Peirce*. New York: Dover Publications.

Pereira, L. M. and Warren, D. H. D. 1980. Definite clause grammars for language analysis—A survey of the formalism and a comparison with augmented transition networks. *Artificial Intelligence* 13, 231–278.

Piaget, J. 1954. *The Construction of Reality in The Child*. New York: Basic Books.

Piaget, J. 1970. *Structuralism*. New York: Basic Books.

Polya, G. 1945. *How to Solve It*. Princeton: Princeton University Press.

Popper, K. R. 1959. *The Logic of Scientific Discovery*. London: Hutchinson.

Posner, Michael I. 1989. *Foundations of Cognitive Science.* Cambridge, MA: MIT Press.

Post, E. 1943. Formal reductions of the general combinatorial problem. *American Journal of Mathematics.* 65: 197–268.

Pratt, T. W. 1984. *Programming Languages: Design and Implementation.* Engelwood Cliffs, N. J.: Prentice-Hall.

Prerau, David, S. 1990. *Developing and Managing Expert Systems: Proven Techniques for Business and Industry* Reading, MA: Addison-Wesley.

Pylyshyn, Z. W. 1973. What the mind's eye tells the mind's brain: a critique of mental imagery. *Psychological Bulletin* 80:1–24.

Pylyshyn, Z. W. 1980. The causal power of machines. *Behavioral and Brain Sciences* 3:442–444.

Pylyshyn, Z. W. 1984. *Computation and Cognition: Toward a Foundation for Cognitive Science.* Cambridge: MIT.

Quillian, M. R. 1967. Word concepts: A theory and simulation of some basic semantic capabilities. In Brachman and Levesque (1985).

Quine, W. V. *From a Logical Point of View,* 2nd Ed. New York: Harper.

Quinlan, J. R. 1983. Learning efficient classification procedures and their application to chess endgames. In Michalski, Carbonell, and Mitchell (1983).

Quinlan, J. R. 1986a. Induction of decision trees. *Machine Learning* 1 (1); 81–106.

Quinlan, J. R. 1986b. The effect of noise on concept learning. In Michalski et al. (1986).

Raphael, B. 1968. SIR: A computer program for semantic information retrieval. In Minsky (1968).

Reddy, D. R. 1976. Speech recognition by machine: A review. *Proceedings of the IEEE 64,* (May).

Reiter, R. 1978. On closed world databases. In Webber and Nilsson (1981).

Reiter, R. 1985. On reasoning by default. In Brachman amd Levesque (1985).

Reiter, R. 1980. A logic for default reasoning. *Artificial Intelligence.* 13:81–132.

Reitman, W. R. 1965. *Cognition and Thought.* New York: Wiley.

Rendell, L. 1986. A general framework for induction and a study of selective induction. *Machine Learning* 1(2).

Rich, Elaine. 1983. *Artificial Intelligence,* 1st Ed, New York: McGraw Hill.

Roberts, D. D. 1973. *The Existential Graphs of Charles S. Pierce.* The Hague: Mouton.

Robinson, J. A. 1965. A machine-oriented logic based on the resolution principle. *Journal of the ACM* 12: 23–41.

Rosch, E. and Lloyd, B. B. ed. 1978. *Cognition and Categorization,* Hillsdale, N. J.:Erlbaum.

Rosch, E. 1978. Principles of categorization. In Rosch and Lloyd (1978).

Rosenblatt, F. 1958. The perceptron: A probablistic model for information storage and organization in the brain. *Psychological Review* 65 : 386–408.

Rosenblatt, F. 1962. *Principles of Neurodynamics.* New York: Spartan.

Rosenbloom, P. S. and Newell, A. 1987. Learning by chunking, a production system model of practice. In Klahr et al. (1987).

Rosenbloom, P. S. and Newell, A. 1986. The chunking of goal hierarchies: A generalized model of practice. In Michalski et al. (1986).

Ross, Peter. 1989. *Advanced PROLOG.* Reading, MA: Addison-Wesley.

Roussel, P. 1975. PROLOG: *Manuel de Reference et d'Utilisation*. Groupe d'Intelligence Artificielle, Universite d'Aix-Marseille, Luminy, France.

Rumelhart, D. E. and Norman, D. A. 1973. Active semantic networks as a model of human memory. *Proceedings IJCAI-3*.

Rumelhart, D. E., Hinton, G. E. and Williams, R. J. 1986. Learning internal representations by error propogation. In McClelland et al. (1986).

Rumelhart, D. E., Lindsay, P. H. and Norman, D. A. 1972. A process model for long-term memory. In Tulving and Donaldson (1972).

Rumelhart, D. E., McClelland, J. L. and The PDP Research Group. 1986. *Parallel Distributed Processing*. Vol. 1. Cambridge, MA: MIT Press.

Russell, S. J. 1989. *The Use of Knowledge in Analogy and Induction*. San Mateo, CA: Morgan Kaufmann.

Sacerdotti, E. D. 1974. Planning in a hierarchy of abstraction spaces. *Artificial Intelligence* 5:115–135.

Sacerdotti, E. D. 1975. The non linear nature of plans. *Proceedings IIJCAI 4*.

Sacerdotti, E. D. 1977. *A Structure of Plans and Behavior*. New York: Elsevier.

Samuel, A. L., 1959, Some studies in machine learning using the game of checkers, *IBM Journal of R & D*, 3: 211–229.

Schank, R. C. 1982. *Dynamic Memory: A Theory of Reminding and Learning in Computers and People*. London: Cambridge University Press.

Schank, R. C. and Colby, K. M., eds. 1973. *Computer Models of Thought and Language*. San Francisco: Freeman.

Schank, R. C. and Nash-Webber, B. L., eds. 1975. *Theoretical Issues in Natural Language Processing*. Association for Computational Linguistics.

Schank, R. C. and Rieger, C. J. 1974. Inference and the computer understanding of natural language. *Artificial Intelligence* 5(4):373–412.

Schank, R. C. and Riesbeck, C. K., eds. 1981. *Inside Computer Understanding: Five Programs Plus Miniatures*. Hillsdale, N. J.: Erlbaum.

Schank, R.C. and Abelson, R. 1977. *Scripts, Plans, Goals and Understanding*. Hillsdale, N.J.: Erlbaum.

Searle, J. 1969. *Speech Acts*. London: Cambridge University Press.

Searle, J. R. 1980. Minds, brains and programs. *The Behavioral and Brain Sciences* 3: 417–424.

Seboek, Thomas A. 1985. *Contributions to the Doctrine of Signs*. Lanham, MD: University Press of America.

Sedgewick, R. 1983. *Algorithms*. Reading, MA: Addison-Wesley.

Sejnowski, Terrence J. and Charles R. Rosenberg. 1987. Parallel networks that learn to pronounce english text. *Complex Systems* 1 : 145–168.

Selfridge, O. 1959. Pandemonium: A paradigm for learning. *Symposium on the Mechanization of Thought*. London: HM Stationery Office.

Selz, O. 1913. *Uber die Gesetze des Geordneten Denkverlaufs*. Stuttgart: Spemann.

Selz, O. 1922. *Zur Psychologie des Produktiven Denkens und des Irrtums*. Bonn: Friedrich Cohen.

Shafer, Glen, Pearl, Judea, eds. 1990. *Readings in Uncertain Reasoning,* Los Altos, CA: Morgan Kaufmann.

Shannon, Claude. 1948. A mathematical theory of communication. *Bell System Technical Journal* :

Shapiro, E. 1987. *Concurrent Prolog: Collected Papers*, Volumes 1 and 2. Cambridge, MA: MIT Press.

Shapiro, S. C., ed. 1987. *Encyclopedia of Artificial Intelligence*. New York: Wiley-Interscience.

Shavlik, Jude W. and Dietterich, Thomas G. ed. 1990. *Readings in Machine Learning*. San Mateo, CA: Morgan Kaufmann.

Shavlik, Jude W., Raymond J. Mooney, and Geoffrey G. Towell. 1991. Symbolic and neural learning algorithms: An experimental comparison. *Machine Learning* 6 (1): 111–143.

Shrager, Jeff and Pat Langley, ed. 1990. *Computational Models of Scientific Discovery and Theory Formation*. San Mateo, CA: Morgan Kaufmann.

Siegler, Robert S., ed. 1978. *Children's Thinking: What Develops*. Hillsdale, N.J.: Erlbaum.

Siekmann, J. H. and Wrightson, G., eds. 1983a. *The Automation of Reasoning: Collected Papers from 1957 to 1970.Vol I*. New York: Springer-Verlag.

Siekmann, J. H. and Wrightson, G., eds. 1983b. *The Automation of Reasoning: Collected Papers from 1957 to 1970, Vol II*. New York: Springer-Verlag.

Simmons, R. F. 1966. Storage and retrieval of aspects of meaning in directed graph structures. *Communications of the ACM* 9:211–216.

Simmons, R. F. 1973. Semantic networks: Their computation and use for understanding english sentences. In Schank (1972).

Simon, D. P. and Simon, H. A. 1978. Individual differences in solving physics problems. In Siegler (1978).

Simon, H. A. 1944. Decision making and administrative organization. *Public Administration Review*, 4: 16–31.

Simon, H. A. 1975. The functional equivalence of problem solving skills. *Cognitive Psychology* 7:268–288.

Simon, H. A. 1981. *The Sciences of the Artificial*, 2nd ed. Cambridge, MA: MIT Press.

Simon, H. A. 1983. Why should machines learn? In Michalski, Carbonell, and Mitchell (1983).

Simon, H. A. 1991. *Models of My Life*. New York: Basic Books.

Sims, M. H. 1987. Empirical and analytic discovery in IL. *Proceedings of the Fourth International Workshop on Machine Learning*. Los Altos, CA: Morgan Kaufmann.

Sleeman, D. 1982. Assessing aspects of competence in basic algebra. In Sleeman and Brown (1982).

Sleeman, D. and Brown, J. S. 1982. *Intelligent Tutoring Systems*. New York: Academic Press.

Sleeman, D. and Smith, M. J. 1981. Modelling students' problem solving. *AI Journal* 1981, 171–187.

Skinner, J. M. & Luger, G. F. 1991. A Synergistic Approach to Reasoning for Autonomous Sattelites, in *Proceedings of Advisory Group for Aerospace Research and Development* (*AGARD 499*), Machine Intelligence for Aerospace Electronic Systems, Neuilly sur Seine France: NATO Publications.

Skinner, J. M. & Luger, G. F. 1992. An Architecture for Integrating Reasoning Paradigms, in B. Nebel, C. Rich, and W. Swartout, Eds, Principles of Knowledge Representation and Reasoning: Proceedings of the Third International Conference (KR92), San Mateo, CA: Morgan Kaufmann.

Smart, G. and Langeland-Knudsen, J. 1986. *The CRI Directory of Expert Systems*. Oxford: Learned Information (Europe) Ltd.

Smith, B. 1985. Prologue to reflection and semantics in a procedural language. In Brachman and Levesque (1985).

Smith, R. G., and Baker, J. D. 1983. The dipmeter advisor system: a case study in commercial expert system development. *Proc. 8th IJCAI* 122–129.

Smoliar, S. W. 1985. A View of Goal-oriented Programming. Schlumberger-Doll Research Note.

Soloway, E., Bachant, J. and Jensen, K. 1987. Assessing the maintainability of XCON-in-RIME: Coping with the problems of a very large rule base. *Proceedings AAAI-87.* Los Altos: Morgan Kaufmann.

Soloway, E., Rubin, E., Woolf, B., Bonar, J. and Johnson, W. L. 1983. MENO-II: an AI-based programming tutor. *Journal of Computer Based Instruction* 10(1,2).

Sowa, J. F. 1984. *Conceptual Structures: Information Processing In Mind and Machine.* Reading, MA: Addison-Wesley.

Steele, G. L. 1990. *Common LISP: The Language,* 2nd Edition. Bedford, MA: Digital Press.

Stefik, M., Bobrow, D., Mittal, S. and Conway, L. 1983. Knowledge programming in LOOPS: Report on an experimental course. *Artificial Intelligence* 4(3).

Sterling, L. and Shapiro, E. 1986. *The Art of Prolog: Advanced Programming Techniques.* Cambridge, MA: MIT Press.

Stern, C. and Luger, G. F. 1993. A Model for Abductive Problem Solving Based on Explanation Templates and Lazy Evaluation, in *International Journal of Expert Systems: Research and Applications,* special edition: Inference and Machine Reasoning.

Sussman, G. J. 1975. *A Computer Model of Skill Acquisition.* Cambridge: MIT.

Tarski, A. 1944. The semantic conception of truth and the foundations of semantics. *Philos. and Phenom. Res.* 4, 341–376.

Tarski, A. 1956. *Logic, Semantics, Metamathematics.* London: Oxford University Press.

Thagard, P. 1988. Dimensions of analogy. In Helman (1988).

Touretzky, D. S. 1986. *The Mathematics of Inheritance Systems.* Los Altos, CA: Morgan Kaufmann.

Touretzky, David. 1990. *Common LISP: A Gentle Introduction to Symbolic Computation.* Redwood City, CA:Benjamin Cummings Publishing.

Tulving, E. and Donaldson, W. 1972. *Organization of Memory.* New York: Academic Press.

Turing, A. A. 1950. Computing machinery and intelligence. *Mind* 59:433–460.

Turner, R. 1984. *Logics for Artificial Intelligence.* Chichester: Ellis Horwood Ltd.

Ullman J. D. 1982. *Principles of Datatbase Systems.* Rockville, MD: Computer Science Press.

Utgoff, Paul E. 1986. Shift of bias in inductive concept learning. In Michalski, Carbonell, amd Mitchell (1986).

Valiant, L. G. 1984. A theory of the learnable. *CACM 27:*1134–1142.

van Emden, M. and Kowalski, R. 1976. The semantics of predicate logic and a programming language. *Journal of the ACM* 23 733–742.

Vere, S. A. 1975. Induction of concepts in the predicate calculus. *Proceedings IJCAI 4.*

Vere, S. A. 1978. Inductive learning of relational productions. In Waterman and Hayes-Roth (1978).

Walker, A., McCord, M., Sowa, J. F. and Wilson, W. G. 1987. *Knowledge Systems and PROLOG: A Logical Approach to Expert Systems and Natural Language Processing.* Reading, Mass: Addison-Wesley.

Warren, D. H. D. 1976. Generating conditional plans and programs. *Proc. AISB Summer Conference,* Edinburgh, pp 334–354.

Warren, D. H. D. 1980. Logic programming and compiler writing. *Software-Practice and Experience* 10(II).

Warren, D. H. D., Pereira, F., and Pereira, L. M. 1979. *User's Guide to DEC-System 10 PROLOG.* Occasional Paper 15, Department of Artificial Intelligence, University of Edinburgh.

Warren, D. H. D., Pereira, L. M., and Pereira, F. 1977. PROLOG-the language and its implementation compared with LISP. *Proceedings, Symposium on AI and Programming Languages,* SIGPLAN Notices, 12:8.

Waterman, D., Hayes-Roth, F. 1978. *Pattern Directed Inference Systems.* New York: Academic Press.

Waterman, D.A. 1968. Machine Learning of Heuristics. Rep. No. STAN-CS-68–118, Computer Science Dept., Stanford University.

Waterman, D.A. 1986. *A Guide to Expert Systems.* Reading: Addison-Wesley.

Webber, B. L. and Nilsson, N. J. 1981. *Readings in Artificial Intelligence.* Los Altos, CA: Tioga Press.

Weiss, Sholom M. and Casimir A. Kulikowski. 1991. *Computer Systems that Learn.* San Mateo, CA: Morgan Kaufmann.

Weizenbaum, J. 1976. *Computer Power and Human Reason.* San Francisco: W. H. Freeman.

Weld, Daniel S. and deKleer, Johan, eds. 1990. *Readings in Qualitative Reasoning about Physical Systems* Los Altos, CA: Morgan Kaufmann.

Welham, R. 1976. *Geometry Problem Solving.* Research Report 14, Department of Artificial Intelligence, University of Edinburgh.

Weyrauch, R., W. 1980. Prolegomena to a theory of mechanized formal reasoning. *Artificial Intelligence* 13(1,2):133–170.

Whitehead, A. N. and Russell, B. 1950. *Principia Mathematica,* 2nd ed. London: Cambridge University Press.

Wilensky, Robert. 1986. *Common LISPCraft,* Norton Press.

Wilks, Y. A. 1972. *Grammar, Meaning and the Machine Analysis of Language.* London: Routledge & Kegan Paul.

Winograd, T. 1972. *Understanding Natural Language.* New York: Academic Press.

Winograd, T. 1973. A procedural model of language understanding. In Schank and Colby (1973).

Winograd, T. 1983. *Language as a Cognitive Process: Syntax.* Reading, MA: Addison-Wesley.

Winograd, T. and Flores, F. 1986. *Understanding Computers and Cognition.* Norwood, N. J.: Ablex.

Winston, P. H. 1975a. Learning structural descriptions from examples. In Winston (1975b).

Winston, P. H., ed. 1975b. *The Psychology of Computer Vision.* New York: McGraw-Hill.

Winston, P. H. 1992. *Artificial Intelligence.* 3d edition. Reading, MA: Addison Wesley.

Winston, P. H. 1986. Learning by augmenting rules and accumulating censors. In Michalski et al. (1986).

Winston, P. H. and Horn, B. K. P. 1984. *LISP.* Reading, MA: Addison-Wesley.

Winston, P. H. and Prendergast, K. A., eds. 1984. *The AI Business.* Cambridge, MA: MIT Press.

Winston, P. H., T. O. Binford, B. Katz, and M. Lowry. 1983. Learning physical descriptions from functional definitions, examples and precedents. *National Conference on Artificial Intelligence in Washington, D. C.*, Morgan Kaufmann, 433–439.

Wirth, N. 1976. *Algorithms + Data Structures = Programs.* Engelwood Cliffs, N. J.: Prentice-Hall.

Wittgenstein, Ludwig. 1953. *Philosophical Investigations.* New York: Macmillan.

Wolstencroft, John. 1989. Restructuring, reminding and repair: What's missing from models of analogy. *AICOM* 2 (2): 58–71.

Woods, W. 1985. What's in a Link: Foundations for Semantic Networks. In Brachman and Levesque (1985).

Wos, L, and Robinson, G. A., 1968, Paramodulation and set of support, *Proceedings of the IRIA Symposium on Automatic Demonstration, Versailles, France*, New York: Springer-Verlag, 367–310.

Wos, L. 1988. *Automated Reasoning, 33 Basic Research Problems.* New Jersey: Prentice Hall.

Wos, L., Overbeek, R., Lusk, E., and Boyle, J. 1984. *Automated reasoning: Introduction and Applications.* Engelwood Cliffs, N. J.: Prentice-Hall.

Young, Richard M. 1976. *Seriation by Children: An Artificial Intelligence Analysis of a Piagetian Task,* Basel: Birkhauser.

Yuasa, T. and Hagiya, M., 1986, *Introduction to Common LISP*, Boston: Academic Press.

Zadeh, L. A. 1983. Commonsense knowledge representation based on fuzzy logic. *Computer* 16: 61–65.

AUTHOR INDEX

SUBJECT INDEX

8 puzzle 82–84, 95, 98, 123–130, 136, 167–171, 304
A* Algorithm 133–137, 149–150, 179
abduction 73, 327
abstract data type 210, 224, 228, 276–277,
ABSTRIPS 433
ACT* 166, 698–699
activation 518–819
activation functions 524–525
activation record 156
active image 538, 682
admissibility 119, 131–135, 150, 482, 691
algorithm A 97, 132–133
algorithm A* 133–137, 149–150, 179
algorithm IDA* 149
alpha-beta pruning 120, 142–145
AM 21, 507–508
American Association for Artificial Intelligence 704
analogy 395, 466, 502–506
analytical engine 7
and elimination 60
and introduction 60
and/or graph 101–113, 148, 162, 322–323, 346, 349,
453–455, 588–590
answer extraction 449–453
applicative programming languages 270
arity 48–50, 53, 543, 546
artificial intelligence—definition 1, 2, 23–24,
689–694
associationist theories of memory 356–378
associative law 45
ATN see augmented transition network parsers
atomic sentence 49
attribute-object-value triples 335–337
augmentations of logic grammars 410
augmented phrase structure grammars 410
augmented transition network parsers 410–419
automated reasoning 14–15, 307, 427–461
    answer extraction 449–453

automated theorem proving see automated
    reasoning, resolution
axon 21, 22

backpropagation 523–527
backtracking 89–92, 103, 114, 156, 164, 168, 214,
220, 279–280, 450, 586, 588
backward chaining see goal driven search
backward search see goal driven search
BACON 508
base level categories 511
Bayes theorem 328–329
Bayesian probability 129, 328–329
beam search 147, 482
best first search 99–100, 117, 120–130, 133, 201,
237–238, 288–289
bi-directional search 175, 475
binary resolution 434, 440–444
binding see unification
blackboard architecture 40, 187–189
blackboard architecture—knowledge source
187–189
blocks world 18, 33–34, 56–57, 180–187, 397–398,
467–471
bottom up parsers 403
branch and bound 85
branching factor 89, 146–147, 175
breadth first search 92–95, 97–98, 132, 201,
235–237, 285–288, 429, 446, 482
bridges of Königsberg 76–78
brittleness 516

candidate elimination 473–483, 571–578
case based reasoning 505–506
case frame 363, 416–419, 467–468, 567–568
case grammars 424
category formation 464, 508–515, 698
category utility 512
certainty theory see confidence measures

727

data driven search 86–89, 104, 127, 172–175, 315, 320–321, 337, 454, 538
data flow diagrams 421
decision tree 483–490, 493
declarative semantics 176, 252, 326
deductive closure 501
default values 355, 379–382, 386–389, 565–566, 681
delayed evaluation 596, 605–609
delta rule 522–523
demodulation 457–459
demons 355, 381, 538, 638, 681–682
deMorgan's law 45
Dempster-Shafer theory of evidence 333–334
DENDRAL 16, 88, 190, 496–497
dendrite 21, 22
depth first search 90–92, 95–99, 154–156, 201, 216–218, 219–222, 234–235, 279–280, 285–288, 550, 585–587, 654, 672
depth first search with iterative deepening 99
derivation 402
difference engine 7
difference lists 548–549
difference reduction tables 430
directed acyclic graph (DAG) 82, 645
discrimination net 696
disjunction 42–44, 50–53, 330, 436, 455
distributed law 45
domain closure axiom 587–588
domain expert 15, 314, 317–320

EBL see explanation based learning
efficiency 30–32, 391–392
embedded language 202, 298
empty clause see null clause
EMYCIN 312
entity relationship diagrams 421
environments see programming environments
EPAM 695–696
epistemology 5–10, 699–703
equality substitution 457–458
equivalence 42–44, 50–53
Euler path 78
evaluation 48
exceptions 355, 392, 387–389
exclusive-or 73
exhaustive search 38, 117, 137–139, 596, 617
existential quantification see quantification
expert systems 15–17, 40, 130–131, 178, 308–350, 541, 551–562, 610–617, 680–682, 692
  and object oriented programming 680–682
  architecture 310–312
  case specific data 309
  conceptual models 17, 178
  confidence measures 130, 329–331, 335–336, 338, 553–554, 556, 610–611
  domain expert 15, 314, 317–320
  evaluation 312–320
  explanations 17, 309, 310, 312, 320, 323–336, 338, 342–344
  exploratory development 317–320

heuristics 130–131, 314
heuristics and control 340
how query 320, 342–344, 552–553, 557–558, 562
hybrid tools 680–682
inference engine 311, 318, 319, 320–323, 326
knowledge acquisition 314–320
knowledge engineering 15–16, 314–317, 323–325
maintenance 130–131
problem selection 323–325
problem types 341
uncertainty 314, 326–334, 335–336, 338
why query 323–334, 335–336, 338, 551–552, 557, 560–562
expert systems shell 312, 320, 326, 536–540, 541, 553–562, 610–617, 680–682
explanation based generalization 497
explanation based learning 21, 464–465, 495, 497–502, 541, 579–582
explanation structure 499–500
exploratory programming 201, 204, 309, 315–316
expressiveness 30–32, 391–392
extensibility 202
extensional definition 354, 509

facets 681–682
factoring 442
falsifiability of models 701
family resemblance categories 511
farmer, wolf, goat and cabbage problem 228–234, 276–281
feature vectors 493, 572–573
FIFO 93
financial advisor 67–72, 108–109, 130–131, 172
first order predicate calculus 8, 13, 33–34, 36, 46–74, 100–110, 156–163, 179–187, 199, 211–212, 320, 326, 354, 356, 360, 428, 436–439, 440–444, 466
  arity 48–50
  atomic sentence 49–50
  completeness 58–61, 428, 434, 436, 446, 449, 457, 459, 583, 585, 586, 587, 690
  conjunction 50–53
  consistency 57–59
  constant 47–49, 53–54
  disjunction 50–53
  equivalence 50–53
  function 47–49, 53–54
  function expression 49
  implication 50–53
  improper symbols 47
  inference 34, 57–72, 396
  inference rules 58–61, 428, 433–453, 582–588
  interpretation 53–61
  logically follows 58–60
  model 59
  negation 50, 53
  predicate 47–49
  proof procedure 59, 440–444
  quantification 50, 54–56, 62, 214, 377–378, 437–438, 451–452

ILLUSTRATION AND TEXT CREDITS

Figure 3.22 from *Problem Solving Methods in Artificial Intelligence* by N. Nilsson. Copyright © 1971 by McGraw-Hill. Reprinted by permission.

Figure 4.22 from *Principles of Artificial Intelligence* by N. Nilsson. Copyright © 1980 by Morgan Kaufmann. Reprinted by permission.

Figure 8.3 from *Building Expert Systems* by F. Hayes-Roth, D. A. Waterman, and D. Lenat. Copyright © 1983 by Addison-Wesley, Reading, Mass., Fig. 1.1 on p. 8. Reprinted by permission.

Figure 9.1 from *Expert Systems: AI in Business* by P. Harmon and D. King. Copyright © 1985 by John Wiley and Sons. Reprinted by permission.

Figures 9.3 and 9.4 from *Word Concepts: A Theory and Simulation of Some Basic Capabilities* by Ross Quillian. Copyright © 1967 by Society of General Systems Research. Reprinted by permission.

Figures 9.6, 9.9, and 9.10 from "Inference and the Computer Understanding of Natural Language" by R. Schank and C. J. Rieger in *Artificial Intelligence*. Copyright © 1974 by Elsevier Science Publishers. Reprinted by permission.

Figure 9.8 from *Computer Models of Thought and Language* by R. Schank and K. Colby. Copyright © 1973 by W. H. Freeman and Co. Reprinted by permission.

Figure 9.25 from "A Framework for Representing Knowledge" by M. Minsky in *Psychology of Computer Vision* by P. Winston. Copyright © 1975 by McGraw-Hill. Reprinted by permission.

Figure 9.26 from *Scripts, Plans, Goals, and Understanding* by R. Schank and R. Abelson. Copyright © 1977 by Lawrence Erlbaum Assoc. Reprinted by permission.

Figure 11.1 from "GPS: A Program that Simulates Human Thought" by A. Newell and H. A. Simon in *Lernende Automaten*. Copyright © 1961 by R. Oldenbourg. Reprinted by permission.

Figure 11.2 from *Computers and Thought*, edited by E. A. Feigenbaum and J. Feldman. Copyright © 1963 by McGraw-Hill. Reprinted by permission.